how
to have a
radical
attitude!

toward God
(and really believe

Spending Prime
Time With God

how
to have a
radical
attitude!
toward God
(and really believe it)

LIZ LEE

BROADMAN
&HOLMAN
PUBLISHERS

Nashville, Tennessee

Dewey Decimal Classification: 242.62
Subject Heading:
DEVOTIONAL LITERATURE //CHILDREN—RELIGIOUS LIFE
Printed in the United States of America

. . . .

This book is dedicated to:

Thomas Micheal Lee
Walter Roy Lee
JoAnna Hope Lee Davis
the children of my life who began my love for children

AND
Jared Lee Davis
John Luke Davis
Morgan Pearce Lee
(and future grandchildren)
who keep the love going in such delightful ways

AND
Robin Pearce Lee
Donna Grimmit Lee
Norman Paul Davis
who love my children and gave me grandchildren

AND
All Children
who give me such a radical attitude for teaching!

Contents

▼

Introduction

▼

Have you ever been told to "take an attitude check"? Perhaps you have been told that your attitude is radical. This book is for you!

A radical attitude about God can and will change your life. As you study the lives of Bible people, you will have an opportunity to discover their **Radical Attitudes**. In each **Investigating** section, you will learn things that students like you believe. In the **Analyzing** section, you can choose what to really believe. Then the final section, **A Faithful Attitude,** provides you an opportunity to express yourself to God.

The Old Testament has many "hidden" heroes. Not all of their attitudes are ones you'll want to possess. As you study the Bible characters and their attitudes—Eliezer, trustworthy; Joshua, daring; Balaam, truthful; Micah, prideful; Abigail, wise; Absalom, deceitful; Caleb, courageous; Jephthah, bartering; Jotham, obedient; Sanballat, taunting; and Hezekiah, prayerful—determine to develop your own faithful attitude.

Be sure you have your Bible, highlighter pens, pencil, and paper (a notebook is great). You can choose to complete a chapter a week or to take longer. I challenge you to SPEND PRIME TIME WITH GOD!

Chapter One

A Trustworthy Attitude

▼

An *attitude* is defined as "posture; a mental position with regard to a fact or state; a feeling or emotion toward a fact or state; a position assumed for a specific purpose." Attitudes often are difficult to talk about because they are abstract. Yet attitudes impact your relationships, behavior, successes, and failures.

In this chapter you will check your attitude of trustworthiness. You will have an opportunity to compare your attitude of trustworthiness with that of Eliezer. Find and read Genesis 24.

Often to be trustworthy is radical. Think about the ways people demonstrate their trustworthiness. Write your answers in the left column that follows. Think about the ways you show trust, and list those ways in the right column. How are the trust you show and the trust shown to you the same? Write the ways common to both in the center column. These are the attitudes you want to practice to have a radical trustworthy attitude.

Ways People Demonstrate Trust	Ways Common to Both	Ways I Show Trust
_____	_____	_____
_____	_____	_____
_____	_____	_____
_____	_____	_____
_____	_____	_____
_____	_____	_____

Abraham was now old and well advanced in years, and the LORD had blessed him in every way. He said to the chief servant in his household, the one in charge of all that he had, "Put your hand under my thigh. I want you to swear by the LORD, the God of heaven and the God of earth, that you will not get a wife for my son from the daughters of the Canaanites, among whom I am living."
— Genesis 24:1–3

So What Difference Does It Make?

Radical Attitude:

Abraham needed someone he trusted very much. He wanted a wife for his son Isaac. He wanted her to be of their same nationality. Abraham needed someone who had a reputation of trust. Highlight the phrase: "the one in charge of all that he had" in the Bible passage.

Abraham turned to a servant: Eliezer (Genesis 15:2). This servant would have inherited all Abraham owned if Isaac had not been born. Eliezer's name meant "God is a helper." Eliezer had shown Abraham for many years that he was truly a trusted servant.

Investigating Attitude:

"It is important that you do your best. We will leave from the church at 5:00 A.M. so be sure to get to bed early," Mr. Thomas said.

With a whoop of joy, the group headed toward the door. They were going to the state park for a day of hiking.

Jeff grabbed Jacob's arm. "Hey, how about a movie tonight? My folks are working late. They gave me money to get pizza."

"Nope, I'm headed home. I want to be rested for tomorrow,"

Jacob answered.

Mr. Thomas smiled. Trust Jacob to think ahead.

The next day everyone set off at a good pace on the hiking trail. The day's climb was going well when, just as Yvette was pulling herself up a rock, her foot slipped. She slid quite a distance before coming to rest against a tree. She lay very still. By the time the group reached her, she was moaning softly. Her leg was twisted under her at an odd angle. It was broken.

Mr. Thomas looked at the group. He needed someone he trusted to go for help. They would go to the ranger station to phone for help. Darkness would come before they could return. Remembering Jacob's remark the night before, Mr. Thomas asked Jacob to go.

Analyzing Attitude:

Think of your actions in the last twenty-four hours. Which ones caused others to think of you as being someone to trust. How are you building a reputation of trust? List your conclusions below. (In the center column, write the actions that are the same as those listed in the two other columns.)

My Actions	Reputation	Trust Actions
_____	_____	_____
_____	_____	_____
_____	_____	_____
_____	_____	_____
_____	_____	_____

A Faithful Attitude:

Dear God, (*write your thoughts here*)

_____

_____

The servant asked him, "What if the woman is unwilling to come back with me to this land? Shall I then take your son back to the country you came from?" "Make sure that you do not take my son back there," Abraham said. "If the woman is unwilling to come back with you, then you will be released from this oath of mine. Only do not take my son back there."

— Genesis 24:5–6,8

Listen Up!

▼

Radical Attitude:

Eliezer was being asked to do something difficult. Abraham could not do the job himself. Eliezer would be doing the job as though he were Abraham. Eliezer thought about what could happen. What if he failed? What if the girl would not come with him? What else could he do? Eliezer listened to Abraham's instructions. He asked questions to be sure he understood. Eliezer knew listening showed trustworthiness.

Investigating Attitude:

Jacob listened to Mr. Thomas. Jacob knew what he must do would not be easy. What if he should fall himself? What if the telephone did not work? What if he should lose his way?

Mr. Thomas was explaining the situation again. "Remember Jacob, we made two turns from the main trail. You will need to be careful to mark these so you can find them. It will be dark when you return. Here is the fluorescent paint. Spray it only at those two places. Remember what you learned during our hiking classes. Pace yourself so that you do not tire and are unable to bring the help back. Just do your best. That is all we expect."

Jacob listened quietly to everything Mr. Thomas said.

Analyzing Attitude:

Perhaps you have never thought of listening as a way to show trust-worthiness. Think about the many times a day you have listened. Think about the way you expressed trust when you listened. Complete the columns. (In the center column list the items that are the same in the other two columns.

Times Listened	When Listening is Shown	Things Listened For
_____	_____	_____
_____	_____	_____
_____	_____	_____
_____	_____	_____
_____	_____	_____
_____	_____	_____

As you work on a radical attitude and believe it, concentrate on the things you listed in the middle column. Notice how people change their behavior toward you as your attitude changes.

A Faithful Attitude:

Dear God, (*write your thoughts here*)

_____

_____

_____

_____

_____

Then the servant took ten of his master's camels and left, taking with him all kinds of good things from his master. He set out for Aram Naharaim and made his way to the town of Nahor. He had the camels kneel down near the well outside the town; it was toward evening, the time the women go out to draw water.
— Genesis 24:10–11

Getting Ready

▼

Radical Attitude:

Eliezer had to find a suitable wife for his master's son, and he had to make a long journey. Added to all of that, Eliezer also had taken an oath. Eliezer had been given much trust!

Highlight Genesis 24:10. Circle the preparation Eliezer made. Abraham's trust in Eliezer required making good preparation.

The custom of the day required parents to arrange for their children's marriages. Assorted gifts were expected during the arrangement process. The gifts were meant to impress the girl's parents with the wealth and generosity of the future groom. Eliezer probably helped Abraham carefully pick the things that he took on the trip. Since Abraham would not be able to go, Eliezer would be acting "the same as" Abraham. The impression he would make might sway the decision. His careful preparation reflected trustworthiness.

Investigating Attitude:

Quickly Jacob was on his feet. He picked up his backpack. Opening the flap, he checked his supplies. Making sure his flashlight worked, he then checked his water bottle and removed everything from the pack he did not need. Finally he retied his hiking boots and tied his jacket around his waist. As he looked around the group, he placed his backpack on and began to walk down the path.

"Hey wait up!" Jeff called. "I'll go with you."

"Thanks," said Jacob. "I'll be glad to have the company."

"Be careful," the group shouted as the boys started down the trail.

Analyzing Attitude:

Too often preparation is thought of only as "putting things together for future use," not as a part of trust. Think about things you do. How does your preparation show your trustworthiness?

Complete the columns. (The center column reflects actions that are the same in the other columns.)

Actions	Results	Preparations
_____	_____	_____
_____	_____	_____
_____	_____	_____
_____	_____	_____
_____	_____	_____
_____	_____	_____
_____	_____	_____

A Faithful Attitude:

Dear God, (*write your thoughts here*)

_____

_____

_____

_____

"Then he prayed, 'O LORD, God of my master Abraham, give me success today, and show kindness to my master Abraham.'"
— Genesis 24:12

Help, I Need Help!

▼

Radical Attitude:

Eliezer had made the journey. We do not know how long he traveled before he arrived in Nahor. We do know that when Eliezer arrived, he had the camels to kneel at the well at the edge of the town. He knew that he would be able to see many of the girls of the town as they came to draw the family's water.

Can't you just picture Eliezer as he sat there? He must have thought, Now what do I do? Which one would my master's son like? Which one will be good for him? How can I know?

Highlight in Genesis 24:12 the words, "Then he prayed." To have a radical attitude for success, remember to practice this phrase. Ask for God's help to be trustworthy.

Investigating Attitude:

Jacob and Jeff kept a good steady pace as they left the group. Soon they could no longer hear the group shouting encouragement to them. It was very quiet. The only sound was their breathing.

"I didn't want the others to know, but I'm afraid," said Jeff as they walked. "What if we lose our way? What if we aren't able to get help?" he asked.

Jacob answered, "I know, I feel the same way. My folks have always told me to pray when I've needed help. I guess I thought that was just a 'parent thing,' but we need help. It is good to know God wants to help us."

"Let's do it," Jeff answered, laughing nervously.

Jacob prayed, "O, Lord, help us to prove the trust Mr. Thomas has placed in us. Help us to not get lost. Keep us safe. Amen."

Analyzing Attitude:

One way to build trust is to ask for help when you need it. God wants you to know you can trust Him for help. He cares about everything you do. In the first column list the times you need help. In the third column list the times you've been trusted to do something. In the middle column list the things from the first and the third columns that are the same.

Times I Need Help	Times Common to Both	Times I've Been Trusted
_____	_____	_____
_____	_____	_____
_____	_____	_____
_____	_____	_____
_____	_____	_____

A Faithful Attitude:

Dear God, (*write your thoughts here*)

_____

_____

_____

_____

"See, I am standing beside this spring, and the daughters of the towns-people are coming out to draw water. May it be that when I say to a girl, 'Please let down your jar that I may have a drink,' and she says, 'Drink, and I'll water your camels too'—let her be the one you have chosen for your servant Isaac. By this I will know that you have shown kindness to my master."
— Genesis 24:13–14

The Plan

▼

Radical Attitude:

Eliezer had taken an oath to find a wife for his master's son. He had traveled to Abraham's homeland to find the right girl. He had made good preparation. He had asked God for help.

Now Eliezer sat by the spring where the girls of the town would come for water. Eliezer had a plan. He would ask for a drink. If the girl gave him the drink and also offered to water his camels, he would know that she was the one God had for his master's son. Before Eliezer finished praying, a girl came to the spring—a beautiful girl who did just as Eliezer had prayed. She even invited him to her home.

Investigating Attitude:

"Let's have a plan," Jacob said to Jeff. "When we come to the turns, we'll spray the arrows like we learned in class. For now we'd better calm down and quit going so fast. We'll tire out! Let's time ourselves. We'll walk for thirty minutes, then rest. Here's some trail mix Mom packed, it will give us energy."

"That's a good plan," answered Jeff. "I feel better already."

Analyzing Attitude:

Trustworthy people seem to have the habit of making plans. Think about some tasks you have to do. Think about the times everything seemed to go right. What did you do? When things seem to go radically wrong, what were your actions? On the line write a task or assignment you have to complete soon: _____ In the first column write all the things you need to do to get the task done. In the third column write what you need to be able to do the things you listed. In the middle column match what you need to do with the things you need and list them. Now number that list in the order you will do them. You now have a plan! Get going!

Things to Do	My Plan	Things I Need
_____	_____	_____
_____	_____	_____
_____	_____	_____
_____	_____	_____
_____	_____	_____
_____	_____	_____
_____	_____	_____

A Faithful Attitude:

Dear God, *(write your thoughts here)*

_____

_____

_____

_____

_____

Then food was set before him but he said, "I will not eat until I have told you what I have to say."
— Genesis 24:33

Staying True

▼

Radical Attitude:

Eliezer had watched Rebekah as she watered the camels. Not only was she beautiful, but she was kind too. When she had shown her family the gifts Eliezer had given to her, they quickly made preparation for Eliezer and those with him. The camels were unloaded and fed. Water was brought for the travelers to wash their feet. Then food was placed before them.

Notice Eliezer was not sidetracked. He would not eat until he told them why he had come. Eliezer showed his trustworthiness by staying true to task. He did not let "things" distract him.

Investigating Attitude:

Jacob and Jeff were about two miles from the ranger station when they met a group of hikers. They were having a picnic. Waving at Jacob and Jeff, one of the girls shouted, "Hey, you look hot, come get a cold drink and rest a bit."

Jeff started toward the group. "Great! Thanks!" he said. "Wait," said Jacob. "We're almost there. If we keep our pace, we'll be able to get help sooner than they expect. Yvette must be in terrible pain."

Shouting to the group, Jeff said, "Thanks anyway! We have a hiker hurt on top of the mountain. We're going for help!"

Analyzing Attitude:

So often trust is broken because someone or something sidetracks you. Think about something you were asked or expected to do recently. In the first column list the things you had to do to accomplish the task. (List them whether you did them or not.) In the third column list the things that did or could have sidetracked you. In the middle column, list the people that trusted you to complete the task. On this line write what Eliezer did and what you need to remember to do when asked to do a job: _____

_____

Things I Did	People Who Trust Me	Things That Sidetrack me:
_____	_____	_____
_____	_____	_____
_____	_____	_____
_____	_____	_____
	_____	_____

A Faithful Attitude:

Dear God, (*write your thoughts here*)

_____

_____

_____

_____

_____

Then Rebekah and her maids got ready and mounted their camels and went back with the man. So the servant took Rebekah and left.
— Genesis 24:61

We Did It!

▼

Radical Attitude:

Success! I Did It! Whoopee, it's done! Eliezer could have made any of these statements. His master had trusted him with an important task. He experienced the results of being trustworthy. Rebekah agreed to go back with him and marry his master's son. Genesis 24:66 tells the completion of the trust Abraham had in Eliezer. "Isaac brought her into the tent of his mother Sarah, and he married Rebekah. So she became his wife, and he loved her." Trustworthiness brings success!

Investigating Attitude:

"You're a fortunate young lady," the doctor said. "Your friends took good care of you and got help quickly. Otherwise there could have been some damage to your leg. Now you'll only have a small scar to remind you of this day!"

Looking up at Jacob and Jeff, Yvette said, "Thanks guys. You did the hard part. All I did was lay there and moan."

Everyone laughed.

"I am proud of this whole group," said Mr. Thomas. "I knew I could trust Jacob. I also appreciate Jeff volunteering to go along with him. I think he also proved to be someone to trust."

Analyzing Attitude:

Sometimes trust is not appreciated until it is lost. Today, a person of trust is wanted by friends, parents, teachers, and employers. Trust is a radical attitude!

In the first column list all of the actions that showed Eliezer was trustworthy. In the third column list all of the actions that showed Jacob was trustworthy. In the middle column list their actions that match trustworthy actions of yours.

Eliezer	You	Jacob
_____	_____	_____
_____	_____	_____
_____	_____	_____
_____	_____	_____
_____	_____	_____
_____	_____	_____

A Faithful Attitude:

Dear God, (*write your thoughts here*)

_____

_____

_____

_____

_____

_____

Chapter Two

A Daring Attitude

▼

In this chapter you will study the Bible person, Caleb. He had a very daring attitude. Perhaps you've thought that to be daring reflects a bad attitude. You may have even gotten into trouble for being daring. As you discover Caleb's daring attitude, consider ways you can become daring in a positive way. Find and read Numbers 13 and 14.

Each session will guide you in discovering the steps Caleb took to have a daring attitude. On the lines that follow, you will find the first letters of several words. Each word will be found in the chapter. When you complete each session, write the key word on the appropriate line. Use these steps in becoming more daring in a positive way.

L _____

P _____

C _____

U _____

P _____

S _____

W _____

Remember: Begin now to develop a daring attitude—it will be radical . . . believe it!

The LORD said to Moses, "Send some men to explore the land of Canaan, which I am giving to the Israelites. From each ancestral tribe send one of its leaders." So at the LORD'S command Moses sent them out from the Desert of Paran. All of them were leaders of the Israelites.
— Numbers 13:1–3

I Dare You!

▼

Radical Attitude:

Finally they were there. The people had been traveling for a long time. They left a land where they were slaves to go to a land they would own. The journey had not been easy.

The leader of the nation, Moses, depended on the Lord to tell him what to do. Moses could hear the voice of the Lord when they talked with each other.

The Lord told Moses to send some men ahead to explore the land. That way they would know what to expect when they arrived.

Circle the word *leader* in the Bible passage. To explore the land took men of daring attitudes. Leaders need daring attitudes.

Investigating Attitude:

There the team sat. With eyes down and heads lowered, they looked totally dejected. They had lost again. That made the fifth game.

Slowly the coach walked toward them. As she stood looking at them, she said, "I want to see your eyes."

One by one they began looking up at her. "I know we lost again, but I dare you to be winners. You have been followers. Let's be leaders!"

Lana jumped up. "I'll take your dare!"

Analyzing Attitude:

Developing a daring attitude involves leadership. Leaders thinks for themselves. Leaders are willing to take a stand for what is right. Leaders will do what others think is impossible. Leaders think good thoughts about themselves. Leaders choose to act according to what is best regardless of outside forces.

Using the letters below, write words that describe you.

_____	L	_____
_____	E	_____
_____	A	_____
_____	D	_____
_____	E	_____
_____	R	_____

A Faithful Attitude:

Dear God, (*write your thoughts here*)

Then Caleb silenced the people before Moses and said, "We should go up and take possession of the land, for we can certainly do it."
— Numbers 13:30

Think Positive

Radical Attitude:
The leaders for the twelve tribes had gone ahead to explore the land. Upon their return, they brought a cluster of grapes so big that two men had to carry it on a pole between them. They also brought other fruit.

The men told the people, "It is a great land. Things grow huge. Everywhere we looked we saw good things, but the men there are giants. We looked like ants!"

The people began to grumble and mumble. Caleb waved his hands to get the people quiet.

In the Bible passage, underline the word that shows Caleb's daring attitude was positive.

Investigating Attitude:
"Just wait," one of the girls said.

"Yes," said another. "Have you forgotten? This IS our fifth loss."

"How do you expect us to be leaders when we're nothing but losers?" said another.

Lana waved her hand. "Listen a minute," she said. "I hear what the coach is saying. We have begun to think of ourselves as losers.

What if we begin to think we're winners? If each of us would concentrate and do the best we can with the things we do best, we could change what's happening. I'm certain!"

Analyzing Attitude:

To develop a daring attitude, the second key word is *positive*. To be positive, you need to be certain. Being certain is being sure of the facts. Being positive is discovering what you do best, then doing it well. Being positive is looking for the possible when others think it is impossible.

Using the letters below, list things you do that are positive.

_____	P	_____
_____	O	_____
_____	S	_____
_____	I	_____
_____	T	_____
_____	I	_____
_____	V	_____
_____	E	_____

A Faithful Attitude:

Dear God, (*write your thoughts here*)

_____

_____

_____

_____

_____

[Joshua and Caleb] said to the entire Israelite assembly. "The land we passed through and explored is exceedingly good. If the LORD is pleased with us, he will lead us into that land, a land flowing with milk and honey, and will give it to us. Only do not rebel against the LORD. And do not be afraid of the people of the land, because we will swallow them up. Their protection is gone, but the LORD is with us. Do not be afraid of them."
— Numbers 14:7–9

Courage to Stand

▼

Radical Attitude:

Read Numbers 14:1–6 to understand the importance of verses 7–9. The twelve men had given their report and shown the things they brought back. Except for Joshua and Caleb, all reported they would be stepped on like they were grasshoppers.

The people began talking among themselves and grumbling against their leaders, Moses and Aaron. They even went so far as to say, "We should just choose a leader and go back to the land we came from!"

What a mess! Then Caleb stepped forward. In the Bible passage, highlight the words that show Caleb's courage.

Investigating Attitude:

As the girls left practice, they were mumbling to one another. They did not look happy.

The next day some of the girls told Lana, "Our parents think we need a new coach. It's her fault we aren't winning. We're tired of all the demands she makes. The other teams aren't having to work as hard. We are ready to quit!"

Lana looked at her teammates in frustration, "I can't believe you!

Mrs. Carrie is giving us a chance to win. What do you do? You blame her for what you are responsible for. The other teams have been working all year. We just got together two months ago. That's why Mrs. Carrie has been working us longer hours. We should thank her, not criticize her! With your attitude, no wonder we continue to lose. I know we can become winners. Now what are YOU going to do?" she challenged.

Analyzing Attitude:

A daring attitude requires courage. Perhaps the most daring thing to do is to stand up for what is right when the majority wants to do wrong. Using the letters below, write words that tell how you can dare to show courage.

_____ C _____

_____ O _____

_____ U _____

_____ R _____

_____ A _____

_____ G _____

_____ E _____

A Faithful Attitude:

Dear God, *(write your thoughts here)*

_____

_____

_____

_____

_____

"Only do not rebel against the LORD. And do not be afraid of the people of the land, because we will swallow them up."
— Numbers 14:9

I'm Not Changing!

▼

Radical Attitude:

Caleb and Joshua were the only ones who stuck to their faith in God. They trusted their leaders. They dared to stand up against all of the people. They dared to stand against the other ten men who had been chosen to explore the land. Caleb and Joshua were taking a great risk. These were their own people, their family. Caleb and Joshua did not change. They did not change their mind about what they saw in the land; their confidence in the people's ability to take the land; their trust in the Lord to help them; or their faith in Moses and Aaron as leaders. These two men realized that to have a daring attitude, you often must be unchanging.

Investigating Attitude:

Mrs. Carrie stood sadly looking at the team. "You really have a chance to win," she said.

One of the girls spoke, "Mrs. Carrie, we think someone else would be better to coach us now."

Lana interrupted, "Wait! Listen, please listen! Mrs. Carrie helped you, Elaine, to hit your jump shots, most of the time. You, Lisa, could hardly make it up and down the court: now look at you. Margie, you were so afraid of the ball, you'd look away when we wanted to throw to you. Every one of you has been helped. Let's not let a little hard work make us quitters. Don't be afraid of Mrs. Carrie because she is strict. I think we can win!"

Analyzing Attitude:

How easy it would have been for Lana to side with the other girls. To have a daring attitude you need to decide those things that are right and choose that which is of real value. People with daring attitudes do not change what they believe is right and of value. A daring attitude is unchanging. Using the letters below, write things that are of value and are right for you.

_____	U	_____
_____	N	_____
_____	C	_____
_____	H	_____
_____	A	_____
_____	N	_____
_____	G	_____
_____	I	_____
_____	N	_____
_____	G	_____

A Faithful Attitude:
Dear God, *(write your thoughts here)*

_____

_____

_____

"Their protection is gone, but the LORD is with us. Do not be afraid of them." But the whole assembly talked about stoning them. Then the glory of the LORD appeared at the Tent of Meeting to all the Israelites.
— Numbers 14:9–10

Quickly Forgotten!

▼

Radical Attitude:

Highlight the phrase that tells where Caleb received his daring attitude. Caleb stood up to the entire nation. He reminded them that they could take the land promised to them even though the men there were like giants. The protection of the Lord would be with them and Caleb knew that was all they would need. A daring attitude recognizes the protection of the Lord.

Investigating Attitude:

"Come on, please give Mrs. Carrie a chance," Lana said.

The girls had turned away. They were still angry. The last week had been the hardest they had ever had. Mrs. Carrie had expected them to be at practice immediately after school. She had kept them an hour longer than they were used to staying. And she had made them work out or play the entire time. Now the team was tired. The game Saturday was against the best team in the city.

"We just don't see any reason for all of this," Betsy said. "We'll just lose anyway."

"Well, I have just never," a voice boomed from the door. "I have never heard such losers. All week I have been watching you practice. You are getting good. I said to myself, 'Now that is a team that will go places.' I guess I am wrong. You have wasted my time and yours!"

Analyzing Attitude:

Some people forget that God allows everyone to make their own choices. Those choices sometimes hurt others who happen just to be near. When disasters surround us, a daring attitude is needed. A daring attitude requires knowing God will protect us, even in death. Using the letters below, write words that tell when you need to feel God's protection.

_____	P	_____
_____	R	_____
_____	O	_____
_____	T	_____
_____	E	_____
_____	C	_____
_____	T	_____
_____	I	_____
_____	O	_____
_____	N	_____

A Faithful Attitude:

Dear God, (*write your thoughts here*)

_____

_____

_____

_____

[The LORD replied] "not one of the men who saw my glory and the miraculous signs I preformed in Egypt and in the desert but who disobeyed me and tested me ten times—not one of them will ever see the land I promised on oath to their forefathers. No one who has treated me with contempt will ever see it."
— Numbers 14:22–23

Losers

▼

Radical Attitude:

A daring attitude can bring suffering. How sad Caleb and Joshua must have felt as they stood with the people listening to God speak. Think about all that the Israelites had been through. In Egypt they were slaves. Then after much cruelty and many false promises, they were free. As they traveled, they were faced with starvation, thirst, and enemies. Yet they made it! Camped near their land of promise, the people made a choice. Their fear kept them from taking the land God promised them.

Now, God spoke so all could hear. None present would see the promised land, except Caleb and Joshua. The Israelites would wander in the wilderness until the last person died.

Despite their stand, Caleb and Joshua had to go with the people. They wandered in the wilderness, too. Their daring attitude did not set them apart so that they would not suffer with the rest.

Investigating Attitude:

Mrs. Carrie said, "I agreed to coach this team because I thought you could win. I knew you had not won a game, but I watched you do so many things right! I thought all you needed was to learn how to work together. Apparently I was wrong. I am sorry you feel I have made you work too hard. I think for the good of the team I need to drop out. I will stay through the game, then step down."

Practice the next two days was quiet; faces were solemn. The game was a hard one. Lana scored more points than she ever had, but they still lost the game.

Analyzing Attitude:

A daring attitude will not keep you from suffering along with the group. Sometimes you may be tempted to think that, if you dare to stand up for what is right, you will not suffer. Caleb and Joshua discovered that is not true. Using the letters below, write words that tell times you have done right, but suffered anyway.

_____	S	_____
_____	U	_____
_____	F	_____
_____	F	_____
_____	E	_____
_____	R	_____
_____	E	_____
_____	D	_____

A Faithful Attitude:

Dear God, (*write your thoughts here*)

_____

_____

_____

_____

"But because my servant Caleb has a different spirit and follows me wholeheartedly, I will bring him into the land he went to, and his descendants will inherit it."
— Numbers 14:24

The Real Winner

▼

Radical Attitude:
Highlight the word that lets you know that even though Caleb would suffer, he would win. Draw a circle around the phrase that describes how God saw Caleb.

What made Caleb different? Think back through the entire incident. (If you have not done so, read Numbers 13 and 14.) How did Caleb practice his daring attitude? Sometimes we feel that if we had lived in Bible times, we would have done the same thing. Or we think the situations in the Bible are not as difficult as those we face today. As you read about Caleb remember:

- Caleb saw the same thing the other men saw.
- The group of people made up a whole nation.
- The people were dependent on what they were told.
- Caleb stayed true to what he knew could happen with God's help.

A daring attitude results in being a winner.

Investigating Attitude:
Sadly the team walked from the court. Lana looked up as Mrs. Stedson walked toward her.

"Lana," Mrs. Stedson said, "You really played a good game today. I liked the way you kept your head during those difficult plays. Would you consider working with me? I coach a group of children who have been in trouble. We are hoping to teach them how to handle pressure as they learn to play ball. I've been watching you for some time, Lana. You handle pressure really well. You're a winner!"

Analyzing Attitude:

Winning is not just scoring points in a game. Winning makes you feel good about yourself. Feeling like a winner is a good reward for daring to do what is right. Using the letters below, write words that tell how you are rewarded when you do right.

_____	R	_____
_____	E	_____
_____	W	_____
_____	A	_____
_____	R	_____
_____	D	_____

A Faithful Attitude:

Dear God, (*write your thoughts here*)

_____

_____

_____

_____

_____

_____

Chapter Three

A Truthful Attitude

▼

Truth can be defined "that which is reliable and can be trusted." Truth is the actual fact over the appearance, assertion, or pretense. In the Bible, God reflects His concept of truth in His commandments. People are able to reflect their concept of truth by the way they live in relationship to God and others.

Perhaps as a young child you were taught to be truthful. Perhaps you even practiced truthfulness then. Now, as an older child, you believe that complete truth does not always help. So you practice truthfulness only when you receive benefit. Truth is heavy "stuff." Practicing truthfulness is radical.

As you study this chapter, there are no pat answers. My prayer for you will be that you discover God's truth. May you acquire a radical truthful attitude—and believe it!

Read Numbers 22—23. Balaam acknowledged God as a powerful God, but he did not believe in the Lord as the only true God. He could have been really great if he had spent the time being truthful, rather than living deceptively.

The Moabites said to the elders of Midiam, "This horde is going to lick up everything around us, . . ." So Balak son of Zippor, who was king of Moab at that time, sent messengers to summon Balaam son of Beor, . . . Balak said: "A people has come out of Egypt; they cover the face of the land and have settled next to me. Now come and put a curse on these people, because they are too powerful for me. Perhaps then I will be able to defeat them and drive them out of the country. For I know that those you bless are blessed, and those you curse are cursed."
— Numbers 22:4–6

Always the Same

▼

Radical Attitude:

Balaam was a sorcerer. People called on him to place curses and blessings on others. Belief in curses and blessings was common in Old Testament times. Balak, the king, thought Balaam had power with the gods. He wanted Balaam to use his powers to place a curse on the Israelites. They had become a great nation of people and were taking possession of the land. The king hoped for magic. He hoped God would turn against His people. Little did he know about God!

Balaam was a successful and highly trusted sorcerer. Highlight the phrase in the Bible passage that indicates Balaam's success. Balak trusted the truth of Balaam.

Investigating Attitude:

Ryan could hardly wait to get off the bus. Ryan needed to talk to his friend, Travis. For nearly a month now, Ryan had been trying to get up enough courage to ask Marissa to go with him to the end-of-school picnic. For most of the sixth graders, the picnic was the first time to ask someone for a date. Sure, parents went along, but they let you act like it was a date. Ryan wanted Travis to tell him if he thought Marissa would say "yes".

Ryan and Travis had been friends since kindergarten. Travis had always told Ryan the truth. Sometimes the truth had hurt, but Ryan knew he could count on Travis.

As usual, Travis was waiting for him by the fence. As the bus began to slow, Travis waved to Ryan.

Analyzing Attitude:

Think of the people in your life that you can count on to be truthful with you. In the box to the left, write their names. In the box on the right, use the letters in their names to write words that tell how they are reliable and can be trusted.

Names of Those Truthful	How They Are Reliable

A Faithful Attitude:

Dear God, (*write your thoughts here*)

_____

_____

_____

_____

_____

But God said to Balaam, "Do not go with them. You must not put a curse on those people, because they are blessed." The next morning Balaam got up and said to Balak's princes, "Go back to you own country, for the Lord has refused to let me go with you."
— Numbers 22:12–13

Misused Truth

▼

Radical Attitude:

Are fortune tellers for real? Balaam would be somewhat like our fortune tellers today. Why would God use Balaam to speak to the Moabites? Highlight the phrase that tells you who made the contact. That is your answer. God used Balaam because the Moabites had already chosen to employ Balaam. He was the one available for God's use. God had a message for the Moabites. Truth cannot be manipulated.

The Israelites were a terrible threat to the Moabites. The Moabite king wanted to have the upper hand. His plan was for Balaam to place a curse on the Israelites. Then the king would be able to fight and drive them from the land. His plan was to manipulate God to win, but God cannot be manipulated.

Investigating Attitude:

The class elections were a week away. Whitney and Stacy were running for class president. They were best friends, and each said they hoped the other would win. So far the campaigns had gone well. It was hard to tell who would win. They both were well liked. On Friday, they would have one last opportunity to sway the class.

Each girl would give a speech at the morning assembly. The class would vote at lunch.

Stacy said, "Whitney, you go first. I've always heard that what people hear first is what they remember. I know I'm risking my chances, but you are my friend."

Analyzing Attitude:

Manipulation and truth cannot exist together in a radical attitude. To manipulate is to exploit, boss, command, control, or take advantage of. Think about times you have acted like you were telling the truth to manipulate. You may find it easier to think of times you've been manipulated. In the box below tell a time you used manipulation.

```
_____

_____

_____

_____

_____

_____
```

A Faithful Attitude:

Dear God, (*write your thoughts here*)

_____

_____

_____

_____

_____

_____

"I will reward you handsomely and do whatever you say. Come and put a curse on these people for me." But Balaam answered them, "Even if Balak gave me his palace filled with silver and gold, I could not do anything great or small to go beyond the command of the LORD my God."
— Numbers 22:17–18

The Bribe

▼

Radical Attitude:

What would you have done if you had been Balaam. The king wanted him to put a curse on a nation whose people who were taking the land all around him. The Israelites had even camped near his border. Balaam refused, not because he loved and followed God, but because he was afraid of God.

Then Balaam was told there would be a great deal of money in it for him if he'd give the curse. Highlight Balaam's answer in the Bible passage. Balaam displayed a radical truthful attitude in refusing to be bribed. Balaam knew in truth that God is powerful.

Investigating Attitude:

Ben and Patrick had been friends for a long time. Hardly a day passed that they did not spend time with each other. In fact, usually they met at one of their houses every afternoon to play video games. That is why Patrick was so hurt now.

For the last month, Ben had frequently been going to Carlos' house. He'd given Patrick some excuse each time.

As Patrick stretched out on his bed, he thought: *Carlos always has money to spend. He is constantly treating Ben to things. Carlos is the first one to get the new video games, the first one to get the trendy clothes, the first one to have . . .*

Analyzing Attitude:

A radical truthful attitude does not allow others to control by buying "things." Perhaps we are not truthful with ourselves when we allow others to control us with "things." Think about Ben. Was he being bribed? In the first box, list the ways Ben was being controlled. Was Patrick being controlled too? List how in the second box.

Ben	Patrick
_____	_____
_____	_____
_____	_____
_____	_____
_____	_____
_____	_____
_____	_____

A Faithful Attitude:

Dear God, (*write your thoughts here*)

_____

_____

_____

_____

_____

_____

*Then the LORD opened the donkey's mouth, and she said to Balaam,
"What have I done to you to make you beat me these times?"*
— Numbers 22:28

When the Truth Hurts

▼

Radical Attitude:

God did finally let Balaam go with Balak's messengers. God knew
Balaam's heart. He knew that Balaam was greedy and that Balaam
wanted the reward very much.

Read Numbers 22:21–30. Picture what happened: Balaam sad-
dled his donkey. In those days donkeys carried loads, plowed fields,
and ground grain. They were highly prized and very dependable.

As they traveled, perhaps Balaam began to think about the
reward. He did not watch where they were going. Suddenly the
donkey turned off into a field. Balaam beat the donkey to move her
back on the road. Soon they passed between two vineyard walls.
The donkey went so close to one wall that Balaam's foot was
pressed against the wall. Balaam beat the donkey again. Later the
donkey lay down. This time Balaam was angry, and he beat the
donkey with his staff.

Suddenly the donkey began to speak. Highlight the words in the
Bible passage that tell you how the donkey was able to talk. The
donkey was smarter than Balaam. The donkey saw the truth. She
saw the angel of the Lord in the path each time. The donkey was
smarter than Balaam because she tried to turn away from the greed

drawing Balaam, to the palace. Yet every time, Balaam beat her. Sometimes those with a radical truthful attitude are hurt.

Investigating Attitude:

Brett walked home alone. He would show them. He didn't need them, he thought as he kicked a rock.

Brett had just moved to Circy. He had finally made some friends. They had been going to one another's houses after school. Today, at Derek's, someone had suggested they take a sample drink from all the liquor in the cabinet. Brett told them he did not think that was a good idea. They had told him to leave.

Analyzing Attitude:

There is an old saying, "The truth hurts." Think of the times you have told the truth and it hurt. Have you decided to not always be truthful? Are there "little" lies? In the box tell a time when you were hurt by being truthful.

A Faithful Attitude:

Dear God, (*write your thoughts here*)

The angel of the LORD asked him, "Why have you beaten your donkey these three times? I have come here to oppose you because your path is a reckless one before me. The donkey saw me and turned away from me these three times. If she had not turned away, I would certainly have killed you by now, but I would have spared her."
— Numbers 22:32–33

Hidden Truth

▼

Radical Attitude:

Balaam did not see the truth right before him. His donkey saved his life three times. Balaam's failure to see the truth caused him to beat his donkey. The donkey was blameless, yet she was hurt.

Why did Balaam not see the angel? Was Balaam looking for the truth about what he was doing? Was Balaam thinking about what he was about to do? Highlight in the Bible passage the phrase that tells you what kind of path Balaam was on. Highlight what would have happened to the donkey had Balaam been killed.

To have a radical truthful attitude you must look for hidden truths.

Investigating Attitude:

Hilary and Brittany were going to the Saturday afternoon movies. They were going to eat at the food court in the mall after the movie. Both girls had been looking forward to their afternoon together.

Later as they sat eating, Hilary said, "That was a great movie. I especially liked it when that guy's ski flew off and hit those people. It was a scream!"

"Yes," said Brittany. "That was hilarious. I thought when the man blew his horn scaring those people, making them drop all their packages and then smashing them with his car, was *the most!*"

As the girls finished their food, they walked away leaving the table a mess.

Analyzing Attitude:

As you read the story, did you find the hidden truths? In the box below, list the truths you discovered.

_____

_____

_____

_____

_____

_____

As you develop a radical truthful attitude, be aware of the hidden truths. Remember, Balaam's donkey's life was spared because she saw the truth.

A Faithful Attitude:

Dear God, (*write your thoughts here*)

_____

_____

_____

_____

_____

_____

Balaam said to the angel of the LORD, "I have sinned. I did not realize you were standing in the road to oppose me. Now if you are displeased, I will go back."
— Numbers 22:34

Confused!

▼

Radical Attitude:

When Balaam saw the angel, he knew the truth. With truth, Balaam saw himself as God saw him. Balaam immediately recognized his sin. He foolishly lashed out at a donkey when he was responsible for the decision to go to the king. The desire for money, possessions, or prestige blinded Balaam.

Investigating Attitude:

Caroline laughed loudly. The boys and girls around her were laughing too.

Katie looked toward the group. "She always has a crowd around her," she said to her friend Molly. "Of course, her makeup is a bit much and just look at her clothes. She thinks she is so popular!" Katie tossed her head and smirked.

"Did you know her mom has cancer? She is really sick and will not live long," Molly whispered.

Analyzing Attitude:

A radical truthful attitude allows you to look past the appeal of popularity and wealth to the long-range benefits of following God.

In the box below, write some benefits of following God.

_____

_____

_____

_____

Have you ever felt foolish when you discovered the truth? Did you think to ask God to forgive you for lashing out? Embarrassment and hurt pride can cause us to strike out at innocent people. To develop a radical truthful attitude, work on the habit of asking, "If I were them, how would my behavior or language hurt?"

In the box, write other things you can do to remember the long-range benefits of following God.

_____

_____

_____

_____

A Faithful Attitude:
Dear God, (*write your thoughts here*)

_____

_____

_____

_____

_____

Then Balak's anger burned against Balaam. He struck his hands together and said to him, "I summoned you to curse my enemies, but you have blessed them these three times. Now leave at once and go home! I said I would reward you handsomely, but the LORD has kept you from being rewarded."
— Numbers 24:10–11

No Reward

▼

Radical Attitude:
Balaam traveled nearly four hundred miles to curse Israel for Balak, the Moabite king. When he arrived at the palace, Balak took Balaam to several places to try to entice him to curse the Israelites. Each time, Balaam blessed them instead. The truth of God's message so filled Balaam that he could only speak that truth.

Balak was so angry, he ordered Balaam to leave immediately without reward. Balaam's truth did not benefit him. A radical truthful attitude can mean no reward!

Investigating Attitude:
The chess game was getting "hot." The competition was keen. For the first time in several years, Jasper High had a chance to be national champions. Todd was leading the team when he realized that his opponent had a chance to win. Todd had left his king open. The next move would bring defeat—if the opponent saw the opening.

Suddenly someone sneezed, causing a chain reaction. The opponent was bumped, and the board and pieces scattered in all directions. By the time things settled down and the board was reset,

Todd realized the pieces were not like they were originally. If he told, his opponent would know about the opening; if he remained quiet, there might be a chance to win.

Analyzing Attitude:

A radical truthful attitude does not always bring reward. On the lines below, write the pros and cons of a radical truthful attitude.

PRO	CON
_____	_____
_____	_____
_____	_____
_____	_____

On the lines below, write what you think Todd did and what you would have done.

Todd:

_____

_____

_____

I would:

_____

_____

_____

A Faithful Attitude:

Dear God, (*write your thoughts here*)

_____

_____

_____

Chapter Four

A Prideful Attitude

▼

In previous chapters you have studied radical attitudes that are worth possessing. In this chapter you will study a radical attitude that can be harmful: pride. Sadly, most of us acquire this attitude easily and hang on to it tightly.

A definition of *pride* is "an undue confidence in and attention to one's own skills, accomplishments, state, possessions, or position." Pride is easy to recognize—especially in others!

Do a self-check now. Put a check in the box next to the words that describe how you feel about yourself, your actions, or your behavior.

❏ arrogant   ❏ cocky
❏ boasting   ❏ haughty
❏ sassy   ❏ conceited
❏ selfish   ❏ confident

The Bible reveals a great deal about pride. Pride is rebellion against God because it credits self with the honor and glory due to God alone. Proud persons do not think it necessary to ask for forgiveness because they do not admit they sin. This attitude is shown in the way others are treated. Pride can cause a low estimate of the ability and worth of others, causing contempt or cruel treatment.

Read Judges 17–18. In these chapters, Micah is not Micah the prophet who foretold of Jesus' birth. This Micah was a good man, but he had a radical prideful attitude.

Now a man named Micah from the hill country of Ephraim said to his mother, "The eleven hundred shekels of silver that were taken from you and about which I heard you utter a curse—I have that silver with me; I took it." Then his mother said, "The LORD bless you, my son!" When he returned the eleven hundred shekels of silver to his mother, she said, "I solemnly consecrate my silver to the LORD for my son to make a carved image and a cast idol. I give it back to you."
— Judges 17:1–3

But It Seems Good!

▼

Radical Attitude:

Micah and his mother seemed to be good and moral. They desired to worship God, but their desire led to disobedience.

The Israelite nation had arrived in the land that God had promised them. They were to take possession of the land by destroying all who lived there and their belongings. God wanted the people to be a nation who loved and worshiped only Him.

We do not know why Micah had taken his mother's money. We do know that it was not uncommon for roaming bandits to rob families.

Micah's mother's gratitude is expressed in her desire to worship God. So when Micah returned the money, she had idols made. Her attitude of pride in possessions led her to do something that appeared right and good. A radical prideful attitude can seem good.

Investigating Attitude:

The sixth-grade class at church was having a contest to earn money for the mission offering. On Saturday they would ride their bikes one mile for each twenty-five dollars pledged to them. The sixth grader with the largest pledge would have a picnic prepared for him or her at the end of the ride. All of the other children would have to bring the food and drinks for the picnic. The spirit of competition was high!

The Sunday before the ride, Mr. Roberts announced the winner. Rosie beamed as her name was called out. The others cheered and whistled.

Analyzing Attitude:

Do you think Rosie was proud? Why? _____

_____

_____

What was wrong with Rosie's pride?_____

_____

_____

What did Rosie do that was good? _____

_____

_____

Was it right for Rosie to be happy about the good things she accomplished? Why or why not?_____

_____

_____

A Faithful Attitude:

Dear God, (*write your thoughts here*)

_____

_____

_____

In those days Israel had no king; everyone did as he saw fit.
— Judges 17:6

Mine!

Radical Attitude:

Who is to say it is wrong? I'll do as I like! That is the attitude of the time in which Micah lived. That kind of attitude is a radical attitude of pride. The people of that time were saying to God, "We will ignore your standards. We will do as we choose and think!"

Micah had a shrine and made an ephod and idols. Then he set up his son as the priest. How proud he must have been of his worship place and things. The words *mine, mine, mine* seem to leap out of the passage.

Micah ignored the rules God had given to the people of Israel long before in the wilderness. He had forgotten the design and order of worship God had given. Micah's radical attitude of pride said, "I'll do as I see fit!"

Investigating Attitude:

Mother had left careful directions. They were having guests that evening for dinner. Miguel and Derek had promised to help. They would make the dessert for mother before she got home from work.

"I forgot that after-school special that was coming on TV," Derek said as they unlocked the door.

"Shucks! We told mother we'd get the dessert made," answered Miguel.

As the boys read the directions for making the dessert, Derek said, "Great, we can watch the movie while we are waiting for the ice cream to soften."

Miguel said, "Sure, we have plenty of time. This doesn't look so hard."

Neither boy paid attention to the line Mother had written in large letters: Do not let ice cream get mushy.

Analyzing Attitude:
How were the boys like Micah? _____

_____

_____

How did the boys say, *mine, mine, mine?* _____

_____

_____

Do some of your behaviors reflect a radical selfish pride? Write them here. _____

_____

_____

A Faithful Attitude:
Dear God, (*write your thoughts here*)

_____

_____

_____

_____

Then Micah installed the Levite, and the young man became his priest and lived in his house. And Micah said, "Now I know that the LORD will be good to me, since this Levite has become my priest."
— Judges 17:12–13

The Fake!

▼

Radical Attitude:

God chose the nation of Israel to be His people to learn about Him, to worship only Him, and to tell others about Him. God had one tribe to serve as priests. The other tribes would support the priests with their tithes.

Possibly the Israelites no longer provided this support because so many of the people did not worship God. The young Levite probably was looking for work when he showed up at Micah's house. He had traveled from his home in Bethlehem. Micah invited the young man to live with them and be their priest.

The young man accepted money, idols, and position in a way that was not consistent with God's laws. The worship was fake. Micah and the young priest allowed their radical attitude of pride to have worship that was fake.

Investigating Attitude:

"Leah, you are the only sixth grader this year who has not joined the church," Mrs. Courtney said. "I will be glad to come see you this week and talk about it."

Mrs. Courtney's words rung in Leah's mind all through the

worship service. She did not hear a word the preacher was saying. All she could think was: *What do my friends think? How could I be the last one? They will think I'm weird. I'm not so bad, I guess it wouldn't hurt anything to join the church. How humiliating to be the last! I guess everyone has been talking. Oh well, so what's the big deal?*

About that time, the congregation stood to sing the invitation hymn. With head down, Leah walked toward the pastor. She thought, *Now I'll be like my friends.*

Analyzing Attitude:
How did Leah's pride cause her to be a fake? _____

_____

_____

How did Mrs. Courtney's pride cause her to be a fake? _____

_____

_____

When has your pride caused you to be a fake? _____

_____

_____

A Faithful Attitude:
Dear God, (*write your thoughts here*)

_____

_____

_____

_____

He told them what Micah had done for him, and said, "He has hired me and I am his priest." Then they said to him, "Please inquire of God to learn whether our journey will be successful." The priest answered them, "Go in peace. Your journey has the LORD's approval."
— Judges 18:4–6

Special Privilege
▼

Radical Attitude:

The priest's radical attitude of pride allowed him to think he had special privileges from God. The priests were to be members of the tribe of Levi. They were to serve the people. They were to teach the people how to worship God, and they were to perform the rituals involved in the worship services at the tabernacle in Shiloh and the designated cities throughout the land. Micah's priest showed disrespect for God. He performed his duties for profit. His pride caused him to feel he had special privileges. God wanted the duties to be performed in the tabernacle or designated cities for the benefit of His people. The priest displayed total disrespect for God by claiming to speak for God when he had not received a message from God. He sure had a radical prideful attitude!

Investigating Attitude:

Cassie was afraid. The newspaper's headlines carried the news: Local Student Has Gun at School. The TV carried the story on the afternoon news. Cassie had classes with the boy. His desk was just three rows away from hers. He had often acted like the teachers owed him special privileges. He frequently showed disrespect toward the teachers and students. Now this!

Analyzing Attitude:

Do you remember the definition of pride given in the introduction to this chapter? Turn to the introduction and highlight the definition.

For all of us, the prideful attitude of others is easier to recognize than our own. List things in others that you help you recognize a disrespectful and prideful attitude.

_____

_____

_____

When has your prideful attitude caused you to be disrespectful?

_____

_____

_____

When has it made you feel you deserve special privileges?

_____

_____

These are behaviors you will want to try to change.

A Faithful Attitude:

Dear God, (*write your thoughts here*)

_____

_____

_____

_____

_____

They answered him, "Be quiet! Don't say a word. Come with us, and be our father and priest. Isn't it better that you serve a tribe and clan in Israel as priest rather than just one man's household?" Then the priest was glad. He took the ephod, the other household gods and the carved image and went along with the people.

— Judges 18:19–20

Looking Out for Number One!

▼

Radical Attitude:

"What goes around, comes around!" Micah discovered the truth of that saying. To satisfy his pride, Micah had set up his own place of worship. A young priest had been paid to stay and serve Micah's household. Then a group of scouts from the tribe of Dan came making the priest an offer to become the priest for the whole tribe.

The priest tried to protest, but the group persuaded him. They appealed to his pride. How great to serve a tribe! *After all*, the priest must have reasoned, *I'd better look out for number one!*

Investigating Attitude:

Taylor's parents had been divorced for several years. She was about to get used to the weekend visits to her mom's. Taylor lived with her dad because he chose to stay in the town where she had grown up. Her mom had moved to another state to begin a great new career. So Taylor's holidays and many weekends were spent with her mom.

"Taylor," her mom said during one visit, "I have some exciting news. I'm going to get married again! We will be moving back. You can come live with me."

Taylor was stunned. Thoughts churned and emotions whirled. "I can't believe what you're saying," Taylor began.

"Shhhh, let me finish," Mom said. "You will have a house with a large room, a swimming pool, and you can have a pet. Since you and your father have been in that apartment, you've been pretty crowded and I know how you miss Puffy. Think of all you can do with your friends. You can still go to your father's anytime. He is just across town."

Analyzing Attitude:

So many situations often appeal to our desire to be number one. That great desire to be "top," "the best," "number one" is a reflection of a radical attitude of pride.

Who in Taylor's family wanted to be number one? Circle your answer and explain why you chose that person.

Mother   Father   Taylor

_____

_____

Tell about a time when you had to make a choice that would make you number one at the expense of someone else.

_____

_____

_____

A Faithful Attitude:

Dear God, (*write your thoughts here*)

_____

_____

_____

He replied, "You took the gods I made, and my priest, and went away. What else do I have? How can you ask, 'What's the matter with you?'" The Danites answered, "Don't argue with us, or some hot-tempered men will attack you, and you and your family will lose your lives." So the Danites went their way, and Micah, seeing that they were too strong for him, turned around and went back home.
— Judges 18:24–26

You Lose!

▼

Radical Attitude:

How could they! The very nerve of them! That is stealing! Surely Micah must have said one or all of these statements.

Micah had made idols and hired a priest to run his personal religion, and now they were gone. The scouts from the tribe of Dan had taken them. Nothing remained.

These things were the pride of Micah's life. After all, he had made and acquired them. He had his own place of worship, so he did not have to go to the places God had commanded. Now they were gone. All that Micah prized the most was lost.

Investigating Attitude:

He was the envy of his class. His collection of baseball cards was the largest. He even had two that were collectors' items. They were each worth more than a thousand dollars. Often everyone had heard him brag about his collection.

Disbelief spread across the class as they heard the news. The principal had called Brian out of class earlier. Now she was telling the class that Brian's house had burned. Nothing remained.

Analyzing Attitude:

When all of your energy is put into "things," an empty shell is left when they are gone. The only way to protect yourself from such loss is to invest your life in God. Remember, what you do for Him can never be taken away.

What do you prize most? (These are things that are most important to you.) List them. _____

_____

_____

Does anything in your life have everlasting value? _____
What do you do for God that will last forever?_____

_____

_____

_____

If you lost all your possessions like Brian did, what would you still have to be thankful for? _____

_____

_____

_____

A Faithful Attitude:

Dear God, (*write your thoughts here*)

_____

_____

_____

_____

Then they took what Micah had made, and his priest, and went on to Laish, against a peaceful and unsuspecting people. They attacked them with the sword and burned down their city.
— Judges 18:27

Pride Hurts

▼

Radical Attitude:
Troops from the tribe of Dan traveled from Zorah and Eshtaol into the hill country of Ephraim. Here they found Micah and his family living very comfortably. They were pleased to find a priest from the tribe of Levi living with Micah. The troops from Dan persuaded the priest to go with them. They then went north to Laish. There the Danites butchered all the citizens and renamed the city Dan. The priest's idols became the new city's focus of worship.

Such a mess for everyone. Highlight all of the people who showed a radical prideful attitude. Circle all of the hurt that was caused because of that pride.

Investigating Attitude:
This chapter has covered the harmful aspects of a radical attitude of pride. Is there such a thing as "good" pride? I think we have been misinformed today in thinking that pride in self is good. Go back to the definition of pride: "an undue confidence in and attention to one's own skills, accomplishments, state, possessions, or position." Thus I must conclude that this type of pride is not good. What do you think?

Analyzing Attitude:
In the space below, write your own debate.

Pride Can Be Good	Pride Is Never Good
_____	_____
_____	_____
_____	_____
_____	_____
_____	_____
_____	_____
_____	_____
_____	_____

Your conclusion:

_____

_____

_____

_____

_____

A Faithful Attitude:
Dear God, (*write your thoughts here*)

_____

_____

_____

Chapter Five

A Wise Attitude

▼

What do you think of when you hear the word *wise?* Who do you know that is wise?

As a child, I often thought wisdom was an "old people thing." I even felt I did not want to acquire a wise attitude. Maybe you've felt like that too.

Being wise and being smart are not the same. To be smart is to be alert, astute, brainy, bright, educated, clever, knowing, and cunning. Wisdom includes all of the qualities of smartness, but it also implies using those qualities to live life successfully.

Read 1 Samuel 25 to discover someone who was wise. The nation of Israel had depended on Samuel for spiritual leadership. Samuel had just died. The king, Saul, had moods of depression. He had threatened David's life. God's plan was for David to be king. Before Samuel died, he had anointed David king. Now Saul was chasing David to kill him. David had about six hundred men who had chosen to follow him.

Abigail was the wife of Nabal. He did not place much value on her yet. Abigail was respected by the others in the household and, in turn, they recognized her radical wise attitude. She showed her wisdom by looking at the big picture and leaving plenty of room for God to be involved. Pay close attention to how Abigail did this.

One of the servants told Nabal's wife Abigail: "David sent messengers from the desert to give our master his greetings, but he hurled insults at them. Yet these men were very good to us. They did not mistreat us, and the whole time we were out in the fields near them nothing was missing. Night and day they were a wall around us all the time we were herding our sheep near them. Now think it over and see what you can do, because disaster is hanging over our master and his whole household. He is such a wicked man that no one can talk to him."
— 1 Samuel 25:14–17

Say What?

▼

Radical Attitude:

David had sent messengers to Nabal asking for food for himself and his men. Nabal rudely refused to feed them.

The custom of that day demanded that Nabal show them hospitality. He was very rich and could have easily fed them. Also, David had been protecting the herdsman of Nabal. Nabal would not have had as many riches if it were not for David and his men. They prevented raiders from taking large numbers of animals.

In sharp contrast to the failure of Nabal to listen, Abigail listened carefully to the servant. Highlight the words that the servant used to give Abigail the "big picture".

A basic for a radical wise attitude is listening.

Investigating Attitude:

Rick turned impatiently to Brett. "I just don't see any need to learn this stuff. Just when do you think we'll ever use it? I'd lots rather be outside."

Brett had been tutoring Rick in algebra every afternoon for a week. Rick wanted to be a building contractor one day.

"Listen," Brett said.

Analyzing Attitude:

You complete the story, remembering that listening helps those with a radical attitude of wisdom to see the big picture.

_____

_____

_____

_____

_____

_____

_____

_____

_____

_____

_____

_____

A Faithful Attitude:

Dear God, (*write your thoughts here*)

_____

_____

_____

_____

_____

Abigail lost no time. She took two hundred loaves of bread, two skins of wine, five dressed sheep, five seahs of roasted grain, a hundred cakes of raisins and two hundred cakes of pressed figs, and loaded them on donkeys.
— 1 Samuel 25:18

Get a Move On!

▼

Radical Attitude:

Highlight the phrase in the Bible passage that tells you Abigail moved quickly. Once she had heard the servant's account of what happened, she immediately took action.

Abigail could imagine David's reaction when he heard how his messengers had been received. Wisely, Abigail lost no time in gathering food. She realized that she must intercept David before he decided to take action against Nabal's household.

Having listened, Abigail saw the big picture. She saw the danger she was in. Now she acted quickly.

Investigating Attitude:

Cassie and Alicia were not speaking. Emily had watched them for a week now. Cassie had gotten up from the lunchroom table when Alicia sat down. Alicia had changed places in science class to keep from sitting next to Cassie. They even turned their backs to each other in the hallway when they met. Things were getting out of hand. The two girls had been friends for several years.

Emily had overheard two teachers talking. "I had planned to take Cassie and Alicia with me to the science convention, but they are treating each other so ugly, I'm about ready to invite two other students."

Quickly Emily . . .

Analyzing Attitude:
Finish the story.

_____

_____

_____

_____

_____

_____

_____

_____

_____

_____

_____

A Faithful Attitude:
Dear God, (*write your thoughts here*)

_____

_____

_____

_____

_____

When Abigail saw David, she quickly got off her donkey and bowed down before David with her face to the ground. She fell at his feet and said: "My lord, let the blame be on me alone. Please let your servant speak to you; hear what your servant has to say."
— 1 Samuel 25:23–24

Whose Fault?

▼

Radical Attitude:

Abigail displayed her radical attitude of wisdom when she was willing to accept the blame for the unwise behavior of her husband. Wisely she appealed in a very humble way to David. She probably could tell that David was very angry and planned to harm Nabal.

How different do you think the account would be if Abigail had loudly declared that David had talked to the wrong person? What if she had told David that he should have known better?

People with radical wise attitudes know when to accept the blame so that they will be allowed to speak what is right.

Investigating Attitude:

The team had practiced hard all week. Spirits were high as the boys yelled back and forth on the bus. As they settled down for the long ride to the playoffs, Paul brought out a deck of cards. Soon a hot game was underway.

Suddenly Scott stood up and shouted, "Sean is cheating!" and tried to hit Sean. A fight quickly began. Sometime later, after peace was restored, the coach began talking. He was very angry.

Paul raised his hand, "Coach, he began, . . .

Analyzing Attitude:
Finish the story.

_____

_____

_____

_____

_____

_____

_____

_____

_____

_____

_____

_____

_____

_____

_____

_____

_____

A Faithful Attitude:
Dear God, (*write your thoughts here*)

_____

_____

_____

_____

_____

"May my lord pay no attention to that wicked man Nabal. He is just like his name—his name is Fool, and folly goes with him. But as for me your servant, I did not see the men my master sent. Now since the LORD has kept you, my master, from bloodshed and from avenging yourself with your own hands, as surely as the LORD lives and as you live, may your enemies and all who intend to harm my master be like Nabal. And let this gift, which your servant has brought to my master, be given to the men who follow you. Please forgive your servant's offense, for the LORD will certainly make a lasting dynasty for my master because he fights the LORD's battles."
— I Samuel 25:25–28

The Truth

▼

Radical Attitude:

Abigail wanted David to know the truth. She reminded David that Nabal lived up to his name, which meant "foolish." She wanted David to know that Nabal's behavior was not hers. People with wise attitudes will make every effort to practice truth. Wise persons do not allow the behavior of those around them to cloud theirs. Abigail wanted David to know she was different.

Investigating Attitude:

Janet sat looking into space. She was thinking about the incident in class that day. A substitute teacher had taught them all week. Each day the class became more unruly. Today the substitute teacher burst into tears as she pleaded with them to do their work. Janet had worked quietly each day because it was important for her to get the information. She was taking an exam Saturday for college entrance. Janet wanted the teacher to know that some students wanted to learn. Would her friends make fun of her? Would they know if she talked to the teacher. Janet's thoughts whirled. Janet decided to . . .

Analyzing Attitude:
Finish the story.

_____

_____

_____

_____

_____

_____

_____

_____

_____

_____

_____

_____

_____

_____

_____

A Faithful Attitude:
Dear God, (*write your thoughts here*)

_____

_____

_____

_____

_____

"When the LORD *has done for my master every good thing he promised concerning him and has appointed him leader over Israel, my master will not have on his conscience the staggering burden of needless bloodshed or of having avenged himself. And when the* LORD *has brought my master success, remember your servant."*
— I Samuel 25:30–31

The Peacemaker

▼

Radical Attitude:

Abigail displayed her wise attitude as peacemaker. She reminded David that one day he would be the king of Israel. People then, as today, expect their leaders to have good and clean reputations. She was saying to David, "Keep a clean conscience." How sad when scandal erupts during a leader's time of service. Abigail wisely reminded David that peace within is of high value. She did not live in a peaceful household, yet she had discovered inner peace. Now with great wisdom, she was passing that discovery on to David. Abigail wanted David to know that a person with a radical attitude of wisdom is a peacemaker.

Investigating Attitude:

"I am going to trash her locker," Patti said to Tim as they walked home from the gym.

Patti and Tim were on a tennis team. They had just finished practice. All week, April had been hitting bad balls to Patti. It seemed she was trying to make Patti look bad so the coach would take her off the team. Now Patti had had enough. She wanted to get back at April.

Tim understood that Patti was angry. If he lost her as his partner, he would have to start over with a new one. He felt anger too.

The two continued to walk. Tim was quiet for almost a block. He looked at Patti's angry face as he said . . .

Analyzing Attitude:
Finish the story.

_____

_____

_____

_____

_____

_____

_____

_____

_____

_____

_____

A Faithful Attitude:
Dear God, (*write your thoughts here*)

_____

_____

_____

_____

_____

"And when the LORD has brought my master success, remember your servant."
— I Samuel 25:31

Looking Ahead!

▼

Radical Attitude:

Abigail had listened to the servant, looked at the big picture, decided a plan, then moved quickly to go talk to David. She then presented the truth as she appealed to David's peaceful nature. Abigail displayed a radical attitude of wisdom. But she was not finished. Wisely, Abigail realized that David would one day rule as king. He would be in a position to share his success with others. She could have asked for specific wealth, a reward, or even a position in the court, but she did not. In the Bible passage, highlight the one word of her request. Circle the word that describes her.

Abigail wisely looked ahead to the time when David would have power. She trusted God to impress David with what would be right for her.

People with radical wise attitudes not only see the big picture, but also they allow God to be involved as He determines the best.

Investigating Attitude:

Jonathan's friends could not understand why he was willing to work so hard at the grocery store. After all, it was not his store. It was only a part-time job. He took the whole thing too seriously.

Frequently some of the other workers would break open a box of cookies or bruise a piece of fruit so they could eat them. When confronted, they always claimed that it was an accident or that, since the food was damaged, they didn't see the harm in eating it.

At the last store meeting Mr. Evans told them he was going to have to let them go. Business had not been good. He could not afford to keep part-time help. "If business is better by the end of the month, I will take one of you back. I would like to talk to each of you today."

Later, seated in Mr. Evans office, Jonathan said, . . .

Analyzing Attitude:
Finish the story.

_____

_____

_____

_____

_____

_____

_____

_____

A Faithful Attitude:
Dear God, (*write your thoughts here*)

_____

_____

_____

_____

_____

David said to Abigail, "Praise be to the LORD, the God of Israel, who has sent you today to meet me. May you be blessed for your good judgment and for keeping me from bloodshed this day and from avenging myself with my own hands. . . .

When David heard that Nabal was dead, he said, "Praise be to the LORD, who has upheld my cause against Nabal for treating me with contempt. He has kept his servant from doing wrong and has brought Nabal's wrongdoing down on his own head."

— 1 Samuel 25:32–33,39

The Winners!

▼

Radical Attitude:

People with radical wise attitudes are winners. Abigail wisely stuck to her plan. Several times she had opportunity to better herself and forget Nabal. Read the entire chapter of 1 Samuel 25. Pencil in a checkmark in the margin each time Abigail could have gotten something only for herself.

David displayed a radical attitude of wisdom as he listened to Abigail. In 1 Samuel 25, highlight David's wisdom as he listened, acted, assumed responsibility, heard the truth, was willing to be peaceful, and looked ahead. These are the qualities of a winning radical attitude of wisdom.

Investigating Attitude

In each of the stories in this chapter, there were people who did not act wisely. Complete the chart below:

Person	Unwise Thought, Feeling, or Behavior
_____	_____
_____	_____

_____   _____
_____   _____
_____   _____
_____   _____
_____   _____

Analyzing Attitude:

In each of the stories in this chapter there were people who used their wisdom. Complete the chart below.

Person   Wise Attitude Shown

_____   _____

_____   _____

_____   _____

_____   _____

_____   _____

_____   _____

A Faithful Attitude:

Dear God, (*write your thoughts here*)

_____

_____

_____

_____

Chapter Six

A Deceitful Attitude

▼

Somewhat like pride, deceit is an attitude we readily recognize in others but do not like to admit in ourselves. Some familiar words that have similar meanings are *falsehood, lying, trickery, cheating,* and *dishonesty.*

Absalom is a Bible character who deceived his father, David. Absalom had his brother Amnon killed, and then he escaped to another country. Although David loved Absalom very much, he would not let Absalom return to Jerusalem for three years. Even then he refused to see Absalom and would not welcome him back to the palace until Absalom finally asked for David's forgiveness. Throughout the time he was separated from his father, Absalom was plotting how to be king.

Read 2 Samuel 13–19 to learn the story of Absalom. In this study we will look primarily at chapter 15. Keep your highlighter near and your Bible open as you study.

As you study this chapter, complete these key words and actions to remind you about the danger of deceit:

C _____

F _____

R _____

L _____

H _____

S _____

G _____

He would get up early and stand by the side of the road leading to the city gate. Whenever anyone came with a complaint to be placed before the king for a decision, Absalom would call out to him, "What town are you from?" He would answer, "Your servant is from one of the tribes of Israel." Then Absalom would say to him, "Look, your claims are valid and proper, but there is no representative of the king to hear you." And Absalom would add, "If only I were appointed judge in the land! Then everyone who has a complaint or case could come to me and I would see that he gets justice."
— 2 Samuel 15:2–4

I Want!

▼

Radical Attitude:

Absalom coveted the throne. He began an elaborate plot to get the throne from his father, David. Covetousness is the beginning of deceit. To covet is to have an excessive desire for something that belongs to someone else. Absalom's strategy was to win the hearts of the people with his good looks, grand entrances, apparent concern for justice, and friendly embraces. A deceitful attitude begins with coveting.

Investigating Attitude:

Jaclyn could not believe what she saw. The dress of her dreams! A *must!* That was absolutely the dreamiest dress she had ever seen. If she could wear that dress to the party, Justin would sure take notice of her. "I just must have it," Jaclyn told her mom.

Her mom agreed to meet her after school to go look at it. "Remember," Mom told her, "We agreed to only spend seventy-five dollars. We can't go over that."

Sadly, she went to her room. Oh, how she wanted that dress! She was almost sure it would cost more than seventy-five dollars. She would just have to think of a way to get it.

Suddenly she had an idea. She would call her father. He was in another state. She'd have him send her money. Then she remembered she had promised her mother not to do that kind of thing. But this was important. Jaclyn decided to tell him to mail the money to her friend's house.

Analyzing Attitude:
How do Jaclyn's plans show a radical deceitful attitude? _____

_____

_____

_____

What other choices does she have? Write them here: _____

_____

_____

_____

What word describes what is causing her to be deceitful? Write that word here: _____

Turn back to the introduction page for this chapter, and write the word in the first blank.

A Faithful Attitude:
Dear God, (*write your thoughts here*)

_____

_____

_____

_____

_____

Also, whenever anyone approached him to bow down before him,
Absalom would reach out his hand, take hold of him and kiss him.
Absalom behaved in this way toward all the Israelites who came to the
king asking for justice, and so he stole the hearts of the men of Israel.
— 2 Samuel 15:5–6

The Fake!

▼

Radical Attitude:

Absalom had begun his plot to become the king. He decided to act like the king.

The practice of that day was to transact business and conduct government affairs at the city gate. Anyone going into the city or leaving the city had to do so through the gate. So merchants set up their tent-shops near the gate entrance. The gate area was the center of city life. The important men and the common men sat together at the gate.

Absalom knew that the king did not make an appearance at the gate very often. He also knew the gate area would be an ideal place to "act like a king." He would win the hearts of the men.

Having a radical deceitful attitude can lead a person to be a fake.

Investigating Attitude:

Philip wanted to go camping with Jeffrey's family. He decided to do all of the things his parents wanted and then he would ask. Philip knew that he had been lax in doing his household jobs. He also had smarted back often. Well, he'd just act the "perfect" son for the next week.

Analyzing Attitude:

How was Philip a fake? Write your answer here:_____

_____

_____

_____

When have you acted fake to get what you wanted? Write your
answer here. _____

_____

_____

_____

How is being fake showing a radical deceitful attitude? Write your
answer here. _____

_____

_____

_____

What word describes Absalom's and Philip's actions? Write the
word here: _____ Write the word on the introductory page.

A Faithful Attitude:

Dear God, (*write your thoughts here*)

_____

_____

_____

_____

_____

At the end of four years, Absalom said to the king, "Let me go to Hebron and fulfill a vow I made to the LORD. While your servant was living at Geshur in Aram, I made this vow: 'If the LORD takes me back to Jerusalem, I will worship the LORD in Hebron.'" The king said to him, "Go in peace." So he went to Hebron.
— 2 Samuel 15:7–9

Acting Religious
▼

Radical Attitude:
Absalom told his father, the king, that he wanted to go to Hebron to worship. He would find his friends at Hebron. They would declare him their king. Absalom knew his father would not deny his request to go worship. He was showing a radical deceitful attitude by acting religious. In other words, he went to church to get what he wanted—to let his friends make him king.

Investigating Attitude:
Zachary liked Lauren very much. She was in several of his classes at school. He had tried to get her attention, but nothing seemed to work.

"I've tried everything," Zachary said to Gary. "I asked her to go with me to Ashley's party. All the guys at school were saying it would be a great party. When I asked Lauren, she said, 'I don't go to parties when the parents are not at home.' Can you believe that?"

"Hey man," Gary said, "Lauren is a Christian. She has said she would not go out with boys who are not Christian, too."

Laughing, Zachary said, "That's no big deal, I'll just go to church. Which one does she go to?"

Analyzing Attitude:

What was the big deal? Write your answer here. _____

_____

_____

_____

Are there times or ways you use going to church to get things you want? What? How? Write your answer here. _____

_____

_____

_____

_____

How would you describe Absalom's radical attitude of deceit? Write your answer here: _____

Turn to this chapter's introductory page. Write the word(s) in the line above on the page that introduces this chapter.

A Faithful Attitude:

Dear God, (*write your thoughts here*)

_____

_____

_____

_____

_____

Then Absalom sent secret messengers throughout the tribes of Israel to say, "As soon as you hear the sound of the trumpets, then say, 'Absalom is king in Hebron.'" Two hundred men from Jerusalem had accompanied Absalom. They had been invited as guests and went quite innocently, knowing nothing about the matter.
— 2 Samuel 15:10–11

The Lie

▼

Radical Attitude:

The "heart" of a radical attitude of deceit is lies. For Absalom to carry out his plan to get the throne away from his father, David, Absalom had to lie. In the previous session in this chapter, Absalom lied about being religious. Now to get others to follow him, he had to lie. In the Bible passage, highlight the one word that tells you that the two hundred who were with him did not know what was happening. Those who deceive others count on having innocent people around them. The innocent are able to make the lie believable.

Investigating Attitude:

The class election was a week away. The campaign had resulted in a runoff between Andrew and Nathan. Andrew had been class president since his sophomore year. He very much wanted to remain president for his senior year.

Nathan had lost to Andrew last year, and he wasn't going to let that happen again. He had to come up with something really good. During the entire campaign, both boys gave good speeches, they had catchy slogans, and they had an even following. Now Nathan knew he had to convince some of Andrew's followers to come over to his side.

"If only I can get William to switch," Nathan told Linda. "William would convince others enough for me to win!"

"Why don't you just begin saying that William is going to vote for you? " Linda said. "I'm having a party tonight. Let's tell a few people there!"

Analyzing Attitude:
What is the lie(s)? Write your answer here. _____

_____

_____

_____

Who is using a radical deceitful attitude? Write your answer here.

_____

_____

When did a lie help you deceive someone? Write your answer here.

_____

_____

What is the "heart" of a radical attitude of deceit? Write your answer here: _____. Write the same word on the introductory page for this chapter.

A Faithful Attitude:
Dear God, (write your thoughts here)

_____

_____

_____

But David continued up the Mount of Olives, weeping as he went; his head was covered and he was barefoot. All the people with him covered their heads too and were weeping as they went up. Now David had been told, "Ahithophel is among the conspirators with Absalom." So David prayed, "O LORD, turn Ahithophel's counsel into foolishness."
— 2 Samuel 15:30–31

The Hurt

▼

Radical Attitude:

David now knew for sure of Absalom's plan to take the throne. To prevent innocent bloodshed, David left Jerusalem. David did not want Jerusalem to be destroyed, so he gave the appearance he was running.

What a heartbreak for David. This son David loved so much and tried so hard not to hurt was now wanting to kill him. Highlight the word in the Bible passage that tells you that David was hurt.

Investigating Attitude:

Mom stopped outside Andrew's door. It sounded like Andrew was crying. Softly she knocked on his door. A muffled, "Come in," answered the knock.

Andrew turned over on his bed. Tears streaked his face. Mom sat on the edge of the bed. "Do you want to talk?" she asked.

With a catch in his voice, Andrew said, "I thought William was my friend. He is voting for Nathan, and now, because he is, others will too. I feel so hurt!"

Analyzing Attitude:
How did a radical deceitful attitude hurt? Write your answer here.

_____

_____

_____

What can Andrew do now? Write your answer here. _____

_____

_____

_____

Have you ever been hurt by a radical deceitful attitude? How? When? Write your answer here. _____

_____

_____

_____

_____

What one word describes the feeling when someone deceives you? Write that word here: _____. Write the same word in the fifth blank on the page that introduces this chapter.

A Faithful Attitude:
Dear God, (*write your thoughts here*)

_____

_____

_____

_____

When David arrived at the summit, where people used to worship God, Hushai the Arkite was there to meet him, his robe torn and dust on his head. David said to him, "If you go with me, you will be a burden to me. But if you return to the city and say to Absalom, 'I will be your servant, O king; I was your father's servant in the past, but now I will be your servant,' then you can help me by frustrating Ahithophel's advice. Won't the priests Zadok and Abiathar be there with you? Tell them anything you hear in the king's palace. Their two sons, Ahimaaz son of Zadok and Jonathan son of Abiathar, are there with them. Send them to me with anything you hear."

— 2 Samuel 15:32–36

Stop It!

▼

Radical Attitude:

The time had come for David to have a plan to stop the deception. He needed spies in Absalom's court. They could then inform David of Absalom's decisions. So David sent Hushai to act like he was a traitor to David.

David hoped to stop Absalom by having Hushai to give advice that contradicted Ahithophel's advice. Hushai would then send word to David about the decision Absalom made.

There always comes a time when a deceitful attitude must be stopped. David knew the time had come for him.

Investigating Attitude:

As Andrew talked to his Mom, he realized that unless the situation was resolved, he would lose the election.

"I'm going to William's," Andrew said as he stood up. "If he says that Nathan has spread a lie, I'm going to ask William to go with me to Nathan. The deceit must be stopped!"

Andrew began putting on his coat. "Thanks, Mom. I think I can handle things from here."

Analyzing Attitude:

What is the best action to take when you are faced with a deceitful attitude? Write your answer here. _____

_____

_____

_____

_____

When you have been deceived, what did you do to stop it? (or what could you have done?) Write your answer here. _____

_____

_____

_____

_____

What words tell you what to do when faced with a radical attitude of deceit? Write your answer here. _____

Write that same action in the sixth blank on the page that introduces this chapter.

A Faithful Attitude:

Dear God, (*write your thoughts here*)

_____

_____

_____

_____

_____

_____

Now Absalom happened to meet David's men. He was riding a mule, and as the mule went under the thick branches of a large oak, Absalom's head got caught in the tree. He was left hanging in midair, while the mule he was riding kept on going. . . .

Joab said, "I'm not going to wait like this for you." So he took three javelins in his hand and plunged them into Absalom's heart while Absalom was still alive in the oak tree. And ten of Joab's armor-bearers surrounded Absalom, struck him and killed him.

— 2 Samuel 18:9, 14–15

Getting What Is Coming to You

▼

Radical Attitude:
David's forces marched against Absalom's. David ordered his men not to harm Absalom.

The armies met in a forest. David's army defeated Absalom's, and many were killed. Absalom saw David's men as he was riding a mule. The mule began to run. Absalom's head—possibly his long beautiful hair—caught in the fork of an oak tree, causing Absalom to hang in midair. While hanging there, David's army captain, Joab, and his armor-bearers killed Absalom.

Because of Absalom's radical deceitful attitude, he planned to kill David. Instead, Absalom got what he intended for his father—death!

Investigating Attitude:
William told Andrew about Linda's party. He told Andrew how several there had told him they had heard he was voting for Nathan.

"I knew it was not true," William said, "So I didn't do anything. I figured everyone would know it was a lie. You and I have been good friends since elementary school."

When William and Andrew got to Nathan's house, no one was home. They decided to confront Nathan at school.

The next day, as William and Andrew were headed to the gym, they saw Nathan. Quickly, Nathan turned and went into a classroom.

As William and Andrew got close to the classroom, they heard Mr. Taylor's voice. "Nathan, I am sad to tell you that you failed the last exam. With the incomplete work on the project, you will get a D this report card. I am really sorry, because now you must withdraw from the class election."

Analyzing Attitude:

How did Nathan's deceitful attitude cause him to get what was coming to him? Write your answer here._____

_____

_____

_____

Have you ever gotten what was coming to you when you have been deceitful? How? When? Write your answer here._____

_____

_____

_____

What words describe a possible outcome of having a deceitful attitude? Write them here: _____
Write the words on the introductory page.

A Faithful Attitude:

Dear God, (*write your thoughts here*)

_____

_____

Chapter Seven

A Courageous Attitude

▼

When you hear the word *courage*, what actions do you picture? Who are some courageous people you know? Are courage and strength the same?

As you study this chapter, challenge yourself to have a radical courageous attitude. Plan to spend time each day reading one devotional section. Put yourself in the place of the Bible person Joshua. He was to lead a nation into a country God promised to them. They were to make it their homeland. Other people already lived in the land. Joshua would have to lead an entire nation in claiming the land. The job would not be easy; it would require courage.

Read Joshua 1, and note Joshua's courageous actions. Also note the childrens' actions in each investigating story that showed great courage. To help you develop a courageous attitude, record the actions in the spaces below. At the end of your study, circle the actions you will begin practicing. Write the actions on cards. Put the cards where you can look at them each day as a reminder to practice them.

Joshua

_____

_____

_____

_____

_____

Children

_____

_____

_____

_____

_____

After the death of Moses the servant of the LORD the LORD said to Joshua son of Nun, Moses' aide: "Moses my servant is dead. Now then, you and all these people, get ready to cross the Jordan River into the land I am about to give to them —to the Israelites. I will give you every place where you set your foot, as I promised Moses.
— Joshua 1:1–3

The Challenge

▼

Radical Attitude:

Joshua had been into this land one time long, long ago. He was one of the spies Moses had sent to look at the land and people, then report back. Joshua and Caleb had encouraged the people to take possession of the land, but the other spies told stories of the people being giants. Because the Israelites were afraid, God said they would wander in the wilderness until all had died. The only two who would see the new land would be Joshua and Caleb.

True to His promise, that generation died. Moses also died. Now Joshua was faced with an enormous challenge. His radical attitude of courage accepted the challenge.

Investigating Attitude:

Matthew had just celebrated his tenth birthday with a party, presents, and a huge cake. Matthew had gotten the baseball bat and glove he had been asking for. He later remembered as he lay in bed that night thinking: *I am so happy, nothing can change this!*

Several weeks later he noticed a bruise on his leg. He showed it to his parents. They asked about it and put some cream on it. Matthew forgot about it.

Some weeks later as Matthew ran to catch a fly ball with his birthday glove, he suddenly fell. He heard a snap and then felt great pain in his leg. The next he knew, he was at the hospital. He'd been poked and jabbed, and finally his leg was placed in a cast.

When Matthew went back to the doctor the next week, the doctor did not look happy. After talking to Matthew's parents, the doctor asked Matthew, "Do you have courage? You are going to have to fight the most difficult fight you've ever had. Matthew, you have cancer of the bone."

After the doctor finished talking, Matthew sat very still for a long time, and then he said, "It is some challenge, isn't it? I'm going to take the challenge and fight."

Analyzing Attitude:

Write about a challenge you are faced with. How will you show courage? _____

_____

_____

_____

_____

_____

A Faithful Attitude:

Dear God, (*write your thoughts here*)

_____

_____

_____

_____

_____

No one will be able to stand up against you all the days of your life. As I was with Moses, so I will be with you; I will never leave you nor forsake you.
— Joshua 1:5

The Source

Radical Attitude:

What a job Joshua had. He was responsible for leading more than two million people into a strange land. They were to conquer it and take it for their own.

Imagine Joshua as he looked out over the sea of tents and heard God say, "Joshua, it is now time to cross the Jordan River and take the land." Think of all the feelings Joshua had as he faced the job. Maybe he wished he could get someone else to do the job for him. Maybe he felt frightened and uncertain.

Then before Joshua could dwell on the impossible, God said, "Remember all I did for Moses? I will be with you, too. I won't ever leave you or forsake you. That is a promise!"

Joshua had the source for a radical attitude of courage.

Investigating Attitude:

Kyle and Samantha watched as their mom and dad walked around what was left of their house. They all cried as Dad gathered them into his arms. "It all seems like a bad dream," Dad kept murmuring.

They were standing outside the charred ruins of their house.

The house had burned the night before. They were grateful that no one was hurt, but they were still in shock at losing all they had.

As they stood huddled together, they did not notice that cars began to stop. One by one, people approached them. Each person had brought something to help: food, clothing, money. Soon the Stevens family was surrounded. As they looked from face to face, they saw the people from their church.

"We wanted you to know right away how sorry we are and how very much we care," Rev. Crete said. "God's great care for us helps us to show that care for you."

The Stevenses drew courage from their friends' help. They had been reminded that God cared for them and would not forsake them.

Analyzing Attitude:
Think about a time you were able to show courage because you knew God was with you. Write about that time here. _____

_____

_____

_____

_____

_____

_____

A Faithful Attitude:
Dear God, (*write your thoughts here*)

_____

_____

_____

_____

"Be strong and courageous, because you will lead these people to inherit the land I swore to their forefathers to give them. Be strong and very courageous. Be careful to obey all the law my servant Moses gave you; do not turn from it to the right or to the left, that you may be successful wherever you go."

— Joshua 1:6–7

Hidden Strength

▼

Radical Attitude:

Joshua had over two million people to lead to the land God had promised their forefathers (ancestors). In the Bible passage, highlight the three things God told Joshua He would do for him. Circle the words that tell what Joshua would need. God knew for Joshua to do his job, Joshua must be strong as well as courageous. This strength would need to be inner strength as well as physical strength.

Investigating Attitude:

Jason and Kelly saw them as they turned the corner. The same four boys that had stopped them last week.

"It's too late to run," Kelly said. "If either one of us can distract them, run in whatever direction you can. We'll meet at my house."

"OK, great idea! Now here they come, quiet!" said Jason.

The boys faced Kelly and Jason. "We have a really good deal for you," one of the boys said. "We have decided to let you be in our gang. We don't usually allow two in at a time, but we've been watching you. You work well together. So what do you say? It had better not be no!"

The other three boys began telling Kelly and Jason some of the things they'd done. They were bragging about damage they had done to the neighborhood.

Jason said, "We are honored that you would want us to be in your gang. There is a problem. We already belong to a gang, it is called Christians' gang."

"Yeah," Kelly added, "To belong, you have to really be strong and have courage. We do things for others that help rather than destroy. That takes strength and courage."

The four boys began to laugh. One had even taken a knife out of his pocket and was beginning to open it.

Without a word, Kelly ran one way and Jason the other.

Analyzing Attitude:
How did Jason and Kelly show strength? When have you had to show strength to get out of a bad situation? Write about it here.

_____

_____

_____

_____

_____

_____

A Faithful Attitude:
Dear God, (*write your thoughts here*)

_____

_____

_____

_____

"Do not let this Book of the Law depart from your mouth; meditate on it day and night, so that you may be careful to do everything written in it. Then you will be prosperous and successful. Have I not commanded you? Be strong and courageous. Do not be terrified; do not be discouraged, for the LORD your God will be with you wherever you go."
— Joshua 1:8–9

Remember the Rules

▼

Radical Attitude:

During the time the nation of Israel wandered in the desert, they obeyed God's laws. They taught the new generation to obey God's laws. God reminded Joshua the way to be courageous is to obey the laws.

Investigating Attitude:

Caroline's class was going white water rafting. Mrs. Davis and the girls had practiced putting their tents up in Mrs. Davis' back yard. Each girl had a specific task to do in preparing the meals. The trip was special.

As the group traveled to the campgrounds, Mrs. Davis reminded the girls of the rules they had made. "We will all have a good safe time if we stick to the rules," Mrs. Davis said.

When they arrived at the canoe area, the girls were assigned a canoe and a guide. Before beginning, the guide said, "Here are the rules. If you fail to abide by them, you could put all of our lives in danger."

Vicki whispered to Caroline, "Rules, rules, rules! That's all I have heard since beginning this trip."

Later as the girls were rafting down the river, all was smooth. Suddenly, around a curve, they hit the rapids. Vicki wasn't paying attention. Then everything happened quickly. Vicki and Caroline were in the water. Vicki did not surface. Caroline abruptly seemed to bounce to the surface. Looking around, she saw Vicki.

Sometime later the girls were resting on the bank. "Thank you, Caroline. How did you get me out?" Vicki asked.

"I almost wasn't able to, and then I remembered the rules. I quit fighting the water and floated to you. Then I remember the rule to check the rock to see if you were hung. The rules saved us both," Caroline said.

Analyzing Attitude:
Write about a time when remembering the rules helped you to be courageous._____

_____

_____

_____

_____

_____

_____

A Faithful Attitude:
Dear God, (*write your thoughts here*)

_____

_____

_____

_____

"Be strong and courageous, because you will lead these people to inherit the land I swore to their forefathers to give them. Be strong and very courageous. Be careful to obey all the law my servant Moses gave you; do not turn from it to the right or to the left, that you may be successful wherever you go. Do not let this Book of the Law depart from your mouth; meditate on it day and night, so that you may be careful to do everything written in it. Then you will be prosperous and successful. Have I not commanded you? Be strong and courageous. Do not be terrified; do not be discouraged, for the LORD your God will be with you wherever you go."
— Joshua 1:6–9

Success with God's Help

▼

Radical Attitude:

Joshua needed courage to succeed in his job. He wanted to be successful. He needed to be successful because of the people who depended on him.

Joshua must have had whirling thoughts as he made the preparation necessary to do his job. How good he must have felt as he listened to God. Yet, how uncertain, too.

Look in the Bible passage to find the three things God said Joshua must do to succeed.

Investigating Attitude:

Zachary had been going to the drug rehab sessions for over a year. He had been on drugs for most of his life. One day he had gone with a youth group on a retreat. For the first time he heard that Jesus Christ had come to give abundant life. Zachary knew that he had always looked for that kind of life in drugs.

The year had been long and hard. Zachary had tried to do everything that was expected. Still he had many ups and downs as he rid his body of the drugs. Always the youth group had given him encouragement and support to follow the rehab rules. Now, as he sat in the last session, joy flooded throughout him. He had completed the course. He had made it!

Analyzing Attitude:

You may think that success is being rich or famous, having power or influence. Success can only be measured by God's standards. God's opinion is the only one that really matters. Think of your successes during the past week. Write about them here. _____

_____

_____

_____

_____

_____

_____

_____

_____

_____

A Faithful Attitude:

Dear God, (*write your thoughts here*)

_____

_____

_____

_____

_____

But to the Reubenites, the Gadites and the half-tribe of Manasseh, Joshua said, "Remember the command that Moses the servant of the LORD gave you: The LORD your God is giving you rest and has granted you this land. Your wives, your children and your livestock may stay in the land that Moses gave you east of the Jordan, but all your fighting men, fully armed, must cross over ahead of your brothers. You are to help your brothers."
— Joshua 1:12–14

Please Help

▼

Radical Attitude:
The tribes of Reuben and Gad and the half-tribe of Manasseh had asked Moses if they could settle just east of the promised land. The land was just what they wanted for their large flocks. Moses agreed to give them the land, but they were to meet one condition. They were to help the others when the time came to conquer the land. After the Israelites were settled, these tribes could then return. Now the time had come. Joshua said to them "Come help your brothers." Joshua realized it takes a radical courageous attitude to ask for help.

Investigating Attitude:
The moving van slowly drove away. Richard and Tammy stood watching. This was not the first time they had moved.

"I really hate to leave," Tammy said.

"I know," Richard answered. "It seems as though every time I really like a place, Dad gets transferred."

"I just feel so lonesome, and I'll never have a best friend," Tammy said, as a tear rolled down her cheek. "It is so scary to start another new school. Oh, Richard, I'm so scared. Please help!"

Analyzing Attitude:

A person with a radical courageous attitude is willing to ask for help. Think about something you need to do. Do you need to ask for help? Write about what you will do here._____

_____

_____

_____

_____

_____

_____

_____

_____

_____

_____

_____

_____

_____

A Faithful Attitude:

Dear God, (*write your thoughts here*)

_____

_____

_____

_____

_____

Then they answered Joshua, "Whatever you have commanded us we will do, and wherever you send us we will go. Just as we fully obeyed Moses, so we will obey you. Only may the LORD your God be with you as he was with Moses. Whoever rebels against your word and does not obey your words, whatever you may command them, will be put to death. Only be strong and courageous!"

— Joshua 1:16–18

Where Does Courage Come From?

▼

Radical Attitude:

Joshua must have asked himself more than once, "Where will I get the courage to do what God wants?"

For Joshua to lead the Israelites into their new land, ALL of the people had to agree to the leader's plan, pledge themselves to obey it, and put his principles into action.

Three times God told Joshua to be strong and courageous. In the Bible passage, highlight what the people said that encouraged Joshua.

Joshua's source of courage was his trust in God.

Investigating Attitude:

Charles had played his best, but they had lost the game. Suddenly he was pushed against the fence.

"You big lug! You hog! You think you're the only one on the team! If you'd get out of the way, some of the rest of us could make some points," Eddie shouted in Charles' face.

Charles could not believe what he was hearing. He did not think he had tried to hog the field. The soccer game had been so fast and close that he had not had time to think about how he had played.

Before Charles could answer, Eddie ran from the field.

Charles spent a restless evening. Finally he told his parents about his encounter with Eddie. They listened and let him express his anger.

"You're the team captain, Charles," his father said. "You are the team leader. The whole team will be watching to see how you handle this."

Later in his room, Charles noticed his Bible on the table beside his bed. "I have my answer," Charles said.

Analyzing Attitude:

As you studied this chapter, you may have discovered, like Joshua, that God is the source of courage.

Courage is a radical attitude that must be developed. Find the verses and match the words by writing the number in the blank to review what you have learned about courage.

1. Joshua 1:1–3 _____ accepts help
2. Joshua 1:5 _____ remembers rules
3. Joshua 1:6–7 _____ depends upon God
4. Joshua 1:8 _____ requires strength
5. Joshua 1:8 _____ is from God
6. Joshua 1:12–14 _____ accepts a challenge
7. Joshua 1:16–18 _____ brings success

Put Joshua's experience to work for you as you work toward a radical courageous attitude.

A Faithful Attitude:

Dear God, (write your thoughts here)

_____

_____

_____

Chapter Eight

A Deal-making Attitude

▼

As you are growing in your relationship with God and others, do you "make deals?" I think we all do! Yet, God's plan for us is to develop radical attitudes that eliminate deals or bargains. To do that, we need to understand the motives or reasons for making deals. We also must be willing to stop making deals and allow God to work His plan. You will not find deal-making habits easy to break. The challenge for a radical attitude that expresses faith is to break the habit!

In this chapter you will find the following pattern for making deals:

1. Desire for success
2. Possible conflict
3. Deal made to achieve goal
4. Success achieved

5. Terms of deal honored (kept)

6. Grief—empty feeling of success

Write this pattern on a card. Put the card where you can be reminded not to make deals.

In preparation for this chapter, read Judges 11. Highlight with a marker the pattern of the deal that Jephthah made.

Jephthah said to them, "Didn't you hate me and drive me from my father's house? Why do you come to me now, when you're in trouble?" The elders of Gilead said to him, "Nevertheless, we are turning to you now; come with us to fight the Ammonites, and you will be our head over all who live in Gilead." Jephthah answered, "Suppose you take me back to fight the Ammonites and the LORD gives them to me—will I really be your head?" The elders of Gilead replied, "The LORD is our witness; we will certainly do as you say."
— Judges 11:7–10

I Want

▼

Radical Attitude:

The nation of Israel had forgotten that God planned for them to have their own land and that they were to tell the rest of their world about God. They were to demonstrate God's desire for an open and loving relationship with Him. They were to demonstrate how to worship and follow God. The account of Jephthah shows how far the people had strayed from God's purposes.

Read Judges 11:1–6 to discover the kind of person Jephthah was. Quite a rebel! Now, because the Ammonites were constantly raiding their cities and taking their possessions, the Israelites in Gilead wanted Jephthah to take command and fight them.

The deal the elders made with Jephthah was: _____

_____

What do you think caused Jephthah to make the deal?

_____

_____

_____

Investigating Attitude:

"I'm so fat!" Jasmine said as she looked at herself in the mirror. "I'd do anything to look like Tara."

Jasmine had not always been fat. She seemed to have put on weight all of a sudden. Her mother said it was a phase and she would lose it. Jasmine thought her mother was just saying that to make her feel good. What if it wasn't a phase? What if she just kept getting bigger? Jasmine was miserable.

Plopping down on the floor with a bowl of popcorn, Jasmine flipped on the TV. As she was flicking the channels, she heard a girl talking about losing weight. Jasmine listened as the girl told of making herself throw up to cause her to eliminate food.

Jasmine stopped listening and thought, *I want to be liked. I want to be chosen for things. I want . . .*

Analyzing Attitude:

Remember the plan for making deals always begins with a desire.

What was Jephthah's desire? _____

_____

What was Jasmine's desire? _____

_____

Make a list of things you desire. _____

_____

_____

A Faithful Attitude:

Dear God, (*write your thoughts here*)

_____

_____

_____

"Now since the LORD, the God of Israel, has driven the Amorites out before his people Israel, what right have you to take it over? Will you not take what your god Chemosh give you? Likewise, whatever the LORD, our God has given us, we will possess. . . . For three hundred years Israel occupied Heshbon, Aroer, the surrounding settlements and all the towns along the Arnon. Why didn't you retake them during that time? I have not wronged you, but you are doing me wrong by waging war against me. Let the LORD, the Judge, decide the dispute this day between the Israelites and the Ammonites."

— Judges 11:23–27

The Attempt

▼

Radical Attitude:

Jephthah sent messengers to the king of the Ammonites to ask why the land of Gilead had been attacked. The king sent word back that the Israelites had stolen the land and he wanted it back. So Jephthah sent another message to the king. In the message, Jephthah gave three arguments against the king's claim for the land. Jephthah tried to solve the problem.

Investigating Attitude:

Mother passed Jasmine's room. She saw Jasmine eating popcorn and watching TV. She also saw the scowl on Jasmine's face.

"Are you all right?" Mother said as she paused at the door.

"Sure. Why?" answered Jasmine.

Mother laughed. "Well, that scowl on you face could stop a train!"

"I'm just so fat, I hate myself," Jasmine replied, with tears beginning to form.

Mother sat down by Jasmine. "Jasmine," she said. "I was fat at your age, too. So was your Dad. Look at us now. You'll outgrow it."

"You keep saying that," Jasmine almost shouted. "I don't want to wait until I'm your age. I'm not getting to do anything now!"

Mother hugged Jasmine to her. "Now, now," she said. "You can do some things now. Why not put the popcorn away? Go ride your bike till time for dinner. You could . . . "

Analyzing Attitude:

How did Jasmine respond to her mother's assurances that Jasmine would outgrow her tendency to be fat? _____

_____

Think about your desires. Do some of them seem unattainable? Has anyone attempted to help you understand how the difficulties might be overcome? List the obstacles to your desires and the suggestions you have been given for overcoming them.

Obstacles	Suggestions
_____	_____
_____	_____
_____	_____
_____	_____
_____	_____
_____	_____

A Faithful Attitude:

Dear God, (*write your thoughts here*)

_____

_____

_____

The king of Ammon, however, paid no attention to the message Jephthah sent him.
— Judges 11:28

Refused!

▼

Radical Attitude:
Jephthah had attempted to resolve the conflict between the Ammonite king and the Israelites. The king refused the peace that was offered, and Jephthah prepared his troops for battle.

At this point, it seems Jephthah was justified totally. These events, however, created a situation where Jephthah was able to make good on his deal to achieve his own desires. (Read Judges 11:7–10 again to remind yourself of the deal Jephthah made with the elders.)

Investigating Attitude:
Mother had been trying to help Jasmine. She knew Jasmine did not like being fat She was suggesting that Jasmine ride her bike before dinner when Jasmine jerked away and stormed out of the house.

Shouting over her shoulder, Jasmine said, "You don't understand at all! Get off my back." The house shook as the door slammed behind Jasmine.

Storming down the sidewalk, Jasmine said, "I'll just show them!"

Analyzing Attitude:

With every deal, there may be conflicts that will have to be handled. What choices did Jasmine have? Put your thoughts here.

_____

_____

_____

Jasmine refused her mother's offer to help, just as the Ammonite king refused, or ignored, Jephthah's attempt to resolve their conflict. Have you refused someone's attempt to help you with a conflict in your life? Write about your refusal here.

_____

_____

_____

Has anyone refused to accept your attempt to smooth out a conflict? _____ How did you respond to that rejection?

_____

_____

_____

In the next session we will see how Jephthah responded to the Ammonite king's refusal by making a deal with God.

A Faithful Attitude:

Dear God, (_write your thoughts here_)

_____

_____

_____

And Jephthah made a vow to the LORD, "If you give the Ammonites into my hands, whatever comes out of the door of my house to meet me when I return in triumph from the Ammonites will be the LORD'S, and I will sacrifice it as a burnt offering."

— Judges 11:30–31

The Deal

▼

Radical Attitude:

We are not told how Jephthah knew about God. However he heard about God, Jephthah recognized the Lord as the people's true leader. He knew God was the only one who could really lead them in conquering their enemies.

Although Jephthah relied on God, he had not learned a valuable truth: Making deals is not necessary for God to provide His help.

Highlight what Jephthah promised God for a victory in battle.

Investigating Attitude:

Jasmine fumed as she walked. "I'll just show her! I'll just show everybody!" she said. "I'll lose weight any way I have to, but I *will* lose it.

As she walked she calmed down. *Dear God,* she thought. *If you will let me lose twenty pounds, I'll go on that mission trip the youth are planning.*

Jasmine felt better. She went to the drugstore and bought some stuff to make her not want to eat. Then she went home and forced herself to vomit.

Analyzing Attitude:

"Wow," you may be saying. "What a dumb thing to do!" Or you may be doing just what Jasmine did. The most dangerous part of a bargaining attitude is making quick promises. Think about your desires. Have you made deals with God? Have you made promises? Complete the chart below:

Desire	Deal	Promise
_____	_____	_____
_____	_____	_____
_____	_____	_____
_____	_____	_____
_____	_____	_____

How serious did you take your promise? Place a check mark next to the promises you have kept. Remember God wants to be very personal to you. *He is for real!* He is not like a fictional character who gives you what you want when you wish real hard and behave real well. He wants to be and work alongside you.

A Faithful Attitude:

Dear God, (*write your thoughts here*)

_____

_____

_____

_____

_____

_____

Then Jephthah went over to fight the Ammonites, and the LORD gave them into his hands. He devastated twenty towns from Aroer to the vicinity of Minnith, and as far as Abel Keramim. Thus Israel subdued Ammon.

— Judges 11:32–34

Success Achieved

▼

Radical Attitude:

Off Jephthah went to fight. Highlight the word in the Bible passage that tells you he was successful. Put yourself in Jephthah's place. Think about what he had won—remember his deal! Be Jephthah. Write a message to the elders of Israel here.

Message:

_____

_____

_____

Investigating Attitude:

"Jasmine," Tara called. "Is that really you? I haven't seen you for months. Wow, you have really lost weight! How did you do it?" Tara had stopped Jasmine when they saw each other at the mall.

"Thanks," Jasmine said. "I've been working on it."

"Well, I'll count on you being on my team Saturday. A bunch of us are getting together. You do look good. Gotta go, I'll see you

Saturday at the soccer field." Tara headed on down the mall.

Jasmine smiled as she continued walking. Others began to comment on how much weight she had lost. She pushed the feeling of dizziness aside. *Everything is great! This is what I wanted,* she thought.

Analyzing Attitude:

A sad fact about making deals is they often bring success. Compare Jephthah's and Jasmine's successes by completing the following:

	Jephthah	Jasmine
Feelings	_____	_____
	_____	_____
	_____	_____
	_____	_____
Actions	_____	_____
	_____	_____
	_____	_____
Reward	_____	_____
	_____	_____
	_____	_____

A Faithful Attitude:

Dear God, (*write your thoughts here*)

_____

_____

_____

When Jephthah returned to his home in Mizpah, who should come out to meet him but his daughter, dancing to the sound of tambourines! She was an only child. Except for her he had neither son nor daughter. When he saw her, he tore his clothes and cried, "Oh! My daughter! You have made me miserable and wretched, because I have made a vow to the LORD that I cannot break.

— Judges 11:34–35

Keeping the Promise

▼

Radical Attitude:

This is one of the saddest accounts in the Bible. Jephthah had fought against a mighty army and won. Spirits were high. The people heard about the victory and knew they would not have to live in constant fear any longer.

Jephthah approached his house with excitement and the thrill of victory. Suddenly he stopped. Highlight in the Bible passage what Jephthah saw.

Jephthah instantly remembered his vow when he saw his only child, his daughter, come dancing from his home. Suddenly he realized the time had come for him to keep his promise to God.

Investigating Attitude:

Jasmine could hardly wait for Saturday. This was the first time Tara had ever asked her to play on her team.

Jasmine hoped that pesky dizziness would go away. Her stomach was churning, but she ignored it. This opportunity to play with Tara was what she had always wanted.

Running toward the field, Jasmine stumbled. Quickly she regained her balance.

"Here she is," called Tara. "See, I told you that you would not know her. Look how thin she is!"

Everyone clustered around Jasmine. They were all telling her how great she looked.

"Hey, let's get going with the game," said Beth. "I have to baby-sit later. I can't stay all day!"

They had been playing about fifteen minutes, when suddenly Jasmine could not seem to focus her eyes. The ball was coming right to her. She wanted to return it, but she could not seem to move. That is the last she remembered.

She awoke to anxious faces. Slowly she realized she was at the hospital.

Analyzing Attitude:

When deals are made, the time comes when the promise must be kept or honored. Often keeping the promise is very costly. Think about what Jephthah's and Jasmine's deals cost them personally, and complete the following

Jephthah's Deals   Cost of Deal

_____   _____

_____   _____

Jasmine's Deals   Cost of Deal

_____   _____

_____   _____

A Faithful Attitude:

Dear God, (*write your thoughts here*)

_____

_____

_____

"My father," she replied, "you have given your word to the LORD. Do to me just as you promised, now that the LORD has avenged you of your enemies, the Ammonites."
— Judges 11:36

A Deal Is a Deal

▼

Radical Attitude:

The Bible leaves out many details that you and I would like to know. Think of what may have happened between Judges 11:35 and 36. Several days may have passed between the verses.

The Bible is an account of real people and real events. Just as God worked in the lives of those real people in the Bible, He wants you to know He will do the same for you. A bargaining attitude results in grief because promises must be kept—a deal is a deal! God does not want promises for the future, He wants you to depend on Him completely.

Investigating Attitude:

Jasmine was in the hospital for a week. She could hardly stand to look at the sadness in her parents' eyes.

"You'll have to come to the clinic once a week," the doctor said. "We want to help you understand the choices you made. We also want you to understand what you did to your body. It will not be easy. It will not be something you can 'undo' quickly. You cannot go anywhere or do anything that will keep you from these appointments."

How sad Jasmine felt. Now she could not go on the mission trip. She could not do anything for the rest of the summer. What a mess she had made. What a lousy deal she had made to become thin!

Analyzing Attitude:
Look back at the pattern for making deals. As you accept the challenge to change a deal-making attitude, look at the possible actions for changing.

Deal-Making Plan	Actions for Radical Change
1. Desire for success	1. List reasons for deal
2. Possible conflict	2. List conflicts/choices
3. Deal made to achieve goal	3. List why you shouldn't make deal
4. Success achieved	4. List cost of success
5. Terms of deal honored	5. List results
6. Grief	6. List hidden grief

Add the actions for a radical change to the back of the card you made at the first of the chapter. Keep the card to remind you each time you are about to make a deal.

A Faithful Attitude:
Dear God, (*write your thoughts here*)

_____

_____

_____

_____

_____

Chapter Nine

A Taunting Attitude

▼

"You'll never make it!"
"I knew I couldn't count on you!"
"You always make me!"
"Can I, can I, can I, can I, huh?"

Taunting can be done in many ways, at any time, and by anyone. Taunting is more than words or actions. It is a desire within the persons doing the taunting to cause harm, and a desire for failure of others so that they themselves can succeed. Taunting reflects a need for recognition or attention.

Taunting almost did not make it into this book, but I began to make a mark in a notebook of all the taunting I saw or heard. In one day, I had over fifty marks. Thus, I felt a need exists for us to study this ugly, unkind, hurting attitude. You see, God tells us when we know about something harmful, and then we have a responsibility to stop.

Your challenge in this chapter is to recognize and then to stop taunting. In the space below, write about taunts you have given and received. You need to include the taunting you've received to understand how hurtful it is.

_____

_____

_____

_____

_____

_____

_____

_____

_____

_____

_____

_____

_____

_____

_____

Read Nehemiah 1—9. Contrast taunting with Nehemiah's behavior as you study. In a notebook, write what you learn about Nehemiah.

But when Sanballat the Horonite, Tobiah the Ammonite official and Geshem the Arab heard about it, they mocked and ridiculed us. "What is this you are doing?" they asked. "Are you rebelling against the king?" I answered them by saying, "The God of heaven will give us success. We his servants will start rebuilding, but as for you, you have no share in Jerusalem or any claim or historic right to it."

— Nehemiah 2:19–20

He's Bugging Me!

▼

Radical Attitude:

Nehemiah had undertaken an impossible task in the eyes of those around him. The walls of Jerusalem had been torn down. Nehemiah received permission from the king to go back and rebuild the walls. Walls were a city's primary means of protection. The walls were often wide enough to drive a chariot and horses on them. Nehemiah's task was not easy.

The neighboring governors heard about Nehemiah's plans. Immediately they began taunting. Their intention was to place doubt. They wanted the king to think these Jews could begin a rebellion. But the real truth was that these governors feared they might lose control of land and their secure positions.

A radical taunting attitude belittles good by placing doubt.

Investigating Attitude:

The history project was due on Monday. Lizabeth had worked hard for several weeks on hers. Her folks had offered suggestions, but they had not done one single thing on it. The whole project was Lizabeth's.

Just as she was putting the last flag in place, she heard Natalie's voice.

"Wow,"Natalie said as she entered the room."Spectacular job. Did your folks do this?"

Quickly Lizabeth assured her that they had not. She even showed Natalie some mistakes she'd had to clean up.

"There is so much here," Natalie said. "Don't you think it's a bit much? It's great! But it is so big!"

Analyzing Attitude:
Remember: A person with a radical taunting attitude places doubt. How did Natalie taunt Lizabeth? _____

_____

_____

_____

To stop a taunting attitude, look at Nehemiah's answer in the Bible passage. Write in the columns below what you've learned about taunting and what you discovered Nehemiah did to stop the taunting. Add how you plan to stop.

Have Learned   How to Stop

_____   _____

_____   _____

_____   _____

_____   _____

A Faithful Attitude:
Dear God, (*write your thoughts here*)

_____

_____

_____

When Sanballat heard that we were rebuilding the wall, he became angry and was greatly incensed. He ridiculed the Jews, and in the presence of his associates and the army of Samaria, he said, "What are those feeble Jews doing? Will they restore their wall? Will they offer sacrifices? Will they finish in a day? Can they bring the stones back to life from those heaps of rubble—burned as they are?" Tobiah the Ammonite, who was at his side, said, "What they are building—if even a fox climbed up on it, he would break down their wall of stones!" Hear us, O our God . . .
— Nehemiah 4:1–4

Ha! Ha! You Can't!

▼

Radical Attitude:

Building the wall was back-breaking, hard work. Picture the people, lifting, scraping, stacking stone after stone. Some mixed the mud, others collected the rocks, others stacked. From sunup to sundown they worked. Then they heard it. Taunting, from all around. Laughing, pointing, and shouting about the hard work they had done. What would you have done? Nehemiah had the secret to face the taunting. Who did he turn to for help?

A radical taunting attitude makes fun of good work.

Write in the space below the ways the good work was made fun of.

_____

_____

Investigating Attitude:

Benjamin and his family looked sleepily at each other as they ate breakfast. The sun had not even begun to rise.

"Remember to get the tools, Ben. Hayley, you get the extra jugs of water we collected last night. Carly, you can bring the sack with the sandwiches. Mom and I will carry the heavy things. Let's finish and get on our way," Dad said.

The Smiths were joining with their neighbors to clean out a vacant lot where trash, broken bottles, and filth had collected. Gangs of children had begun to hang out there. Now the neighborhood had decided to make it a park. It would be a hard and dirty job.

The sun beat down on the small group that worked. The progress was slow, yet they worked on.

"Hey," a voice shouted. "Just what do you think you are doing? Making mud pies? Ha, Ha, Ha," they taunted.

"Yeah, look at them," another voice said. "Little good they can do!"

Analyzing Attitude:

Remember: A person with a radical taunting attitude makes fun of good work. How were the workers taunted? Write your answer here.

_____

_____

To stop a taunting attitude, remember Nehemiah's answer. Write what you learned about taunting in this session. How will you stop taunting?

What I Have Learned   How to Stop

_____   _____

_____   _____

_____   _____

_____   _____

A Faithful Attitude:

Dear God, (*write your thoughts here*)

_____

_____

When word came to Sanballat, Tobiah, Geshem the Arab and the rest of our enemies that I had rebuilt the wall and not a gap was left in it . . . Sanballat and Geshem sent me this message: "Come, let us meet together in one of the villages on the plain of Ono." But they were scheming to harm me; so I sent messengers to them with this reply: "I am carrying on a great project and cannot go down. Why should the work stop while I leave it and go down to you?"

— Nehemiah 6:1–3

False Peace

▼

Radical Attitude:

Sanballat and Tobiah realized the wall was almost complete. They were desperate! All their efforts to stop the work had failed to this point. They would try a new approach. They would act like friends. They would offer to make peace.

The plain of Ono was about twenty miles northwest of Jerusalem. If they could get Nehemiah to go there, they could ambush him on the way. Without their leader, the people would quit the work.

A person with a taunting attitude will offer false peace. In the space, write why the peace offered Nehemiah was false.

Investigating Attitude:

"Sisters! They are such a pain!" Richard said disgustedly. "I can't do anything without getting fussed at. It's all her doing. She expects me to let her do everything I do! Sisters, yuck!"

John and Richard were late for ball practice. Richard had been receiving a "talking to" from his mom. Now as the boys were hurrying along, Richard was telling John what happened.

"We went along with Mom to the grocery store. I needed some things for school. Otherwise I would not have gone. She started it in the car. She started begging to go with me to the game. I tried to explain, but she wouldn't listen. All I did was call her a few names! Copycat, baby, monkey see, monkey do . . . nothing really bad! Besides, I said I was sorry before we got out at the grocery. Now I'm in big trouble! Sisters, yuck!"

Analyzing Attitude:

Remember: A person with a radical taunting attitude offers false peace. How was the peace Richard offered to his sister false? Put your answer here. _____

_____

_____

Look at Nehemiah's response to false peace. He kept focused on his responsibility. As you have studied about false peace and taunting, write what you have discovered. Write how you plan to stop.

What I Have Learned	How to Stop
_____	_____
_____	_____
_____	_____
_____	_____

A Faithful Attitude:

Dear God, (*write your thoughts here*)

_____

_____

Then the fifth time, Sanballat sent his aide to me with the same message, and in his hand was an unsealed letter in which was written: "It is reported among the nations—and Geshem says it is true—that you and the Jews are plotting to revolt, and therefore you are building the wall. Moreover, according to these reports you are about to become their king and have even appointed prophets to make this proclamation about you in Jerusalem: 'There is a king in Judah!' Now this report will get back to the king; so come, let us confer together." I sent him this reply: "Nothing like what you are saying is happening; you are just making it up out of your head."
— Nehemiah 6:5–8

The Lie

▼

Radical Attitude:

Nehemiah's enemies had made fun of the good, they had ridiculed the work, and they had made an attempt to make false peace. Now they began to taunt the person of Nehemiah. They planted rumors, deceit, and false reports. Nothing hurts worse than to receive personal, unjustified criticism.

A radical taunting attitude attacks by lying.

Investigating Attitude:

Juan, Vincent, and Jesse were sitting in the principal's office. Juan's heart was beating fast. He had never been involved in anything like this. He did not know what to do. Here's how it began.

English class was a drag. They were reading poems and most of the students were not "getting into" poetry. The teacher had worked hard to make the subject interesting. She had divided the class into smaller groups. Each group was to act out their assigned poem. That part had gone great. Juan, Vincent, and Jesse had gotten a standing ovation for their group's presentation. Then the disaster struck!

Mrs. Lutz gave a pop quiz. Mrs. Lutz had suddenly called Juan,

Vincent, and Jesse out of the room. She was holding a note. She looked sad.

"Boys," Mrs. Lutz said. "This note says that you boys have a secret signal system for giving each other the answers on tests. I am so very disappointed in all of you. You are all making nearly the same grades and have been all year. I just don't know what to believe."

The three boys had tried to tell her the note was not true. They all were shocked that someone would tell such a lie. Yet here they sat!

Analyzing Attitude:
Remember: A person who has a radical taunting attitude will lie. What was the lie about Juan, Vincent, and Jesse? _____

_____

_____

Write what you have learned and how to stop a taunting attitude that resorts to lying.

What I Have Learned	How to Stop
_____	_____
_____	_____
_____	_____
_____	_____

A Faithful Attitude:
Dear God, (*write your thoughts here*)

_____

_____

_____

I sent him this reply: "Nothing like what you are saying is happening; you are just making it up out of your head." They were all trying to frighten us, thinking, "Their hands will get too weak for the work, and it will not be completed." But I prayed, "Now strengthen my hands."

— Nehemiah 6:8–9

The Truth!

▼

Radical Attitude:

Nehemiah was facing a most difficult situation. His enemies were taunting him with a rumor that Nehemiah had led the people to proclaim him as their king. Nothing was farther from the truth. Yet what could he do?

A radical taunting attitude should be answered with a strong refusal. Nehemiah could have taken time from the work to answer or to fight the rumor. Nehemiah could have gathered his people around and let them fight the rumor with him. What did Nehemiah choose to do? Put your answer here.

Investigating Attitude:

Juan, Vincent, and Jesse were in a real mess. As they sat outside the principal's office, they knew they were in big trouble. The worst part about the whole thing was the whole thing was a lie!

The boys had made several attempts to comfort each other, but they were told not to talk. Finally the door opened. The principal told them to go into his office.

After many questions and much stress, Juan said, "Mr. Todd, I know it looks bad for us. We have tried to tell you the truth, but even the truth makes us look guilty. We can't fight a lie. Just look at our work. All year we have done well in all of our subjects. We are not in every class together. Look at our work. Then watch what we do the rest of the year. This will hurt us, but please give us a chance."

Analyzing Attitude:
Remember: A radical taunting attitude should be answered with a strong refusal (reply). How did Juan reply? Write your answer here.

_____

_____

To stop a radical taunting attitude, you must know your strengths. Look at Nehemiah's reply in the Bible passage. Complete the following by writing what you learned about taunting in this session. Then write how to stop taunting. Be sure to add how you plan stop taunting others.

What I Have Learned	How to Stop
_____	_____
_____	_____
_____	_____
_____	_____

A Faithful Attitude:
Dear God, (*write your thoughts here*)

_____

_____

_____

So the wall was completed on the twenty-fifth of Elul, in fifty-two days. When all our enemies heard about this, all the surrounding nations were afraid and lost their self-confidence, because they realized that this work had been done with the help of our God.
— Nehemiah 6:15–16

The Loser

▼

Radical Attitude:

The impossible task was finished. Not only was the wall rebuilt, but they completed it in fifty-two days. During all of the work the taunting went on. Picture the people working. Visualize the constant taunting. How the fifty-two days must have seemed like forever! How often the taunting must have made the people feel depressed!

Highlight in the Bible passage what was lost as a result of taunting.

Taunting behavior results in failure (loss). How did Sanballat, Tobiah, and Geshem's taunting fail? What was their loss? Write your answer here. _____

_____

_____

Investigating Attitude:

Go back in each session of this chapter and list below the taunting that took place. Name the person or persons who ridiculed Nehemiah and the Jews who helped him. Next to their names, write the taunting insults.

Session	Person(s)	Taunting
_____	_____	_____
_____	_____	_____
_____	_____	_____
_____	_____	_____
_____	_____	_____

Analyzing Attitude:

Remember: A person with a radical taunting attitude often fails. Look at the people in each session who taunted. How did they fail (lose)? Put your answer here._____

_____

_____

To stop a radical taunting attitude, you must remember that taunting fails. Write in the columns what you have discovered about taunting and how to stop it.

What I Have Learned	How to Stop
_____	_____
_____	_____
_____	_____
_____	_____

A Faithful Attitude:

Dear God, (*write your thoughts here*)

_____

_____

_____

So on the first day of the seventh month Ezra the priest brought the Law before the assembly, which was made up of men and women and all who were able to understand. He read it aloud from daybreak till noon as he faced the square before the Water Gate in the presence of the men, women and others who could understand. And all the people listened attentively to the Book of the Law.
—Nehemiah 8:2–3

The Right Answer!

▼

Radical Attitude:

Often the person telling the story of Nehemiah stops when the wall was complete. The best is yet to come!

The people gathered in the center of Jerusalem to hear Ezra read the Book of the Law. To be able to correctly answer taunts and insults, the people needed to know God's instruction. So Ezra, the priest, read aloud God's instruction. Can you imagine standing from daybreak till noon listening to the Bible being read aloud?

A radical taunting attitude can only be stopped with the right answers from God's Word. What word indicates that what was read was serious and meant to be kept?
Write that word here: _____

Investigating Attitude:

Write here about the last time you were guilty of taunting.

_____

_____

_____

Analyzing Attitude:

Remember: To stop a radical taunting attitude, you must know God's Word. Find these verses. Next to each one, write how it will stop a taunt.

Exodus 20:12 _____

Psalm 145:21 _____

Proverbs 8:7 _____

Luke 6:31 _____

Hebrews 13:17_____

1 John 4:11 _____

A Faithful Attitude:
Dear God, (write your thoughts here)

_____
_____
_____
_____
_____

Chapter Ten

A Prayerful Attitude

▼

Prayer is talking to God. That is such a simple statement, yet praying can be hard to do.

The development of a radical attitude of prayer is directly related to how you think about God. In the box, write your description of God. Describe fully how you think He looks, thinks, and the kind of being He is.

In this chapter you will explore how a radical prayerful attitude is helpful, what it can do for you, and why it is necessary to have a fun, exciting, and successful life.

Hezekiah was a great and good king, but he failed to be recorded as a mighty king like David, because he did not consider the future. Yet Hezekiah had a radical attitude of prayer. Read 2 Kings 18—20 to have the whole picture.

Your understanding of God will lead to a radical prayerful attitude. It is in prayer that you will gain understanding of His will and plan for you.

In the third year of Hoshea son of Elah king of Israel, Hezekiah son of Ahaz king of Judah began to reign. He was twenty-five years old when he became king, and he reigned in Jerusalem twenty-nine years. His mother's name was Abijah daughter of Zechariah. He did what was right in the eyes of the LORD, just as his father David had done. He removed the high places, smashed the sacred stones and cut down the Asherah poles. He broke into pieces the bronze snake Moses had made, for up to that time the Israelites had been burning incense to it. (It was called Nehushtan.)
— 2 Kings 18:1–4

The Only One!

▼

Radical Attitude:

What a person Hezekiah was. Use your highlighter to mark the following facts about Hezekiah in the Bible passage: parents, age, length of reign, and what he did.

When Hezekiah became king, the people had almost forgotten God. This is the same nation that God had chosen to be His people. The generations before had actually heard God's voice and seen His presence in visual ways. Little of God was evident in their worship now. Idols, buildings, and symbols from the past were being worshiped.

Hezekiah began his reign as king by destroying these visible attachments. He knew the people could not see God if they were looking at these.

Hezekiah took a stand. He was the only one at that time who dared to remove such massive religious symbols.

A radical prayerful attitude will help you take a stand for God, even when you are the only one to do so.

Investigating Attitude:

Dustin walked up to the group of boys gathered. "Hey, Dustin,"

Thomas said. "Come look. Joseph brought the new issue of the magazine with the girls in swim suits. His brother gave it to him."

Dustin looked at the pictures Thomas held out to him. As he looked, he felt strange.

"I'm sorry, I do not want to stay and look. I don't think God made our bodies to be used in contest. I don't feel very clean when I look at these. See you later."

Thomas caught up with Dustin. "Aw, Dustin, there is nothing wrong with looking. You are the only one that thinks like that. Now the other guys will think you're a wimp!"

Analyzing Attitude:

Do you agree with Dustin or Thomas? Put your answer here.

_____

_____

Look at your description of God, and tell why you agreed with Dustin or Thomas. _____

_____

_____

Dustin and Hezekiah were alone in their stand for what they thought was right. Have you ever been the only one to stand up for what was right? Describe the situation here. _____

_____

_____

A Faithful Attitude:

Dear God, (*write your thoughts here*)

_____

_____

_____

Hezekiah trusted in the LORD, the God of Israel. There was no one like him among all the kings of Judah, either before him or after him. He held fast to the LORD and did not cease to follow him; he kept the commands the LORD had given Moses.
— 2 Kings 18:5–6

Remembering to Do Right!

▼

Radical Attitude:

Highlight the phrase, "He held fast to the Lord and did not cease to follow him." Here is Hezekiah's secret to a radical prayerful attitude. Even though God had ceased talking out loud to the leaders, Hezekiah knew God was present in a real way.

Hezekiah trusted in God and followed Him. He remembered the commandments God had given to the Israelites through Moses. He remembered God had said the people were to worship no gods but Him, the one true God. Hezekiah remembered what was right.

Investigating Attitude:

Marissa squeezed in beside Ryan. The organ was playing and the choir had just entered.

"Hi," Marissa said. "I thought Mr. Davis would never hush. Why weren't you in class?"

Before Ryan could answer, someone behind them said, "Shhh."

During the hymns Marissa talked to Ryan. She even leaned past him to talk to Kathy. Several near them gave her angry looks, but she continued her conversations.

During the sermon, she tore strips of paper from the bulletin and passed notes up and down the bench. At one point, the preacher even paused and looked her way.

Analyzing Attitude:
Look at your description of God. In the box below, write all of the ways Marissa did not do what was right.

In your description of God, what have you written that indicates that God deserves that which is right? Put your answer here.

Is church the only place you can show God that He is worthy of you doing what is right? Where and when else? Put your answer here.

A Faithful Attitude:
Dear God, (*write your thoughts here*)

And the LORD was with him; he was successful in whatever he undertook. He rebelled against the king of Assyria and did not serve him.
— 2 Kings 18:7

The Trust

▼

Radical Attitude:

Hezekiah became king when the people were not used to being treated right. Hezekiah's father, King Ahaz, was exactly the opposite of Hezekiah. For every good word you could use to describe Hezekiah, you would need to use the opposite to describe Ahaz.

The land Hezekiah ruled was between two world powers. Both wanted to control Israel and Judah. When Hezekiah became king, Assyria controlled Judah. With great courage, Hezekiah stood up to this mighty empire. He put his faith in God's strength, not his own. He obeyed God's commands. Hezekiah put his total being and faith in God. He knew a radical prayerful attitude reflects total faith in God.

Investigating Attitude:

Holly and Derek could not understand the serious look on their mom's face. Her eyes were red. She had been crying.

"I have something to tell you that makes me very sad," Mother began. "You father and I are getting a divorce. We love both of you very much and that will not change. We have not been getting along for months now. We have decided it is better this way."

Holly and Derek just sat there. Holly began to whimper. "Will we ever see Daddy? I don't like this, I want Daddy here," Holly cried.

Later as Derek sat in his room, he was shocked. Then he began to feel guilty. He had been really hard to get along with lately. He had not been doing well in school. Then he became angry. "How dare they," he thought. "They are not thinking about anyone but themselves. I'll never trust them again. Who can you trust?"

Analyzing Attitude:

Look at your description of God. What makes Him trustworthy?

_____

_____

Look at Hezekiah. How did he show that he had put his faith in God?

_____

_____

Look at Derek. Where had he put his faith?

_____

_____

Why is it important to be able to put your faith in God? _____

_____

_____

A Faithful Attitude:

Dear God, (write your thoughts here)

_____

_____

_____

_____

In the fourteenth year of King Hezekiah's reign, Sennacherib king of Assyria attacked all the fortified cities of Judah and captured them. So Hezekiah king of Judah sent this message to the king of Assyria at Lachish; "I have done wrong. Withdraw from, and I will pay whatever you demand of me." The king of Assyria exacted from Hezekiah king of Judah three hundred talents of silver and thirty talents of gold. So Hezekiah gave him all the silver that was found in the temple of the LORD and in the treasuries of the royal palace.
— 2 Kings 18:13–15

When Right Is Right

▼

Radical Attitude:

These verses refer to something that happened many years before Hezekiah became king. It was the custom for surrounding stronger nations to charge a tribute (fee) to smaller, weaker nations. The fee served as a promise that the larger nation would not attack the smaller one.

When Hezekiah became king, he did not pay the fee. Refusal to pay the tribute was a form of rebellion, and so Assyria attacked Judah.

Hezekiah and the area where he lived were not bothered by the attack, but Hezekiah realized he had done wrong.

Investigating Attitude:

Shona had just crawled into bed. It had been such a good day. Everything seemed to go well. She had worn her new sweater. She had gotten compliments all day. That cute boy, Sam, that she had been wanting to notice her told her she looked nice. Shona stretched her legs and felt good as she lay thinking over the day.

Suddenly Shona remembered something. She tried to shove the thoughts away. She even turned over and shut her eyes real tight.

The thoughts would not leave. She was remembering the terrible fight she had with her mother over the sweater. "Money is tight," Mom had said. Shona had acted so ugly, Mother had given in.

Analyzing Attitude:
Hezekiah and Shona both had done something wrong. What was it?

_____

_____

_____

_____

What caused them to realize their wrong?

_____

_____

_____

Look at your description of God. What characteristics does He have that make you know when you have done wrong? _____

_____

_____

_____

A Faithful Attitude:
Dear God, (*write your thoughts here*)

_____

_____

_____

_____

Hezekiah received the letter from the messengers and read it. Then he . . . spread it out before the LORD. And Hezekiah prayed to the Lord: "O LORD, God of Israel, enthroned between the cherubim, you alone are God over all the kingdoms of the earth. You have made heaven and earth. Give ear, O LORD, and hear; open your eyes, O LORD, and see; listen to the words Sennacherib has sent to insult the living God. It is true, O LORD, that the Assyrian kings have laid waste these nations and their lands. Now, O LORD our God, deliver us from his hand, so that all kingdoms on earth may know that you alone, O LORD, are God."
— 2 Kings 19:14–19

It's Your Responsibility

▼

Radical Attitude:

Big trouble! Sennacherib's armies had captured many of the walled cities of Judah. Now Hezekiah received a message to surrender. The situation seemed hopeless. What could Hezekiah do?

Hezekiah demonstrated his radical attitude of prayer in the Bible passage. He did not take God for granted. He did not assume that God would take care of things. He did not say the situation was hopeless, so there was no need to involve God. No, Hezekiah spread the message out before God. Then in prayer, Hezekiah first recognized God's power and his kingdom's total dependence on God. It was with great respect that Hezekiah asked God's help.

Investigating Attitude:

Ken finally got his motor bike going. He had worked hard all day. Just about dark, it cranked. Off Ken rode to give it a try. As he pulled into the drive, Mom called him to eat. Hurriedly, Ken put the tools away.

About a month later, Dad asked Ken about one of the tools. Ken said he had remembered using it to fix his bike. "Yes, I know," Dad said. "I found the tool in the yard while I was mowing. It is so rusted, we cannot use it anymore. You will have to buy a new one to replace it. It is pretty expensive, too."

Ken argued with his father. He had been saving his money to upgrade his bike with a new one. The tool would take all of his savings. Ken tried to reason with his Dad. In his anger, Ken said, "I think you are not fair. After all, it is your responsibility to provide and care for me. It was your tool, not mine!"

Analyzing Attitude:

A radical prayerful attitude does not take God for granted. Compare Hezekiah's attitude with Ken's. Put your answers here:

Hezekiah	Ken
_____	_____
_____	_____
_____	_____
_____	

Are there ways that you act that make God think you take Him for granted? How? _____

_____

_____

_____

A Faithful Attitude:

Dear God, (*write your thoughts here*)

_____

_____

_____

_____

In those days Hezekiah became ill and was at the point of death. The prophet Isaiah son of Amoz went to him and said, "This is what the LORD says: Put your house in order, because you are going to die; you will not recover." Hezekiah turned his face to the wall and prayed to the LORD, "Remember, O LORD, how I have walked before you faithfully and with wholehearted devotion and have done what is good in your eyes." And Hezekiah wept bitterly.
— 2 Kings 20:1–3

It's the Pits!

▼

Radical Attitude:

Hezekiah could very well have said, "It's the pits," after Isaiah's visit. What did he do? The real test of a radical attitude of prayer comes through.

In the Bible passage, highlight Hezekiah's prayer. What base did Hezekiah give to God for making him well? _____

_____

Did Hezekiah think God did not know of Hezekiah's faithfulness?

_____

Was Hezekiah trying to bribe God with all the good things he had done? If not, what?_____

_____

Hezekiah had such a personal relationship with God that he was sad to think it would end. Remember, Jesus had not come at this point and the knowledge of the resurrection had not been taught.

A person with a radical prayerful attitude has a growing relationship with God.

Investigating Attitude:

Vanessa felt hopeless. She had AIDS. Her mother had the virus and passed it to Vanessa at birth. Her mother had died the year before, and now Vanessa was afraid. She did not want to die. She was angry sometimes because her Mother had given it to her. She felt left out of everything because the children her age were afraid of her. Even though the AIDS had not become "full blown," Vanessa knew it could. Maybe it would be better if she got it and died. This sure wasn't living!

Analyzing Attitude:

Can prayer help Vanessa? How? Put your answer below. _____

_____

_____

If you were Vanessa how would you pray? _____

_____

_____

Look at your description of God. What have you written that tells you He can handle Vanessa's problem?_____

_____

_____

Remember that God is a personal God. He knows and can do what is best for you. He wants you to acknowledge Him by praying to Him and telling Him your needs.

A Faithful Attitude:

Dear God, (*write your thoughts here*)

_____

_____

Before Isaiah had left the middle court, the word of the LORD came to him: "Go back and tell Hezekiah, the leader of my people, 'This is what the LORD, the God of your father David, says: I have heard your prayer and seen your tears, I will heal you. On the third day from now you will go up to the temple of the LORD.'"
— 2 Kings 20:4–5

He Hears!

▼

Radical Attitude:

When God answers, He does not drag around. Right away, before Isaiah had gotten out of the palace, the answer was given. In the Bible passage, highlight God's answer.

Remember, in a radical attitude of prayer, do not confuse the answer with an action. Sometimes when we pray, God says, "Wait!" But when God does take action, it can be instantaneous.

Investigating Attitude:

I must share something that happened to me when I was your age. My father is a preacher. One night after we had gone to sleep, a church member came to our door.

"I have a group from the church here. We want you and your family to come pray with us. My wife is having a baby, and they both will die if something doesn't change. I know prayer is the only thing left."

Quickly we went to the church with our night clothes still on. The ten or fifteen there began to pray, sometimes out loud, sometimes in silence. I must confess that as a child, I dozed some. Yet just as the sun broke through, the phone rang. "All is well," came the answer.

Analyzing Attitude:

Prayer is not magic. Prayer does not require special words, times, or people. Prayer does not manipulate. A radical prayerful attitude recognizes the realness of God.

Look at your description of God. What words did you use to tell that He is real? _____

_____

_____

_____

As a result of this study, write another description of God here.

_____

_____

_____

What have you learned about God to help you develop a radical prayerful attitude?_____

_____

_____

_____

A Faithful Attitude:

Dear God, (*write your thoughts here*)

_____

_____

_____

_____

_____

Chapter Eleven

A Leadership Attitude

▼

Have you ever played "Follow the Leader?" In the game, you walk behind the leader and do everything exactly as he or she does. You copy every look, every movement, and every word that is said. In many ways that game is an example of the radical attitude of leadership. The key is the *leader* you choose to follow, to act like, and to look and talk like.

One of the most outstanding leaders in the Bible was Deborah, a wife, prophetess, and judge. Unlike the "Follow the Leader" game, Deborah led through other people. She wisely was able to see the big picture, thus helping others to accomplish great work. Deborah's strong leadership skills came from the one she followed—God. Because she was available to God for His use, she was able to settle disputes; advise an army general, predict the outcome of a nation, acquire respect, and serve as a role model for those of her day and ours. To learn the whole story of Deborah, read Judges 4—5.

List leaders you know in the first column. In the second column write what makes them good leaders.

Leaders	Qualities of Good Leaders
_____	_____
_____	_____
_____	_____
_____	_____
_____	_____
_____	_____

Deborah, a prophetess, the wife of Lappidoth, was leading Israel at that time. She held court under the Palm of Deborah between Ramah and Bethel in the hill country of Ephraim, and the Israelites came to her to have their disputes decided.

— Judges 4:4–5

Break It Up!

▼

Radical Attitude:

The period of Bible history when the events in the Book of Judges occurred was just after Joshua led the people into the promised land. Things should have been perfect for the Israelites. Instead the people did not know what to do or how to act. They forgot God. They had no leader. During this time, the people turned to wise people who were able to settle disputes. Deborah was just such a wise person.

Highlight in the Bible passage why the people came to her.

A radical attitude of leadership settles disputes.

Investigating Attitude:

Perhaps you have been involved in a dispute recently. Imagine you are as wise as Deborah. Complete the following report.

Name: _____

Date: _____

Location of dispute: _____

Persons involved: _____

What caused the dispute: _____

Analyzing Attitude:
Could the dispute have been prevented? _____ If yes, how?

_____

_____

_____

How was the dispute settled? _____

_____

_____

_____

Could the dispute have been settled differently? _____ If yes, how?

_____

_____

_____

How can the dispute be prevented in the future? _____

_____

_____

_____

What three things could you do to always prevent disputes? _____

1. _____

2. _____

3. _____

A Faithful Attitude:
Dear God, (*write your thoughts here*)

_____

_____

She sent for Barak son of Abinoam from Kedesh in Naphtali and said to him, "The LORD, the God of Israel, commands you: 'Go, take with you ten thousand men of Naphtali and Zebulun and lead the way to Mount Tabor. I will lure Sisera, the commander of Jabin's army, with his chariots and his troops to the Kishon River and give him into your hands.'"

— Judges 4:6–7

Take Action!

▼

Radical Attitude:

Deborah was not a woman wanting power. She wanted to serve God. So when God told her He would help the Israelites win a battle, she sent for Barak to lead the army.

A person with a radical leadership attitude involves others in the action.

Investigating Attitude:

Amber's parents had invited a large group of parents to talk about the dangers at school. Little things had happened all year: a ceiling tile had fallen on a pupil, windows had been broken, and the playground's trees had been cut down. Finally last week a pupil had pulled a gun on a teacher. The gun was a fake, but the fear was not. The parents were angrily talking about what they were going to do.

Amber asked her dad if she could speak. Nervously she cleared her throat and said, "I think you need to help the students handle the problem, rather than doing it for us."

The parents were excited about Amber's suggestions. They decided to form an organization called "Take Action" that would be made up of students. The students would begin to be observant and turn in anyone who violated rules or destroyed property. The penalty to the person breaking rules or destroying property would be to spend an appropriate number of work hours cleaning and repairing the school. The parents would supervise the work so the teachers would not have to.

Analyzing Attitude:

Begin your radical attitude of leadership by taking action. What can you do to make these places better?

Home: _____

_____

School: _____

_____

Church: _____

_____

Play area: _____

_____

Your room: _____

_____

Your yard: _____

_____

A Faithful Attitude:

Dear God, (*write your thoughts here*)

_____

_____

_____

Barak said to her, "If you go with me, I will go; but if you don't go with me I won't go." "Very well," Deborah said, "I will go with you. But because of the way you are going about this, the honor will not be yours, for the LORD will hand Sisera over to a woman." So Deborah went with Barak to Kedesh, where he summoned Zebulun and Naphtali. The thousand men followed him, and Deborah also went with him.

— Judges 4:8–10

I'll Help!

▼

Radical Attitude:

Even today, the idea of women going to battle is offensive to some. Deborah did not sign up to go to battle with Barak. She did not tell Barak he would only win if she were along. The Bible does not tell why Barak insisted on Deborah going along, but he refused to go without her.

Deborah could have refused to go. Her husband could have forbidden her to go. Yet none of this happened because Deborah, the leader, was willing to help.

(Special note: Deborah was not the woman who received the honor. Read Judges 4:17-22.)

Investigating Attitude:

Brooke looked up. Mrs. Phillips, the special education teacher, was walking across the gym to where they were waiting to catch the school busses. One of her pupils was in a wheelchair. Several of the pupils had difficulty walking. Mrs. Phillips was trying to help them.

"Look," said Amy. "Aren't they gross? I don't see how anyone can work with them. I sure couldn't!"

Brooke heard the rain as it poured against the building. Without a word, she got up and hurried over to Mrs. Phillips.

"Here, I'll take Kate out to her bus. Tell me the number and what I need to do!"

Analyzing Attitude:

A person with a radical attitude of leadership looks for ways to help—without being asked or without expecting praise.

Think back over helpful actions you have taken. Complete the chart.

When	What	Where	To whom

Place a check by each action that was done without being asked, expected, or rewarded.

A Faithful Attitude:

Dear God, (*write your thoughts here*)

_____

_____

_____

_____

_____

Deborah, a prophetess, the wife of Lappidoth, was leading Israel at that time. She held court under the Palm of Deborah between Ramah and Bethel in the hill country of Ephraim, and the Israelites came to her to have their disputes decided. She sent for Barak son of Abinoam from Kedesh in Naphtali and said to him, "The LORD, the God of Israel, commands you: 'Go, take with you ten thousand men of Naphtali and Zebulun and lead the way to Mount Tabor. I will lure Sisera, the commander of Jabin's army, with his chariots and his troops to the Kishon River and give him into your hands.'"

— Judges 4:4–7

All Ears!

▼

Radical Attitude:

Deborah listened to God. Deborah listened to the people. Deborah was a good listener. She recognized the importance of listening to develop an attitude of leadership.

In the Bible passage, highlight the phrase that tells you how much trust the people placed in Deborah. As their leader, how did she help them? Write your answer here. _____

_____

_____

A person with a radical attitude of leadership listens.

Investigating Attitude:

Mrs. Hayley seemed to always have a student coming from her room. She was surrounded with pupils everywhere she went. What was her secret?

Mr. Justin's team always seemed to be winning. It was hard to understand. The boys seemed to be such unlikely winners. Most were not well-groomed or well-dressed, yet they were winners.

What was his secret? _____

The Wilson family was often seen together. They were usually laughing and having a good time. Most often the parents were seen out walking with their children. What was their secret?

Brad had many friends. He treated each one the same. They all liked to go to Brad's house. One of his friends said, "I sure like Brad. You can tell him anything." What was the secret?

Analyzing Attitude:
Write the secret for:

Mrs. Hayley _____

_____

Mr. Justin _____

_____

The Wilson family _____

_____

Brad _____

_____

What would you tell someone who really listened to you? _____

_____

_____

_____

A Faithful Attitude:
Dear God, (*write your thoughts here*)

_____

_____

_____

On that day Deborah and Barak son of Abinoam sang this song:
"When the princes in Israel take the lead,
when the people willingly offer themselves—
praise the LORD!"
— Judges 5:1–2

Real Praise

▼

Radical Attitude:

Israel's culture treasured music and singing. The song given in Judges 5 probably was composed and sung by Deborah and Barak. The song retells the story of the victory.

Deborah knew her people's love of music. To help them give the praise where the praise was due, she sang a song about the victory. Once again Deborah's radical attitude of leadership is evident. Radical leadership gives praise where deserved.

Investigating Attitude:

Nicholas could not believe the noise. It sounded like everyone in the world was clapping and yelling. Finally, the fact begin to sink in. He had won. He was the winner of the computer competition.

Nicholas had worked hard for this day. Just a year ago, he had been told it could not be done. Nicholas is blind!

As Nicholas stepped up to accept the award, he told not of his struggle to get to compete. He told of the people who had helped prepare and those who had fought to have rules changed so he could be there. Nicholas gave praise to those who helped him.

Analyzing Attitude:

Think about those who help you each day. Complete the following:

Action   Those who helped

_____   _____

_____   _____

_____   _____

_____   _____

Think about ways you can give praise to those who help. Write your plans here. _____

_____

_____

_____

Is God your leader? How do you give Him praise? Write your answer here. _____

_____

_____

_____

_____

A Faithful Attitude:

Dear God, (*write your thoughts here*)

_____

_____

_____

_____

"Hear this, you kings! Listen, you rulers!
I will sing to the LORD, I will sing;
I will make music to the LORD, the God of Israel.
"O LORD, when you went out from Seir,
when you marched from the land of Edom,
the earth shook, the heavens poured,
the clouds poured down water.
The mountains quaked before the LORD, the One of Sinai,
before the LORD, the God of Israel.
— Judges 5:3–5

The Leader

▼

Radical Attitude:

Deborah began her song by recognizing her Leader. She reminded the people of God's greatness and presence.

People with leadership attitudes know their Leader is God.

Investigating Attitude:

Jimmy was in trouble again. For the second time that week he had been sent to detention. Everything seemed to go against him. His home life wasn't much. He seldom saw his parents. When they weren't working, they were at the nearby bar, drinking.

Mr. Craig was walking down the hall when he saw Jimmy.

"Jimmy, meet me right here after class. I have a surprise for you," Mr. Craig said.

That was the beginning of many afternoons spent with Mr. Craig. After a snack, they spent time with Jimmy's homework. They were both happy when he had a C in every class. Jimmy said he did not know anything but Fs.

One afternoon, Mr. Craig told Jimmy about God. "With God, you always have a good Leader," Mr. Craig told Jimmy.

Analyzing Attitude:

A person with a radical attitude of leadership recognizes God as *the* Leader. Think about your days. Do you let God lead you in everything you do? In the time schedule below, tell how God leads you.

5:00 A.M. _____

6:00 _____

7:00 _____

8:00 _____

9:00 _____

10:00 _____

11:00 _____

Noon _____

1:00 P.M. _____

2:00 _____

3:00 _____

4:00 _____

5:00 _____

6:00 _____

7:00 _____

8:00 _____

9:00 _____

10:00 _____

A Faithful Attitude:

Dear God, (*write your thoughts here*)

_____

_____

"In the days of Shamgar son of Anath,
in the days of Jael, the roads were abandoned;
travelers took to winding paths. Village life in Israel ceased,
ceased until I, Deborah, arose, arose a mother in Israel.
When they chose new gods, war came to the city gates,
and not a shield or spear was seen among forty thousand in Israel.
My heart is with Israel's princes,
with the willing volunteers among the people.
Praise the LORD!"

— Judges 5:6–9

Respected Leader

▼

Radical Attitude:

As the song continued, Deborah reminded the people of what life was like before the victory. "Remember," she said, "people were afraid to travel on the roads. They chose new gods; they had no weapons. The times were not good."

Deborah was not singing her own praises when she said "she arose." The people had chosen her to lead them because she had earned their respect. To become a judge did not require that they run for the position. It was not a political slot. Respect for Deborah placed her in the position.

To become a radical leader, a person must be respected.

Investigating Attitude:

Respect cannot be given; it must be earned. Think again about the leaders you know. Are they people you respect? Write a description of a leader you know, and tell how he or she earned your respect.

Analyzing Attitude

Is it really hard for you to compliment yourself? You may have been taught it is wrong to do so. Deborah taught us a valuable lesson. When sharing in a success, you need to include yourself. Complete the following about your accomplishments:

Name: _____

Age: _____ Date: _____

Last week I did these things really well: _____

_____

_____

_____

When I did them, I felt: _____

_____

_____

The people around me did this: _____

_____

_____

I was told: _____

_____

_____

_____

A Faithful Attitude:
Dear God, (write your thoughts here:)

_____

_____

_____

Chapter Twelve

An Obedient Attitude

▼

What if you could only remember one thing, had only one person to listen to, and were responsible only to obey that individual—could you? To have a radical obedient attitude, you only have one responsibility. You are to hear (read) God's Word and act accordingly. Stop here and think about just obeying God's Word. Radical! God's Word describes proper behavior for every situation and for every person.

In this chapter you will study a different Bible person each day. Each person faced different situations. Each person acted in a different way, but *every* person *obeyed God*.

Today many people around you may not feel they are subject to anyone or anything. You yourself may have more opportunities to disobey than to obey. Or you may have already realized that God's way is the the only right way; yet you struggle to obey.

As you study this chapter, keep your notebook near. Be ready to write the behavior you discover in each of the Bible persons that you want to practice. Then each day begin to copy that behavior. Record in your notebook the difference in the way you are treated. Remember, to radically obey will have its ups and downs. Those around you may not believe you're for real at first, but don't quit!

The LORD spoke to Manasseh and his people, but they paid no attention. So the LORD brought against them the army commanders of the king of Assyria, who took Manasseh prisoner, put a hook in his nose, bound him with bronze shackles and took him to Babylon. In his distress he sought the favor of the LORD his God and humbled himself greatly before the God of his fathers. And when he prayed to him, the LORD was moved by his entreaty and listened to his plea; so he brought him back to Jerusalem and to his kingdom. Then Manasseh knew that the LORD is God.

— 2 Chronicles 33:10–13

The Punishment

▼

Radical Attitude:

The Books of Chronicles record the events of the nation of Israel. With each turn of the page, you will read that the people quickly forgot God. Yet God kept attempting to accomplish His will and plan.

Manasseh was twelve years old when he became king. That in itself could be used as an excuse for his actions, but that excuse was unacceptable to God. Manasseh's behavior was sickening. He did everything in direct disobedience to God.

In the Bible passage highlight how God punished Manasseh. Imagine having a hook placed in your nose and being led off like an animal. What an embarrassment to God Manasseh's behavior had been. Now think of Manasseh's embarrassment!

Thankfully the story does not end with the punishment. With Manasseh's repentance (deep sorrow), God forgave. Still the story does not end. With forgiveness, Manasseh became obedient.

Sometimes in developing a radical attitude of obedience, we suffer punishment first.

Investigating Attitude:

Below are some facts. Using the information, write a story in your notebook.

Characters: a group of four children your age.

Setting: a party.

Plot: The children decide to play a trick on people by throwing water balloons. A driver swerves, hits a curb and some bushes, and glass breaks. A sliver of glass puts an eye out.

Punishment: The children have to go to a juvenile center.

Results: The children learned to be obedient.

Analyzing Attitude:

Think about punishment you have received during the last month. Did you repent or were you just sorry you got caught? Did the punishment cause you to decide to change your behavior? Complete the following:

Punishment	Repented	Obedience

Remember: All behavior should be based on what God would want you to do. When punishment causes changed behavior, it can lead to a radical attitude of obedience.

A Faithful Attitude:

Dear God, (*write your thoughts here*)

_____

_____

_____

_____

Josiah was eight years old when he became king . . . . He did what was right in the eyes of the LORD . . . . The king . . . renewed the covenant in the presence of the LORD—to follow the LORD and keep his commands, regulations and decrees with all his heart and all his soul, and to obey the words of the covenant written in this book. Then he had everyone in Jerusalem and Benjamin pledge themselves to it; . . . . As long as he lived, they did not fail to follow the Lord.
— 2 Chronicles 34:1–2, 31–33

Keep Your Word

▼

Radical Attitude:

Josiah was another young king, but his story is far different from Manasseh's. Josiah began from the beginning to seek God. During the cleaning out of the temple, a Book of the Law was found. When the words were read, Josiah realized he and the people had forgotten the covenant made between God and their forefathers. In the Bible passage highlight the covenant Josiah made. He promised to keep and to obey the words in the Book of Law.

Josiah realized a radical attitude of obedience involves keeping your word. To be able to keep your word, you must know God's word.

Investigating Attitude:

Write a story in your notebook using the following facts:

Characters: two best friends and one of their parents
Setting: house of one of the friends
Plot: The parents must be out of town for two days. The child may invite a friend to stay with him. The next door neigh bors will check on them frequently. The children have an

important project to complete. The child has promised
(coveted) to complete the project.
Results: The child is obedient. He keeps his word.

Analyzing Attitude:

When you accept Jesus Christ as your Savior and Lord, you enter a
covenant relationship with Him. You are now His child.

Read Josiah's covenant with God. Write yours here. _____

_____

_____

_____

_____

_____

_____

_____

_____

_____

_____

A Faithful Attitude:

Dear God, (*write your thoughts here*)

_____

_____

_____

_____

They assembled at Jerusalem in the third month of the fifteenth year of Asa's reign. At that time they sacrificed to the LORD seven hundred head of cattle and seven thousand sheep and goats from the plunder they had brought back. They entered into a covenant to seek the LORD, the God of their fathers, with all their heart and soul. . . .

King Asa also deposed his grandmother Maacah from her position as queen mother, because she had made a repulsive Asherah pole. Asa cut the pole down, broke it up and burned it in the Kidron Valley.

— 2 Chronicles 15:10–12,16

Don't Blame Me!

▼

Radical Attitude:

Would you be willing to stand up to your family to obey God? Asa did.

Asa had led the people in a very successful battle. The victory meant the Israelites would be safe from invaders. They were happy and very grateful that God had been with them. In the Bible passage highlight the amount that was sacrificed.

During the sacrifice, a covenant was made with the Lord. All would seek God and obey Him. Anyone who failed to keep the covenant would be put to death.

Later Asa learned that his own grandmother had made a repulsive idol to a fertility goddess. Asa kept his promise to God. Highlight the verse in the Bible passage that tells what Asa did.

A person with a radical attitude of obedience will obey God even when family does not.

Investigating Attitude:

Use these facts to write a story in your notebook.

Characters: a child and her family.

Setting: mealtime.

Plot: The child has a main part in a play at church. The family
has a family reunion to attend.

Results: The girl learns that obedience to God sometimes
conflicts with family wants and needs. (Remember, one of
God's rules is to obey your parents.)

Analyzing Attitude:

We need to be very careful about the promises we make to God.
God keeps His promises and He expects us to do so, too. How can
you obey God and family if your family does not believe in God?

Find these verses. Next to each verse write the word that tells
you how to obey God and parents.

James 5:16 _____

1 John 3:18 _____

Ephesians 4:25 _____

2 Corinthians 5:9 _____

Proverbs 3:5–6 _____

Psalm 119:11 _____

A Faithful Attitude:

Dear God, (*write your thoughts here*)

_____

_____

_____

_____

_____

"You will not have to fight this battle. Take up your positions; stand firm and see the deliverance the Lord will give you, O Judah and Jerusalem. Do not be afraid; do not be discouraged. Go out to face them tomorrow, and the LORD will be with you."...

Early in the morning they left for the Desert of Tekoa. As they set out, Jehoshaphat stood and said, "Listen to me, Judah and people of Jerusalem! Have faith in the LORD your God and you will be upheld; have faith in his prophets and you will be successful.
— 2 Chronicles 20:17,20–21

Who Is in Charge?

▼

Radical Attitude:

Once again the people were having to face their enemy. Word had come to Jehoshaphat that a vast army was approaching. The message said the army was not far away.

Jehoshaphat did two things: He called the people to fast (do without food), and he went to the temple to talk to God.

God told Jehoshaphat to take his army and go out, but He (God) would fight the battle.

In the Bible passage, highlight this statement, "Do not be afraid; do not be discouraged. Go out to face them tomorrow, and the Lord will be with you." This would be a good verse to memorize.

Jehoshaphat knew he must obey. God would take care of tomorrow. People with radical attitudes of obedience know that God is in charge (present) with them.

Investigating Attitude:

Write a story in your notebook using the following facts.
Characters: group of children from church.
Setting: church.
Plot: The class had been learning how to tell others about Jesus.

The teacher had a list of names of children who do not go to church. The class was to visit those on the list on Saturday.

Results: The children learn that obeying God is not always easy, but He is always present with those who seek to obey Him.

Analyzing Attitude:

Complete the following:

List of Things I Must Do Tomorrow

_____

_____

_____

_____

How can God help you accomplish each task? _____

_____

_____

_____

How do you know God will help you? _____

_____

_____

A Faithful Attitude:

Dear God, (*write your thoughts here*)

_____

_____

_____

Uzziah was sixteen years old when he became king, and he reigned in Jerusalem fifty-two years. His mother's name was Jecoliah; she was from Jerusalem. He did what was right in the eyes of the LORD, just as his father Amaziah had done. He sought God during the days of Zechariah, who instructed him in the fear of God. As long as he sought the LORD, God gave him success. . . .

But after Uzziah became powerful, his pride led to his downfall. He was unfaithful to the LORD his God, and entered the temple of the LORD to burn incense on the altar of incense.

— 2 Chronicles 26:3–5,16

The Downfall!

▼

Radical Attitude:

Uzziah was good, real good! He was so good, in fact, he decided he could go offer the incense offering. The incense offering was a daily offering made in the temple, but the priest was the only one who was supposed to make the offering.

From the beginning God gave very specific directions for conducting worship. Since Jesus had not come to earth yet, God gave instructions for sacrifices. Each day the priest was to offer an offering of incense. The sweet smell was pleasant. It would remind the people of the sweetness of God's fellowship.

There is no doubt that Uzziah loved and obeyed God. But Uzziah let his pride get in the way. He felt as qualified to offer the incense offering as the priest—after all he was the king!

Caution must be used so that an obedient attitude does not lead to pride.

Investigating Attitude:

Write a story in your notebook using the following facts.

Characters: three children your age.

Setting: schoolroom.

Plot: One child does everything right. She always obeys. The teacher shows partiality. The other children would like to have the teacher notice them. They have their chance when the girl "messes up."

Results: The children discovered that disobedience and pride in accomplishments can lead to mistakes.

Analyzing Attitude:

Is there such a thing as being "too perfect"? _____

Defend your answer here. _____

_____

_____

_____

What can you do to keep a good balance of obedience and pride? _____

_____

_____

_____

_____

A Faithful Attitude:

Dear God, (*write your thoughts here*)

_____

_____

_____

_____

_____

Jotham was twenty-five years old when he became king, and he reigned in Jerusalem sixteen years. His mother's name was Jerusha daughter of Zadok. He did what was right in the eyes of the LORD, just as his father Uzziah had done, but unlike him he did not enter the temple of the LORD. The people, however, continued their corrupt practices. Jotham grew powerful because he walked steadfastly before the LORD his God.

— 2 Chronicles 27:1–2,6

It's Tough!

▼

Radical Attitude:

Jotham is a good example of someone who obeys when everyone else does not.

Jotham must have paid attention as his father Uzziah ruled. In the Bible passage, highlight the words that tell you Jotham obeyed God.

You would think with good kings like Uzziah and now Jotham, the people would serve God, too. Highlight the words that tell you what the people did.

Do you think it was easy for Jotham to serve God when the people did not? Write your answer here. (Why or why not?) _____

_____

_____

What could Jotham have done about the people? _____

_____

Why didn't he? _____

_____

People with radical attitudes of obedience will obey even when no one else does.

Investigating Attitude:

Write a story in your notebook using these facts.

Characters: Children your age (you choose how many).

Setting: Life.

Plot: You choose a situation when a child obeys, but no one else does.
Be sure to include the feelings and the choices that are faced.

Results: The children learn that having a radical attitude of
obedience means they must obey even when others do not.

Analyzing Attitude:

Follow the directions for each box.

List all situations when you need to obey.

List reasons for obedience.
Put a check mark beside the reasons that help develop a radical obedient attitude.

List reasons not to obey.

A Faithful Attitude:

Dear God, (*write your thoughts here*)

The thief comes only to steal and kill and destroy; I have come that they may have life, and have it to the full.
— John 10:10

A Full Life

▼

Radical Attitude:

The ultimate example of obedience is Jesus. God gave you His Word, the Bible, so you would know how to obey Him. God does not try to trick you. He does not set traps for you. He has done everything within His power to give you all the information possible. He has provided an account of the lives of people so you could have examples. He has a plan for you and your life. He wants your obedience. God gave His only son to die to show you that His love for you is real. What He asks in return is a radical attitude of obedience.

Investigating Attitude:

Accepting Jesus Christ as your Lord and Savior is telling God you want to have a radical obedient attitude. Match the following definitions:

1. ___ Lost   *a.* a deep hurting, sorrow for sin
2. ___ Sin   *b.* removal of sin that separates
3. ___ Repentance   *c.* separated from God

4. __ Forgiveness

d. acceptance of forgiveness and commitment to be obedient

5. __ Accepting Christ

e. thought, feeling, attitude, or behavior that separates a person from God

Analyzing Attitude:

If you have accepted Christ and committed yourself to live like God plans for you to live, sign your name and the date here.

_____

If you have not repented of your sins, asked for forgiveness, and accepted Christ as your Savior, find these verses in your Bible. After you read them, tell God what you want to do. Then tell an adult you trust. That person will help you know what to do next.

1. Acts 4:13   2. Acts 3:19   3. Romans 10:9
4. 1 John 1:9   5. Ephesians 2:10

A Faithful Attitude:

If you have accepted Christ as your Savior and Lord, ask Him to help you with your radical attitude of obedience. If you want to accept Christ, tell Him of your repentance and ask Him for forgiveness. Write your thoughts here.

_____

_____

_____

_____

_____

_____

Fodor's 2023

LONDON

Welcome to London

History and tradition greet you at every turn in London; it's also one of the coolest, most modern cities in the world. If London contained only landmarks such as Westminster Abbey and Buckingham Palace, it would still rank as one of the world's great destinations, but Britain's capital is much more. People come to glimpse the royals and take in theater and trendy shops, to sample tea and cutting-edge cuisine. When you need a break from the action, pop into a pub, relax in a park—or take a walk and make the city your own. As you plan your upcoming travels to London, please confirm that places are still open and let us know when we need to make updates by writing to us at editors@fodors.com.

TOP REASONS TO GO

★ **Architectural icons:** The Tower of London and Big Ben are quintessential London.

★ **Art museums:** From the National Gallery to Tate Modern, a visual feast awaits.

★ **Top theater:** Whether it's Shakespeare or avant-garde drama, the play's the thing.

★ **City of villages:** Unique neighborhoods, from Mayfair to the East End, invite discovery.

★ **Shopping:** Fun markets mix it up with famous flagship department stores and chic boutiques.

★ **Parks and squares:** Distinctive green spaces large and small are civilized retreats.

Contents

Fodor's Features

MAPS

Chapter 1

EXPERIENCE LONDON

20 ULTIMATE EXPERIENCES

London offers terrific experiences that should be on every traveler's list. Here are Fodor's top picks for a memorable trip.

1 Big Ben and the Houses of Parliament

The neo-Gothic Houses of Parliament contains the Houses of Commons and Lords (the legislative bodies of the United Kingdom's government) and the giant clock tower known as Big Ben (one of London's most-beloved icons). *(Ch. 3)*

2 Drinking in Historic Pubs

The history of London's taverns and pubs is the history of the city itself. Grab a pint or a gin cocktail, and get to know how the locals live. *(Ch. 3–14)*

3 British Museum

It would take a lifetime to do justice to the extraordinary collection (spanning 8 million artifacts from over 2 million years) at Britain's most-visited museum. *(Ch. 6)*

4 Hampton Court Palace

One of Britain's grandest royal palaces, Hampton Court contains some of the finest Tudor architecture in the world and is imbued with an overwhelming sense of history. *(Ch. 14)*

5 Gallery-Hopping in East London

With one of the highest concentrations of artists in Europe, East London is fertile ground for some serious contemporary art gallery hopping, from Whitechapel to Hackney. *(Ch. 8)*

6 Hyde Park and Kensington Gardens

London is famous for its awesome Royal Parks, and contiguous Hyde Park and Kensington Gardens are perfect for escaping the hustle and bustle of the city. *(Ch. 10)*

7 The Markets

From gourmet food to antiques, you can find nearly everything at London's most famous street markets: Portobello Road Market in Notting Hill and Borough Market on the South Bank. *(Ch. 9, 11)*

8 London Eye

For an unrivaled bird's-eye view of the metropolis and beyond, take a ride on one of the world's tallest observation wheels. *(Ch. 9)*

9 Afternoon Tea

For a quintessential English ritual, enjoy a pot of tea served in bone china alongside finger sandwiches, fruit scones, and cakes at one of the city's fanciest hotels. *(Ch. 1)*

10 Shakespeare's Globe

A replica of the original Globe Theatre just yards from where Shakespeare's Elizabethan playhouse stood, the modern-day Globe still hosts open-air performances of the Bard's plays. *(Ch. 9)*

11 Indian Food on Brick Lane

Thanks to successive waves of immigrants, Whitechapel's Brick Lane is famous for London's highest concentration of curry houses and some of the best Indian food outside India. *(Ch. 8)*

12 Victoria and Albert Museum

With a vast collection of 2.3 million objects, the V&A is one of the world's greatest museums of decorative arts and design. *(Ch. 10)*

13 Tate Modern

A must-visit for global art lovers, Tate Modern wows with its extensive collection of constantly rotating modern art. *(Ch. 9)*

14 St. Paul's Cathedral

With the second-largest cathedral dome in the world, St. Paul's is a towering masterpiece of English Baroque design, both inside and out. *(Ch. 7)*

15 Covent Garden

Covent Garden is considered the heart of London, thanks to its markets, pubs, restaurants, museums, theaters, boutiques, street entertainers, and more. *(Ch. 5)*

16 Buckingham Palace

The official residence of the British monarch is opulently filled with priceless tapestries, artwork, and marble and gilt galore. *(Ch. 3)*

17 Theater in the West End

Thanks to some of the world's best actors and directors (and the most historic theaters), London's contributions to the theater world give Broadway a run for its money. *(Ch. 5)*

18 National Gallery

With more than 2,300 of the world's masterpieces, this museum is considered Britain's greatest art collection. *(Ch. 3)*

19 Tower of London

With a gory 950-year history of beheadings, imprisonments, and torture, myths and legends shroud England's most perfect medieval fortress and home of the Crown Jewels. *(Ch. 7)*

20 Westminster Abbey

The site of all but two royal coronations since 1066, the Abbey is steeped in history—from tombs of monarchs to monuments for nobles, statesmen, and poets. *(Ch. 3)*

WHAT'S WHERE

1 **Westminster and St. James's.** This is the place to embrace your inner tourist. Snap pictures of the mounted Horse Guards, watch kids clambering onto the monumental bronze lions in Trafalgar Square, and visit stacks of world-class art in the fantastic national galleries. Brave the crowds to peruse historic Westminster Abbey and its ancient narrative in stone.

2 **Mayfair and Marylebone.** You may not have the wallet for London's most prestigious shops, but remember window-shopping in historic Mayfair is free. Meanwhile, chic boutiques in Marylebone are a refreshing change from gaudy Oxford Street a few blocks south.

3 **Soho and Covent Garden.** More sophisticated than seedy these days, the heart of London puts Theatreland, strip joints, Chinatown, and the trendiest of film studios side by side. Hold tight through the hectic hordes in Leicester Square. Covent Garden's historic paved piazza is one of the most raffishly enjoyable parts of the city.

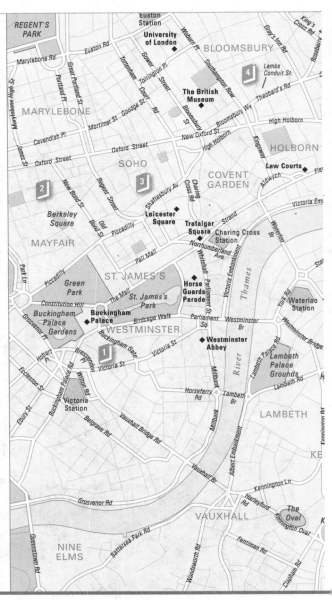

4 Bloomsbury and Holborn. Once the bluestocking and intellectual center of London, elegant 17th- and 18th-century Bloomsbury is now also a mixed business district. The British Museum has enough amazing objets d'art and artifacts to keep you busy for a month; the Law Courts, the University of London, and quaint, trendy Lamb's Conduit Street are worth a gander.

5 The City. London's Wall Street might be the oldest part of the capital, but thanks to new skyscrapers and a sleek Millennium Bridge, it also looks like the newest. History fans won't be short-changed, however: head for St. Paul's Cathedral, Tower Bridge, and the Tower of London.

6 East London. Once famed for the 19th-century slums immortalized by Charles Dickens and Jack the Ripper, today the area is a fulcrum of London's contemporary art scene and a hip party zone. Dive headfirst into the eclectic wares at Spitalfields Market and along Brick Lane, and take in Columbia Road's much-loved early-morning flower market.

WHAT'S WHERE

7 South of the Thames. The South-bank Centre—including the National Theatre and Royal Festival Hall, plus nearby Shakespeare's Globe and Tate Modern—showcases the capital's crowning artistic glories. Or put it all in aerial perspective from the 72nd floor of the Shard.

8 Kensington, Chelsea, Knightsbridge, and Belgravia. Although the many boutiques of King's Road have lost much of their heady '60s swagger, the free museums are as awe-inspiring as ever. Kensington High Street is slightly more affordable than King's Road; otherwise, flash your cash at London's snazziest department stores, Harrods and Harvey Nichols.

9 Notting Hill and Bayswater. North of Kensington, around Portobello Road, Notting Hill Gate is a trendsetting couple of square miles of photographers' galleries, indie bookshops, fashionable boutiques, and hip restaurants. Nearby, Bayswater mixes eclectic fashions, fresh organic food shops, and gaudy Middle Eastern and Chinese restaurants.

10 Regent's Park and Hampstead with Primrose Hill and Camden Town. Surrounded by elegant, stucco-fronted "terraces"—mansions as big as palaces—designed by 19th-century architect John Nash, Regent's Park is a Regency extravaganza. The nearby ancient hilltop villages of Hampstead and Primrose Hill attract celebrity residents, while Camden Town provides the area with a much needed hip, alternative bent.

11 Greenwich. The Royal Observatory, Sir Christopher Wren's architecture, the Old Royal Naval College, British clipper ship *Cutty Sark*, and the prime meridian all add up to one of the best Thames-side excursions beyond central London.

12 The Thames Upstream. As an idyllic retreat from the city, stroll around London's historic gardens and enjoy the stately homes of Chiswick, Kew, and Richmond. Better yet, take a gentle river cruise and end up at famous Hampton Court Palace.

London Today

Majestic London has always been a great city in flux, and these days it's hard to turn a corner without stumbling into some work-in-progress crater so vast you can only imagine what was there before. New neighborhoods continually bubble up and burst to the fore—for example, a visit to Shoreditch at the eastern edge of The City should provide you with your quotient of London hipness. The anything-goes creative fervor that swirls through London like a fog shows up in DIY art galleries, cutting-edge boutiques, pop-up restaurants, nighttime street-food markets, and slick hipster hotels.

Discovery can take a bit of work, however. Modern London still largely reflects its medieval layout, a difficult tangle of streets and alleys. Even Londoners get lost in their own city. But London's bewildering street pattern will be a plus for the visitor who wants to experience its indefinable historic atmosphere. London is a walker's city and will repay every moment you spend exploring on foot.

Although many images are seared on your consciousness before you arrive—the guards at Buckingham Palace, the big red double-decker buses, Big Ben, and the River Thames—time never stands still in this ancient and yet gloriously contemporary city. Instead, London is in permanent revolution, and evolves, organically, mysteriously, historically through time.

ARCHITECTURE

With the exceptions of Canary Wharf, 30 St Mary Axe (more commonly known as "the Gherkin"), the Lloyd's of London building, and the London Eye, London's skyline has traditionally been low-key, with little of the skyscraping swagger of, say, Manhattan, Hong Kong, or Shanghai. But a spectacular crop of soaring new office towers with wonderful monikers—the Quill, the Shard, the Pinnacle, the Cheese Grater, and the Walkie-Talkie—is taking over.

With an astonishing 250-odd new skyscrapers being planned or built, opinions are split. Not everyone loves Renzo Piano's spire-like Shard and its 95-floor cloud-piercing "Vertical City" at London Bridge, which has stunning viewing galleries on the 68th, 69th, and 72nd floors. Nevertheless, once you whiz up and enjoy the 40-mile views, your take on the vast immensity of London is transformed forever.

IMMIGRATION

There's no doubt that London was built on immigration and is now one of the most diverse cities on Earth, with 300 languages spoken on the streets and nearly every world religion practiced at its places of worship. Immigrants make up over a third of the population and "white Britons" are in the minority for the first time, representing 45% of London's population of 8.9 million. The largest first-generation immigrant communities are from India, Poland, Ireland, Nigeria, Pakistan, Bangladesh, and Jamaica.

To Londoners, this is no big deal, as this has always been a city of immigrants—from invaders like the Romans, Anglo-Saxons, Vikings, and Normans to those seeking sanctuary like the French Huguenots and eastern European Jews, along with those seeking their postwar fortunes from Caribbean islands, the Indian subcontinent, and the rest of the British Commonwealth. Despite the populist tendencies sprouting up in other parts of the United Kingdom and Europe (and an anti-immigration prime minister in the form of Boris Johnson), London remains proud of its immigrant heritage and welcoming to any who wish to call themselves a Londoner.

ARTS AND CULTURE

Have you scanned a free copy of the daily London *Evening Standard* newspaper lately? It's full of listings for world-class shows, plays, jazz performances, readings, recitals, concerts, fashion follies, lectures, talks, tastings, cabarets, burlesque, and art auctions and exhibitions. Whether it's modern art and rare Old Masters paintings at the Frieze London art fair in Regent's Park or an all-day feast of food and diverse events at Mercato Metropolitano in Elephant and Castle, London is one of the most happening places on the planet.

PUBLIC TRANSPORTATION

Despite being horribly expensive, you'll notice that the public transport in London is generally nicer and more reliable than mass transit in other major cities. The much-delayed, £19 billion high-speed Crossrail underground railway—known as the Elizabeth line, after Queen Elizabeth II—is an epic feat of engineering that shortens the journey time for east to west trips. With 10 new stations and quick trips linking Paddington Station with Heathrow Airport and Canary Wharf in the east, even the notorious over-congestion eased when it finally opened in 2022. In addition, the Night Tube now runs around-the-clock on weekends on five key Underground lines.

Don't miss London's popular bike-sharing program, Santander Cycles, which has more than 11,000 bikes at some 700-odd central London docking stations, with unlimited short rides costing just £2 over a 24-hour period.

POLITICS

With its heady mix of modernity, migrants, and money, London is historically a pretty liberal city. It elected its first Muslim mayor in 2016, Sadiq Khan, a former London MP, human rights lawyer, and son of a London bus driver, but the city keeps adjusting to the fallout from the 2016 Brexit vote. The majority of Londoners voted to remain in the European Union, and many of the city's EU-origin residents, students, and workers have been affected by the changes to their legal rights to live, work, and study in the United Kingdom post-Brexit. Most Londoners were not pleased when pro-Brexit, anti-immigration former mayor Boris Johnson became prime minister in 2019 following Theresa May's resignation. But whatever the ongoing fallout from the United Kingdom's departure from the EU, London carries on as ever—vibrant, vital, diverse, and open for business.

NEW UPGRADES AND EXHIBITS

Some of London's top cultural attractions seem to be caught in an arts-upgrade arms race and are investing heavily in new galleries, exhibits, and extensions, plus assorted shiny new bells and whistles. Although COVID-19 has pushed back the Victoria and Albert Museum's ambitious new project, V&A East, in its Queen Elizabeth Olympic Park location, the currently shuttered National Portrait Gallery is set to complete its refurbishment in time to deliver a new wing and fresh presentation of its exquisite collection for spring 2023.

In the meantime, you can already appreciate the major £56 million revamp of the eminent Royal Academy of Arts in Piccadilly, which includes extended public galleries and a slick new bridge. After a three-year-long top-down renovation, the recently reopened Museum of the Home (formerly the Geffrye Museum) has returned with a slew of new spaces that tackle the evolution of home interiors along with a new program of events that takes in everything from community-focused talks to weekend yard sales.

What to Eat and Drink in London

FULL ENGLISH BREAKFAST
Consisting of eggs (usually fried or scrambled), sausages, bacon, fried tomatoes, black pudding, baked beans, mushrooms, and toast, the classic Full English Breakfast is best enjoyed with a classic builder's tea on the side to cut through the greasy, calorific mass.

FISH-AND-CHIPS
England's most famous dish is available throughout the city and comes in many shapes and sizes. Best enjoyed out of a hot paper wrap from a typical fish-and-chips shop, aka a chippy (and generally takeaway only), the meal should be eaten with a miniature wooden fork for extra authenticity. The fish is usually cod (but haddock, skate, and rock are not uncommon), covered in a crispy deep-fried batter. Chips are thick-cut fried potatoes, and sides can include anything from pickles and pickled eggs to mushy peas and curry sauce.

AFTERNOON TEA
Typically enjoyed between an early lunch and late dinner, Afternoon Tea is a very British way to spend your midday. A true Afternoon Tea consists of cakes, pastries, finger sandwiches sans crusts, and scones with jam and clotted cream displayed on a tiered stand and served with pots of loose-leaf tea. In many establishments, you can expect a tea menu (and the fanciest might even have a tea sommelier) where you can consider the likes of Earl Grey and Assam (the Queen's favorite teas), Darjeeling, and Ceylon.

CURRY
The 1970s saw a wave of Bangladeshi immigrants arriving in London and setting up restaurants along Brick Lane and in the surrounding area; competition clearly (and luckily for London diners) bred success. These days, there's a mix of Indian, Bangladeshi, and Pakistani restaurants, all serving some of the finest curry anywhere outside Asia. Aside from classics like vindaloo (super-hot), madras, and tandoori meats, the range of sweet, salty, spicy, and sour curries makes it one of London's best-loved cuisines.

CRAFT BEER
Although real ale (which is relatively flat and warm) still has its fans, the craft beer revolution has been the heart of London's beer scene for the last decade. Inspiration from American IPAs and their heady hops awakened London's senses, leading to a mass of new breweries supplying the demand for eclectic brews.

SUNDAY ROAST
Roast potatoes, roasted meat (chicken, beef, pork, or lamb), assorted vegetables, cauliflower cheese, Yorkshire pudding, and assorted condiments, like mint sauce, bread sauce, English mustard, horseradish, and cranberry jelly, make up some of the most important elements of a traditional Sunday roast, a meal that should leave you ready to sleep within 30 minutes of eating it.

Every pub in London serves a Sunday roast—and if it doesn't, then it can hardly call itself a pub—and the quality ranges dramatically depending on the establishment.

PIMM'S CUP
Best enjoyed while outside in the sun, Pimm's is a gin-based liqueur typically mixed with lemonade and ice, then filled with sliced strawberries, cucumber, and mint (and orange if you're feeling fancy). Popular at weddings, regattas, Wimbledon, horseracing tracks, and cricket matches, it is the British version of the Aperol Spritz and even more refreshing than water.

SRI LANKAN HOPPERS
A relatively new craze in London, the Sri Lankan hopper was always destined for great things in the city—who could resist the concept of a rice and coconut pancake filled with curry, relish, and fried eggs? Find them in Paradise, a hip restaurant in the heart of Soho.

GIN
Historically London's most popular spirit, gin has been rejuvenated over the last decade thanks to a range of small-batch distilleries joining the likes of established London brands like Hendrick's, Tanqueray, and Sipsmith. The "ginaissance" is very much in vogue, and visitors can expect to find full-on gin menus and a variety of tonics.

SALT BEEF BEIGELS
Cured in brine and slow-boiled for hours, the delicacy of salt beef belongs sandwiched between two beigel (yes, that's bagel to you Americans) halves, slathered in hot English mustard, and topped with pickles. The sandwich is available throughout the city in locations like the famous Brass Rail in Selfridges department store or at Brick Lane's historic 24-hour Beigel Bake, where every beigel comes with a dollop of East London charm.

PASTA FROM PADELLA
Although pasta in London is well regarded, it's unusual to see huge crowds lining up for the chance to sample well-crafted ravioli. But that's the story at Padella, the Borough Market restaurant whose legendary pasta has inspired levels of hysteria not seen in the city in several years. After trying the beef shin pappardelle and simple tagliarini with garlic and chilli, you'll be ready and willing to line up to try out the rest of the menu in no time.

TURKISH FOOD
London's huge Turkish community is responsible for gifting the city one of its favorite dishes—the *döner* kebab, a huge hunk of meat roasted on a revolving spit. Although Londoners love stopping off for late-night döner after a night of drinking, that's just one way to consume Turkish food. For those with more sophisticated palates, head

Gin

to one of the city's many excellent Turkish *ocakbasi* (grill restaurants) and opt for *shish* (large cubes of chicken or lamb cooked on the grill), *beyti* (ground lamb or beef wrapped in lavash bread and topped with yogurt), and plenty of roasted red onions and pomegranate.

DIM SUM DUMPLINGS
Although Soho has lost much of its independent dining scene, next-door Chinatown is much the same as it has always been, aside from the odd new bubble tea shop or Sichuan joint. That means reliably good dim sum can be found throughout the neighborhood in any one of Gerard Street's litany of restaurants; look out for the ubiquitous all-day dumpling menu.

What to Buy in London

Vintage shopping at Camden and Spitalfields markets

BESPOKE SUITS

Arguably the most famous road in men's fashion, Savile Row in Mayfair is the classic destination for all your bespoke suiting needs. A made-to-measure suit from the likes of Gieves & Hawkes or Ozwald Boateng might be quite the investment, but the quality and craftsmanship ensure a purchase that will stand the test of time.

VINTAGE SHOPPING

The booming London vintage scene is proof that one person's trash is another's treasure, with plenty of shops, markets, and warehouses around the city selling preloved clothing, shoes, and accessories. Head to Camden Market, Spitalfields Market, and best of all, Brick Lane and adjoining Cheshire Street, for the finest vintage finds in the city.

BOROUGH MARKET

Borough Market in London is like nowhere else, and the most important thing to remember before visiting is to arrive on an empty stomach. Between the coffee, deli meats, exotic vegetables, fresh bread, oysters, and cheese stands, you can almost fill up on samples alone. There are also plenty of condiments, jams, spices, and snacks to bring home with you.

James Smith & Sons

TOYS FROM BENJAMIN POLLOCK'S TOYSHOP
Though no child can say no to a visit to toy megastore Hamleys, adults will prefer the vintage appeal of Benjamin Pollock's Toyshop. This boutique is all about beautiful pop-up books, wooden yo-yos, and classic games.

UMBRELLAS FROM JAMES SMITH & SONS
Although stories of relentless London rainfall are exaggerated, it's fair to say an umbrella will still come in handy on a trip here. If you'd rather skip the flimsy hotel parasol for a refined brolly, perhaps with a chic polished-elm handle and a sturdy steel frame, you'll find the emblematic James Smith & Sons a dream come true. The Smith family has been keeping Londoners dry since 1830.

ANTIQUE BOOKS
The famous bookshop Foyles might have once used its old books in place of sandbags to protect its roof during the Blitz, but today the city has nothing but respect for the treasures found in its many rare and used-book shops. Still an exceptional store, Foyles has left antiquarian titles behind, but bibliophiles can source rare treasures in the likes of Hatchards, Maggs Bros. Ltd., and Peter Harrington.

PORTOBELLO ROAD MARKET
Portobello Road Market is a hodgepodge street sale selling everything from vintage clothes to fruit and vegetables, but the glue that holds it all together is the always interesting antiques section that commands big crowds. Every Saturday, a parade of stalls line up to sell antique goods with a sometimes dramatic range in quality—the fun is finding the best bits and engaging in a little haggling.

TEA FROM FORTNUM & MASON
If it's good enough for the Queen, then the tea selection at Fortnum & Mason should suffice for everyone else. The range of loose-leaf teas at this gourmet department store can seem endless, but keep in mind Her Majesty loves the Assam and Earl Grey. Available in tin boxes, hampers, and selection packs, tea from Fortnum & Mason makes the perfect gift.

Best Museums in London

THE NATURAL HISTORY MUSEUM

Undoubtedly the museum to have inspired more future paleontologists than any other, the Natural History Museum is the spiritual home of dinosaurs in London. The star attractions among the dino collection include a full fossil of a *Tyrannosaurus rex* and the skull of a *Triceratops*.

THE V&A MUSEUM

As the largest museum of art and design in the world, the Victoria and Albert Museum will greet you with intricate ceramic staircases, marble vaulted ceilings, and frescoed walls, all before you even begin thinking about the museum's collection of decorative arts.

TATE BRITAIN

All regal grandeur and impressive portico architecture, the classy—not to mention super-old—Tate Britain was opened in 1897 and owns a collection spanning 500 years, with some works dating back to 1500.

THE BRITISH MUSEUM

The biggest museum in London, the British Museum is also the most popular thanks to its eclectic collection of art, curiosities, and artifacts from around the world. Covering nearly 19 acres, the space contains everything from the riches of the Roman Empire to the largest collection of Egyptian artifacts outside Egypt—and yes, that includes a 5,000-year-old mummy.

TATE MODERN

Housed in a vast former power station on the south bank of the Thames, the towering structure of Tate Modern dominates its particular section of riverfront real estate. On top of the impressive collection of modern and contemporary artists—like Picasso, Francis Bacon, David Hockney, and Duchamp—on display in the main gallery, there's the imposing Turbine Hall and its interactive installations.

THE NATIONAL GALLERY

Instantly recognizable by its portico pillars overlooking Trafalgar Square, the National Gallery is probably the square's second most popular cultural attraction—placing close behind its handsome lions, of course. A grand gallery that shuns contemporary art in favor of masterpieces dating from the 1300s to the 1900s, the museum's permanent collection includes paintings by da Vinci, Caravaggio, Titian, Michelangelo, Raphael, and van Gogh.

IWM London, Imperial War Museum's flagship outpost

THE NATIONAL PORTRAIT GALLERY

It may reside in the physical shadow of the larger National Gallery just around the corner, but the National Portrait Gallery is no less of a draw. Start in the Tudor and Stuart rooms, where you'll find a lineup of all the kings and queens of England and Scotland. Don't miss Graham Sutherland's Churchill, the Darnley portrait of Queen Elizabeth I, and the only portrait of Shakespeare ever painted from life.

SIR JOHN SOANE'S MUSEUM

A cult institution that has gained mainstream popularity in recent years, Sir John Soane's Museum is a museum with a difference, in that it's a loving memorial to the late, great British architect in the shape of the perfect preservation of his former home in the heart of Holborn. A four-story town house, the home has been left untouched in accordance with Soane's wishes upon his death in 1837.

IMPERIAL WAR MUSEUMS

Consisting of Churchill's War Rooms; the decommissioned HMS *Belfast* battleship on the Thames; and the original Imperial War Museum (now IWM London), with exhibits featuring everything from Holocaust remembrance tours to war photography, the city's outposts of the national IWM collection create a comprehensive and thoughtful take on the theme of modern conflict without necessarily celebrating war.

THE SCIENCE MUSEUM

Between learning about the amazing intricacies of superviruses, embarking on a journey into space via VR, and tracing back the history of flight, there's not a lot left uncovered by the Science Museum.

Best Royal Sights in London

THE TOWER OF LONDON

A royal residence, longtime vault for the Crown Jewels, and gory location of more beheadings than you could count, the Tower of London has been a little bit of everything over the years.

BUCKINGHAM PALACE

Originally built in 1703, the palace has had significant upgrades over the last 300 years to make it fit for lavish royal living. Synonymous with both Queen Victoria (the first monarch to live here) and its current resident, Queen Elizabeth II, Buckingham Palace remains a working palace, although visitors can book guided tours of the state rooms in summer.

HAMPTON COURT PALACE

One of only two surviving palaces owned by Henry VIII, Hampton Court Palace was the home of Tudor royalty. The palace's serene location on the Thames, amazing gardens (including the famous maze), and dramatic interiors (be sure to see the famous Great Hall) make the short trip to Hampton well worth taking.

WESTMINSTER ABBEY

Royals never have to worry about securing a wedding venue because Westminster Abbey is always ready and waiting. Since the first in 1100, 16 royal weddings have taken place amidst the stained-glass windows, weathered oil paintings, and incredible Gothic stonework of the interior. The abbey has also been the site of all but two royal coronations since 1066.

THE HOUSEHOLD CAVALRY MUSEUM

If you miss the Changing the Guard ceremony, the next best thing is a visit to the Household Cavalry Museum. Here you can see the living, working routines of the Queen's Household Cavalry—the commissioned soldiers in full ceremonial regalia that you see at the Changing the Guard ceremony—as they go about their day.

KENSINGTON PALACE

Kensington Palace has had some of the royal family's biggest names as residents, with William, Kate, and their three children continuing to call it home today. You can explore the Sunken Garden, the Queen's State Apartments, and the King's State Apartments on a visit.

ST. JAMES'S PALACE

While no king or queen has lived in St. James's Palace since King William IV in the 1830s, the Tudor palace is older than Buckingham Palace and represents the most senior royal residence in the country.

KEW PALACE

Once home to King George III and Queen Charlotte, Kew Palace has been restored to its former glory and the private redbrick retreat makes for a picturesque sight surrounded by the manicured hedges and bucolic gardens of Kew. It may be the smallest of the royal palaces, but the English country house interiors are nothing short of charming.

THE QUEEN'S GALLERY

Housed within Buckingham Palace, the Queen's Gallery displays the Royal Family's downright huge and important collection of art, held in trust for the nation. The gallery is an amassed assortment of paintings, photography, antique furniture, and decorative arts that span the ages.

CLARENCE HOUSE

Built by John Nash, Clarence House is today home to the Prince of Wales and the Duchess of Cornwall, Charles and Camilla. The impressive whitewashed facade of the aristocratic town house mansion stands out from the crowd in its picturesque location beside St. James's Palace and The Mall.

Best Parks and Gardens in London

ST. JAMES'S PARK
Bordered by Buckingham Palace, The Mall, and Horse Guards, St. James's Park is London's most whimsical royal green space. Roam the gardens, tour the lakes, and observe their own lively pod of pelicans (residents here for more than 400 years).

RICHMOND PARK
Once a favorite hunting ground of Henry VIII, Richmond Park covers close to 2,500 acres of grasslands and forest, making it the biggest of London's Royal Parks. Any given weekend sees a rush of cyclists pushing themselves around the undulating 6.7-mile road that circles the park's perimeter, while others enjoy walking, running, and all manner of group activities across the meadows.

KEW GARDENS
Home to some of the world's rarest threatened species and most elusive plants, the Royal Botanic Gardens are more than just an attraction, they are a sanctuary, with a historic Victorian glasshouse at their heart. The range of exhibitions, installations, themed gardens, tropical greenhouses, and treetop walkways are way more than you can fit into a day, so start your explorations early.

HAMPSTEAD HEATH
It's the sign of a good London summer day when the bathing ponds of Hampstead Heath are packed with fair-weather locals and tourists alike, mixing it up with the ducks. But the real allure of Hampstead Heath is its wild, roaming grassland, wooded copses, and stunning views of the city, which combine to lend the heath an unmistakable literary quality.

KENSINGTON GARDENS
Annexed from Hyde Park by the Serpentine Lake, Kensington Gardens have a quieter, more intimate appeal compared to their larger neighbors. Here you'll find the Diana Memorial Playground, the famous bronze statue of Peter Pan, and, of course, the historic royal residence of Kensington Palace.

HYDE PARK
London's most popular park, Hyde Park is home to the Serpentine Galleries and the annual Pavilion art installation, plus boating lakes, the Albert Memorial, and Speakers' Corner.

REGENT'S PARK
On top of the gorgeous gardens, the picturesque lake and its pedalo boats, and an impressive collection of fountains and statues, Regent's Park is also home to London Zoo.

GREENWICH PARK
There's no park in London like Greenwich Park—after all, this is the only one of the city's green spaces that gives visitors the chance to pose with legs astride the prime meridian line. Located outside the Royal Observatory and its planetarium, the prime meridian establishes the reference for Greenwich Mean Time and the area's maritime history. In addition, there are green fields, orchards, stunning gardens, and some truly spectacular views of London and its Docklands.

HOLLAND PARK
A grand expanse of manicured lawns, nature trails, paths, and woodland surround the proud remains of a Jacobean mansion at the heart of Holland Park. The building suffered bomb damage during World War II, but the remaining front terrace provides a spectacular backdrop to the summertime open-air plays staged in the park. Be sure to check out the stunning Kyoto Garden, where Japanese maple trees, dahlias, and a tiered waterfall with a koi pond are some of the highlights.

Best Historic Pubs in London

THE DOG AND DUCK, SOHO

Elbow room is scant at this cramped Soho pub, but it's well worth pushing inside to take a look around. The beautiful Victorian tiles, plush red-leather banquets, imposing double-decker bar, polished chessboard floor, and vintage mirrors will appeal to literary history hunters looking for the spirit of George Orwell's "down and out in London."

THE SPANIARDS INN, HAMPSTEAD

Hampstead Heath has a smattering of pubs surrounding its boundaries, but none carry the history of The Spaniards Inn, where poets Byron and Keats were once locals. There's also a resident ghost.

THE LAMB, BLOOMSBURY

Close enough to the West End that it can form a part of any day trip around the major sites of central London, The Lamb on Lamb's Conduit Street is one of Bloomsbury's finest. Walking through the door here is like entering a time warp that transports you to a simpler time when the cell phone was but a twinkle in the eye of its inventor and the art of conversation ruled.

THE GEORGE INN, THE SOUTH BANK

The only pub in London owned by the National Trust, The George Inn is a fully functioning historic relic, dating back to somewhere around 1543. Not only is it one of the oldest pubs in London, but The George Inn is also the only original galleried coach house left in the city.

YE OLDE CHESHIRE CHEESE, THE CITY

Rebuilt after the 1666 Great Fire of London, Ye Olde Cheshire Cheese is so old that it actually deserves its moniker. And with age comes beauty in this pub that attracted a literary crowd centuries before it became a home away from home to Fleet Street's journalists.

THE HARP, COVENT GARDEN

A traditional West End pub that has changed with the times is The Harp, which supplements its physical charms with a range of about 20 real ales and craft beers on tap. There is an upstairs lounge here, but the cramped bar space below is way more fun.

Lamb & Flag

**THE DOVE,
HAMMERSMITH**
London's oldest riverside
pub north of the Thames
is one of the city's finest
and perfect for a whimsical
wander along the river path
west of central London.
With low-beamed ceilings,
grand brick fireplaces, and
secret rooms, The Dove
couldn't be cozier if it tried.

**LAMB & FLAG,
COVENT GARDEN**
Tucked away in a hidden
courtyard in the heart of
Covent Garden, The Lamb
& Flag is a beautiful old pub
established in 1772 and once
nicknamed "The Bucket
of Blood" on account of
the bare-knuckle fights it
hosted in its upstairs room.

**THE BLACKFRIAR,
THE CITY**
This is a quirky wedge
of a local pub filled with
religious iconography, art
nouveau flourishes, and a
roaring fire. A touch Bavar-
ian in theme, it dates back
to 1875 and sits on the site
of a former friary, hence the
name.

Under-the-Radar Things to Do in London

THE MUSEUM OF THE HOME
A museum of many facets, the Museum of the Home (formerly the Geffrye Museum) in Hoxton is a nostalgic exploration of home life through the ages, from 1600 to the present day. Preserved rooms fill the quaint building and include a 1745 parlor, a re-created living room from 1935, an 1890 drawing room, and a 1630 hallway.

HORNIMAN MUSEUM WALRUS
A resident of the Horniman Museum for more than a century, London's favorite walrus is a taxidermy specimen who doesn't quite live up to his real-life counterparts. Prepared in the 19th century when taxidermists didn't have the luxury of the Internet for reference, the lovingly idiosyncratic and overstuffed walrus is synonymous with this charming natural history museum that sits at the top of Forest Hill. Full of educational and evocative pieces, the permanent collection features everything from ancient tribal art to man-made mermaids.

BERMONDSEY BEER MILE
Around 15 independent craft breweries and bottle shops are housed in the old brick railway arches of Bermondsey, and their close proximity and the decision to synchronize opening times on Saturday has led to the birth of the Bermondsey Beer Mile. Start at Brew by Numbers Tasting Room on Enid Street.

PRINCE CHARLES CINEMA
Surrounded by the multiplexes of Leicester Square, the Prince Charles caters to cinephiles who pine for the old, the odd, and the celebrated, showing classic double-billings, quote-along screenings, all-night movie marathons, and cult movies in their original 35 mm formats.

REGENT'S CANAL
Dotted with stylish cafés, pubs, breweries, and one whimsical floating bookshop, the length of Regent's Canal between Angel and Hackney Wick is an ideal way to explore the East End.

Barbican Centre

HIGHGATE CEMETERY
Highgate is the most famous of London's Victorian cemeteries, and locals love exploring its flora and fauna and finding an appealingly atmospheric—not to mention beautiful—place to wander. It's the final resting place for the likes of Karl Marx, Malcolm McLaren, and George Eliot.

BARBICAN CENTRE
Having recently enjoyed something of a renaissance, it's now acceptable to enjoy the bold, rigid lines of this Brutalist masterpiece, which houses Europe's largest performing arts center. With a cinema, theater, library, and exhibition spaces, the Barbican Centre is a haven of creativity and artistic expression.

VICTORIA AND ALBERT MUSEUM AFTER-HOURS
The Victoria and Albert Museum was one of the first in London to host regular after-hours events. The Friday Late series runs on the last Friday of every month, when DJs, pop-up cocktail bars, artists, and designers help create one of the best free nights out in town.

London's Royal Legacy

THE ROCKY MONARCHY

From medieval castles and keeps to Royal Parks, palaces, pageants, ceremonies, and processions, London has had a tumultuous and sometimes bloody royal history, which can still be encountered at practically every turn. London has been the royal capital of England since 1066, when the Norman king William the Conqueror began the tradition of royal coronations at Westminster Abbey. All but two reigning monarchs since then—from Richard I (the "Coeur de Lion") in 1189 to the current Queen Elizabeth II in 1953—have been crowned at the Abbey.

Many of England's illustrious—and sometimes downright notorious—kings and queens have left a legacy or their majestic mark on the city. You'll find many of the finest places have royal associations: William I subjugated London with the imposing Tower of London, Henry VIII hunted deer at Hampton Court, Elizabeth I enjoyed bear-baiting in Southwark, and Charles I was publicly executed on Whitehall. Tyrannical but weak monarchs like King John (1199–1216) granted the City of London extra power under the Magna Carta, while the first "Parliament" sat at the Royal Palace of Westminster in 1265 under Henry III. The late medieval Tudors, however, rarely brooked dissent: Elizabeth I's half-sister, "Bloody" Mary I (1553–58), burned heretic Protestant bishops at the stake, and traitors were hung, drawn, and quartered, with their heads stuck on pikes on London Bridge.

A CULTURAL RENAISSANCE

From 1558 to 1601, peace under Elizabeth I ("the Virgin Queen") led to a cultural renaissance and the great flowering of English theater, poetry, letters, music, and drama, centered on Shakespeare's Globe and the open-air playhouses of Southwark. Charles I was later captured by the formidable Puritan Oliver Cromwell during the English Civil War and beheaded on a freezing day outside the Banqueting House in Westminster in 1649.

Although the Interregnum lasted only 16 years (outlawing simple pleasures, such as dancing and theater), the Restoration of Charles II in 1660 and subsequent monarchs saw London grow and transform into a teeming metropolis. These monarchs included the Dutch Protestant William III and Mary II—who moved into Kensington Palace, now the home of the Duke and Duchess of Cambridge—and the House of Hanover's four Georgian kings and later Queen Victoria.

THE MODERN ROYALS

Besides the color, pageantry, and marching bands of the Changing the Guard ceremony at Buckingham Palace, there's also a rich calendar of royal ceremonies. The Ceremony of the Keys to lock up the Tower of London has taken place at 9:53 pm each night for more than 700 years (bar the odd bombing during the Blitz), and you can see the monarch take the Royal Salute from the Household Division at the annual Trooping the Colour march from Horse Guards Parade to St. James's Park. The Queen is also drawn by four horses in the dazzling Irish State Coach from Buckingham Palace to the Palace of Westminster in a huge royal procession for the State Opening of Parliament each autumn, and you can see her pay homage to the war dead at the Cenotaph on Remembrance Sunday.

These days, you might spot the Duke and Duchess of Cambridge (Prince William and Kate Middleton) walking in Kensington Gardens with their three young children.

Sports in London

Sports in the capital are probably best watched rather than participated in. If you're lucky enough to score a ticket for a Premier League football match, you'll experience a seething mass of jeering, mockery, and tribal chanting. Rugby, tennis, horseracing, and cricket also impinge on Londoners' horizons at crucial times of the year, but you're unlikely to see grown men crying at the outcome of the Wimbledon Men's Final.

CRICKET

At its best, cricket can be a slow build of smoldering tension and unexpected high-wire excitement. At its worst, it can be too slow and uneventful for the casual observer, as five-day games crawl toward a draw or as rain stops play. But try to visit Lord's—known as the home of cricket—on match days, just to hear the *thwack* of leather on willow and to see the English aristocracy and upper-middle class on full display.

Lord's. Lord's Cricket Ground—home of the venerable Marylebone Cricket Club, founded in 1787 and whose rules codified the game—has been hallowed cricketing turf since 1814. Tickets for major test matches are hard to come by: obtain an application form online and enter the ballot (lottery) to purchase them. ⊠ *Marylebone Cricket Club, Lord's Cricket Ground, St. John's Wood Rd., St. John's Wood* ☎ *020/7432–1000* ⊕ *www. lords.org* Ⓜ *St. John's Wood.*

FOOTBALL

London's top soccer teams—Chelsea, Tottenham Hotspur, Arsenal, and West Ham—are world-class outfits and the first three often progress in the Europe-wide Champions League. It's unlikely you'll get tickets for anything except the least popular Premier League games during the August–May season, despite the high ticket prices—£50 for a walk-up

match-day seat at Chelsea, and £97 for the most expensive tickets at Arsenal.

ROWING

The Boat Race. Join more than a quarter of a million merry devotees along the banks of the River Thames between Putney and Mortlake for a glimpse of the annual Oxford and Cambridge Boat Races, held on the last Saturday of March or the first Saturday of April. Sink a few pints and soak up the tweed-cap-and-Barbour-clad atmosphere as these heavyweight eight-man university crews clash oars and tussle head-to-head for supremacy. First raced in 1829, the 4-mile route is a picturesque stretch between Putney and Chiswick bridges. The Men's and Women's Boat Races are held on the same day. ⊠ *Putney Bridge, Putney* ⊕ *www. theboatraces.org.*

RUNNING

TCS London Marathon. The London Marathon starts at 9:30 am on a Sunday in mid-April, with more than 35,000 athletes running from Blackheath or Greenwich to The Mall. Happy crowds throng the route to cheer the runners along. ⊕ *www.tcslondonmarathon.com.*

TENNIS

Wimbledon Lawn Tennis Championships. The All England Club's Wimbledon Lawn Tennis Championships are famous for Centre Court, strawberries and cream, a gentle spot of rain, and a nostalgic old-school insistence on players wearing white. Thankfully, the rain has been banished on Centre Court by the nifty retractable roof, but whether you can get tickets for Centre Court all comes down to the luck of the draw—there's a ballot system for advance purchase (see their website for more details). ⊠ *The All England Lawn Tennis Club, Church Rd., London* ☎ *020/8971–2473 for general inquiries* ⊕ *www.wimbledon.com.*

Free and Cheap

The exchange rate may vary, but there is one conversion that will never change: £0 = $0. Here are our picks for the top free (and cheap) things to do in London.

CONCERTS

St. Martin-in-the-Fields, St Stephen Walbrook, St Olaves in The City, and St James's Church in Piccadilly all host free lunchtime concerts and recitals, as does St. George's in Bloomsbury on Sunday afternoon. There are also regular organ recitals at Westminster Abbey.

Of the elite music colleges, the Royal Academy of Music, the Royal College of Music, Guildhall, Trinity College, and the Royal Opera House offer free recitals. For contemporary ears, there's free jazz and classical music on an exquisite 1897 Bechstein on the first Sunday of the month at The Dysart Petersham restaurant (✉ *135 Petersham Rd.* ☎ *07967/481–625*) in Richmond and live jazz at The Blue Posts (✉ *28 Rupert St.* ☎ *07921/336–010*) in Soho, starting at 3 pm every Sunday. For free blues Sunday–Thursday or before 8:30 pm on Friday and Saturday, head to the Ain't Nothin' But... blues bar in Soho (✉ *20 Kingly St.* ☎ *020/7287–0514*).

FILM, THEATER, AND OPERA

Both the National Theatre and the Royal Opera House release a number of Friday Rush tickets at £10 each. These tickets are for a range of performances and can also include sold-out shows, so it is always worth setting your alarm and joining the online queue at 1 pm on Friday (for both venues).

There are 400 £5 standing-room tickets available for every performance at the Shakespeare's Globe theater, as well as £10 standing-room tickets for magical candlelit plays and concerts at the adjacent indoor Sam Wanamaker Playhouse. At Sloane Square, the Royal Court Theatre offers all tickets at £12 on Monday for all performances in the Jerwood Theatre Downstairs.

SIGHTSEEING

Prop yourself on the top deck of a red double-decker bus for a fantastic sightseeing tour through the most scenic parts of the city. With all buses now cashless, you can instead use your Oyster card or buy tickets from machines at bus stops for the following routes:

Bus 11: King's Road, Sloane Square, Victoria Station, Westminster Abbey, Houses of Parliament and Big Ben, Whitehall, Trafalgar Square, the Strand, Royal Courts of Justice, Fleet Street, and St. Paul's Cathedral.

Bus 19: Sloane Square, Knightsbridge, Hyde Park Corner, Green Park, Piccadilly Circus, Shaftsbury Avenue, Bloomsbury, Angel, and Islington.

Bus 88: Oxford Circus, Conduit Street, Piccadilly Circus, Haymarket, Trafalgar Square, Whitehall, Horse Guards Parade, Westminster Station, Westminster Abbey, Horseferry Road, and Tate Britain.

London with Kids

ACTIVITIES

Ride the London Eye. Europe's largest observation wheel looks like a giant fairground ride, and you can see across what seems like half of London from the top.

Pose with a Queen's Horse Guard. There's always the Queen's mounted guards in uniform by the entrance to Horse Guards on the Trafalgar Square end of Whitehall. They don't mind posing for pictures, but they're not allowed to smile.

Ice-skating at Somerset House. Send your kids whizzing, arms whirling, across ice from mid-November to January at this spotlighted open-air ice rink in a former Renaissance royal palace.

Pedalo on the Serpentine. Pack a picnic and take a blue pedalo out into the middle of Hyde Park's famed Serpentine lake; settle back and tuck in to lunch.

Lose the kids at Hampton Court Maze. The topiary might be more than 300 years old, but the quest to reach the middle of Hampton Court's world-famous trapezoid-shape yew hedge maze remains as challenging as ever.

West End musicals. Foot-stompingly good West End musicals and shows like *Les Misérables, Mary Poppins, Matilda, Mamma Mia!, The Lion King, Oliver!, Grease,* and *Harry Potter and the Cursed Child* will captivate the over-seven crowd.

EDUCATION WITHOUT YAWNS

Kew Gardens. The Royal Botanic Gardens in Kew are great for young ones, and the huge Children's Garden features a 60-foot-high treetop Sky Walk, trampolines, scramble slides, and children's trails; it's free for kids under four.

The London Dungeon. It's guts and gore galore at this top South Bank attraction that plunges you into the blood-soaked depths of London history, with tales from a gruesome Jack the Ripper pub, Sweeney Todd barbers, and Mrs. Lovett's infamous pie shop.

London Zoo. Disappear into the animal kingdom among the enclosures, complete with sessions for kids about all kinds of bugs and spiders in this popular animal retreat in Regent's Park.

The Natural History Museum. It doesn't get more awe-inspiring than bloodsucking bats, a cabinet of hummingbirds, simulated Kobe earthquakes, and a life-size blue whale. Just make sure you know your dodo from your *Daspletosaurus.*

The Science Museum. Special effects, virtual space voyages, 800 interactive exhibits, puzzles, and mysteries from the world of science can keep kids effortlessly engaged all day.

The Tower of London. Perfect for playing prince and princess in front of the Crown Jewels, but not so perfect for imagining what becomes of the fairy tale—watch your royal necks.

PERFORMANCES

Covent Garden street performers. You can't beat the open-air gaggle of jugglers, fire-eaters, unicyclists, mime artists, and human statues tantalizing crowds at Covent Garden Piazza.

Regent's Park Open Air Theatre. Welcome to the land of fairy dust and magic. Don't miss an evening performance under the stars of *A Midsummer Night's Dream* in high summer.

What to Read and Watch

THE CROWN

Since it debuted on Netflix in November 2016, this historical drama about the reign of Queen Elizabeth II has picked up a host of accolades and awards, from Emmys to Golden Globes. Although you're unlikely to bump into Liz on your visit to England, you might well visit some of the many palaces, castles, and other locations featured in the show.

FLEABAG

Probably the most talked-about British TV show of the late 2010s, this award-winning comedy-drama follows creator Phoebe Waller-Bridge's titular character as she attempts to cope with life and love in London, all while coming to terms with a recent tragedy.

CALL THE MIDWIFE

This BBC period drama, which follows a group of nurse midwives working in the East End of London in the 1950s and '60s, has been widely praised for tackling subjects like miscarriage, abortion, and female genital mutilation.

CHEWING GUM

Written by and starring Michaela Coel, this cult British sitcom (which has since reached a larger international audience through Netflix) features 24-year-old shop assistant Tracey Gordon, who wants to break free of her strict religious upbringing and learn more about the modern world. Coel also brought her talent to the television screen with her 2020 HBO limited series *I May Destroy You*, which explored a young woman in London rebuilding her life in the aftermath of a rape.

THE GREAT BRITISH BAKING SHOW

A quaint television baking competition has became an international phenomenon. Every season, a fresh-faced group of 12 amateur bakers are set a series of baking challenges over several weeks to determine the ultimate winner. *The Great British Bake Off* (as it was known originally) has spawned dozens of international versions all over the world, including *The Great American Baking Show* on ABC, but the original remains the best.

LOVE ACTUALLY

Since it was released in 2003, this romantic comedy has become a staple of Christmases all over the world. The movie follows the loosely interconnected love stories of several characters in London, played by a who's who of British acting royalty, including Colin Firth, Kiera Knightley, Chiwetel Ejiofor, Emma Thompson, and Hugh Grant.

THE HARRY POTTER SERIES BY J. K. ROWLING

The best-selling book series in history, J. K. Rowling's epic fantasy novels chronicle the lives of young wizard Harry Potter and his friends Hermione and Ron as they attend the Hogwarts School of Witchcraft and Wizardry. Visitors to London can find a photo op at Platform 9¾ at King's Cross train station, where Harry and company board the Hogwarts Express in the books.

THE ADVENTURES OF SHERLOCK HOLMES BY ARTHUR CONAN DOYLE

First published in the 1890s, these short stories about fictional private detective Sherlock Holmes, who uses observation, deduction, and logical reasoning to crack seemingly unsolvable cases, have fascinated audiences ever since. The recent BBC series *Sherlock,* based on the stories and starring Benedict Cumberbatch and Martin Freeman as modern versions of Sherlock and his assistant Watson, has breathed new life into the character. In the books, Holmes resides at 221B Baker Street in London, which in real life is now the address of the Sherlock Holmes Museum.

OLIVER TWIST BY CHARLES DICKENS

Charles Dickens's second novel is perhaps his most famous, recounting the story of orphan Oliver Twist and his life as a juvenile pickpocket for the criminal Fagin. It offers a fascinating, unflinching insight into the criminal gangs and cruel treatment of orphans in London during the mid-19th century.

WHITE TEETH BY ZADIE SMITH

This award-winning 2000 novel focuses on the lives of two best friends—Samad Iqbal and Archie Jones—and their families in North London. The book, which was Zadie Smith's debut, deftly explores themes of cultural identity, faith, race, and gender in modern England.

BRICK LANE BY MONICA ALI

Set on the eponymous Brick Lane, the heart of London's Bangladeshi community, this novel follows the life of Nazneen, an 18-year-old Bangladeshi woman who struggles to adapt to life in England after marrying an older man.

WILLIAM SHAKESPEARE'S HISTORIES

The Bard's series of historical plays chronicle the lives of four centuries of English monarchs, including King John, Henry V, and Richard III. Although widely regarded as Tudor propaganda (Shakespeare lived during the reign of Elizabeth I, the last Tudor monarch), the histories are hugely entertaining and informative, too. Many take place in historical spots around London, including the Tower of London, and if you're lucky, you might even catch one of them being performed at the Globe Theatre.

Afternoon Tea

AN AGE-OLD TRADITION

So what is Afternoon Tea, *exactly*? Well, it is real loose-leaf tea—Earl Grey, English Breakfast, Ceylon, Darjeeling, or Assam—brewed in a silver or porcelain pot and served with fine bone-china cups and saucers, milk or lemon, and silver spoons, taken between noon and 6 pm. For the traditional full English experience, there should be elegant finger foods on a three-tier silver cake stand: finely cut crustless finger sandwiches on the bottom; scones with Cornish clotted cream and strawberry preserves in the middle; and rich English fruitcake, shortbread, pastries, macarons, and dainty *petits gateaux* on top.

CLASSIC CHOICES

The Savoy on the Strand offers one of the most beautiful settings for Afternoon Tea. The Thames Foyer, a symphony of grays and golds centered on a winter garden wrought-iron gazebo and great glass cupola, is just the place for the house pianist to accompany you as you enjoy 72 rare house teas along with finger sandwiches, homemade scones, and pastries. A traditional Afternoon Tea here is £65.

Setting the standard in its English Tea Room for some of London's best-known traditional teas, **Brown's Hotel** in Mayfair offers Afternoon Tea for £65 in an Agatha Christie–esque wood-paneled salon or, if you wish to splurge, Champagne Afternoon Tea for £75.

If you seek timeless chic, the art deco dining room at **The Wolseley** on Piccadilly remains a deeply classy hangout. The silver service teas here—light Cream Tea is £9.50, Classic Afternoon Tea is £33, and Champagne Tea, £44.50—are divine, and the café can present a vegan alternative with prior notice.

SOMETHING DIFFERENT

Camp it up in India Mahdavi's golden space, with site-specific works by British-Nigerian artist yinka shobinare, in the high-ceilinged **Gallery** at **Sketch,** where Afternoon Tea (£65) is tweaked with malt, pumpernickel, and white-bread finger sandwiches, from Scottish smoked salmon topped with dill and roe to Norfolk goose egg and mayo with quail's egg on top, as well as warm scones and *petits gateaux,* such as lemon and Mara des Bois strawberry Battenberg cake.

Alternatively, you can sample finger sandwiches and sip fine English sparkling wine while looking out onto the immaculate lawns of the **Kensington Palace Pavilion,** the site of William and Kate's marriage proposal within resplendent Kensington Gardens. Afternoon Tea is £34, and a suitably Royal Afternoon Tea (with a glass of English sparkling wine) is £45.

With hip, art deco interiors, **Brasserie of Light** (handily located within Selfridges department store for post-shopping refreshments) serves a luxurious take on the classic Afternoon Tea with its Pegasus Afternoon Tea (£70), quite possibly the most Instagrammable tea in London.

AN EDWARDIAN ESCAPE

For some gilt-edged rococo grandeur, few can compete with Afternoon Tea at **The Ritz** on Piccadilly. It's served in the stunning Palm Court, replete with linen-draped tables, Louis XIV chaise lounges, sparkling chandeliers, resplendent bouquets, and discrete musical accompaniment; it's a true taste of Edwardian London in the 21st century. Afternoon Tea is £62, and Celebration Champagne Tea is £86. There are five sittings from 11:30 am to 7:30 pm; be sure to book three months ahead, and men should wear a jacket and tie.

TRAVEL SMART

Updated by
James O'Neill

★ **CAPITAL:**
London

👫 **POPULATION:**
8,962,000

💬 **LANGUAGE:**
English

$ **CURRENCY:**
Pound sterling

☎ **COUNTRY CODE:**
44

⚠ **EMERGENCIES:**
999

🚗 **DRIVING:**
On the left

⚡ **ELECTRICITY:**
220–240V/50Hz; Continental-style plugs, with two or three round prongs

⊗ **TIME:**
5 hours ahead of New York

🌐 **WEB RESOURCES:**
www.visitbritain.com
www.visitlondon.com
www.standard.co.uk
www.timeout.com/london

Know Before You Go

As one of the largest cities in the world, London can be overwhelming for a first-time visitor. Here are some key tips to help you navigate your trip, whether it's your first time visiting or your 21st.

DIVERSITY

London is among the most diverse cities on Earth. With 300 languages spoken on its streets and nearly every world religion practiced at its places of worship, immigrants make up over a third of the population, and "white Britons" are now in the minority for the first time in history. Most Londoners embrace this diversity, and indeed some of the best neighborhoods to visit are thriving immigrant communities. The highest populations of immigrants come from India, Pakistan, Poland, Romania, Ghana, and Turkey.

BREXIT

The 2016 referendum saw Britain vote by a slender margin to leave the European Union. Problem is, London voted overwhelmingly to remain. Consequently, Prime Minister Boris Johnson's decision, upon gaining power in 2019, to pursue a hardline Brexit has further riled the citizens of this outward-looking, multicultural city. What's more, six years on from the referendum, U.K.–EU talks on the more problematic aspects of Brexit are still ongoing. Johnson's a deeply unpopular figure in London, so too is Brexit. So just keep that all in mind if you decide to risk talking politics on a trip here.

THE ROYAL FAMILY

The Royal Family remains a key feature of, if not British life, then certainly the British tabloids. It has to be said that not all Londoners are fans of the Windsors, with the exception of the widely respected Queen. One consistent complaint is the taxpayer-funded royal lifestyle. Another has been the family's perceived treatment of Meghan Markle, the Duchess of Sussex. What can't be denied though, is that the Royal Family continues to be a major draw for many visitors to London, thanks in no small part to the success of shows like Netflix's The Crown. Maybe just don't expect a local to gush over Prince Louis as much as you do.

BRITISH VERSUS AMERICAN LINGO

Nearly everyone knows that Brits have different words for certain things than Americans do. But some knowledge of the British-English dialect is essential for a trip to London: a lift is an elevator; instead of waiting in line, you queue; pants are actually underpants (what Americans consider pants are trousers); chips are french fries; crisps are potato chips; and the bathroom is known as the toilet or the loo (or even, in some public spaces, the W/C, or water closet). The list is a long one, but a final good word to remember is "cheers," which is used when toasting with drinks but also often employed when saying "goodbye" or "thank you."

BANK HOLIDAYS

Several national "bank" holidays are celebrated throughout the year in the United Kingdom: May Day (the first Monday in May), at Easter time, the last Monday in May, the last Monday in August, Boxing Day (December 26), and New Year's Day. On these days many stores and some attractions might be closed, while restaurants and museums may be much busier than usual. Do check to see if your trip falls during a bank holiday, so you can plan accordingly.

SAVING MONEY

There's no denying London is an expensive city, but there are plenty of ways to save money. Most major museums in London are free, and those that aren't are often covered under the London Pass. With a variety of prices and durations (from 1 day for £62 to 5 days for £131), you'll get access to nearly every major London attraction.

PUB LIFE

The pub is the lifeblood of London's social life. Expect noisy after-work crowds, especially on days of soccer or rugby matches. The drinking age in England is 18, and while not explicitly legal *everywhere*, alcohol can be consumed in public areas within reason; so don't be afraid to put together a gin-heavy Pimm's punch for your picnic. Smoking is banned in all indoor public spaces in London. Currently marijuana is not legal in the United Kingdom.

PUBLIC TRANSIT

Renting a car during your time in London is a downright horrible idea. Both taxis and rideshare programs are widely available, although these can get pricey and the traffic in the city can be notoriously bad depending on the time of day (Uber is indeed still up-and-running in the city after a 2018 lawsuit from London cabbies almost succeeded in banning the rideshare app). But the best way to get around London during your trip is by using buses and the underground Tube system.

The Tube now runs 24 hours a day on weekends on five major lines: Piccadilly, Victoria, Northern, Central, and Jubilee. Night buses do run from midnight to 5 am, but they're infrequent and probably best avoided. When traveling the city via public transportation, be sure to purchase an Oyster card, a smart card that can be charged with a cash value and then used for discounted travel throughout London. Buy your Oyster card for £5 when you first arrive, and then prepay any amount you wish for your expected travel while here.

Two important things to remember when traveling on the city's public transit; first, always stand to the right on escalators; second, the consumption of alcohol is banned within London's TfL network (Transport for London; think Underground and buses), but not on national rail lines that link to the city.

NAVIGATING LONDON

London is a confusing city to navigate, even for people who've visited it a few times. Its streets are arranged in medieval patterns that no longer make much sense, meaning that you can't always use logic to find your way around. A good map is essential, and public transportation can be a lifesaver: buses will take you magically from point A to point B, and the Tube is often the quickest way to reach your destination.

Although free tourist maps can be handy, they're usually quite basic and include only major streets. If you're going to be doing lots of wandering around, buy the pocket-size map book *London A–Z*, which is sold in bookstores and Tube and train stations throughout the city. Its detailed maps are invaluable. To find your way, look for tall landmarks near where you are headed: the London Eye, for example, or the cross atop St. Paul's Cathedral— or the most obvious of all, Big Ben. If you get properly lost, the best people to ask are the Londoners hustling by you, who know the area like nobody else.

Central London and its surrounding districts are divided into 32 boroughs (33, counting the City of London). More useful for finding your way around, however, are the subdivisions of London into postal districts. The first one or two letters give the location: N means north, NW means northwest, and so on. Don't expect the numbering to be logical, however. You won't, for example, find W2 next to W3. The general rule is that the lower numbers, such as W1 or SW1, are closest to Buckingham Palace, but it is not consistent—SE17 is closer to the city center than SE2, for example.

Getting Here and Around

Air

Flying time to London is about 6½ hours from New York, 7½ hours from Chicago, 11 hours from San Francisco, and 21½ hours from Sydney.

For flights out of London, the general rule is that you should be at the airport at least one hour before your scheduled departure time for domestic flights and two to three hours before international flights.

AIRPORTS

Most international flights to London arrive at either Heathrow Airport (LHR), 15 miles west of London, or at Gatwick Airport (LGW), 27 miles south of the capital. Most flights from the United States go to Heathrow, which is divided into five terminals, with Terminals 3–5 handling transatlantic flights. Gatwick is London's second gateway. It has grown from a European airport into an airport that also serves dozens of U.S. destinations.

A third airport, Stansted (STN), is 35 miles northeast of the city; it handles European and domestic traffic. Three smaller airports, Luton (LTN), 30 miles north of town, Southend (SEN), 40 miles to the east, and business-oriented London City (LCY), in east London E16, mainly handle flights to Europe.

GROUND TRANSPORTATION

London has excellent if pricey bus and train connections between its airports and central London. If you're arriving at Heathrow, you can pick up a map and fare schedule at the Transport for London (TfL) Information Centre, in the Underground station serving Terminals 2–3. Train service can be quick, but the downside (for trains from all airports) is that you must get yourself and your luggage to the train via a series of escalators and connecting trams. Airport link

From Heathrow to Central London

TRAVEL MODE	TIME	COST
Taxi	1 hour–plus	£49–£92 (depending on traffic)
Heathrow Express train	15 minutes	From £25 (£37 round-trip), £32 for first class
Underground	50 minutes	£6 one-way (less with Oyster card)
National Express bus	1 hour	From £5 one-way

buses (generally National Express airport buses) may ease the luggage factor and drop you off closer to central hotels, but they're subject to London traffic, which can be horrendous and make the trip drag on for hours. Taxis can be more convenient than buses, but beware that prices can go through the roof.

Heathrow by bus: National Express buses take one hour to reach the city center (Victoria) and cost from £5 one-way and £10 round-trip (book online for best prices). The National Express Hotel Hoppa service runs from all airports to 30 hotels near the airport (from £4.50). Heathrow Shuttle offers a shared minibus service between Heathrow and more than 500 London hotels starting from £23.

The N9 night bus runs to Aldwych every 30 minutes midnight–5 am; it takes just over an hour and costs £1.55 (you need to pay with an Oyster card or a contactless debit/credit card). Please note: the N9 doesn't stop at Terminal 4; take Bus Nos. 490 or 482 to Terminal 5 and catch it there.

Heathrow by Tube and train: The cheap, direct route into London is via the Piccadilly line of the Underground (London's extensive subway system, or "Tube"). Trains normally run every four to eight minutes from all terminals from early morning until just before midnight. The 50-minute trip into central London costs £6 one-way and connects with other central Tube lines. The Heathrow Express train is comfortable and convenient, if costly, speeding into London's Paddington Station in 15 minutes. Standard one-way tickets cost £25 (£37 round-trip) and £32 for first class (£55 round-trip), but tickets booked online and 90 days in advance can cost as little as £5.50. In all cases, children under 15 travel free. There's daily service 5:10 am (6:10 am on Sunday) to 11:25 pm, with departures usually every 15 minutes.

Local trains to Paddington can be a cheaper alternative to the Heathrow Express (one-way tickets start at £11.20). However, these trains take a little longer (34 minutes), are less frequent (two per hour), and make six stops en route. They also have no first-class carriages.

Heathrow by taxi: Taking a taxi from the airport into the city is an expensive and time-consuming option. The city's congestion charge (£15) may be added to the bill if your hotel is in the charging zone; you run the risk of getting stuck in traffic; and if you take a taxi from the stand, the price will be even more expensive (whereas a minicab booked ahead is a set price). The trip can take more than an hour and can cost in the region of £75, depending on time of day.

Gatwick by bus: An hourly National Express bus service runs from Gatwick's north and south terminals to London's Victoria Station. The journey takes upward of 90 minutes (depending on time of day) and costs from £7 one-way.

The easyBus service runs to west London (Earl's Court) from as little as £4 if booked in advance; the later the ticket is booked online, the higher the price (up to £12 on board).

Gatwick by train: The fast, nonstop Gatwick Express leaves for Victoria Station every 15 minutes, 6 am–11:10 pm. The 30-minute trip costs from £19.90 one-way, and £38.90 round-trip (slightly cheaper tickets are available online).

Thameslink Railway runs nonexpress services that are cheaper. Thameslink trains run regularly throughout the day to St. Pancras International, London Bridge, and Blackfriars stations; departures are every 15 minutes (hourly during the night), and the journey takes 45–55 minutes. Tickets are from £12.40 one-way to St. Pancras International.

Stansted by bus: Hourly service on National Express Airport bus A6 (24 hours a day) to Victoria Coach Station costs from £8 one-way, £16 round-trip, and takes about 1 hour 45 minutes (again, the cheapest tickets are only available online and in advance). Stops include Golders Green, Finchley Road, St. John's Wood, Baker Street, Marble Arch, and Hyde Park Corner. The easyBus service to Victoria via Baker Street costs from £6 one-way, but book early and online for best prices.

Stansted by train: The Stansted Express to Liverpool Street Station (with a stop at Tottenham Hale) runs daily every 20 minutes or so, 5:30 am–12:30 am. If booked online and in advance, the 50-minute trip costs from £9.70 one-way and £19.40 round-trip; tickets cost more when purchased on board or nearer travel time.

Luton by bus and train: An airport shuttle runs from Luton Airport to the nearby Luton Airport Parkway Station, from which you can take a train or bus into London (this shuttle is free if you have

Getting Here and Around

bought a rail ticket in advance; otherwise it's £2.40 one-way). From there, Thameslink train service runs to St. Pancras, Farringdon, Blackfriars, and London Bridge. The journey takes about 30 minutes. Trains leave every 20 minutes or so during the day, and hourly during the night. Single tickets cost from £15.90 one-way, if booked in advance. The Green Line 757 bus service from Luton to Victoria Station runs every hour, takes about 90 minutes, and costs from £11.50 one-way, if booked in advance.

TRANSFERS BETWEEN AIRPORTS
Allow at least two to three hours for an interairport transfer. The cheapest option—but most complicated—is public transportation: from Gatwick to Stansted, for instance, you can catch the nonexpress commuter train from Gatwick to Victoria Station, take the Tube to Liverpool Street Station, then catch the train to Stansted from there. To get from Heathrow to Gatwick by public transportation, take the Tube to King's Cross, then change to the Victoria line, get to Victoria Station, and then take the commuter train to Gatwick.

The National Express airport bus is the most direct option. Between Gatwick and Heathrow, buses pick up passengers every hour from 3:50 am to 10:50 pm from both airports. The trip takes around 75 minutes, and the fare is from £20 one-way, but it's advisable to book tickets in advance. National Express buses between Stansted and Gatwick depart every hour or so at peak times and can take 3–4½ hours, depending on traffic. The adult one-way fare is from £14, if booked in advance. Some airlines may offer shuttle services as well—check with your airline in advance of your journey.

Bicycle

Nicknamed "Boris bikes" after the former mayor, dedicated cyclist, and current prime minister Boris Johnson, a 24-hour bike-rental program called Santander Cycles enables Londoners to pick up a bicycle at one of more than 750 docking stations and return it at another. The first 30 minutes are free, then it's £2 for every 30-minute period thereafter. There is also a £2-per-day access charge. You pay at the docking station, using credit or debit cards only (cash is not accepted)—simply follow the instructions on the touch screen and away you go.

Bus

ARRIVING AND DEPARTING
National Express is the biggest British long-distance bus operator and the nearest equivalent to Greyhound. It's not as fast as traveling by train, but it's comfortable (with bathrooms on board). Services depart mainly from Victoria Coach Station, a well-signposted short walk behind the Victoria mainline train station. The departures point is on the corner of Buckingham Palace Road; this is also the main information point. The arrivals point is opposite, at Elizabeth Bridge. National Express buses travel to all large and midsize cities in southern England and the Midlands. Scotland and the north are not as well served. The station is extremely busy around holidays and weekends. Arrive at least 30 minutes before departure so you can find the correct exit gate.

Another bus company, Megabus, offers cross-country fares for as little as £1 per person. The company's single- and double-decker buses serve an extensive array of cities across Great Britain with a cheerful budget attitude. In London, buses for all destinations depart from the Green Line bus stand at Victoria Station. Megabus does not accommodate wheelchairs, and the company strictly limits luggage to one piece per person checked, and one piece of hand luggage.

Green Line serves the counties surrounding London, as well as airports. Bus stops (there's no central bus station) are on Buckingham Palace Road, between the Victoria train station and Victoria Coach Station.

Tickets on many long-distance routes are cheaper if purchased in advance, and traveling midweek costs less than over weekends and at holiday periods.

GETTING AROUND LONDON

Although London is famous for its double-decker buses, the old beloved rattletrap Routemasters, with the jump-on, jump-off back platforms, have finally gone to that great big bus depot in the sky. The modernized Routemaster buses that have taken their place are more accessible and comfortable, and yet retain echoes of the iconic design of their illustrious predecessors.

Bus stops are clearly indicated; signs at bus stops feature a red TfL symbol on a plain white background. You must flag the bus down at some stops. Each numbered route is listed on the main stop, and buses have a large number on the front with their end destination. Not all buses run the full route at all times; check with the driver to be sure. You can pick up a free bus guide at a TfL Travel Information Centre (at Euston, Liverpool Street, Piccadilly Circus, King's Cross, and Victoria Tube stations and at Heathrow Airport).

Buses are a good way of seeing the town, particularly if you plan to hop on and off to cover many sights, but don't take a bus if you're in a hurry, as traffic can really slow them down. To get off,

press the red "Stop" buttons mounted on poles near the doors. You will usually see a "Bus Stopping" sign light up. Expect to get sardined during rush hour, 8–9:30 am and 4:30–6:30 pm.

Night buses, denoted by an "N" before their route numbers, run midnight–5 am on a more restricted route than day buses. However, some night-bus routes should be approached with caution, and the top deck avoided (the danger is that muggings are most likely to occur there, since it's farthest from both the exit doors and the driver). All night buses run by request stop, so flag them down if you're waiting, or push the button if you want to alight.

All London buses are now cash-free, which means you must buy your ticket *before* you board the bus. There are a number of ways to do this. One-day paper bus passes are available at underground and rail stations as well as TfL Visitor Centres and cost £5.20. An easier, and cheaper, option is to pay by prepaid Oyster card or "contactless" bank card. Visitor Oyster cards must be purchased before you arrive; they cost £5 (plus postage), but a day's bus travel is capped at £4.65. Normal Oyster cards (also £5) are available from ticket desks at all major airports or at any Tube station and are transferable if you have money left over. Contactless cards are increasingly being used for London travel: you touch a compatible debit or credit card on a bus or Tube-station reader, and the fare is automatically debited from your bank account.

One alternative is to buy a one- or seven-day Travelcard, which is good for both Tube and bus travel. Travelcards can be bought at Tube stations, rail stations, and travel information centers. However, note that seven-day Travelcards bought in London *must be loaded onto an Oyster card*. Although using a Travelcard may save you some money, it might be

Getting Here and Around

easier to just add additional money to your Oyster card as needed, since there are machines at all Tube stations and at lots of London newsagents. A seven-day paper Travelcard can only be purchased in advance, online.

However you buy your ticket, just make sure you have one: traveling without a valid ticket makes you liable for a significant fine (£80). Buses are supposed to swing by most stops every five or six minutes, but in reality you often end up waiting a bit longer, although those in the city center are quite reliable.

 Car

The best advice on driving in London is this: don't. London's streets are a winding mass of chaos, made worse by one-way roads. Parking is also restrictive and expensive, and traffic is tediously slow at most times of the day; during rush hours (8–9:30 am and 4:30–6:30 pm) it often grinds to a standstill, particularly on Friday, when everyone wants to leave town. Avoid city-center shopping areas, including the roads feeding Oxford Street, Kensington, and Knightsbridge. Other main roads into the city center are also busy, such as King's Cross and Euston in the north. Watch out also for cyclists and motorcycle couriers, who weave between cars and pedestrians who seem to come out of nowhere, and you may get a heavy fine for straying into a bus lane during its operating hours—check the signs.

If you are staying in London for the duration of your trip, there's virtually no reason to rent a car because the city and its suburbs are widely covered by public transportation. However, you may want a car for day trips to castles or stately homes out in the countryside. Consider renting your car in a medium-size town in the area where you'll be traveling, journeying there by train and picking up the car once you arrive. Rental rates are generally reasonable, and insurance costs are lower than in comparable U.S. cities. Rates generally begin at £20 per day for a small economy car (such as a subcompact General Motors Vauxhall Corsa or Renault Clio), usually with manual transmission. Air-conditioning and unlimited mileage generally come with the larger-size automatic cars.

In London your U.S. driver's license is acceptable (as long as you are over 23 years old, with no driving convictions). If you have a driver's license from a country other than the United States, it may not be recognized in the United Kingdom. An International Driver's Permit is a good idea no matter what; it's available from the American or Canadian Automobile Association (AAA and CAA, respectively) and, in the United Kingdom, from the Automobile Association (AA) or Royal Automobile Club (RAC). International permits are universally recognized, and having one may save you a problem with the local authorities.

Remember that Britain drives on the left, and the rest of Europe on the right. Therefore, if you cross the Channel into Britain in a right-side rental, you may want to leave it there and pick up a left-side rental.

CONGESTION CHARGE

Designed to reduce traffic through central London, a congestion charge has been instituted. Vehicles (with some exemptions) entering central London on weekdays 7 am–6 pm (excluding public holidays) have to pay £15 per day; it can be paid up to 90 days in advance, or on the day of travel, or on the following "charging day," when the fee goes up to £17.50. Day-, month-, and yearlong passes are available on the Congestion Charge page of the Transport for London website, at gas stations and parking lots (car parks), by mail, by phone, and by SMS text message. Traffic signs designate the entrance to congestion areas, and cameras read car license plates and send the information to a database. Drivers who don't pay the congestion charge by midnight of the next charging day following the day of driving are penalized £160, which is reduced to £80 if paid within 14 days.

On top of the congestion charge, the entire Greater London area has been designated a Low Emissions Zone, which means that all older and pollution-heavy vehicles will be levied with an extra daily charge of £12.50. However, this will almost certainly not apply to rented cars (which tend to be newer and therefore greener), but it's smart to check with the rental company first.

GASOLINE
Gasoline (petrol) is sold in liters and is expensive (at this writing about £1.46 per liter—around $6.57 per gallon). Unleaded petrol, denoted by green pump lines, is predominant. Premium and Super Premium are the two varieties, and most cars run on regular Premium. Supermarket pumps usually offer the best value. You won't find many service stations in the center of town; these are generally on main, multilane trunk roads away from the city center. Service is self-serve, except in small villages, where gas stations are likely to be closed on Sunday and in the late evening. Most stations accept major credit cards.

PARKING
During the day—and probably at all times—it's safest to believe that you can park nowhere except at a meter, in a pay-and-display bay, or in a garage; otherwise, you run the risk of an expensive ticket, plus possibly even more expensive clamping and towing fees (some boroughs are

clamp-free). Restrictions are indicated by the "No Waiting" parking signpost on the sidewalk (these restrictions vary from street to street), and restricted areas include single yellow lines or double yellow lines, as well as Residents' Parking bays. Parking at a bus stop is prohibited, and parking in bus lanes is restricted. On Red Routes, indicated by red lines, you are not allowed to park or even stop. It's illegal to park on the sidewalk, across entrances, or on white zigzag lines approaching a pedestrian crossing.

Meters have an insatiable hunger in the inner city—20p may buy you just three minutes—and many will permit only a maximum two-hour stay. Coin meters (which take 10p, 20p, 50p, £1, and £2 coins) are being phased out. Some meters take payment by credit card, but increasingly meters in central London require payment by cell phone. You will need to set up an account to do this (which can be done in a matter of minutes). Meter parking is usually free after 6:30 or 8:30 in the evening, on Sunday, and on holidays; always check the sign. In the evening, after restrictions end, meter bays are free. After meters are free, you also can park on single yellow lines—but not double yellow lines. In the daytime, take advantage of the many NCP parking lots in the center of town (from about £5 per hour, but cheaper prices are available if booked in advance).

RULES OF THE ROAD
London is a mass of narrow, one-way roads and narrow, two-way streets no bigger than the one-way roads. The speed limit is either 20 or 30 mph—unless you see the large 40 mph signs found only in the suburbs. Speed bumps are sprinkled about with abandon in case you forget. Speed is strictly controlled and cameras, mounted on lampposts, photograph speeders for ticketing.

Getting Here and Around

Medium-size circular intersections are often designed as "roundabouts" (marked by signs in which three curved arrows form a circle). On these, cars travel left in a circle and incoming cars must yield to those already on their way around from the right. Make sure you're in the correct lane when approaching a roundabout—this will make leaving the roundabout at your desired exit easier. Stay in the left lane if you wish to go left, the middle lane for going straight ahead, and the right-hand lane for turning right. Signal when about to leave the roundabout.

Jaywalking is not illegal in London and everybody does it, despite the fact that striped crossings with blinking yellow lights mounted on poles at either end—called "zebra crossings"—give pedestrians the right-of-way to cross. Cars should treat zebra crossings like stop signs if a pedestrian is waiting to cross or already starting to cross. It's illegal to pass another vehicle at a zebra crossing. At other crossings (including intersections) pedestrians must yield to traffic, but they do have the right-of-way over traffic turning left at controlled crossings.

Traffic lights sometimes have arrows directing left or right turns; try to catch a glimpse of the road markings in time, and don't get into the turn lane if you mean to go straight ahead. Turning on a red light is not permitted. Signs at the beginning and end of designated bus lanes give the time restrictions for use (usually during peak hours); if you're caught driving on bus lanes during restricted hours, you will be fined. By law, seat belts must be worn in the front and back seats. Drunk-driving laws are strictly enforced, and it's safest to avoid alcohol altogether if you'll be driving. The legal limit is 80 milligrams of alcohol per 100 milliliters

of blood, which roughly translated means two units of alcohol—two small glasses of wine, one pint of beer, or one glass of whiskey.

🚈 DLR: Docklands Light Railway

For reaching destinations in east London, the quiet, driverless Docklands Light Railway (DLR) is a good alternative, with interesting views of the area.

The DLR connects with the Tube network at Bank and Tower Hill Stations as well as at Canary Wharf. It goes to London City Airport, the Docklands financial district, and Greenwich, running 5:30 am–12:30 am Monday–Saturday, 7 am–11:30 pm Sunday. The DLR takes Oyster cards, contactless bank cards, and Travelcards, and fares are the same as those on the Tube.

🚢 River Bus

One legacy of the 2012 Olympics was a renewed push to develop river travel as part of London's overall public transportation system. The service, operated by Thames Clippers under the name Uber Boat, stops at eight piers between London Eye/Waterloo and Greenwich, with peak-time extensions to Putney in the west and Woolwich Arsenal in the east. The Waterloo–Woolwich commuter service runs 7:16 am–10:29 pm on weekdays, 8:27 am–10:50 pm on weekends (peak-time frequency: every 20 minutes). Tickets are £7.30, with a one-third discount for Travelcard holders and a 20% discount for Oyster card holders. When there are events at the O2 (North Greenwich Arena), a half-hourly express service runs to and from Waterloo starting three hours before the event. Thames Clippers also operates the special Tate to Tate Boat, a 15-minute trip between Tate Modern and Tate Britain that costs £8.70 one-way. Boats run every 20–30 minutes, from 10 to 4 on weekdays and 9 to 7 on weekends. A River Roamer ticket (from £18.40 per day if booked online) offers unlimited river travel after 9 am.

 Taxi

Universally known as "black cabs" (even though many of them now come in other colors), the traditional big black London taxicabs are as much a part of the city's streetscape as red double-decker buses, and for good reason: the unique, spacious taxis easily hold five people, plus luggage. To earn a taxi license, drivers must undergo intensive training on the history and geography of London. The course, and all that the drivers have learned in it, is known simply as "the Knowledge." There's almost nothing your taxi driver won't know about the city. Partly because of lobbying efforts by the black cab industry, rideshare companies, such as Uber, have yet to make significant inroads into the London market, although the battle is ongoing.

Hotels and main tourist areas have cabstands (just take the first in line), but you can also flag one down from the roadside. If the orange "For Hire" sign on the top is lighted, the taxi is available. Cab drivers sometimes cruise at night with their signs unlighted so that they can choose their passengers and avoid those they think might cause trouble. If you see an unlighted, passengerless cab, hail it: you might be lucky.

Fares start at £3.20 and charge by the minute—a journey of a mile (which might take 6–13 minutes) will cost £6.20–£9.60 (the fare goes up 10 pm–5 am—a system designed to persuade more taxi drivers to work at night). A surcharge of £2 is applied to a telephone booking and £2.80 for journeys that start from the Heathrow Airport taxi ranks. At Christmas and New Year's, there is an additional surcharge of £4. You may, but do not have to, tip taxi drivers 10% of the tab. Usually passengers round up to the nearest pound.

Minicabs, which operate out of small, curbside offices throughout the city, are generally cheaper than black cabs, but they are less reliable and less trustworthy. These are usually unmarked passenger cars, and their drivers are often not native Londoners and do not have to take or pass "the Knowledge" test. Still, Londoners use them in droves because they are plentiful and cheap. If you choose to use them, do not ever take an unlicensed cab: anyone who curb-crawls looking for customers is likely to be unlicensed. Unlicensed cabs have been associated with many crimes and can be dangerous. All cab companies with proper dispatch offices are likely to be licensed. Look for a small purple version of the Underground logo on the front or rear window with "private hire" written across it.

There are plenty of trustworthy and licensed minicab firms. For London-wide service, try Addison Lee, which uses comfortable minivans but requires that you know the full postal code for both your pickup location and your destination. When using a minicab, always ask the price in advance when you phone for the car, then verify with the driver before the journey begins. Alternatively, there's always your Uber app.

Getting Here and Around

🚊 Train

The National Rail Enquiries website is the clearinghouse for information on train times and fares as well as the main place for booking rail journeys around Britain— and the earlier the better. Tickets bought two to three weeks in advance can cost a quarter of the price of tickets bought on the day of travel. However, journeys within commuting distance of city centers are sold at unvarying set prices, and those can be purchased on the day you expect to make your journey without any financial penalty. You may also be able to purchase a PlusBus ticket, which adds unlimited bus travel at your destination. Note that, in busy city centers such as London, all travel costs more during morning rush hour. You can purchase tickets online, by phone, or at any train station in the United Kingdom.

Check the website or call the National Rail Enquiries line to get details of the train company responsible for your journey and have them give you a breakdown of available ticket prices. Regardless of which train company is involved, many discount passes are available, such as the 16–25 Railcard (for which you must be under 26 and provide a passport-size photo), the Senior Railcard, and the Family & Friends Railcard, which can be bought from most mainline stations. But if you intend to make several long-distance rail journeys, it can be a good idea to invest in a BritRail Pass, available to non-U.K. residents (which you must buy before you leave home).

You can get a BritRail Pass valid for London and the surrounding counties, for England, for Scotland, or for all of Britain. Discounts (usually 20%–25%) are offered if you're between 16 and 25, over 60, traveling as a family or a group, or accompanied by a British citizen. The pass includes discounts on the Heathrow Express and Gatwick Express. BritRail Passes come in two basic varieties. The Consecutive Pass allows travel on consecutive days while the Flexi Pass allows a number of travel days within a set period of time. Prices of a BritRail Consecutive Pass adult ticket range from around $350 for an 8-day pass in standard class (around $500 in first class) to $650 for 22 days (around $1,000 in first class). The BritRail Flexi Pass adult ticket costs from $300 standard ($450 first class) for 4 days within one month all the way up to around $650 ($950 first class) for 15 days within two months. Prices drop by about 20% for off-peak travel passes November–February.

Most long-distance trains have refreshment carriages, called buffet cars. Most trains these days also have "quiet cars," where the use of cell phones and music devices is banned. Smoking is forbidden in all railcars.

Generally speaking, rail travel in the United Kingdom is expensive and the ticketing system unnecessarily convoluted: for instance, a round-trip ticket to Bath from London can cost more than £150 per person at peak times, although for an off-peak ticket purchased far enough in advance, that price can drop to £20 or even less. It's best to avoid the frantic business commuter rush (before 9:30 am and 4:30–7 pm). Credit cards are accepted for train fares paid in person, by phone, and online.

Delays are not uncommon, but they're rarely long. You almost always have to go to the station to find out if there's going to be one (because delays tend to happen at the last minute). Luckily, most stations have coffee shops, restaurants, and pubs where you can cool your heels while you wait for the train to get rolling. National Rail Enquiries provides an up-to-date state-of-the-railroads schedule.

Most of the time, first-class train travel in England isn't particularly first class. Some train companies don't offer at-seat service, so you still have to get up and go to the buffet car for food or drinks. First class is generally booked by business travelers on expense accounts because crying babies and noisy families are quite rare in first class and quite common in standard class.

Short of flying, taking the Eurostar train through the Channel Tunnel is the fastest way to reach the continent: it's 2 hours 16 minutes from London's St. Pancras International to Paris's Gare du Nord. You can also go from St. Pancras to Midi Station in Brussels in just under two hours, or to Amsterdam in 3 hours 50 minutes. If purchased in advance, round-trip tickets from London to Belgium, Holland, or France cost from as little as £39, especially if you travel in the very early or very late hours of the day. If you want to bring your car over to France (ask the rental company if this is permitted), you can use the Eurotunnel Shuttle, which takes 35 minutes from Folkestone to Calais, plus at least 30 minutes to check in. The Belgian border is just a short drive northeast of Calais.

⊙ Underground/The Tube

London's extensive Underground train system (the Tube) has color-coded routes, clear signage, and many connections. Trains run out into the suburbs, and all stations are marked with the London Underground circular symbol. (Do not be confused by similar-looking signs reading "subway," which is British for "pedestrian underpass.") Trains are all one class; smoking isn't allowed on board or in the stations. There is also an Overground network serving the farther reaches of Inner London.

Some lines have multiple branches (Central, Circle, District, Northern, Metropolitan, and Piccadilly), so be sure to check which branch is needed for your particular destination. Do this by noting the end destination on the lighted sign on the platform, which also tells you how long you'll have to wait until the train arrives. Compare that with the end destination of the branch you want. When the two match, that's your train.

London is divided into six concentric zones (ask at Underground ticket booths for a map and booklet, which give details of the ticket options), so be sure to buy a ticket for the correct zone or you may be liable for an on-the-spot fine of £80. Don't panic if you do forget to buy a ticket for the right zone: just tell a station attendant that you need to buy an "extension" to your ticket. Although you're meant to do that in advance, if you're an out-of-towner, they generally don't give you a hard time. You also can pay your fare using an Oyster card or a contactless debit or credit card.

Oyster cards are "smart cards" that can be charged with a cash value and then used for discounted travel throughout the city. A Visitor Oyster card, which you must buy before arriving in the United Kingdom, costs £5. Normal Oyster cards also cost £5, and you can open an Oyster account online or pick up an Oyster card at any London Underground station and then prepay any amount you wish for your expected travel while in the city. Each time you take the Tube or bus, you place the blue card on the yellow reader at the entrance and the amount of your fare is deducted.

Passengers using Oyster cards pay lower rates. For one-way Tube fares paid in cash, a flat £5.50 price per journey now applies across all central zones (1–2), whether you're traveling 1 stop or 12. However, the corresponding Oyster card fare is £3.

Getting Here and Around

One-day Travelcards used to be a good value for the money, but now, costing from £13.90 per card, they're a much less attractive option. If you're planning several trips in one day, it's much cheaper to buy an Oyster card: because of the system's daily "cap," you can make as many journeys as you want in Zones 1–2 for just £7.40 (or in Zones 1–3 for £8.70). If you're going to be in town for several days, a seven-day Travelcard gives you the same value as an Oyster card (£37 for Zones 1–2, £67.70 for Zones 1–6).

Children aged 11–15 can travel at discounted rates on the Tube and travel free on buses and trams with an Oyster photocard (must be ordered online at least four weeks before date of travel), while those under 11 travel free on all buses and on the Tube if accompanied by an adult or with an Oyster photocard. Young people aged 16–18 and students over 18 get discounted Tube fares with an Oyster photocard. Oyster card Tube fares start at £2 and go up depending on the number of zones you're covering, the time of day, and whether you're traveling into Zone 1.

Nevertheless, although Oyster cards sound like the way of the future, they will soon be a thing of the past. Moves are underway to gradually phase out Oyster cards and to encourage passengers to move to a system of direct payments using their bank debit card or credit card instead. In practice, this means swiping a "contactless" bank card instead of your Oyster card at ticket barriers. The cheaper fares available to Oyster card holders are the same as for those who pay by contactless cards.

Tube trains now run for 24 hours a day on weekends on five major lines: Piccadilly, Victoria, Northern, Central, and Jubilee. On all other lines the usual timetable still applies, with trains running from just after 5 am Monday to Saturday, and with the last services leaving central London between midnight and 12:30 am. On Sunday, trains start an hour later and finish about an hour earlier. The frequency of trains depends on the route and the time of day, but normally you should not have to wait more than 10 minutes in central areas.

For helpful advice on getting from A to B, just ask a member of the Tube station staff, who tend to have an encyclopedic knowledge of the network they're only too willing to impart. For more detailed questions on travel in London, as well as tourist offers and tickets to many of the city's key attractions, visit one of the three conveniently located TfL Visitor Centres. The Centres at St. Pancras International and Victoria are open Wednesday–Saturday from 9:30 am to 4:45 pm, while the one at Piccadilly Circus is open Thursday–Saturday from 9:30 am to 4:45 pm.

Important note: you need to have your ticket (Oyster card, Travelcard, regular ticket, or contactless debit/credit card) handy in order to exit the turnstiles of the Tube system, not just to enter them.

Essentials

Customs and Duties

You're always allowed to bring goods of a certain value back home without having to pay any duty or import tax. But there's a limit on the amount of tobacco and liquor you can bring back duty-free, and some countries have separate limits for perfumes; for exact figures, check with your customs department. The values of so-called duty-free goods are included in these amounts. When you shop abroad, save all your receipts, as customs inspectors may ask to see them as well as the items you purchased. If the total value of your goods is more than the duty-free limit, you'll have to pay a tax (most often a flat percentage) on the value of everything beyond that limit.

One of the many casualties of Brexit has been the generous duty-free allowances that visitors to the United Kingdom arriving from an EU country used to enjoy. Now, there are very strict limits on the amount of tobacco and alcohol you can bring into the country with you.

With tobacco, you may import only one of the following duty-free: 200 cigarettes or 100 cigarillos or 50 cigars or 250 grams of tobacco or 200 sticks of tobacco for electronic heated tobacco devices. You may split this allowance (e.g., 100 cigarettes and 25 cigars, which would be half your allowance for each).

When it comes to alcohol, you should not exceed 42 liters of beer or 18 liters of still wine. On top of that, you may bring with you 4 liters of spirits and liquors with over 22% alcohol or 9 liters of sparkling wine or fortified wine (e.g., sherry, port) and other alcoholic drinks containing up to 22% alcohol. Again, with this latter category, you can split your allowance (e.g., 4.5 liters of sherry and 2 liters of spirits).

Pets (dogs and cats) can be brought into the United Kingdom from the United States without six months' quarantine, provided that the animal meets all the PETS (Pet Travel Scheme) requirements, including microchipping and vaccination. Other pets have to undergo a lengthy quarantine, and penalties for breaking this law are severe and strictly enforced.

Fresh meats, vegetables, plants, and dairy products may be imported from within the European Union. Controlled drugs, switchblades (aka flick knives), obscene material, counterfeit or pirated goods, and self-defense sprays may not be brought into the United Kingdom; firearms (both real and imitation) and ammunition, as well as souvenirs made from endangered plants or animals, are barred except with relevant permits.

Dining

British food hasn't always had the best reputation, but nowhere in the country is that reputation being completely upturned more than in London. The city has zoomed up the global gastro charts, and can now seriously compete with the world's top culinary heavyweights. The truth is that no other city—barring New York—has the immense range of global cuisines that London has to offer. Standards have rocketed at all price points, and every year it seems like the London restaurant scene is better than ever.

To appreciate how far London has risen in the food game, just look back to the days of Somerset Maugham, who was once justified in warning, "To eat well in England, you should have breakfast three times a day." Change was slow after World War II, when it was understood that the British ate to live, while the French lived to eat. When people thought

Essentials

of British cuisine, fish-and-chips—a greasy grab-and-gulp dish that tasted best wrapped in yesterday's newspaper—first came to mind. Then there was always shepherd's pie, ubiquitously found in smoke-filled pubs, though not made, according to Sweeney Todd, "with real shepherd in it."

These days, standards are miles higher and shepherd's pie has been largely replaced by the city's unofficial dish, Indian curry. London's restaurant revolution is built on its extraordinary ethnic diversity, and you'll find the quality of other global cuisines has grown immeasurably in recent years, with London becoming known for its Chinese, Japanese, Indian, Thai, Spanish, Italian, French, Peruvian, and West African restaurants. Thankfully, pride in the best of British food—local, seasonal, wild, and foraged—is enjoying quite the renaissance, too.

Prices in the reviews are the average cost of a main course at dinner or, if dinner is not served, at lunch. Note: If a restaurant offers only prix-fixe (set-price) meals, it has been given the price category that reflects the full prix-fixe price.

WHAT IT COSTS in Pounds

$	$$	$$$	$$$$
RESTAURANTS			
Under £16	£16–£23	£24–£31	Over £31

🛏 Lodging

If your invitation from Queen Elizabeth still hasn't shown up in the mail, no worries—staying at one of London's grande dame hotels is the next best thing to being a guest at the palace, and some say it's even better. Luckily there is

no dearth of options where friendliness outdistances luxe; London has plenty of atmospheric places that won't cost a king's ransom.

That noted, until fairly recently it was extremely difficult to find a decent hotel in the center of town for less than £150 per night. Things have improved, thanks to a flurry of new mid-priced hotels that have sprung up in recent years. You'll still have to shop around for deals—never assume you'll be able to find somewhere good *and* cheap on short notice.

Of course, it's very different if money is no object. London has some of the very best and most luxurious hotels in the world. Freshly minted millionaires favor the rash of super-trendy hot spots like Corinthia or ME London, while fashionistas gravitate toward Kit Kemp's stylish hotels like Covent Garden and Charlotte Street. But even these places have deals, and you can sometimes snag a bargain within reach of mere mortals, particularly in the off-season, or just be a spectator to all the glamour by visiting for Afternoon Tea, the most traditional of high-society treats.

Meanwhile, several mid-range hotels have dropped their average prices in response to the choppy waters of the global economy, especially in the midst of the COVID-19 pandemic, which has pulled some fantastic places, such as Hazlitt's, The Rookery, and Town Hall, back into the affordable category. There's also a clutch of hip, affordable hotels that are a real step forward for the city. The downside is that these places tend to be a little out of the way, but that's often a price worth paying. Another attractive alternative includes hotels in the Premier and Millennium chains, which offer sleek, modern rooms, lots of up-to-date conveniences, and sales that frequently bring room prices well below £100 a night.

Where Should I Stay?

	NEIGHBORHOOD VIBE	PROS	CONS
Westminster and St. James's	Historic and home to major tourist attractions.	Central area; easy Tube access; safe.	Expensive lodging; few good restaurants and entertainment venues.
Mayfair and Marylebone	Traditional, old money; a mixture of the business and financial set with fashionable shops.	In the heart of the action; excellent hotels.	Pricey; peace and quiet hard to come by.
Soho and Covent Garden	A tourist hub with endless entertainment.	Buzzing area with plenty to see and do; late-night entertainment abounds; wonderful shopping district.	London's busiest (and noisiest) district after dark; few budget hotels.
Bloomsbury and Holborn	Diverse area that is part bustling business center and part tranquil respite.	Easy access to Tube; major sights like the British Museum.	Busy and noisy streets; the area around King's Cross can be sketchy—particularly at night.
The City	London's financial district.	Extremely central with easy transportation access and great hotel deals.	Can be as quiet as a tomb on weekends—even the pubs close.
East London	One of London's trendiest areas, with a great arts scene.	Great for art lovers, shoppers, and business execs with meetings in Canary Wharf.	Parts can be a bit dodgy at night; 20-minute Tube ride from central London.
South of the Thames	A vibrant cultural hub.	London's unofficial cultural quarter, walking distance from the West End theaters.	Close to some iffy areas.
Kensington, Chelsea, Knightsbridge, and Belgravia	Upscale neighborhoods and a hub of London's tourist universe.	Diverse hotel selection; great area for meandering urban walks; London's capital of high-end shopping.	Depending on where you are, the nearest Tube might be a hike; might be too quiet for some.
Notting Hill and Bayswater	An upscale, trendy area favored by locals.	Affordable; gorgeous greenery.	Not all hotels are great; residential area may be quiet.
Regent's Park and Hampstead	A mix of arty, fashionable districts with a villagelike feel.	Some of London's most fashionable neighborhoods.	Some distance from center; lack of hotel options.

Essentials

At the budget level, London has come a long way in the last couple of years, with a familiar catch: to find a good, reasonably priced bed-and-breakfast, you must be prepared to look outside the very center of town. This means that you have to weigh the city's notoriously high transport costs against any savings—but on the plus side, the Tube can shuttle you out to even some far-flung suburbs in less than 20 minutes. If you're prepared to be just a little adventurous with your London base, you will be rewarded by a collection of unique and interesting B&Bs and small boutique hotels, in the kinds of neighborhoods real Londoners live in. If you're willing to fend for yourself, the city also has some great rental options.

But if you are interested in luxury, London is just the place. Although the image we love to harbor about Olde London Towne may be fast fading in the light of today's glittering city, when it comes time to rest your head, the old-fashioned clichés remain enticing. Choose one of London's heritage-rich hotels—Claridge's supplies perfect parlors; the Savoy has that river view—and you'll find that these fantasies can, and always will, be fulfilled.

RESERVATIONS

Yes, hotel reservations are an absolute necessity when planning your trip to London, so book your room as far in advance as possible. The further in advance you can book, the better a deal you're likely to get. Just watch out if you change your mind—cancellation fees can be hefty. On the other hand, it is possible to find some amazing last-minute deals at mid- to high-range places, but this is a real gamble, as you could just as easily end up paying full rate. Fierce competition means properties undergo frequent improvements, so when booking inquire about any ongoing renovations that may interrupt your stay.

Prices in the reviews are the lowest cost of a standard double room in high season, including a 20% V.A.T.

WHAT IT COSTS in Pounds			
$	$$	$$$	$$$$
HOTELS			
Under £125	£125–£250	£251–£400	Over £400

Nightlife

There isn't *a* London nightlife scene—there is a multitude of them. As long as there are crowds for obscure teenage rock bands, Dickensian-style pubs, comedy cabarets, cocktail lounges, and swing dance nights, someone will create clubs and venues for them in London. The result? London has become a veritable utopia for excitement junkies, culture fiends, and those who—simply put—like to party.

Nearly everyone who visits London these days is mesmerized by the city's energy, which reveals itself in layers. Whether you prefer rhythm and blues with fine French food, the gritty guitar-riff music of Camden Town, the craft beers of East London, a pint and a gourmet pizza at a local gastropub, or swanky heritage cocktails and sushi at London's sexiest subterranean lair, the scene is sure to feed your fancy.

London's nightlife has been given a big boost with five Night Tube lines serving central London (see ⊕ *www.tfl.gov.uk* for details) that run all night on Friday and Saturday, making getting home after a night out cheaper and easier than ever before. The rest of the network stops running around 12:30 am Monday through Saturday and midnight on Sunday. Night buses are largely safe (especially on the lower deck) and reliable but far slower than taxis, as you'd expect.

The best place to hail a black taxi is at the front door of one of the major hotels; or find a licensed local minicab firm on the Transport for London website. Avoid unlicensed taxis or minicabs that tout for business around closing time.

PUBS

Pubs are where Londoners go to hang out, see and be seen, act out the drama of life, and, for some, drink themselves into varying degrees of oblivion. The pub is still a vital part of London life, though many of the traditions of the pub experience are evolving. There are few better places to meet Londoners in their local habitat. There are somewhere around 4,000 pubs in London; some are dark and woody, others plain and functional, and a few still have original Victorian etched glass, Edwardian panels, and art nouveau carvings.

Not long ago, before the smoking ban, pubs tended to be smoky, male-dominated places with a couple of standard beers on tap and the only available food a packet of salt-and-vinegar-flavor crisps (potato chips). All that has changed. Gastropub fever swept through London around the turn of the 21st century, and at many places, charcoal grills are installed in the kitchen and inventive pub grub is on the menu. A new wave of enthusiasm for craft beers and microbreweries is now having a similar effect on the liquid offerings.

The big decision is what to drink. The beer of choice among Britons has traditionally been "bitter," lightly fermented, with an amber color, and getting its bitterness from hops. It's usually served at cellar temperature (that is, cooler than room temperature but neither chilled, nor, as common misconception

would have it, warm). Real ales, served from wooden kegs and made without chilling, filtering, or pasteurization, are flatter than other bitters and are enjoying a renaissance. Many small London breweries have sprung up in recent years, and bottled designer and American beers can be found in most bars across London. Stouts, like Guinness, are a meal in themselves and something of an acquired taste—they have a dark, caramel-infused flavor and look like thickened flat Coke with a frothy top. Chilled continental lagers, most familiar to American drinkers, are light in color and carbonated.

■TIP→ **The most commonly served lagers in Britain are from continental Europe.**

Many English pubs are owned by chains, such as Fullers, Nicholson's, or Samuel Smith's, and are tenanted, meaning that they are run on a sort of franchise basis. Most are not obviously branded and retain at least some independence. Independently owned pubs, sometimes called "free houses," tend to offer a more extensive selection of beer. Other potations available include apple-based ciders, ranging from sweet to dry and from alcoholic to very alcoholic (Irish cider, served over ice, is now also commonplace), and shandies, a refreshing mix of beer and lemonade. Friendly pubs will usually be happy to give you a taste of the brew of your choice before you order.

NIGHTCLUBS

Because today's cool spot is often tomorrow's forgotten or closed venue, check the weekly listings in the *Evening Standard* (⊕ *www.stand-ard.co.uk*) and especially *Time Out* (⊕ *www.timeout.com/london*). Other websites to consult are ⊕ *www.london-town.com* and ⊕ *www.designmynight.com*.

Essentials

com. Although most clubs are frequented by those under 30, there are plenty of others that are popular with patrons of all ages and types. One particularly useful website for clubs and club nights is ⊕ *www.residentadvisor.net/guide/uk/london.*

Performing Arts

"All the world's a stage," said Shakespeare, immortal words heard for the first time right here in London. And whether you prefer your theater, music, and art classical or modern, or as contemporary twists on time-honored classics, you'll find that London's vibrant cultural scene more than holds its own on the world stage.

Divas sing original-language librettos at the Royal Opera House, Shakespeare's plays are brought to life at the reconstructed Globe Theatre, and challenging new writing is produced at the Royal Court. Whether you feel like basking in the lighthearted extravagance of a West End musical or taking in the next shark-in-formaldehyde at the White Cube gallery, the choice is yours.

There are international theater festivals, innovative music festivals, and critically acclaimed seasons of postmodern dance. Short trip or long, you'll find the cultural scene in London is ever-changing, ever-expanding, and ever-exciting.

THEATER

The website ⊕ *www.whatsonstage.com* is an invaluable resource for theater listings.

Safety

The rules for safety in London are the same as in New York City or any big metropolis. The most important rule is to use common sense. In central London, nobody will raise an eyebrow at tourists studying maps on street corners, and don't hesitate to ask for directions. Nevertheless, outside the center, exercise general caution about the neighborhoods you walk in: if they don't look safe, take a cab. After midnight, outside the center, take cabs rather than wait for a night bus. Although London has plenty of so-called minicabs—normal cars driven by self-employed drivers in a cab service—don't ever get into an unmarked car that pulls up offering you "cab service." Take a licensed minicab only from a cab office, or, preferably, a normal London "black cab," which you flag down on the street.

London is one of the most diverse cities in the world and, as such, is a safe and attractive destination for LGBTQ+ travelers. Popular gay-friendly neighborhoods include slap-bang-in-the-middle-of-things Soho as well as just-south-of-the-river Vauxhall, which is a mile or so west of the London Eye. With the usual precautions (avoid deserted ill-lit sidestreets and less central neighborhoods altogether after dark), solo female travelers will also find London safe and welcoming.

COVID-19

COVID 19 has disrupted travel since March 2020, and travelers should expect sporadic ongoing issues. Always travel with a mask in case it's required, and keep up to date on the most recent testing and vaccination guidelines for London.

🛍 Shopping

The keyword of London shopping has always been "individuality," whether expressed in the superb custom tailoring of Savile Row, the nonconformist punk roots of quintessential British designer Vivienne Westwood, or the unique small stores that purvey their owners' private passions—be they paper theaters, toy soldiers, or buttons. This tradition is under threat from the influx of chains (global luxury, domestic mid-market, and international youth), but the distinctively British mix of quality and originality, tradition and character remains.

You can try on underwear fit for a queen at Her Majesty's lingerie supplier, track down a leather-bound Brontë classic at an antiquarian bookseller, or find a bargain antique on Portobello Road. Whether you're just browsing—there's nothing like the size, variety, and sheer theater of London's street markets to stimulate the acquisitive instinct—or on a fashion-seeking mission, London shopping offers something for all tastes and budgets.

Although it's impossible to pin down one particular look that defines the city, London style tends to fall into two camps: one is the quirky, somewhat romantic look exemplified by homegrown designers like Matthew Williamson, Jenny Packham, Vivienne Westwood, and Lulu Guinness; the other reflects Britain's celebrated tradition of classic knitwear and suiting, with labels like Jaeger, Pringle, and Brora, while Ozwald Boateng, Paul Smith, and Richard James take tradition and give it a very modern twist. Traditional bespoke men's tailoring can be found in the upscale gentlemen's shops of Jermyn Street and Savile Row—there's no better place in the city to buy custom-made shirts and suits—while the

handbags at Mulberry, Asprey, and Anya Hindmarch are pure classic quality. If your budget can't stretch that far, no problem; the city's mid-market chains, such as Reiss, Jigsaw, and L.K. Bennett, offer smart design and better quality for the more discerning shopper.

If there's anything that unites London's designers, it's a commitment to creativity and originality, underpinned by a strong sense of heritage. This combination of posh and rock and roll sensibilities turns up in everyone from Terence Conran, who revolutionized product and houseware design in the '60s, to Alexander McQueen, who combined the punk aesthetic with the rigor of couture. You'll see it in fanciful millinery creations by Philip Treacy and Stephen Jones and in the work of imaginative shoemakers Nicholas Kirkwood, United Nude, and Terry de Havilland—and it keeps going, right through to current hot designers Erdem, Christopher Kane, and Victoria Beckham and up-and-coming names like Shrimps, Duro Olowu, and Molly Goddard.

One reason for London's design supremacy is the strength of local fashion college Central Saint Martin's, whose graduates include Conran, Kane, McQueen, McQueen's successor at his eponymous label—and designer of the Duchess of Cambridge's wedding dress—Sarah Burton, and Stella McCartney's equally acclaimed successor at Céline, Phoebe Philo.

To find the McQueens and McCartneys of tomorrow, head for the independent boutiques of the East End and Bermondsey. If anything, London is even better known for its vibrant street fashion than for its high-end designers. Stock up from the stalls at Portobello Road, Camden, and Spitalfields markets.

Essentials

Aside from bankrupting yourself, the only problem you may encounter is exhaustion. London's shopping districts are spread out over the city, so do as savvy locals do: plan your excursion with military precision, taking in only one or two areas in a day and stopping for lunch with a glass of wine or for a pint at a pub.

💲 Taxes

Departure taxes are divided into two bands. The Band A tax on a per-person economy fare for flights of under 2,000 miles is £13; Band B, for everything over, is £84. The fee is subject to government tax increases.

The British sales tax (V.A.T., value-added tax) is 20%. The tax is almost always included in quoted prices in shops, hotels, and restaurants.

Most travelers can get a V.A.T. refund (no minimum amount is required) by either the Retail Export or the more cumbersome Direct Export method. Many, but not all, large stores provide these services, but only if you request them; they will handle the paperwork.

For the Retail Export method, you must ask the store for Form V.A.T. 407 when making a purchase (you must have identification—passports are best). Some retailers will refund the amount on the spot, but others will use a refund company or the refund booth at the point when you leave the country. For the latter, have the form stamped like any customs form by U.K. customs officials when you leave the country. After you're through passport control, take the form to a refund-service counter for an on-the-spot refund (which is usually the quickest and easiest option), or mail it to the address on the form (or the envelope with it) after you arrive home. You receive the total refund stated on the form (the retailer or refund company may deduct a handling fee), but the processing time can be long, especially if you request a credit-card adjustment. This may be preferable to a check, however, as U.S. banks will charge a fee for depositing a check in a foreign currency.

With the Direct Export method, the goods are shipped directly to your home. You must have a Form V.A.T. 407 certified by customs, the police, or a notary public when you get home and then send it back to the store, which will refund your money. For inquiries, contact Her Majesty's Revenue & Customs office.

Global Blue (formerly, Global Refund) is a worldwide service with 270,000 affiliated stores and more than 200 refund offices. Its refund method, called a Tax Free Form, is the most common across the European continent. The service issues refunds in cash or to your credit card.

📞 Tipping

Tipping is done in Britain just as in the United States, but at a lower level. Tipping less than you would back home in restaurants—and not tipping at all in pubs—is not only accepted, but standard. Do not tip movie or theater ushers, elevator operators, or bar staff in pubs—although you can always offer to buy the latter a drink.

Tipping Guidelines for London

Bartender	In cocktail bars, if you see a tip plate, it's fine to leave £1–£2. For table service, tip 10% of the cost of the bill. But the gratuity is often included in the check at more expensive bars.
Bellhop	£1 per bag, depending on the level of the hotel.
Hotel concierge	£5 or more, if a service is performed for you.
Hotel housekeeper	It's extremely rare for housekeepers to expect a tip; £1–£2 would be generous.
Porter at airport or train station	£1 per bag.
Taxi driver	Optional 10%–12%, perhaps a little more for a short ride.
Tour guide	Tipping optional; £1–£2 would be generous.
Server	10%–15%, with 15% being the norm at high-end restaurants; nothing additional if a service charge is added to the bill.

◉ Visitor Information

You can get good information at the Travel Information Centre near the Eurostar arrivals area at St. Pancras International train station and also at Victoria rail station (opposite platform 8). Both these centers are open Wednesday through Saturday from 9:30 am to 4:45 pm. A third visitor center is located on the concourse of the Piccadilly Circus Tube station (Thursday through Saturday, 9:30 am to 4:45 pm).

▦ When to Go

The heaviest tourist season runs April through September, with another peak around Christmas. Late spring is the time to see the Royal Parks and gardens at their freshest; fall brings autumnal beauty and fewer people. Summer gives the best chance of good weather, although the crowds are intense. Winter can be dismal—it's dark by 5—but all the theaters, concerts, and exhibitions go full speed ahead, and Christmas lights bring a major touch of festive magic.

Weather-wise, winter is cold and wet with occasional light snow, and spring is colorful and fair. June through August can range from a total washout to a long, hot summer and anything in between. Autumn ranges from warm to cool to mild. It's impossible to forecast London weather, but you can be certain that it will not be what you expect.

The October "half-term," when schools in the capital take a break for a week or two, results in most attractions being overrun by children. The start of August can be a very busy time, and hot weather makes Tube travel a sweltering and sweaty nightmare. Air-conditioning is far from the norm in London, even in hotels; although it rarely tops 90°F, it can feel much hotter. And festive shopping in central London just before Christmas borders on the insane.

Great Itineraries

London in 1 Day

Do a giant best-of loop of the city by open-top boat and bus through six key districts, with a stop at the Tower of London, now almost 1,000 years old, and fun in Soho at the end. Start early, with the first ride of the London Eye at 10 am; you'll have the rest of the day to explore at whatever pace you wish, but be sure to get to Buckingham Palace before the sun sets or you'll miss out on some great photo opportunities.

On your morning ride on the **London Eye,** you'll be able to get an unrivaled bird's-eye view of the city. Then launch from the Eye's namesake pier for a swivel-eyed Thames River cruise past four famous bridges and Traitors' Gate before landing in front of the unmissable **Tower of London.**

Once inside the Tower, take in the Crown Jewels and gory royal history on a Yeoman Warder's tour, before jumping on a double-decker bus over **Tower Bridge,** past Monument, the Embankment, Park Lane, Oxford, and Piccadilly circuses and stopping at **Trafalgar Square,** where you can glimpse **Big Ben** and the **Houses of Parliament,** before stopping for lunch at a historic Westminster pub. Then take a walk over to **Westminster Abbey,** where a self-guided tour will take you through centuries of British history within one awe-inspiring building (note that the Abbey closes early on Saturday). Then take another short stroll through **St. James's Park** to **Buckingham Palace**; you'll have missed the daily Changing the Guard ceremony, but that

means the palace grounds will be less crowded, with more photo ops. End the day by meandering over to the hip Soho neighborhood, where foodies will find endless eclectic restaurants for dinner and partygoers will find some of the city's best nightlife.

London in 5 Days

DAY 1: BUCKINGHAM PALACE, TRAFALGAR SQUARE, AND THE NATIONAL PORTRAIT GALLERY

Start Day 1 with coffee in a Dickensian alleyway just north of **St. James's Palace,** before being first into the 19 impossibly grand state rooms at **Buckingham Palace.** Afterward, join the crowds outside the palace to watch a sea of bearskin foot guards perform the **Changing the Guard** ceremony, held 11:30 am most days. Some palace tickets include tours of the **Queen's Gallery,** which showcases top Old Masters art from the Royal Collection. Then take a stroll through **St. James's Park** before lunch at a historic Pall Mall pub. It's a short walk to the **National Gallery** at **Trafalgar Square.** Hit its quieter Sainsbury Wing, pick up an audio guide, and hunt down a few choice early Renaissance masterpieces. Enjoy stern portraits of Tudor monarchs at the **National Portrait Gallery** next door, before browsing the antiquarian booksellers on Charing Cross Road or Cecil Court and enjoying fresh handmade dim sum in **Chinatown.**

DAY 2: WESTMINSTER ABBEY, THE HOUSES OF PARLIAMENT, AND THE EAST END

Devote the early morning of Day 2 to a 90-minute verger-guided tour of solemn **Westminster Abbey.** Then investigate the **Houses of Parliament.** If in session, you can attend a debate in the public galleries or take a 75-minute tour of both houses. The stately **Members' and Strangers' Dining Rooms** in the House of Commons are occasionally open to the public for lunch; otherwise have a ploughman's lunch at a historic pub. Take pics of the newly restored **Big Ben** and walk up Whitehall to the gates of **No. 10 Downing Street,** the prime minister's residence. For a complete change of tune, take the Tube over to the gritty yet hip East End and Bangladeshi-influenced Brick Lane, where you can stroll along the art galleries and have a classic Indian curry for dinner.

DAY 3: THE SOUTH BANK

Start with a ride on the **London Eye** for eye-popping city panoramas. Take a long walk along the Thames, popping into any galleries, cinemas, or shops that catch your eye, like the excellent **Hayward Gallery.** Eventually meander along to **Tate Modern** for a modern art fix, stopping for lunch nearby. Then enjoy a Shakespeare hit with tours of the replica Elizabethan **Shakespeare's Globe.** Wiggle along for venison burgers and foodie stall heaven at **Borough Market** before backtracking over the pedestrian **Millennium Bridge** for a stunning approach to **St. Paul's Cathedral.** Hopefully you'll catch choral evensong there at 5 pm; then head east toward Bow Lane alleyway for a customary pub fish-and-chips dinner in The City.

DAY 4: THE BRITISH MUSEUM AND SOHO

On Day 4, start early at the **British Museum** in Bloomsbury and leave a few hours to explore hits like the Egyptian mummies, Rosetta Stone, and 7th-century Anglo-Saxon Sutton Hoo treasures. Afterward, Tube it to restaurant-mad **Soho,** where you can stop for Sri Lankan rice-and-curry at Hoppers, before browsing **Carnaby Street** and the surrounding indie fashion boutiques. Cut across Regent Street via the dapper gentlemen's tailors of **Savile Row** and head south for **Fortnum & Mason** and the old-world gentlemen's outfitters and bespoke shoe shops on Jermyn Street. Work back through the twinkly Regency red-carpet **Burlington Arcade** and pop into the **Royal Academy** gallery before taking Afternoon Tea at the cozy Brown's Hotel in Mayfair.

DAY 5: KENSINGTON'S MUSEUMS, PICCADILLY, AND THE WEST END

Finally, on Day 5, start with a one-hour tour of **The V&A,** the renowned museum of decorative arts and design, whose collection ranges from rare Persian rugs to Tudor chalices. Once out, refuel with a crepe on pedestrianized Exhibition Road near the South Kensington Tube, then choose either all things science at the **Science Museum** or the *T. rex* dinosaur trail at the **Natural History Museum.** Then stroll up Knightsbridge to **Harrods'** famous Food Halls, where you can drool over salamis and people-watch to your heart's content. Either duck in for the ace fashion at **Harvey Nichols** or sip early cocktails at **The Ritz** at Green Park. Then enjoy the giant neon lights of **Piccadilly Circus** and **Leicester Square** before having a pretheater dinner in **Covent Garden** and then catching a West End play or musical.

Best Festivals in London

World renowned for its thriving culture scene, London unsurprisingly keeps a packed annual arts calendar filled with festivals of all shapes and sizes, many of which include free events that are open to everyone. From movies on the South Bank to dance at Sadler's Wells, London's parade of festivals takes over swaths of the city's most interesting and eclectic venues throughout the year. Attending one is a great way to step out of your comfort zone and experience something new that you'll likely only find in London.

SPRING

Underbelly Festival
ART FESTIVALS | Running April through September, Underbelly offers a packed calendar of stand-up comedy, cabaret, and circus from its pop-up location in Cavendish Square, just north of Oxford Street. The range of shows caters to all ages, from family-friendly daytime events to risqué after-hours parties. Shows take place in the self-contained, inflatable cow-shape venue (hence the name of the festival). Tickets can be purchased in advance, or you can stop in and see what's available on any given day, which can be part of the fun. ⊠ *Cavendish Square, South Bank* ☎ *084/4545–8252* ⊕ *www.underbellyfestival.com* 🎫 *Free–£25* Ⓜ *Oxford Circus.*

SUMMER

Film4 Summer Screen
FILM FESTIVALS | Every year, Film4 Summer Screen gives Londoners the chance to watch a collection of classic and cult movies—as well as exclusive premieres—under the stars in the sumptuous courtyard of Somerset House, one of the city's most beautiful neoclassical buildings. Pack a blanket and an umbrella (this is London after all) and enjoy fine film, food, and wine on select dates throughout August. ⊠ *Somerset House, Strand, Covent Garden* ☎ *033/3320–2836* ⊕ *www.somersethouse.org* 🎫 *From £20* Ⓜ *Charing Cross.*

Meltdown Festival
MUSIC FESTIVALS | The wildly eclectic and very cool Meltdown generally takes place in June at the Southbank Centre. It's curated by a different big-name artist each year (e.g., Robert Smith in 2018, Nile Rodgers in 2019, and Grace Jones in 2022), so you never have any idea what to expect until the program comes out. ⊠ *Belvedere Rd., South Bank* ☎ *020/3879–9555* ⊕ *www.southbankcentre.co.uk* 🎫 *Free–£90* Ⓜ *Waterloo, Embankment.*

The Proms
CONCERTS | Hosted predominantly in the epic Royal Albert Hall, The BBC Proms is an eight-week-long festival of classical concerts that takes place every summer. More than 100 years old, the festival is considered an institution, but the lineup doesn't shy away from embracing the new and quirky aspects of classical music. Expect to find the likes of children's concerts, classic film scores, and avant-garde African salsa on the bill. Standing tickets of £6 are available for most performances. ⊠ *Royal Albert Hall, Kensington Gore, South Kensington* ☎ *020/7589–8212* ⊕ *www.royalalberthall.com* 🎫 *From £6.*

FALL

BFI London Film Festival

FILM | More than 200 feature films, many of them world or European premieres, plus shorts and artist talks, grace the program of the BFI London Film Festival, which takes place over 12 days every October. The big movie theaters in Leicester Square are the focus for the galas and major releases, but you can catch screenings at a total of 14 other venues across town, including locations like the Institute of Contemporary Arts. Booking ahead is advised. ⊠ *London* ☎ *020/7928–3232* ⊕ *www.bfi.org.uk* ▧ *From £12.*

Dance Umbrella

CULTURAL FESTIVALS | The biggest annual performing arts event in London is Dance Umbrella, a 20-day festival that hosts international and British-based artists at venues across the city. ⊠ *London* ☎ *020/7257–9380* ⊕ *www.danceumbrella.co.uk* ▧ *Free–£35.*

Frieze London

ART FESTIVALS | A glamorous contemporary art fair, Frieze London brings the crème de la crème of the international art world to London each October. Its sister show, Frieze Masters, is a 15-minute walk across Regent's Park and focuses on art from the ancient world through the late 20th century. For the two events combined, hundreds of galleries exhibiting thousands of artworks—everything from Old Masters to Rachel Whiteread—fill two huge pop-up spaces in the park.

The food and drink available on-site are pricey but excellent, and there's a compelling program of artist and curator talks. Catch the free Frieze Sculpture Park in Regent's Park between July and October. ⊠ *Regent's Park, Regent's Park* ☎ *020/3372–6111* ⊕ *www.frieze.com/fairs/frieze-london* ▧ *Combined ticket £82* Ⓜ *Regent's Park, Baker St., Great Portland St.*

London Jazz Festival

MUSIC FESTIVALS | Come November, international jazz superstars rub shoulders with emerging local talent and cutting-edge bands at more than 50 venues across the city during the 10 days of the London Jazz Festival. A varied program of around 350 performances, including free concerts and gigs for toddlers, means both jazz connoisseurs and those new to the genre will find plenty to enjoy. ⊠ *London* ⊕ *www.efglondonjazzfestival.org.uk* ▧ *Free–£70.*

WINTER

Vault Festival

ART FESTIVALS | This seven-week extravaganza of fringe theater and stand-up comedy is a chance to see some of the United Kingdom's most innovative and engaging performers. The atmosphere in the eerie tunnels beneath Waterloo Station (where the Vault Festival takes place) is always buzzing. ⊠ *The Vaults, Leake St., South Bank* ☎ *020/8050–9241* ⊕ *www.vaultfestival.com* ▧ *From £6* Ⓜ *Waterloo.*

Best Tours in London

With its crooked medieval streets, layers of history, and atmospheric buildings, London is a true walking city often best explored on a guided tour. Tours are a great way to investigate out-of-the-way, hidden, historic, and secret districts; to get an insider's eye on where locals like to eat, drink, and be merry; and to learn all the interesting and infamous aspects of London's history, architecture, and inhabitants.

BOAT TOURS

City Cruises. In nice weather, an open top-deck ride from Westminster, the London Eye, or Tower Piers to the ancient royal romping ground of Greenwich along the Thames River is one of the best ways to get acquainted with the city. You'll pass sights like Tower Bridge, the Tower of London, and St. Paul's Cathedral, all with a chirpy Cockney boatman running commentary. Lunch, Afternoon Tea, and nighttime cruises are also available. ⊠ *Cherry Garden Pier, Cherry Garden St., London* ☎ *020/7740–0400* ⊕ *www. citycruises.com* ✉ *From £10.50.*

Thames RIB Experience. Make like James Bond in an exhilarating special forces–style inflatable speedboat as you whiz past the MI6 building, Shakespeare's Globe, and Tower Bridge on a high-speed 50-minute round-trip to Canary Wharf. There are also 40-minute roller-coaster blasts to the O2 Arena in Greenwich and 75-minute round-trips from Tower Pier to the Thames Barrier. ⊠ *Embankment Pier, London* ☎ *020/3613–7838* ⊕ *www. thamesribexperience.com* ✉ *From £28.*

BUS TOURS

Golden Tours. Various hop-on, hop-off open-top double-decker tours with this company take in the main sites on three key loops. With 60 drop-off points and 48-hour passes, they also offer discount tickets to attractions like the Tower of London and the London Dungeon, as well as nighttime tours, free walking tours, and boat rides on the Thames. ⊠ *London* ☎ *020/7630–2028* ⊕ *www. goldentours.com* ✉ *From £26.*

The Original Open-Air Tourist Bus. This one-day, hop-on-hop-off, open-top bus tour with over 80 stops along six different routes takes in major landmarks like the Houses of Parliament, Westminster Abbey, Trafalgar Square, the British Museum, the Tower of London, and, of course, Buckingham Palace, as well as more off-the-beaten-path sites like Lambeth Palace (home of the Bishop of London). Tickets are good for the entire day and for all routes. ⊠ *London* ☎ *020/8877–1722* ⊕ *www.tootbus.com* ✉ *From £29.*

FREE TOURS

Guides to The City. The City Guides (or, to give them their full name, The City of London Guide Lecturers Association) are the official guides to the City of London, "The City" being not the entire metropolis but the "Square Mile" historic financial district. They offer two highly informed daily walks, one at 11 am and one in the afternoon, that cover essential sights like Guildhall (The City's town hall), Mansion House, the Bank of England, and the Royal Exchange.

More specialized walks offered by the Museum of London focus on topics like Samuel Johnson's London, the gardens of The City, the Great Fire of London, Roman London, and the churches of Christopher Wren, most notably his magnificent St. Paul's Cathedral. ⊕ *www. cityoflondonguides.com* ✉ *Free - £16.*

Sandemans New Europe—PleaLondon. It seems almost too good to be true: Sandemans offers an excellent, free, 2½-hour Royal London walking tour daily, which winds from Buckingham Palace to Big Ben. Tours are also available in Spanish and while free, tips are the expected way to show your appreciation (along with a round of applause at the finish).

Led by wisecracking actors, poets, and esteemed art historians, paid walks on offer include a boozy five-stop pub crawl and spooky East End's Dark Secrets tours. ☎ *074/4729–3760* ⊕ *www. neweuropetours.eu/london* ✉ *Free.*

SPECIALTY TOURS

Brit Movie Tours. See the exterior of Grantham House and the spot where Branson first confesses his love for Lady Sybil on this insiders' central London tour of *Downton Abbey* filming locations. Other tours focusing on James Bond, *Sherlock, The Da Vinci Code,* and Harry Potter filming locations, among many others, are also available. ☎ *0844/247–1007* ⊕ *www. britmovietours.com* ✉ *From £15.*

London Food Lovers Food Tours. London's a top global foodie city now, and the London Food Lovers walking tour of Soho is a fascinating way to explore the capital's gastro delights. Well-led and synchronized throughout, the four-hour walk kicks off with Hawaiian blueberry pancakes at burger bar KuaAina and takes in offbeat stops for truffle pumpkin ravioli at Soho's retro Italian delicatessen Lina Stores, a hot-chocolate tasting at a local chocolatier, and a sit-down lunch of fish-and-chips and Indian pale ale in quaint Soho pub The Dog and Duck. You'll also stop in Chinatown to sample steamed-prawn dim sum at Beijing Dumpling and spot celebrities amid the Afternoon Tea crowds at the Maison Bertaux French patisserie and tearoom. The tour ends with a dessert and wine pairing in the Dickensian underground cellar vaults of the 1890s Gordon's Wine Bar. There are various versions of the Soho tour, as well as a Jack the Ripper Happy Hour Tasting Tour. ✉ *Islington* ☎ *0777/4099–306* ⊕ *www.londonfood-lovers.com* ✉ *From £64.*

WALKING TOURS

Context Travel. This company takes a highbrow approach to its intellectually curious small-group walks program, providing PhD- and MA-level scholars, authors, architects, and historians to lead walks of no more than six people. Lasting up to three hours, walks include the evolution of London theater to Charles Dickens and Victorian London. ⊕ *www.contexttravel. com/cities/london* ✉ *From £90.*

London Walks. With London's oldest established walking tours, there's no need to book ahead; instead, just turn up at the meeting point at the allotted hour and pay £15 for a first-rate, guided two-hour walk with themes like Secret London, Literary London, Harry Potter film locations, Haunted London, and much more. Top crime historian and leading Ripper authority Donald Rumbelow often leads the 7:30 pm Jack the Ripper walk in Whitechapel. ☎ *020/7624–3978* ⊕ *www.walks.com* ✉ *From £15.*

Sophie Campbell. Travel journalist and former BBC *Travel Show* broadcaster Sophie Campbell specializes in exhaustive and exhausting London walks. Full-day walks include the chance to explore the elegance of Kensington and the wares of Portobello Market or make your way from Hampton Court Palace to Richmond Palace via the noble palazzi of the nontidal Thames. Half-day hikes include a wander through Royal London or a fascinating whirl through Covent Garden and London's theater-heavy West End. ⊕ *www.sophiecampbell.london* ✉ *From £230.*

Contacts

✈ Air Travel

AIRPORTS Gatwick Airport. ☎ *0344/892–0322* ⊕ *www.gatwickairport. com.* **Heathrow Airport.** ☎ *0844/335–1801* ⊕ *www. heathrow.com.* **London City Airport.** ☎ *020/7646–0000* ⊕ *www.londoncityairport.com.* **Luton Airport.** ☎ *01582/405100* ⊕ *www.london-luton. co.uk.* **Southend Airport.** ☎ *01702/538500* ⊕ *www.southendairport. com.* **Stansted Airport.** ☎ *0808/169–7030* ⊕ *www. stanstedairport.com.*

GROUND TRANSPORTATION easyBus. ⊕ *www. easybus.com.* **Gatwick Express.** ☎ *0345/850–1530* ⊕ *www.gatwickexpress. com.* **Heathrow Express.** ☎ *0345/600–1515* ⊕ *www.heathrowexpress.com.* **Heathrow Shuttle.** ☎ *020/3026–7368* ⊕ *www.heathrowshuttle. com.* **National Express.** ☎ *0871/781–8181* ⊕ *www.nationalexpress. com.* **Stansted Express.** ⊕ *www.stanstedexpress. com.* **Thameslink.** ⊕ *www. thameslinkrailway.com.*

⚓ Boat Travel

Thames Clippers. ⊕ *www. thamesclippers.com.* **Transport for London.** ☎ *0343/222–1234* ⊕ *www.tfl.gov.uk.*

🚌 Bus Travel

LONG-DISTANCE BUS CONTACTS easyBus. ⊕ *www.easybus.com.* **Green Line.** ☎ *0344/801– 7261* ⊕ *www.greenline.co.uk.* **Megabus.** ☎ *0900/160–0900* ⊕ *www.megabus. com.* **National Express.** ☎ *0871/781–8181* ⊕ *www.nationalexpress. com.* **Transport for London.** ☎ *0343/222–1234* ⊕ *www.tfl.gov.uk.* **Victoria Coach Station.** ✉ *164 Buckingham Palace Rd., Victoria* ☎ *0343/222–1234* Ⓜ *Victoria.*

🚕 Taxi Travel

Addison Lee. ☎ *020/7387– 8888* ⊕ *www.addisonlee.com.* **Dial-a-Cab.** ☎ *020/7253–5000 for cash bookings, 020/7251–0581 for inquiries* ⊕ *www. dialacab.co.uk.*

🚆 Train Travel

BritRail Travel. ☎ *866/938– 7245 in U.S. and Canada* ⊕ *www.britrail.net.* **Eurostar.** ☎ *03432/186186* ⊕ *www.eurostar.com.* **Eurotunnel.** ☎ *0344/335– 3535* ⊕ *www.eurotunnel. com.* **National Rail Enquiries.** ☎ *0345/748–4950* ⊕ *www.nationalrail.co.uk.*

🚇 Tube Travel

Transport for London. ☎ *0343/222–1234* ⊕ *www.tfl.gov.uk.*

📍 Visitor Information

Official websites
www.visitbritain.com
www.visitlondon.com
Other websites
www.londontown.com
www.standard.co.uk
www.bbc.co.uk
Entertainment information
www.timeout.com/london
www.officiallondontheatre.co.uk

Chapter 3

WESTMINSTER AND ST. JAMES'S

3

Updated by
Jo Caird

 Sights
★★★★★

 Restaurants
★★★☆☆

 Hotels
★★☆☆☆

 Shopping
★★☆☆☆

 Nightlife
★★☆☆☆

WESTMINSTER AND ST. JAMES'S SNAPSHOT

TOP REASONS TO GO

Westminster Abbey: This Gothic church was not only the site of William and Kate's marriage in 2011 but also has seen 38 coronations, starting with William the Conqueror in 1066.

Buckingham Palace: Even if you miss the palace's summer opening, keep pace with the marching soldiers as they enact the time-honored Changing the Guard.

The National Gallery: The works of Leonardo, Raphael, van Eyck, Rembrandt, and many other artistic greats are shown off in the gorgeous rooms at the National Gallery.

Churchill War Rooms: Listen to Churchill's radio addresses to the British people as you explore this atmospheric underground wartime hideout.

Big Ben: London's most famous photo op is looking splendid as ever following the completion in 2022 of a multiyear renovation project.

MAKING THE MOST OF YOUR TIME

■ For royal pageantry, begin with Buckingham Palace, Westminster Abbey, and the Household Cavalry Museum, followed by the Houses of Parliament and Big Ben. For art, the National Gallery, Tate Britain, and the Queen's Gallery top anyone's list.

NEAREST PUBLIC RESTROOMS

■ Paid restrooms (50 pence) are across the street from Westminster Abbey at the bottom of Victoria Street. The Queen's Gallery has elegant restrooms.

GETTING THERE

Trafalgar Square is in the center of the action. Take the Tube to Embankment (Northern, Bakerloo, District, and Circle lines) and walk north until you cross the Strand, or exit to Northumberland Avenue at Charing Cross (Bakerloo and Northern lines). Buses are another great option, as almost all roads lead to Trafalgar Square.

Two Tube stations are right in the heart of St. James's: Piccadilly Circus (Piccadilly and Bakerloo lines) and Green Park (Piccadilly, Victoria, and Jubilee lines).

This is postcard London at its best. Crammed with historic churches, grand state buildings, and some of the world's best art collections, Royal London and Westminster unite politics and high culture. (Oh, and the Queen lives here, too.) The places you'll want to explore are grouped into four distinct areas—Trafalgar Square, Whitehall, St. James's, and Buckingham Palace—each nudging a corner of triangular St. James's Park. There is as much history in these few acres as in many whole cities, so pace yourself—this is concentrated sightseeing.

Westminster

Home to London's most photogenic pigeons, **Trafalgar Square** is the official center of the district known as **Westminster,** nominally a separate city but in fact the official center of London. What will bring you here are the two magnificent museums on the northern edge of the square, the **National Gallery** and the **National Portrait Gallery** (just note that the latter is closed for refurbishment until 2023). From the square, two boulevards lead to the seats of different areas of governance. The avenue called **Whitehall** drops south to the neo-Gothic **Houses of Parliament,** where members of both (Commons and Lords) hold debates and vote on pending legislation. Just opposite, **Westminster Abbey** is a monument to the nation's history and for centuries the scene of coronations and royal weddings as well as daily worship. Poets, political leaders, and 17 monarchs are buried in this world-famous, 13th-century Gothic building. Sandwiched between the two is the **Jewel Tower,** the only surviving part of the medieval Palace of Westminster (a name still given to Parliament and its environs). Halfway down Whitehall, **10 Downing Street** is both the residence and the office of the prime minister. One of the most celebrated occupants, Winston Churchill, is commemorated in the **Churchill War Rooms,** his underground wartime headquarters off Whitehall. Just down the road is the **Cenotaph,** built for the dead of World War I and since then a focal point for the annual remembrance of those lost in war.

The Mall, a wide elegant avenue beyond the stone curtain of **Admiralty Arch,** heads southwest from Trafalgar Square toward the **Queen Victoria Memorial** and **Buckingham Palace,** the sovereign's official London residence. The building and its grand gardens are open to the public only in summer (and for tours on select dates throughout the year), but you can see highlights of the royal art collection in the **Queen's Gallery** and spectacular ceremonial coaches in the **Royal Mews,** both open all year. Farther south toward Pimlico, **Tate Britain** focuses on prominent British artists from 1500 to today.

The main drawback to sightseeing here is that half the world is doing it at the same time. So, for a large part of the year a lot of Royal London is floodlit at night (when there's more elbow room), adding to the theatricality of the experience.

◉ Sights

Carlton House Terrace
NOTABLE BUILDING | Architect John Nash designed Carlton House, a glorious example of the Regency style, under the patronage of the Prince Regent (later George IV), who ruled in place of George III while the "mad king" was considered too unstable to rule. Carlton House was considered a most extravagant building for its time; it was demolished after the prince's accession to the throne in 1820. In its place Nash built Carlton House Terrace—no less imposing, with white-stucco facades and massive Corinthian columns. Carlton Terrace was a smart address, home to a number of the 19th-century's greatest luminaries—including two prime ministers, William Gladstone (1856) and Lord Palmerston (1840–46). Today Carlton House Terrace

houses the Royal Society (No. 6–9), Britain's most prestigious society of scientific minds; still active, its previous members have included Isaac Newton and Charles Darwin. ⊠ *The Mall, St. James's* Ⓜ *Charing Cross.*

★ Churchill War Rooms
HISTORY MUSEUM | FAMILY | It was from this small warren of underground rooms—beneath the vast government buildings of the Treasury—that Winston Churchill and his team directed troops in World War II. Designed to be bombproof, the whole complex has been preserved almost exactly as it was when the last light was turned off at the end of the war. Every clock shows almost 5 pm, and the furniture, fittings, and paraphernalia of a busy, round-the-clock war office are still in situ, down to the colored map pins.

During air raids, the leading government ministers met here, and the Cabinet Room is arranged as if a meeting were about to convene. In the Map Room, the Allied campaign is charted on wall-to-wall maps with a rash of pinholes showing the movements of convoys. In the hub of the room, a bank of differently colored phones known as the "Beauty Chorus" linked the War Rooms to control rooms around the nation. Spot the desk from which the PM made his morale-boosting broadcasts; the Transatlantic Telephone Room (a converted broom cupboard) has his hotline to FDR. You can also see the restored rooms that the PM used for dining and sleeping. Telephonists (switchboard operators) and clerks who worked 16-hour shifts slept in lesser quarters in unenviable conditions.

An excellent addition to the War Rooms is the Churchill Museum, a tribute to the great wartime leader himself. ⊠ *Clive Steps, King Charles St., Westminster* ☎ *020/7416–5000* ⊕ *www.iwm.org. uk/visits/churchill-war-rooms* ⊠ *£25* Ⓜ *Westminster.*

A Brief History of Westminster

The Romans may have shaped The City, but England's royals created Westminster. Indeed, it's still technically a separate city—notice it reads "City of Westminster" on street signs, not "City of London"—although any formal divide between the two vanished centuries ago, along with the open countryside that once lay between them. Edward the Confessor started the first Palace of Westminster in the 11th century; in the 1040s, he also founded Westminster Abbey, where every British coronation has taken place.

The district became the focus of political power in England after the construction of Whitehall Palace in the 16th century; a vast and opulent building, it was the official residence of the monarch until it burned down in 1698. It survives both as the name of Westminster's most important road, and as a term still used in Britain to refer to the seat of government in

general. The first Parliament building was part of the same complex; it, too, was nearly destroyed, by the Gunpowder Plot of 1605 (the foiling of which is still commemorated annually on November 5, Guy Fawkes Day), eventually succumbing to fire in 1834.

The Westminster we see today took shape during the Georgian and Victorian periods, as Britain reached the zenith of its imperial power. Grand architecture sprang up, and Buckingham Palace became the principal royal residence in 1837, when Victoria acceded to the throne. Trafalgar Square and Nelson's Column were built in 1843, to commemorate Britain's most famous naval victory, and the Houses of Parliament were rebuilt in the 1840s in the trendy neo-Gothic style of the time. The illustrious Clarence House, built in 1825 for the Duke of Clarence (later William IV), is now the home of Prince Charles and Camilla, Duchess of Cornwall.

Downing Street

GOVERNMENT BUILDING | Were it not for the wrought-iron gates and armed guards that block the entrance, you'd probably miss this otherwise unassuming Georgian side street off Whitehall—but this is the location of the famous No. 10, London's modest equivalent of the White House. The Georgian entrance to the mid-17th-century mansion is deceptive; it's actually a huge complex of discreetly linked buildings. Since 1732 it has been the official home and office of the prime minister—the last private resident was the magnificently named Mr. Chicken (the current prime minister actually lives in the private apartments above No. 11, traditionally the residence of the Chancellor of the Exchequer, the head of the Treasury). There are no public

tours, but the famous black front door to No. 10 is clearly visible from Whitehall. Keep your eyes peeled for Larry the cat, whose official title is Chief Mouser to the Cabinet Office.

Just south of Downing Street, in the middle of Whitehall, is the Cenotaph, a stark white monolith built to commemorate the 1918 armistice. On Remembrance Day (the Sunday nearest November 11), it's strewn with red poppy wreaths to honor the dead of both world wars and all British and Commonwealth soldiers killed in action since; the first wreath is always laid by the Queen. A hundred yards farther, toward Parliament, is the Monument to the Women of World War II. The prominent black marble sculpture uses a string of empty uniforms to

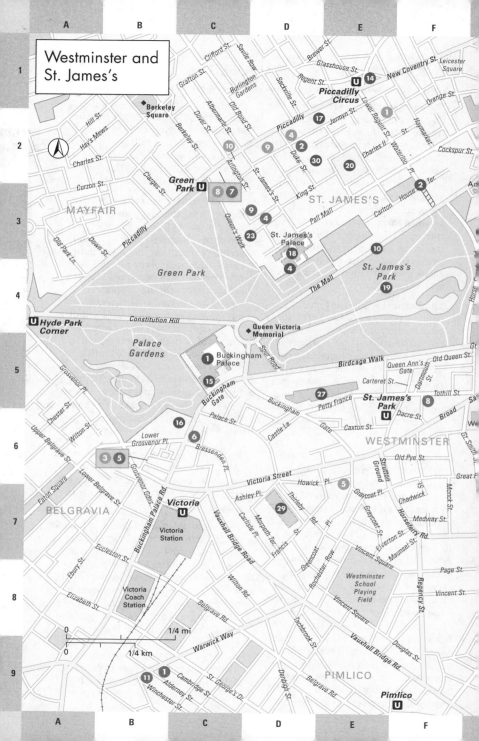

Sights ▼

1 Buckingham Palace.....**C5**
2 Carlton House Terrace...**F2**
3 Churchill War Rooms... **G4**
4 Clarence House......... **D4**
5 Downing Street......... **G4**
6 Horse Guards Parade.. **G3**
7 Household Cavalry Museum **G3**
8 Houses of Parliament .. **H5**
9 The Jewel Tower **G6**
10 The Mall **E3**
11 National Gallery......... **G2**
12 National Portrait Gallery **G1**
13 Parliament Square...... **G5**
14 Piccadilly Circus......... **E1**
15 The Queen's Gallery:....**C5**
16 Royal Mews **C6**
17 St. James's Church **D2**
18 St. James's Palace **D3**
19 St. James's Park **E4**
20 St. James's Square..... **E2**
21 St. Margaret's Church **G5**
22 St. Martin-in-the-Fields..................... **G1**
23 Spencer House **D3**
24 The Supreme Court..... **G5**
25 Tate Britain **G9**
26 Trafalgar Square........ **G2**
27 Wellington Barracks and the Guards Chapel....... **E5**
28 Westminster Abbey **G5**
29 Westminster Cathedral **D7**
30 White Cube.............. **D2**

Restaurants ▼

1 Aquavit................... **E1**
2 Boyds Grill and Wine Bar................. **G2**
3 The Dining Room at The Goring.............. **B6**
4 45 Jermyn St **D2**
5 Iris & June................ **E6**
6 Kerridge's Bar & Grill... **H2**
7 Notes Music and Coffee............... **G1**
8 The Ritz Restaurant...... **C2**
9 Wiltons................... **D2**
10 The Wolseley............ **C2**

Hotels ▼

1 Artist Residence **B9**
2 The Cavendish **D2**
3 The Corinthia............ **H2**
4 Dukes Hotel **D3**
5 The Goring............... **B6**
6 Hotel 41 .... **C6**
7 The Ritz **C2**
8 Sanctuary House Hotel **F5**
9 The Stafford London ... **D3**
10 The Westminster London, Curio Collection by Hilton **G8**
11 Windermere Hotel...... **B9**

3

Westminster and St. James's WESTMINSTER

KEY

① Sights
① Restaurants
① Hotels

symbolize the vital service of women in then-traditionally male jobs during the war, as well as in frontline roles, such as medics and auxiliary officers. ✉ *Whitehall* Ⓜ *Westminster.*

Horse Guards Parade

OTHER ATTRACTION | FAMILY | Once the tiltyard for jousting tournaments, Horse Guards Parade is best known for the annual Trooping the Colour ceremony, in which the Queen takes the salute on her official birthday, on the second Saturday in June. (Though it's called a birthday, it's actually the anniversary of her corona-tion—her real birthday is April 21.) It's a must-see if you're around, with marching bands and throngs of onlookers. Through-out the rest of the year, the changing of two mounted sentries known as the Queen's Life Guard at the Whitehall facade of Horse Guards provides what may be London's most popular photo opportunity. The ceremony takes place daily from April to July, and on alternate days from August to March (usually odd numbered days, but check the monthly schedule at ⊕ *www.householddivision. org.uk/changing-the-guard-calendar*). It starts at 10:30 am at St. James's Palace, where the guard begins its march to Buckingham Palace, and the new guards take up their posts in a ceremony at 11. (It's sometimes cancelled in bad weather.)

At 4 pm daily is the dismounting cere-mony, aka the 4 O'Clock Parade, during which sentries are posted and horses are returned to their stables. It began in 1894, when Queen Victoria discovered the guards on duty drinking and gam-bling. As a punishment she decreed that the regiment should be inspected every day at 4 pm for the next 100 years—by the time 1994 swung around they decid-ed to continue the tradition indefinitely. ✉ *Whitehall* ⊕ *www.householddivision. org.uk/changing-the-guard* 🎫 *Free* Ⓜ *Westminster.*

Household Cavalry Museum

OTHER MUSEUM | FAMILY | Hang around Horse Guards for even a short time and you'll see a member of the Household Cavalry on guard, or trotting past on horseback, resplendent in a bright crim-son uniform with polished brass armor. Made up of soldiers from the British Army's most senior regiments, the Life Guard and the Blues and Royals, mem-bership is considered a great honor; they act as the Queen's official bodyguards and play a key role in state occasions (they also perform the famed Changing the Guard ceremony).

Housed in the cavalry's original 17th-cen-tury stables, the museum has displays of uniforms and weapons going back to 1661 as well as interactive exhibits on the regiments' current operational roles. In the tack room you can handle saddles and bridles, and try on a trooper's uni-form, including a distinctive brass helmet with horsehair plume. You can also observe the working horses being tend-ed to in their stable block behind a glass wall. ✉ *Horse Guards Parade, Whitehall* ☎ *020/7930–3070* ⊕ *www.householdcav-alrymuseum.co.uk* 🎫 *£9.50* Ⓜ *Charing Cross, Westminster.*

★ Houses of Parliament

GOVERNMENT BUILDING | The Palace of Westminster, as the complex is called, was first established on this site by Edward the Confessor in the 11th centu-ry. William II built a new palace in 1097, and this became the seat of English pow-er. A fire destroyed most of the palace in 1834, and the current complex dates largely from the mid-19th century. The best view is from the opposite (south) bank of the Thames, across Lambeth Bridge. It is most dramatic at night when lighted green and gold.

The Visitors' Galleries of the House of Commons provide a view of democracy in action when the benches are filled by opposing MPs (members of Parlia-ment). Debates are formal but raucous, especially during Prime Minister's Questions (PMQs), when any MP can put a question to the nation's leader. Tickets to PMQs are free but highly sought after, so the only way for non-U.K. citizens to gain access is by lining up on the day and hoping for returns or no-shows—expect to wait for up to two hours, with no guarantee of entry. The action starts at noon every Wednesday when Parliament is sitting, and the whole shebang is broadcast live on television. For non-PMQ debates, Embassies and High Commissions have a quota of tickets available to their citizens, which can help you avoid long lines. The easiest time to get into the Commons is during an evening session—Parliament is still sitting if the top of the Clock Tower is illuminated. There are also Visitors Galleries for the House of Lords.

The Clock Tower—renamed Elizabeth Tower in 2012, in honor of the Queen's Diamond Jubilee—was completed in 1858, and contains the 13-ton bell known as Big Ben. Just note that renovations of the tower are scheduled through the end of 2022, with scaffolding somewhat marring photo ops during this period, although Big Ben has been revealed in all its refurbished glory. At the southwest end of the main Parliament building is the 323-foot-high Victoria Tower. The Queen uses the Sovereign's Entrance, at its base, when visiting Parliament.

Engaging guided and audio tours of Parliament are available on Saturday and weekdays when Parliament isn't sitting, but sell out six months in advance. ⊠ *St. Stephen's Entrance, St. Margaret St., Westminster* ☎ *020/7219–4114 for public tours* ⊕ *www.parliament.uk/visiting* 🎫 *Free; tours from £22* ⊘ *Closed Sun.* Ⓜ *Westminster.*

The Jewel Tower

NOTABLE BUILDING | Overshadowed by the big-ticket attractions of Parliament to one side and Westminster Abbey to the other, this is the only significant portion of the Palace of Westminster complex to have survived intact from medieval times. Built in the 1360s to contain treasures belonging to Edward III, it once formed part of the palace's defensive walls—hence the fortresslike appearance. Check out the original ribbed stone ceiling on the ground floor; look up to see the carved stone images of men and beasts. The Jewel Tower was later used as a records office for the House of Lords, but hasn't served any official function since the rest of the old palace was destroyed by fire in 1834 and the ancient documents were moved to the greater safety of the Tower of London. Today it contains an exhibition on the history of the building. This is a great option for those looking for a slice of British political history on days Parliament tours are sold out. ⊠ *Abingdon St., Westminster* ☎ *020/7222–2219* ⊕ *www.english-heritage.org.uk/visit/places/jewel-tower* 🎫 *£6.60* ⊘ *Closed Mon. and Tues. in summer and weekdays in winter* Ⓜ *Westminster.*

★ National Gallery

ART GALLERY | FAMILY | Anyone with even a passing interest in art will want to put this near the top of their to-do list while visiting London, for it is truly one of the world's great art museums. More than 2,300 masterpieces are on show here, including works by Michelangelo, Leonardo, Turner, Monet, van Gogh, Picasso, and more. Enter through the grand portico overlooking the north side of Trafalgar Square to delve headlong into the highlights of the collection, although the Sainsbury Wing (the modern building immediately to the left), which focuses mainly on medieval art, is invariably less crowded.

You could easily spend all day discovering what the National Gallery has to offer, but among the best-known highlights are *The Ambassadors* by Hans Holbein (1497–1543), a portrait of two wealthy visitors from France, surrounded by objects laden with enough symbolism to fill a book—including, most beguilingly, a giant

Did You Know?

After an 1834 fire, Parliament was rebuilt, combining Renaissance and Gothic styles. Then, when the bomb-damaged House of Commons was redone after World War II, some of its ornamental flourishes were toned down.

skull at the base, which only takes shape when viewed from an angle; *The Arnolfini Portrait* by Jan van Eyck (1390–1441), in which a solemn couple holds hands, the fish-eye mirror behind them mysteriously illuminating what can't be seen from the front view; *The Virgin of the Rocks* by Leonardo da Vinci (1452–1519), a magnificently sculpted altarpiece commissioned in 1480; and *Rain, Steam, and Speed—The Great Western Railway* by J. M. W. Turner (1775–1851), which seems, in its mad whirl of rain, steam, and mist, to embody the mystical dynamism of the steam age (spot the fleeing hare).

Special exhibitions, of which there are several every year, tend to be major events. Generally they're ticketed, so booking is advisable if it's a big name. The permanent collection, however, is always free. Guided tours of the collection and curator's talks take place regularly, both in the gallery and online; check the website for details. ☒ *Trafalgar Sq., Westminster* ☎ *020/7747–2885* ⊕ *www.nationalgallery.org.uk* ☒ *Free; special exhibitions from £7* Ⓜ *Charing Cross, Embankment, Leicester Sq.*

★ **National Portrait Gallery**
ART GALLERY | FAMILY | The National Portrait Gallery was founded in 1856 with a single aim: to gather together portraits of famous (and infamous) Britons throughout history. More than 150 years and 200,000 portraits later, it is an essential stop for all history and literature buffs. If you visit with kids, ask at the desk about the excellent Family Trails, which make exploring the galleries with children much more fun.

Galleries are arranged clearly and chronologically, from Tudor times to contemporary Britain. The enormous portrait of Elizabeth I—bejeweled and literally astride the world in a powerful display of imperial intent—may be the most impressive image in the Tudor Gallery, but there are plenty of contenders for that title. The huge permanent collections include portraits of Shakespeare, the Brontë sisters, and Jane Austen. Look for Stuart Pearson Wright's portrait of a seated J. K. Rowling and Annie Leibovitz's striking photograph of Queen Elizabeth II. Temporary exhibitions can be explored on the first three floors, particularly in the Wolfson and Porter galleries on the ground floor. On the top floor, the Portrait Restaurant has one of the best views in London—a panoramic vista of Nelson's Column and the backdrop along Whitehall to the Houses of Parliament. ⚠ **The National Portrait Gallery is closed for renovations until spring 2023.** ☒ *St. Martin's Pl., Westminster* ☎ *020/7306–0055* ⊕ *www. npg.org.uk* ☒ *Free; special exhibitions from £6* Ⓜ *Charing Cross, Leicester Sq.*

Parliament Square
PLAZA/SQUARE | Accessing Parliament Square, the green space opposite the Palace of Westminster, isn't always easy—it's regularly filled with protestors hoping to get the attention of the lawmakers across the road. But it's worth the effort to get a closer look at the statues of political figures that line the square. Notable among the 12 are Winston Churchill; Sir Robert Peel, the 19th-century prime minister who created the modern police force (it's because of him that British police officers are known as "bobbies"); U.S. president Abraham Lincoln (this statue is a replica of the one in Chicago's Lincoln Park); Nelson Mandela; and Mahatma Gandhi. The newest statue, erected in 2018 as part of celebrations of the centenary of British women being granted the right to vote, portrays the women's rights campaigner Millicent Fawcett and is the first statue of a woman in the square; it was designed by Turner Prize–winning artist Gillian Wearing. ☒ *Parliament Sq., Westminster* ☒ *Free* Ⓜ *Westminster.*

Tate Britain showcases British art from the last 500 years, including contemporary works.

St. Margaret's Church

CHURCH | Dwarfed by its neighbor, Westminster Abbey, St. Margaret's was probably founded in the 11th century and rebuilt between 1482 and 1523. It's the unofficial parish church of the House of Commons—Winston Churchill tied the knot here in 1908, and since 1681, a pew off the south aisle has been set aside for the Speaker of the House (look for the carved portcullis). Samuel Pepys and John Milton also worshipped here. The stained glass in the north windows is classically Victorian, facing abstract glass from the 20th-century artist John Piper in the south, while the east windows date from the early 16th century. These were to replace the originals, which were ruined in World War II. Opening times can be irregular, so it's smart to call before your visit. ✉ *St. Margaret's St., Parliament Sq., Westminster* ☎ *020/7222–5152* ⊕ *www.westminster-abbey.org/st-margarets-church* 🎫 *Free* ☉ *Closed Sat.* Ⓜ *Westminster.*

St. Martin-in-the-Fields

CHURCH | **FAMILY** | One of London's best-loved and most welcoming of churches is more than just a place of worship. Named after St. Martin of Tours, known for the help he gave to beggars, this parish has long been a welcome sight for the homeless, who have been given soup and shelter at the church since 1914. The church is also a haven for music lovers; the internationally known Academy of St. Martin-in-the-Fields Chamber Ensemble was founded here, and a popular program of concerts continues today. (many of the shows are free, although some do charge an entry fee). The crypt is a hive of activity, with a popular café and shop. Here you can also make your own life-size souvenir knight, lady, or monarch from replica tomb brasses, with metallic waxes, paper, and instructions. ✉ *Trafalgar Sq., Westminster* ☎ *020/7766–1100* ⊕ *www.smitf.org* 🎫 *Free; brass rubbing from £5* Ⓜ *Charing Cross, Leicester Sq.*

The Supreme Court

GOVERNMENT BUILDING | The highest court of appeal in the United Kingdom is a surprisingly young institution, only having heard its first cases in 2009. Visitors are welcome to drop by and look at the three courtrooms, housed in the carefully restored Middlesex Guildhall, including the impressive Court Room 1, with its magnificent carved wood ceiling. Court is in session Monday through Thursday, and since space in the public galleries is limited, you'll want to arrive early. The Court's art collection, on permanent display, includes portraits by Thomas Gainsborough and Joshua Reynolds. Guided tours are available on Friday at 2 pm. There is a café downstairs. ⊠ *Parliament Sq., Westminster* ☎ *020/7960–1500* ⊕ *www. supremecourt.uk* ⊠ *Free; guided tour £10* ⊙ *Closed weekends* Ⓜ *Westminster.*

★ Tate Britain

ART GALLERY | FAMILY | First opened in 1897, and funded by the sugar magnate Sir Henry Tate, this stately neoclassical institution may not be as ambitious as its Bankside sibling, Tate Modern, but its bright galleries lure only a fraction of the Modern's overwhelming crowds and are a great place to explore British art from 1500 to the present. The museum includes the Linbury Galleries on the lower floors, which stage temporary exhibitions, and a permanent collection on the upper floors. And what a collection it is—with classic works by John Constable, Thomas Gainsborough, Francis Bacon, and an outstanding display from J. M. W. Turner in the Clore Gallery. Sumptuous Pre-Raphaelite pieces are a major draw, while more recent art historical periods are represented with works by artists such as Rachel Whiteread, L. S. Lowry, Vanessa Bell, Duncan Grant, Barbara Hepworth, and David Hockney. Tate Britain also hosts the annual Turner Prize exhibition, with its accompanying furor over the state of contemporary art, from about October to January each year.

There's a good little café, and the excellent Rex Whistler Restaurant has been something of an institution since it first opened in 1927. Look out for semiregular Late at Tate Friday evening events, when the gallery is open late for talks or performances; check the website for details.

Craving more art? Head down the river on the Tate Boat (£9.10 one-way) to Tate Modern; it runs between the two museums every 20 to 40 minutes. ⊠ *Millbank, Westminster* ☎ *020/7887–8888* ⊕ *www. tate.org.uk/britain* ⊠ *Free; special exhibitions from £13* Ⓜ *Pimlico.*

★ Trafalgar Square

PLAZA/SQUARE | This is officially the center of London: a plaque on the corner of the Strand and Charing Cross Road marks the spot from which distances on U.K. signposts are measured. (London's *actual* geographic center is a rather dull bench on the Victoria Embankment.) Medieval kings once kept their aviaries of hawks and falcons here; today the humbler gray pigeons flock en masse to the open spaces around the ornate fountains (feeding them is banned).

The square was designed in 1830 by John Nash, who envisaged a new public space with striking views of the Thames, the Houses of Parliament, and Buckingham Palace. Of those, only Parliament is still clearly visible from the square, but it remains an important spot for open-air concerts, political demonstrations, and national celebrations, such as New Year's Eve. Dominating the square is 168-foot Nelson's Column, erected as a monument to the great admiral in 1843. Note that the lampposts on the south side, heading down Whitehall, are topped with ships—they all face Portsmouth, home of the British navy. The column is flanked on either side by enormous bronze lions. Climbing them is a very popular photo op, but be extremely careful, as there are no guardrails and it's a long fall onto concrete if you slip. Four plinths border the square; three contain militaristic statues, but one was left empty—it's now used for contemporary art installations, often with a wry and controversial edge. Surprisingly enough, given that this was a square built to honor British military victories, the lawn at the north side, by the National Gallery, contains a statue of George Washington—a gift from the state of Virginia in 1921.

At the southern point of the square is the equestrian statue of Charles I. After the Civil War and the king's execution, Oliver Cromwell, the antiroyalist leader, commissioned a brazier, John Rivett, to melt the statue down. The story goes that Rivett instead merely buried it in his garden. He made a fortune peddling knickknacks wrought, he claimed, from its metal, only to produce the statue miraculously unscathed after the restoration of the monarchy—and then made another fortune reselling it. In 1675 Charles II had it placed where it stands today, near the spot where his father was executed in 1649. Each year, on January 30, the day of the king's death, the Royal Stuart Society lays a wreath at the foot of the statue. ⊠ *Westminster* ▣ *Free* Ⓜ *Charing Cross.*

Wellington Barracks and the Guards Chapel
MILITARY SIGHT | These are the headquarters of the Guards Division, the Queen's five regiments of elite foot guards (Grenadier, Coldstream, Scots, Irish, and Welsh), who protect the sovereign and, dressed in tunics of gold-purled scarlet and tall bearskin caps, patrol her palaces. Guardsmen alternate these ceremonial postings with serving in current conflicts, for which they wear more practical uniforms. The Guards Museum has displays on all aspects of a guardsman's life in conflicts dating back to 1642, but it's currently closed for renovation. The Guards Chapel, the spiritual home of the Household Division, dates to 1962, the previous chapel having been destroyed during World War II. ⊠ *Birdcage Walk, Westminster* ☎ *020/7414-3428* ⊕ *www.*

theguardsmuseum.com ▣ *Free* ⊙ *Closed Sat.* Ⓜ *St. James's Park, Green Park.*

★ **Westminster Abbey**
CHURCH | Steeped in hundreds of years of rich and occasionally bloody history, Westminster Abbey is one of England's iconic buildings. An abbey has stood here since the 10th century, although the current building mostly dates from the 1240s. It has hosted 38 coronations—beginning in 1066 with William the Conqueror—and no fewer than 16 royal weddings, the latest being that of Prince William and Kate Middleton in 2011. But be warned: there's only one way around the abbey, and it gets very crowded, so you'll need to be alert to catch the highlights.

The Coronation Chair, which you'll find in St. George's Chapel by the east door, has been used for nearly every coronation since Edward II's in 1308, right up to Queen Elizabeth II's in 1953. Farther along, the exquisite confection of Henry VII's Lady Chapel is topped by a magnificent fan-vaulted ceiling. The tomb of Henry VII lies behind the altar. Elizabeth I is buried above her sister "Bloody" Mary I in the tomb in a chapel on the north side, while her arch enemy, Mary Queen of Scots, rests in the tomb to the south. The Chapel of St. Edward the Confessor contains the shrine of the pre-Norman king, who reigned from 1042 to 1066. Because of its great age, you must join a verger-guided tour to be admitted to the chapel (£10; book at the admission desk). To the left, you'll find Poets' Corner. Geoffrey Chaucer was the first poet to be buried here, and other statues and memorials include those to William Shakespeare, D. H. Lawrence, T. S. Eliot, and Oscar Wilde.

The medieval Chapter House is adorned with 14th-century frescoes and a magnificent 13th-century tiled floor, one of the finest in the country. Near the entrance is Britain's oldest door, dating from the

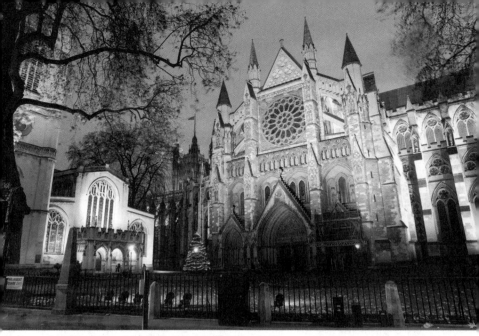

One of London's most famed sites, Westminster Abbey contains more than 600 monuments and memorials and serves as the final resting place of some of England's most famous citizens.

1050s. If you walk toward the West Entrance, you'll see a plaque to Franklin D. Roosevelt—one of the abbey's very few tributes to a foreigner. The poppy-wreathed Grave of the Unknown Warrior commemorates soldiers who lost their lives in both world wars.

With a separate timed ticket (£5), you can visit the Queen's Diamond Jubilee Galleries located 52 feet above the abbey floor; it's worth it for the views onto the abbey's interior below alone, but it also gets you access to a remarkable collection of historical objects that tell the story of the building, including its construction and relationship to the monarchy. Don't miss the Duke and Duchess of Cambridge's marriage license, the bright white vellum it's written on in stark contrast to the aged documents elsewhere on display.

Exact hours for the various parts of the abbey are frustratingly long and complicated, and can change daily, so it's important to check before setting out, particularly if you're visiting early or late in the day, or off-season. The full schedule is posted online daily (or you can call). Certain areas of the abbey are completely inaccessible to wheelchair users; however, you will get free entry for yourself and one other. ⊠ *Broad Sanctuary, Westminster* ☎ *020/7222–5152* ⊕ *www.westminster-abbey.org* ✆ *£24* ⊗ *Closed Sun., except for worship and the gift shop* Ⓜ *Westminster, St. James's Park.*

Westminster Cathedral

CHURCH | Tucked away on traffic-clogged Victoria Street lies this remarkable neo-Byzantine gem, seat of the Archbishop of Westminster, head of the Roman Catholic Church in England and Wales. Faced with building a church with Westminster Abbey as a neighbor, architect John Francis Bentley looked to the east for inspiration, to the basilicas of St. Mark's in Venice and the Hagia Sofia in Istanbul. The asymmetrical redbrick edifice, dating to 1903, is banded with stripes of Portland stone and abutted by a 272-foot bell tower at the northwest corner, ascendable by elevator for sterling views.

The interior remains incomplete, the unfinished overhead brickwork of the ceiling lending the church a dark brooding intensity. The side chapels, including the Chapel of the Blessed Sacrament and the Holy Souls Chapel, are beautifully finished in glittering mosaics. The Lady Chapel—dedicated to the Virgin Mary—is also sumptuously decorated. Look out for the Stations of the Cross, done here by Eric Gill, and the striking baldachin—the enormous stone canopy standing over the altar with a giant cross suspended in front of it. The nave, the widest in the country, is constructed in green marble, which also has a Byzantine connection—it was cut from the same place as the marble used in the Hagia Sofia, and was almost confiscated by warring Turks as it traveled west. All told, more than 100 different types of marble can be found within the cathedral's interior. There's a café in the crypt. ✉ *Ashley Pl., off Victoria St., Westminster* ☎ *020/7798–9055* 🌐 *www.westminstercathedral.org.uk* 🎫 *Free* [M] *Victoria.*

🍴 Restaurants

Given the huge range of excellent dining options in nearby St. James's and Covent Garden, Westminster itself has surprisingly few restaurants of note, with mostly chain sandwich and quick-bite joints dominating the busy touristy landscape. The good news is that the handful that do exist can be relied upon to serve up high-quality ingredients in often rather chic surroundings.

Boyds Grill & Wine Bar
$ | INTERNATIONAL | One of those restaurants you could never hope to find unless you were looking for it, Boyds occupies a ravishing, marble-clad dining room on the premises of an otherwise nondescript Northumberland Avenue business hotel. Meat is the focus on an international menu that puts simplicity over innovation, with satisfying results. **Known for:** wide range of wines, including English wines, available by the glass; comfort food such as burgers and sausages; excellent location within spitting distance of Trafalgar Square. [$] *Average main: £15* ✉ *8 Northumberland Ave., Trafalgar Sq.* ☎ *020/7808–3344* 🌐 *www.boydsgrillandwinebar.co.uk* 🕒 *No lunch weekends, no dinner Sun.* [M] *Charing Cross, Embankment.*

★ The Dining Room at The Goring
$$$$ | BRITISH | *Downton Abbey* meets *The Crown* at this quintessentially English, old-school dining salon located within an Edwardian-era hotel down the road from Buckingham Palace. A favorite with royalty and courtiers, here you can enjoy daily specials like traditional beef Wellington or antediluvian quirks such as Eggs Drumkilbo (a hard-boiled egg/lobster seafood cocktail with caviar)—a onetime favorite of the late Queen Mother. **Known for:** royal history and pedigree; plush salon designed by Viscount David Linley; glazed lobster omelet with duck fat chips. [$] *Average main: £37* ✉ *The Goring, Beeston Pl., Victoria* ☎ *020/7396–9000* 🌐 *www.thegoring.com* 🕒 *No lunch Sat.* [M] *Victoria.*

Iris & June
$ | BRITISH | The area between Victoria and Westminster is something of a wasteland in terms of independent quick-bite eateries, but this minimalist café serves excellent coffee, salads, wraps, and more. Peak office lunchtimes can get pretty busy, so aim to avoid the rush if you want to dine in. **Known for:** indulgent treats like buttermilk banana bread; vegetable peels and trimmings made into soups, stocks, and pickles to minimize waste; frequently changing lunch menu. [$] *Average main: £8* ✉ *1 Howick Pl., Victoria* 🌐 *www.irisandjune.com* 🕒 *No dinner* [M] *Victoria.*

Kerridge's Bar & Grill
$$$$ | **BRITISH** | Tom Kerridge made his name earning Michelin stars at rural gastropubs, and there's still a sense of pub grub about the menu here, at his first London restaurant, despite the glamorous high-ceilinged dining room, flawless service, and rather steep prices. That's no bad thing, however, when you've got a chef as skilled as Kerridge—think rich, meat-focused dishes served alongside unusual twists, such as gherkin ketchup or black cabbage purée. **Known for:** atmospheric views of Northumberland Avenue; inventive use of rotisserie cooking, from steak to cauliflower; playful presentation, from irreverant pastry additions to pour-it-yourself sauces. [$] *Average main: £40* ✉ *10 Northumberland Ave., Trafalgar Sq.* ☎ *020/7321–3244* 🌐 *www.kerridgesbarandgrill.co.uk* [M] *Embankment, Charing Cross.*

Notes Music and Coffee
$ | **CAFÉ** | Located next door to the London Coliseum (home of English National Opera), this hip café serves some of the best sandwiches, salads, and coffee in the neighborhood. In the evening (it's open until 9 pm), there's more of a wine-bar vibe. **Known for:** industrial chic decor; good-quality wines available by the glass; friendly staff that doesn't rush you. [$] *Average main: £8* ✉ *31 St. Martin's La., Westminster* ☎ *020/7240–0424* 🌐 *www.notescoffee.com* [M] *Charing Cross.*

Hotels

Staying in the capital's most central neighborhood is ideal if you like stepping out of the lobby onto more or less the doorstep of fantastic galleries, government buildings, and green spaces.

★ **Artist Residence**
$$$ | **HOTEL** | As packed with bohemian character as they come, this small boutique hotel oozes retro charm. **Pros:** great staff; quirky charm; excellent breakfasts. **Cons:** most rooms have a shower only; stairs to upper floors; some rooms on the small side. [$] *Rooms from: £295* ✉ *52 Cambridge St., Pimlico* ☎ *020/7931–8946* 🌐 *www.artistresidencelondon.co.uk* 🛏 *10 rooms* 🍴 *No Meals* [M] *Victoria, Pimlico.*

★ **The Corinthia**
$$$$ | **HOTEL** | The London outpost of the exclusive Corinthia chain is design heaven-on-earth, with levels of service that make anyone feel like a VIP. **Pros:** excellent fine-dining options; so much luxury and elegance you'll feel like royalty; exceptional spa with indoor pool. **Cons:** air-conditioning and lighting are difficult to use; not many special offers; prices jump to the stratosphere once the least expensive rooms sell out. [$] *Rooms from: £715* ✉ *Whitehall Pl., Westminster* ☎ *020/7930–8181* 🌐 *www.corinthia.com* 🛏 *283 rooms* 🍴 *No Meals* [M] *Embankment.*

The Goring
$$$$ | **HOTEL** | With Buckingham Palace just around the corner, this hotel, built in 1910 and now run by third-generation Gorings, has always been a favorite among discreet VIPs—including Kate Middleton's family on the night before her marriage to Prince William in 2011. **Pros:** great attention to detail; elegant spacious rooms; overlooks Buckingham Palace. **Cons:** the basic gym is small; interior's a bit fussy; price is still too high for what you get. [$] *Rooms from: £455* ✉ *15 Beeston Pl., Grosvenor Gardens, Westminster* ☎ *020/7396–9000* 🌐 *www.thegoring.com* 🛏 *69 rooms* 🍴 *Free Breakfast* [M] *Victoria.*

★ **Hotel 41**
$$$$ | **HOTEL** | With faultless service, sumptuous designer furnishings, and a sense of fun to boot, this impeccable hotel breathes new life into the cliché "thinks of everything," yet the epithet is really quite apt. **Pros:** Buckingham Palace is on your doorstep; impeccable service; beautiful and stylish. **Cons:** the private bar can feel stuffy; expensive; unusual design is not

for everyone. Ⓢ *Rooms from: £473* ✉ *41 Buckingham Palace Rd., Westminster* ☎ *020/7300–0041* ⊕ *www.41hotel.com* ⤳ *28 rooms* ¶◯¶ *No Meals* Ⓜ *Victoria.*

The Sanctuary House Hotel

$$ | **B&B/INN** | This is a classic example of what the British mean when they refer to an "inn"—a pub with bedrooms, albeit one of better-than-average quality for London. **Pros:** "wow" location right in the heart of Westminster; cozy, authentic London feel; friendly staff. **Cons:** dining options are limited; after-work crowd keeps the pub busy; noise from pub. Ⓢ *Rooms from: £233* ✉ *33 Tothill St., Westminster* ☎ *020/7799–4044* ⊕ *www. sanctuaryhousehotel.co.uk* ⤳ *35 rooms* ¶◯¶ *Free Breakfast* Ⓜ *St. James's Park.*

The Westminster London, Curio Collection by Hilton

$$ | **HOTEL** | **FAMILY** | Spectacular views of the river, Big Ben, and the London Eye fill the floor-to-ceiling windows in this rather stark, steel-and-glass building steps from Tate Britain. **Pros:** can be surprisingly affordable for the location; amazing views; free daily newspaper to your room. **Cons:** some noise from neighboring rooms; tiny bathrooms; small bedrooms. Ⓢ *Rooms from: £239* ✉ *30 John Islip St., Westminster* ☎ *020/7630–1000* ⊕ *www.hilton.com* ⤳ *464 rooms* ¶◯¶ *No Meals* Ⓜ *Westminster, Pimlico.*

The Windermere

$$ | **HOTEL** | **FAMILY** | This sweet and rather elegant old hotel, on the premises of one of London's first B&Bs (1881), is a decent, well-situated option. **Pros:** good amenities for an old hotel of this size, including air-conditioning and an elevator; good location close to Victoria Station; free Wi-Fi. **Cons:** many major attractions are a 20-minute walk away; traditional decor might not suit all tastes; rooms and bathrooms are tiny. Ⓢ *Rooms from: £161* ✉ *142–144 Warwick Way, Pimlico* ☎ *020/7834–5163* ⊕ *www.winder-mere-hotel.co.uk* ⤳ *19 rooms* ¶◯¶ *Free Breakfast* Ⓜ *Victoria.*

 # Nightlife

BARS

Cinnamon Club

BARS | On the ground floor of what was once the Reading Room of the Old Westminster Library, the book-lined Library Bar of this contemporary Indian restaurant (the curries are superb) has Indian-theme cocktails (mango mojitos, "Delhi mules"), delicious bar snacks, and a clientele that includes young politicos. The bar is sometimes used for private events, so it can be a good idea to call before you visit. ✉ *The Old Westminster Library, 30–32 Great Smith St., Westminster* ☎ *020/7222–2555* ⊕ *www. cinnamonclub.com* Ⓜ *St James's, Westminster.*

★ Gordon's Wine Bar

WINE BARS | Nab a rickety candlelit table in the atmospheric, 1890s, low-slung, brick-vaulted cellar interior of what claims to be the oldest wine bar in London, or sit outdoors in the long pedestrian-only alley garden that runs alongside it. There are no reservations, so be prepared to line up outside during busy periods, like after work and on sunny afternoons. Either way, the mood is always cheery as a diverse crowd sips on more than 70 different wines, ports, and sherries. Tempting cheese and meat plates are great for sharing. ✉ *47 Villiers St., Westminster* ☎ *020/7930–1408* ⊕ *www. gordonswinebar.com* Ⓜ *Charing Cross, Embankment.*

PUBS

The Red Lion

PUBS | Given its proximity to both the Houses of Parliament and Downing Street, it's no surprise that this traditional old boozer should be so popular with politicos of all stripes. Portraits of former prime ministers—several of whom also drank here—line the walls, and the bar room is one of a handful of premises outside the Palace of Westminster fitted with a "division bell" that recalls members of Parliament to the chamber for important votes. ⊠ *48 Parliament St., Westminster* ☎ *020/7930–5826* ⊕ *www.redlionwestminster.co.uk* Ⓜ *Westminster.*

🎭 Performing Arts

St. John's Smith Square

CONCERTS | Chamber music, organ recitals, and orchestral concerts are held at this Baroque church behind Westminster Abbey. There are three or four lunchtime recitals a month. ⊠ *Smith Sq., Westminster* ☎ *020/7222–1061* ⊕ *www.sjss.org. uk* Ⓜ *Westminster.*

St. James's

As a fitting coda to all of Westminster's pomp and circumstance, St. James's—packed with old-money galleries, restaurants, and gentlemen's clubs that embody the history and privilege of traditional London—is found to the south of Piccadilly and north of The Mall.

When Whitehall Palace burned down in 1698, all of London turned its attention to St. James's Palace, the new royal residence. In the 18th and 19th centuries, the area around the palace became the place to live, and many of the estates surrounding the palace disappeared in a building frenzy, as mansions were built and streets laid out. Most of the homes here are privately owned and therefore closed to visitors, but there are some treasure houses that you can explore (such as Spencer House), as well as many fancy shops that have catered to the great and good for centuries. Today St. James's contains some interesting art galleries and antiques shops.

In one corner is St. James's Park, framed on its western side by the biggest monument in the area: Buckingham Palace, the official London residence of the Queen. The smaller St. James's Palace is where much of the office work for the House of Windsor gets done; nearby is Clarence House, London home of Prince Charles and his wife, Camilla.

👁 Sights

★ Buckingham Palace

CASTLE/PALACE | If Buckingham Palace were open year-round, it would be by far the most visited tourist attraction in Britain; as it is, the Queen's main residence, home to every British monarch since Victoria in 1837, opens its doors to the public only in the summertime, with a handful of other dates throughout the year. The Queen is almost never there at the time—traditionally she heads off to Scotland for a couple of months every summer, where she takes up residence at Balmoral Castle. (Here's a quick way to tell if the Queen's at home: if she's in residence, the Royal Standard flies above the palace; if not, it's the more famous red, white, and blue Union Jack.)

The tour covers the palace's 19 State Rooms, with their fabulous gilt moldings and walls adorned with Old Masters. The Grand Hall, followed by the Grand Staircase and Guard Room, are visions in marble and gold leaf, filled with massive, twinkling chandeliers. Don't miss the theatrical Throne Room, with the original 1953 coronation throne, or the sword in the Ballroom, used by the Queen to bestow knighthoods and other honors with a touch on the recipient's shoulders. Royal portraits line the State Dining Room, and the Blue Drawing Room is dazzling in its splendor. The bow-shape Music Room features lapis lazuli columns between arched floor-to-ceiling windows, and the alabaster-and-gold plasterwork of the White Drawing Room is a dramatic statement of wealth and power.

Admission is by timed-entry ticket every 15 minutes throughout the day. It's also worth adding a guided tour of the sprawling gardens to your visit; the gardens are

A classic photo op: cavalry from the Queen's Life Guard at Buckingham Palace

also available as a standalone tour. Allow up to two hours to take it all in. Changing the Guard remains one of London's best free shows and culminates in front of the palace. Marching to live military bands, the old guard proceed up The Mall from St. James's Palace to Buckingham Palace. Shortly afterward, the new guard approach from Wellington Barracks. Then within the forecourt, the captains of the old and new guards symbolically transfer the keys to the palace. Get there early for the best view. ⊠ *Buckingham Palace Rd., St. James's* ☎ *030/3123–7300* ⊕ *www. rct.uk/visit/buckingham-palace* ✉ *£30; garden highlights tour £24.50* ⊗ *Closed Oct.–July except on selected dates* Ⓜ *Victoria, St. James's Park, Green Park.*

Clarence House

HISTORIC HOME | The London home of the Queen Mother for nearly 50 years until her death in 2002, Clarence House is now the residence of Charles, the

Prince of Wales, and his wife, Camilla, the Duchess of Cornwall. The Regency mansion was built in 1828 by John Nash for the Duke of Clarence (later to become William IV) who considered next-door St. James's Palace to be too cramped for his liking, although postwar renovation work means that little remains of Nash's original. Since then it has remained a royal home for princesses, dukes, and duchesses, including the present monarch, Queen Elizabeth II, as a newlywed before her coronation.

The rooms have been sensitively preserved to reflect the Queen Mother's taste, with the addition of many works of art from the Royal Collection, including works by Winterhalter, Augustus John, and Sickert. Clarence House is usually open only for the month of August, and tickets must be booked in advance. ⊠ *St. James's Palace, The Mall, St. James's* ☎ *030/3123–7300* ⊕ *www.*

Royalty Watching

You've seen Big Ben, the Tower, and Westminster Abbey. But somehow you feel something is missing: a close encounter with Britain's most famous attraction—Her Royal Majesty, Elizabeth II. The Queen and the Royal Family attend hundreds of functions a year, and if you want to know what they are doing on any given date, turn to the Court Circular, printed in the major London dailies, or check out the Royal Family website (⊕ *www.royal. uk*) for the latest events on the Royal Diary.

Trooping the Colour is usually held on the second Saturday in June, to celebrate the Queen's official birthday. This spectacular parade begins when she leaves Buckingham Palace in her carriage and rides down The Mall to arrive at Horse Guards Parade at 11 am exactly. To watch, just line up along The Mall with your binoculars.

Another time you can catch the Queen in all her regalia is when she rides in state to open the Houses of Parliament. The famous black and gilt-trimmed Irish State Coach travels from Buckingham Palace—on a clear day, it's to be hoped, for this ceremony takes place in late October or early November. The Gold State Coach, an icon of fairy-tale glamour, is used for coronations and jubilees only.

But perhaps the most relaxed, least formal time to see the Queen is during Royal Ascot, held at the famous racetrack near Windsor Castle—a short train ride out of London— usually during the third week of June (Tuesday–Saturday). The Queen and members of the Royal Family are driven down the track to the Royal Box in an open carriage, giving spectators a chance to see them. After several races, the famously horse-loving Queen invariably walks down to the paddock, greeting racegoers as she proceeds. If you meet her, the official etiquette is to first make a short bow or curtsy, and then to address her first as "Your Majesty," and then "Ma'am" thereafter.

royalcollection.org.uk 🖾 *£11* ⊘ *Closed Sept.–July* Ⓜ *Green Park.*

The Mall

PROMENADE | This stately, 115-foot-wide processional route sweeping toward Trafalgar Square from the Queen Victoria Memorial at Buckingham Palace is an updated 1911 version of a promenade laid out around 1660 for the game of *paille-maille* (a type of croquet crossed with golf), which also gave the parallel road Pall Mall its name. (That's why Mall is pronounced to rhyme with "pal," not "ball.") The tarmac is colored red to represent a ceremonial red carpet. During state visits, several times a year, The Mall is traditionally bedecked with the flag of the visiting nation, alongside the Union Jack. The Duke of York Memorial up the steps toward stately John Nash–designed Carlton House Terrace (worth a look in itself) is a towering column dedicated to George III's second son, who was further immortalized in the English nursery rhyme "The Grand Old Duke of York." Be sure to stroll along The Mall on Sunday when the road is closed to traffic, or catch the bands and troops of the Household Division on their way from St. James's Palace to Buckingham Palace for the Changing the Guard ceremony.

At the northernmost end of The Mall is Admiralty Arch, a stately gateway named after the adjacent Royal Navy headquarters. It was designed by Sir Aston Webb and built in 1910 as a memorial to Queen Victoria. Actually comprising five arches—two for pedestrians, two for traffic, and the central arch, which is only opened for state occasions—it was a government building until 2012, and has even served as an alternative residence for the prime minister while Downing Street was under renovation. It is currently being transformed into a luxury hotel. Look out for the bronze nose grafted onto the inside wall of the right-hand traffic arch (when facing The Mall); it was placed there in secret by a mischievous artist in 1997 and has been allowed to remain. ⊠ *St. James's* Ⓜ *Charing Cross, Green Park.*

Piccadilly Circus

PLAZA/SQUARE | The origins of the name "Piccadilly" relate to a humble 17th-century tailor from the Strand named Robert Baker who sold piccadills—stiff ruffled collars all the rage in courtly circles— and built a house with the proceeds. Snobs dubbed his new-money mansion Piccadilly Hall, and the name stuck. Pride of place in the circus—a circular junction until the construction of Shaftesbury Avenue in 1886—belongs to the statue universally referred to as Eros, dating to 1893 (although even most Londoners don't know that it is, in reality, a representation of Eros's brother Anteros, the Greek god of requited love). The other instantly recognizable feature of Piccadilly Circus is the enormous bank of lit-up billboards on the north side; if you're passing at night, frame them behind the Tube entrance sign on the corner of Regent Street for a classic photograph. ⊠ *St. James's* Ⓜ *Piccadilly Circus.*

★ The Queen's Gallery

ART GALLERY | Technically speaking, the sovereign doesn't "own" the rare and exquisite works of art in the Royal Collection: she merely holds them in trust for the nation—and what a collection it is. Only a selection is on view at any one

time, presented in themed exhibitions. Let the excellent (and free) audio guide take you through the elegant galleries filled with some of the world's greatest artworks.

A rough timeline of the major royal collectors starts with Charles I (who also commissioned Rubens to paint the Banqueting House ceiling). An avid art enthusiast, Charles established the basis of the Royal Collection, purchasing works by Raphael, Titian, Caravaggio, and Dürer. During the Civil War and in the aftermath of Charles's execution, many masterpieces were sold abroad and subsequently repatriated by Charles II. George III, who bought Buckingham House and converted it into a palace, scooped up a notable collection of Venetian (including Canaletto), Renaissance (Bellini and Raphael), and Dutch (Vermeer) art, and a large number of Baroque drawings, in addition to patronizing English contemporary artists, such as Gainsborough and Beechey. The Prince Regent, later George IV, had a particularly good eye for Rembrandt, equestrian works by Stubbs, and lavish portraits by Lawrence. Queen Victoria had a penchant for Landseer animals and landscapes, and Frith's contemporary scenes. Later, Edward VII indulged Queen Alexandra's love of Fabergé, and many royal tours around the empire produced gifts of gorgeous caliber, such as the Cullinan diamond from South Africa and an emerald-studded belt from India. Tickets are valid for one year from the date of entry. ⊠ *Buckingham Palace, Buckingham Palace Rd., St. James's* ☎ *030/3123–7300* ⊕ *www.rct.uk* 🎟 *£17* Ⓜ *Victoria, St. James's Park, Green Park.*

Royal Mews

HISTORIC SIGHT | **FAMILY** | Fairy-tale gold-and-glass coaches and sleek Rolls-Royce state cars emanate from the Royal Mews, next door to the Queen's Gallery. Designed by John Nash, the Mews serves as the headquarters for Her Majesty's travel department (so beware of closures for state visits), complete with the Queen's own special breed of horses, ridden by wigged postilions decked in red-and-gold regalia. Between the stables and the riding school arena are exhibits of polished saddlery and riding tack. The highlight of the Mews is the splendid Gold State Coach, a piece of art on wheels, with its sculpted tritons and sea gods. There are activities for children, and free guided tours are available April through October (daily at 10:15, then hourly 11–4). ⊠ *Buckingham Palace, Buckingham Palace Rd., St. James's* ☎ *030/3123–7300* ⊕ *www.rct.uk* 🎫 *£14* ◷ *Closed Dec. and Jan.* Ⓜ *Victoria, St. James's Park.*

Spencer House

HISTORIC HOME | Ancestral abode of the Spencers—Princess Diana's family—this is perhaps the finest extant example of an elegant 18th-century London town house. Reflecting his passion for the Grand Tour and classical antiquities, the first Earl Spencer commissioned architect John Vardy to adapt designs from ancient Rome for a magnificent private palace. Vardy was responsible for the exteriors, including the gorgeous west-facing Palladian facade, its pediment adorned with classical statues, and the ground-floor interiors, notably the lavish Palm Room, with its spectacular screen of columns covered in gilded carvings that resemble gold palm trees. The lavish style was meant not only to attest to Spencer's power and wealth but also to celebrate his marriage, a love match then rare in aristocratic circles (the palms are a symbol of marital fertility).

Midway through construction—the house was built between 1756 and 1766—Spencer changed architects and hired James "Athenian" Stuart, whose designs were based on a classical Greek aesthetic, to decorate the gilded State Rooms on the first floor. These include the Painted Room, the first completely neoclassical room in Europe. Since the

1940s, the house has been leased by the Spencers to a succession of wealthy residents. Entry is by tours only, which occur on Sunday only. ■TIP→ **Note that children under 10 are not allowed inside.** ⊠ *27 St. James's Pl., St. James's* ☎ *020/7514–1958* ⊕ *www.spencerhouse.co.uk* 🎫 *£15* ◷ *Closed Mon.–Sat. and Aug.* Ⓜ *Green Park.*

St. James's Church

CHURCH | Bombed by the German Luftwaffe in 1940 and not restored until 1954, this was one of the last of Sir Christopher Wren's London churches—and his favorite. Completed in 1684, it contains one of the finest works by the master carver Grinling Gibbons (1648–1721): an ornate limewood reredos (the screen behind the altar). The church is a lively place, with all manner of lectures and concerts (some are free). A café occupies a fine location right alongside the church, while a small sedate garden is tucked away at the rear. There's a market in the pretty courtyard out front on Tuesday and Thursday. A major renovation project will close the whole site for several months at some point in 2023 (dates yet to be confirmed), so check ahead of your visit. ⊠ *197 Piccadilly, St. James's* ☎ *020/7734–4511* ⊕ *www.sjp.org.uk* 🎫 *Free* Ⓜ *Piccadilly Circus, Green Park.*

St. James's Palace

CASTLE/PALACE | Commissioned by Henry VIII, this Tudor brick palace was the residence of kings and queens for more than 300 years; indeed, while all monarchs have actually lived at Buckingham Palace since Queen Victoria's day, it is still one of the official residences of the Royal Family. (This is why foreign ambassadors are received by the "Court of St. James.") Today it contains various royal apartments and offices, including the working office of Prince Charles. The palace is not open to the public, but the surprisingly low-key Tudor exterior is well worth the short detour from The Mall. Friary Court out front is a splendid setting for Trooping the Colour, part of the Queen's official birthday celebrations. Everyone loves to take a snapshot of the scarlet-coated guardsman standing sentry outside the imposing Tudor gateway. Note that the Changing the Guard ceremony at St. James's Palace occurs only on days when the guard at Buckingham Palace is changed. ⊠ *Friary Ct., St. James's* Ⓜ *Green Park.*

★ St. James's Park

CITY PARK | FAMILY | There is a story that, many years ago, a royal once inquired of a courtier how much it would cost to close St. James's Park to the public. "Only your crown, ma'am," came the reply. Bordered by three palaces—Buckingham, St. James's, and the governmental complex of the Palace of Westminster—this is one of London's loveliest green spaces. It's also the oldest; the former marshland was acquired by Henry VIII in 1532 as a nursery for his deer. Later, James I drained the land and installed an aviary, which gave Birdcage Walk its name, and a zoo (complete with crocodiles, camels, and an elephant). When Charles II returned from exile in France, where he had been hugely impressed by the splendor of the gardens at the Palace of Versailles, he transformed the park into formal gardens, with avenues, fruit orchards, and a canal. Lawns were grazed by goats, sheep, and deer, and, in the 18th century, the park became a different kind of hunting ground, for wealthy lotharios looking to pick up nighttime escorts. A century later, John Nash redesigned the landscape in a more naturalistic, romantic style, and if you gaze down the lake toward Buckingham Palace, you could easily believe yourself to be on a country estate.

A large population of waterfowl—including pelicans, geese, ducks, and swans (which belong to the Queen)—breed on and around Duck Island at the east end of the lake. From March to October, the deck chairs (charge levied) come out,

crammed with office workers at midday, eating lunch while being serenaded by music from the bandstands. One of the best times to stroll the leafy walkways is after dark, with Westminster Abbey and the Houses of Parliament rising above the floodlit lake. ⊠ *The Mall or Horse Guards approach or Birdcage Walk, St. James's* ⊕ *www.royalparks.org.uk* Ⓜ *St. James's Park, Westminster.*

St. James's Square

PLAZA/SQUARE | One of London's oldest squares, St. James's was first laid out in the 1660s. It soon became the capital's most fashionable address; by 1720, it was home to 14 dukes and earls. These days you're more likely to find it populated with office workers eating their lunches under the shade of its leafy old trees on a warm summer's day, but it still has some prestigious residents. Most famous among them is The London Library, at No. 14, one of several 18th-century residences spared by World War II bombs. Founded by Thomas Carlyle, it contains a million or so volumes, making it the world's largest independent lending library, and is also considered the best private humanities library in the land. Nonmembers can take free evening tours of the library which must be booked in advance; check the website for dates and times. ⊠ *St. James's* Ⓜ *Piccadilly Circus.*

White Cube

ART GALLERY | The English role in the exploding contemporary art scene has been major, thanks in good portion to Jay Joplin's influential gallery, which has regularly moved around London since 1993. Its latest site, this striking modern concrete structure was the first freestanding building to be built in the area for 30 years when it opened in 2006. It is home base for an array of British artists who have won the Turner Prize, including Damien Hirst, Tracey Emin, and Antony Gormley. ⊠ *25–26 Mason's Yard, St. James's* ☎ *020/7930–5373* ⊕ *www.*

whitecube.com ✉ *Free* ⊙ *Closed Sun.
and Mon.* Ⓜ *Green Park, Piccadilly Circus.*

🍴 Restaurants

It's no surprise, given the illustrious
royal residents of this neighborhood,
that so many of its restaurants feel fit
for a future king. This is where you'll
find London's top-end eateries—dining
experiences that are geared toward a
well-heeled, deep-pocketed clientele.
You should make reservations well in
advance to dine at any of these restaurants for dinner (or reserve a table for
the earlier or later parts of the evening,
when demand is lower). Keep in mind
that no-shows mean last-minute tables
often crop up, and having lunch here can
be a great money-saving strategy. Dress
codes are usually stricter than elsewhere
in town; if in doubt, men should opt for a
jacket and tie.

Aquavit

$$$ | SCANDINAVIAN | There's a hygge-style
glow at this ritzy New Nordic emporium
off Piccadilly Circus. Swedish designer
Martin Brudnizki pulls out all the best
Scandinavian design stops, while a hip,
upscale crowd dish over the pickled
matjes herring from the small-jars
smorgasbord and pair Swedish meatballs
with mash and lingonberries. **Known
for:** sea bass with creamy Sandefjord
sauce; nifty Nordic smorgasbord starters;
soaring Scandinavian design showcase.
ⓢ *Average main: £29* ✉ *St. James's
Market, 1 Carlton St., Piccadilly Circus*
☎ *020/7024–9848* ⊕ *www.aquavitres-
taurants.com* ⊙ *Closed Sun. and Mon.*
Ⓜ *Piccadilly Circus.*

45 Jermyn St.

$$$$ | BRASSERIE | FAMILY | A sophisticat-
ed crowd enjoys the clubhouse vibe at
this classic brasserie at the back of the
Queen's grocer, Fortnum & Mason. An
old-school trolley trundles up table-side
to serve Siberian Sturgeon caviar with
scrambled eggs, baked new potatoes,

and blinis, while creamy beef Stroganoff
and whole duck with elderberry sauce
get the full table-side-flambé treatment.
Known for: collection of boozy ice-cream
floats; unique caviar trolley; glamorous
decor. ⓢ *Average main: £35* ✉ *45 Jermyn
St., St. James's* ☎ *020/7205–4545* ⊕ *ww-
w.45jermynst.com* ⊙ *No dinner Sun.*
Ⓜ *Green Park.*

The Ritz Restaurant

$$$$ | BRITISH | London's most opulent
dining salon here at The Ritz would
impress even Marie Antoinette with its
sumptuous Gilded Age Rococo Revival
trompe-l'oeil frescoes, tasseled silk dra-
pery, and towering marble columns. Sit
at the late Margaret Thatcher's favorite
seat overlooking Green Park (Table 1)
and luxuriate in unreconstructed British
haute cuisine, such as Bresse chicken
with black Périgord truffles or beef
Wellington carved table-side. **Known for:**
legendary traditional Afternoon Tea in the
Palm Court; luxurious dining made for
the British elite; possibly London's best
beef Wellington. ⓢ *Average main: £55*
✉ *The Ritz, 150 Piccadilly, St. James's*
☎ *020/7493–8181* ⊕ *www.theritzlondon.
com* 🍴 *Jacket and tie* Ⓜ *Green Park.*

Wiltons

$$$$ | BRITISH | Lords, ladies, and
other assorted aristocrats blow the
family bank at this Edwardian bastion
of traditional English fine dining on
Jermyn Street (the place first opened
near the Haymarket as a shellfish stall
in 1742). Posh patrons tend to order
half a dozen oysters, followed by grilled
Dover sole, Blythburgh pork from the
carving trolley, or fabulous native game,
such as roast partridge, grouse, or teal.
Known for: Bordeaux-heavy wine menu;
traditional English dining focused on
shellfish and game; waiter service that
would put Jeeves to shame. ⓢ *Average
main: £40* ✉ *55 Jermyn St., St. James's*
☎ *020/7629–9955* ⊕ *www.wiltons.co.uk*
⊙ *Closed Sun. and bank holidays. No
lunch Sat.* 🍴 *Jackets encouraged, no*

sneakers, open-toe shoes, sportswear or short-sleeve tops M *Green Park.*

The Wolseley

$$$ | AUSTRIAN | FAMILY | A glitzy procession of famous faces, media moguls, and hedge-funders comes for the spectacle, swish service, and soaring elegance at this bustling Viennese-style grand café on Piccadilly. Located in a former Wolseley Motors luxury-car showroom, this brasserie begins its long decadent days with breakfast at 7 am (8 am on weekends) and serves Dual Monarchy delights until 11 pm (10 pm on Sunday). **Known for:** classic grand café setting; old-country central European delights; afternoon tea with a Viennese twist. $ *Average main: £28* ✉ *160 Piccadilly, St. James's* ☎ *020/7499–6996* ⊕ *www.thewolseley.com* M *Green Park.*

🛏 Hotels

Some of the best, most discreet, and (unsurprisingly) most expensive hotels in London can be found in St. James's. As with restaurants in this area, think traditional, service-oriented establishments with a timeless feel and plenty of luxurious touches.

The Cavendish

$$ | HOTEL | Located across the road from Fortnum & Mason (one of the most luxurious department stores in the world), it seems appropriate that the Cavendish comes with a touch of Gilded Age history, a whiff of historical scandal, and a pleasant air of joie de vivre. **Pros:** unbeatable location; sophisticated yet relaxed; great service. **Cons:** rooms near the elevator can be particularly noisy; some street noise; guest rooms are small. $ *Rooms from: £238* ✉ *81 Jermyn St., St. James's* ☎ *020/7930–2111* ⊕ *www.thecavendish-london.co.uk* ⇄ *230 rooms* ❢❂ *No Meals* M *Piccadilly.*

Dukes Hotel

$$$$ | HOTEL | At this small exclusive hotel in a discreet cul-de-sac, ample natural light brightens the classically elegant rooms. **Pros:** excellent restaurant; famous martini bar; peaceful setting in a central location. **Cons:** cheapest rooms book up well in advance; price is still rather high for what's available; maybe a bit too quiet for some. $ *Rooms from: £416* ✉ *35 St. James's Pl., St. James's* ☎ *020/7941–4840, 800/381–4702 in U.S.* ⊕ *www.dukeshotel.com* ⇄ *87 rooms* ❢❂ *Free Breakfast* M *Green Park.*

The Ritz

$$$$ | HOTEL | If you're wondering if the *Downton Abbey*–style world of the old British upper class still exists, look no further than here; The Ritz is as synonymous with London's high society and decadence today as it was when it opened in 1906. **Pros:** iconic restaurant and bar; historic luxury hotel; service at every turn. **Cons:** located on a congested road; tediously old-fashioned dress code; sometimes snooty service. $ *Rooms from: £595* ✉ *150 Piccadilly, St. James's* ☎ *020/7493–8181* ⊕ *www.theritzlondon.com* ⇄ *136 rooms* ❢❂ *No Meals* M *Piccadilly Circus.*

★ The Stafford London

$$$ | HOTEL | This is a rare find: a posh hotel that's equal parts elegance and friendliness, and located in one of the few peaceful spots in the area, down a small lane behind Piccadilly. **Pros:** quiet location; great staff; home to one of London's original "American Bars". **Cons:** some rooms can feel small; perks in the more expensive rooms could be more generous (free airport transfer, but one-way only; free clothes pressing, but only one item per day); traditional style of most rooms may not be to all tastes. $ *Rooms from: £350* ✉ *16–18 St. James's Pl., St. James's* ☎ *020/7493–0111* ⊕ *www.thestaffordlondon.com* ⇄ *107 rooms* ❢❂ *No Meals* M *Green Park.*

Nightlife

BARS

★ American Bar

BARS | FAMILY | Festooned with a chin-dropping array of old club ties, vintage celebrity-signed photographs, sporting mementos, model airplanes, and baseball caps, this sensational hotel cocktail bar has superb martinis and Manhattans. The name dates from the 1930s, when hotel bars in London started to cater to growing numbers of Americans crossing the Atlantic in ocean liners. The collection of paraphernalia was started in the 1970s when a customer left a small carved wooden eagle. ⊠ *The Stafford, 16–18 St. James's Pl., St. James's* ☎ *020/7493–0111* ⊕ *www.thestaffordlondon.com* Ⓜ *Green Park.*

PUBS

The Red Lion

PUBS | There's been a tavern with this name on this site since 1788, but the interior of the current pub dates back to the 19th century; its specially commissioned engraved glass panels and dark wood detailing are a perfect example of Victorian pub decor. You'll find a few wines available by the glass, but the star here, as is the case at most traditional pubs, is cask beer. For those on the hunt for a simple, inexpensive meal (no mean feat in this part of town), classic pub grub is served until 5 pm each day. The leather banquettes fill up fast when the after-work crowd descends. ⊠ *2 Duke of York St., St. James's* ☎ *020/7321–0782* ⊕ *www.redlionmayfair.co.uk* Ⓜ *Piccadilly Circus.*

 Performing Arts

Institute of Contemporary Arts (*ICA*)

ARTS CENTERS | You would never suspect that behind the stately white John Nash–designed stucco facade in the heart of Establishment London, you'll find a champion of the avant-garde. Since 1947, the ICA has been pushing boundaries in visual arts, performance, theater, dance, and music. There are two movie theaters, a performance theater, three galleries, a highbrow bookstore, a reading room, and a café-bar. ⊠ *The Mall, St. James's* ☎ *020/7930–3647* ⊕ *www.ica.art* 🖵 *Exhibitions £5, cinema tickets from £13* Ⓜ *Charing Cross, Piccadilly Circus.*

Shopping

ACCESSORIES

★ Lock & Co. Hatters

HATS & GLOVES | Need a silk top hat, a flat-weave Panama, or a traditional tweed flat cap? Or, for ladies, an occasion hat? This wood-paneled shop has been providing hats since 1676 (the oldest in London, they claim) for customers ranging from Admiral Lord Nelson, Oscar Wilde, and Frank Sinatra to, more recently, Robert Downey Jr., Guy Ritchie, and Kate Middleton, as well as trendsetting musicians and models. ⊠ *6 St. James's St., St. James's* ☎ *020/7930–8874* ⊕ *www.lockhatters.co.uk* Ⓜ *Green Park.*

★ Swaine Adeney Brigg

OTHER SPECIALTY STORE | Providing practical supplies for country pursuits since 1750, Swaine Adeney Brigg carries beautifully crafted umbrellas, walking sticks, and hip flasks, or ingenious combinations, such as the umbrella with a slim tipple-holding flask secreted inside the stem. The same level of quality and craftsmanship applies to the store's leather goods, which include attaché cases (you can buy the "Q Branch" model that James Bond carried in *From Russia with Love*) and wallets. You'll find scarves, caps, and the Herbert Johnson "Poet Hat," the iconic headgear (stocked since 1890) worn by Harrison Ford in every Indiana Jones film. ⊠ *7 Piccadilly Arcade, St. James's* ☎ *020/7409–7277* ⊕ *www.swaineadeney-brigg.com* Ⓜ *Green Park.*

ANTIQUES AND COLLECTIBLES

The Armoury of St. James's

ANTIQUES & COLLECTIBLES | **FAMILY** | Besides fine toy soldiers in lead or tin representing conflicts ranging from the Crusades through World War II, with prices starting at £15 and going into four figures, the shop has regimental brooches and drums, historic orders and medals, royal memorabilia, and military antiques. ⊠ *17 Piccadilly Arcade, St. James's* ☎ *020/7493–5082* ⊕ *www.armoury.co.uk* Ⓜ *Piccadilly Circus.*

BEAUTY

Floris

PERFUME | What did Queen Victoria, Mary Shelley, and Marilyn Monroe have in common? They all used products from Floris, one of the most beautiful shops in London, with gleaming glass-and-Spanish-mahogany showcases salvaged from the Great Exhibition of 1851. In addition to scents for both men and women (including the current queen), Floris has been making its own shaving products—plus combs, brushes, and fragrances—since 1730 (and is still owned by the same family, nine generations later), reflecting its origins as a barbershop. Other gift possibilities include a famous rose-scented mouthwash and beautifully packaged soaps and bath essences. ⊠ *89 Jermyn St., St. James's* ☎ *0330/134–0180* ⊕ *www.florislondon.com* Ⓜ *Piccadilly Circus, Green Park.*

BOOKS

★ Hatchards

BOOKS | This is the United Kingdom's oldest bookshop, open since 1797 and beloved by writers themselves—customers have included Oscar Wilde, Rudyard Kipling, and Lord Byron. Despite its wood-paneled, "gentleman's library"

atmosphere and eclectic selection of books, Hatchards is now owned by the large Waterstones chain. Nevertheless, the shop still retains its period charm, aided by the staff's old-fashioned helpfulness and expertise. Look for the substantial number of books signed by notable contemporary authors on the well-stocked shelves. There's another branch in the St. Pancras International train station. ⊠ *187 Piccadilly, St. James's* ☎ *020/7439–9921* ⊕ *www.hatchards.co.uk* Ⓜ *Piccadilly Circus.*

CLOTHING

Dover Street Market

MIXED CLOTHING | With its creative displays and eclectic, well-chosen mix of merchandise, this four-floor emporium is as much art installation as store. The merchandise and its configuration change every six months, so you never know what you will find, which is half the fun. The creation of Comme des Garçons' Rei Kawakubo, Dover Street Market showcases all the label's collections for men and women alongside a changing roster of other ultrafashionable designers, including Gucci, Raf Simons, Balenciaga, Loewe, Wales Bonner, and Molly Goddard, all of whom have their own customized miniboutiques—plus sneaker and denim collaborations, eyeglass frames, and jewelry. An outpost of Rose Bakery on the top floor makes for a good break. ⊠ *18–22 Haymarket, St. James's* ☎ *020/7518–0680* ⊕ *london.doverstreetmarket.com* Ⓜ *Piccadilly Circus.*

Turnbull & Asser

MEN'S CLOTHING | The Jermyn Street store sells luxurious jackets, cashmere sweaters, suits, ties, pajamas, ready-to-wear shirts, and accessories perfect for the man who has everything. The brand is best known for its superb custom-made shirts—worn by Prince Charles and every James Bond to appear in film, to name a few. These can be ordered at the nearby

Bury Street or Davies Street branches, which are devoted to bespoke wear. At least 18 separate measurements are taken, and the cloth, woven to the company's specifications, comes in 1,000 different patterns—the cottons feel as good as silk. The first order must be for a minimum of four shirts, which start at £325 each. ⊠ *71–72 Jermyn St., St. James's* ☎ *020/7808–3000* ⊕ *www. turnbullandasser.co.uk* Ⓜ *Green Park.*

FOOD

★ Berry Bros. & Rudd

WINE/SPIRITS | Nothing matches Berry Bros. & Rudd for rare offerings and a unique shopping experience. A family-run wine business since 1698 (Lord Byron was a customer), BBR stores more than 4,000 vintage bottles and casks in vaulted cellars that are more than 300 years old. The in-house wine school offers educational tasting sessions, while the dedicated spirits room also has an excellent selection of whiskeys, cognacs, rums, and more. The shop has a quirky charm, and the staff are extremely knowledgeable—and not snooty if you're on a budget. ⊠ *63 Pall Mall, St. James's* ☎ *800/280–2440* ⊕ *www.bbr.com* Ⓜ *Green Park.*

★ Fortnum & Mason

FOOD | Although F&M is jokingly known as "the Queen's grocer," and the impeccably mannered staff still wear traditional tailcoats, its celebrated food hall stocks gifts for all budgets, including irresistibly packaged luxury foods stamped with the gold "By Appointment" crest for under £5. Try the teas, preserves (including the unusual rose-petal jelly), condiments, or Gentleman's Relish (anchovy paste). The store's famous hampers are always a welcome gift.

The gleaming food hall spans two floors and incorporates a sleek wine bar, with the rest of the store devoted to upscale housewares, men's and women's

accessories and toiletries, a dedicated candle room, and a jewelry department featuring exclusive designs by break-through talent. If you start to flag, take a break in the tea salon, the Gallery café offering tastes of the food hall, the contemporary 45 Jermyn St. restaurant (the three-course set menu is a good value), or an indulgent ice-cream parlor, where you can find decadent treats like a banana split or a less-traditional gin-and-tonic float. There's another branch at St. Pancras International train station. ⊠ *181 Piccadilly, St. James's* ☎ *020/7734–8040* ⊕ *www.fortnumandmason.com* Ⓜ *Green Park, Piccadilly Circus.*

Paxton & Whitfield

FOOD | In business for more than 200 years, this venerable and aromatic London shop stocks hundreds of the world's greatest artisan cheeses, particularly British and French varieties (a homesick General de Gaulle shopped here during World War II). The cheeses are laid on straw on refrigerated shelves, with tasting samples set out on a marble-top counter. You can pick up some ham, pâté, condiments, preserves, wine, or port, as well as cheese-related accessories like boards or knives. There's another branch in Chelsea. ⊠ *93 Jermyn St., St. James's* ☎ *020/7930–0259* ⊕ *www.paxtonandwhitfield.co.uk* Ⓜ *Piccadilly Circus, Green Park.*

JEWELRY

Wartski

JEWELRY & WATCHES | This family-run specialist in antique jewelry and precious objects boosted its fortunes when the founder's canny son-in-law snapped up confiscated treasures from the Bolshevik government after the Russian Revolution of 1917. As a result, this is the place to come if you're looking for a miniature carved Fabergé Easter Bunny, 1920s Cartier stickpin, art nouveau necklace by Lalique, or 17th-century gold signet ring. Even if you're not in the market to buy but are just interested in the history of jewelry, it's worth a visit. You can also order handmade wedding rings—Wartski created the engagement ring Prince William gave Kate Middleton. ⊠ *60 St. James's St., St. James's* ☎ *0207/493–1141* ⊕ *www.wartski.com* ◐ *Closed weekends* Ⓜ *Piccadilly.*

SHOES
Loake Shoemakers

SHOES | Long established in England's Midlands and a provider of boots to the British armed forces in both world wars, this family-run firm specializes in classic handcrafted men's shoes. Whether you're after brogues, loafers, or deck shoes, the staff will take the time to ensure you have the right fit. In terms of quality and service, Loake represents real value for money, though they definitely aren't inexpensive. There are other branches in London: three in The City and one by Old Spitalfields Market. ⊠ *39C Jermyn St., St. James's* ☎ *020/7734–8643* ⊕ *www. loake.co.uk* Ⓜ *Piccadilly.*

SPECIALTY STORES
★ Geo F. Trumper

OTHER SPECIALTY STORE | If you don't have the time for an old-fashioned hot-towel shave at this "traditional gentlemen's barbers" established in 1875, pick up a razor, a shaving brush, or other men's grooming accessories to take home for yourself or as a gift. The Extract of Limes Skin Food is a popular, zingy aftershave, and the Coconut Oil Hard Shaving Soap, which comes in a hand-turned wooden bowl, is a classic. There is also a store at 9 Curzon Street in Mayfair. ⊠ *1 Duke of York St., St. James's* ☎ *020/7734–6553* ⊕ *www. trumpers.com* Ⓜ *Piccadilly Circus.*

Chapter 4

MAYFAIR AND MARYLEBONE

Updated by
Toby Orton

◉ Sights	🍴 Restaurants	🛏 Hotels	🛍 Shopping	🍸 Nightlife
★★★★☆	★★★★☆	★★★★☆	★★★★☆	★☆☆☆☆

MAYFAIR AND MARYLEBONE SNAPSHOT

TOP REASONS TO GO

The Duke of Wellington's home: The Iron Duke's Apsley House is filled with splendid salons lined with grand Old Master paintings.

Fashion galore: There's great shopping aplenty on Bond and Mount streets, where the likes of McQueen and McCartney will keep your credit card occupied, but don't forget stylish, gigantic Selfridges.

London's most charming shopping arcade: Built for Lord Cavendish in 1819, the beautiful Burlington Arcade is right out of a Victorian daguerreotype.

The Wallace Collection: Savor room after room of magnificent furniture, porcelain, silver, and top Old Master paintings in the former residence of the Marquesses of Hertford.

Claridge's: Afternoon Tea at this sumptuous Art Deco gem is the perfect end to a shopping spree in Mayfair.

GETTING THERE

Three Tube stations on the Central line are handy for reaching these neighborhoods: Marble Arch, Bond Street (also on the Jubilee line), and Oxford Circus (also on the Victoria and Bakerloo lines).

You can also take the Piccadilly or Bakerloo line to the Piccadilly Circus Tube station, the Piccadilly line to the Hyde Park Corner station, or the Piccadilly, Victoria, or Jubilee line to the Green Park station.

The best buses are the 22, which takes in Green Park, Berkeley Square, and New Bond Street, and the 9—London's oldest existing bus route—which runs along Piccadilly.

MAKING THE MOST OF YOUR TIME

■ Set aside at least a day to experience Mayfair and Marylebone. Leave enough time for shopping and also to wander casually through the streets and squares. The only areas to avoid are the Tube stations at rush hour, and Oxford Street if you don't like crowds. At all costs, stay away from Oxford Circus around 5 pm, when the commuter rush can, at times, resemble an East African wildebeest migration—but without the charm. The area becomes quiet at night, so plan to party elsewhere.

Mayfair forms the core of London's West End, the city's most stylish central area. This neighborhood exudes class and old-school style. The sense of being in one of the world's most wealthy and powerful cities is palpable as you wander along its grand and graceful streets. Scoot across the district's one exception to all this elegance—Oxford Street—and you'll discover the pleasant thoroughfares of Marylebone, the most central of London's many "villages."

Mayfair

Ultra-ritzy Mayfair, lined with beautiful 18th-century mansions (along with Edwardian apartment buildings made of deep-red brick), is the address of choice for many of London's wealthiest residents—note the number of Rolls-Royces, Bentleys, and Jaguars on the streets. Even the delivery vans all seem to bear some royal coat of arms, advertising that they've been purveyors of fine goods for as long as anyone can remember.

The district can't claim to be stuffed with must-sees, but that is part of its appeal. There is no shortage of history and gorgeous architecture; the streets here are custom-built for window-shopping, expansive strolling, and getting a peek into the lifestyles of London's rich and famous, past and present. Mayfair is primarily residential, so its homes are off-limits except for one satisfyingly grand example: **Apsley House,** the Duke of Wellington's home, built by Robert Adam in the 1770s and once known as No. 1, London; nearby **Wellington Arch** also commemorates the great hero.

Despite being bordered by four of the busiest streets in London—the busy budget-shopping mecca Oxford Street (to the north), the major traffic artery Park Lane (to the west), and the bustling Regent Street and Piccadilly (to the east and south, respectively)—Mayfair itself is remarkably traffic-free and a delight to explore. Starting at **Selfridges,** on Oxford Street, a southward stroll will take you through quiet streets lined with Georgian town houses (the area was largely developed in the 17th and 18th centuries). From there, with a bit of artful navigating, you can reach four pleasant patches of green: **Grosvenor Square, Berkeley Square, Hanover Square,** with its splendid **St. George's**

Church where Handel worshipped, and the quiet **St. George's Gardens,** bounded by a maze of streets and mews. Some of London's most exclusive shopping destinations are here, including **Mount Street, Bruton Street, Savile Row,** and the **Burlington Arcade.** The **Royal Academy of Arts** is at the southern fringe of Mayfair on Piccadilly, beyond which begins the more sedate St. James's.

Sights

★ **Apsley House**

HISTORIC HOME | Apsley House was built by Robert Adam in the 1770s and was bought by the Duke of Wellington two years after his famous victory over Napoléon at the Battle of Waterloo in 1815. Long known simply as No. 1, London, on account of its being the first mansion at the old tollgate from Knights-bridge village, the Duke's old regency abode continues to look quite grand. Victory over the French made Wellington the greatest soldier and statesman in the land. The so-called Iron Duke lived here from 1817 until his death in 1852, and, although the 7th Duke of Wellington gave the house to the nation, the family retained some residential rights.

As you'd expect, the mansion has many uniforms and weapons on display, but it also houses a celebrated art collection, the bulk of which was once owned by Joseph Bonaparte, onetime King of Spain and older brother of Napoléon. With works by Brueghel, van Dyck, and Rubens, as well as the Spanish masters Velázquez and Murillo (note the former's famous portrait of Pope Innocent X), the collection also includes a Goya portrait of the duke himself on horseback. An 11-foot-tall statue of a nude (fig-leafed) Napoléon looms over you as you approach the grand central staircase. The statue was taken from the Louvre and given as a gift to Wellington from the grateful British government in 1816. ✉ 149 Piccadilly,

Hyde Park Corner, Mayfair ☎ 0207/499-5676 ⊕ www.english-heritage.org.uk ✉ From £12.50 ⏱ Closed Mon. and Tues. Ⓜ Hyde Park Corner.

Bond Street

STREET | This world-class shopping haunt is divided into northern "New" (1710) and southern "Old" (1690) halves. You can spot the juncture by a bronzed bench on which Franklin D. Roosevelt sits companionably next to Winston Churchill. At No. 34–35, on New Bond Street, you'll find **Sotheby's,** the world-famous auction house, as well as upscale retailers like Asprey's, Burberry, Louis Vuitton, and Church's. You'll find even more opportunities to flirt with financial ruin on Old Bond Street, with flagship boutiques of top-end designers like Prada, Gucci, and Yves Saint Laurent; an array of fine jewelers including Tiffany & Co.; and art dealers Richard Green, Richard Nagy, and Trinity Fine Art. **Cork Street,** which parallels the top half of Old Bond Street, is where many top dealers in contemporary art have their galleries. ✉ Mayfair ⊕ www.bondstreet.co.uk Ⓜ Bond St., Green Park.

★ **Burlington Arcade**

PEDESTRIAN MALL | With ceilings and lights now restored to how they would have looked when it was built in 1819, Burlington Arcade is the finest of Mayfair's enchanting covered shopping alleys. Originally built for Lord Cavendish, it was meant to stop commoners from flinging garbage into his garden at next-door Burlington House. Top-hatted watchmen called beadles—the world's smallest private police force—still patrol, preserving decorum by preventing you from singing, running, or carrying an open umbrella. The arcade is also the main link between the Royal Academy of Arts and its extended galleries at 6 Burlington Gardens. ✉ Piccadilly, Mayfair ☎ 020/7493-1764 ⊕ www.burlingtonarcade.com Ⓜ Green Park, Piccadilly Circus.

Marble Arch was originally a gateway to Buckingham Palace before it was moved to the corner of Hyde Park.

David Zwirner

ART GALLERY | This is just one of several influential New York gallerists to open a London space in Mayfair in recent years, a trend that has revitalized an area that's been losing ground to edgier neighborhoods like Bethnal Green. Zwirner's roster contains the likes of Bridget Riley and Jeff Koons, and modern masters such as Piet Mondrian are exhibited in this grand converted town house, too. ⊠ *24 Grafton St., Mayfair* ☎ *020/3538–3165* ⊕ *www. davidzwirner.com* ✉ *Free* ☉ *Closed Sun.* Ⓜ *Green Park.*

Grosvenor Square

PLAZA/SQUARE | Pronounced "*Grove*-na," this leafy square was laid out in 1721–31 and is as desirable an address today as it was then. Americans have certainly always thought so—from John Adams, the second president, who as ambassador lived at No. 38, to Dwight D. Eisenhower, whose wartime headquarters was at No. 20. The entire west side of the square was home to the U.S. Embassy for more than 50 years until its relocation south of the river. In the square itself stand memorials to Franklin D. Roosevelt and those who died on September 11, 2001. Grosvenor Chapel, completed in 1730 and used by Eisenhower's men during World War II, stands a couple of blocks south of the square on South Audley Street, with the entrance to pretty **St. George's Gardens** to its left. ⊠ *Mayfair* ⊕ *www.royalparks.org.uk* Ⓜ *Bond St.*

Handel & Hendrix in London

OTHER MUSEUM | This fascinating museum celebrates the lives of not one, but two, musical geniuses: classical composer George Frideric Handel and rock guitar legend Jimi Hendrix. Comprising two adjoining buildings, the bulk of the museum centers on the life and works of Handel, who lived at No. 25 for more than 30 years until his death in 1759. In rooms decorated in fine Georgian style, you can linger over original manuscripts and gaze at portraits. Some of the composer's most famous pieces were created here, including *Messiah* and *Music for the Royal Fireworks*. Fast-forward 200 years or so, and the apartment on the upper floors of No. 23 housed one of rock's great innovators, Jimi Hendrix, for a short but creative period in the late 1960s. The apartment has been lovingly restored, complete with replica furniture, fixtures, and fittings from Hendrix's heyday. ⊠ *23–25 Brook St., entrance in Lancashire Court, Mayfair* ☎ *020/7495–1685* ⊕ *www.handelhendrix.org* 🚇 *£10* ⊘ *Closed Sun.* Ⓜ *Bond St.*

Marble Arch

MONUMENT | John Nash's 1827 arch, moved here from Buckingham Palace in 1851, stands amid the traffic whirlpool where Bayswater Road segues into Oxford Street, at the top of Park Lane. The arch actually contains three small chambers, which served as a police station until the mid-20th century. Search the sidewalk on the traffic island opposite the movie theater for the stone plaque recalling Tyburn Tree, an elaborately designed gallows that stood here for 400 years, until 1783. The condemned would be conveyed here in their finest clothes from Newgate Prison in The City, and were expected to affect a casual indifference or face a merciless heckling from the crowds. Towering across the grass from the arch toward Tyburn Way is *Still Water,* a vast patina-green statue of a horse's head by sculptor Nic Fiddian-Green. Cross over (or under) to the northeastern corner of Hyde Park for Speakers' Corner, a parcel of land long-dedicated to the principle of free speech. On Sunday, people of all views—or none at all—come to pontificate, listen, and debate about everything under the sun. ⊠ *Park La., Mayfair* Ⓜ *Marble Arch.*

Marlborough Gallery

ART GALLERY | This veteran of the Mayfair art scene has been presenting exhibitions by masters old and new since it was founded in 1946. Great living artists, like Paula Rego and Frank Auerbach, plus exhibitions of graphic works from a whole host of starry names are showcased in the main first floor space, while the contemporary gallery on the second floor puts the spotlight on a younger generation of artists from the United Kingdom and abroad. ⊠ *6 Albermarle St., Mayfair* ☎ *020/7629–5161* ⊕ *www.marlboroughgallerylondon.com* 🚇 *Free* ⊘ *Closed Sun. and Mon.* Ⓜ *Green Park, Piccadilly Circus.*

★ Royal Academy of Arts

ART MUSEUM | Burlington House was built in 1664, with later Palladian additions for the 3rd Earl of Burlington in 1720. The piazza in front dates from 1873, when the Renaissance-style buildings around the courtyard were designed by Banks and Barry to house a gaggle of noble scientific societies, including the Royal Society of Chemistry and the Royal Astronomical Society. .

The house itself is home to the Royal Academy of Arts and an ambitious redevelopment for the academy's 250th anniversary in 2018 has meant that even more of its 46,000 treasures are now on display. The statue of the academy's first president, Sir Joshua Reynolds, palette in hand, stands prominently in the piazza. Free tours show off part of the collection and the excellent temporary exhibitions. Every June through August, the RA puts on its Summer Exhibition, a huge and eclectic collection of art by living Royal Academicians and many other contemporary artists. ⊠ *Burlington House, Piccadilly, Mayfair* ☎ *020/7300–8090* ⊕ *www.royalacademy.org.uk* 🚇 *Free; certain exhibits £22* Ⓜ *Piccadilly Circus, Green Park.*

Wellington Arch

MONUMENT | Opposite the Duke of Wellington's mansion, Apsley House, this majestic stone arch surveys the traffic rushing around Hyde Park Corner. Designed by Decimus Burton and completed in 1828, it was created as a grand entrance to the west side of London and echoes the design of that other landmark gate, Marble Arch. Both were triumphal arches commemorating Britain's victory

Each June for the past 240 years, the iconic Royal Academy of Arts has put on its Summer Exhibition, a huge draw for art-loving visitors and Londoners alike.

against France in the Napoleonic Wars. Atop the building, the Angel of Peace descends on the quadriga, or four-horse chariot of war. Inside the arch, three floors of permanent and temporary exhibits reveal the monument's history. From the balconies at the top of the arch you can peek into the Queen's back garden at across-the-road Buckingham Palace. ✉ *Hyde Park Corner, Mayfair* ☎ *020/7930–2726* 🌐 *www.english-heritage.org.uk* 🎫 *From £6.50* [M] *Hyde Park Corner.*

🍴 Restaurants

Between its grand dame institutions, deluxe steak houses, and contemporary A-list eateries, Mayfair's restaurant scene is all about fine dining, with something to suit all tastes—provided you are willing to pay big for it. With more Michelin stars than any other neighborhood in the city, Mayfair is the epicenter of London dining royalty.

★ Alain Ducasse at The Dorchester

$$$$ | **FRENCH** | One of only three three-Michelin-starred restaurants in the city, Alain Ducasse at The Dorchester achieves the pinnacle of classical French haute cuisine in a surprisingly fun, lively, and unstuffy salon. Diners feast on a blizzard of beautifully choreographed dishes, including classic rum baba with Chantilly cream, sliced open and served in a silver domed tureen. **Known for:** signature sautéed lobster with chicken quenelles; impeccable five-star service; surprisingly unstarchy vibe. [$] *Average main: £45* ✉ *The Dorchester, 53 Park La., Mayfair* ☎ *020/7629–8866 for reservations only* 🌐 *www.alainducasse-dorchester.com* 🕓 *Closed Sun. and Mon. No lunch* [M] *Marble Arch, Green Park.*

Cecconi's

$$$$ | **MODERN ITALIAN** | Revel with the A-listers in the glamorous buzz at this upscale Italian brasserie wedged between Cork Street, Savile Row, and the Royal Academy of Arts. It's perfect for a pit stop during a West End shopping

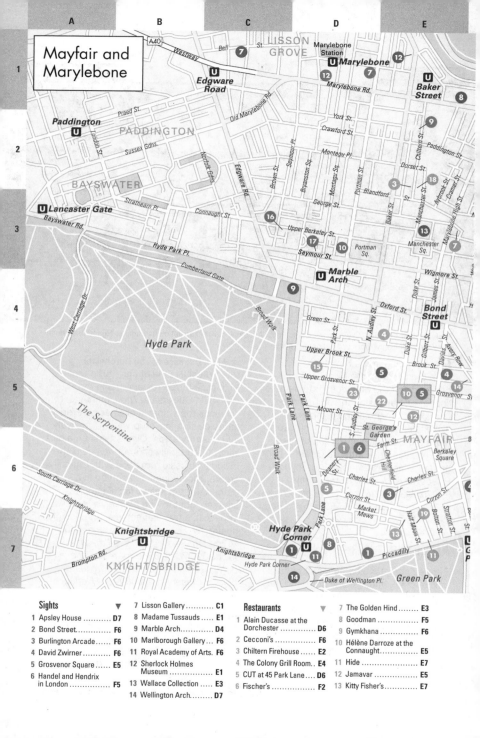

Mayfair and Marylebone

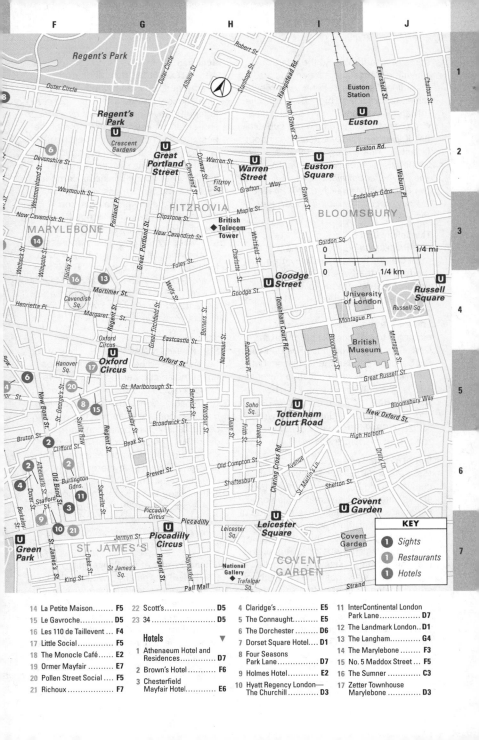

F	G	H	I	J

Regent's Park

Outer Circle

Regent's Park U

Crescent Gardens

Great Portland Street U

MARYLEBONE

Devonshire St.

Weymouth St.

New Cavendish St.

Wimpole St.

Harley St.

Portland Pl.

Great Portland St.

Mortimer St.

Cavendish Sq.

Henrietta Pl.

Margaret St.

Oxford Circus U

Hanover Sq.

Oxford Circus

New Bond St.

Bruton St.

Clifford St.

Albemarle St.

Dover St.

Old Bond St.

Stafford St.

Berkeley St.

Burlington Gdns.

Sackville St.

Green Park U

ST. JAMES'S

King St.

Duke St.

St. James's St.

Regent St.

Jermyn St.

Piccadilly Circus U

Piccadilly

St. James's Sq.

Pall Mall

Haymarket

National Gallery ◆ Trafalgar

Outer Circle

Robert St.

Albany St.

Stanhope St.

Hampstead Rd.

North Gower St.

Euston Station

U Euston

Eversholt St.

Chalton St.

Euston Rd.

Euston Square U

Warren St. U

Warren St.

Conway St.

Cleveland St.

Fitzroy Sq.

Grafton

Way

Gower St.

Woburn Pl.

FITZROVIA

British Telecom Tower ◆

Clipstone St.

New Cavendish St.

Maple St.

Whitfield St.

BLOOMSBURY

Endsleigh Gdns.

Foley St.

Charlotte St.

Goodge St. U

Goodge Street

Gordon Sq.

0   1/4 mi
0   1/4 km

Wells St.

Mortimer St.

Great Titchfield St.

Eastcastle St.

Oxford St.

Berners St.

Newman St.

Rathbone Pl.

Tottenham Court Rd.

University of London

Russell Sq.

Russell Square U

Montague Pl.

British Museum

Montague St.

Great Russell St.

Bloomsbury St.

Gt. Marlborough St.

Berwick St.

Wardour St.

Dean St.

Soho Sq.

Greek St.

Frith St.

Tottenham Court Road U

Carnaby St.

Broadwick St.

Beak St.

Brewer St.

Old Compton St.

Shaftesbury

Charing Cross Rd.

Avenue

St. Martin's Ln.

Bloomsbury Way

New Oxford St.

High Holborn

Shelton St.

Drury Ln.

Covent Garden U

Covent Garden

Piccadilly Circus

Leicester Sq.

Leicester Square U

COVENT GARDEN

Strand

KEY
❶ Sights
❶ Restaurants
❶ Hotels

spree or after browsing the nearby Mayfair galleries and auction houses, with diners spilling out onto pavement tables for breakfast, brunch, and *cicchetti* (Italian tapas)—and then returning later in the day for something more substantial. **Known for:** all-day jet-setter hangout; favorite of nearby Vogue House staff and Sotheby's clientele; popular veal Milanese. [$] *Average main: £32* ✉ *5A Burlington Gardens, Mayfair* ☎ *020/7434–1500* 🌐 *www.cecconis.co.uk* [M] *Green Park, Piccadilly Circus.*

The Colony Grill Room

$$$$ | AMERICAN | Glide past the parked royal-blue Armstrong Siddeley, through the foyer of the five-star hotel The Beaumont, and into the swank art deco–inspired dining salon of The Colony grill room. Fans of 1920s New York will admire the throwback decor, before digging into classics like steak tartare, Caesar salad, and bananas Foster. **Known for:** bespoke sundae menu; classic buttermilk fried chicken; evocative American 1920s panache and glamour. [$] *Average main: £36* ✉ *The Beaumont, 8 Balderton St., Brown Hart Gardens, Mayfair* ☎ *020/7499–9499* 🌐 *www.colonygrillroom.com* [M] *Marble Arch.*

CUT at 45 Park Lane

$$$$ | STEAKHOUSE | Austrian-born star chef Wolfgang Puck amps up the stakes at this ultraexpensive steak house on Park Lane. Set against a luxe backdrop of Damien Hirst artwork and globe lights, carnivores go crazy for the pricey prime cuts from England, Australia, Japan, and the United States. **Known for:** art gallery–like interior; rare Kagoshima Wagyu beef steaks; celebrity chef hot spot. [$] *Average main: £60* ✉ *45 Park La., Mayfair* ☎ *020/7493–4545 for reservations only* 🌐 *www.dorchestercollection.com* [M] *Marble Arch, Hyde Park Corner.*

Goodman

$$$$ | STEAKHOUSE | This Manhattan-themed, Russian-owned swanky steak house, named after Chicago jazz legend Benny Goodman, has everyone in agreement: these truly are some of the best steaks in town. USDA-certified, 150-day corn-fed, and on-site dry-aged Black Angus T-bones, rib eye, porterhouse, and New York bone-in sirloins compete for taste and tenderness with heavily marbled grass-fed prime cuts from Scotland and the Lake District. **Known for:** long list of classy Coravin-extracted red wines by the glass; truly impressive steaks; specially imported Josper oven for smoky charcoal cooking. [$] *Average main: £40* ✉ *24–26 Maddox St., Mayfair* ☎ *020/7499–3776* 🌐 *www.goodmanrestaurants.com* 🕒 *Closed Sun.* [M] *Oxford Circus, Piccadilly Circus.*

★ Gymkhana

$$$ | MODERN INDIAN | The last days of the Raj are invoked here at one of London's finest Indian curry emporiums, where top choices include dosas with fennel-rich Chettinad duck and the famed suckling pig vindaloo. Diners admire the whirring ceiling fans, rattan chairs, and other decor inspired by the colonial-era gymkhana sporting clubs of yesteryear. **Known for:** signature kid goat methi keema; unusual game curries; Indian punches in the basement private dining booths. [$] *Average main: £28* ✉ *42 Albemarle St., Mayfair* ☎ *020/3011–5900* 🌐 *www.gymkhanalondon.com* 🕒 *Closed Sun.* [M] *Green Park.*

Hélène Darroze at The Connaught

$$$$ | FRENCH | The city's wealthy flock to French virtuoso Hélène Darroze's restaurant at The Connaught for her dazzling regional French haute cuisine, served up in a stylish Edwardian wood-paneled dining salon. Taking inspiration from the Les Landes region in southwestern France, Darroze sallies forth with a procession of magnificent dishes, like Robert Dupérier foie gras with fig and port and Limousin sweetbreads with Jerusalem artichokes. **Known for:** relatively affordable three-course set lunch; sumptuous dining salon; classy French haute dishes. [$] *Average main: £40* ✉ *The Connaught, Carlos Pl., Mayfair* ☎ *020/3147–7200 for reservations only* 🌐 *www.the-connaught.co.uk* 🕓 *Closed Sun. and Mon.* 👔 *Jacket required* [M] *Green Park.*

Hide

$$$$ | **MODERN BRITISH** | Mayfair is home to more than its share of fussy fine dining restaurants, so Hide is a welcome alternative, charming with experimental dishes that make the new-Nordic, produce-focused modern European menu shine. Look out for art-like dishes strewn with wildflowers on the seasonal eight-course tasting menus served in a fairy-tale setting. **Known for:** bespoke interiors, including a gorgeous oak spiral staircase; intimate basement bar for cocktails and dining; vast wine collection is the largest of any restaurant in the country. [$] *Average main: £42* ✉ *85 Piccadilly, Mayfair* ☎ *020/3146–8666* 🌐 *www.hide.co.uk* [M] *Green Park.*

Jamavar

$$$ | **INDIAN** | There is no finer fish dish in town than the Malai stone bass tikka at this upmarket Indian restaurant. The food and spices here are so authentic that it regularly buzzes with Bollywood stars, wealthy Mayfair moguls, and the entire well-heeled Indian diaspora. **Known for:** glossy, luxurious Indian crowd; stunning interior of dark wood, marble, and Indian artwork; unmissable Malai stone bass tikka. [$] *Average main: £25* ✉ *8 Mount St., Mayfair* ☎ *020/7499–1800* 🌐 *www.jamavarrestaurants.com* [M] *Bond St., Green Park.*

Kitty Fisher's

$$$ | **MODERN BRITISH** | Named after an infamous 18th-century courtesan, Kitty Fisher's is situated in a tiny, creaky Georgian town house in Mayfair's Shepherd Market. Crammed with antique prints, portraits, and silver candelabras, here you can sample some of the finest wood-grill and smokehouse fare around. **Known for:** high-end showbiz and politico diners; cozy and candlelit town-house setting; incredible steaks from the grill. [$] *Average main: £29* ✉ *10 Shepherd Market, Mayfair* ☎ *020/3302–1661* 🌐 *www.kittyfishers.com* 🕓 *Closed Sun. and Mon.* [M] *Green Park.*

La Petite Maison (LPM)

$$$$ | **FRENCH** | **FAMILY** | With the legend "*Tous Célèbres Ici*" ("All Famous Here") boldly etched on the front doors, the delightful LPM boasts an impressively well-sourced and balanced French Mediterranean, Ligurian, and Provençal menu based on the relaxed Riviera style of the original La Petite Maison in Nice. Try the soft burrata cheese with a sweet Datterini tomato and basil spread or aromatic baked turbot with artichokes, chorizo, five spices, and white wine sauce. **Known for:** whole roast black-leg chicken; light French Riviera–inspired dining; excellent selection of rosé wines. [$] *Average main: £35* ✉ *53–54 Brook's Mews, Mayfair* ☎ *020/7495–4774* 🌐 *www.lpmlondon.co.uk* 🕓 *Closed Mon.* [M] *Bond St., Oxford Circus.*

Le Gavroche

$$$$ | **FRENCH** | Masterchef Michel Roux Jr. works the floor in the old-fashioned proprietorial way at this old-school Mayfair basement institution—established by his father and uncle in 1967—which many still rate as the best formal dining in London. Roux's mastery of classical French haute cuisine hypnotizes with signature dishes like foie gras with cinnamon-scented crispy duck pancake and

saddle of rabbit with Parmesan cheese. **Known for:** tasty soufflé Suissesse; swanky Mayfair basement setting; luxurious tasting menu. $ *Average main: £44* ✉ *43 Upper Brook St., Mayfair* ☎ *020/7408–0881* ⊕ *www.le-gavroche. co.uk* ⊗ *Closed Sun. and Mon. No lunch.* ⌂ *Jacket required* Ⓜ *Bond St., Marble Arch.*

Little Social

$$$ | **MODERN BRITISH** | Part of Michelin-starred chef Jason Atherton's dining dynasty, Little Social backs its elegant, modernist dining room with a menu of adventurous dishes celebrating the joy of British produce. Expect to find a range of prime cuts straight from the Josper grill, and pay special attention to the maple-glazed pork rib eye with charred cabbage and pomme purée. **Known for:** chic cocktail bar; relaxed mid-century modern setting; great value set menu. $ *Average main: £27* ✉ *5 Pollen St., Mayfair* ☎ *020/7870–3730* ⊕ *www.littlesocial. co.uk* ⊗ *Closed Sun. and Mon.* Ⓜ *Oxford Circus, Piccadilly Circus.*

Ormer Mayfair

$$$$ | **BRITISH** | Hidden away in the depths of a Mayfair hotel, Ormer delivers modern British cooking at its finest. In the art deco–inspired basement haven, you can indulge on elegant dishes from executive chef Sofian Msetfi, which celebrate the seasonal and the foraged. **Known for:** great vegetarian and vegan fine-dining options; range of tasting menus; excellent wine selection with sharp focus on British fizz. $ *Average main: £34* ✉ *Flemings Hotel, 7–12 Half Moon St., Mayfair* ☎ *020/7016–5601 for reservations only* ⊕ *www.flemings-mayfair.co.uk/fine-dining-london/ormer-mayfair-restaurant* ⊗ *Closed Sun.–Tues.* Ⓜ *Green Park.*

Pollen Street Social

$$$$ | **MODERN EUROPEAN** | Gastro god Jason Atherton may not man the stoves here anymore, but his flagship in a cute Dickensian alleyway off Regent Street still knocks the London dining scene for a loop. Fans can enjoy refined small and large dishes ranging from a "Fruite of the Sea" appetizer to sublime suckling pig belly with lemon, parsnip, and yogurt. **Known for:** vegan and vegetarian tasting menus; Michelin-star riffs on classic British dishes; focus on locally sourced ingredients. $ *Average main: £35* ✉ *8–10 Pollen St., Mayfair* ☎ *020/7290–7600* ⊕ *www.pollenstreetsocial.com* ⊗ *Closed Sun. and Mon.* Ⓜ *Oxford Circus, Piccadilly Circus.*

Richoux

$ | **BISTRO** | This has been an affordable refuge from busy Piccadilly for more than a century. Simple but well-executed French bistro food and assorted classic British dishes are served all day, as is scrumptious Afternoon Tea. **Known for:** traditional service; combined Anglo-French menu; elegant interiors. $ *Average main: £12* ✉ *172 Piccadilly, Mayfair* ☎ *020/7493–2204* ⊕ *www.richoux.co.uk* Ⓜ *Green Park, Piccadilly Circus.*

Scott's

$$$$ | **SEAFOOD** | Imposing doormen in bowler hats greet visitors with a wee nod at this ever-fashionable seafood haven on Mount Street in Mayfair. Originally founded in 1851 in the Haymarket, and a former haunt of James Bond author Ian Fleming (he apparently enjoyed the potted shrimps), Scott's draws the wealthiest of London, who come for the fresh Lindisfarne oysters, Dover sole, and tasty shrimp burgers. **Known for:** extravagant prices; possibly London's most magnificent crustacean bar; huge platters of fresh fruits de mer. $ *Average main: £37* ✉ *20 Mount St., Mayfair* ☎ *020/7495–7309 for reservations only* ⊕ *www.scotts-restaurant.com* Ⓜ *Green Park, Bond St.*

34

$$$ | **INTERNATIONAL** | A-listers head straight for 34, off Grosvenor Square in Mayfair, simply because all the other celebrities seem to hang out here, too. It must be the plush Edwardian and

art deco dining salon, the neat fish, game, and steak-focused menu, and the smooth Upper Manhattan–style service. **Known for:** live jazz; an endless procession of Hollywood stars; impressive global meats off an Argentine-inspired grill. *$ Average main: £30 ✉ 34 Grosvenor Sq., entrance on S. Audley St., Mayfair ☎ 020/3350–3434 🌐 www.34-restaurant.co.uk [M] Marble Arch.*

Hotels

The Athenaeum Hotel and Residences
$$$$ | **HOTEL** | This grand hotel overlooking Green Park offers plenty for the money: rooms are both comfortable and lavishly decorated, with deeply cushy Hypnos beds, plasma-screen TVs, luxurious fabrics, and original contemporary artworks. **Pros:** an excellent Afternoon Tea; peaceful park views; central location. **Cons:** only some rooms come with park views; some rooms can feel tiny; bathrooms are almost all small. *$ Rooms from: £405 ✉ 116 Piccadilly, Mayfair ☎ 020/7499–3464 🌐 www.athenaeumhotel.com 🛏 164 rooms 🍴 No Meals [M] Green Park.*

Brown's Hotel
$$$$ | **HOTEL** | Founded in 1837 by James Brown, Lord Byron's "gentleman's gentleman," this hotel occupying 11 Georgian town houses holds a treasured place in London society. **Pros:** good Afternoon Tea; elegant spaces; attentive service. **Cons:** low availability for the most basic rooms; renovation detracted from the hotel's historic atmosphere; even the most basic room is very pricey. *$ Rooms from: £580 ✉ 34 Albemarle St., Mayfair ☎ 020/7493–6020, 888/667–9477 in U.S. 🌐 www.roccofortehotels.com 🛏 148 rooms 🍴 No Meals [M] Green Park.*

The Chesterfield
$$$ | **HOTEL** | Deep in the heart of Mayfair, the former town house of the Earl of Chesterfield welcomes guests in wood-and-leather public rooms that match the dark-wood furnishings in the bedrooms—small but looking like fashion magazine spreads, with bold designer wallpaper or tones of fawn and gray. **Pros:** fabulous Afternoon Tea; laid-back atmosphere; attentive service. **Cons:** restaurant is very expensive; some rooms are tiny; prices rise sharply if you don't get the cheapest rooms. *$ Rooms from: £290 ✉ 35 Charles St., Mayfair ☎ 020/7491–2622, 877/955–1515 in U.S. 🌐 www.chesterfieldmayfair.com 🛏 107 rooms 🍴 No Meals [M] Green Park.*

★ Claridge's
$$$$ | **HOTEL** | **FAMILY** | The well-heeled have been meeting—and eating—at Claridge's for generations, and the tradition continues in the original art deco public spaces of this super glamorous London institution. **Pros:** famed history; see-and-be-seen dining and drinking; serious luxury everywhere—this is an old-money hotel. **Cons:** to protect the privacy of guests, photographs are prohibited in some areas; all that luxury means an expensive price tag; better pack your designer wardrobe if you want to fit in with the locals. *$ Rooms from: £650 ✉ Brook St., Mayfair ☎ 020/7629–8860, 866/599–6991 in U.S. 🌐 www.claridges.co.uk 🛏 203 rooms 🍴 No Meals [M] Bond St.*

★ The Connaught
$$$$ | **HOTEL** | **FAMILY** | A huge favorite of the "we wouldn't dream of staying anywhere else" monied set since its opening in 1917, The Connaught has many dazzlingly modern complements to its famously historic delights. **Pros:** Michelin-starred dining; legendary hotel; great for star-spotting. **Cons:** the superior king room is small for the price; bathrooms are small; history comes at a price. *$ Rooms from: £660 ✉ Carlos Pl., Mayfair ☎ 020/7499–7070, 866/599–6991 in U.S. 🌐 www.the-connaught.co.uk 🛏 121 rooms 🍴 No Meals [M] Bond St.*

One of Mayfair's most famous and historic hotels, Claridge's also offers one of the city's most authentic high-class Afternoon Teas.

★ The Dorchester

$$$$ | **HOTEL** | Few hotels this opulent manage to be as personable as The Dorchester, which opened in 1939 and boasts a prime Park Lane location with unparalleled glamour; gold leaf and marble adorn the public spaces, and guest quarters are awash in English country house–meets–art deco style. **Pros:** excellent spa; historic luxury in 1930s building; lovely views of Hyde Park. **Cons:** some rooms are disappointingly small; prices are sky-high; traditional look is not to all tastes. $ *Rooms from: £750* ✉ *53 Park La., Mayfair* ☎ *020/7629–8888* ⊕ *www.dorchestercollection.com* ⤴ *250 rooms* ⫼○⫼ *No Meals* Ⓜ *Marble Arch, Hyde Park Corner.*

Four Seasons Park Lane

$$$$ | **HOTEL** | A racy departure for the Four Seasons, this hotel has an English clubhouse look with a dose of boudoir. **Pros:** lovely location next to Hyde Park; highly elegant rooms; excellent spa. **Cons:** breakfast is an additional fee; haute design comes with high prices; not for strict traditionalists. $ *Rooms from: £800* ✉ *Hamilton Pl., Park La., Mayfair* ☎ *020/7499–0888* ⊕ *www.fourseasons.com/london* ⤴ *193 rooms* ⫼○⫼ *No Meals* Ⓜ *Hyde Park Corner.*

InterContinental London Park Lane

$$$$ | **HOTEL** | Overlooking busy Hyde Park Corner and the grounds of Buckingham Palace (much to the Queen's chagrin, allegedly), this hotel's luxurious rooms are aimed at high-end business travelers. **Pros:** good business facilities; great location; feel-like-a-million-dollars service. **Cons:** without the wow factor or history of some similarly priced Park Lane hotels; prices sky-high in midsummer; no park views with standard rooms. $ *Rooms from: £500* ✉ *1 Hamilton Pl., Park La., Mayfair* ☎ *020/7409–3131* ⊕ *parklane.intercontinental.com* ⤴ *447 rooms* ⫼○⫼ *No Meals* Ⓜ *Hyde Park Corner.*

★ The Langham

$$$$ | HOTEL | Hotel pedigrees don't come much greater than this one: built in 1865, The Langham was *the* original luxury hotel in the city, all but inventing the very image of what a great London hotel looked like. **Pros:** great restaurant and bar; beautiful historic building; gorgeous and peaceful pool. **Cons:** some modernized rooms don't share the building's historic charm; need to book ahead for the wildly popular Artesian Bar; price rises considerably once cheapest rooms sell out. [$] *Rooms from: £549* ✉ *1C Portland Pl., Mayfair* ☎ *020/7636–1000* 🌐 *www.langhamhotels.co.uk* 🛏 *380 rooms* 🍴 *No Meals* [M] *Oxford Circus.*

No.5 Maddox Street

$$$ | APARTMENT | FAMILY | Just five minutes' walk from Oxford Street, this is a great option for those who tire of traditional hotels: 12 luxury suites—some with balconies and working fireplaces—filled with everything you could ever need, including a handy kitchen. **Pros:** guests have access to nearby health club; cozy and private; room service will deliver meals from local restaurants. **Cons:** two-night minimum stay; no communal lobby can make you feel isolated; no elevator. [$] *Rooms from: £300* ✉ *5 Maddox St., Mayfair* ☎ *020/7647–0200* 🌐 *www.living-rooms.co.uk/hotel/no5maddoxstreet* 🛏 *12 suites* 🍴 *No Meals* [M] *Oxford Circus.*

Nightlife

Bars in this upscale central neighborhood—many of which can be found within luxury hotels—attract a polished crowd. Cocktails, fine wines, and rare aged spirits are the tipples of choice. Even the pubs tend to be as upscale as the people who frequent them, but you'll also find plenty of informal establishments with a lot of character.

BARS

Claridge's Bar

BARS | This elegant Mayfair meeting place remains unpretentious even when it brims with beautiful people. The bar has an art deco heritage made hip by the sophisticated touch of designer David Collins. A library of rare champagnes and brandies as well as a delicious choice of traditional and exotic cocktails—try the Flapper or the Black Pearl—will occupy your taste buds. Request a glass of vintage Cristal in the darkly moody, leather-walled, 36-seat Fumoir. ✉ *Claridge's, 55 Brook St., Mayfair* ☎ *020/7629–8860* 🌐 *www.claridges.co.uk* [M] *Bond St.*

★ The Connaught Bar

BARS | The walls are platinum silver leaf and everything's all buffed and burnished at this glamorous David Collins–designed 1920s cocktail lounge at The Connaught. Hail the famous martini trolley for a classic dry martini or sip signatures like a Ron Zacapa rum–based Vieux Connaught, which is presented on a mirrored tray with a swirl of saffron smoke. ✉ *The Connaught, Carlos Place, Mayfair* ☎ *020/7314–3419* 🌐 *www.the-connaught.co.uk* ☞ *No reservations* [M] *Green Park, Marble Arch.*

★ Mr Fogg's Residence

BARS | Explorers of all stripes will be captivated by this Jules Verne–inspired cocktail parlor, which is chock-full of the weathered maps, hunting trophies, taxidermy, suspended penny-farthings, and *Around the World in 80 Days* globe-trotting items of eccentric fictional Victorian British adventurer, Phileas J. Fogg. Expect Victorian tipples and gin-based afternoon "Tipsy Teas" from staff in bow ties and other old-fashioned getups. ✉ *15 Bruton La., Mayfair* ☎ *020/7036–0608* 🌐 *www.mr-foggs.com* [M] *Green Park, Oxford Circus.*

★ sketch

BARS | FAMILY | One seat never looks like the next at this downright extraordinary collection of esoteric living-room bars off Savile Row. The exclusive Parlour, a patisserie during the day, exudes plenty of rarefied charm; the intimate East Bar at the back is reminiscent of a sci-fi film set; the Gallery is a shocking-pink wonderland; and in the Glade it's permanently sunset in an enchanted forest. The space-age dinosaur egg–pod-shape restrooms are definitely London's quirkiest. ⊠ *9 Conduit St., Mayfair* ☎ *020/7659–4500* ⊕ *www. sketch.london* Ⓜ *Oxford Circus.*

PUBS

The Punch Bowl

PUBS | In a quiet corner of Mayfair, the cozy little Punch Bowl dates to 1729 and the interior remains steadfastly old-fashioned, with a painting of Churchill, candles, polished dark wood, and engraved windows. Try the place's own ale, made specially in Scotland by Caledonian. A dining area at the rear buzzes at lunchtime with locals who come for the upscale English pub food, and there's a fancier restaurant upstairs. ⊠ *41 Farm St., Mayfair* ☎ *020/7493–6841* ⊕ *www. punchbowllondon.com* Ⓜ *Green Park, Bond St.*

Ye Grapes

PUBS | Like any London neighborhood, Mayfair has its fair share of pubs but few can compare to the charm and location of Ye Grapes. Poised in the heart of the delightfully quaint Shepherd Market, the place sells itself almost entirely on atmosphere alone. The bar serves a comfortingly familiar list of ales, beers, and wines—and there's an excellent Thai food menu—but it is the village-style location and warm local crowd that warrant seeking it out when in need of liquid refreshment. ⊠ *16 Shepherd Market, Mayfair* ☎ *020/7493–4216* ⊕ *www.shannon-pubs. com/ye-grapes-1* Ⓜ *Green Park.*

Shopping

ACCESSORIES

Mulberry

HANDBAGS | Staying true to its rural Somerset roots, this luxury goods company epitomizes *le style anglais,* a sophisticated take on the earth tones and practicality of English country style. Best known for highly desirable luxury handbags—such as the Lily, Chiltern, and Bayswater models—the company also produces gorgeous leather accessories, from wallets to luggage, as well as shoes and clothing for men and women. Aside from the New Bond Street flagship, there are branches in Knightsbridge, Covent Garden, Heathrow, and the Westfield centers, along with Mulberry concessions in most of the major upscale department stores. The small store on St. Christopher's Place in Marylebone stocks accessories only. ⊠ *50 New Bond St., Mayfair* ☎ *020/7491–3900* ⊕ *www. mulberry.com* Ⓜ *Bond St.*

ANTIQUES

Grays Antique Centre

ANTIQUES & COLLECTIBLES | There are approximately 200 dealers here, specializing in everything from Bakelite items to Mughal art. The majority focus on jewelry, ranging from contemporary to antique. Bargains are not out of the question, and proper pedigrees are guaranteed. Be sure to go on a weekday as the store is closed Saturday and Sunday. ⊠ *58 Davies St., Mayfair* ☎ *020/7629–7034* ⊕ *www. graysantiques.com* Ⓜ *Bond St.*

BOOKS AND STATIONERY

★ Heywood Hill

BOOKS | Open since 1936, this is considered by some to be the best small bookstore in the English-speaking world—John Le Carré, who set a scene in *Tinker Tailor Soldier Spy* here, was a long-standing customer. Browse for a leather-bound volume on architecture, gardening, natural history, or topography—just some of the topics in which the antiquarian collection specializes. The contemporary selection emphasizes literature, history, biography, travel, architecture, and children's books, and the knowledgeable staff is happy to provide advice. During World War II, author Nancy Mitford helped keep the bookstore going. Today, the 12th Duke of Devonshire, a descendant of her brother-in-law, the 11th Duke, is the owner. ⊠ *10 Curzon St., Mayfair* ☎ *020/7629–0647* ⊕ *www. heywoodhill.com* Ⓜ *Green Park.*

Smythson of Bond Street

STATIONERY | No hostess of any standing would consider having a leather-bound guest book made by anyone besides this elegant stationer, and the shop's social stationery and distinctive diaries with their pale-blue pages are the epitome of British good taste. These, along with other made-in-Britain leather goods, including a small line of handbags, backpacks, and luggage tags, can be personalized. There are branches in Chelsea, Notting Hill, and Heathrow, plus concessions in leading department stores. ⊠ *131–132 New Bond St., Mayfair* ☎ *020/3535–8009* ⊕ *www.smythson.com* Ⓜ *Bond St., Oxford Circus.*

Waterstones

BOOKS | At this megabookshop (Europe's largest, with more than 8 miles of bookshelves) in a former art deco department store near Piccadilly Circus, browse for your latest purchase, attend one of the frequent meet-the-author events, or enjoy a coffee in the café in the basement. Waterstones is the country's leading book chain, and it's pulled out all the stops to make its flagship as welcoming as a bookstore can be. There are several smaller branches throughout the city. ⊠ *203–206 Piccadilly, Mayfair* ☎ *0207/851–2400* ⊕ *www.waterstones. com* Ⓜ *Piccadilly Circus.*

CLOTHING

Alexander McQueen

MIXED CLOTHING | Since the legendary designer's untimely death in 2010, his right-hand woman, Sarah Burton, has been at the helm, receiving raves for continuing his tradition of theatrical, darkly romantic, and beautifully cut clothes incorporating corsetry, lace, embroidery, and hourglass silhouettes, all of which were exemplified in Burton's celebrated wedding dress for Kate Middleton. Can't afford a gala gown? Go home with a skull-print silk scarf. ⊠ *27 Old Bond St., Mayfair* ☎ *020/7355–0088* ⊕ *www.alexandermcqueen.com* Ⓜ *Bond St.*

Belstaff

LEATHER GOODS | For years the purveyors of Britain's coolest motorcycle leathers, Belstaff has expanded into dresses, skirts, and handbags, as well as knitwear, boots, tops, and trousers for men, women, and children. Outerwear in general and leather jackets in particular remain a strength. All the items reflect the brand's functional yet unconventional heritage. Previous customers include Lawrence of Arabia, Amelia Earhart, Steve McQueen, and Che Guevara. ⊠ *203 Regent St., Mayfair* ☎ *020/7734–1339* ⊕ *www. belstaff.co.uk* Ⓜ *Oxford Circus.*

Browns

MIXED CLOTHING | A trendsetting boutique since it opened in the 1970s, this shop occupying interconnecting town houses has been reinvigorated after a purchase by luxury e-tailer Farfetch.com. Browns focuses on well-established international luxury designers, such as Vetements, Valentino, Marques'Almeida, and Saint Laurent. The menswear, footwear, and accessories collections are equally well chosen. A Shoreditch branch showcases new design talent, and if you're about to go down the aisle, check out the appointment-only bridal boutique at 12 Hinde Street in Marylebone. ⊠ *39 Brook St., Mayfair* ☎ *020/7514–0016* ⊕ *www. brownsfashion.com* Ⓜ *Bond St.*

Burberry

MIXED CLOTHING | Known for its trademark tartan, this company has cultivated an edgy, high-fashion image in recent years, and creative director and former Givenchy designer Riccardo Tisci is pushing the boundaries even more, bringing in a street-style influence. For those who prefer the traditional Burberry look, the raincoats are still a classic buy, along with handbags and plaid scarves in every color imaginable. If you're up for a trek, there's a huge factory outlet in Hackney on Chatham Place that has clothes and accessories for men, women, and children at half price or less. There are also branches in Knightsbridge, Chelsea, and the Westfield shopping center in addition to this spectacular flagship store. ☒ *121 Regent St., Mayfair* ☎ *020/7806–8904* ⊕ *uk.burberry.com* Ⓜ *Piccadilly Circus.*

Isabel Marant London

MIXED CLOTHING | The first London store from Marant, a favorite of French fashion editors, this airy skylit space is full of her signature slim-cut pants, slouchy knits, wedge sneakers, and rock-chick miniskirts, all exuding Left Bank boho cool. ☒ *29 Bruton St., Mayfair* ☎ *020/7499–7887* ⊕ *www. isabelmarant.com* Ⓜ *Bond St.*

Matches Fashion

MIXED CLOTHING | Housed within a beautiful six-story Mayfair town house, Matches Fashion's flagship store is so much more than just a retail destination. Designed to create a bricks-and-mortar location that delivers the ultimate contemporary shopping experience, this is a multifaceted emporium in which the ground floor fashion retail space is complemented by an in-house garden, exhibition spaces, multimedia studios, and a calendar of curated talks and events. Whether this is the future of fashion retail is still to be seen, but at the very least it's a lovely place to shop for brands from Gucci to Jil Sander. ☒ *5 Carlos Pl., Mayfair* ☎ *020/3907–8590* ⊕ *www. matchesfashion.com* Ⓜ *Green Park.*

Stella McCartney

WOMEN'S CLOTHING | It's not easy emerging from the shadow of a Beatle father, but Stella McCartney is a major force in fashion in her own right. Her signature jumpsuits and tuxedo pantsuits embody her design philosophy, combining minimalist tailoring with femininity and sophistication with ease of wear. Her love of functionality and clean lines has led to her branching off into lingerie, accessories, swimwear, and sportswear, designing a line for Adidas. A vegetarian like her parents, she refuses to use fur or leather, making her a favorite with similarly minded fashionistas. ☒ *23 Old Bond St., Mayfair* ☎ *020/7518–3100* ⊕ *www. stellamccartney.com* Ⓜ *Bond St.*

Victoria Beckham

WOMEN'S CLOTHING | Many were dubious when the former Spice Girl launched herself as a high-end designer, but her elegant yet wearable clothes soon made her a favorite with influencers and customers alike. This, her only stand-alone boutique, carries all the Beckham lines: the VVB diffusion line, the main collection, and accessories like bags, shoes, and eyewear, all displayed like artwork in the gallery-like space. ☒ *36 Dover St., Mayfair* ☎ *020/7042–0700* ⊕ *www.victoriabeckham.com* Ⓜ *Green Park, Piccadilly.*

Vivienne Westwood

WOMEN'S CLOTHING | From her beginnings as the most shocking and outré designer around, Westwood (now Dame Vivienne) has become a standard-bearer for high-style British couture. At the Chelsea boutique where she first sold the lavish corseted ball gowns, dandified nipped-waist jackets, and tartan-meets-punk daywear that formed the core of her signature look, you can still buy ready-to-wear—mainly items from the more casual Anglomania diffusion line and the exclusive Worlds End label, which draws from her archives. The small Davies Street boutique is devoted to couture (plus bridal), while the flagship Conduit

Street store carries all of the above. There's also a men's collection at 18 Conduit Street. ⊠ *44 Conduit St., Mayfair* ☎ *020/7439–1109* ⊕ *www.viviennewestwood.com* Ⓜ *Oxford Circus.*

DEPARTMENT STORES

★ Fenwick

DEPARTMENT STORE | A manageably sized department store, Fenwick is a welcome haven of affordability in a shopping area where stratospheric prices are the norm. The store is particularly strong on accessories (notably lingerie, wraps, and hats), cosmetics, perfumes, and chic, wearable fashion by both big names and more niche designers such as Goat, J Brand, and Tory Burch. There are also three small spas (Chantecaille, La Prairie, and a Blink waxing room), various beauty services (including a hair salon, nail bar, and Blink brow bar), and three restaurants, plus a men's department in the basement. ⊠ *63 New Bond St., Mayfair* ☎ *020/7629–9161* ⊕ *www.fenwick.co.uk* Ⓜ *Bond St.*

Thomas Goode

DEPARTMENT STORE | This spacious luxury housewares shop has been at the same smart Mayfair address since 1845. The china, silver, crystal, and linen, whether from the store's own line or from luxury brands like Christofle and Puiforcat, are simply the best that money can buy, a legacy of its original customer base of international royals and heads of state. The store still holds two royal warrants, but anyone who can afford it can commission their own bespoke set of china. If such luxury is beyond you, visit anyway for the shop's small museum of plates, either antique or designed for royalty, including some created for Princess Diana's wedding. ⊠ *19 South Audley St., Mayfair* ☎ *020/7499–2823* ⊕ *www.thomasgoode.co.uk* Ⓜ *Green Park.*

FOOD

Charbonnel et Walker

CHOCOLATE | Established in 1875, this master chocolatier's Mayfair shop specializes in traditional handmade chocolates (rose-petal creams and champagne truffles, for example) and has been creating these beautifully packaged, high-quality candies from long before most of today's fashionable brands appeared. Their drinking chocolate—coarsely grated fine chocolate in a tin—is worth carrying home in a suitcase. ⊠ *One The Royal Arcade, 28 Old Bond St., Mayfair* ☎ *020/7318–2075* ⊕ *www.charbonnel.co.uk* Ⓜ *Green Park.*

JEWELRY

Asprey

JEWELRY & WATCHES | The company's "global flagship" store displays exquisite jewelry—as well as silver and leather goods, watches, china, and crystal—in a discreet, very British setting that epitomizes quality, expensive good taste, and hushed comfort. If you're in the market for an immaculate 1930s cigarette case, a silver cocktail shaker, a pair of pavé diamond and sapphire earrings, or a ladylike handbag, you won't likely be disappointed. And, for the really well-heeled, there's custom service available as well (Ringo Starr had a chess set made here). Having been at its original location since 1847 (some 66 years after Asprey was established in 1781), the company celebrated its 240th birthday in 2021 with a move to a new flagship store just around the corner on Bruton Street. ⊠ *36 Bruton St., Mayfair* ☎ *020/7493–6767* ⊕ *www.asprey.com* Ⓜ *Green Park.*

Garrard

JEWELRY & WATCHES | The oldest jewelry house in the world, Garrard has been in business since 1735. Between 1843 and 2007, the company was responsible for the upkeep of the Crown Jewels in the Tower of London and for creating several royal crowns (you can see some on display in the Tower). Today the focus is on precious gems in simple, classic settings, along with silver accessories. Although some collections are definitely contemporary (with items like minimalist hoop earrings or two-finger rings), many of the designs are traditional and impressive—which will be handy should you be in the market for an old-school diamond tiara. ⊠ *24 Albemarle St., Mayfair* ☎ *020/7529–7605* ⊕ *www.garrard. com* Ⓜ *Green Park.*

MEN'S CLOTHING
Alfred Dunhill
MEN'S CLOTHING | For more than 100 years, Dunhill has been synonymous with the most luxurious and sophisticated men's goods, including accessories, briefcases, and superbly tailored clothes. This Georgian mansion, their flagship, also features a barbershop, cellar bar, courtyard restaurant, and bespoke services, where you can order custom-fitted menswear or unique versions of the brand's celebrated leather goods. The smaller, original St. James's shop has been on Jermyn Street since 1906. ⊠ *Bourdon House, 2 Davies St., Mayfair* ☎ *020/3425–7313* ⊕ *www. dunhill.com* Ⓜ *Bond St.*

Gieves & Hawkes
MEN'S CLOTHING | One of the grand men's tailoring houses of Savile Row, this company made its name outfitting British royals who served as officers in the armed forces. The company still supplies custom-made military uniforms, as well as beautifully tailored formal and civilian wear for clients who have included Winston Churchill and Ian Fleming. Prices for a bespoke suit start around £5,000 and made to measure at £1,150, but you can find ready-made versions from around £900 (separates from £200), while a new line of casual wear has several items under £200. Custom-made shoes are also available. ⊠ *1 Savile Row, Mayfair* ☎ *020/7434–2001* ⊕ *www.gievesand-hawkes.com* Ⓜ *Piccadilly Circus.*

Ozwald Boateng
MEN'S CLOTHING | The dapper menswear by Ozwald Boateng (pronounced *bwa*-teng) combines contemporary funky style with traditional Savile Row quality. His made-to-measure suits have been worn by the dandyish likes of Jamie Foxx, Mick Jagger, and Laurence Fishburne, who appreciate the sharp cuts, luxurious fabrics, and occasionally vibrant colors (even the more conservative choices have jacket linings in bright silk). ⊠ *30 Savile Row, Mayfair* ☎ *020/7437–2030* ⊕ *www.ozwald-boateng.co.uk* Ⓜ *Piccadilly Circus.*

SHOES
Rupert Sanderson
SHOES | Designed in London and made in Italy, Sanderson's elegant shoes have been a huge hit in fashion circles with their lavish ornamentation on heels and flats alike. Red-carpet-ready high heels—worn by celebs, including Claire Danes, Nicole Kidman, and Sandra Bullock—come in gorgeous colors and prints; peep toes are signature elements. The high prices reflect the impeccable craftsmanship. ⊠ *19 Bruton Pl., Mayfair* ☎ *07585/708–172* ⊕ *www.rupertsander-son.com* Ⓜ *Bond St., Green Park.*

Marylebone

A favorite of newspaper style sections everywhere, Marylebone High Street forms the heart of Marylebone Village (pronounced *marr*-le-bone), a vibrant, upscale neighborhood that encompasses the squares and streets around High Street and nearby Marylebone Lane. The district took its name from a church dedicated to St. Mary and the *bourne* (another word for "stream") that ran through the original village. Nowadays, it's hard to believe you're just a few blocks north of gaudy Oxford Street as you wander in and out of Marylebone's small shops and boutiques, the best of which include Cadenhead's Whisky Shop and Tasting Room (⊠ *26 Chiltern Street*);

At 221B Baker Street, you can immerse yourself in the world of one Mr. Sherlock Holmes.

La Fromagerie (✉ *2–6 Moxon Street*), an excellent cheese shop; Daunt Books (✉ *Nos. 83–84 Marylebone High Street*), a superlative travel bookshop; and a large farmers' and artisan food market (Sunday 10–2) in a parking lot on Cramer Street, just behind High Street. But some memorable sights await, too, including the best remnant of ancien régime France in London, the fabled Wallace Collection.

⊙ Sights

Lisson Gallery
ART GALLERY | Owner Nicholas Logsdail represents about 50 blue-chip artists, including the minimalist Sol LeWitt and performance artist Marina Abramović, at one of the most respected art galleries in London. The gallery is most associated with New Object sculptors like Anish Kapoor and Richard Deacon, many of whom have won the Turner Prize. There's another branch down the road at 27 Bell Street. ✉ *67 Lisson St., Marylebone* ☎ *020/7724–2739* ⊕ *www.lissongallery.*

com ✉ *Free* ⊙ *Closed Sun. and Mon.* Ⓜ *Edgware Rd., Marylebone.*

Madame Tussauds
OTHER ATTRACTION | **FAMILY** | One of London's busiest tourist attractions, this is nothing less than the world's most famous exhibition of lifelike waxwork models of celebrities. Madame T. learned her craft while making death masks of French Revolution victims, and in 1835 she set up her first show of the famous ones near this spot. While top billing once went to the murderers and ghouls in the Chamber of Horrors, that era has passed and it's the limited exhibitions that feature characters from the Star Wars universe and Marvel movies that now steal the show. ■**TIP**➔ **Beat the crowds by booking timed-entry tickets in advance. You can also buy nondated, "priority access" tickets via the website (at a premium).** ✉ *Marylebone Rd., Regent's Park* ☎ *0871/894–3000* ⊕ *www.madametussauds.com* ✉ *From £30.50 (advance ticket)* Ⓜ *Baker St.*

Sherlock Holmes Museum

OTHER MUSEUM | FAMILY | Outside Baker Street Station, by the Marylebone Road exit, is a 9-foot-high bronze statue of Arthur Conan Doyle's celebrated detective, who "lived" around the corner at number 221B Baker Street—now a museum to all things Sherlock. Inside, Mrs. Hudson, Holmes's housekeeper, guides you into a series of Victorian rooms where the great man lived, worked, and played the violin. It's all carried off with such genuine enthusiasm and attention to detail that you could be forgiven for thinking that Mr. Holmes actually *did* exist. ⊠ *221B Baker St., Regent's Park* ☎ *020/7224–3688* ⊕ *www.sherlock-holmes.co.uk* 🎫 *£15* Ⓜ *Baker St.*

★ The Wallace Collection

ART MUSEUM | FAMILY | With its Great Gallery stunningly refurbished, there's even more reason to visit this exquisite gem of an art gallery—although housing one of the world's finest assemblies of Old Master paintings is reason enough. This glorious collection and the 18th-century mansion in which it's located were bequeathed to the nation by Lady Julie-Amélie-Charlotte Wallace, the widow of Sir Richard Wallace (1818–90). Wallace's father, the 4th Marquess of Hertford, took a house in Paris after the French Revolution and set about snapping up paintings by what were then dangerously unpopular artists.

Frans Hals's *The Laughing Cavalier* is probably the most famous painting here, or perhaps Jean-Honoré Fragonard's *The Swing*. The full list of painters in the collection reads like a "who's who" of classical European art—from Rubens, Rembrandt, and van Dyck to Canaletto, Titian, and Velázquez. English works include paintings by Gainsborough and Turner. There are also fine collections of furniture, porcelain, Renaissance gold, and majolica (15th- and 16th-century Italian tin-glazed pottery). With craft activities, hands-on sessions, and the "Little Draw" drawing workshops, as well as the chance to try on a suit of armor in the "Arms and Armour" collection, there's plenty to keep kids occupied, too.

The conditions of the bequest mean that no part of the collection can leave the building; this is the only place in the world you'll ever be able to see these works. ⊠ *Hertford House, Manchester Sq., Marylebone* ☎ *020/7563–9500* ⊕ *www.wallacecollection.org* 🎫 *Free* Ⓜ *Bond St.*

🍽 Restaurants

If you're looking for something more wallet-friendly than what's on offer in Mayfair, head north to Marylebone, formerly dowdy but now prized for its ultrachic, village-like feel. Here you'll find an array of low-key little cafés, boîtes, and tapas bars, champagne-and-hot-dog joints, and the odd world-class sizzler, offering everything from Moroccan and Spanish to Thai and Japanese.

Chiltern Firehouse

$$$ | ECLECTIC | It can be quite tricky to get into Chiltern Firehouse, but if you do snag a table, you're in for a treat. Set inside a sensationally converted 1888 redbrick fire station, this place sets the bar for glamour-chic dining. **Known for:** slider-style crabmeat "donuts"; legendary buttermilk pancakes; exclusive celeb-heavy crowd. 💲 *Average main: £29* ⊠ *1 Chiltern St., London* ☎ *020/7073–7676 for reservations only* ⊕ *www.chilternfirehouse.com* Ⓜ *Baker St., Bond St.*

Fischer's

$$ | AUSTRIAN | FAMILY | It almost feels like Sigmund Freud or Gustav Klimt might doff their Homburg hats and shuffle into a dark leather banquette at this evocative, early-20th-century–style Viennese neighborhood café on Marylebone High Street. Savor the antique light fittings and distressed wallpaper before diving into a rye *brötchen* (bread roll) sandwich with chopped chicken livers and dill. **Known for:**

decadent strudels and ice cream coupes; evocative turn-of-the-20th-century Old Vienna café decor; some of London's best breaded Wiener schnitzel. $ *Average main: £21* ⊠ *50 Marylebone High St., Marylebone* ☎ *020/7466–5501* ⊕ *www. fischers.co.uk* Ⓜ *Baker St., Bond St.*

The Golden Hind
$ | **SEAFOOD** | **FAMILY** | You'll land some of the best fish-and-chips in town at this British chippy in a retro 1914 art deco café. Marylebone locals and satisfied tourists alike hunker down for the neatly prepared and decidedly nongreasy deep-fried or steamed battered cod, haddock, and plaice; the classic hand-cut Maris Piper chips; and the traditional mushy peas and homemade tartar sauce. **Known for:** huge portions; some of the city's best deep-fried battered cod and chips; hard-to-find traditional mushy peas. $ *Average main: £14* ⊠ *71A–73 Marylebone La., Marylebone* ☎ *020/7486–3644* ⊕ *www. goldenhindrestaurant.com* ☉ *Closed Sun. No lunch Sat.* Ⓜ *Bond St.*

Les 110 de Taillevent
$$$ | **FRENCH** | Dazzling classic French dishes mark out Les 110 de Taillevent as the city's top French *brasserie de luxe.* Housed in a chic former Coutts bank on Cavendish Square, diners and oenophiles delight in the exquisite cuisine and accompanying master list of 110 fine wines by the glass. **Known for:** haunt for wine experts and merchants; soaring traditional dining salon; brilliant list of paired fine wines by the glass. $ *Average main: £28* ⊠ *16 Cavendish Sq., Marylebone* ☎ *020/3141–6016* ⊕ *www.les-110-taillevent-london.com* ☉ *Closed Sun. and Mon.* Ⓜ *Bond St., Oxford Circus.*

The Monocle Café
$ | **CAFÉ** | As the name suggests, The Monocle Café isn't quite a restaurant, but thanks to its sheer weight of personality, it still lends itself as an important Marylebone food stop. Salads, bagels, open sandwiches, and breakfasts represent a diverse menu of international

bites that can always be accompanied by something from the drink menu, whether that's artisan coffee or something stronger like the yuzu gin and tonic. **Known for:** in-house pop-up shop; serious intellectual credentials (it's run by Monocle magazine); excellent snacks and takeaway treats. $ *Average main: £8* ⊠ *18 Chiltern St., Marylebone* ☎ *0020207/7135–2040* ⊕ *cafe.monocle.com* Ⓜ *Baker Street.*

🛏 Hotels

★ Dorset Square Hotel
$$$ | **HOTEL** | This fashionable boutique hotel occupies a charming old town house in one of London's most upscale neighborhoods. **Pros:** good Afternoon Tea; ideal location; lovely design. **Cons:** no gym; no bathtub in some rooms; some rooms are small. $ *Rooms from: £252* ⊠ *39 Dorset Sq., Marylebone* ☎ *020/7723–7874* ⊕ *www.firmdalehotels.com* ⤴ *38 rooms* 🍽 *No Meals* Ⓜ *Baker St.*

Holmes Hotel
$$$ | **HOTEL** | Named in honor of the fictional detective who had his home on Baker Street, rooms here have a masculine edge with plenty of nods to Mr. Holmes himself (along with hypermodern bathrooms stocked with fluffy bathrobes). **Pros:** fun literary theme that doesn't go overboard; chic decor; fun bar on-site. **Cons:** rooms on the small side; street noise reaches rooms that could be more soundproof; have to walk through the bar to get to reception. $ *Rooms from: £260* ⊠ *83 Chiltern St., Marylebone* ☎ *0333/400–6138* ⊕ *www.holmeshotel.com* ⤴ *118 rooms* 🍽 *No Meals* Ⓜ *Baker St.*

Hyatt Regency London—The Churchill
$$$ | **HOTEL** | Even though it's one of London's largest hotels, The Churchill is always abuzz with guests smiling at the perfection they find here, including warmly personalized service and calmly alluring guest rooms. **Pros:** central location; comfortable and stylish; great dining and drinking, including a bottomless

brunch. **Cons:** prices are steep; lots of renovations going on; feels more geared to business than leisure travelers. Ⓢ *Rooms from: £369* ✉ *30 Portman Sq., Marylebone* ☎ *020/7486–5800* ⊕ *www.hyatt.com/en-US/hotel/england-united-kingdom/hyatt-regency-london-the-churchill/lonch* ⌁ *440 rooms* ⦿ *No Meals* Ⓜ *Marble Arch.*

The Landmark London

$$$ | **HOTEL** | A glass-covered, eight-story atrium sets the scene at this truly grand hotel, where the huge bedrooms are richly furnished and have marble bathrooms; odd-numbered rooms overlook the Winter Garden restaurant beneath the glass roof. **Pros:** good discounts are available; amazingly luxurious; one of the few really posh London hotels that doesn't make you dress up. **Cons:** the spa can get busy; the stunning atrium is usually filled with Instagrammers; two-night minimum stay at certain times. Ⓢ *Rooms from: £320* ✉ *222 Marylebone Rd., Marylebone* ☎ *020/7631–8000* ⊕ *www.landmarklondon.co.uk* ⌁ *346 rooms* ⦿ *No Meals* Ⓜ *Marylebone.*

The Marylebone

$$$ | **HOTEL** | Capitalizing on its location in central London's most intimate, village-like neighborhood, The Marylebone features contemporary designer rooms and drinking and dining options that match the boutique elements of its surroundings. **Pros:** two penthouse suites come with stunning rooftop terraces; lively location in the heart of Marylebone; access to the in-house Third Space gym and spa with pool. **Cons:** guests share the spa with non-guest users; surrounding streets get busy, especially in summer; prices are high for the smaller standard rooms. Ⓢ *Rooms from: £375* ✉ *47 Welbeck St., Marylebone* ☎ *020/7486–6600* ⊕ *www.doylecollection.com/hotels/the-marylebone-hotel* ⌁ *250 rooms* ⦿ *No Meals* Ⓜ *Bond St.*

The Sumner

$$ | **HOTEL** | You can feel yourself relaxing the minute you enter this elegant Georgian town house. **Pros:** great value; excellent location for shopping; small enough that the staff know your name. **Cons:** street noise can be a minor issue; some rooms are small; services are limited. Ⓢ *Rooms from: £140* ✉ *54 Upper Berkley St., Marble Arch, Marylebone* ☎ *020/7723–2244* ⊕ *www.thesumner.com* ⌁ *20 rooms* ⦿ *Free Breakfast* Ⓜ *Marble Arch.*

★ **The Zetter Townhouse Marylebone**

$$$ | **HOTEL** | No matter how hip the crowd here gets, the clientele is never likely to distract from the sumptuous decor of this boutique hotel that is equal parts Tudor-style and Georgian flair, with a pinch of steampunk for good measure. **Pros:** gorgeous rooms that feel like you're on a movie set; beautiful interior design; cocktail bar that makes repeat visits a must. **Cons:** neighborhood can be too quiet on weekends; prices are high considering the amenities; atmosphere can feel too trendy at times. Ⓢ *Rooms from: £320* ✉ *28–30 Seymour St., Marylebone* ☎ *020/7324–4544* ⊕ *www.thezettertownhouse.com/marylebone* ⌁ *24 rooms* ⦿ *No Meals* Ⓜ *Marylebone.*

🎭 Performing Arts

CLASSICAL MUSIC

★ **Wigmore Hall**

CONCERTS | **FAMILY** | London's most beautiful venue for chamber music also happens to boast near-perfect acoustics. The hall has a rich history, including hosting the premieres of a number of works by the British composer Benjamin Britten, and today attracts leading ensembles from all over the world. The varied program contains lunchtime and Sunday morning concerts plus workshops, as well as concerts for babies and toddlers. ✉ *36 Wigmore St., Marylebone* ☎ *020/7935–2141* ⊕ *www.wigmore-hall.org.uk* ⌁ *From £18* Ⓜ *Bond St.*

⬤ Shopping

ANTIQUES

Alfies Antique Market

ANTIQUES & COLLECTIBLES | This four-story, bohemian-chic labyrinth is London's largest indoor antiques market, housing more than 75 dealers specializing in art, lighting, glassware, textiles, jewelry, furniture, and collectibles, with a particular strength in vintage clothing and 20th-century design. Come here to pick up vintage (1900–70) clothing, accessories, and luggage from Tin Tin Collectables; antique and vintage glassware and vases at Robinson Antiques; or a spectacular mid-20th-century Italian lighting fixture at Vincenzo Caffarella. The atmosphere may be funky, but the prices are not. There's also a rooftop café with free Wi-Fi if you need a coffee break. In addition to the market, this end of Church Street is lined with excellent antiques shops. ✉ *13–25 Church St., Marylebone* ☎ *020/7723–6066* ⊕ *www.alfiesantiques. com* Ⓜ *Marylebone.*

BOOKS

★ Daunt Books

BOOKS | An independent bookstore chain (there are additional branches in Belsize Park, Chelsea, Hampstead, Holland Park, and Cheapside), Daunt favors a thoughtful selection of contemporary and classic fiction and nonfiction. The striking Marylebone branch is an original Edwardian bookstore, where a dramatic room with a long oak-paneled gallery under lofty skylights houses the noted travel section, which includes not only guidebooks but also related literature and poetry. The Hampstead branch is strong on children's books. ✉ *83 Marylebone High St., Marylebone* ☎ *020/7224–2295* ⊕ *www.dauntbooks.co.uk* Ⓜ *Baker St.*

CLOTHING

Matches Fashion

MIXED CLOTHING | This carefully curated boutique carries fashion from a selection of 400 designers both rising and established, including Christopher Kane, Erdem, J. W. Anderson, Proenza Schouler, Vetements, McCartney, McQueen, Balenciaga, Balmain, Valentino, Saint Laurent, Marni, and Duro Olowu. There's also an equally stylish menswear department, plus jewelry, lingerie, footwear, and accessories. Other branches can be found in Mayfair and Wimbledon. ✉ *87 Marylebone High St., Marylebone* ☎ *020/7487–5400* ⊕ *www.matchesfashion.com* Ⓜ *Regent's Park, Baker St.*

Reiss

MIXED CLOTHING | With an in-house design team whose experience includes stints at Gucci and Calvin Klein and customers like Beyoncé and the Duchess of Cambridge, who wore a Reiss dress for her official engagement picture, this reliable chain brings luxury standards of tailoring and details to mass-market womens- and menswear. The sleek and contemporary style doesn't come cheap, but does offer value for money. There are branches in Knightsbridge, The City, Covent Garden, Chelsea, Hampstead, Islington, Soho, Kensington, and basically all over London. ✉ *10 Barrett St., Marylebone* ☎ *020/7486–6557* ⊕ *www.reiss.com* Ⓜ *Oxford St.*

DEPARTMENT STORES

Marks & Spencer

DEPARTMENT STORE | You'd be hard-pressed to find a Brit who doesn't have something in the closet from Marks & Spencer (or M&S, as it's popularly known). This major chain is famed for its classic dependable clothing for men, women, and children—affordable cashmere and lamb's wool sweaters are particularly good buys—and occasionally scores a fashion hit. The food department at

M&S is consistently good, especially for frozen food, and a great place to pick up a sandwich or premade salad on the go (look for M&S Simply Food stores all over town). The flagship branch at Marble Arch and the Pantheon location at 173 Oxford Street have extensive fashion departments. ⊠ *458 Oxford St., Marylebone* ☎ *020/7935–7954* ⊕ *www.marksandspencer.com* Ⓜ *Marble Arch.*

★ **Selfridges**

DEPARTMENT STORE | This giant bustling store (the second largest in the United Kingdom after Harrods) gives Harvey Nichols a run for its money as London's most fashionable department store. Packed to the rafters with clothes ranging from mid-price lines to the latest catwalk names, the store continues to break ground with its innovative retail schemes, especially the ground-floor Wonder Room (for extravagant jewelry and luxury watches), a dedicated Denim Studio, a Fragrance Bar where you can create custom perfume, an array of pop-ups ranging from spaces for designers such as Jil Sander to a healthy shot bar (if you need some colloidal silver to keep you going) or a collaboration with boutique boxing club BXR. The giant accessories hall has miniboutiques dedicated to top-end designers such as Chanel, Gucci, and Vuitton, while the new Corner Shop offers U.K.-theme gifts and souvenirs at all price points.

There are so many zones that merge into one another—from youth-oriented Miss Selfridge to audio equipment to the large, comprehensive cosmetics department—that you practically need a map. Don't miss the Shoe Galleries, the world's largest shoe department, which is filled with more than 5,000 pairs from 120 brands, displayed like works of art under spotlights. Take a break with a glass of wine at the rooftop restaurant or pick up some tea in the Food Hall as a gift. ⊠ *400 Oxford St., Marylebone* ☎ *020/7160–2222* ⊕ *www.selfridges.com* Ⓜ *Bond St.*

JEWELRY

Kabiri

JEWELRY & WATCHES | A carefully curated array of exciting contemporary jewelry by emerging and established designers from around the world is packed into this small shop. There is something to suit most budgets and tastes, though understated minimalism predominates. You can score an elegant, one-of-a-kind piece here for a very reasonable price. ⊠ *94 Marylebone La., Marylebone* ☎ *020/7317–2150* ⊕ *www.kabiri.co.uk* Ⓜ *Baker St.*

Chapter 5

SOHO AND COVENT GARDEN

Updated by
Alex Wijeratna

● Sights	🏛 Restaurants	🛏 Hotels	🛍 Shopping	🍸 Nightlife
★★★☆☆	★★★★☆	★★☆☆☆	★★★☆☆	★★★★★

SOHO AND COVENT GARDEN SNAPSHOT

TOP REASONS TO GO

Newburgh Quarter: Head to this adorable warren of cobblestone streets for stylish boutiques, edgy stores, and young indie upstarts.

Dining: London has fallen in love with its chefs, and Soho is home to many of the most talked-about restaurants in town.

Covent Garden Piazza: Eliza Doolittle's former backyard has been taken over by boutiques and street performers who play to the crowds from morning to night.

Royal Opera House: Even if you're not going to the opera or ballet, take in the beautiful architecture and sense of history.

West End theater: Shaftesbury Avenue is the heart of London's theater district, where more than 50 West End venues pull in the crowds with a mix of extravagant musicals, plays, and performances.

GETTING THERE

Almost all Tube lines cross the Covent Garden and Soho areas, so it's easy to hop off for dinner or a show in one of the hippest parts of London. For Soho, take any train to Piccadilly Circus, Leicester Square, Oxford Circus, or Tottenham Court Road. For Covent Garden, get off at Covent Garden Station on the Piccadilly line. (It may be easier to exit the Tube at Leicester Square or Holborn and walk.) Thirty buses connect to the Covent Garden area from all over London; check out the area's website (⊕ *www. coventgarden.london*).

MAKING THE MOST OF YOUR TIME

■ You can comfortably tour all the sights around Soho and Covent Garden in a day. Make sure to leave plenty of time to watch street entertainment or shop at the stalls around Covent Garden Piazza or in the fashion boutiques of Soho in the afternoon. Save some energy for a night on the town in Soho.

LGBTQ+ LONDON

■ Old Compton Street in Soho is the historical epicenter of London's proud, stylish, and flamboyant LGBTQ+ scene. There are some fun and outrageous nightclubs and drinking dens in the area, with crowds forming in Soho Square, south of Oxford Street. Some of the more well-known clubs and bars in the area include The Friendly Society, Ku Bar, and She.

A red-light district no more, today's Soho is more stylish than seedy and offers some of London's best bars, live music, restaurants, and theaters. By day, this hotbed of film and media production reverts to the business side of its renowned late-night scene. If Soho is all about showbiz, neighboring Covent Garden is devoted to culture. Both districts offer an abundance of narrow Georgian and Victorian streets packed with one-off shops and oodles of historic character.

Soho

Soho, which, along with Covent Garden, is now loosely known as the "West End" has long been known as the entertainment and arts quarter of London's center. Bordered by Oxford Street to the north, Regent Street to the west, and Chinatown and Leicester Square to the south, the narrow Georgian streets of Soho are unabashedly devoted to pleasure. Wardour Street bisects the neighborhood, with tons of interesting boutiques and some of London's best-value restaurants to the west (especially around Foubert's Place and on Brewer and Lexington streets). Most nightlife lies to the east—including the LGBTQ+ clubs on or near Old Compton Street—and beyond that is the city's densest collection of theaters, on Shaftesbury Avenue. London's compact Chinatown is wedged between Soho and Leicester Square. A bit of erudition surfaces to the east of the square on Charing Cross Road, famous for its secondhand bookshops, and on tiny Cecil Court, a pedestrianized passage lined with small antiquarian booksellers and curiosity shops specializing in vintage film posters, first editions, and West End theaterland paraphernalia.

Sights

★ Newburgh Quarter

PEDESTRIAN MALL | FAMILY | Want to see the hip style of today's London? Find it one block east of famed Carnaby Street—where the look of the '60s "Swinging London" was born—an adorable warren of cobblestone streets now lined with specialty boutiques and edgy stores. A check of the ingredients

A Brief History of Soho

Almost as soon as a 17th-century housing development covered what had been Henry VIII's royal hunting grounds, Soho (named after wealthy local landowner the Duke of Monmouth's "So Ho!" battle cry at the Battle of Sedgemoor in 1685) earned a reputation for louche living, bohemianism, and cosmopolitan liberality. When the authorities adopted a zero-tolerance policy toward soliciting in 1991 (the most recent of several attempts to end Soho's sex trade), they cracked down on an enduring neighborhood vice that has continually resurfaced throughout the ages.

Briefly popular with the aristocracy, successive waves of foreign refugees—French Huguenots in the 1680s, followed by Germans, Russians, Jews, Poles, Greeks, Italians, and Chinese—settled here and brought their skills, trades, and national cuisines with them. When dining out became popular after World War I, Soho was the natural place for cafés and restaurants to flourish (as they continue to do today).

Among the luminaries who have made Soho home are landscape painter John Constable; the womanizer Casanova; Canaletto, the great painter of Venice; the visionary poet William Blake; and political theorist Karl Marx. In the 1950s and '60s, densely packed Soho was London's artists' (and gangsters') quarter and the place to find jazz clubs, dance halls, and bordellos.

Nearby, the outlines of present-day Covent Garden took shape in the 1630s, when architect Inigo Jones turned what had been agricultural land into Britain's first planned public square. After the Great Fire of 1666, it became the site of England's largest fruit and vegetable market (the flower market arrived in the 19th century). The district's many theaters, taverns, and coffee shops gave the area a rowdy reputation, and after the produce market relocated in 1973, the surviving buildings were set for demolition. A local campaign saved them, and the restored market opened in 1980 and continues to thrive spectacularly to this day.

reveals one part '60s London, one part futuristic fetishism, one part steampunk, and one part London street swagger. The New Bohemian look best flourishes in shops like Raeburn, an ethical boutique crowded with fashion mavens who dig Raeburn's reworked 1950s Yugoslav military camouflage puffer coats, joggers, and hoodies. Quality coffee shops abound—take a break at Department of Coffee and Social Affairs, where you can also browse for home coffee-making equipment. ✉ *Newburgh St., Foubert's Pl., Marshall St., and Carnaby St., Soho* ⊕ *www.carnaby.co.uk* Ⓜ *Oxford Circus, Tottenham Court Rd.*

★ **The Photographers' Gallery**
ART GALLERY | FAMILY | London's first gallery dedicated to photography offers cutting-edge and provocative exhibitions. Open since 1980, the space has shown everyone from Robert Capa and Sebastião Salgado to Nick Knight and Corinne Day. The prestigious Deutsche Börse Photography Foundation Prize is exhibited and awarded here annually. The gallery also has a print salesroom, an archive, a well-stocked bookstore, and a nice café-bar—a great spot to chat photography and escape the mania of nearby Oxford Circus. ✉ *16–18 Ramillies St., Soho* ☎ *020/7087–9300* ⊕ *www.*

thephotographersgallery.org.uk 🎟 *£2.50–£5* ⏲ *Closed Mon.* [M] *Oxford Circus, Tottenham Court Rd.*

Sadie Coles HQ
ART GALLERY | Showcasing the work of important British and international artists such as Sarah Lucas and Martine Syms, this all-white and light-filled art space overlooking busy Regent Street is a major expansion for respected British gallerist Sadie Coles. A second Sadie Coles exhibition space operates nearby at Davies Street in Mayfair, while a third is also close, found on Bury Street in St. James's. ✉ *62 Kingly St., Soho* ☎ *020/7493–8611* 🌐 *www.sadiecoles.com* ⏲ *Closed Sun. and Mon.* [M] *Oxford Circus, Piccadilly Circus.*

🍴 Restaurants

Soho and Covent Garden are the city's historic playground and pleasure zone, an all-day, all-night jostling neon wonderland of glitz, glamour, grime, and greasepaint. This area is London's cultural heart, with old and new media companies, late-night dive bars, cabaret, street performers, West End musicals, and world-class theater, ballet, and opera. Rising rents have forced out many of Soho's seedier red-light businesses and ushered in edgier, top-notch restaurants. Just follow your nose in Covent Garden, Chinatown, and Theatreland to find copious and increasingly excellent options for pre- and post-theater dining.

Andrew Edmunds
$$ | **MEDITERRANEAN** | Candlelit at night, with a haunting Dickensian vibe, Andrew Edmunds is a permanently packed, old-school Soho dining institution. Tucked away behind Carnaby Street in an 18th-century town house, it's a cozy favorite whose unpretentious and keenly priced dishes draw on the tastes of Ireland, the Mediterranean, and the Middle East. **Known for:** bargains galore on the acclaimed wine list; deeply romantic, Georgian-era town house setting; unpretentious daily changing handwritten menus. [$] *Average main: £19* ✉ *46 Lexington St., Soho* ☎ *020/7437–5708* 🌐 *www.andrewedmunds.com* [M] *Oxford Circus, Piccadilly Circus.*

★ **Bancone**
$ | **ITALIAN** | **FAMILY** | Fabulous fresh pasta at affordable prices characterizes this groovy Italian eatery off Soho's Golden Square. Sit at the bustling chef's counter to sample options like bucatini cacio e pepe or pork, fennel, and 'nduja ragù with twirly ribbons of mafalde pasta. **Known for:** upbeat atmosphere; Instagram-famous "silk handkerchiefs" sheets of pasta with confit egg yolk; top-value pasta dishes from 20 Italian regions. [$] *Average main: £14* ✉ *8-10 Lower James St., Soho* ☎ *020/3034–0820* 🌐 *www.bancone.co.uk* [M] *Piccadilly Circus, Oxford Circus.*

BAO
$ | **TAIWANESE** | **FAMILY** | Lines form daily to secure a prized seat, perch, or stool at this no-reservations 32-seater from a crack team of Taiwanese steamed bao bun specialists. The gloriously plump milk-based, rice flour bao buns—stuffed with organic Cornish braised pork, peanut powder, and fermented greens—are the undisputed stars of the show. **Known for:** bao bun with Horlicks ice cream for dessert; long lines for the steamed, stuffed Taiwanese bao buns; highly Instagram-able pig's blood cake. [$] *Average main: £9* ✉ *53 Lexington St., Soho* 🌐 *www.baolondon.com* ⏲ *No dinner Sun.* [M] *Oxford Circus, Piccadilly Circus, Tottenham Court Rd.*

★ **Bar Italia**
$ | **ITALIAN** | **FAMILY** | This legendary Italian coffee bar on Frith Street is Soho's unofficial beating heart and a 22-hours-a-day classic institution. Established in 1949 during the postwar Italian coffee bar craze and still run by the founding Polledri family, today most regulars grab an espresso or cappuccino made from the vintage Gaggia coffee machine, and wolf

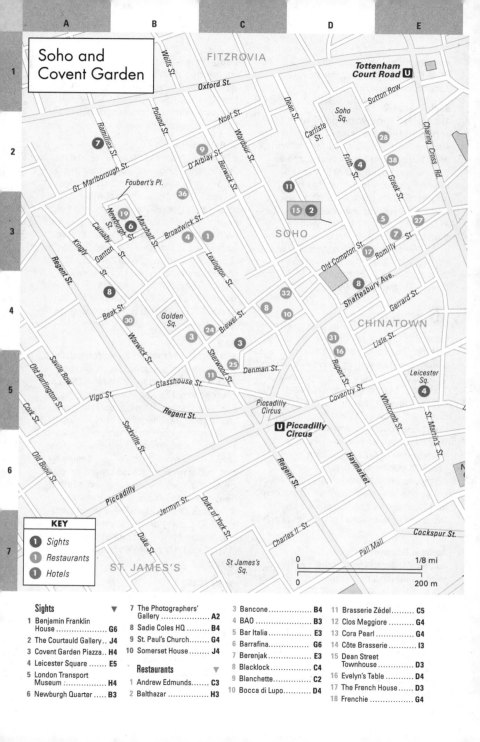

Soho and Covent Garden

FITZROVIA

Tottenham Court Road U

SOHO

CHINATOWN

ST. JAMES'S

Piccadilly Circus

Leicester Sq.

Soho Sq.

St James's Sq.

KEY
- Sights
- Restaurants
- Hotels

0 — 1/8 mi
0 — 200 m

Sights

1 Benjamin Franklin House **G6**
2 The Courtauld Gallery .. **J4**
3 Covent Garden Piazza... **H4**
4 Leicester Square **E5**
5 London Transport Museum **H4**
6 Newburgh Quarter **B3**
7 The Photographers' Gallery **A2**
8 Sadie Coles HQ **B4**
9 St. Paul's Church........ **G4**
10 Somerset House **J4**

Restaurants

1 Andrew Edmunds....... **C3**
2 Balthazar **H3**
3 Bancone **B4**
4 BAO **B3**
5 Bar Italia **E3**
6 Barrafina............... **G6**
7 Berenjak **E3**
8 Blacklock **C4**
9 Blanchette............. **C2**
10 Bocca di Lupo........... **D4**
11 Brasserie Zédel......... **C5**
12 Clos Maggiore **G4**
13 Cora Pearl **G4**
14 Côte Brasserie **I3**
15 Dean Street Townhouse **D3**
16 Evelyn's Table **D4**
17 The French House **D3**
18 Frenchie **G4**

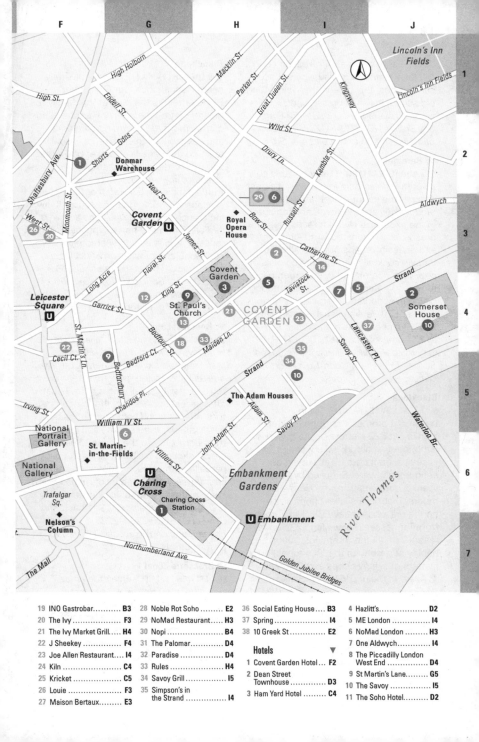

down a snack at the mirrored bar counter. **Known for:** sturdy sausage or bacon sandwiches; tiny hole-in-the-wall setting; old-school Italian espresso and sliced pizza. $ *Average main: £8* ✉ *22 Frith St., Soho* ☎ *020/7734–4737* ⊕ *www. baritaliasoho.co.uk* Ⓜ *Leicester Sq.*

★ **Berenjak**

$$ | **MIDDLE EASTERN** | **FAMILY** | At this cult favorite Persian hole-in-the-wall, it's best to sit at the counter overlooking the tandoor grill and clay oven and indulge in the expansive meze spreads, sesame breads, and marinated lamb, chicken, and poussin kebabs. You can also sip Persian cocktails and sharbat cordials in cozy side booths and in the green backroom snug. **Known for:** sociable outdoor dining in spring/summer; celeb sightings; popular £20 Persian kebab specials for Friday lunches. $ *Average main: £19* ✉ *27 Romilly St., Soho* ☎ *020/3319–8120* ⊕ *www.berenjaklondon.com* ◔ *Closed Sun.* Ⓜ *Tottenham Court Rd, Oxford Circus, Piccadilly Circus.*

Blacklock

$ | **STEAKHOUSE** | **FAMILY** | Set in a former basement brothel, this Soho meatopia cranks out £22 platters of chargrilled lamb, beef, and pork skinny chops and juice-soaked flatbread, all served on antique pearlware. Supplied by Philip Warren butchers from the Cornwall moors, Blacklock's killer chops sizzle on the grill under heavy Blacklock irons from Tennessee. **Known for:** £22 Sunday roasts with all the trimmings; young and bubbly service with top '80s tunes; huge platters of skinny chops and flatbread. $ *Average main: £15* ✉ *The Basement, 24 Great Windmill St., Soho* ☎ *020/3441–6996* ⊕ *www.theblacklock.com/restaurants/blacklock-soho* ◔ *No dinner Sun.* Ⓜ *Piccadilly Circus, Oxford Circus.*

Blanchette

$$ | **FRENCH** | **FAMILY** | French tapas may sound sacrilegious, but Gallic gem Blanchette hits the spot at this family-run hipster bistro where jazzy French sounds complement the charming bare-brick and oak table candlelit interior. Visually feast on the Paris flea market bric-a-brac and then order a host of small plates to share, like the crispy frogs' legs and truffle *saucisson* (sausage) or baked scallops with Café de Paris sauce. **Known for:** crunchy French frogs' legs and wild sea bass with sea herbs; unusual French tapas-style dishes and shared plates; cool Soho crowd with romantic, jazzy soundtrack. $ *Average main: £20* ✉ *9 D'Arblay St., Soho* ☎ *020/7439–8100* ⊕ *www.blanchettesoho.co.uk* Ⓜ *Tottenham Court Rd, Oxford Circus.*

★ **Bocca di Lupo**

$$ | **ITALIAN** | This upscale Italian institution is always crowded and the tables are crammed too close together, but everyone still adores the glorious spread of regional Italian small plates here. Located off Shaftesbury Avenue, the famous trattoria offers magnificent peasant-based pasta, stews, fritti, salumi, and raw crudi from Lombardy to the Veneto. **Known for:** crowd-pleasing Sicilian lobster and pappardelle with venison ragù; open chef's counter serving a medley of rustic Italian small plates; exceptional all-Italian wine list. $ *Average main: £22* ✉ *12 Archer St., Soho* ☎ *020/7734–2223* ⊕ *www. boccadilupo.com* Ⓜ *Piccadilly Circus, Oxford Circus.*

★ **Brasserie Zédel**

$$ | **FRENCH** | **FAMILY** | Enjoy the amazing-value, prix-fixe menus of classic French dishes at Piccadilly's ever-bustling subterranean Parisian-style brasserie. Dripping with beaux-arts gilt mirrors and monumental marble pillars, you can enjoy French standards like steak haché, choucroute, Niçoise salad, and

crème brûlee. **Known for:** nightly live music, cabaret, comedy, and burlesque; London's largest and most spectacular beaux-arts basement brasserie; fantastically cheap set-meal deals. $ *Average main: £18* ✉ *20 Sherwood St., Piccadilly Circus* ☎ *020/7734–4888* ⊕ *www.brasseriezedel.com* Ⓜ *Piccadilly Circus, Oxford Circus.*

Dean Street Townhouse

$$$ | **BRITISH** | **FAMILY** | Everyone feels 10 times more glamorous just stepping inside this candlelit restaurant attached to the swanky Georgian-era hotel of the same name. Straightforward but fun retro-British favorites include pea and ham soup, primary school–style mince and potatoes, smoked haddock soufflé, and tasty sherry trifle. **Known for:** cheery Afternoon and High Teas; classy candlelit dining salon with British art on the walls; highly professional service. $ *Average main: £24* ✉ *69–70 Dean St., Soho* ☎ *020/7434–1775* ⊕ *www.deanstreettownhouse.com* ☾ *No dinner Sun.* Ⓜ *Oxford Circus, Tottenham Court Rd.*

★ **Evelyn's Table**

$$$ | **JAPANESE** | Hidden beneath The Blue Posts pub in Chinatown, you'll find an intimate speakeasy vibe at Evelyn's Table, specializing in set tasting menus based on top British produce, Japanese technique, and classical French training. A secret door with a peephole reveals a small but passionate chef's kitchen counter where the three Selby brother chefs serve dishes like barbecued monkfish dashi or hand-dived Devon scallop sashimi. **Known for:** superb soundtracks curated by ex-DJ and current co-owner Layo Paskin; secret and cozy beer cellar venue; wonderfully fresh Cornish day-boat fish and bivalves. $ *Average main: £26* ✉ *The Blue Posts, 28 Rupert St., Soho* ☎ ⊕ *www.theblueposts.co.uk/evelyns-table* ☾ *Closed Sun. and Mon.* Ⓜ *Piccadilly Circus, Leicester Sq.*

★ **The French House**

$$$ | **FRENCH** | Black-and-white photos of legendary The French House regulars like artists Francis Bacon and Lucian Freud beam down at this disarmingly charming old-school Soho hangout. Set on the first floor of the famous pub of the same name and run by a former cabaret artist, you can sip Ricard pastis or bargains from the all-French wine list before embracing superb French classics like salt cod beignets, calves brain with brown butter, or slow-braised navarin of lamb with *aligot* mash (cheese-blended potatoes). **Known for:** no music, no phone, and no laptops policy; storied home to Soho's actors, artists, and bohemians; French classics like whole roast garlic bulb on toast. $ *Average main: £24* ✉ *49 Dean St., Soho* ☎ *020/7437–2477* ⊕ *www.frenchhousesoho.com* ☾ *Closed Sun. and Mon. No dinner Sat.* Ⓜ *Piccadilly Circus, Leicester Sq., Tottenham Court Rd.*

★ **INO Gastrobar**

$ | **GREEK** | London's modern Greek food scene is flourishing, and tiny INO Gastrobar on cobblestoned Newburgh Street is leading the charge. Take a seat at the chef's counter overlooking the charcoal grill and enjoy beautifully updated dishes, such as a deconstructed traditional *kakavia* (Greek fisherman's stew)—which arrives as grouper sashimi with a dipping bowl of fish broth—and other standouts, like sliced soy and olive oil tuna *tataki* topped with charred green beans and shimeji mushrooms. **Known for:** all-Greek wine list; modernized and deconstructed takes on traditional Greek favorites; chargrilled lamb chops, octopus tacos, and spanakopita (spinach/feta pie). $ *Average main: £13* ✉ *4 Newburgh St., Soho* ⊕ *www.inogastrobar.com* ☾ *Mon.* Ⓜ *Oxford Circus, Tottenham Court Rd.*

★ **Kiln**

$ | THAI | Earthy northern Thai cuisine bursts out of the charcoal-fired kiln and hot clay pots at this barbecue-focused wonderland in Soho. Take a look at the tiny open kitchen and you'll see sizzling cumin-dusted hogget skewers and chargrilled chicken thigh bites, along with other Thai village-style dishes that show influences from Laos, Myanmar, and the Yunnan province of China. **Known for:** popular cumin-dusted aged hogget skewers; open-kitchen setup with charcoal grill and hot clay pots; array of Cornish-grown Thai, Burmese, and other Asian herbs and spices. [$] *Average main: £11* ✉ *58 Brewer St., Soho* ☎ 🌐 *www.kilnsoho.com* [M] *Oxford Circus, Piccadilly Circus.*

Kricket

$ | INDIAN | FAMILY | Large dishes of Indian street food fly from the open kitchen at this Piccadilly party spot. Sit at the L-shape, lava-topped counter and watch the chefs haul out bone marrow–smeared *kulcha* (flatbreads) from the blazing clay tandoor alongside a heap of other funky dishes. **Known for:** hip, young crowds; pepped-up Indian street food faves; colonial cocktails in the raucous downstairs dining den. [$] *Average main: £14* ✉ *12 Denman St., Soho* ☎ *020/3019–8120* 🌐 *www.kricket.co.uk/soho* 🕒 *Closed Sun.* [M] *Piccadilly Circus, Oxford Circus.*

★ **Maison Bertaux**

$ | CAFÉ | FAMILY | Romantics and Francophiles cherish this quirky 1871 French patisserie, vintage tea parlor, and occasional pop-up art space, where nothing seems to have changed since the 1940s. Colorful pastries, tarts, croissants, and sweet cakes are well loved and baked on-site. **Known for:** old-fashioned collection of creamy French pastries; mesmerizing vintage French interiors; retro Afternoon Tea. [$] *Average main: £8* ✉ *28 Greek St., Soho* ☎ *020/7437–6007* 🌐 *www.maisonbertaux.com* [M] *Leicester Sq.*

★ **Noble Rot Soho**

$$$$ | FRENCH | Fans of French food and wine flock to this gorgeous wood-paneled Georgian town house for dishes like roast chicken with morel mushrooms and creamy *vin jaune* sauce along with the wonderful 28-page French-focused wine menu. Dark oak floors, brass lights, and cut-crystal glass decanters help oenophiles bliss out on one of London's finest and surprisingly most accessible wine lists, with numerous rare gems available by the glass. **Known for:** incredible wine selection; boisterous atmosphere; bargain £22 three-course set lunches. [$] *Average main: £35* ✉ *2 Greek St., Soho* ☎ *020/7183–8190* 🌐 *www.noblerot.co.uk/soho-restaurant* 🕒 *Closed Sun.* [M] *Tottenham Court Rd, Oxford Circus.*

Nopi

$$ | MODERN ISRAELI | FAMILY | Israeli-born star chef and global cookbook sensation Yotam Ottolenghi cleans up at his flagship vegetable-centric restaurant on the edge of Soho. Mixing densely flavored small dishes from the Middle East, Asia, and the Mediterranean, diners here can jump around from courgette (zucchini) and manouri cheese fritters to harissa-marinated octopus and Persian love rice to carob and coconut ice cream. **Known for:** popular shakshuka and scrambled tofu–laden breakfasts; vegetable-focused classics like roast eggplant, pomegranate seeds, and feta yogurt; healthy offerings like rainbow trout with koji and sheep's labneh. [$] *Average main: £21* ✉ *21–22 Warwick St., Soho* ☎ *020/7494–9584* 🌐 *www.ottolenghi.co.uk/restaurants/nopi* [M] *Oxford Circus, Piccadilly Circus.*

★ **The Palomar**

$$ | MIDDLE EASTERN | It's Jerusalem meets Palestine meets Beirut at this funky Israeli-Arab spot off Chinatown. Sit at the zinc open kitchen counter and down shots of arak while trading quips with the brilliant Middle Eastern chefs, who offer an exuberant medley of Levantine delights, including Yemeni Jewish *kubaneh* (a light, fluffy pull-apart bread), Palestinian steak tartare, Jerusalem truffled mushroom polenta, and paprika-rich pork belly tajine with Israeli couscous. **Known for:** popular Persian oxtail stew and sumac-rich fattoush salad; fun Middle Eastern party atmosphere and free arak shots; lively chefs at the open kitchen counter. $ *Average main: £16* ✉ *34 Rupert St., Soho* ☎ *020/7439–8777* 🌐 *www.thepalomar.co.uk* [M] *Piccadilly Circus, Leicester Sq.*

★ Paradise

$ | SRI LANKAN | FAMILY | London's top contemporary Sri Lankan spot dazzles with fiery deviled prawns, Aylesbury duck-leg rolls, authentic egg hoppers, and char-smoked curries. Located on Rupert Street in the heart of Soho, the diminutive space is focused on tropical modernism: a sleek mix of concrete walls, brown leather cushions, stainless steel counters, handwoven batiks, and bespoke Sinhala/Tamil typographed clay tableware. **Known for:** Sri Lankan family recipes with Portuguese, Malay, South Indian, and Dutch influences; Sri Lanka–sourced fruit, vegetables, and spices combined with top British produce; punchy Colombo-style cocktails and gutsy house infusions. $ *Average main: £14* ✉ *61 Rupert St., Soho* 🌐 *www.paradisesoho.com* 🕒 *Closed Sun.* [M] *Piccadilly Circus, Oxford Circus.*

★ Social Eating House

$$$ | FRENCH | FAMILY | At Jason Atherton's underrated but brilliant French bistronomie Soho hangout, witty dishes like smoked duck's ham (made from cured duck's breast) and Scotch egg–and-chips are served alongside accomplished classics like charred Cumbrian pork with mustard jelly. The moodily lit bare-brick salon is nicely decorated with dark parquet floors, antique mirrored ceilings, and comfy red leather banquettes. **Known for:** vintage and heritage cocktails at the upstairs speakeasy; extravagant tasting menus at the open chef's table; popular set lunch menu. $ *Average main: £31* ✉ *58 Poland St., Soho* ☎ *020/7993–3251* 🌐 *www.socialeatinghouse.com* 🕒 *Closed Sun.* [M] *Oxford Circus, Tottenham Court Rd.*

★ 10 Greek Street

$$$ | MODERN EUROPEAN | There may only be 28 table seats and nine counter stools at this stripped-back Modern European eatery, but the consistently great and unpretentious food, cheap wine, affable prices, and tremendous service more than make up for it. Once seated, expect deceptively simple starters and mains like butternut ravioli with sage, slow-braised beef ribs, or slip sole with lemon butter. **Known for:** generous platters of house-cured charcuterie and gravlax; buzzed-up foodie atmosphere in a pared-back dining space; speciality slow roasts and gutsy seasonal Modern European mains. $ *Average main: £24* ✉ *10 Greek St., Soho* ☎ *020/7734–4677* 🌐 *www.10greekstreet.com* [M] *Oxford Circus, Tottenham Court Rd.*

🛏 Hotels

★ Dean Street Townhouse

$$$ | HOTEL | Discreet and unpretentious—and right in the heart of Soho—this oh-so-stylish Georgian town house has a chic bohemian vibe and an excellent Modern British restaurant decorated with fun pieces by renowned artists like Peter Blake and Tracey Emin. **Pros:** great location in central Soho; ultracool vibe; resembles an upper-class pied-à-terre. **Cons:** the crowd can often feel cooler-than-thou; rooms at the front of the building can be noisy, especially on weekends; some rooms are small. $ *Rooms from: £330* ✉ *69–71 Dean St., Soho* ☎ *020/7434–1775* 🌐 *www.deanstreettownhouse.com* 🛏 *39 rooms* 🍴 *Free Breakfast* [M] *Leicester Sq., Tottenham Court Rd., Oxford Circus.*

★ **Ham Yard Hotel**

$$$ | **HOTEL** | **FAMILY** | Colorful, luxurious, playful, and riotously good fun, Ham Yard is another winner from the stable of London hotel designer extraordinaire Kit Kemp. **Pros:** fun facilities, including an authentic Texas 10-pin bowling alley; great modern British design; excellent service throughout. **Cons:** with a cinema, bowling alley, and spa on-site, you might not leave the hotel; some will find the lobby scene a little too trendy; room rates can be pricey. [$] *Rooms from: £400* ✉ *1 Ham Yard, Soho* ☎ *020/3642–2000* 🌐 *www.firmdalehotels.com/hotels/london/ham-yard-hotel* 🛏 *91 rooms* 🍴 *No Meals* [M] *Piccadilly Circus, Oxford Circus.*

★ **Hazlitt's**

$$$ | **HOTEL** | **FAMILY** | This disarmingly friendly place, full of personality, elegant antiques, old portraits, and claw-foot bathtubs, occupies three connected early 18th-century town houses, one of which was the last home of prolific English essayist William Hazlitt (1778–1830). **Pros:** truly beautiful and relaxed setting; great for bibliophiles and lovers of English antiques and old masters–style paintings; historic atmosphere with lots of small sitting rooms and wooden staircases. **Cons:** no elevators; breakfast costs extra; no in-house restaurant. [$] *Rooms from: £265* ✉ *6 Frith St., Soho* ☎ *020/7434–1771* 🌐 *www.hazlittshotel.com* 🛏 *30 rooms* 🍴 *No Meals* [M] *Tottenham Court Rd., Oxford Circus.*

The Piccadilly London West End

$$$ | **HOTEL** | **FAMILY** | This hotel could not be better situated for theater lovers; it's right in the famed West End district, with three such venues within sight of the front door alone. **Pros:** attentive staff; unbeatable location on Theatreland's Shaftesbury Avenue; some thoughtful extras like free earplugs. **Cons:** rooms are compact; you're paying for the location rather than the amenities, and it shows; noise is unavoidable. [$] *Rooms from: £295* ✉ *65–73 Shaftesbury Ave., Soho* ☎ *020/7871–6000, 877/898–1586 in U.S.* 🌐 *www.thepiccadillywestend.co.uk* 🛏 *67 rooms* 🍴 *No Meals* [M] *Piccadilly Circus, Leicester Square.*

The Soho Hotel

$$$ | **HOTEL** | **FAMILY** | A mecca for film, media, and fashion folk, this super-trendy hotel personifies Soho's enduring hipness with its artsy, urban-chic vibe. **Pros:** great restaurant; small, arty, and sophisticated; excellent service. **Cons:** a bit expensive for a boutique hotel; some lower-level rooms lack the amenities of pricier rooms; bar can be crowded and noisy on weeknights. [$] *Rooms from: £345* ✉ *4 Richmond Mews, off Dean St., Soho* ☎ *020/7559–3000* 🌐 *www.firmdalehotels.com/hotels/london/the-soho-hotel* 🛏 *96 rooms* 🍴 *No Meals* [M] *Tottenham Court Rd., Oxford Circus.*

Nightlife

The center of town is famous for its vibrant LGBTQ+ scene, atmospheric music, cabaret venues, and acclaimed comedy clubs. Traditional British "boozers" stand side by side with informal continental-style drinking dens. Drop in for a late drink and you may find yourself rubbing shoulders with musicians and actors from the West End's 50-odd theaters.

BARS

★ **Bar Américain**

COCKTAIL LOUNGES | The beaux-arts interior of this popular subterranean bar just north of Piccadilly Circus is so opulent that you'd be forgiven for thinking it had been here since the 1890s. In fact it's a relatively new revival and has been a hit since it was reconverted in 2012, along with the cavernous Parisian-inspired Brasserie Zédel and racy Crazy Coqs cabaret, which share the premises. The nifty cocktails cover Pre-Prohibition, Prohibition, and Post-Prohibition standards, with additional special menus on occasion. ✉ *20 Sherwood St., Soho*

☏ *020/7734–4888* ⊕ *www.brasse-riezedel.com/bar-americain* Ⓜ *Piccadilly Circus, Leicester Square.*

★ The Blind Pig

COCKTAIL LOUNGES | Chances are you won't have heard of half the ingredients on the cocktail menu at this dark and sultry bar above Social Eating House, famed TV chef Jason Atherton's restaurant, but the sense of mystery only adds to the experience. So, too, do the antique mirrored ceilings and copper-topped bar, the delectable small plates (like black pepper prawn crackers and macaroni and cheese with shaved mushroom)—and the knowledge that you've nabbed a seat at one of the coolest spots in Soho. ✉ *58 Poland St., Soho* ☏ *020/7993–3251* ⊕ *www.socialeatinghouse.com* Ⓜ *Oxford Circus, Tottenham Court Rd.*

★ Experimental Cocktail Club

COCKTAIL LOUNGES | It's easy to miss the unmarked shabby-chic black door with a scuffed wash of red paint on Chinatown's hectic Gerrard Street, but once you find it and make your way past the sometimes hard-to-please doorman, you'll be in a secret three-floor speakeasy that is also one of London's coolest cocktail joints. With a lively crowd, heavenly cocktails, moody lighting, and a DJ spinning smooth jazz sounds, the vibe is laid-back, sexy, Parisian cool. ✉ *13A Gerrard St., Chinatown* ✥ *Look for unmarked scuffed black-and-red door* ☏ *020/7434–3559* ⊕ *www.chinatownecc.com* Ⓜ *Leicester Sq., Piccadilly Circus.*

COMEDY

★ Amused Moose Comedy

COMEDY CLUBS | This roving West End comedy-night group is often considered the best way to see new talent as well as established household names doing "secret" shows. Famous British comedians like Ricky Gervais, Eddie Izzard, and Russell Brand are among those who have graced an Amused Moose stage, and every summer a handful of the Edinburgh Fringe comedians preview with them.

They keep the bar open late (and serve food), and there's a DJ and dancing after the show. Tickets are often discounted with a printout from their website, and shows are mainly on Monday, Wednesday, and weekends. ✉ *Townsend House, 22-25 Dean St., Soho* ☏ *020/7287–3727* ⊕ *www.amusedmoose.com* Ⓜ *Oxford Circus, Tottenham Court Rd.*

★ The Comedy Store

COMEDY CLUBS | Before heading off to prime time, some of the United Kingdom's funniest stand-ups cut their teeth here, at what's considered the birthplace of alternative comedy in Britain. The Comedy Store Players, a team with six resident comedians doing improv based on audience suggestions, perform on Sunday; the King Gong open mic and Old Rope sessions showcase new material on Monday; and Thursday, Friday, and Saturday have the best stand-up acts. There's also a bar with food. Note you must be over 18 to enter. ✉ *1A Oxendon St., Soho* ☏ *020/7024–2060 for tickets and booking* ⊕ *www.thecomedystore. co.uk* Ⓜ *Leicester Sq., Piccadilly Circus.*

LGTBQ+

The Friendly Society

BARS | An unremarkable-looking door in a Soho alleyway leads down some dingy steps into one of the most fun LGBTQ+ joints in the neighborhood. Hopping with activity almost any night of the week, the place is known for its welcoming atmosphere to everyone—gay, trans, questioning, or straight. The interior alone—including garden gnome stools and a ceiling covered in Barbie dolls and disco balls—is enough to lift the spirits. ✉ *79 Wardour St., Soho* ☏ *020/7434–3804* Ⓜ *Leicester Sq., Tottenham Court Rd., Oxford Circus.*

Ku Bar

BARS | A deliciously camp vibe, toned bar staff, and a friendly atmosphere make this one of Soho's most popular LGBTQ+ bars. The crowd is mostly male, but women are very welcome. Head to the quieter upstairs lounge bar for a more laid-back mood, or dance the night away at Ku Klub in the basement. There's a second branch around the corner on Lisle Street, near Chinatown and Leicester Square. ✉ *25 Frith St., Soho* ☎ *020/7437–4303* ⊕ *www.ku-bar.co.uk* Ⓜ *Leicester Sq., Tottenham Court Rd.*

She
DANCE CLUBS | This female-focused basement club, part of the popular Ku group of LGBTQ+ venues, is a standout on the Soho scene. It welcomes a mostly lesbian and nonbinary LGBTQ+ crowd for informal cocktails early in the evening, followed by dancing—of the pop and house variety—later on. The vibe is fun, open, and friendly, especially on the last Thursday of each month, when She hosts London's only drag-king open mic night. ✉ *23a Old Compton St., Soho* ☎ *020/7437–4303* ⊕ *www.she-soho.com* Ⓜ *Tottenham Court Rd., Piccadilly Circus.*

LIVE MUSIC

Ain't Nothin' But…
LIVE MUSIC | This sweaty and fun venue off Carnaby Street does exactly what its name suggests. Local blues musicians, as well as some notable names, squeeze onto the tiny stage, and there's good bar food of the chili-and-gumbo variety. Most weekday nights, there's no cover. ✉ *20 Kingly St., Soho* ☎ *020/7287–0514* ⊕ *www.aintnothinbut.co.uk* Ⓜ *Oxford Circus, Piccadilly Circus.*

★ The 100 Club
LIVE MUSIC | Since this legendary live music venue opened on Oxford Street in 1942, many of the greats have played here, from swing and jazz stars Glenn Miller and Louis Armstrong to punk bands the Sex Pistols and The Clash. Host to the first-ever punk festival in 1976, The 100 Club was saved from closure in 2010 by Paul McCartney, and the fabled basement venue still rocks and reverberates today to all shades of jazz, blues, funk, ska, and soul. ✉ *100 Oxford St., Soho* ⊕ *www.the100club.co.uk* Ⓜ *Oxford Circus, Tottenham Court Rd.*

★ The Phoenix Arts Club
THEMED ENTERTAINMENT | Thankfully, by booking online, nonmembers can gain entry to this legendary West End open mic, musical theater, cabaret, and late-night private members' club. Frequented by a colorful crew of Theatreland thespians, writers, and critics, you might catch a raunchy burlesque, see a theater star belt it out at the Thursday open mic night, or be mesmerized by a monologue from a once-famous global movie star. ✉ *1 Phoenix St., Soho* ☎ *020/7836–1077* ⊕ *www.phoenixartsclub.com* Ⓜ *Covent Garden, Tottenham Court Rd, Leicester Square.*

★ Pizza Express Jazz Club
LIVE MUSIC | FAMILY | One of the United Kingdom's most ubiquitous pizza chains also runs a leading jazz venue in Soho. Established in 1976, the dimly lit basement restaurant hosts both established and emerging local and international jazz acts every night, with food available about 90 minutes before stage time. The thin-crust pizzas are always popular, but it's the exceptional live sets that draw in London's hip jazz lovers. ✉ *10 Dean St., Soho* ☎ *020/7439–4962 for jazz club, 020/7437–9595 for restaurant* ⊕ *www.pizzaexpresslive.com/venues/soho-jazz-club* Ⓜ *Tottenham Court Rd., Oxford Circus.*

★ Ronnie Scott's
LIVE MUSIC | Britain's most famous jazz club has attracted the biggest names—from Stan Getz to Ella Fitzgerald and Jimi Hendrix—since opening nearby on Gerrard Street in 1959 (moving to its current location in 1965). It's usually dark, hot, and crowded, and thankfully the food and table service are now up to par. The ultra-cool James Bond mood can't be beat, despite the sad departure of the eponymous founder and saxophonist, Ronnie Scott, who died in 1996. A full program of free-form jazz sets and shows take

place every night, with additional late gigs on Friday and Saturday. Reservations are recommended. ✉ *47 Frith St., Soho* ☎ *020/7439–0747* ⊕ *www.ronniescotts. co.uk* Ⓜ *Leicester Sq., Tottenham Court Rd. Oxford Circus.*

PUBS

★ The Coach & Horses

PUBS | On the corner of Greek Street, Soho's most famous pub is as authentic as they come, complete with light oak screens and fittings, spittoon troughs, sturdy bar stools, and singalongs around the piano. Established in 1840, this was a post-war haunt for satirical *Private Eye* writers, poets, and painters—from Lucian Freud to Dylan Thomas. Today, you can still down pints of London Pride here and booze with the best of Soho's modern-day habituées and pretenders. ✉ *29 Greek St., Soho* ☎ *020/7437–5920* ⊕ *www.coachandhorsessoho.pub* Ⓜ *Leicester Square, Tottenham Court Rd.*

The Dog and Duck

PUBS | **FAMILY** | A beautiful example of a High Victorian pub, The Dog and Duck has a majestic interior overflowing with thousands of ornate glazed tiles, etched mirrors, chandeliers, and polished wood, although it's often so packed it can be hard to get a proper look. There's a fine selection of real ales at the bar and a restaurant serving superb pale ale–battered fish-and-chips with mushy peas. Originally built in 1734 and patronized by painters and poets like John Constable and Dante Gabriel Rossetti, the cozy upstairs dining room is named for writer and Dog and Duck regular George Orwell. ✉ *18 Bateman St., Soho* ☎ *020/7494–0697* ⊕ *www.nicholsonspubs.co.uk* Ⓜ *Oxford Circus, Tottenham Court Rd.*

🎭 Performing Arts

London's hip center has it all, from multiplexes playing the biggest global blockbuster movies to niche contemporary art galleries tucked away in backstreets and from world-famous opera houses to sultry cabaret joints.

FILM

★ Curzon Soho

FILM | **FAMILY** | Opened in 1959 and now a Soho institution, this three-screen independent cinema runs a vibrant program of first-run arthouse and mainstream films, along with an engaging calendar of director talks, Q&As, festival events, and other cinephile shindigs. The first-floor mezzanine bar is great for a quiet drink, even when Soho is heaving with people. There are other wonderful Curzon cinemas in Mayfair, Bloomsbury, and Victoria. ✉ *99 Shaftesbury Ave., Soho* ☎ *01233/555–644* ⊕ *www.curzon.com/ venues/soho* ☒ *From £13* Ⓜ *Tottenham Court Rd., Piccadilly Circus, Leicester Sq.*

The Prince Charles Cinema

FILM | **FAMILY** | This quirky two-screen repertory movie theater just north of Leicester Square offers you a chance to catch up with indie arthouse films, documentaries, and even classic blockbusters you may have missed. A second screen upstairs shows newer movies at more typical West End prices. With 300 velvet seats, this is where London's "Singalong Screenings" took off; come in character and sing along to the likes of *The Sound of Music, Grease, The Rocky Horror Picture Show,* and other cult classics. ✉ *7 Leicester Pl., Soho* ☎ *020/7494–3654* ⊕ *www.princecharlescinema.com* ☒ *From £5; sing-alongs £17* Ⓜ *Leicester Sq., Piccadilly Circus.*

THEATER

Soho Theatre

THEATER | This popular playhouse is devoted to finding, commissioning, and fostering new work and talent, and therefore is a prolific presenter of plays by young, emerging, and established writers. With three performance spaces, it also puts on its fair share of comedy, cabaret, drag, and dance shows, and unsurprisingly the bar is always buzzing. ⊠ *21 Dean St., Soho* ☎ *020/7478–0100* ⊕ *www.sohotheatre.com* ✉ *From £7* Ⓜ *Tottenham Court Rd., Oxford Circus.*

Shopping

BOOKS

★ Foyles

BOOKS | **FAMILY** | Founded in 1903 by the Foyle brothers after they failed the Civil Service exams, this family-owned bookstore and literary landmark is in a 1930s Art Deco building, once the home of the renowned art college Central Saint Martins. One of London's best sources for textbooks and the United Kingdom's largest retailer of foreign language books, with more than 200,000 titles on its four miles of bookshelves, Foyles also stocks everything from popular fiction to military history, sheet music, medical tomes, graphic novels, and illustrated fine arts books. It also offers the in-store Ray's Jazz (one of London's better outlets for music) and a cool jazz café. Foyles also has branches in the Royal Festival Hall at the Southbank Centre and at Waterloo Station. ⊠ *107 Charing Cross Rd., Soho* ☎ *020/7437–5660* ⊕ *www.foyles.co.uk* Ⓜ *Leicester Sq., Tottenham Court Rd.*

CLOTHING

★ Agent Provocateur

LINGERIE | Created by fashion designer Vivienne Westwood's son and daughter-in-law, this line of lingerie in gorgeous fabrics, silks, latex, and lace tends toward the kind of risqué underwear that is both provocative and practical. The original boudoir-like shop is staffed by assistants in prim pink uniforms in what was Soho's red-light district, but the brand has gone a bit more mainstream and now also sells bathing suits, nightwear, jewelry, and luggage in multiple locations in Knightsbridge, Mayfair, Victoria, and Notting Hill. ⊠ *6 Broadwick St., Soho* ☎ *020/7439–0229* ⊕ *www.agentprovocateur.com* Ⓜ *Oxford Circus, Tottenham Court Rd.*

Wolsey

MEN'S CLOTHING | **FAMILY** | Specializing in men's knitwear since 1755, this long-established company sells rugged but stylish outerwear, sweaters, shirts, hats, scarves, socks, T-shirts, sweatshirts, sleepwear, and underwear (the undies of choice for polar explorers Roald Amundsen, Captain Robert Scott, and Ernest Shackleton). The company also supplied woolen garments to British troops in 1914. It's not all heritage, though; Wolsey makes hoodies as well, and its padded jackets and vests employ the latest in thermal wear technology. The interior reflects this blend of the traditional and the contemporary, with exposed brick walls, brushed steel beams, and photographs of expeditions the brand has outfitted. ⊠ *83a Brewer St., Soho* ☎ *020/7434–4257* ⊕ *www.wolsey.com* Ⓜ *Piccadilly Circus, Oxford Circus.*

DEPARTMENT STORES

★ Liberty

DEPARTMENT STORE | **FAMILY** | Its distinctive black-and-white Tudor-style facade, created from the timbers of two Royal Navy men-o'-war ships, reflects this department store's origins in the late Victorian Arts and Crafts movement. Leading designers were recruited to create the classic Liberty silk prints that are still a signature of the brand, gracing everything from cushions and kimonos to photo albums and stationary. Inside, Liberty is a wood-paneled labyrinth of rooms stocked with well-chosen merchandise, including niche beauty, perfume, footwear, and housewares lines such as Soho Home, which features furniture and textiles from the membership club. Clothes for both men and women focus on high quality and high fashion, with labels like Rixo and Roland Mouret. The store regularly commissions new prints from contemporary designers, and it sells both these and its classic patterns by the yard. If you're not so handy with a needle, an interior design service will create soft furnishings for you. There's also a florist, a hair salon, a men's barber, beauty treatment rooms, a brow bar, a foot spa, and a body piercing studio. ⊠ *Regent St., Soho* ☎ *020/3893–3062* ⊕ *www.liberty-london.com* Ⓜ *Oxford Circus, Piccadilly Circus.*

FOOD

The Vintage House

WINE/SPIRITS | If Scottish whisky or Irish whiskey is more to your taste than wine, visit family-run The Vintage House on Soho's main drag, Old Compton Street, which has the country's largest selection of single malts (over 1,350), including many rare bottles, some exclusive to the shop. You'll also find more than 100 tequilas, plus choice rums, liqueurs, ports, and Armagnacs, as well as Cuban Habanos cigars. The shop is open until 11 pm (10 pm on Sunday). ⊠ *42 Old Compton St., Soho* ☎ *020/7437–2592* ⊕ *www.vintage-house.london* Ⓜ *Tottenham Court Rd., Leicester Sq. Oxford Circus.*

MUSIC

★ Reckless Records

MUSIC | Open since 1984, Soho's longest-standing secondhand vinyl store has seen the reign of cassette tapes, CDs, Napster, and Spotify, and arguably has massively helped contribute to vinyl's recent revival. Come here to leaf through the racks for rare vinyl finds and classic albums, spanning everything from rock and roll and New Wave to electro, heavy metal, and drum and bass. If the shop front itself looks familiar, that's because it was featured on the cover of Oasis's 1995 hit album *(What's the Story)*

Morning Glory? ⊠ *30 Berwick St., Soho* ☎ *020/7437–4271* ⊕ *www.reckless.co.uk* Ⓜ *Oxford Circus, Piccadilly Circus, Tottenham Court Rd.*

TOYS

Hamleys

TOYS | FAMILY | When British children visit London, this institution—the oldest toy store in the world—is at the top of their agenda. Its six floors hold 50,000 lines of the latest dolls, soft toys, video games, and technological devices, as well as old-fashioned items like train sets, Subbuteo, drum kits, and magic tricks, plus every must-have on the preteen shopping list (some parents may find the offerings to be overly commercialized, as they're heavy on movie and TV tie-ins). Hamleys is a bit of a madhouse at Christmas time, but Santa's Grotto is one of the best in town. ⊠ *188–196 Regent St., Soho* ☎ *020/7479–7398* ⊕ *www.hamleys.com* Ⓜ *Oxford Circus, Piccadilly Circus.*

Covent Garden

To the east of Charing Cross Road lies Covent Garden, the famous Georgian marketplace–turned–shopping mall. Although bougie boutiques and haute fashion shops line the surrounding streets, many Londoners come to Covent Garden for its two outposts of culture: the resplendent **Royal Opera House** and the nonprofit **Donmar Warehouse,** one of London's best and most innovative theaters. The area becomes more sedate just to the east, at the end of Wellington Street, where semicircular Aldwych is lined with grand buildings, and from there the Strand leads to the huge stately piazza of **Somerset House,** a vibrant center of contemporary arts and home to the many masterpieces on view at the **Courtauld Gallery.** You'll get a sense of old-fashioned London just behind the Strand, where its small lanes are little changed since the 18th century. On the way to the verdant **Embankment Gardens** bordering the Thames, you may pass **Benjamin Franklin House,** where the noted statesman lived in the years leading up to the American Revolution.

Covent Garden joins Soho as the arts-and-entertainment center of the city, popularly referred to as the West End. The neighborhood centers on the covered market piazza, site of the original 1670s Covent Garden market. High Holborn to the north, Kingsway to the east, and the Strand to the south form its other boundaries.

◉ Sights

★ Benjamin Franklin House

HISTORIC HOME | FAMILY | This architecturally significant 1730 town house is the only surviving residence of American statesman, scientist, writer, and inventor Benjamin Franklin, who lived and worked here for 16 years preceding the American Revolution. The restored Georgian home has been left unfurnished, the better to show off the original features: 18th-century paneling, stoves, beams, bricks, and windows. Visitors are led around the house by the costumed character of Polly Hewson, the daughter of Franklin's landlady, who interacts with engaging video projections and recorded voices (weekends only). On Friday you can take a guided tour focusing on the architectural details of the building, and a walking tour of the surrounding area lasting up to 90 minutes sets off from the house at noon. ✉ *36 Craven St., Covent Garden* ☎ *020/7839–2006* ⊕ *www.benjamin-franklinhouse.org* 🎫 *Historical experience £8; architectural tour £6* ⊗ *Closed Mon.–Thurs.* ⚠ *Reservations essential* Ⓜ *Charing Cross, Embankment.*

★ The Courtauld Gallery

ART MUSEUM | One of London's most beloved art collections, The Courtauld is to your right as you pass through the archway into the grounds of the beautifully restored, grand 18th-century neoclassical Somerset House. Founded in 1931 by the textile magnate Samuel Courtauld to house his remarkable private collection, this is one of the world's finest impressionist and post-impressionist galleries, with artists ranging from Bonnard to van Gogh. A déjà-vu moment with Cézanne, Degas, Seurat, Monet, and more awaits on every wall (Manet's *Bar at the Folies-Bergère* and van Gogh's *Self-Portrait with Bandaged Ear* are two of the stars). Botticelli, Bruegel, Tiepolo, and Rubens are also represented, thanks to the exquisite bequest of Count Antoine Seilern's Princes Gate collection. German Renaissance paintings include the sublime *Adam and Eve* by Lucas Cranach the Elder. The second floor has a more provocative, experimental feel, with masterpieces such as Modigliani's famous *Female Nude*. Look out for a full program of additional blockbuster one-off exhibitions, and don't miss the little café downstairs, a perfect place for a spot of tea. ✉ *Somerset House, Strand, Covent Garden* ☎ *020/3947–7711* ⊕ *www. courtauld.ac.uk* 🎫 *£9 weekdays, £11 weekends; additional charge for special exhibits* Ⓜ *Covent Garden, Charing Cross.*

★ Covent Garden Piazza

MARKET | FAMILY | Once home to London's main flower market, where *My Fair Lady's* Eliza Doolittle peddled her blooms, the square around which Covent Garden pivots is known as the Piazza. In the center, the fine old market building now houses stalls and shops selling expensive clothing, plus several restaurants and cafés, and knickknacks stores that are good for gifts. One particular gem is Benjamin Pollock's Toyshop at No. 44 in the market. Established in the 1880s, it sells delightful toy theaters. The Apple Market has good crafts stalls on most days, too. On the south side of the Piazza, the indoor Jubilee Market, with its stalls of clothing, army surplus gear, and more crafts and knickknacks, feels a bit like a flea market.

Leicester Square is home to many movie theaters and a half-price theater ticket booth.

In summer it may seem that everyone in the huge crowds around you in the Piazza is a fellow tourist, but there's still plenty of office life in the area. Londoners who shop here tend to head for Neal Street and the area to the north of Covent Garden Tube station, rather than the market itself. In the Piazza, street performers—from global musicians to jugglers and mimes—play to the crowds, as they have done since the first English *Punch and Judy* show, staged here in the 17th century. ⊠ *Covent Garden Piazza, Covent Garden* ⊕ *www.coventgarden.london* Ⓜ *Covent Garden, Holborn.*

Leicester Square
PLAZA/SQUARE | FAMILY | Looking at the neon of the major movie houses, the fast food outlets, and the casino and disco entrances, you'd never guess that this square (pronounced "Lester") was a model of formality and refinement when it was first laid out around 1670. By the 19th century, the square was already bustling and disreputable, and although it's not a threatening place, you

should still be on your guard, especially at night—any space so full of people is bound to attract pickpockets, and Leicester Square certainly does.

Although there's a bit of residual glamour (major red-carpet blockbuster film premieres often happen here), Londoners generally tend to avoid the place, though it's worth a visit for its hustle and bustle, its mime artists, and the pleasant modern fountain at its center. Also in the middle is a famous statue of a sulking William Shakespeare, perhaps remembering the days when the movie houses were live theaters—burlesque houses, but live all the same. On the northeast corner, in Leicester Place, stands the church of Notre Dame de France, with a wonderful mural by Jean Cocteau in one of its side chapels. For more in the way of atmosphere, head north and west from here, through Chinatown and the narrow Georgian streets of Soho. ⊠ *Leicester Square, Covent Garden* ⊕ *www.leicestersquare.london* Ⓜ *Leicester Sq. Piccadilly Circus, Charing Cross.*

London Transport Museum

CHILDREN'S MUSEUM | FAMILY | Housed in the old flower market at the southeast corner of Covent Garden, this fun museum is filled with highly impressive vehicle, poster, and photograph collections. As you watch the crowds drive a Tube train simulation and gawk at the Victorian steam locomotives and horse-drawn trams (and the piles of detritus that remained behind), it's unclear who's enjoying it more: children or adults. Best of all, the kid-friendly museum (under 18s admitted free, and there's a play area) has a multilevel approach to education, including clear information for the youngest visitors and transit aficionados alike. Food and drink are available at the Upper Deck café, and the shop has numerous good options for gifts. Tickets are valid for unlimited entry for 12 months. ✉ *Covent Garden Piazza, Covent Garden* ☎ *0343/222–5000* ⊕ *www.ltmuseum. co.uk* 🎫 *£18.50* Ⓜ *Covent Garden, Holborn, Leicester Sq.*

★ **Somerset House**

ARTS CENTER | FAMILY | This majestic former royal palace—rebuilt by Sir William Chambers (1723-96) during the reign of George III to house offices of the Navy Board—has been transformed from dusty government offices into one of the capital's most buzzing centers of arts and culture, often hosting several fabulous exhibitions at once. The cobblestone Italianate Fountain Court, where Admiral Nelson used to walk, makes a fitting setting for 50-odd playful fountains and is transformed into an ice rink in winter; the grand space is also the venue for outdoor concerts and film screenings in the summer. The Courtauld Gallery and its world-class impressionist art collection occupy most of the north building, facing the Strand.

Across the courtyard are the barrel-vaulted Embankment Galleries, with a lively program of fashion, design, architecture, and photography exhibitions. The

Ice-Skating at Somerset House 🏃

It's hard to beat the skating experience at Somerset House's Fountain Court, where from mid-November to mid-January a rink is erected in the grand courtyard of this central London former royal palace. Check the website for current prices; its popularity is enormous, and if you can't get a ticket, other atmospheric venues, such as Hampton Court, the Tower of London, the London Eye, and the Natural History Museum, are following Somerset House's lead in having temporary winter rinks.

East Wing has another small exhibition space, and events are also held in the atmospheric cellars below the Fountain Court. The Eat Ten café is a great spot for a low-emission plant-forward meal or snack, while the high-profile Spring restaurant is all wildflowers, zero waste, and biodynamic vegetables. In summer, eating and drinking spill out onto the large terrace overlooking the Thames. ✉ *Strand, Covent Garden* ☎ *0333/320– 2836* ⊕ *www.somersethouse.org.uk* 🎫 *Embankment Galleries price varies, other areas free* Ⓜ *Charing Cross, Covent Garden, Holborn, Temple.*

St. Paul's Church

CHURCH | FAMILY | If you want to commune with the spirits of Vivien Leigh, Noël Coward, Gracie Fields, and Charlie Chaplin, this is the place. Memorials to them and myriad other theater and movie greats are found in this 1633 work of the renowned Inigo Jones, who, as Surveyor of the King's Works, designed the whole of Covent Garden Piazza. St. Paul's Church has been known as "the Actors' Church" since the Restoration, thanks to the bawdy neighboring theater district and St. Paul's prominent parishioners

(well-known actors often read the lessons at services, and the church still hosts concerts and small-scale productions.) Fittingly, the opening scene of Shaw's *Pygmalion* takes place under its Tuscan portico.

Today, the western end of the Piazza is a prime pitch for street entertainers, but if they're not to your liking, you can repair to the serenity of the walled garden, entered from King or Bedford streets. Enchanting open-air performances of Shakespeare plays and other works are staged here in the summertime. ✉ *Bedford St., Covent Garden* ☎ *020/7836–5221* 🌐 *www.actorschurch.org* [M] *Covent Garden, Leicester Sq.*

🍴 Restaurants

★ Balthazar

$$$ | FRENCH | FAMILY | British restaurateur Keith McNally recreates his famed New York Parisian-style brasserie at this busy corner spot off Covent Garden. The soaring grand café setting creates an enchanting white-tablecloth backdrop to enjoy the classic French brasserie menu, including dishes like duck and beef pie, *moules marinière* (mussels with cream and white wine), and ox cheek bourguignon (stew). **Known for:** vegan and vegetarian options; Parisian-style grand café setting; handy prix fixe, weekend brunch, children's, and Afternoon Tea menus. [$] *Average main: £26* ✉ *4–7 Russell St., Covent Garden* ☎ *020/3301–1155* 🌐 *www.balthazarlondon.com* [M] *Covent Garden, Holborn.*

★ Barrafina

$$$ | TAPAS | One of London's favorite Spanish tapas bars, modeled after famed Cal Pep in Barcelona, has only a few raised bar stools within the open counter kitchen off Trafalgar Square. Lunchtime lines form starting at noon daily for a succession of impeccably sourced small plates ranging from giant Spanish *carabineros* (red prawns) and Iberian pork cheeks to black squid ink risotto with cuttlefish. **Known for:** top Cava and Spanish sherry selection; long lines starting at noon; intriguing offal dishes like milk-fed lamb's kidneys. [$] *Average main: £26* ✉ *10 Adelaide St., Covent Garden* 🌐 *www.barrafina.co.uk* [M] *Charing Cross, Covent Garden, Leicester Sq.*

★ Clos Maggiore

$$$$ | FRENCH | FAMILY | Insist on a table in the dreamy, white blossom–filled conservatory at this warm, cozy, and seriously romantic Provençal country-style inn off Covent Garden. Once inside, you'll be won over by the old-fashioned but refined French cuisine. **Known for:** lunch and pre- and post-theater meal deals; regularly voted one of London's most romantic restaurants; warren of blossom-filled conservatories and candle-lit hideaways. [$] *Average main: £34* ✉ *33 King St., Covent Garden* ☎ *020/4580–1174* 🌐 *www.closmaggiore.com* 👔 *Smart casual* [M] *Covent Garden.*

Cora Pearl

$$$ | MODERN BRITISH | British comfort food like ham-and-cheese toasties, bubble and squeak, and even the mighty potato chip are transformed into showstoppers at this classy Covent Garden town house. Triple-cooked chips are squeezed, sliced, buttered, and deep-fried to perfection, while the famous crustless toasties are all succulent ham hock, Montgomery cheddar, and tangy house pickle. **Known for:** classy pre-theater option; elegant decor and upmarket atmosphere; buffed-up British comfort food dishes. [$] *Average main: £26* ✉ *30 Henrietta St., Covent Garden* ☎ *020/7324–7722* 🌐 *www.corapearl.co.uk* 🕒 *Closed Mon. No dinner Sun.* [M] *Covent Garden, Holborn.*

Côte Brasserie

$ | BISTRO | FAMILY | Where else can you find an amazing three-course French meal right by Covent Garden for £21? The Côte Brasserie chain does just the trick, offering a pleasing menu loaded with classic French favorites: crêpes with mushrooms and Gruyère cheese, boeuf bourguignon, moules marinière, and iced berries and white chocolate sauce. **Known for:** reliable French classics like moules marinières; part of a dependable chain of French brasseries; very reasonable pre- and post-theater deals. $ *Average main: £15* ⊠ *17–21 Tavistock St., Covent Garden* ☎ *020/7379–9991* ⊕ *www.cote.co.uk/restaurant/covent-garden* Ⓜ *Covent Garden.*

Frenchie

$$$ | FRENCH | FAMILY | With three popular restaurants in Paris, star French chef Grégory Marchand brings his highly colorful and daring dishes to London at this sleek eatery not far from the historic Covent Garden Piazza. Everyone loves the effortlessly ebullient offerings like stone bass, bisque, and borlotti beans or Welsh lamb with sweet corn three ways, all served in a bustling, modern brasserie setting. **Known for:** adventurous wine list stacked with small, artisan, and eco-friendly producers; eclectic French dishes like duck foie gras pressé with sour black cherries, almonds, and elderflower; flavor-packed puddings like lemon curd, olive shortbread, and rosemary ice cream. $ *Average main: £30* ⊠ *16 Henrietta St., Covent Garden* ☎ *020/7836–4422* ⊕ *www.frenchiecoventgarden.com* ⊗ *Closed Mon. and Tues.* Ⓜ *Charing Cross, Embankment.*

★ The Ivy

$$$ | MODERN BRITISH | FAMILY | London's onetime most famous celebrity haunt and West End landmark is still so popular it receives over a thousand calls a day. Established as an Italian café in 1917, today it's still where London's wealthiest dine on haddock, mushy peas and chips, Thai baked sea bass, and evergreen English classics like shepherd's pie and baked Alaska. **Known for:** discrete service and great people-watching; celebrity-filled history; famed house staples like grilled calf's liver and Dover sole. $ *Average main: £24* ⊠ *1–5 West St., Covent Garden* ☎ *020/7836–4751* ⊕ *www.the-ivy.co.uk* Ⓜ *Covent Garden, Tottenham Court Rd.*

★ The Ivy Market Grill

$$ | BRASSERIE | Scrub up like Eliza Doolittle and perch at the pewter bar sipping a dreamy My Fair Lady (with house-made gin and orange blossom) at this laid-back little sister to the flagship The Ivy restaurant. You'll find bargains galore here on the something-for-everyone brasserie menu—from crispy duck salad and poached lobster cocktail to chicken Milanese and blackened cod. For dessert, be sure to try the chocolate bombe, a chocolatey mush of milk foam, vanilla ice cream, and gooey hot salted caramel sauce. The salon atmosphere is amplified by the mottled green leather banquettes and dark timber floors and tables are stunningly set off by late 19th-century brass lamps and chandeliers. **Known for:** Vespar Martinis at the sizzling central bar; enticing green leather booths;all-day weekend brunch menu. $ *Average main: £18* ⊠ *1A Henrietta St., Covent Garden* ☎ *020/3301–0200* ⊕ *www.theivymarketgrill.com* ⟡ *Reservations essential* Ⓜ *Leicester Sq., Covent Garden.*

★ J Sheekey

$$$ | SEAFOOD | Open since 1896, this timelessly chic seafood haven is a discreet alternative to the more celeb-focused eateries nearby. Dripping with vintage black-and-white photos of famous West End stars, J Sheekey charms with a ravishing menu of fresh Atlantic prawns, pickled Arctic herrings, shrimps, scallops, salmon burgers, and the famous Sheekey Fish Pie. **Known for:** glamorous art deco oyster bar; low-key celebrity hideaway; old-school seafood menu. $ *Average main: £28*

✉ *28–32 St. Martin's Ct., Covent Garden* ☎ *020/7240–2565* 🌐 *www.j-sheekey.co.uk* [M] *Leicester Sq., Covent Garden, Charing Cross.*

★ Joe Allen

$$ | AMERICAN | FAMILY | It seems like everyone involved in the West End theater world swarms this legendary subterranean spot for its enchanting blend of American brasserie comfort food, live piano music, and wall-to-wall theater posters, pics, and memorabilia. Established nearby in 1977, enduring classics include Joe's slow-braised smoked baby back ribs, New York strip steak, a not-so-secret off-menu burger, and a classic PB&J ice cream sandwich. **Known for:** resident jazz pianists nightly; theater world regulars like Judy Dench and Ian McKellen; speakeasy cocktail bar vibe. [$] *Average main: £19* ✉ *2 Burleigh St., Covent Garden* ☎ *020/7836–0651* 🌐 *www.joeallen.co.uk* [M] *Charring Cross, Covent Garden, Leicester Square.*

★ Louie

$$$$ | CREOLE | There's a distinct Roaring Twenties vibe here at Louie, set in a glamorous town house with a collection of unique dining rooms and terraces. Exceptional Mississippi-inspired Creole delights include seafood gumbo, oysters Rockefeller, and New Orleans barbecued lobster with Creole-spiced butter, but it's the eccentric cocktails and hedonistic crowds that truly make a visit here memorable. **Known for:** impossibly cool music and funky live sets; Louisiana and Deep South–inspired Creole dishes; very hip atmosphere. [$] *Average main: £35* ✉ *13-15 West St., Covent Garden* ☎ *020/8057–6500* 🌐 *www.louie-london.com* ⏲ *Closed Sun.* [M] *Tottenham Court Rd, Leicester Square.*

★ NoMad Restaurant

$$$$ | AMERICAN | FAMILY | One of London's most spectacular dining rooms is set in a glass-ceilinged atrium at the boho-chic NoMad London hotel, located opposite Covent Garden's famed Royal Opera House. Don't miss the signature roast chicken with foie gras and black truffle or the leisurely weekend brunch where you can enjoy simple eggs Benedict or chili avocado toast. **Known for:** exclusive nightlife scene with great cocktails; historic building from 1740; glamorous hotel atmosphere. [$] *Average main: £39* ✉ *NoMad London, 28 Bow St., Covent Garden* ☎ *020/3906–1600* 🌐 *www.thenomadhotel.com/london* [M] *Covent Garden, Holborn.*

★ Rules

$$$ | BRITISH | FAMILY | Opened by Thomas Rule in 1798, London's oldest restaurant is still perhaps its most beautiful. Resembling a High Victorian bordello overflowing with taxidermy, here you can indulge in traditional British fare like jugged hare, steak-and-kidney pie, or roast beef and Yorkshire pudding. **Known for:** traditional British game-focused fare; famous diners from Charles Dickens to Evelyn Waugh; the oldest restaurant in London. [$] *Average main: £31* ✉ *35 Maiden La., Covent Garden* ☎ *020/7836–5314* 🌐 *www.rules.co.uk* 👔 *Smart dress, no shorts or sportwear* [M] *Covent Garden, Holborn.*

Savoy Grill

$$$$ | BRITISH | FAMILY | You can feel the history at this 1889 art deco powerhouse, which has wined and dined everyone from Oscar Wilde and Winston Churchill to Liz Taylor and Marilyn Monroe. Nowadays it caters to business barons and well-heeled West End visitors, who come for the Grill's famed table-side silver serving trolley, which might trundle up laden with roasts like beef Wellington, rack of pork, or saddle of lamb. **Known for:** signature glazed omelet Arnold Bennett; ravishing old-school dining salon; beef Wellington from the daily carving trolley service. [$] *Average main: £45* ✉ *The Savoy, 100 Strand, Covent Garden* ☎ *020/7592–1600 for reservations only* 🌐 *www.gordonramsayrestaurants.com/savoy-grill* [M] *Charing Cross, Covent Garden.*

★ Simpson's in the Strand

$$$ | **BRITISH** | **FAMILY** | Head straight for the 30-day roast rib of Scottish beef and Yorkshire puddings carved table-side at this magnificent 1848 oak-paneled dining institution on the Strand. Originally a Victorian cigar lounge, a coffeehouse, and later a famed chess venue (known as the Grand Cigar Divan), it was once frequented by the likes of Charles Dickens and Vincent van Gogh. **Known for:** roast Welsh lamb and Scottish beef served from the famous silver-domed carving trolley; one of the city's grandest and most historic taverns; traditional Sunday roasts with Yorkshire pudding and all the trimmings. Ⓢ *Average main: £29* ✉ *100 Strand, Covent Garden* ☎ *020/7420–2111 restaurant reservations only* ⊕ *www.simpsonsinthestrand.co.uk* Ⓜ *Charing Cross, Leicester Sq.*

★ Spring

$$$$ | **ITALIAN** | **FAMILY** | Trailblazing Australian chef Skye Gyngell worships the four seasons at her pastel-hued dining destination in majestic Somerset House off the Strand. Housed in the building's 1865 neoclassical New Wing, Spring offers root-to-stem, produce-driven Italian dishes in an airy light-drenched dining salon. **Known for:** biodynamic Fern Verrow Farm salads; highly seasonal, sustainable, and ingredient-driven dishes; eco-friendly ethos. Ⓢ *Average main: £33* ✉ *Somerset House, New Wing, Lancaster Pl., Covent Garden* ☎ *020/3011–0115* ⊕ *www.springrestaurant.co.uk* ☽ *Closed Sun.–Tues.* Ⓜ *Charing Cross, Holborn.*

🏨 Hotels

★ Covent Garden Hotel

$$$ | **HOTEL** | **FAMILY** | It's little wonder this is now the London home-away-from-home for off-duty celebrities, A-list actors, and various style mavens, with its unbeatable Covent Garden location in a former French hospital and stylish guest rooms that use mix-and-match couture fabrics and one-off pieces to stunning effect. **Pros:** plush basement cinema for movie buffs; great for star-spotting; opulent English baronial country house setting. **Cons:** only some rooms come with balcony views; location in Covent Garden can be boisterous; room prices are quite high. Ⓢ *Rooms from: £340* ✉ *10 Monmouth St., Covent Garden* ☎ *020/7806–1000, 888/559–5508 in U.S.* ⊕ *www.firmdalehotels.com/hotels/london/covent-garden-hotel* ⇨ *58 rooms* ⑩ *No Meals* Ⓜ *Covent Garden, Holborn.*

★ ME London

$$$ | **HOTEL** | **FAMILY** | A shiny fortress of luxury, ME brings a splash of modern cool to a rather stuffy patch of the Strand. **Pros:** stunning London views from rooftop bar; convenient, fashionable location; full of high-tech comforts and gadgets. **Cons:** rooftop bar can get uncomfortably busy; small closets and in-room storage areas; design can sometimes verge on form over function. Ⓢ *Rooms from: £265* ✉ *336–337 The Strand, Covent Garden* ☎ *020/7395–3400* ⊕ *www.melia.com* ⇨ *157 rooms* ⑩ *No Meals* Ⓜ *Covent Garden, Charing Cross, Holborn.*

★ NoMad London

$$$ | **HOTEL** | **FAMILY** | London's hottest hotel sits opposite the famed Royal Opera House and while a bit austere from the outside, inside it's all deluxe boho-chic, with dark mahoganies, worn rugs, velvet sofas, embroidered damasks, and hand-painted wallpapers. **Pros:** fabulous location opposite Covent Garden's Royal Opera House; set in London's historic 1740 magistrates' court; hip on-site drinking and dining. **Cons:** high prices; rooms overlooking the Atrium restaurant can be a bit noisy. Ⓢ *Rooms from: £280* ✉ *28 Bow St., Covent Garden* ☎ *020/3906–1600* ⊕ *www.thenomadhotel.com/london* ⇨ *91 rooms* ⑩ *No Meals* Ⓜ *Covent Garden, Holborn.*

One Aldwych

$$$ | HOTEL | FAMILY | A fine Edwardian building, with an artsy lobby and an understated blend of contemporary and classic, provides pure modern luxury in a great location for theaters and shopping. **Pros:** good deals and special offers, including big advance-booking discounts; understated luxury; ultracool atmosphere. **Cons:** rooms are relatively plain; fashionable ambience is not always relaxing; all this luxury doesn't come cheap. [$] *Rooms from: £375* ✉ *1 Aldwych, Covent Garden* ☎ *020/7300–1000* 🌐 *www.onealdwych.com* 🛏 *105 rooms* 🍴 *Free Breakfast* [M] *Charing Cross, Covent Garden, Holborn.*

★ **The Savoy**

$$$$ | HOTEL | FAMILY | One of London's most famous hotels maintains its status at the top with winning attributes of impeccable service, stunning decor, and a desirable location on the Strand. **Pros:** Thames-side location; one of the absolute top hotels in Europe; unbeatable pedigree and illustrious history. **Cons:** some may find it over-the-top; street noise is surprisingly problematic, particularly on lower floors; everything comes with a price tag. [$] *Rooms from: £504* ✉ *The Strand, Covent Garden* ☎ *020/7836–4343, 888/265–0533 in U.S.* 🌐 *www.thesavoylondon.com* 🛏 *268 rooms* 🍴 *Free Breakfast* [M] *Covent Garden, Charing Cross.*

St Martin's Lane

$$$ | HOTEL | Hip travelers come to this Philippe Starck–designed spot positioned artfully between Trafalgar Square and Covent Garden. **Pros:** guests enjoy free entry to adjacent Gymbox gym; ultracool lobby, restaurant, bar, and secret speakeasy; funky color-your-mood bedroom lighting system. **Cons:** some find it cooler-than-thou; noise from St Martin's Lane inevitable; rooms can be small. [$] *Rooms from: £290* ✉ *45 St Martin's Ln., Covent Garden* ☎ *020/7300–5500* 🌐 *www.sbe.com/hotels/originals/st-martins-lane* 🛏 *204 rooms* 🍴 *No Meals* [M] *Charing Cross, Leicester Sq.*

Nightlife

BARS

★ **Beaufort Bar**

BARS | Things could hardly get more glamorous than at the Savoy's lesser-known Beaufort Bar—a black-and-gold art deco master class with dramatic low lighting that has vintage champagne and a spread of heritage cocktails. Dark and sultry and with a rising cabaret stage once graced by Gershwin and Josephine Baker, this venue has nightly live jazz piano music beginning at 7 pm. ✉ *The Savoy, Strand, Covent Garden* ☎ *020/7420–2111 for reservations only* 🌐 *www.thesavoylondon.com/restaurant/beaufort-bar* [M] *Charing Cross, Covent Garden.*

★ **Le Bar at Louie**

COCKTAIL LOUNGES | On any given night, ace jazz player Trombone Shorty might work his way through this beyond cool New Orleans voodoo cocktail lounge on the second floor of Louie restaurant off Cambridge Circus. Even if he's not there playing tunes, the staff dish out deviled eggs, truffle pizzas, and theme cocktails in a rising fever dream delirium until 2 am five nights a week. ✉ *13–15 West St., Covent Garden* ☎ *020/8057–6500* 🌐 *www.louie-london.com* 🕓 *Closed Sun.–Mon.* [M] *Covent Garden, Tottenham Court Rd, Leicester Square.*

★ **Upstairs at Rules**

COCKTAIL LOUNGES | Discretion's the word at this under-the-radar cocktail lounge on the first floor above Rules, London's oldest restaurant (established in 1798). In rooms where Edward VII used to dine with his socialite mistress Lillie Langtry, old-school bartenders serve traditional English cocktails (martinis are stirred, never shaken). The decor reflects a more bygone era, with royal portraits, mounted antlers, patterned carpets, and copious Edwardian hunting scenes. ⊠ *Rules, 34–35 Maiden La., Covent Garden* ☎ *020/7836–5314* ⊕ *www.rules.co.uk* Ⓜ *Covent Garden, Leicester Sq., Holborn.*

LGBTQ+

Heaven

DANCE CLUBS | Offering the best light show on any London dance floor, Heaven is unpretentious, loud, and huge, with a labyrinth of rooms, bars, and live-music parlors. Thursday through Saturday nights it's all about the G-A-Y club and comedy nights. Check in advance about live performances—they can take place any night of the week. If you go to just one gay club in London, Heaven should be it. ⊠ *Under the Arches, Villiers St., Covent Garden* ☎ *0844/847–2351 24-hr ticket line* ⊕ *www.heavenlive.co.uk* Ⓜ *Charing Cross, Embankment.*

PUBS

The Harp

PUBS | FAMILY | This is the sort of friendly flower-decked locale you might find on some out-of-the-way backstreet, except that it's right in the middle of town, between Trafalgar Square and Covent Garden. As a result, The Harp can get crowded, but the squeeze is worth it for the excellent beer and cider (there are usually 10 carefully chosen ales, often including a London microbrew, plus 10 ciders and perries) and a no-frills menu of high-quality British sausages, cooked behind the bar. ⊠ *47 Chandos Pl., Covent Garden* ☎ *020/7836–0291* ⊕ *www. harpcoventgarden.com* Ⓜ *Charing Cross, Covent Garden.*

★ The Lamb & Flag

PUBS | FAMILY | This refreshingly ungentrified 17th-century pub was once known as "The Bucket of Blood" because the upstairs room and front yard were used

as a ring for winner-takes-all, bare-knuckle fights—a form of live entertainment back in the day. Now it's a much friendlier place, serving British food and real ale. It's on the edge of Covent Garden, up a hidden alley off Garrick Street. ⊠ *33 Rose St., Covent Garden* ☎ *020/7497–9504* ⊕ *www.lambandflagcoventgarden.co.uk* Ⓜ *Covent Garden.*

🎭 Performing Arts

OPERA

★ Royal Opera House

OPERA | FAMILY | Along with Milan's La Scala, New York's Metropolitan, and the Palais Garnier in Paris, this is one of the world's great opera houses. First established in 1732, the Royal Opera House has staged countless spectacular performances during its illustrious history, while recent shows have tended toward a more contemporary repertoire. Whatever the style, the extravagant 2,250-seat auditorium delivers a serious dose of gilt and glamour. The famed Royal Ballet performs classical and contemporary repertoire here, too, and smaller-scale works of both opera and dance are presented in the Linbury Theatre and Clore Studio. A small allocation of tickets for each performance of main stage productions for the week ahead—even those that are sold out—goes on sale online at 1 pm every Friday.

If you wish to see the famed auditorium but are not able to procure a ticket, you can join a backstage tour or one of the less frequent tours of the auditorium; they book up several weeks in advance. ⊠ *Bow St., Covent Garden* ☎ *020/7304–4000* ⊕ *www.roh.org.uk* 🎟 *Performances from £7; tours from £16* Ⓜ *Covent Garden.*

158

PERFORMING ARTS CENTERS
London Coliseum
ARTS CENTERS | FAMILY | An architectural extravaganza of Edwardian style, the baroque-style theater has a magnificent 2,350-seat auditorium and a rooftop glass dome with a bar and great views. As one of the city's most venerable venues, the Coliseum functions mainly as the home of the English National Opera, which produces innovative opera, sung in English, for lower prices than the nearby Royal Opera House. In recent years the company also has presented musicals, sometimes featuring star opera singers. During opera's off-season (including summertime and during winter holidays), the house hosts the English National Ballet and other troupes. Guided tours offering fascinating insights into the architecture and history of the building take place on selected dates at 11 am. ✉ *St Martin's La., Covent Garden* ☎ *020/7845–9300* ⊕ *www.londoncoliseum.org* ▣ *Opera from £10, ballet from £14, tours £12* Ⓜ *Charing Cross, Leicester Sq.*

THEATER
The Donmar Warehouse
THEATER | FAMILY | Hollywood stars often perform at this not-for-profit theater in diverse and daring new works, bold interpretations of the classics, and small-scale musicals. Heavy-hitters like Nicole Kidman, Gwyneth Paltrow, and Ewan McGregor have all graced the stage. ✉ *41 Earlham St., Seven Dials, Covent Garden* ☎ *020/3282–3808* ⊕ *www.donmarwarehouse.com* Ⓜ *Covent Garden.*

Shopping

BOOKS AND PRINTS
Grosvenor Prints
ART GALLERIES | FAMILY | London's largest collection of 17th- to early 20th-century prints focuses on views of London and its architecture and denizens, as well as royal, sporting, and decorative motifs. From master printmaker William Hogarth to caricaturist James Gillray, the

somewhat higgledy-piggledy selection is hugely eclectic, with prices ranging from £20 into the thousands. Staff will happily ship globally; just note that it's closed on weekends. ✉ *19 Shelton St., Covent Garden* ☎ *020/7836–1979* ⊕ *www.grosvenorprints.com* ◷ *Closed Sat.–Sun.* Ⓜ *Covent Garden, Leicester Sq. Holborn.*

★ Stanfords
OTHER SPECIALTY STORE | FAMILY | When it comes to encyclopedic coverage, there is simply no better map and travel shop on the planet. Trading in Covent Garden since 1853, Stanfords is packed with a comprehensive selection of travel books and travel accessories, as well as ordinance surveys, cycle route maps, travel adaptors, globes, replicas of antique maps, mosquito nets, and more. Even the floor is decorated with giant maps. Whether you're planning a day trip to Dorset or a serious adventure to the Kalahari Desert, this should be your first stop. ✉ *7 Mercer Walk, Covent Garden* ☎ *020/7836–1321* ⊕ *www.stanfords.co.uk* Ⓜ *Covent Garden, Holborn, Leicester Sq.*

CLOTHING
★ Blackout II
SECOND-HAND | FAMILY | Escape the bustle of Covent Garden's Neal Street here at one of London's top vintage clothing shops. Its two small floors are overflowing with high-end vintage dresses, coats, suits, costume jewelry, shoes, and more from the 1920s to the 1970s. With that much to choose from, you'll be hard-pressed to leave without finding something to sharpen up your look. ✉ *51 Endell St., Covent Garden* ☎ *020/7240–5006* ⊕ *www.blackout2.com* Ⓜ *Covent Garden, Holborn, Leicester Sq.*

Jack Wills
MIXED CLOTHING | FAMILY | The British heritage and country sports–inspired styles here have a wholesome yet sexy edge to them. Crowds of teens don't mind the pumping music while they browse the collection of parkas, jeans, dresses, polos, athleisure, and more. The store

also carries backpacks, baseball hats, branded water bottles, and other youthful lifestyle items. You can find another branch at Westfield White City. ⊠ *136 Long Acre, Covent Garden* ☎ *0343/909–2259* ⊕ *www.jackwills.com* Ⓜ *Leicester Sq., Covent Garden, Holborn.*

★ Paul Smith

MIXED CLOTHING | FAMILY | British classics with an irreverent twist define esteemed designer Paul Smith's collections for women, men, and children. Beautifully tailored suits for men and women take hallmarks of traditional British style and turn them on their heads with humor and color, combining exceptional fabrics with flamboyant linings or unusual detailing. Gift ideas abound—wallets, scarves, phone cases, and distinctive belts and socks—all in Smith's signature rainbow stripes. There are several branches throughout London, in Notting Hill, Soho, Marylebone, Southwark, and Canary Wharf, plus a Mayfair shop that includes mid-century furniture. ⊠ *40–44 Floral St., Covent Garden* ☎ *020/7379–7133* ⊕ *www.paulsmith.com* Ⓜ *Covent Garden, Leicester Sq., Holborn.*

Walker Slater

MIXED CLOTHING | Edinburgh tailor and Scottish tweed specialists Walker Slater step back in time at this men and women's tweed cornucopia near the Royal Opera House. The myriad selection of Border and hand-woven Harris tweed from Scotland's Outer Hebrides ranges from three-piece turn-up bottom and riding jacket—inspired tailcoats to over-the-knee herringbone, as well as sturdy Williamsburg, Kintyre, and Kirk caps. ⊠ *19 Great Queen St., Covent Garden* ☎ *020/3831–9144* ⊕ *www.walkerslater. com* Ⓜ *Covent Garden, Holborn.*

FOOD

★ Neal's Yard Dairy

FOOD | FAMILY | Magnificent stacks of ⹁ Britain's finest farmhouse cheeses fill the racks at this renowned cheesemonger and artisan cheese lovers' paradise off Seven Dials. Ever pungent and matured on-site, browse the rare raw milk Stilton-esque Stichelton blue cheese from Welbeck in Nottinghamshire or the 65 other small-batch, British-made creations like Montgomery cheddar, Camembert-style Tunworth, and a lactic goat's cheese Innes Log. ⊠ *17 Shorts Gardens, Covent Garden* ☎ *020/7500–7520* ⊕ *www.nealsyarddairy.co.uk* Ⓜ *Covent Garden, Holborn.*

MARKETS

★ Covent Garden Market

MARKET | FAMILY | Established in the 1670s as a thriving fruit, herb, and flower market, this popular historic piazza now has three separate market areas: the Apple Market, the East Colonnade Market, and the Jubilee Market. In the main covered area originally designed by Inigo Jones and known as the Apple Market, 40 stalls sell handcrafted jewelry, prints, clothes, ceramics, and crafts from Tuesday through Sunday, while Monday is given over to antiques, curios, and collectibles. The East Colonnade Market has stalls with mostly handmade specialty items like soaps and jewelry, as well as housewares, accessories, and magic tricks. The Jubilee Market, in Jubilee Hall toward Southampton Street, tends toward kitschy T-shirts and cheap household goods Tuesday through Friday but has vintage antiques and collectibles on Monday and handmade goods on weekends.

Largely aimed at the tourist trade in the past, Covent Garden Market continues its ascent, introducing a more sophisticated image (and correspondingly higher prices) with the opening of upscale restaurants and chains in the surrounding arcades, including a huge Apple Store; beauty outlets like Chanel, M.A.C., and Dior; and boutiques for top brands like Mulberry and N.Peal. ■TIP→ **Don't miss the magicians, musicians, jugglers, and escape artists who perform in the open-air piazza; the performances are free (though contributions are welcome).** ✉ *The Piazza, off Wellington St., Covent Garden* ⊕ *www.coventgarden.london* Ⓜ *Covent Garden.*

TOYS

★ Benjamin Pollock's Toyshop

TOYS | FAMILY | This landmark toy shop still carries on the tradition of its eponymous founder, who sold miniature theater stages made from richly detailed paper from the late 19th century until his death in 1937. Among his admirers was author Robert Louis Stevenson, who wrote, "If you love art, folly, or the bright eyes of children, speed to Pollock's." Today the mesmerizing antique model theaters are expensive, but there are plenty of magical reproductions for less than £10. There's also an extensive selection of nostalgic puppets, marionettes, teddy bears, Victorian paper dolls, spinning tops, jack-in-the-boxes, and similar traditional children's toys from the days before batteries were required (or toys were even run on them). ✉ *44 The Market, Covent Garden* ☎ *020/7379–7866* ⊕ *www.pollocks-coventgarden.co.uk* Ⓜ *Covent Garden, Leicester Sq., Holborn.*

The Tintin Shop

TOYS | Before there was Harry Potter, there was Tintin. Created by the Belgian cartoonist Hergé, the story of the fictional boy detective and his intrepid dog, Snowy, has been a cult favorite for generations. At this namesake shop devotees can find Tintin-related books, posters, T-shirts, metal and resin figurines, die-cast model airplanes, alarm clocks, and more. ✉ *34 Floral St., Covent Garden* ☎ *020/7836–1131* ⊕ *thetintinshop.uk.com* Ⓜ *Covent Garden, Leicester Sq., Holborn.*

Chapter 6

BLOOMSBURY AND HOLBORN

Updated by
James O'Neill

● Sights	🍴 Restaurants	🛏 Hotels	● Shopping	🍸 Nightlife
★★☆☆☆	★★☆☆☆	★★★★☆	★★☆☆☆	★★☆☆☆

BLOOMSBURY AND HOLBORN SNAPSHOT

TOP REASONS TO GO

The British Museum: From the Rosetta Stone to the Elgin Marbles, the British Museum is a wondrous vault of priceless treasures seized over centuries by the British Empire.

The Inns of Court: The quiet courts, leafy gardens, and magnificent halls that make up the heart of Holborn are the closest thing to the spirit of Oxbridge in London.

Sir John Soane's Museum: Quirky and enchanting, the former home of the celebrated 19th-century architect is a delightful treasure trove of antiquities and oddities.

The British Library: In keeping with Bloomsbury's literary spirit, this world-renowned archive holds everything from Shakespeare's *First Folio* to original, handwritten Beatles lyrics.

Charles Dickens: The famed author's former residence—he wrote *Oliver Twist* while living here—is now a fascinating museum.

GETTING THERE

The Russell Square Tube stop on the Piccadilly line leaves you right at the corner of Russell Square. The best Tube stops for the Inns of Court are Holborn on the Central and Piccadilly lines or Chancery Lane on the Central line. Tottenham Court Road on the Northern and Central lines is best for the British Museum. Once you're in Bloomsbury, you can easily get around on foot.

MAKING THE MOST OF YOUR TIME

If you plan to visit the Inns of Court as well as the British Museum, and you'd like to get a feel for the neighborhood, devote an entire day to this literary and legal enclave. An alternative scenario is to set aside a separate day for a visit to the British Museum, which can easily consume as many hours as you have to spare. It's a pleasure to wander through the leafy squares at your leisure, examining historic Blue Plaques or relaxing at a street-side café.

PAUSE HERE

■ In a neighborhood blessed with so many open green spaces, nothing quite beats the simple splendor of secluded **St. George's Gardens**. Located northeast of the Russell Square Tube station, this former 18th-century cemetery is Bloomsbury's best-kept secret, known only to those who live and work locally. With three discreet entrances (on Handel Street, Sidmouth Street, and Heathcote Street), most Londoners aren't even aware of this delightful 3-acre green oasis. Whether you choose to relax on a bench or peruse the weather-worn gravestones (Oliver Cromwell's granddaughter is buried here), it's the perfect place to catch your breath and recharge your batteries.

With the British Library, the British Museum, and countless departments of the University of London among its residents, Bloomsbury might appear all bookish and cerebral—but fear not, it's much more than that. There's a youthfulness about its buzzing thoroughfares, and this vitality extends from down-by-the-Thames Holborn—once Dickens territory, now the heartbeat of legal London—way up to revamped King's Cross and classy Islington to the north and out to cool Clerkenwell to the east.

Bloomsbury

A neighborhood of pretty squares and handsome thoroughfares, Bloomsbury is the intellectual heart of London. Once the epicenter of the Bloomsbury Group, an elite ensemble of artists and writers who converged on the area in the early 20th century, it's also home to the **University of London.** The university's vast campus stretches from Gower Street down across a series of elegant squares: Tavistock Square, **Russell Square** with its delightful gardens, and peaceful **Gordon Square,** which, aptly, was the home of Bloomsbury Group stalwarts Virginia Woolf (No. 46), John Maynard Keynes (also No. 46), and Lytton Strachey (No. 51). The **British Library,** with its vast treasures, is a few blocks north, across busy Euston Road.

Bloomsbury is bordered by Tottenham Court Road on the west, Euston Road on the north, Woburn Place (which becomes Southampton Row) on the east, and New Oxford Street on the south.

The area from Somerset House on the Strand, all the way up Kingsway to Euston Road, is known as London's **Museum Mile** for the myriad historic houses and museums that dot the area. The **Charles Dickens Museum,** in the house where the author wrote *Oliver Twist,* pays homage to the master, and artists' studios and design shops share space near the majestic **British Museum.** And guaranteed to raise a smile from the most blasé and footsore tourist is **Sir John Soane's Museum,** where the colorful collection reflects the eclectic interests of its namesake founder.

Sights

British Library

LIBRARY | FAMILY | With a collection totaling more than 150 million items, plus 3 million new additions every year, the British Library is a world-class repository of knowledge. Its greatest treasures are on view to the general public in the Sir John Ritblat Gallery: the Magna Carta, the Codex Sinaiticus (an ancient bible containing the oldest complete copy of the New Testament), Jane Austen's writings, and Shakespeare's *First Folio*, as well as musical manuscripts by Handel and Beethoven and original, handwritten lyrics by the Beatles. ⊠ *96 Euston Rd., Bloomsbury* ☎ *0330/333–1144* ⊕ *www.bl.uk* ✉ *Free, donations appreciated; charge for special exhibitions* Ⓜ *Euston, Euston Sq., King's Cross St. Pancras.*

★ British Museum

HISTORY MUSEUM | FAMILY | The sheer scale and importance of the British Museum's many treasures are impossible to overstate or exaggerate; it truly is one of the world's great repositories of human civilization. Established in 1753 and initially based on the library and "cabinet of curiosities" of the royal physician Sir Hans Sloane, the collection grew exponentially over the following decades, partly due to bequests and acquisitions, but also as a result of plundering by the burgeoning British Empire.

The neoclassical grandeur of the museum's Great Russell Street entrance befits what lies in wait inside. Here you'll find the Rosetta Stone, whose inscriptions were key to deciphering hieroglyphics (Room 4); the controversial but exquisite Elgin Marbles (aka the Parthenon Sculptures) that once stood on the Acropolis in Athens (Room 18); the remarkable 7th century BC masterpieces of Assyrian sculpted reliefs, the lion hunts (Room 10a); and stunning fragments and friezes from the Mausoleum of Halikarnassos (aka one of the Seven Wonders of the Ancient World; Room 21).

Other perennial favorites include the Egyptian mummies (Rooms 62–63); the colossal Statue of Ramesses II, dating to circa 1270 BC and weighing in at just over 7 tons (Room 4); and the splendid 8th-century Anglo-Saxon Sutton Hoo treasures, with magnificent helmets and jewelry aplenty (Room 41).

Leave time for exploring the glass-covered Great Court designed by celebrated architect Norman Foster at the turn of the present millennium—it has become a focal point of the museum. Likewise, don't miss the revered circular Reading Room where Karl Marx wrote *Das Kapital* under the beautiful blue-and-gold papier-mâché dome. And keep an eye out for the museum's excellent temporary exhibitions, which have featured exhibits on Stonehenge and influential Japanese artist Hokusai.

If it all seems a little overwhelming or if you're pushed for time, try one of the excellent museum tours. Eye-opener Tours (free; 30–40 minutes) focus on 14 individual galleries each day, while the 90-minute Highlights Tour covers all the major exhibits plus a few lesser-known ones, beginning at 11:30 am and 2 pm on Friday and weekends (£14; book online or at the ticket desk in the Great Court). ⊠ *Great Russell St., Bloomsbury* ☎ *020/7323–8000* ⊕ *www.britishmuseum.org* ✉ *Free (except for temporary exhibitions); donations encouraged* Ⓜ *Russell Sq., Holborn, Tottenham Court Rd.*

Charles Dickens Museum

OTHER MUSEUM | This is one of the few London houses Charles Dickens

(1812–70) inhabited that is still standing, and it's the place where he wrote *Oliver Twist* and *Nicholas Nickleby*. The house looks exactly as it would have in Dickens's day, complete with first editions, letters, and a tall clerk's desk (Dickens wrote standing up). Catch the fascinating Housemaid's Tour (£15) in which you're taken back in time to 1839 by Dickens's housemaid, who reveals the private lives of the great author and his family; note that it's only available select Sunday mornings and must be booked in advance. ✉ *48 Doughty St., Bloomsbury* ☎ *020/7405–2127* ⊕ *www.dickensmuseum.com* ☒ *£9.50* ⊗ *Closed Mon. and Tues.* Ⓜ *Chancery La., Russell Sq.*

Lamb's Conduit Street

STREET | If you think Bloomsbury is about all things intellectual, then think again. Lamb's Conduit Street, a pedestrian-only street of gorgeous Georgian town houses nestled to the east of Russell Square, is building a reputation as one of the capital's most charming—and fashionable—shopping thoroughfares. Avail yourself of what the boutiques have to offer, from fashion to ceramics, flowers to jewelry, fine art to wine; there's even an excellent run-by-locals food cooperative called The People's Supermarket. Alternatively, you could just window-shop your way down to The Lamb, a Victorian-era pub whose patrons have included Ted Hughes, Sylvia Plath, and Mr. Dickens himself. ✉ *Bloomsbury* Ⓜ *Russell Sq.*

Petrie Museum

HISTORY MUSEUM | If you don't get your fill of Egyptian artifacts at the British Museum, you can see more in the neighboring Petrie Museum, located on the first floor of the D. M. S. Watson Building, home to the UCL (University College London) Science Library. The museum houses an outstanding collection of Egyptian, Sudanese, and Greco-Roman archaeological objects, including jewelry, art, toys, and some of the world's oldest garments. ✉ *Malet Pl., Bloomsbury*

☎ *020/3108–9000* ⊕ *www.ucl.ac.uk/ museums/petrie* ☒ *Free, donations appreciated* ⊗ *Closed Sun. and Mon.* Ⓜ *Euston Sq., Goodge St.*

★ Sir John Soane's Museum

HISTORIC HOME | Sir John (1753–1837), architect of the Bank of England, bequeathed his eccentric house to the nation on one condition: that nothing be changed. It's a house full of surprises. In the Picture Room, two of Hogarth's famous *Rake's Progress* paintings swing away to reveal secret gallery recesses where you can find works by Canaletto and Turner. Everywhere, mirrors play tricks with light and space, and split-level floors worthy of a fairground funhouse disorient you. Soane's lovingly restored private apartments are also open to the public, but they can only be viewed as part of a guided tour, which must be booked in advance. Although entry to the house is free (with a suggested donation), you must book timed tickets at least a day in advance online or over the phone. ✉ *13 Lincoln's Inn Fields, Bloomsbury* ☎ *020/7405–2107* ⊕ *www.soane.org* ☒ *Free; guided tours £15* ⊗ *Closed Mon. and Tues.* Ⓜ *Holborn.*

Wellcome Collection

OTHER MUSEUM | If you fancy something unconventional, sample this collection by U.S. pharmaceutical millionaire and philanthropist Henry Wellcome (1853–1936), which explores the connections between medicine, life, and art (some exhibits may not be suitable for younger children). Comprising an estimated 1 million items, the collection includes Napoléon's elegant silver gilt–handled toothbrush, Horatio Nelson's razor, and Charles Darwin's walking stick. There are also anatomical models, Peruvian mummies, and Japanese sex toys, as well as two fascinating permanent exhibitions, "Medicine Man" and "Being Human." Keep an eye out for an original Picasso in the lobby just above the entrance when you enter. ✉ *183 Euston Rd., Bloomsbury*

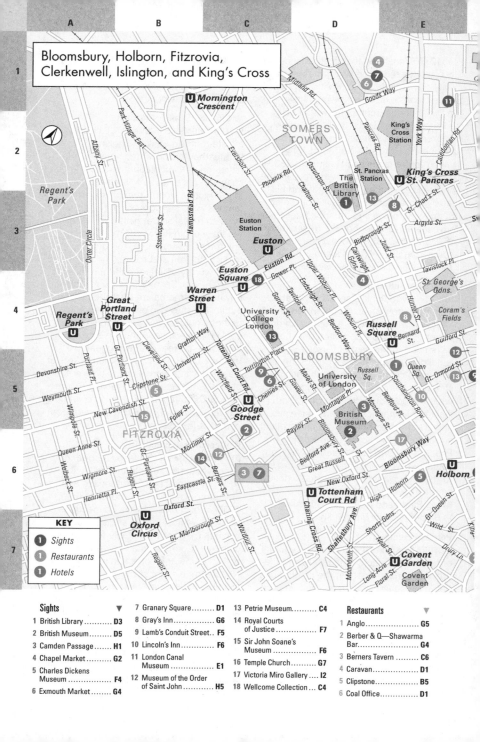

Bloomsbury, Holborn, Fitzrovia, Clerkenwell, Islington, and King's Cross

KEY

- ● Sights
- ● Restaurants
- ● Hotels

☎ 020/7611–2222 ⊕ www.wellcome-collection.org ⚑ Free ⊘ Closed Mon. Ⓜ Euston Sq., Euston.

 Restaurants

The literary giants of the Bloomsbury set—from Virginia Woolf to E. M. Forster and Vanessa Bell—may be long gone, but this bluestocking enclave (centered on the University of London and the British Library) still excels at a cultured and pleasure-loving dining scene.

The Hare and Tortoise Dumpling & Noodle Bar

$ | ASIAN | This informal eatery serves scrumptious Asian fast food in generous portions at reasonable prices. Popular with students from the many nearby universities, the accent is on freshly prepared, flavorful fare—from sushi and ramen to tempura and delicious noodle and rice dishes. **Known for:** tasty, well-priced sushi boxes; friendly staff; tempting array of starters and side dishes, such as panko honey king prawns. ⓢ *Average main: £10* ✉ *11–13 Brunswick Shopping Centre, Brunswick Sq., Bloomsbury* ☎ *020/7278–9799* ⊕ *www.hareandtortoise.co.uk/bloomsbury* Ⓜ *Russell Sq.*

Master Wei

$ | CHINESE | FAMILY | Deepest Bloomsbury might be the last place to expect superior Chinese street food, but think again. Tucked down an alleyway just off Southampton Row, this unpretentious eatery features the spicy, surprising cuisine of Xi'an, the city in northwest China that's home to the famed Terracotta Army statues (pictures of which hang above the bar). **Known for:** prompt, efficient service; flat, wide biang biang noodles, served in a variety of sumptuous broths and sauces; authentic, fresh, and flavorful Chinese cuisine. ⓢ *Average main: £10* ✉ *13 Cosmo Pl., Bloomsbury* ☎ *020/7209–6888* ⊕ *www.master-wei.com* Ⓜ *Russell Sq.*

★ Noble Rot

$$$ | BRITISH | There's an old Amsterdam coffeehouse vibe at this dark and creaky wine bar and restaurant on historic Lamb's Conduit Street in Bloomsbury. Run by two wine buffs and cult wine magazine publishers, you'll find deceptively simple ingredient-driven British dishes like Whitstable oyster and Cornish turbot braised in oxidized 1998 Bâtard-Montrachet Grand Cru. **Known for:** neat combos like leeks vinaigrette and Brixham crab; paradise for oenophiles; unpretentious seasonal British and French wine-friendly fare. ⓢ *Average main: £26* ✉ *51 Lamb's Conduit St., Bloomsbury* ☎ *020/7242–8963* ⊕ *www.noblerot.co.uk* ⊘ *Closed Sun.* Ⓜ *Holborn.*

Truckles of Pied Bull Yard

$ | WINE BAR | This wine bar and café serves up tasty modern British food within a stone's throw of the British Museum. Weather permitting, sit in its pretty Georgian courtyard. **Known for:** handsome Georgian courtyard oasis in the heart of the city; diverse wine list; traditional English favorites such as bangers and mash. ⓢ *Average main: £15* ✉ *Off Bury Pl., Bloomsbury* ☎ *020/7404–5338* ⊕ *www.davy.co.uk/truckles* ⊘ *Closed Sun.*

 Hotels

Celtic Hotel

$ | HOTEL | A stone's throw from the Russell Square Tube station, this is a reliable budget choice whose key attraction is its proximity to the West End and the British Museum. **Pros:** bargain rates; free Wi-Fi; good location. **Cons:** not all rooms have private bathrooms; no elevator; no-frills approach means few extras. ⓢ *Rooms from: £100* ✉ *62 Guilford St., Bloomsbury* ☎ *020/7837–6737* ⊕ *www.stmargaretshotel.co.uk* ⌨ *35 rooms* ⓧ *Free Breakfast* Ⓜ *Russell Sq.*

The Grange Blooms

$$ | **HOTEL** | Originally built as a Georgian town house, this charming hotel is just around the corner from the British Museum, and all its 26 rooms are fully ensuite and come with a variety of modern amenities, including TVs and complimentary Wi-Fi. **Pros:** excellent rates if you book early through the website; great location; good value. **Cons:** street noise in some rooms; no air-conditioning; guests can be bumped to sister hotel if fully booked. [$] *Rooms from: £150* ✉ *7 Montague St., Bloomsbury* ☎ *020/7323–1717* 🌐 *www.grangehotels.com* 🛏 *26 rooms* 🍴 *No Meals* [M] *Russell Sq.*

The Harlingford

$$ | **HOTEL** | Set in a handsome Georgian crescent, this family-run hotel offers quiet and comfortable accommodations with excellent amenities. **Pros:** private garden; good location; free Wi-Fi. **Cons:** no elevator; no air-conditioning; not great for those with cat and dog allergies. [$] *Rooms from: £130* ✉ *61–63 Cartwright Gardens, Bloomsbury* ☎ *020/7387–1551* 🌐 *www.harlingfordhotel.com* 🛏 *43 rooms* 🍴 *Free Breakfast* [M] *Russell Sq.*

Jesmond Hotel

$ | **B&B/INN** | This friendly family-run B&B is a great value given the location: it's only a short walk from the British Museum, Soho, and Covent Garden. **Pros:** free Wi-Fi; great location; friendly, helpful staff. **Cons:** no elevator; nearly half have shared bathrooms; some rooms are very small. [$] *Rooms from: £95* ✉ *63 Gower St., Bloomsbury* ☎ *020/7636–3199* 🌐 *www.jesmondhotel.org.uk* 🛏 *15 rooms* 🍴 *Free Breakfast* [M] *Goodge St., Euston Sq., Warren St., Russell Sq.*

The Megaro

$$ | **HOTEL** | Located right by St. Pancras International station, this colorful, snazzily designed hotel offers guests rooms with a chic contemporary vibe and all the latest amenities, from espresso machines to Bluetooth speakers. **Pros:** short hop on the Tube to city center; comfortable beds; great location for Eurostar travelers. **Cons:** interiors may be a bit stark for some; situated on a busy road, so it can get noisy; immediate neighborhood isn't interesting. [$] *Rooms from: £200* ✉ *1 Belgrove St., King's Cross* ☎ *020/7843–2222* 🌐 *www.hotelmegaro.co.uk* 🛏 *57 rooms* 🍴 *Free Breakfast* [M] *King's Cross St. Pancras.*

The Ridgemount Hotel

$ | **B&B/INN** | Mere blocks from the British Museum and London's West End theaters, this handsomely fronted guesthouse has clean, neat, and plainly decorated rooms at bargain rates. **Pros:** family rooms (accommodating up to five) are an excellent value; free Wi-Fi; helpful staff. **Cons:** cheapest rooms have shared bathrooms; no elevator; decoration is basic. [$] *Rooms from: £90* ✉ *65–67 Gower St., Bloomsbury* ☎ *020/7636–1141* 🌐 *www.ridgemounthotel.co.uk* 🛏 *32 rooms* 🍴 *Free Breakfast* [M] *Goodge St.*

★ **St. Pancras Renaissance Hotel**

$$$ | **HOTEL** | This stunningly restored Victorian landmark—replete with gingerbread turrets and neo-Gothic flourishes—started as a love letter to the golden age of railways, and now it's one of London's most sophisticated places to stay. **Pros:** close to the train station; unique and beautiful; faultless service. **Cons:** free Wi-Fi only in the lobby and public areas; streets outside are busy 24/7; very crowded bar and restaurant. [$] *Rooms from: £290* ✉ *Euston Rd., King's Cross* ☎ *020/7841–3540* 🌐 *www.marriott.com/hotels/travel/lonpr-st-pancras-renaissance-hotel-london* 🛏 *245 rooms* 🍴 *No Meals* [M] *King's Cross St. Pancras. National Rail: Kings Cross, St. Pancras.*

Continued on page 178

THE BRITISH MUSEUM

Anybody writing about the British Museum had better have a large stack of superlatives close at hand: most, biggest, earliest, finest. This is the golden hoard of nearly three centuries of the Empire, the booty brought from Britain's far-flung colonies.

The first major pieces, among them the Rosetta Stone and the Parthenon Sculptures (Elgin Marbles), were "acquired" from the French, who "found" them in Egypt and Greece. The museum has since collected countless goodies of worldwide historical significance: the Black Obelisk, some of the Dead Sea Scrolls, the Lindow Man. And that only begins the list.

The British Museum is a vast space split into 94 galleries, generally divided by continent or period of history, with some areas spanning more than one level. There are marvels wherever you go, and—while we don't like to be pessimistic—it is, yes, impossible to fully appreciate everything in a day. So make the most of the tours, activity trails, and visitors guides that are available.

The following is a highly edited overview of the museum's greatest hits, organized by area. Pick one or two that whet your appetite, then branch out from there, or spend two straight hours indulging in the company of a single favorite sculpture. There's no wrong way to experience the British Museum, just make sure you do!

✉ Great Russell St., Bloomsbury WC1

☎ 020/7323–8000

🌐 www.britishmuseum.org

🎫 Free; donations encouraged. Tickets for special exhibits vary in price.

Ⓤ Russell Square, Holborn, Tottenham Court Rd.

(Left) The Great Court
(Top) Cradle to Grave by Pharmacopoeia

MUSEUM HIGHLIGHTS

Ancient Civilizations

The Rosetta Stone. Found in 1799 and carved in 196 BC by decree of Ptolemy V in Egyptian hieroglyphics, demotic, and Greek, it was this multilingual inscription that provided French Egyptologist Jean-François Champollion with the key to deciphering hieroglyphics. *Room 4.*

Colossal statue of Ramesses II. A member of the 19th dynasty (ca. 1270 BC), Ramesses II commissioned innumerable statues of himself—more than any other preceding or succeeding king. This one, a 7-ton likeness of his perfectly posed upper half, comes from his mortuary temple, the Ramesseum, in western Thebes. *Room 4.*

(Top) Portland vase
(Bottom) Colossal statue of Ramesses II

The Parthenon Sculptures. Perhaps these marvelous treasures of Greece shouldn't be here—but while the debate rages on, you can steal your own moment with the Elgin Marbles. Carved in about 440 BC, these graceful decorations are displayed along with an in-depth, high-tech exhibit of the Acropolis; the handless, footless Dionysus who used to recline along its east pediment is especially well known. *Room 18.*

Mausoleum of Halikarnassos. All that remains of this, one of the Seven Wonders of the Ancient World, is a fragmented form of the original "mausoleum," the 4th-century tomb of Maussollos, King of Karia. The highlight of this gallery is the marble forepart of the colossal chariot horse from the *quadriga. Room 21.*

The Egyptian mummies. Another short flight of stairs takes you to the museum's most popular galleries, especially beloved by children: the Roxie Walker Galleries of Egyptian Funerary Archaeology have a fascinating collection of relics from the Egyptian realm of the dead. In addition to real corpses, wrapped mummies, and mummy cases, there's a menagerie of animal companions and curious items that were buried alongside them. *Rooms 62–63.*

Portland Vase. Made in Italy from cameo glass at the turn of the first century, it is named after the Dukes of Portland, who owned it from 1785 to 1945. It is considered a technical masterpiece—opaque white mythological figures cut by a gem-cutter are set on cobalt-blue background. *Room 70.*

The **Enlightenment Gallery** should be visited purely for the fact that its antiquarian cases hold the contents of the British Museum's first collections—Sir Hans Sloane's natural-history loot, as well as that of Sir Joseph Banks, who acquired specimens of everything from giant shells to fossils to rare plants to exotic beasts during his voyage to the Pacific aboard Captain Cook's *Endeavour. Room 1.*

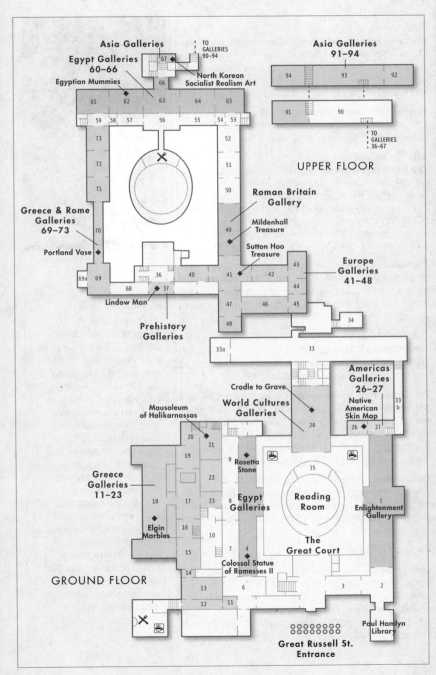

Asia Galleries

Egypt Galleries
60–66

Egyptian Mummies

67

TO
GALLERIES
90–94

North Korean
Socialist Realism Art

66

Asia Galleries
91–94

94   93   92

91   90

TO
GALLERIES
36–67

61   62   63   64   65

59 58 57   56   55   54 53

73   52

72   51

71   50

UPPER FLOOR

Greece & Rome
Galleries
69–73

Portland Vase

70

Roman Britain
Gallery

49   Mildenhall
Treasure

Sutton Hoo
Treasure

69a 69   36   40   41   42   43

68   37   44

Lindow Man   47   46   45

Prehistory
Galleries

48

Europe
Galleries
41–48

34

33a   33

Cradle to Grave

World Cultures
Galleries

Mausoleum
of Halikarnassos

Americas
Galleries
26–27

Native
American
Skin Map

33
b

26   27

20   21

19   9 Rosetta
Stone

24

Greece
Galleries
11–23

18   17   22   23   8   Egypt
Galleries

35

Reading
Room

1
Enlightenment
Gallery

Elgin
Marbles

16   10

15   7   4

The
Great Court

14   Colossal Statue
of Ramesses II

GROUND FLOOR

13   6

12   11

3   2

Paul Hamlyn
Library

Great Russell St.
Entrance

174

Asia

The Korea Foundation Gallery. Delve into striking examples of North Korean Socialist Realism art from the 1950s to the present and a reconstruction of a sarangbang, a traditional scholar's study, complete with hanji paper walls and tea-making equipment. *Room 67.*

The Percival David Collection. More than 1400 pieces of Chinese ceramics (the most comprehensive collection outside China) are on display. *Room 95.*

World Cultures

The North American Gallery. This is one of the largest collections of native culture outside North America, going back to the earliest hunters 10,000 years ago. Here a 1775 native American skin map serves as an example of the importance of such documents in the exploration and cartography of North America. Look for the beautifully displayed native American costumes. *Room 26.*

The Mexican Gallery. The most alluring pieces sit in this collection side by side: a 15th-century turquoise mask of Xiuhtecuhtli, the Mexican Fire God and Turquoise Lord, and a double-headed serpent from the same period. *Room 27.*

Britain and Europe

The Mildenhall Treasure. This glittering haul of 4th-century Roman silver tableware was found beneath the sod of a Suffolk field in 1942. *Room 49.*

The Sutton Hoo Treasure. Next door to the loot from Mildenhall—and equally splendid, including brooches, swords, and jewel-encrusted helmets—the treasure was buried at sea with (it is thought) Redwald, one of the first English kings, in the 7th century, and excavated from a Suffolk field in 1938–39. *Room 41.*

Lindow Man. "Pete Marsh"—so named by the archaeologists who unearthed the body from a Cheshire peat marsh—was ritually slain, probably as a human sacrifice, in the 1st century and lay perfectly pickled in his bog until 1984. *Room 50.*

Theme Galleries

Living & Dying. The "Cradle to Grave" installation pays homage to the British nation's wellbeing—or ill-being, as it were. More than 14,000 drugs (the number estimated to be prescribed to every person in the U.K. in his lifetime) are displayed in a colorful tapestry of pills and tablets. *Room 24.*

Colossal chariot horse from the quadriga of the Mausoleum of Halikarnassos

LOWER GALLERY

The three rooms that comprise the **Sainsbury African Galleries** are of the main interest here: together they present a staggering 200,000 objects, featuring intricate pieces of old ivory, gold, and wooden masks and carvings—highlighting such ancient kingdoms as the Benin and Asante. The displays include a collection of **55 throwing knives**; ceremonial garments including a dazzling pink and green **woman's coif** (*qufiya*) from Tunisia made of silk, metal, and cotton; and the *Oxford Man, a* 1992 woodcarving by Owen Ndou, depicting a man of ambiguous race clutching his Book of Knowledge.

DID YOU KNOW?

Galleries help divide this sprawling space into manageable sizes for visitors. The Sainsbury African Galleries are just some of the 94 galleries; the British Museum's collection totals more than 7 million objects.

THE NATION'S ATTIC: A HISTORY OF THE MUSEUM

The collection began when Sir Hans Sloane, physician to Queen Anne and George II, bequeathed his personal collection of curiosities and antiquities to the nation. The collection quickly grew, thanks to enthusiastic klepto-maniacs after the Napoleonic Wars—most notoriously the seventh Earl of Elgin, who obtained the marbles from the Parthenon and Erechtheion on the Acropolis in Athens during his term as British ambassador in Constantinople.

Soon thereafter, it seemed everyone had something to donate—George II gave the old Royal Library, Sir William Hamilton gave antique vases, Charles Townley gave sculptures, the Bank of England gave coins. When the first exhibition galleries opened to visitors in 1759, the trustees agreed to admit only small groups guided by curators. The British Museum quickly became one of the most fashionable places to be seen in the capital, and tickets, which had to be booked in advance, were treated like gold dust.

The museum's holdings quickly outgrew their original space in Montague House. After the addition of such major pieces as the Rosetta Stone, other Egyptian antiquities (spoils of the Napoleonic War), and the Parthenon Sculptures, Robert Smirke was commissioned to build an appropriately large and monumental building on the same site. It's still a hot ticket: the British Museum now receives more than 6 million visitors every year.

THE GREAT COURT AND THE READING ROOM

The museum's classical Greek-style facade features figures representing the progress of civilization, and the focal point is the awesome Great Court, a massive glass-roofed space. Here is the museum's inner courtyard (now the largest covered square in Europe) that, for more than 150 years, had been used for storage.

The 19th-century Reading Room, an impressive 106-foot-high blue-and-gold-domed library, forms the centerpiece of the Great Court. H. G. Wells, Thomas Hardy, Lord Tennyson, Oscar Wilde, George Orwell, T. S. Elliot, and Beatrix Potter are just a few writers who have used this space as a literary and academic sanctuary over the past 150 years or so.

(Top) Reading Room

PLANNING YOUR VISIT

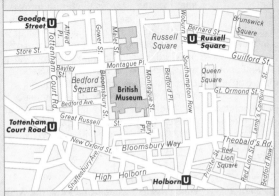

Tours

The **30–40 minute Eye-opener tour (free)** by Museum Guides does just what it says; ask for details at the information desk. After this tour, you can then dip back into the collections that most captured your imagination at your leisure.

An excellent **multimedia guide** is a good way to explore the galleries at your own pace, via a series of differently-themed tours.

Alternatively, the **Visitor's Guide** gives a brief but informative overview of the museum's history and is, again, divided into self-guided themed tours.

Before you go, take a look at the online **COMPASS tour** using the museum's navigation tool (⊕ *www.thebritishmuseum.org/compass*), which allows users to browse past and present exhibits as well as search for specific objects. A children's version can also be found here. Computer stations in the Reading Room offer onsite access to COMPASS.

■ TIP→ **The closest underground station to the British Museum is Russell Square on the Piccadilly line. However, since you will be entering via the back entrance on Montague Place, you will not experience the full impact of the museum's grand facade. To do so, alight at Holborn on the Central and Piccadilly lines or Tottenham Court Road on the Central and Northern lines. The walk from these stations is about 10 minutes.**

WITH KIDS

■ Take a look at the "Family Visits" page online for the top 12 objects to see with children.

■ The Families Desk in the Great Court has trails for kids ages 3 to 5 and 6 to 11. The Ford Centre for Young Visitors has free activity backpacks.

■ Art materials are available for free from information points, where you can also find out about workshops, performances, storytelling sessions, and other free events.

■ Around the museum, there are Hands On desks open daily 11–4, which let visitors handle objects from the collections.

WHERE TO REFUEL

The British Museum's self-service **Gallery Café** gets very crowded but serves an acceptable menu beneath a plaster cast of a part of the Parthenon frieze that Lord Elgin didn't remove. It's open daily, but isn't particularly family friendly.

The **café in the Great Court** keeps longer hours and is a great place to people-watch and admire the spectacular glass roof while you eat your salad and sandwich.

If the weather is nice, exit the museum via the back entrance on Montague Place and amble over to **Russell Square**, which has grassy lawns, water fountains, and a glass-fronted café for post-sandwich coffee and ice cream.

Nightlife

The gorgeous pubs of Bloomsbury attract tourists in the daytime and huge crowds of after-work drinkers in the early evening. They tend to quiet down as the night advances, making this a great spot for a relaxing night out. The redevelopment of the area around King's Cross St. Pancras Station has especially invigorated the nightlife scene here. Fitzrovia, meanwhile, manages to blend sophistication and informality in a way that's not found elsewhere in the center of town.

Exmouth Market and Upper Street are the main nightlife hot spots in Islington, just north and east of central London. The fun informal bars here make it a reliable choice for going out.

PUBS

Bloomsbury Tavern

PUBS | FAMILY | Located between the British Museum and the West End, this pretty Victorian-era pub and its stained-glass windows and varnished wooden floors and paneling is the perfect place for a pit stop. Legend says it was the final watering hole for condemned criminals en route to Tyburn gallows at Marble Arch. There's a good selection of pub fare and beers on tap. ⊠ *236 Shaftesbury Ave., Holborn* ☎ *020/7379–9811* ⊕ *www.bloomsburytavern.co.uk* Ⓜ *Holborn, Tottenham Court Rd.*

The Lamb

PUBS | FAMILY | Charles Dickens and his contemporaries drank here, but today's enthusiastic clientele make sure this intimate and eternally popular pub avoids the pitfalls of feeling too old-timey. One interesting feature: for private chats at the bar, you can close a delicate etched-glass "snob screen" to the bar staff, opening it only when you fancy another pint. ⊠ *94 Lamb's Conduit St., Bloomsbury* ☎ *020/7405–0713* ⊕ *www.thelamblondon.com* Ⓜ *Russell Sq.*

Museum Tavern

PUBS | FAMILY | Across the street from the British Museum in Bloomsbury, this friendly and classy Victorian pub makes an ideal resting place after the rigors of the culture trail. Karl Marx unwound here after a hard day in the British Museum Library. If he visited today, he could spend his *kapital* on its excellent selection of craft beers and spirits. ⊠ *49 Great Russell St., Bloomsbury* ☎ *020/7242–8987* ⊕ *www.greeneking-pubs.co.uk/pubs/greater-london/museum-tavern* Ⓜ *Tottenham Court Rd., Holborn.*

The Queens Larder

PUBS | FAMILY | Queen Charlotte, the wife of "mad" King George III, is said to have stored food for him here in the basement while he was being treated nearby. The interior of this tiny pub preserves its antique feel, with dark wood and old posters, and in the evenings fills up quickly with office workers, pediatricians, and students. In good weather, you might prefer to grab one of the seats outdoors. ⊠ *1 Queen's Sq., Bloomsbury* ☎ *020/7837–5627* ⊕ *www.queenslarder. co.uk* Ⓜ *Russell Sq., Holborn.*

🎭 Performing Arts

Once the heart of fashionable literary London, there's still an air of refinement about this neighborhood. A handful of small theaters with links to the colleges with campuses in the area create a vibrant small-scale performance scene with theater, dance, and stand-up comedy. It's also home to the world famous acting school, RADA (Royal Academy of Dramatic Art).

The Place

MODERN DANCE | This is London's only theater dedicated solely to contemporary dance, and with tickets often under £20, it's a good value, too. The Resolution festival, held in May and June, is the United Kingdom's biggest platform event for new choreographers. There's also an excellent bar and café. ✉ *17 Duke's Rd., Bloomsbury* ☎ *020/7121–1100* ⊕ *www. theplace.org.uk* ⌛ *From £17* Ⓜ *Euston.*

🛍 Shopping

ACCESSORIES

⭐ **James Smith & Sons Ltd.**

OTHER SPECIALTY STORE | Stepping into this gorgeous Victorian-era umbrella shop is like stepping back in time. Open since 1857, this family-run emporium sells every kind of umbrella, parasol, cane, and walking stick under the sun (including some containing a small flask or a corkscrew or that fold out into a seat). Rumored to have been the inspiration behind Ollivanders Wand Shop in the Harry Potter series, the interior of the shop is almost unchanged since it first opened its doors. Prices range from about £35 for a modest folding umbrella to more than £400 for a classic blackthorn root-knob solid stick brolly, to thousands for bespoke items. If the umbrella prices are too steep, smaller accessories like ox horn shoehorns or pocket combs make perfect gifts. ✉ *Hazelwood House, 53 New Oxford St., Bloomsbury* ☎ *020/7836–4731* ⊕ *www.james-smith. co.uk* ☉ *Closed Sun.* Ⓜ *Tottenham Court Rd., Holborn.*

BOOKS

Gay's The Word

BOOKS | Open since 1979, this is London's leading gay and lesbian bookshop. Thousands of titles, from literature and thoughtful nonfiction to erotica and pro-diversity children's books, fill the shelves. The shop is a well-loved fixture on the scene (it features prominently in the 2014 movie *Pride*) and often hosts discussion groups, readings, and other events. ✉ *66 Marchmont St., Bloomsbury* ☎ *020/7278–7654* ⊕ *www.gaystheword. co.uk* Ⓜ *Russell Sq.*

⭐ **Maggs Bros. Ltd.**

BOOKS | A bibliophile's heaven, this bookshop was first established in 1853 by the wonderfully Dickensian-sounding Uriah Maggs, who passed the business onto his four sons. Still one of the most important sellers of rare antiquarian books today, Maggs famously negotiated the purchase of a Gutenberg Bible from cash-starved Stalinist Russia, as well as the priceless Codex Sinaiticus (the oldest copy of the New Testament) that now sits on display in the nearby British Library.

The staff are expert enough to advise important collectors but are friendly and helpful to all interested visitors. Maggs is also an authority on works on counter-culture, subversion, punk, and the occult. There are occasional exhibitions of man-uscripts and rare editions, plus a sister shop on Curzon Street in Mayfair. ✉ *48 Bedford Sq., Bloomsbury* ☎ *020/7493–7160* ⊕ *www.maggs.com* Ⓜ *Goodge St., Tottenham Court Rd.*

Holborn

Southeast of Bloomsbury and west of The City, Holborn may appear to be little more than a buffer zone between the two—but although it may lack the panache of its neighbors, don't under-estimate this varied slice of the capital. Home to legal London and the impres-sive Inns of Court, this is also Charles Dickens territory, with The Old Curiosity Shop snug within its borders and the Charles Dickens Museum close by. Add to that its fair share of churches and quirky places of interest, and you'll soon discover that Holborn can be a rewarding place to while away an afternoon.

Holborn's massive Gothic-style **Royal Courts of Justice** ramble all the way to the Strand, and the **Inns of Court**—Gray's Inn, Lincoln's Inn, Middle Temple, and Inner Temple—are where most British trial law-yers have offices to this day. Geograph-ically, Holborn's borders are probably best defined as: west, Kingsway; north,

Theobald's Road; east, Gray's Inn Road; south, where the Strand becomes Fleet Street. In the 14th century, the Inns were lodging houses where barristers lived so that people would know how to easily find them (hence, the label "inn").

 Sights

Gray's Inn

NOTABLE BUILDING | Although the least architecturally interesting of the four Inns of Court and the one most heavily damaged by German bombs in the 1940s, Gray's still has romantic associations. In 1594 Shakespeare's *Comedy of Errors* was performed for the first time in the hall, which was restored after World War II and has a fine Elizabethan screen of carved oak. You must make advance arrangements to view the hall, but the secluded and spacious gardens, first planted by Francis Bacon in 1597, are open to the public. ⊠ *Gray's Inn Rd., Holborn* ☎ *020/7458–7800,* ⊕ *www.graysinn.org.uk* ⊠ *Free* ⊘ *Closed weekends* Ⓜ *Holborn, Chancery La.*

Lincoln's Inn

NOTABLE BUILDING | There's plenty to see at one of the oldest, best preserved, and most attractive of the Inns of Court— from the Chancery Lane Tudor brick gatehouse to the wide-open, tree-lined, atmospheric Lincoln's Inn Fields and the 15th-century chapel remodeled by Inigo Jones in 1620. The chapel and the gardens are open to the public, but to see more you must reserve a place on one of the official tours. But be warned: they tend to prefer group bookings of 15 or more, so it's best to check the website or call for details. ⊠ *Chancery La., Holborn* ☎ *020/7405–1393* ⊕ *www.lincolnsinn.org.uk* ⊠ *Free* ⊘ *Closed weekends* Ⓜ *Chancery La.*

Royal Courts of Justice

GOVERNMENT BUILDING | Here is the vast Victorian Gothic pile of 35 million bricks containing the nation's principal law courts, with 1,000-odd rooms running off 3½ miles of corridors. This is where the most important civil law cases—that's everything from divorce to fraud, with libel in between—are heard. You can sit in the viewing gallery to watch any trial you like, for a live version of Court TV; the more dramatic criminal cases are heard at the Old Bailey. Other sights are the 238-foot-long Great Hall and the compact exhibition of judges' robes. Guided tours must be booked online and in advance, and include a chance to view original court documents relating to a certain Guy Fawkes. ⊠ *The Strand, Holborn* ⊕ *www.theroyalcourtsofjustice.com* ⊠ *Free, tours £14* ⊘ *Closed weekends* Ⓜ *Temple, Holborn, Chancery La.*

Temple Church

CHURCH | As featured in *The Da Vinci Code,* this church was built by the Knights Templar in the late 12th century. The Red Knights held their secret initiation rites in the crypt here. Having started poor, holy, and dedicated to the protection of pilgrims, they grew rich from showers of royal gifts until, in the 14th century, they were stripped of their wealth, charged with blasphemy and sodomy, and thrown into the Tower. ⊠ *King's Bench Walk, The Temple, Holborn* ☎ *020/7353–3470* ⊕ *www.templechurch.com* ⊠ *£5* ⊘ *Closed weekends* Ⓜ *Temple.*

🍴 Restaurants

★ The Delaunay

$$$ | AUSTRIAN | FAMILY | It's all fin de siècle Vienna at this evocative art deco–style grand café on Aldwych near Covent Garden. Dishes on the majestic Middle European menu would do the Austro-Hungarian Empire proud—think Wiener schnitzel, Hungarian goulash, beef Stroganoff, and wonderful *würstchen* (frankfurters and hot dogs) served with sauerkraut and onions. **Known for:** excellent wine list; elegant old-world Austro-Hungarian vibe; proper Holstein schnitzel and frankfurters. $ *Average main: £25* ⊠ *55 Aldwych, Holborn* ☎ *020/7499–8558* ⊕ *www.thedelaunay. com* Ⓜ *Covent Garden, Holborn.*

 Hotels

The Hoxton

$$ | HOTEL | FAMILY | The emphasis here is on modest-size rooms elegantly appointed and decorated with a chic eye for detail. **Pros:** fab restaurant and bar; good value for money; great location close to the West End and the British Museum. **Cons:** hotel lobby becomes a co-working space during the day and can get noisy; smallest rooms are on the tiny side; breakfast isn't inclusive and is a rather meager affair. $ *Rooms from: £140* ⊠ *199–206 High Holborn, Holborn* ☎ *020/7661–3000* ⊕ *www.the-hoxton.com* ⌁ *174 rooms* ‖O‖ *No Meals* Ⓜ *Holborn.*

★ **Rosewood London**

$$$$ | HOTEL | Exuding an understated grandeur, this luxurious hotel is a relaxing, indulgent sanctuary in the heart of the city. **Pros:** great spa; gorgeous romantic space; excellent restaurant. **Cons:** the rooms can't quite match the splendor of the public areas; the area can be quiet on weekends; luxury comes at a price. $ *Rooms from: £500* ⊠ *252 High Holborn, Holborn* ☎ *020/7781–8888, 888/767–3966 in U.S.* ⊕ *www.rosewoodhotels.com/en/london* ⌁ *306 rooms* ‖O‖ *No Meals* Ⓜ *Holborn.*

SACO Holborn

$$ | APARTMENT | FAMILY | Down a charming backstreet a 10-minute walk from the British Museum, these serviced one- and two-bedroom apartments (some of the latter sleep up to six people) are spacious, modern, and well equipped, including kitchens with dishwashers and washing machines. **Pros:** on-site parking; more independence than hotels; pleasant and spacious accommodations. **Cons:** the area is empty on weekends; responsible

for your own dining; exterior is dated. $ *Rooms from: £250* ⊠ *Spens House, 72–84 Lamb's Conduit St., Holborn* ☎ *0330/202–0505* ⊕ *www.sacoapartments.co.uk* ⌁ *32 apartments* ‖O‖ *No Meals* Ⓜ *Russell Sq.*

 Nightlife

BARS

★ **Scarfes Bar**

BARS | FAMILY | Named after renowned London-born artist and caricaturist Gerald Scarfe (whose work adorns the walls), the Rosewood's seductively glamorous bar is one part Edwardian gentleman's club to two parts *Downton Abbey* drawing room. Recline on sofas by a roaring log fire or sink into velvet armchairs and explore the bar's impressive collection of fine wines, cocktails, and spirits (there are more than 180 single malt whiskies alone to choose from). Bar snacks are restaurant-standard dishes, and there's complimentary jazz most nights. ⊠ *The Rosewood, 252 High Holborn, Holborn* ☎ *020/3747–8670* ⊕ *www.scarfesbar. com* Ⓜ *Holborn.*

PUBS

Princess Louise

PUBS | FAMILY | This fine pub, popular with academics from the nearby British Museum and King's College London, is an exquisite museum piece of a Victorian interior, with glazed tiles and intricately engraved glass screens that divide the bar area into cozy little annexes. There's an excellent selection of real ales on tap, too. ⊠ *208 High Holborn, Holborn* ☎ *020/7405–8816* Ⓜ *Holborn.*

The Seven Stars

PUBS | Originally established in 1602 to cater to Dutch sailors, this charming hostelry somehow survived the Great Fire of London to become the little gem it is today. Located at the rear of the Royal Courts of Justice, you can often find barristers and their clients celebrating or drowning their sorrows. Scrumptious pub food is also served. ✉ *53 Carey St., Holborn* ☎ *020/7242–8521* 🌐 *www.thesevenstars1602.co.uk* [M] *Chancery Lane, Holborn.*

Performing Arts

Peacock Theatre

MODERN DANCE | Sadler's Wells's West End annex, this modernist theater near the London School of Economics (which sometimes uses it as a lecture hall during the day) focuses on younger companies and features popular dance genres like flamenco, tango, and hip-hop. ✉ *Portugal St., Holborn* ☎ *020/7863–8198* 🌐 *www.peacocktheatre.com* 🎟 *From £15* [M] *Holborn.*

Shopping

ANTIQUES

The London Silver Vaults

ANTIQUES & COLLECTIBLES | Originally opened in 1885 as Britain's first safe deposit building, this extraordinary space five floors beneath ground level has been converted to more than 30 small shops (or "vaults" as they're called) that house silver dealers, the majority of which are family businesses. Products range from 16th-century items to contemporary pieces (with everything in between), and from the spectacularly over-the-top costing thousands to smaller items—like teaspoons, candlesticks, or a Victorian serving tray—at £30. ✉ *53–64 Chancery La., Holborn* ☎ *020/7242–3844* 🌐 *www.silvervaultslondon.com* [M] *Chancery La.*

Fitzrovia

To the north of Soho, on the other side of Oxford Street, is Fitzrovia, famed for its dining and drinking. It is known affectionately by some as "Noho." Like its brasher southern sibling, it has some excellent bars and restaurants (especially on Charlotte Street) but more breathing space and fewer crowds. Its name most likely derives from nearby Fitzroy Square. Originally designed by the Adam brothers, the square and its environs quickly became fashionable for haute bohemia; George Bernard Shaw and James McNeill Whistler lived here. To the west, Great Portland Street separates it from Marylebone, while Tottenham Court Road marks its eastern border, beyond which is Bloomsbury. Busy Euston Road (and the Circle line beneath it) is its northern extent.

Restaurants

Berners Tavern

$$$$ | **MODERN BRITISH** | **FAMILY** | All the cool cats swing by this grand brasserie at Ian Schrager's insanely trendy London Edition hotel near Tottenham Court Road. Enter the monumental Edwardian dining salon, where you might swoon over a Herdwick lamb rump with mashed potatoes and white onion purée. **Known for:** legendary Buccleuch Estate steaks; knockout dining salon; cool backlit cocktail bar. [$] *Average main: £35* ✉ *The London Edition, 10 Berners St., Fitzrovia* ☎ *020/7908–7979* 🌐 *www.bernerstavern.com* [M] *Oxford Circus, Tottenham Court Rd.*

★ **Clipstone**

$$$ | **FRENCH** | Flavorful, inventive dishes elevate this hipster casual joint to the top rank of London's midrange gastro titans. With a focus on in-house curing, pickling, smoked meats, and heritage vegetables, expect a cavalcade of unlikely combinations and classic gastronomy specialties. **Known for:** good-value set lunches; fine dining without the fuss; lots of homemade, pickled, fermented, or cured extras. [$] *Average main: £28* ✉ *5 Clipstone St., Fitzrovia* ☎ *020/7637–0871* 🌐 *www.clipstonerestaurant.co.uk* 🕓 *Closed Mon.* [M] *Great Portland St., Warren St.*

★ Newman Arms

$ | MODERN BRITISH | Glimpse the future of British cuisine at this rickety wood-paneled dining salon at the atmospheric 1730 Newman Arms pub in Fitzrovia. A one-time haunt of Dylan Thomas and George Orwell (it's even mentioned in *1984*), the menu showcases the finest Cornish- and Devon-sourced meat, vegetables, and fresh fish with a rare instinctive ease. $ *Average main: £14* ⊠ *23 Rathbone St., Fitzrovia* ☎ *0020/3643–6285* ⊕ *www.newmanarmspub.com* Ⓜ *Goodge St.*

★ Portland

$$$$ | MODERN EUROPEAN | Consistently brilliant modern European fare in a low-key setting characterizes this restaurant located just northeast of Oxford Circus. Marvel at the chef's brigade in the open kitchen busily turning the inventive seasonal produce–driven menu into delicious reality. **Known for:** good-value tasting menus; vegetarian- and vegan-friendly menu; excellent wine list. $ *Average main: £45* ⊠ *113 Great Portland St., Fitzrovia* ☎ *020/7436–3261* ⊕ *www.portlandrestaurant.co.uk* ☻ *Closed Sun. and Mon.* Ⓜ *Oxford Circus.*

 Hotels

★ Charlotte Street Hotel

$$$ | HOTEL | Superstar London hotel designer Kit Kemp has taken the fabled Bloomsbury Group as her inspiration for this supremely stylish boutique hotel, which, if anything, feels more like a private members' club. **Pros:** excellent, lively location; elegant and luxurious; great attention to detail. **Cons:** some rooms are small considering the price; reservations essential for the restaurant; the popular bar can be noisy. $ *Rooms from: £340* ⊠ *15–17 Charlotte St., Fitzrovia* ☎ *020/7806–2000, 888/559–5508 in U.S.* ⊕ *www.firmdalehotels.com* ⇝ *52 rooms* ¶◯¶ *No Meals* Ⓜ *Goodge St.*

★ The London EDITION

$$$$ | HOTEL | Style and image are the draw at the London EDITION Hotel, where Michelin-starred chefs and hip bars complement the boutique property's sleek, contemporary design. **Pros:** beautifully designed bedrooms; very trendy; great bars. **Cons:** can at times feel more like an event space than a hotel; lobby can get crowded with trendsetters descending upon the bars; rooms may feel small to some. $ *Rooms from: £420* ⊠ *10 Berners St., Fitzrovia* ☎ *020/7781–0000* ⊕ *edition-hotels.marriott.com/london* ⇝ *173 rooms* ¶◯¶ *Free Breakfast* Ⓜ *Oxford Circus.*

Sanderson London

$$$ | HOTEL | Originally designed by French designer Philippe Starck, the style of this fashionable, quirky hotel is part surrealist Baroque, part Alice in Wonderland; sleigh beds are positioned in the middle of bedrooms at playful angles, and so are the freestanding bathtubs and wash basins—indeed, everything is off-center. **Pros:** unique Afternoon Tea; excellent design; your every whim gratified. **Cons:** you need to book far in advance to get lower rates; bar and restaurant are so exclusive it's hard to get in; glass walls and sheer curtains are all that separate the bathroom in some rooms. $ *Rooms from: £290* ⊠ *50 Berners St., Fitzrovia* ☎ *020/7300–1400* ⊕ *www.sanderson-london.com* ⇝ *150 rooms* ¶◯¶ *No Meals* Ⓜ *Oxford Circus, Tottenham Court Rd.*

 Nightlife

BARS

★ Artesian

BARS | They don't take reservations at this jewel box of a cocktail bar at The Langham hotel, but you can order a drink while you wait for a chic mirror-top table surrounded by some of London's most beautiful people. The innovative, creative cocktails involve exotic ingredients, like aromatic bitters all the way from Marrakesh, and are simply unforgettable, if pricey. Service is also top-notch, making this a nightlife treat. ⊠ *The Langham, 1C Portland Pl., Fitzrovia* ☎ *020/7636–1000* ⊕ *www.artesian-bar.co.uk* Ⓜ *Oxford Circus, Goodge St.*

★ The London EDITION

BARS | Visitors to Ian Schrager's London EDITION hotel are spoiled for choice when it comes to bars. High ceilings, eclectic artwork, and innovative cocktails can be found at the all-day Berners Tavern and in the Lobby Bar, which opens in the evening. You'll need a reservation to get into the cozy wood-paneled and open-fire Punch Room, but the bar's reinventions of traditional punches (the type favored by pirates and privateers) and the exemplary service are well worth the extra effort. ⊠ *10 Berners St., Fitzrovia* ☎ *020/7781–0000* ⊕ *www.editionhotels. com/london* Ⓜ *Tottenham Court Rd., Oxford Circus.*

Shopping

CLOTHING

★ So Tiny London

CHILDREN'S CLOTHING | This small store has loads of imaginative clothes for babies and young children, such as T-shirts emblazoned with Union Jacks and phrases like "Darth Vader Is My Father" and "Baby Gaga," as well as the utterly inspired baby onesie decked out in classic black-and-white prison stripes with the caption "Been Inside for 9 Months." There are also pretty dresses with English Rose prints, dragon costumes for dress-up, and great gifts for the little ones in your life, like dinosaur hand puppets or a knitted gold crown. ⊠ *64 Great Titchfield St., Fitzrovia* ☎ *020/7636–3501* ⊕ *www.sotinylondon.com* Ⓜ *Oxford Circus.*

Clerkenwell

Once home to medieval religious orders such as the Knights Hospitallers of St. John of Jerusalem, Clerkenwell later became an epicenter of the Industrial Revolution in the capital and, subsequently, of political radicalism (a young Joseph Stalin is said to have met a young Vladimir Lenin at The Crown Tavern pub in Clerkenwell Green). The monks are long gone—so, too, the communists—and the neighborhood's warehouses and factory floors are now home to cutting-edge design agencies, new media start-ups, and ubertrendy apartments. With its fashionable boutiques, bars, and restaurants, Clerkenwell can be a pleasant place to spend a few hours. Like its neighbor immediately to the east, The City, this area can be quite deserted on weekends.

Sights

Exmouth Market

PEDESTRIAN MALL | At this charming pedestrianized thoroughfare, trendy clothing boutiques, jewelers, beauty salons, gift shops, and even a tattoo parlor all jostle for space with Exmouth Market's excellent cafés and restaurants, many of which offer outdoor seating. At its southern end is the 19th-century Church of Our Most Holy Redeemer, the only Italian basilica–style church in London. There's also a vibrant food market on weekdays serving gourmet street food. Look out for the brilliantly named barber shop, Barber Streisand. ⊠ *Exmouth St., Clerkenwell* ⊕ *www.exmouth.london* Ⓜ *Farringdon, Angel.*

Museum of the Order of St. John

OTHER MUSEUM | This fascinating museum tells the story of the Knights Hospitallers of St. John, from the order's 11th-century Crusader origins in Jerusalem to its present-day incarnation as the St. John Ambulance service. The museum is spread across two adjacent sites: the arched St. John's Gatehouse, which dates back to 1504, and the Priory Church with its atmospheric Norman crypt. An excellent interactive display explores the order's past, both as a military force and a religious institution that cared for sick pilgrims, and the eclectic variety of objects on display reflects that colorful history: from antique medicinal jars and medical equipment to pieces of armor worn by the knights when they defended Malta from the Ottomans in the 16th century, as well as a bronze cannon given by Henry VIII before he dissolved the order altogether a few years later. ⊠ *St. John's Gate, St. John's La., Clerkenwell* ☎ *020/7324–4005* ⊕ *www. museumstjohn.org.uk* ⊠ *Free, guided tours £5 suggested donation* ⊙ *Closed Sun. Oct.–June* Ⓜ *Farringdon.*

🍴 Restaurants

Anglo

$$$$ | **MODERN BRITISH** | Mark Jarvis's cool, unpretentious fine-dining establishment in the historic Hatton Garden jewelry quarter in Farringdon is focused on food that is both seasonal and ethically and locally produced. Five- or seven-course tasting menus are offered at lunch and dinner, with each dish as much a feast for your eyes as for your palate. **Known for:** inventive desserts like frozen chocolate-and-water mousse with apple chips; well-priced tasting menus for lunch and dinner; signature grated cheese and onion on malt toast. $ *Average main: £40* ⊠ *30 St Cross St., Clerkenwell* ☎ *020/7430–1503* ⊕ *www.anglorestaurant.com* ⊙ *Closed Sun. and Mon.* Ⓜ *Farringdon.*

Berber & Q—Shawarma Bar

$$ | **ISRAELI** | **FAMILY** | Every night feels as bustling as downtown Tel Aviv at Exmouth Market's superb and hip shawarma bar. Enjoy challah toast with tahini-rich meze before delving into slow-cooked, harissa-heavy lamb shawarmas and the best *mejadera* (rice with lentils

and onions) this side of the Middle East. **Known for:** unmissable barbecued cauliflower shawarma; Tel Aviv–style trendy hangout; wondrous chargrilled lamb and beef shawarmas. $ *Average main: £16* ⊠ *46 Exmouth Market, Clerkenwell* ☎ *020/7837–1726* ⊕ *www.shawarmabar. co.uk* ⊙ *Closed Mon.* Ⓜ *Farringdon.*

★ Luca

$$$$ | **MODERN ITALIAN** | This winning mix of modern Italian classics is made from the very best in British seasonal produce. Add to that the super-chic setting—from the art deco–esque dining salon to the marble-top bar and the stunning glass-walled conservatory—and this popular Clerkenwell haunt is very much a case of both style *and* substance. **Known for:** to-die-for fluffy parmesan fries; edgy Italian pastas; cool and glamorously designed brasserie. $ *Average main: £35* ⊠ *88 St John St., Clerkenwell* ☎ *020/3859–3000* ⊕ *www.luca.restaurant* ⊙ *Closed Sun.* Ⓜ *Farringdon.*

Moro

$$$ | **MOROCCAN** | **FAMILY** | Exmouth Market today is a magnet for fine indie-spirited restaurants and it all began with this one back in 1997. Lovingly nurtured by husband-and-wife chefs Sam and Sam Clark, the menu features a mélange of Spanish and Moroccan dishes, all packed with flavor and perfectly seasoned and spiced. **Known for:** house yogurt cake with pistachios and pomegranate; loud and buzzy dining room with booming acoustics; expressive Moorish delights. $ *Average main: £25* ⊠ *34–36 Exmouth Market, Clerkenwell* ☎ *020/7833–8336* ⊕ *www. moro.co.uk* Ⓜ *Farringdon, Angel.*

★ St. John

$$$ | **MODERN BRITISH** | **FAMILY** | Global foodie fanatics join Clerkenwell locals for the pioneering nose-to-tail cuisine at this high-ceilinged, converted smokehouse near Smithfield Market. Here the chef uses all scraps of a carcass—from tongue and cheeks to tail and trotters—so brace for radically stark signatures like

bone-marrow-and-parsley salad. **Known for:** great wine list; crispy pig's-skin appetizer; ground zero of influential Modern British nose-to-tail dining. *[$] Average main: £24 ✉ 26 St. John St., Clerkenwell ☎ 020/7251–0848 🌐 www.stjohnrestaurant.com 🕑 No dinner Sun. [M] Farringdon, Barbican.*

Hotels

★ The Rookery

$$$ | HOTEL | A stylish period masterpiece in the heart of laid-back Clerkenwell, The Rookery is a luxury boutique hotel with a hefty dollop of *Downton Abbey* charm. **Pros:** good deals in the off-season; charming decor; free Wi-Fi. **Cons:** neighborhood can get noisy on weekends; no restaurant in the hotel; breakfast costs extra. *[$] Rooms from: £260 ✉ 12 Peter's La., at Cowcross St., Clerkenwell ☎ 020/7336–0931 🌐 www.rookeryhotel.com 🛏 33 rooms 🍴 No Meals [M] Farringdon.*

★ The Zetter

$$ | HOTEL | The five-story atrium, art deco staircase, and slick European restaurant hint at the delights to come in this converted warehouse—a breath of fresh air with its playful color schemes, elegant wallpapers, and wonderful views of the city from the higher floors. **Pros:** free Wi-Fi; huge amounts of character; big rooms. **Cons:** the property's best bar is across the street at the Zetter Townhouse; the contemporary style won't appeal to everyone; rooms with good views cost more. *[$] Rooms from: £140 ✉ 86–88 Clerkenwell Rd.,. Clerkenwell ☎ 020/7324–4444 🌐 www.thezetter.com 🛏 59 rooms 🍴 Free Breakfast [M] Farringdon.*

Nightlife

Cafe Kick

BARS | Perfect for a midafternoon pick-me-up or late-night drinks, this quirky, friendly bar has a continental feel and a sporty vibe. Soccer memorabilia and bank notes from across the globe line the walls while formica furniture and not one, but two foosball tables fill out the space. World beers and cocktails are the drinks of choice (the caipirinhas are legendary), and simple but tasty pub fare is served all day. *✉ 43 Exmouth Market, Clerkenwell ☎ 020/7837–8077 🌐 www.cafekick.co.uk [M] Farringdon, Angel.*

The Craft Beer Co.

BARS | FAMILY | With 37 beers on tap and 350 more in bottles (one brewed exclusively for The Craft Beer Co.), the main problem here is knowing where to start. Luckily, friendly and knowledgeable staff are happy to advise or give tasters—or why not sign up for a guided tasting session? A huge chandelier and a mirrored ceiling lend antique charm to the interior, and a smattering of tourists and beer pilgrims break up the crowds of Leather Lane workers and locals. Just note that (oddly for a bar), they are closed on weekends. *✉ 82 Leather La., Clerkenwell ☎ 020/7404–7049 🌐 www.thecraftbeerco.com [M] Chancery La.*

★ The Holy Tavern

BARS | FAMILY | Loved by Londoners and owned by the well-respected St. Peter's Brewery in Suffolk, The Holy Tavern is one-of-a-kind: small, historic, atmospheric, and endearingly eccentric. Antique Delft-style tiles meld with wood and concrete in a converted watchmaker and jeweler's shop dating back to the 18th century. The beer, both bottled and on tap, is some of the best available anywhere in London. It's often busy, especially after work, but is closed on weekends. *✉ 55 Britton St., Clerkenwell*

☎ *020/7490–4281* 🌐 *www.stpetersbrewery.co.uk/london-pub* [M] *Farringdon.*

Islington

Islington is one of the most fashionable of London's villagelike neighborhoods. Upper Street, with its high-street stores, independent boutiques, and myriad restaurants and bars, is where most of the action takes place. But wander off the main drag and you'll discover elegant residential streets and squares, as well as bustling charming markets. You'll also find a handful of top-flight Off West End theaters and music venues in the area, including Almeida Theatre, the hugely atmospheric Union Chapel, and—down on Islington's border with Clerkenwell—the renowned contemporary dance venue Sadler's Wells.

Sights

Camden Passage

STREET | A pretty pedestrian thoroughfare just off Upper Street, Camden Passage is famous for its many antiques shops selling everything from vintage furniture to period jewelry to timeless timepieces. In recent years, a sprinkling of independent boutiques, delis, and cafés has given the passage an eclectic vibrant feel. Check out the antiques market held on Wednesday and from Friday through Sunday. ✉ *Islington* 🌐 *www.camdenpassageislington.co.uk* [M] *Angel.*

Chapel Market

NEIGHBORHOOD | Chapel Market is what Islington used to be: an unpretentious, working-class enclave. Like lots of areas in London, gentrification continues apace, but there's still a lively food market that runs for half the length of the street every day except Monday—just listening to the stallholders advertising their wares can be entertainment enough. ✉ *Chapel Market, Islington* [M] *Angel.*

Victoria Miro

ART GALLERY | This large, important commercial gallery, in a former furniture factory, has exhibited some of the biggest names on the British contemporary art scene: Grayson Perry, Chris Ofili, the Chapman Brothers, Paula Rego, and many others. Some exhibitions spill out into the gallery's garden. It also brings in exciting talent from abroad. ✉ *16 Wharf Rd., Islington* ☎ *020/7336–8109* 🌐 *www.victoria-miro.com* 🎫 *Free* 🕒 *Closed Sun. and Mon.* [M] *Old St., Angel.*

Restaurants

Ottolenghi

$ | **CAFÉ** | **FAMILY** | The original outpost of the ever-expanding Ottolenghi empire, this spot is a foodie's heaven. With the accent on North African and Eastern Mediterranean cuisine, the inventive, tasty, and healthy veg-centric dishes, along with fresh salads, flaky pastries, and artisan cakes, make this deli-bakery-café worth an hour of anyone's time. **Known for:** weekend brunches; zingy veg-centric Middle Eastern salad combos; fabulous meringue-filled window displays. [$] *Average main: £15* ✉ *287 Upper St., Islington* ☎ *020/7288–1454* 🌐 *www.ottolenghi.co.uk* [M] *Angel.*

Nightlife

BARS

The Bar with No Name

BARS | This elegant faux-speakeasy might be London's tiniest cocktail lounge. Book one of the handful of tables or a seat at the diminutive bar to sample perfectly made twists on classic cocktails, like the Heather Negroni which adds heather flowers to the traditional recipe. ✉ *69 Colebrooke Row, Islington* ☎ *07540/528–593* 🌐 *www.69colebrookerow.com* [M] *Angel.*

LIVE MUSIC
★ Union Chapel

LIVE MUSIC | FAMILY | The beauty of this sublime old chapel and its impressive multicultural not-for-profit programming make this spot one of London's best musical venues, especially for acoustic shows. A variety of star names have played here in recent years (including Kris Kristofferson, Björk, and Beck) along with alternative country, world music, and jazz performers. There are also poetry and literary events, film screenings, and stand-up comedy gigs. Tickets are only available online. ✉ *Union Chapel, Compton Terr., Islington* ☎ *020/7226–1686 for venue (no box office; ticket sales numbers vary with each event)* ⊕ *www.unionchapel.org.uk* Ⓜ *Highbury & Islington.*

 Performing Arts

Close to central London, yet with its own unique atmosphere, this neighborhood is home to a handful of renowned theaters and music venues that make the short journey northeast well worth the effort.

DANCE
★ Sadler's Wells

MODERN DANCE | FAMILY | If you're into leading classical and contemporary dance companies, head to this purpose-built complex, which opened in 1998 and is the sixth theater on this site in its 300-year history. Choreographers like Matthew Bourne and Hofesh Shechter often bring their work here. The smaller Lilian Baylis Studio hosts avant-garde work. ✉ *Rosebery Ave., Islington* ☎ *020/7863–8000* ⊕ *www.sadlerswells.com* 🚇 *From £15* Ⓜ *Angel.*

THEATER
Almeida Theatre

THEATER | This Off West End venue, helmed by artistic director Rupert Goold, premieres excellent new plays and exciting twists on the classics, often featuring high-profile actors. A good café-bar serves tasty food, wine, and cocktails.

King's Cross Station

Sick of living in the shadow of its sumptuously renovated next-door neighbor, St. Pancras Station, King's Cross—and the area behind it—has undergone a major makeover of its own, with bars, restaurants, shops, cultural venues, and a stunning fountain display for all to enjoy. It's also a place dear to Harry Potter fans everywhere because it was from the imaginary platform 9¾ that our hero boarded the *Hogwarts Express* (the station has helpfully put up a sign for platform 9¾ if you want to take a picture there).

✉ *Almeida St., Islington* ☎ *020/7359–4404* ⊕ *almeida.co.uk* 🚇 *From £10* Ⓜ *Angel, Highbury & Islington.*

Little Angel Theatre

PUPPET SHOWS | FAMILY | Innovative puppetry performances for children and adults have been taking place in this adorable former temperance hall since 1961. ✉ *14 Dagmar Passage, Islington* ☎ *020/7226–1787* ⊕ *www.littleangeltheatre.com* 🚇 *From £8* Ⓜ *Angel, Highbury & Islington.*

Shopping

HOUSEHOLD GOODS
★ twentytwentyone

HOUSEWARES | This furniture, lighting, and accessories store is a must-see if you're into mid-century and modernist design. It carries an enormous selection of 20th-century classics, including pieces from Eames, Noguchi, Wegner, Aalto, Prouvé, Saarinen, and the husband-and-wife team Robin and Lucienne Day, both in the form of original pieces and licensed reissues. You can also find contemporary products from modern masters like Tom

Centered on the train station made most famous as the fictional gateway to Hogwarts, King's Cross has seen a bevy of new dining and nightlife openings in the past few years.

Dixon, Thomas Heatherwick, and Marc Newson. Small accessories like tote bags and bath mats will easily fit into your luggage. ⊠ *274–275 Upper St., Islington* ☎ *020/7288–1996* ⊕ *www.twentytwenty-one.com* Ⓜ *Highbury & Islington.*

King's Cross

The transformation of King's Cross to a traffic-free cultural, culinary, and shopping oasis has taken twenty years and billions of pounds, but it's been well worth it. On what was once postindustrial wasteland and railroad yards, the 67-acre site is now populated by bars, restaurants, street-food vendors, and shops, including the stylish Coal Drops Yard shopping center designed by Thomas Heatherwick (of the famed London 2012 Olympic cauldron).

It's also home to the capital's premier art college, University of the Arts London, which now occupies an entire former grain warehouse in Granary Square, as well as an arts cinema and other cultural venues. If all that weren't enough, you've still got the gentle waters of Regent's Canal rolling by.

 Sights

Granary Square

PLAZA/SQUARE | Now the heart of King's Cross, Granary Square is one of London's liveliest open spaces. Pride of place is given to the ever-changing 1,000-strong fountain display, which is even more spectacular by night when lights accompany the choreography. It's also home to The Outside Project (essentially a permanent alfresco art space) as well as the immense, six-story granary building—designed in 1852 to store wheat for London's bakers—that now houses University of the Arts London, plus a small selection of excellent bars and eateries. The square's south-facing steps double as an amphitheater for site-specific art events. ⊠ *King's Cross* Ⓜ *King's Cross St. Pancras.*

London Canal Museum

OTHER MUSEUM | FAMILY | This delightful museum, dedicated to the rise and fall of London's once-extensive canal network, is based in the former warehouse of ice-cream maker Carlo Gatti (hence it also partly features the ice-cream trade as well as London's canals). Children enjoy the activity zone and learning about Henrietta, the museum's horse. Outside, on the Battlebridge Basin, you'll find the painted narrow boats of modern canal dwellers—a stone's throw from the hustle and bustle of the King's Cross redevelopment. You can walk to the museum along the towpath from Camden Lock; download a free audio tour from the museum's website to accompany the route. ✉ *12–13 New Wharf Rd., King's Cross* ☎ *020/7713–0836* 🌐 *www.canalmuseum.org.uk* 🎟 *£5* 🕒 *Closed Mon. and Tues.* [M] *King's Cross.*

🍴 Restaurants

Caravan

$$ | ECLECTIC | FAMILY | Set in a corner of what was once a vast Victorian warehouse, this airy eatery is open from early morning to late at night, serving great food and freshly roasted coffee (you'll pass by the giant coffee roaster en route to the bathroom). The focus is on world cuisine (the jalapeño cornbread is a perennial favorite), and the all-day menu features shared plates as well as sourdough pizzas. **Known for:** great cocktails; delicious selection of tapas-style plates; informal, buzzy vibe. [$] *Average main: £18* ✉ *1 Granary Sq., King's Cross* ☎ *020/7101–7661* 🌐 *www.caravanrestaurants.co.uk* [M] *King's Cross St. Pancras.*

Coal Office

$$$ | MODERN ISRAELI | Styled as a collaboration between star designer Tom Dixon and chef/entrepreneur Assaf Granit, this delightful restaurant is full of infectious joie de vivre and, most important, to-die-for food. With a mix of shared plates and main courses, the menu is a playful celebration of Israeli cuisine, with dishes from *the* most delicious cured trout to shawarma with tender bavette and bone marrow. **Known for:** grilled beef and lamb with tahini and chickpeas; ancient Levantine bread with za'atar and olive oil; bar seating where the chefs often give tasting samples. [$] *Average main: £25* ✉ *2 Bagley Walk, King's Cross* ☎ *020/3848–6086* 🌐 *coaloffice.com* 🕒 *No lunch Mon.–Wed.* [M] *King's Cross St. Pancras.*

🍸 Nightlife

The Betjeman Arms

PUBS | Inside St. Pancras International's renovated Victorian station, this pub is the perfect place to grab a pint and some superior pub fare. ✉ *Pancras Rd., Unit 53, King's Cross* ☎ *020/7923–5440* 🌐 *www.thebetjemanarms.co.uk* [M] *King's Cross St. Pancras.*

🎟 Performing Arts

Kings Place

CONCERTS | The cultural jewel of the King's Cross transformation, this airy concert venue is the headquarters of the London Sinfonietta. Its resident orchestra, Aurora Orchestra, is the world's first professional orchestra to perform whole symphonies by the likes of Mozart and Beethoven without sheet music. There's a varied cultural calendar here, including jazz, comedy, folk, and political and literary lectures, plus two gallery spaces. ✉ *90 York Way, King's Cross* ☎ *020/7520–1490* 🌐 *www.kingsplace.co.uk* 🎟 *Free–£70* [M] *King's Cross.*

THE CITY

7

Updated by
Toby Orton

👁 **Sights**   🍴 Restaurants   🛏 Hotels   💼 Shopping   🍸 Nightlife
★★★★★   ★★★☆☆   ★★★☆☆   ★☆☆☆☆   ★★☆☆☆

THE CITY SNAPSHOT

TOP REASONS TO GO

St. Paul's Cathedral: Although the cathedral is increasingly surrounded by skyscrapers, the beauty of Sir Christopher Wren's 17th-century masterpiece nevertheless remains undiminished.

The Millennium Bridge: Travel from past to present on this promenade between St. Paul's and Tate Modern—and get a great river view, too.

The Tower of London: This medieval complex is home to atmospheric towers, the dazzling Crown Jewels, and hundreds of years of history.

The Museum of London: From skimpy leather briefs dating to Roman times and Queen Victoria's crinolines to Selfridges's Art Deco elevators and a diorama of the Great Fire (including sound effects and flickering flames), this gem of a museum has got it all.

GETTING THERE

The City is well served by a concentration of Tube stations—St. Paul's and Bank on the Central line, and Mansion House, Cannon Street, and Monument on the District and Circle lines. Liverpool Street and Aldgate border The City's eastern edge, while Chancery Lane and Farringdon lie to the west. Barbican and Moorgate provide easy access to the theaters and galleries of the Barbican, and Blackfriars, to the south, leads to Ludgate Circus and Fleet Street.

MAKING THE MOST OF YOUR TIME

■ The City is also known as the "Square Mile," which hints at how compact it is with little distance between points of interest. For full immersion in the Tower of London, set aside half a day, especially if seeing the Crown Jewels is a priority. Allow an hour minimum each for the Museum of London, St. Paul's Cathedral, and Tower Bridge. On weekends, without the workers who make up 90% of the daytime population, The City is nearly deserted and many affordable lunch places are closed—and yet this is when the major attractions are at their busiest.

A GOOD WALK

■ Crossing the Millennium Bridge from Tate Modern to St. Paul's is one of the finest walks in London—with the river to either side and Christopher Wren's iconic dome gleaming at one end.

The capital's fast-beating financial heart, The City is associated with power and pomp, embodied in the three institutions at its epicenter: the Bank of England, the Royal Exchange, and Mansion House. The site of the original Roman settlement from which all of London grew, the "Square Mile" has statement skyscrapers cheek-by-jowl with some of London's most recognizable historic buildings, from Wren's uplifting St. Paul's Cathedral to the Tower of London, a royal fortress, prison, and jewel house surrounded by a moat.

Home to both the latest financial high-tech and the descendants of medieval guilds, The City is where the historic past and fast-moving present collide. Begin your explorations on **Fleet Street,** the site of England's first printing press and the undisputed seat of British journalism until the 1980s. Nestled behind Fleet Street is **Dr. Johnson's House,** where the noted lexicographer, famous for asserting "when a man is tired of London, he is tired of life," compiled the original *Dictionary of the English Language.* Nearby **St. Bride's,** a Wren gem recognizable by its tiered-wedding-cake steeple, is still known as "the journalists' church" while to the east is Wren's masterpiece of the English Baroque, **St. Paul's Cathedral.**

Legacies of London's past are everywhere: at the **Central Criminal Court,** better known as the Old Bailey (and, in its various incarnations, the venue for many of London's most notorious criminal trials); the soaring Victorian **Smithfield Market,** built on a site where livestock has been sold since the 14th century and where a dusk-to-dawn wholesale meat market—the largest in Britain—still operates; the Romanesque church **St. Bartholomew the Great** and next to it **St. Bartholomew's Hospital,** both begun in 1123 at the eastern end of Smithfield; the **Guildhall,** from whose Gothic Great Hall The City was governed and where you can see recently excavated remains of the only Roman amphitheater in London; the church of **St. Mary-le-Bow,** home of the "Bow Bells," of which true Cockneys are supposedly born within earshot; and the maze of charmingly old-fashioned, narrow streets around **Bow Lane.**

To the south is another Wren edifice, the **Monument,** begun in 1671 to commemorate the Great Fire of London five years earlier, while farther east is the historically rich **Tower of London,** which has dominated the riverbank for over a thousand years. Looking toward the river, you'll immediately spot the Victorian Gothic **Tower Bridge,** one of London's most recognizable landmarks. You can put all this history into context at the **Museum of London,** where the archaeological displays include a segment of the **Roman Wall** that ringed The City when it was known to Romans as "Londinium."

The City is also home to some of London's most distinctive contemporary architecture. To the north of Smithfield is the **Barbican Centre,** a Brutalist concrete complex of arts venues and apartments that was controversial when it was built between 1965 and 1976 but has since become an indispensable part of the London streetscape. A plethora of distinctive new structures now tower over The City, not all of which are popular; bold designs, such as **20 Fenchurch Street** (aka the Walkie Talkie) and **30 St. Mary Axe** (the Gherkin), are almost as contentious today as the Barbican was 40 years ago (but several have top-floor restaurants, where you can take in superb views). They all add to the mix in this constantly evolving area, and whenever you return—whether in months or years—The City is guaranteed not to be the same as when you saw it last.

 # Sights

Bank of England

BANK | Since its establishment in 1694 as England's central bank, the role of the "Old Lady of Threadneedle Street" (a political cartoon caption that stuck) has grown to include managing foreign exchanges, issuing currency, storing the nation's gold reserves, and regulating the United Kingdom's banking system. Since 1997, it has had operational responsibility for Britain's monetary policy, most visibly setting interest rates (similar to the Federal Reserve in the United States).

The 3-acre site is enclosed in a massive, neoclassical curtain wall designed by Sir John Soane. This 1828 windowless outer wall is all that survives of Soane's original bank building, which was demolished in 1925. You can discover more about the bank's history in the surprisingly varied Bank of England Museum (the entrance is around the corner on Bartholomew Lane). In addition to the bank's original Royal Charter, there's a lively program of special exhibitions, plus interactive displays (you can even try your hand at controlling inflation). The most popular exhibit remains the solid-gold bar in the central trading hall that you can actually hold—but before you get any ideas, there's security everywhere. ✉ *Threadneedle St., City of London* ☎ *020/3461–4878* ⊕ *www.bankofengland.co.uk* 🎫 *Free* ☾ *Closed weekends and bank holidays* Ⓜ *Bank, Monument.*

Dr. Johnson's House

HISTORIC HOME | Built in 1700, this elegant Georgian residence, with its restored interiors, paneled rooms, and period furniture, is where Samuel Johnson lived between 1748 and 1759, compiling his landmark *A Dictionary of the English Language* in the garret as his health deteriorated. There's a research library with two early editions on view, along

A Brief History of London

Although there is evidence of scattered Celtic rural settlements on the north bank of the Thames, London truly begins with the Romans, who established an outpost of the empire called Londinium (which was about the size of Hyde Park) in AD 47. In AD 60, the warrior queen Boudicca led an uprising of the native Iceni, burning the city to the ground, but the Romans soon regained control, adding a defensive wall. Not much is known of what happened to the city after the Romans left in the fifth century (while England as a whole suffered successive invasions by the Angles, Saxons, Jutes, and Vikings), beyond the establishment of a seventh-century cathedral dedicated to Saint Paul (the famous one now stands on the same site).

After the Norman invasion of 1066 and William the Conqueror's building of the fortress-cum-castle that became known as the Tower of London, the city started to prosper again within those old Roman walls. By the early 13th century, King John acknowledged the city's importance by granting it the right to elect a Lord Mayor. During the Middle Ages, powerful guilds took root that helped nurture commerce, and in the Tudor era, London became the center of both government and trade, reaching a population of some 200,000 people. Dockyards were built to service the British ships that plied lucrative new trade routes, both to the New World and India, laying the foundations for London's role as the world's premier city for the next three centuries.

After the Restoration of 1660, London immediately faced two disasters: the Great Plague of 1665, which killed almost a quarter of the city's population, and then, in 1666, the Great Fire, which destroyed most of its old medieval wood structures. But the reconstruction gave rise to buildings created by one of Britain's greatest architects, Sir Christopher Wren. He, along with John Nash in the 18th century, gave shape to much of the city we see today. Subsequent Regency and Victorian expansion created the characteristic look of new neighborhoods to the west and north like Kensington, Notting Hill, Camden, and Hampstead. Another disaster befell London, particularly in the East End and The City, when Luftwaffe bombs rained down relentlessly during World War II (a destruction equalled by, some argue, the unimaginative urban planners of the 1960s and 1970s). Nevertheless, as the plethora of shiny new skyscrapers attest, the capacity for reinvention that has enabled this city to thrive for 2,000 years remains undimmed.

with other mementos of Johnson and his friend and biographer, James Boswell, one of literature's greatest diarists. After your visit, enjoy more 17th-century atmosphere around the corner in Wine Office Court at the venerable pub **Ye Olde Cheshire Cheese,** once Johnson and Boswell's favorite watering hole. ✉ 17 Gough Sq., City of London ☎ 020/7353–3745 ⊕ www.drjohnsonshouse.org

🖥 £8 ⊘ Closed Sun. and bank holidays ☞ Admission is cash-only Ⓜ Holborn, Chancery La., Temple.

Guildhall

NOTABLE BUILDING | For centuries, this building has been the administrative and ceremonial base of the Corporation of London, the world's oldest continuously elected municipal governing authority

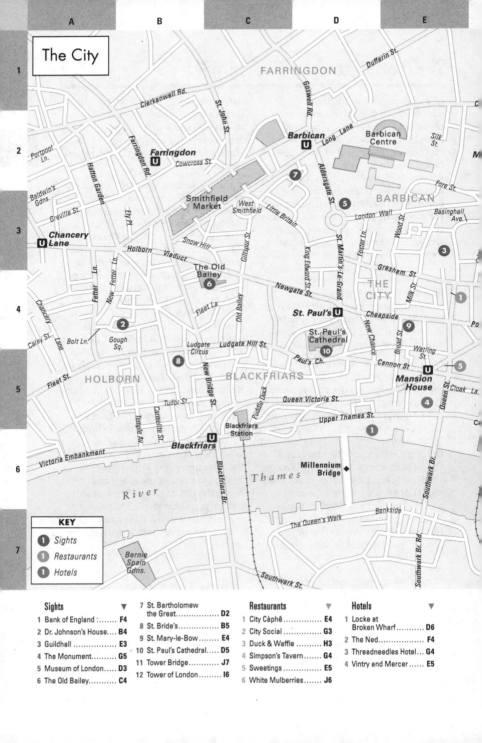

The City

	A	B	C	D	E
1				FARRINGDON	
2		Farringdon U		Barbican U	Barbican Centre
3	Chancery U Lane				BARBICAN
4				St. Paul's U	THE CITY
5		HOLBORN	BLACKFRIARS	St. Paul's Cathedral	Mansion House U
6		Blackfriars U		Millennium Bridge	
7					

Clerkenwell Rd. · St. John St. · Goswell Rd. · Dufferin St. · Long Lane · Silk St. · Cowcross St. · Farringdon Rd. · Portpool Ln. · Baldwin's Gdns. · Hatton Garden · Greville St. · Ely Pl. · Snow Hill · Smithfield Market · West Smithfield · Little Britain · Aldersgate St. · Fore St. · London Wall · Wood St. · Basinghall Ave. · St. Martin's-Le-Grand · Foster Ln. · Gresham St. · Milk St. · Holborn · Viaduct · The Old Bailey · Gutspur St. · Newgate St. · Cheapside · Bread St. · Watling St. · Fetter Ln. · New Fetter Ln. · Fleet La. · Old Bailey · King Edward St. · New Change · Cannon St. · Queen St. · Cloak La. · Chancery Ln. · Carey St. · Bolt Ln. · Gough Sq. · Ludgate Circus · Ludgate Hill St. · St. Paul's Ch. · Paul's Ch. · Fleet St. · New Bridge St. · Tudor St. · Carmelite St. · Temple Av. · Queen Victoria St. · Upper Thames St. · Southwark Br. · Blackfriars Station · Victoria Embankment · Blackfriars Br. · River · Thames · The Queen's Walk · Bankside · Southwark Br. Rd. · Bernie Spain Gdns. · Southwark St.

KEY

- ① Sights
- ① Restaurants
- ① Hotels

Sights ▼

1 Bank of England : **F4**
2 Dr. Johnson's House.... **B4**
3 Guildhall **E3**
4 The Monument......... **G5**
5 Museum of London..... **D3**
6 The Old Bailey........... **C4**
7 St. Bartholomew the Great................. **D2**
8 St. Bride's............... **B5**
9 St. Mary-le-Bow....... **E4**
10 St. Paul's Cathedral..... **D5**
11 Tower Bridge............ **J7**
12 Tower of London......... **I6**

Restaurants ▼

1 City Càphê **E4**
2 City Social **G3**
3 Duck & Waffle **H3**
4 Simpson's Tavern **G4**
5 Sweetings **E5**
6 White Mulberries....... **J6**

Hotels ▼

1 Locke at Broken Wharf........... **D6**
2 The Ned................. **F4**
3 Threadneedles Hotel... **G4**
4 Vintry and Mercer **E5**

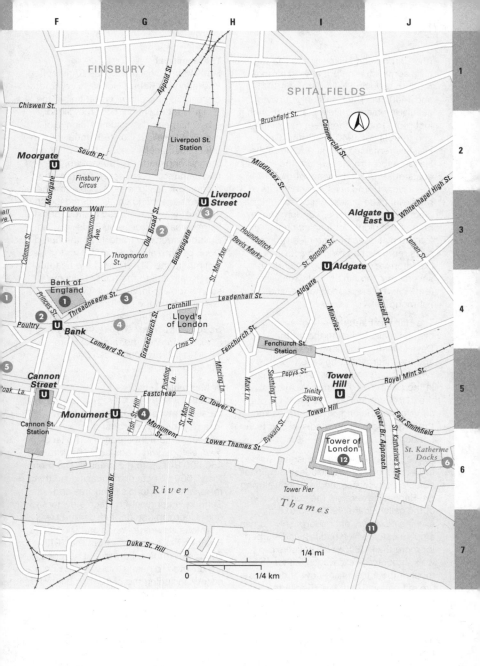

(the Corporation still oversees The City's civic administration but now in a more modern building). Built between 1411 and 1440, it is The City's only surviving secular medieval building, and although it lost roofs to both the Great Fire of 1666 and the Blitz of 1940, its Gothic Great Hall has remained intact. Adding to the Hall's period atmosphere are the colorful coats of arms and banners of the 110 City Livery Companies, descendants of medieval trade guilds, which still officially elect the Lord Mayor of London. These range from older Companies originally formed by trades of yesteryear to new ones representing modern activities like information technology, along with several that remain eternally relevant (e.g., carpenters, upholsterers, and fishmongers).

The Hall has been the site of several historic trials, including that of the "Nine Days Queen" Lady Jane Grey in 1553 and the landmark *Zong* case (1783), which helped end Britain's involvement in the slave trade. Even more ancient are the 11th Century East and West Crypts, survivors of the original Saxon Hall and the largest remaining medieval crypts in London.

To the right of Guildhall Yard is the Guildhall Art Gallery, which includes portraits of notables, cityscapes, and a slightly cloying pre-Raphaelite section. The construction of the gallery in the 1980s led to the exciting discovery of London's only Roman amphitheater, which had lain undisturbed for more than 1,800 years. Visitors can walk through the excavation, although most of the artifacts are now at the Museum of London. There are 75-minute guided tours on select Thursdays when the city council meets at 10:45 am (advance booking required); check the website for dates. ⊠ *Off Guildhall Yard, Gresham St., City of London* ☎ *020/7332–1313* ⊕ *www. cityoflondon.gov.uk* ✉ *Guildhall tours £10* ⊗ *Closed Aug.* Ⓜ *St. Paul's, Moorgate, Bank, Mansion House.*

The Monument

MONUMENT | Designed by Sir Christopher Wren and Dr. Robert Hooke to commemorate 1666's "dreadful visitation" of the Great Fire of London (note the gilded orb of flame at the column's pinnacle), the world's tallest isolated stone column offers spectacular views of the city from the viewing platform 160 feet up. The two architects were asked to erect the monument as close as possible to where the fire began, and so it's located exactly 202 feet from the alleged point of origin, Farrier's baking house on Pudding Lane. Built between 1671 and 1677, the fluted Doric column also stands 202 feet tall, so if climbing the 311 steps of the beautiful spiral staircase to the public balcony seems too arduous, you can watch a live view from the platform played on a screen at the entrance. ⊠ *Monument St., City of London* ☎ *020/7403–3761* ⊕ *www.themonument.info* ✉ *From £5.40* ☞ *Admission is cash only* Ⓜ *Monument.*

★ Museum of London

HISTORY MUSEUM | **FAMILY** | This fascinating museum reveals London in its many incarnations, from its first days as a Roman settlement around AD 50 (and even before, with finds going back to 450,000 BC) up to the present. The more than 7,000 objects encompass everything from Queen Victoria's crinolines and Selfridges's original Art Deco elevators to grim Georgian iron doors from the city's infamous Newgate Prison and Thomas Heatherwick's cauldron from the 2012 London Olympics. Permanent galleries are devoted to nearly every era of English history, including the current globalized megalopolis period.

The Roman London collection contains some extraordinary gems, including an astonishingly well-preserved floor mosaic uncovered just a few streets away; don't miss the outstanding Bronze Age and Roman artifacts unearthed during construction of the new Crossrail underground railway. There are also themed temporary exhibitions, themed walking tours (such as "Hogarth's London"), and an offshoot branch (Museum of London Docklands) near Canary Wharf devoted to the history of the area and the River Thames. ⊠ *150 London Wall, City of London* ☎ *020/7001–9844* ⊕ *www. museumoflondon.org.uk* ✉ *Free* ⊙ *Closed Mon. and Tues.* Ⓜ *Barbican, St. Paul's.*

The Old Bailey

GOVERNMENT BUILDING | Visitors are allowed into the public galleries of the 16 courtrooms at London's Central Criminal Court (universally known as "the Old Bailey," a reference to the street where it's located, which follows the line of the original fortified city wall, or "bailey" in Middle English). Historically it has been the venue for many of Britain's most famous criminal trials. It was here that Oscar Wilde was condemned for "gross indecency" in 1895, where notorious murderers like the Kray twins in the 1960s and the Yorkshire Ripper in the 1980s were convicted, and, more recently, where high-profile terrorism cases have been tried.

Originally the site of a medieval courthouse destroyed in the Great Fire, a courthouse was built here next to the grim Newgate Prison, the poor man's version of the Tower, in 1673. The building went through two more incarnations before the present Edwardian Baroque building opened in 1907 (it was rebuilt again after the Blitz). Until 1868, executions were held on the street outside (a great public attraction), and you can still see the "Dead Man's Walk" along which condemned prisoners were taken from their cells to the gallows under a series of ever-narrowing arches. Note the 12-foot gold-leaf statue of Lady Justice at the top of the dome, not wearing a blindfold as she is usually portrayed.

Visitors are only allowed access to the public galleries to view trials; there is no visitor access to the rest of the

building. Trials take place from 10 am to 1 pm and 2 pm to 4:30 pm. There are security restrictions, and children under 14 and overly casual dress are not allowed. ⊠ *The Old Bailey, City of London* ☎ *020/7248–3277* ⊕ *www.cityoflondon. gov.uk* ✉ *Free* ⊙ *Closed weekends, bank holidays, and when court not in session.* Ⓜ *St. Paul's.*

★ St. Bartholomew the Great

CHURCH | Originally founded in 1123 as part of an Augustinian monastery, this is one of the oldest churches in London and one of the city's few surviving Norman buildings. Although much of the church has been destroyed or demolished over the centuries, with restoration only beginning in the mid-19th century (it even saw use as a stable and a factory in the interim), it nevertheless remains perhaps the best preserved example of Romanesque architecture in London. Most notable are the 13th-century arch with a half-timbered gatehouse at the entrance and the fine Romanesque chancel, apse, and triforium at the east end of the interior. The artist William Hogarth was baptized in the font, which dates back to 1404. The redolent atmosphere has made it a favorite filming location, and you can see it in *The Other Boleyn Girl, Four Weddings and a Funeral,* and *Shakespeare in Love,* to name just a few. ⊠ *Cloth Fair, West Smithfield, City of London* ☎ *020/7600–0440* ⊕ *www. greatstbarts.com* ✉ *£5 (free for prayer in the chapel), photography £2* Ⓜ *Barbican, Farringdon.*

St. Bride's

CHURCH | Located just off Fleet Street in the city's former epicenter of English print and newspapers, St. Bride's is known as "the journalists' church," and indeed a small altar in the north aisle marks a memorial dedicated to the sadly ever-growing list of reporters, photographers, and crew who have lost their lives covering 21st-century conflicts. St. Bride's is another of Sir Christopher

Wren's English Baroque gems, built nine years after the Great Fire of 1666. The distinctively tiered steeple, Wren's highest, for which Benjamin Franklin designed a lightning rod, allegedly inspired a baker parishioner to make a similarly shaped tiered cake for his own wedding, thus creating the modern wedding cake design.

This is thought to be the eighth church on the site (there's still a medieval chapel in the northeast corner), with the first one built during the seventh century. Evidence for this, along with a section of a Roman mosaic sidewalk, was discovered in the crypt, where you can now see the many archaeological finds unearthed from the thousands of coffins there. Ninety-minute guided tours are held on Tuesday afternoon starting at 2:15 pm; the church also hosts regular free lunchtime concert recitals. ⊠ *Fleet St., City of London* ☎ *020/7427–0133* ⊕ *www. stbrides.com* ▱ *Free; guided tours £6* Ⓜ *St. Paul's, Blackfriars.*

St. Mary-le-Bow

CHURCH | Founded around 1080 as the Archbishop of Canterbury's London seat, this church is a survivor; it collapsed and was rebuilt three times before being completely destroyed in the Great Fire of 1666. Once again, Sir Christopher Wren was called in, creating a new building that was completed in 1673, but sadly this, too, was destroyed, during the Blitz. The version you see today is a re-creation of Wren's design that was reconsecrated in 1965. According to tradition, only Londoners born within earshot of the church's famous "Bow Bells" (which used to echo more widely than they do now) can be considered true Cockneys, a concept that may date back to the 9 pm curfew bells rung during the 14th century.

The Norman crypt is the oldest parochial building in London still in use, and you can see the bow-shape arches from which the church takes its name.

The garden contains a statue of former parishioner Captain John Smith, the founder of the Virginia Colony. Opening times on weekends and holidays are irregular, so calling ahead is advised. Guided tours available by arrangement. Classical music concerts are held here regularly; check the website for listings. ⊠ *Cheapside, City of London* ☎ *020/7248–5139* ⊕ *www.stmarylebow. co.uk* ▱ *Free* ☽ *Closed most weekends* Ⓜ *Mansion House, St. Paul's.*

★ St. Paul's Cathedral

CHURCH | For centuries, this iconic building has represented London's spirit of survival and renewal, and it remains breathtaking, inside and out. Sir Christopher Wren started planning the current cathedral in 1666, immediately after the previous medieval building, founded in 1087, was destroyed in the Great Fire, hence the word *resurgam* ("I shall rise again") inscribed on the pediment of the south door. St. Paul's again became a symbol of the city's resilience during the Blitz, when local volunteers risked death to put out a blaze on the dome (despite these efforts, much of the cathedral's east end and its high altar were destroyed). It has often been the scene of great state occasions, such as Winston Churchill's funeral and the wedding of Prince Charles and Princess Diana.

Construction started in 1675 and took 35 years to finish. It was actually Wren's third design: the first was rejected for being too modern; the second for being too modern *and* too Italian, that is, Catholic (you can see the 20-foot "Great Model" of this design in the crypt). Despite mollifying the Anglican clergy with the promise of a traditional English spire, Wren installed a neoclassical triple-layered dome, the second-largest cathedral dome in the world after St. Peter's in Rome.

The interior is a superb example of the English Baroque. Climb 257 steps up the Geometric Staircase, a perfectly

Walking over the Millennium Bridge takes you to St. Paul's Cathedral, the Sir Christopher Wren–designed masterpiece that is one of the most beautiful cathedrals in England.

engineered stone spiral, to the Whispering Gallery, so named because a whisper against one wall can be heard on the wall 112 feet opposite. Another 119 steps up is the Stone Gallery, which encircles the exterior of the dome and provides panoramic views over London. If you have a head for heights, tackle another 152 steps to the small Golden Gallery, an observation platform at the dome's highest point. At 278 feet above the cathedral floor, it offers even more spectacular vistas. Back on the ground, in the south choir aisle, you'll find the grave of John Donne, the poet who was dean of St. Paul's from 1621 until his death in 1631. His marble effigy is the oldest memorial in the cathedral and one of the few to survive the Great Fire. The intricate lively figures on the choir stall nearby are the work of master carver Grinling Gibbons, who also embellished the Wren-designed great organ. Behind the high altar is the American Memorial Chapel, dedicated to the 28,000 American GIs stationed in the United Kingdom during World War II. Among the notables buried in the crypt

are the Duke of Wellington, Admiral Lord Nelson, Sir Joshua Reynolds, Henry Moore, and Wren himself. The Latin epitaph above his tomb fittingly reads, "Reader, if you seek his monument, look around you."

Free, introductory, 20-minute talks are offered regularly throughout the day. Free, 60-minute, guided tours take place Monday through Saturday at 10, 11, 1, and 2; reserve a place at the welcome desk when you arrive. Save £3 per admission ticket and get fast-track entry by booking online. ⊠ *St. Paul's Churchyard, City of London* ☎ *020/7246–8350* ⊕ *www.stpauls.co.uk* ✉ *£21* ⊘ *Closed Sun. except for services* Ⓜ *St. Paul's.*

Tower Bridge

BRIDGE | FAMILY | Despite its medieval appearance, London's most famous bridge was actually built at the tail end of the Victorian era in the then-popular neo-Gothic style, first opening to traffic in 1894. With a latticed steel construction clad in Portland stone, the bridge is known for its enormous bascules—the 1,000-ton "arms" that open to allow ships taller than its normal 28-foot clearance to glide beneath. The steam-powered bascules were a marvel of Victorian engineering when they were created (you can still visit the Engine Room, now with explanatory films and interactive displays), and required 80 people to raise and lower. Initially, heavy river traffic meant this happened 20 to 30 times a day, but it's now reduced to a number of days per month, with greater frequency depending on the time of year (see the Bridge's website for a schedule).

The family-friendly Tower Bridge Exhibition includes the ground-level Engine Room, displays in the North Tower documenting the bridge's history, access to the east and west walkways that run alongside the road between the turrets and provide views over the river and city, and for those untroubled by vertigo, a transparent walkway 138 feet up between the towers that lets you look down on the traffic or, if the bascules are raised, the ships below. ☒ *Tower Bridge Rd., City of London* ☎ *020/7403–3761* ⊕ *www.towerbridge.org.uk* ✉ *From £10.60* Ⓜ *Tower Hill.*

★ The Tower of London

CASTLE/PALACE | **FAMILY** | Nowhere else in London does history seem so vividly alive as in this minicity begun by the Normans more than 1,000 years ago. In its time, the Tower has been a fortress, a mint, a palace, an archive, and the Royal Menagerie (which formed the kernel of London Zoo). Most of all, however, it has been known as a place of imprisonment and death. Thousands of unfortunate souls, including numerous aristocrats and even a few sovereigns (some notorious traitors, some complete innocents), spent their last days here, several etching their final recorded thoughts onto their cell walls, and pints of royal blood have been spilled on its stones. Executions at the Tower were reserved for the nobility, with the most privileged beheaded in the privacy of Tower Green instead of before the mob at Tower Hill. In fact, only seven people received this dubious "honor," among them Anne Boleyn and Catherine Howard, two of Henry VIII's six wives.

The White Tower, the oldest building in the complex (which is actually made up of 20 towers, not just one) is also its most conspicuous. Begun by William the Conqueror in 1078 and whitewashed (hence the name) by Henry III (1207–72), it contains the Armouries, a splendid collection of arms and armor. Across the moat to the right is the riverside Traitors' Gate, to which the most famous prisoners were rowed to bring them to their impending doom.

Opposite is the Bloody Tower, where the "little princes in the Tower"—the uncrowned boy king Edward V and his brother—were consigned by their wicked uncle, who then took the crown for himself, thus becoming Richard III. The boys were never seen again, widely assumed to have been murdered in their tower prison. Also not-to-be-missed are the gorgeous Crown Jewels in the Jewel House. The original crown, orb, and scepter, symbols of monarchial power, were destroyed during the English Civil War; the ones you see here date back to after the Restoration in 1661. The most impressive gems were added only in the 20th century, when their countries of origin were part of the British Empire. Free 60-minute tours of the Tower depart every half hour or so (until midafternoon) from the main entrance. They are conducted by the Yeoman Warders, more popularly known as Beefeaters, who have guarded the Tower since Henry VII appointed them in 1485. Veterans of Britain's armed forces, they're easy to spot in their resplendent navy-and-red Tudor uniforms (scarlet-and-gold on special occasions). Keep an eye out for the ravens upon whose residency of the Tower, legend has it, the safety of the kingdom depends.

Continued on page 210

THE TOWER OF LONDON

The Tower is a microcosm of the city itself—a sprawling, organic hodgepodge of buildings that inspires reverence and terror in equal measure. See the block on which Anne Boleyn was beheaded, marvel at the Crown Jewels, and pay homage to the ravens who keep the monarchy safe.

An architectural patchwork of time, the oldest building of the complex is the fairytale White Tower, conceived by William the Conqueror in 1078 as both a royal residence and a show of power to the troublesome Anglo-Saxons he had subdued at the Battle of Hastings. Today's Tower has seen everything, as a palace, barracks, a mint for producing coins, an armoury, and the Royal menagerie (home of the country's first elephant). The big draw is the stunning opulence of the Crown Jewels, kept on-site in the heavily fortified Jewel House. Most of all, though, the Tower is known for death: it's been a place of imprisonment, torture, and execution for the realm's most notorious traitors as well as its martyrs. These days, unless you count the killer admission fees, there are far less morbid activities taking place in the Tower, but it still breathes London's history and pageantry from its every brick and offers hours of exploration.

TOURING THE TOWER

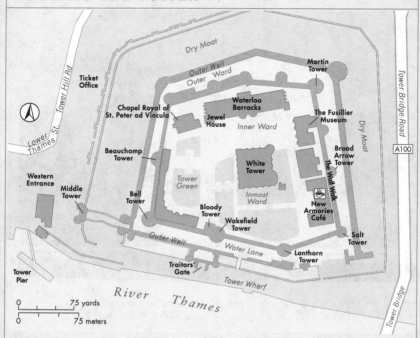

Entry to the Tower is via the **Western Entrance** and the **Middle Tower,** which feed into the outermost ring of the Tower's defenses.

Water Lane leads past the dread-inducing **Traitors' Gate,** the final point of entry for many Tower prisoners.

Toward the end of Water Lane, the **Lanthorn Tower** houses by night the ravens rumored to keep the kingdom safe, and by day a timely high-tech reconstruction of the Catholic Guy Fawkes's plot to blow up the Houses of Parliament in 1605.

The **Bloody Tower** earned its name as the apocryphal site of the murder of two young princes, Edward and Richard, who disappeared from the Tower after being put there in 1483 by their uncle, Richard III. Two little skeletons (now in Westminster Abbey) were found buried close to the White Tower in 1674 and are thought to be theirs.

The **Beauchamp Tower** housed upper-class miscreants: Latin graffiti about Lady Jane Grey can be glimpsed today on its walls.

GOLD DIGGER?

Keep your eyes peeled as you tour the Tower: according to one story, Sir John Barkstead, goldsmith and Lieutenant of the Tower under Cromwell, hid £20,000 in gold coins here before his arrest and execution at the Restoration of Charles II.

Like a prize gem set at the head of a royal crown, the **White Tower** is the centerpiece of the complex. Its four towers dominate the Inner Ward, a fitting and forbidding reminder of Norman strength at the time of the conquest of England.

Tower of London exterior

ROYAL BLING

The Crown of Queen Elizabeth, the Queen Mother, from 1937, contains the exotic 105-carat Koh-i-Noor (Mountain of Light) diamond.

TIME KILLERS

Some prisoners managed to keep themselves plenty amused: Sir Walter Raleigh grew tobacco on Tower Green, and in 1561 suspected sorcerer Hugh Draper carved an intricate astronomical clock on the walls of his Salt Tower cell.

Once inside the White Tower, head upstairs for the **Armouries,** where the biggest attraction, quite literally, is the suit of armor worn by a well-endowed Henry VIII. There is a matching outfit for his horse.

Other fascinating exhibitsw include the set of Samurai armor presented to James I in 1613 by the emperor of Japan, and the tiny set of armor worn by Henry VIII's young son Edward.

The **Jewel House** in **Waterloo Block** is the Tower's biggest draw, perfect for playing pick-your-favorite-crown from the wrong side of bulletproof glass. Not only are these crowns, staffs, and orbs encrusted with heavy-duty gems, they are invested with the authority of monarchical power in England, dating back to the 1300s.

Outside, pause at **Tower Green**, permanent departure point for those of noble birth. The hoi polloi were dispatched at nearby Tower Hill. The Tower's most famous female victims—Anne Boleyn, Margaret Countess of Salisbury, Catherine Howard, and Lady Jane Grey—all went this privileged way.

Behind a well-kept square of grass stands the **Chapel Royal of St. Peter ad Vincula**, a delightful Tudor church and final resting place of six beheaded Tudor bodies.

■TIP→ **Visitors are welcome for services and can also enter after 4:30 pm daily.**

The **Salt Tower**, reputedly the most haunted corner of the complex, marks the start of the **Wall Walk**, a bracing promenade along the stone spiral steps and battlements of the Tower that looks down on the trucks, taxis, and shimmering high-rises of modern London.

The Wall Walk ends at the **Martin Tower**, former home of the Crown Jewels and now host to the crowns and diamonds exhibition that explains the art of fashioning royal headwear and tells the story of some of the most famous stones.

On leaving the Tower, browse the **gift shop,** and wander the wharf that overlooks the Thames, leading to a picture-postcard view of Tower Bridge.

WHO ARE THE BEEFEATERS?

First of all, they're Yeoman Warders, but probably got the nickname "beefeater" from their position as Royal Bodyguards which entitled them to eat as much beef as they liked. Part of the "Yeoman of the Guard," started in the reign of Edmund IV, the warders have formed the Royal Bodyguard as far back as 1509 when Henry VIII left a dozen of the Yeoman of the Guard at the Tower to protect it.

Originally, the Yeoman Warders also served as jailers of the Tower, doubling as torturers when necessary. (So it would have been a Beefeater tightening the thumb screws, or ratchetting the rack another notch on some unfortunate prisoner. Smile nicely.) Today 36 Yeoman Warders (men and women since 2007), along with the Chief Yeoman Warder and the Yeoman Gaoler, live within the walls of the Tower with their families, in accommodations in the Outer Ward. They stand guard over the Tower, conduct tours, and lock up at 9:53 pm every night with the Ceremony of the Keys.

■ TIP→ **Free tickets to the Ceremony of the Keys are available by writing several months in advance; check the Tower Web site for details.**

HARK THE RAVENS!

Legend has it that should the hulking black ravens ever leave, the White Tower will crumble and the kingdom fall. Charles II, no doubt jumpy after his father's execution and the monarchy's short-term fall from grace, made a royal decree in 1662 that there should be at least six of the carrion-eating nasties present at all times. There have been some close calls. During World War II, numbers dropped to one, echoing the precarious fate of the war-wracked country. In 2005, two (of eight) died over Christmas when Thor—the most intelligent but also the largest bully of the bunch—killed new recruit Gundolf, named after the Tower's 1070 designer. Pneumonia put an end to Bran, leaving lifelong partner Branwen without her mate.

rabbit, and scraps from the mess kitchen that keeps them coming back. Their lifting feathers on one wing are trimmed, meaning they can manage the equivalent of a lop-sided airbound hobble but not much more. In situ they are a territorial lot, sticking to Tower Green and the White Tower, and lodging nightly by Wakefield Tower. They've had free front-row seats at all the most grisly moments in Tower history—Anne Boleyn's execution included.

■ DID YOU KNOW? **In 1981 a raven named Grog, perhaps seduced by his alcoholic moniker, escaped after 21 years at the Tower. Others have been banished for "conduct unbecoming."**

The six that remain, each one identified by a colored band around a claw, are much loved for their fidelity (they mate for life) and their cheek (capable of 440 noises, they are witty and scolding mimics). It's not only the diet of blood-soaked biscuits,

■ TIP→ **Don't get too close to the ravens: they are prone to pecking and not particularly fond of humans, unless you are the Tower's Raven Master.**

AND WHAT ARE THEY WEARING?

A **pike** (or halberd), also known as a partisan, is the Yeoman Warder's weapon of choice. The Chief Warder carries a staff topped with a miniature silver model of the White Tower.

Anyone who refers to this as a costume will be lucky to leave the Tower with head still attached to body: this is the ceremonial uniform of the Yeoman Warders, and it comes at a cool £13,000 a throw.

The black Tudor **bonnet** is made of velvet; the blue undress consists of a felt top hat, with a single Tudor rose in the middle.

This **Tudor-style ruff** helps date the ceremonial uniform, which was first worn in 1552.

Insignia on a Yeoman Warder's upper right arm denote the rank he carried in the military.

The **medals** on a Yeoman Warder's chest are more than mere show: all of the men and women have served for at least 22 years in the armed forces.

Slits in the **tunic** date from the times when Beefeaters were expected to ride a horse.

The **red lines down the trousers** are a sign of the blood from the swords of the Yeoman Warders in their defense of the realm.

This version of the **royal livery** bears the insignia of the current Queen ("E" for Elizabeth) but originally dates from Tudor times. The first letter changes according to the reigning monarch's Christian name; the second letter is always an "R" for *rex* (king) or *regina* (queen).

Red socks and **black patent shoes** are worn on special occasions. Visitors are more likely to see the regular blue undress, introduced in 1858 as the regular working dress of the Yeoman Warders.

(IN)FAMOUS PRISONERS OF THE TOWER

Anne Boleyn   Lady Jane Grey   Sir Walter Raleigh

Sir Thomas More. A Catholic and Henry VIII's friend and chancellor, Sir Thomas refused to attend the coronation of Anne Boleyn (Henry VIII's second wife) or to recognize the multi-marrying king as head of the Church. Sent to the Tower for treason, More was beheaded in 1535.

Anne Boleyn. The first of Henry VIII's wives to be beheaded, Anne, who failed to provide the king with a son, was accused of sleeping with five men, including her own brother. All six got the chop in 1536. Her severed head was held up to the crowd, and her lips were said to be mouthing prayer.

Margaret, Countess of Salisbury. Not the best-known prisoner in her lifetime, she has a reputation today for haunting the Tower. And no wonder: the elderly 70-year-old was condemned by Henry VIII in 1541 for a potentially treacherous bloodline (she was the last Plantagenet princess) and hacked to death by the executioner after she refused to put her head on the block like a common traitor and attempted to run away.

Queen Catherine Howard. Henry VIII's fifth wife was locked up for high treason and infidelity and beheaded in 1542 at age 20. Ever-eager to please, she spent her final night practicing how to lay her head on the block.

Lady Jane Grey. The Nine-Day Queen lost her head in 1554 at age 16. Her death was the result of sibling rivalry gone seriously wrong, when Protestant Edward VI slighted his Catholic sister Mary in favor of Lady Jane as heir, and Mary decided to have none of it.

Guy Fawkes. The Roman Catholic soldier who tried to blow up the Houses of Parliament and kill the king in the 1605 Gunpowder plot was first incarcerated in the chambers of the Tower, where King James I requested he be tortured in ever-worsening ways. Perhaps unsurprisingly, he confessed. He met his seriously grisly end in the Old Palace Yard at Westminster, where he was hung, drawn, and quartered in 1607.

Sir Walter Raleigh. Once a favorite of Elizabeth I, he offended her by secretly marrying her maid of honor and was chucked in the Tower. Later, as a conspirator against James I, he paid with his life. A frequent visitor to the Tower (he spent 13 years there in three stints), he managed to get the Bloody Tower enlarged on account of his wife and growing family. He was finally executed in 1618 in Old Palace Yard, Westminster.

Josef Jakobs. The last man to be executed in the Tower was caught as a spy when parachuting in from Germany and executed by firing squad in 1941. The chair he sat in when he was shot is preserved in the Royal Armouries' artifacts store.

FOR FURTHER EVIDENCE . . .

A trio of buildings in the Inner Ward, the **Bloody Tower, Beauchamp Tower,** and **Queen's House,** all with excellent views of the execution scaffold in Tower Green, are the heart of the Tower's prison accommodations and home to a permanent exhibition about notable inmates.

TACKLING THE TOWER (WITHOUT LOSING YOUR HEAD)

MAKING THE MOST OF YOUR TIME:
Without doubt, the Tower is worth two to three hours. A full hour of that would be well spent by joining one of the Yeoman Warders' tours (included in admission). It's hard to better their insight, vitality, and humor—they are knights of the realm living their very own fairytale castle existence.

The Crown Jewels are worth the wait, the White Tower is essential, and the Medieval Palace and Bloody Tower should at least be breezed through.

■TIP➜ **It's best to visit on weekdays, when the crowds are smaller.**

WITH KIDS: The Tower's centuries-old cobblestones are not exactly stroller-friendly, but strollers are permitted inside most of the buildings. If you do bring one, be prepared to leave it temporarily unsupervised (the stroller, that is—not your child) outside the White Tower, which has no access. There are baby-changing facilities in the Brick Tower restrooms behind the Jewel House. Look for regular free children's events such as the Knight's school where children can have a go at jousting, sword-fighting, and archery.

■TIP➜ **Tell your child to find one of the Yeoman Warders if he or she should get lost; they will in turn lead him or her to the Byward Tower, which is where you should meet.**

IN A HURRY? If you have less than an hour, head down the Wall Walk, through a succession of towers, which eventually spit you out at the Martin Tower. The view over modern London is quite a contrast.

TOURS: Tours given by a Yeoman Warder leave from the main entrance near Middle Tower every half-hour from 10–4, and last about an hour. Beefeaters give occasional 30-minute talks in the Lanthorn Tower about their daily lives. Both tours are free. Check the Tower of London Web site for talks and workshops

Avoid lines by buying a ticket in advance online, by phone, or from the automatic kiosks on Tower Hill. For free tickets to the 700-year-old Ceremony of the Keys (the locking of the main gates, nightly between 9:30 and 10), write several months in advance; check the Tower website for details. ✉ *Tower Hill, City of London* ☏ *020/3166–6000* ⊕ *www.hrp. org.uk* 🎫 *£32.90* Ⓜ *Tower Hill.*

🍴 Restaurants

The City caters overwhelmingly to traditional business-focused dining.

City Càphê

$ | **VIETNAMESE** | This unpretentious but charming family-run Vietnamese street-food café offers delicious quick bites and takeout dishes for lunch. Try the pho, banh mi, or spring rolls. **Known for:** excellent pho noodles; great value; lunchtime lines. 💲 *Average main: £8* ✉ *17 Ironmonger La., City of London* ⊕ *www. citycaphe.com* 🕐 *Closed Fri.–Sun.* Ⓜ *Mansion House, Bank.*

City Social

$$$$ | **MODERN BRITISH** | A largely corporate crowd comes here for the Manhattan-esque views of The City and chef Jason Atherton's masterful but straightforward cuisine. Impressed diners look out from Level 24 of Tower 42 on a majestic panorama that takes in illustrious buildings like the Gherkin and the Walkie Talkie. **Known for:** suited financiers and corporate dealmaker crowd; majestic panoramas of The City; gutsy steak and fish standards. 💲 *Average main: £36* ✉ *Tower 42, 25 Old Broad St., City of London* ☏ *020/7877– 7703* ⊕ *www.citysociallondon.com* 🕐 *Closed Sun. and Mon. No lunch Sat.* Ⓜ *Liverpool St.*

★ Duck & Waffle

$$$ | **MODERN BRITISH** | **FAMILY** | Zoom up to the 40th floor of 110 Bishopsgate and head straight for the cult signature dish of confit duck leg, Belgium waffle, fried duck egg, and mustard maple syrup for

a taste of foodie bliss. Open 24/7, with spectacular panoramas of The City, you might satisfy the munchies with a foie gras breakfast, served all day, alongside streaky bacon and homemade Nutella or an Elvis PB&J waffle with banana brûlée. **Known for:** eponymous duck-and-waffle dish; rare-to-London 24-hour service; awe-inspiring panoramas of London's skyline. 💲 *Average main: £25* ✉ *Heron Tower, 110 Bishopsgate, City of London* ☏ *020/3640–7310* ⊕ *www.duckandwaffle.com* Ⓜ *Liverpool St.*

★ Simpson's Tavern

$ | **BRITISH** | **FAMILY** | The City's oldest tavern and chop house was founded in 1757 and undoubtedly is every bit as raucous now as the day it opened. Approached via a cobbled alleyway, it draws diners who revel in the old boarding school surroundings and are eager to down oodles of claret and English tavern-style grub. **Known for:** charming but old-fashioned service; lots of history, with past diners from diarist Samuel Pepys to Charles Dickens; signature stewed cheese on toast. 💲 *Average main: £12* ✉ *Ball Court, 38½ Cornhill, City of London* ☏ *020/7626–9985* ⊕ *www.simpsonstavern.co.uk* 🕐 *Closed weekends. No dinner* Ⓜ *Bank.*

Sweetings

$$$ | **SEAFOOD** | Established in 1889 not far from St. Paul's Cathedral, little seems to have changed since the height of the British Empire at this quirky eatery. Although there are some things Sweetings doesn't do (dinner, reservations, coffee, or weekends), it does, mercifully, do great seafood. **Known for:** popular potted shrimp and Dover sole; fresh Billingsgate fish served at raised linen-covered counters; tankards of "Black Velvet" Guinness and champagne. 💲 *Average main: £30* ✉ *39 Queen Victoria St., City of London* ☏ *020/7248–3062* ⊕ *www.sweetingsrestaurant.co.uk* 🕐 *Closed weekends. No dinner* Ⓜ *Mansion House.*

White Mulberries
$ | **CAFÉ** | This friendly coffeeshop at St. Katharine Docks serves outstanding breakfasts (with fresh juices and baked goods) plus homemade soups, cakes, and light bites for lunch. In an area too readily associated with chains, this charming independent eatery is a breath of fresh air, particularly for long, leisurely brunches when the sun is shining. **Known for:** delicious breakfast bowls; charming waterside location; weekend brunch. [$] *Average main: £8* ✉ *D3 Ivory House, St. Katharine Docks, City of London* 🌐 *www.whitemulberries.com* [M] *Tower Hill, Tower Gateway (DLR).*

Hotels

Locke at Broken Wharf
$$ | **APARTMENT** | Somewhere between hotel and serviced apartment, Locke at Broken Wharf offers the freedom of a personal home from which you can explore The City. **Pros:** great views of the river; restaurant and co-working space on-site; all rooms come with kitchenettes. **Cons:** some may not enjoy the design emphasis on "hip"; area is very quiet on weekends; rooms book up fast. [$] *Rooms from: £145* ✉ *Broken Wharf House, 2 Broken Wharf, City of London* ☎ *0330/124–4676* 🌐 *www.lockeliving.com/en/london/locke-at-broken-wharf* 🛏 *113 rooms* 🍴 *No Meals* [M] *Blackfriars.*

★ **The Ned**
$$$ | **HOTEL** | Bursting with eye-catching art deco design and achingly hip interiors, The Ned is as close to the glamour of the 1920s Jazz Age as you'll find in contemporary London. **Pros:** beautiful interiors in all rooms; amazing variety of bars and restaurants, all of high quality; rooftop pool with views of St. Paul's Cathedral. **Cons:** also doubles as a private members club, so the vibe can get snooty; neighborhood is deserted on weekends; location in The City means public spaces get very busy after work. [$] *Rooms from: £275* ✉ *27 Poultry, City of London* ☎ *020/3828–2000* 🌐 *www.thened.com* 🛏 *250 rooms* 🍴 *No Meals* [M] *Bank.*

Threadneedles Hotel
$$$ | **HOTEL** | The elaborate building housing this grand hotel in the financial district is a former bank, and the vast old banking hall—beautifully adapted as the lobby, with luxurious marble and mahogany panels—really sets the scene. **Pros:** a good variety of drinking and dining options; lap of luxury; excellent service. **Cons:** neighborhood is quiet at night; can be at least three times more expensive weekdays; a bit stuffy for some tastes. [$] *Rooms from: £250* ✉ *5 Threadneedle St., City of London* ☎ *020/7657–8080* 🌐 *www.hotelthreadneedles.co.uk* 🛏 *74 rooms* 🍴 *No Meals* [M] *Bank.*

Vintry & Mercer
$$ | **HOTEL** | Located close to the London Stock Exchange, merchant banks, hedge funds, and The City's oldest guilds, the luxury boutique hotel Vintry & Mercer offers a nod to tradition, then proceeds to deliver a chic, colorful, and contemporary experience that stands out in this neighborhood. **Pros:** some rooms have stunning views of The City; rooms with gorgeous fabrics and chic wallpapers; excellent on-site izakaya restaurant. **Cons:** slightly removed from the sights of the West End; neighborhood is extremely quiet on weekends; predominantly business crowd dominates the bar and restaurant. [$] *Rooms from: £204* ✉ *19–20 Garlick Hill, City of London* ☎ *020/3908–8088* 🌐 *www.vintryandmercer.com* 🛏 *92 rooms* 🍴 *No Meals* [M] *Monument.*

Nightlife

Workers from The City's many finance firms pour into the neighborhood's pubs at the end of the day, but by 8 pm the party is pretty much over and you'll have no trouble finding a place to sit. It's always worth ducking down a side street, as this is where some of the area's most interesting drinking establishments can be found.

BARS

The Anthologist

BARS | In a neighborhood filled with financial institutions, ancient church-es, and ye olde pubs, The Anthologist makes for a pleasantly light-hearted, energetic place to drink, eat, and dance the day away. The City is famous for its sleepy weekends, but this is when The Anthologist comes into its own, closing on Saturdays to save its energy for its famed Sunday boozy brunch, which often comes backed by the likes of live gospel choirs and international DJs. The venue doubles as an all-day restaurant but tends to get most lively during the evening. ✉ *58 Gresham St., City of London* ☎ *020/7726–8711* ⊕ *www.drakeandmorgan.co.uk/the-anthologist* Ⓜ *Bank.*

DANCE CLUBS

fabric

DANCE CLUBS | This sprawling subterrane-an club opposite Smithfield Meat Market is a firm fixture on the London scene and is regularly voted one of the top clubs in the world. The "fabriclive" series hosts drum and bass, dubstep, and hip-hop crews and live acts on Friday; international big-name DJs play slow, sexy bass lines and cutting-edge music on Saturday. The devastating sound system ensures that bass riffs vibrate through your entire body. Get there early to avoid a lengthy line, and don't wear a suit. Expect a mainly young crowd. ✉ *77A Charterhouse St., City of London* ☎ *020/7336–8898* ⊕ *www.fabriclondon. com* Ⓜ *Farringdon.*

PUBS

★ The Blackfriar

PUBS | FAMILY | A step from Blackfriars Tube station, this spectacular pub has an Arts and Crafts interior that is entertain-ingly, satirically ecclesiastical, with inlaid mother-of-pearl, wood carvings, stained glass, and marble pillars all over the place. Under finely lettered temperance tracts on view just below the reliefs of monks, fairies, and friars, there is a nice group of ales on tap from independent brewers. The 20th-century poet Sir John Betjeman once led a successful cam-paign to save the pub from demolition. ✉ *174 Queen Victoria St., City of London* ☎ *020/7236–5474* ⊕ *www.nicholsons-pubs.co.uk* Ⓜ *Blackfriars.*

Ye Olde Cheshire Cheese

PUBS | This wonderfully higgledy-piggledy, multilevel inn on Fleet Street was built in 1667, but the basement bar is centuries older, lending credence to its claim as London's oldest pub. The list of famous people who've imbibed here is like a "who's who" of London history, including the likes of Samuel Pepys, Charles Dick-ens, and Samuel Johnson. ✉ *145 Fleet St., City of London* ☎ *020/7353–6170* Ⓜ *St. Paul's.*

Ye Olde Mitre

PUBS | FAMILY | Hidden off the side of 8 Hatton Gardens (and notoriously hard to find), this cozy pub's roots go back to 1546, though it was rebuilt around 1782. Originally built for the staff of the Bishop of Ely, whose London residence was next door, it remained officially part of Cambridgeshire until the 20th century. Elizabeth I was once spotted dancing round a cherry tree here with a dashing young beau. Now it's a friendly little labyrinthine place, with a fireplace, well-kept ales, wooden beams, and traditional bar snacks. ✉ *1 Ely Ct., City of London* ⊹ *Off 8 Hatton Gardens* ☎ *020/7405–4751* ⊕ *www.yeoldemitreholburn.co.uk* Ⓜ *Chancery La.*

Ye Olde Watling

PUBS | FAMILY | This busy corner pub has been rebuilt at least three times since 1666. One of its incarnations was as the drawing office for Sir Christopher Wren, who used it while building nearby St. Paul's Cathedral. The ground floor is a laid-back pub, while the upstairs houses an atmospheric restaurant, complete with wooden beams and trestle tables, offering a basic English pub menu, such as fish-and-chips and Gloucester old-spot sausages. ✉ *29 Watling St., City of London* ☎ *020/7248–8935* ⊕ *www.nicholsonspubs.co.uk* Ⓜ *Mansion House.*

Performing Arts

It may seem at first glance like the denizens of London's financial center are far too busy to take time out for culture, but look a little closer: arts events are taking place all over, courtesy of a number of acclaimed annual festivals. Art exhibits in empty offices and chamber performances in historic churches are regular occurrences.

★ Barbican Centre

ARTS CENTERS | FAMILY | Opened in 1982, The Barbican is an enormous Brutalist concrete maze that Londoners either love or hate—but its importance to the cultural life of the capital is beyond dispute. At the largest performing arts center in Europe, you could listen to Elgar, see 1960s photography, and catch German animation with live accompaniment, all in one day. The main concert hall, known for its acoustics, is most famous as the home of the London Symphony Orchestra. The Barbican is also a frequent host to the BBC Symphony Orchestra. Architecture tours take place several times a week. ✉ *Silk St., City of London* ☎ *020/7638–4141* ⊕ *www.barbican.org.uk* Art exhibits free–£15, cinema from £6, theater and music from £10, tours £15 Ⓜ *Barbican.*

The Bridge Theatre

THEATER | This gleaming theater on the banks of the River Thames by Tower Bridge is the brainchild of director Nicholas Hytner and producer Nick Starr, who together oversaw a golden age at the National Theatre before handing over the reins of The Bridge to current artistic director Rufus Norris. The program at this totally adaptable space is a blend of the classics (Hytner's *Julius Caesar* was a huge hit in 2018) and riskier new works, though big-name actors (e.g., Ben Whishaw, Laura Linney) are a constant. ✉ *3 Potters Fields Park, London Bridge* ☎ *033/3320–0052* ⊕ *www.bridgetheatre.co.uk* From £15 Ⓜ *London Bridge, Tower Hill.*

EAST LONDON

Updated by
Jo Caird

◉ Sights	🍴 Restaurants	🛏 Hotels	🛍 Shopping	🍸 Nightlife
★★★☆☆	★★★★☆	★★★☆☆	★★★★☆	★★★★★

EAST LONDON SNAPSHOT

TOP REASONS TO GO

Dennis Severs' House: The atmospheric set pieces in this Georgian town house use visuals, sounds, and aromas to evoke the lives of its fictional previous inhabitants.

Broadway Market: Check out more than 100 (mainly) food stalls here on Saturday, offering everything from cheeses to oysters.

London's hottest art scene: Edgy galleries mix with large collections.

Jack the Ripper: Track Britain's most infamous serial killer through streets that were part of a major slum area in Victorian times.

The ArcelorMittal Orbit: This enormous sculpture offers great views over London and a rush of adrenaline if you take the quick route back down to Earth via the slide.

GETTING THERE

The London Overground, with stops at Shoreditch High Street, Hoxton, Whitechapel, Dalston Junction, Dalston Kingsland, London Fields, Hackney Central, and Hackney Wick is the easiest way to reach East London. Alternatively, the best Tube stations to use are Old Street on the Northern line, Bethnal Green on the Central line, and Liverpool Street on the Metropolitan and Circle lines.

MAKING THE MOST OF YOUR TIME

To experience East London at its most lively, visit on the weekend. Spitalfields Market bustles all weekend, while Brick Lane and Columbia Road are best on a Sunday morning and Broadway Market on Saturday. If you're planning to explore East London's art galleries, pick up a free map at the Whitechapel Gallery (which you can also view online). As for the area's booming nightlife scene, there's no time limit: you'll find people partying pretty much every night of the week.

SAFETY

■ Around Shoreditch, Spitalfields, and Brick Lane, streets are largely safe during daylight hours. Be cautious on the rougher streets of Whitechapel, Bethnal Green, and Hackney at night.

PAUSE HERE

■ Escape the hubbub of nearby Shoreditch with a visit to **Hoxton Square**. Laid out in 1683, it's thought to be one of the oldest public garden squares in London. Join the local office workers lunching on the grass or just swing by to admire the massive London plane trees and the eclectic mix of architecture that lines the square.

Made famous by Dickens and infamous by Jack the Ripper, East London is one of the city's most enduringly evocative neighborhoods, rich in popular history, architectural gems, and artists' studios. Since the early 1990s, au courant gallerists, designers, and new-media entrepreneurs have colonized its handsome Georgian buildings and converted industrial lofts. Today, this collection of neighborhoods lays claim to being London's hippest area.

The British equivalent of parts of Brooklyn, East London is a patchwork of districts encompassing struggling artists, multicultural enclaves, and upscale professionals occasionally teetering, like its New York equivalent, on the edge of self-parody. The vast area ranges from gentrified districts like Spitalfields, where bankers and successful artists live in desirable renovated town houses, to parts of Hackney, where seemingly derelict, graffiti-covered industrial buildings are hives of exciting creative activity. It remains a little rough around the edges, so stick to busier streets at night.

At the start of the new millennium, Hoxton, an enclave of Shoreditch, became the glossy hub of London's buzzing contemporary art scene, which accelerated the gentrification process. Some artists, such as Tracey Emin and Gilbert & George, long-term residents of Spitalfields' handsome Georgian terraces—and successful enough to still afford the area—have remained.

One such residence, **Dennis Severs' House,** was transformed two decades ago by the eponymous American artist into a unique "living house museum" that evokes how past generations of a fictional Huguenot family might have lived there. Not far away, **Spitalfields Market** offers an ever-changing selection of crafts and funky clothes stalls under a glass roof in what was once a Victorian produce market. Across from the market, **Christ Church Spitalfields,** Nicholas Hawkmoor's masterpiece, soars above Fournier Street.

In the last decade, streets around the Old Street roundabout (as well as converted warehouses in Hackney and Dalston) have flourished with start-ups, with attendant stylish boutiques (especially on Redchurch Street), destination restaurants, and hipster bars, as part of a government initiative to attract IT-oriented businesses to the neighborhood. Old and new Shoreditch meet on **Brick Lane,** the heart of the Bangladeshi community, lined with innumerable curry houses and glittering sari shops, plus vintage-clothing emporia. Here you'll also find **The Truman Brewery,** an East London landmark converted into a warren of street fashion and pop-up galleries. On Sunday, the Columbia Road Flower Market to the north of Brick Lane becomes a colorful, fragrant oasis of greenery.

As property prices have climbed, up-and-coming artists have sought more affordable studio spaces in former industrial buildings eastward toward Whitechapel and Bethnal Green, where there are also some notable galleries. Here you'll find the **Whitechapel Gallery,** a leading center for contemporary art, and—a design connoisseur's favorite— the **Museum of the Home,** a collection of domestic interiors throughout the ages that occupies a row of early 18th-century almshouses.

Probably the best start to an East London tour is via the London Overground, getting off at Shoreditch High Street Station. Immediately northwest of the station, on the west side of Shoreditch High Street, is the heart of the neighborhood that aspires to be the U.K. equivalent to Silicon Valley. To the northeast is Shoreditch's boutique, gallery, and restaurant zone. The subneighborhood of Hoxton is located just above Shoreditch, north of the Old Street roundabout. To the southeast of the station are the handsome Georgian streets of Spitalfields. Bethnal Green is due east, past busy Brick Lane. Whitechapel, formerly Jack the Ripper's patch, is to the south of Spitalfields. All these neighborhoods are within what is traditionally referred to as the "East End," although East London extends farther to the north and east.

Sights

Bevis Marks Synagogue

SYNAGOGUE | This is Britain's oldest synagogue still in use and is certainly its most splendid. It was built in 1701, after Jewish people, having been expelled from England in 1290, were allowed to return under Cromwell in 1656. Inspired by the Spanish and Portuguese Great Synagogue of Amsterdam, the interior is embellished with rich woodwork, seven hanging brass candelabra (representing the seven days of the week), and 12 trompe-l'oeil wood columns painted to look like marble. The magnificent Ark, which contains the sacred scrolls of the five books of Moses, is modeled on contemporary Wren neoclassical altarpieces, with oak doors and Corinthian columns. In 1992 and 1993 the synagogue was seriously damaged by IRA bombs, but it was subsequently completely restored. It's closed to visitors during Jewish holidays, so check the website before visiting. ⊠ *Bevis Marks, Whitechapel* ☎ *020/7621–1188* ⊕ *www. sephardi.org.uk/bevis-marks* ⊠ *£6* ⊗ *Closed Sat. and bank holiday Mon.* Ⓜ *Aldgate, Liverpool St.*

Christ Church Spitalfields

CHURCH | This is the 1729 masterpiece of Sir Christopher Wren's associate Nicholas Hawksmoor, one of his six London churches and an example of English Baroque at its finest. It was commissioned as part of Parliament's 1711 Fifty New Churches Act, passed in response to the influx of immigrants with the idea of providing for the religious needs of the "godless thousands"—and to help ensure they joined the Church of England, as opposed to such nonconformist denominations as the Protestant Huguenots. (It must have worked; you can still see gravestones with epitaphs in French in the crypt.) As the local silk industry declined, the church fell into disrepair, and by 1958 the structure was crumbling, with the looming prospect of demolition. But after 25 years—longer than it took to build the church—and a huge local fundraising effort, the structure was meticulously restored and is a joy to behold, from the colonnaded Doric portico and tall spire to its soaring, heavily ornamented plaster ceiling. Its excellent acoustics make it a superb concert venue. There's also a café in the crypt. ✉ Commercial St., Spitalfields ☎ 020/7377–2440 ⊕ www.ccspits.org ☑ Free ⊘ Closed weekdays Ⓜ Overground: Shoreditch High St.

★ **Dennis Severs' House**

HISTORIC HOME | The remarkable interiors of this extraordinary time machine of a house are the creation of Dennis Severs (1948–99), a performer-designer-scholar from Escondido, California, who dedicated his life to restoring this Georgian terraced house. More than that, he created "still-life dramas" using sight, sound, and smell to evoke the world of a fictitious family of Huguenot silk weavers, the Jervises, who might have inhabited the house between 1728 and 1914. Each of the 10 rooms has a distinctive compelling atmosphere that encourages visitors to become lost in another time, deploying evocative design details like rose-laden Victorian wallpaper, Jacobean paneling, Georgian wingback chairs, Baroque carved ornaments, rich "Catholic" wall colors downstairs, and more sedate "Protestant" shades upstairs.

The Silent Night candlelight tour offered Friday evenings, a stroll through the rooms with no talking allowed, is the most theatrical and memorable way to experience the house. The Denis Severs Tour (Thursday, Saturday, and Sunday evenings) draws upon recently discovered recordings and writings to recreate the tours that the artist himself gave when he first opened the house in 1980. ✉ 18 Folgate St., Shoreditch ⊕ www.dennissevershouse.co.uk ☑ £15 weekends, £20 Fri. evenings, £70 Thurs., Sat., and Sun. evenings ⊘ Closed Mon.–Wed. Ⓜ Overground: Shoreditch High St.

East End Tours

The two-hour **Jack the Ripper Walk** (⊕ www.walks.com) departs from Tower Hill Tube station daily at 7:30 pm, plus Saturday at 3. The same company also offers an **Unknown East End** walk, a more comprehensive look at the history of the area. It departs at 2:30 pm from the Whitechapel Tube station every Sunday.

Maureen Paley

ART GALLERY | Inspired by the DIY punk aesthetic and the funky galleries of New York's Lower East Side, Maureen Paley started putting on exhibitions in her East End home back in 1984, when it was virtually the only gallery in the area. Since then, this American artist and gallerist has shown such respected contemporary artists as Gillian Wearing, Helen Chadwick, Jenny Holzer, Peter Fischli, and Wolfgang Tillmans, and today she is considered the doyenne of East End gallerists. Paley now has two London spaces, one in the midst of a cluster of galleries in Bethnal Green and another in a former school building in Shoreditch. ✉ 60 Three Colts La., Bethnal Green ☎ 020/7729–4112 ⊕ www.maureenpaley.com ☑ Free ⊘ Closed Mon. and Tues. Ⓜ Bethnal Green.

★ **Museum of the Home**

HISTORY MUSEUM | **FAMILY** | In contrast to the West End's grand aristocratic town houses, this charming museum is devoted to the life of the city's middle class over the years. Originally a row of almshouses built in 1714, it now contains a series of 11 rooms that re-create everyday domestic interiors from the Elizabethan period through the 1950s to the present day. The Home Galleries, located in the basement of the museum, puts it all in context with a wider history of the

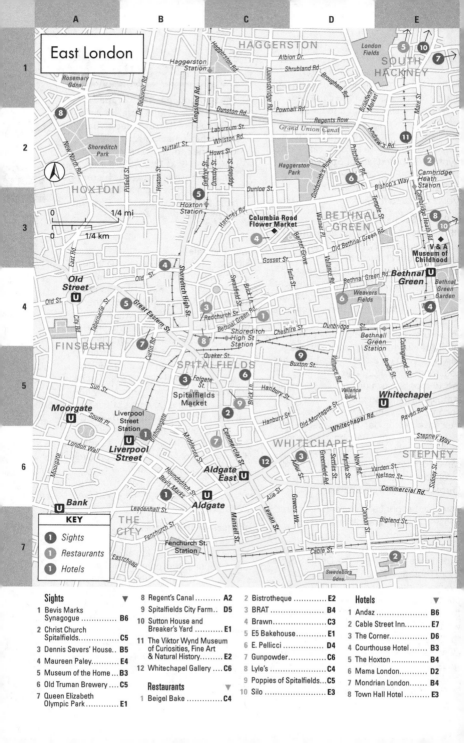

East London

Key

- **1** Sights
- **1** Restaurants
- **1** Hotels

The East End's Famous Streets

Brick Lane and the narrow streets running off it offer a paradigm of East London's development. Its population has moved in waves: communities seeking refuge, others moving out in an upwardly mobile direction.

Brick Lane has seen the manufacture of bricks (during the 16th century), beer, and bagels, but nowadays it's primarily known as the heart of Banglatown—Bangladeshis make up one-third of the population in this London borough, and you'll see that the names of the surrounding streets are written in Bengali—where you find many kebab and curry houses along with shops selling DVDs, colorful saris, and stacks of sticky sweets. On Sunday, cars aren't allowed on the upper section of the street. Shops and cafés are open, and several stalls are set up, creating a companion market to the one on nearby **Petticoat Lane.**

Fournier Street contains fine examples of the neighborhood's characteristic Georgian terraced houses, many of them built by the richest of the early-18th-century Huguenot silk weavers (note the enlarged windows on the upper floors to maximize light for the intricate work). Most of those along the north side of Fournier Street have since been restored.

Wilkes Street, with more 1720s Huguenot houses, is north of Christ Church Spitalfields, and neighboring **Princelet Street** was once important to East London's Jewish community. Where No. 6 stands now, the first of several thriving Yiddish theaters opened in 1886. **Elder Street**, just off Folgate, is another gem of original 18th-century houses.

On the south and east sides of Spitalfields Market are yet more time-warp streets that are worth a wander, such as **Gun Street**, where artist Mark Gertler (1891–1939) was born, at No. 16.

8

East London

concept of home that includes plenty of interactive exhibits.

Outside, a series of gardens charts the evolution of the town garden over the past 400 years; next to them is a walled herb garden. In the museum's front garden, you'll find a statue of Sir Robert Geffreye, the English merchant who founded the almshouses; the museum used to bear his name, but in the wake of the Black Lives Matter movement and the acknowledgment of Geffreye's connections with the transatlantic slave trade, the museum has been renamed. The future of the statue itself is still under consideration. Molly's Café, the excellent on-site eatery, provides appropriately homely lunches and snacks. ⊠ *136 Kingsland Rd., Hoxton* ⊕ *www.*

museumofthehome.org.uk ⊠ *Free (charge for special exhibitions)* ⊗ *Closed Mon.* Ⓜ *Overground: Hoxton.*

Queen Elizabeth Olympic Park

CITY PARK | FAMILY | Built for the London 2012 Olympic and Paralympic Games, this 560-acre parkland still boasts some of the city's best sporting arenas. The London Stadium, site of the London 2012 athletics competitions, is now home to local soccer team Westham United; it also hosts major athletic events. In addition, it's open for behind-the-scenes tours; check the website for dates. You can try four types of cycling (track, road racing, BMX, and mountain biking) at the Lee Valley VeloPark, or go for a swim in the magnificent pool within the London

Aquatics Centre, while the Copper Box Arena hosts basketball, netball, and volleyball contests.

The ArcelorMittal Orbit, an enormous sculpture, is well worth a visit—the views across London from the top are terrific. It's open daily in the summer and during school holidays and Friday through Sunday the rest of the year. Thrill seekers have a couple of options when it comes to getting back down: a gasp-inducing slide that twists its way around the outside of the structure (art buffs might recognize it as the work of German-Belgian artist Carsten Höller) or via vertical rappelling (available on selected dates, advance booking essential). The latest arrival in the park is ABBA Voyage, a live music experience that includes avatars of the Swedish pop group in their heyday. ⊠ East End ☎ 800/0072–2110 ⊕ www.queenelizabetholympicpark. co.uk ⊡ From £13, stadium tours £19 Ⓜ Stratford, Hackney Wick, Pudding Mill Lane, Leyton.

★ Regent's Canal

BODY OF WATER | The 19th-century waterway known as Regent's Canal officially starts in Little Venice in West London, but you'll find this quirky section east of City Road Basin. Join the towpath, where horses once walked as they pulled barges carrying all manner of cargo, at Wharf Road in Islington (N1), then head east on foot or by bike to experience the East End from an unusual perspective. What was once a no-go area is now a route lined with trendy cafés, floating bookshops, and a distinct community of water-dwelling Londoners. Regent's Canal runs through Hackney, before heading south through Bethnal Green and Mile End, ending up at Limehouse Basin and the River Thames. Or you can continue eastward by turning off along the Hertford Union Canal at Victoria Park, a route that eventually leads to Queen Elizabeth Olympic Park. ⊠ East End.

Spitalfields City Farm

FARM/RANCH | **FAMILY** | An oasis of rural calm in an urban landscape, this little community farm raises a variety of animals, including some rare breeds, to help educate city kids about life in the country. A tiny farm shop sells freshly laid eggs, along with organic seasonal produce, while the Tea Hut is a nice spot for a cup of coffee and a snack. ⊠ Buxton St., Spitalfields ☎ 020/7247–8762 ⊕ www. spitalfieldscityfarm.org ⊡ Free ⊘ Closed Mon.; Tea Hut closed Jan. and Feb. Ⓜ Overground: Shoreditch High St.

Sutton House and Breaker's Yard

HISTORIC HOME | **FAMILY** | Built by a courtier to King Henry VIII, this Tudor mansion has since been home to merchants, Huguenot silk weavers, and, in the 1980s, a group of arty squatters. The house dates back to 1535, when Hackney was a village on the outskirts of London surrounded by fields. Later, in 1751, it was split into two self-contained houses. Its oak-paneled rooms, tranquil courtyard, and award-winning community garden are an unexpected treat in an area that's yet to entirely shake off its grit. Visits to the house are by prebooked guided tour only. They take place on Wednesday, Friday, and Sunday at 11 am and 2 pm, plus 3:30 pm on Sunday. ⊠ 2–4 Homerton High St., Hackney ☎ 020/8986–2264 ⊕ www.nationaltrust.org.uk/sutton-house ⊡ £8 ⊘ Closed Mon., Tues., Thurs., and Sat. Ⓜ Overground: Hackney Central.

The Truman Brewery

PEDESTRIAN MALL | **FAMILY** | The last old East End brewery still standing—a handsome example of Georgian and 19th-century industrial architecture, and in late Victorian times the largest brewery in the world—has been transformed into a cavernous hipster mall housing galleries, record shops, fashion-forward boutiques, bars, clubs, and restaurants, along with an array of international street-food vendors. There's also a fantastic—and absolutely sprawling—vintage-clothing

The East End Art Scene

Banksy, the Bristol-based artist and provocateur who has maintained his anonymity despite works that now command six figures, is widely credited with making Londoners see street art as more than mere vandalism. He first came to public attention in the East End in the late '80s, and the area continues to attract new talent from around the globe today. Unfortunately, much of Banksy's early work has been lost, either from being covered over by local councils and building owners, defaced by other graffiti artists, or removed by profiteers. Currently murals remain at Rivington Street near Old Street (in the garden of Cargo bar and nightclub) and at Stoke Newington Church Street. There's more to the street art scene than Banksy though, so take the time to notice the extraordinarily varied range of work on display when strolling through Shoreditch.

Today East London is a global hotbed of contemporary art, but its avant-garde roots go way back. Shoreditch's cheap industrial units and Georgian–Victorian terraced streets have attracted artists since the 1960s, when op-art pioneer Bridget Riley established a service to find affordable studio space for her contemporaries. In the early '90s it gained new notoriety when Young British Artists Sarah Lucas and Tracey Emin began selling their own and their friends' work in The Shop, joining Maureen Paley's influential Bethnal Green gallery and the long-established Whitechapel Gallery, where many leading abstract expressionists and pop artists had their first U.K. shows. Hoxton truly became a destination for well-heeled collectors when Jay Jopling, the most important modern-art dealer in town, set up his White Cube gallery in 2000 (it's now in Bermondsey, with a second location at Mason's Yard in Westminster), followed by Kate MacGarry's gallery in 2002.

Priced out by the area's fashionability, the emerging artists themselves have relocated farther off the beaten path to edgier neighborhoods such as Hackney, with several trendsetting galleries found clustered around Cambridge Heath Road and Herald Street.

market in the basement, trendy retailers at street level, and offices and studios on the upper floors. Events include fashion shows for both new and established designers, excellent sample sales, art installations, and, on weekends, a food hall and market stalls selling both new and vintage clothing. The brewery itself shut down in 1989. ✉ *91 Brick La., Spitalfields* ☎ *0207/770–6000* ⊕ *www.trumanbrewery.com* Ⓜ *Overground: Shoreditch High St.*

★ **The Viktor Wynd Museum of Curiosities, Fine Art & Natural History**

OTHER MUSEUM | This tiny basement establishment professes to be a museum but feels more like an art installation, with real historical and occult artifacts (the range of taxidermy is astonishing) displayed alongside satirical items like celebrity poops, all accompanied by serious handwritten description cards. It's a hoot, especially following a visit to the upstairs cocktail bar, which specializes in absinthe. The museum is sometimes hired out for private events, so check before you visit. ✉ *11 Mare St., Hackney* ☎ *020/8533–5297* 🌐 *www.thelasttuesdaysociety.org* 🎟 *£10; £5 if visiting the cocktail bar* ⏲ *Closed Mon. and Tues.* [M] *Overground: Cambridge Heath.*

★ Whitechapel Gallery

ART GALLERY | Founded in 1901, this internationally renowned gallery mounts exhibitions that rediscover overlooked masters and showcase tomorrow's legends. Painter and leading exponent of abstract expressionism Jackson Pollock was exhibited here in the 1950s as was pop artist Robert Rauschenberg in the 1960s; the 1970s saw a young David Hockney's first solo show. The exhibitions continue to be on the cutting edge of contemporary art. The gallery also hosts talks, film screenings, workshops, and other events; First Thursdays is a regular event designed to highlight monthly openings at over 150 local galleries, with the Whitechapel offering curated tips about where to visit on the first Thursday of the month. Pick up a free East London art map (also available online) to help you plan your visit to the area. Townsend, the gallery's on-site restaurant, serves good quality modern British food in a bright and pretty room. ✉ *77–82 Whitechapel High St., Whitechapel* ☎ *020/7522–7888* 🌐 *www.whitechapelgallery.org* ⏲ *Closed Mon.* [M] *Aldgate East.*

🍴 Restaurants

An invasion of hipsters and foodies has transformed the once-bleak East End food scene into the city's most daring dining zone. Seek out new British breakout stars like BRAT or Lyle's in Shoreditch, or hunt down a nighttime food truck for an irreverent taste of the foodie underground.

★ Beigel Bake

$ | JEWISH DELI | Locals are keen to proclaim the virtues of their favorite Brick Lane bagel emporium, but to be perfectly honest, there's not much true competition aside from this spot and its two-doors-down neighbor, the Beigel Shop. Both serve delicious fresh beigels (the traditional European spelling) 24 hours a day, seven days a week (at just 40 pence each); both date back to when Brick Lane was home to a largely Jewish immigrant community, and both are family-owned (two branches of the same family, in fact). **Known for:** brusque service; classic hot salt beef beigel sandwich; lively, often drunk, clientele. [$] *Average main: £6* ✉ *155 Brick Ln., Shoreditch* ☎ *020/7729–0616* 🌐 *www.bricklanebeigel.co.uk* [M] *Shoreditch.*

Bistrotheque

$$ | MODERN EUROPEAN | FAMILY | You'll need some help finding this East End fashionista headquarters located down a side alley in happening Bethnal Green. Once inside, check out the striking loft dining space and the bar, Manchichi, in its post-industrial chic setting, before polishing off light French and English dishes. **Known for:** resident pianist at brunch; classic choices like steak tartare and Croque Madame; weekend brunch with pancakes and maple syrup. [$] *Average main: £20* ✉ *23–27 Wadeson St., Bethnal Green* ☎ *020/8983–7900* 🌐 *www.bistrotheque.com* ⏲ *Closed Mon.–Wed. No lunch Thurs. and Fri. No dinner Sun.* [M] *Bethnal Green.*

★ BRAT

$$$$ | SPANISH | Welsh chef Tomos Parry brings his signature wood-grilled, whole roast Cornish turbot to this Basque-inspired hipster restaurant. Expect other live-fire smashes like aged Jersey beef chops and seared leeks. **Known for:** heritage Welsh grain flour breads; meat-heavy dishes grilled in a variety of ways; noisy hipster atmosphere. [$] *Average main: £40* ✉ *1st fl., 4 Redchurch St., Shoreditch* 🌐 *www.bratrestaurant.com* [M] *Liverpool St., Overground: Shoreditch High St.*

Brawn

$$$ | EUROPEAN | This unpretentious neighborhood restaurant serves inventive modern European cuisine—think rabbit, pork, and pistachio terrine or brill, mussels, and fennel in a bouillabaisse sauce—alongside some of the best natural wines you'll find in London. **Known for:** welcoming vibe; industrial look; orange wines by the glass. $ *Average main: £25* ✉ *49 Columbia Rd., Shoreditch* ☎ *020/7729–5692* ⊕ *www.brawn.co* ☾ *Closed Sun. No lunch Mon.* Ⓜ *Bethnal Green, Overground: Shoreditch High Street, Bethnal Green.*

★ **e5 Bakehouse**

$ | CAFÉ | This bakery, which supplies bread to many of East London's top eateries, has a friendly café and deli on-site, where you can sample some of the tastiest toasted sandwiches in the city, plus pizzas on Sunday. The shop also stocks a concise range of elegant household items. **Known for:** house-milled flour; secret courtyard garden in back; fantastic daylong sourdough-making classes that sell out months in advance. $ *Average main: £8* ✉ *Mentmore Terr., Arch 395, Dalston* ☎ *020/8525–2890* ⊕ *www.e5bakehouse.com* ☾ *No dinner* Ⓜ *Overground: London Fields.*

★ **E. Pellicci**

$ | CAFÉ | FAMILY | It's all Cockney banter and full English breakfasts at this tiny family-run café and one-time gangsters' lair near Brick Lane and Columbia Road Markets. The atmosphere may be rowdy, but it's all good-natured, with greasy fry-ups (think eggs, bacon, sausages, baked beans, toast, tomatoes, fried mushrooms, black pudding, and cabbage and mash) served alongside homemade Italian classics like lasagna and cannelloni and British classics like pies and roast dinners, all courtesy of matriarch Mama Maria. **Known for:** cash-only cheap dishes; full cast of East End Cockney characters; copious full English breakfasts and builder's brew tea. $ *Average main: £10* ✉ *332 Bethnal Green Rd., Bethnal Green* ☎ *020/7739–4873* ⊕ *epellicci.co.uk* ▭ *No*

credit cards ☾ *Closed Sun. and Aug. No dinner* Ⓜ *Bethnal Green.*

Gunpowder

$$ | INDIAN | Eschew the myriad copy-and-paste curry houses of Brick Lane and opt instead for this broom cupboard–size Spitalfields restaurant serving flawless small-plate Indian cuisine. The charming waitstaff is happy to offer guidance when it comes to the menu, with its highly original takes on authentic flavor combinations from the subcontinent. **Known for:** rasam ke bomb, a puff of spiced potato served atop a flavorful Bloody Mary–style shot; ingredients not normally found on Indian menus, such as duck or sea bass; good value multidish "feast" menus. $ *Average main: £20* ✉ *11 White's Row, Spitalfields* ⊕ *www.gunpowderrestaurants.com* ☾ *Closed Sun.* Ⓜ *Liverpool St.*

★ **Lyle's**

$$ | MODERN BRITISH | Globally acclaimed Brit chef and co-owner James Lowe forsakes heavy sauces and sorcery at this stripped-back, informal British dining mecca in Shoreditch. Stark but highly inventive locally sourced dishes may include house-cured cod with radiant nasturtium flowers or 24-hour Cornish Helford Estuary monkfish with wood sorrel and pick-your-own East Sussex greengages. **Known for:** excellent cheese plates and wines by the glass; highly modern and airy dining space; serious new-wave British neo-bistronomy. $ *Average main: £20* ✉ *Tea Bldg., 56 Shoreditch High St., East End* ⊕ *Entrance on Bethnal Green Rd.* ☎ *020/3011–5911* ⊕ *www.lyleslondon.com* ☾ *Closed Sun. and bank holiday Mon.* Ⓜ *Shoreditch High St.*

Poppies of Spitalfields

$$ | SEAFOOD | FAMILY | This eatery strikes a balance between trendy and traditional with retro-diner style and efficient service. The specialty is fish-and-chips, but if fish isn't your thing, try the free-range grilled chicken. **Known for:** walls covered with fun mix of maritime and rock and roll paraphernalia; wider range of fish

than at most traditional fish-and-chip places; wine, beer, and cocktails available (uncommon for a chip shop). $ *Average main: £16* ✉ *6–8 Hanbury St., Spitalfields* ☎ *020/7247–0892* ⊕ *www.poppiesfishandchips.co.uk* Ⓜ *Shoreditch High St.*

★ Silo

$$$ | BRITISH | If you've ever wondered what the future tastes like, it might just be the 12-course tasting menu here at Silo, a sleek zero-waste restaurant opened by pioneering chef Douglas McMaster in this on-trend area of East London. Clever use of techniques like smoking and dehydration will change how you think about everyday ingredients like carrots and potatoes, while the occasional meat dishes—game and offal feature often—are melt-in-the-mouth delectable (those not in the mood for the full 12 courses can go à la carte with the small plates menu). **Known for:** atmospheric views of London Stadium and the ArcelorMittal Orbit tower; innovative design is full of surprises, including a bar made of recycled Italian shoe leather; ingredients like house-churned butter and house-rolled oats that typify the zero-waste philososphy. $ *Average main: £25* ✉ *Unit 7 Queens Yard, Hackney* ☎ *020/7993–8155* ⊕ *www.silolondon. com* ◷ *Closed Sun.–Tues. No lunch Wed.–Fri.* Ⓜ *Overground: Hackney Wick.*

Hotels

What was once a lodging no-man's land is fast becoming the hippest place to stay in London. Hotels tend to be quirky and design-led, attracting a crowd keen to make the most of the excellent food and drink, culture, and shopping opportunities available in the East End.

Andaz

$$$ | HOTEL | Swanky and upscale, this hotel sports a modern masculine design and an enjoyable check-in ritual—guests are offered a glass of prosecco on arrival.

Pros: complimentary "healthy minibars" are stocked with nuts, fruit, and yogurt; nice attention to detail; bath products from REN. **Cons:** busy, sometimes hectic neighborhood; rates rise significantly for midweek stays; sparse interior design is not for all. $ *Rooms from: £320* ✉ *40 Liverpool St., East End* ☎ *020/7961–1234* ⊕ *www.andaz.hyatt.com* ⇄ *267 rooms* ⦿ *No Meals* Ⓜ *Liverpool St.*

★ Cable Street Inn

$$ | B&B/INN | Wonderful modern art lines the walls of this former Victorian pub a mile east of the Tower of London, which has been beautifully restored and converted into a modern bed-and-breakfast. **Pros:** wonderful host; true one-of-a-kind place; beautiful art. **Cons:** with only three rooms, availability can be low; historic nature of the building makes it unsuitable for those with mobility problems; 20-minute journey by DLR then Tube to the center. $ *Rooms from: £140* ✉ *232 Cable St., East End* ☎ *020/7790–4019* ⊕ *www. cablestreetinn.co.uk* ⇄ *3 rooms* ⦿ *Free Breakfast* Ⓜ *DLR: Shadwell.*

The Corner

$ | HOTEL | A contrast to the wildly expensive business hotels that proliferate in this part of the East End, right on the edge of The City, the Corner is a modern and surprisingly affordable option in a trendy area of town. **Pros:** environmentally friendly; free bike rentals; great value for money. **Cons:** cheapest rooms have no windows; not everyone will love the style; a bit out of the way. $ *Rooms from: £80* ✉ *42 Adler St., Whitechapel* ☎ *020/3021–1440* ⊕ *www.thecornerlondoncity.co.uk* ⇄ *183 rooms* ⦿ *No Meals* Ⓜ *Aldgate East.*

Courthouse Hotel—Shoreditch

$$$ | HOTEL | Housed within a beautifully restored former courthouse, this hip Shoreditch hotel contributes its own contemporary flair to the grand architectural style of the original building, with chic rooms that provide the perfect base to

explore the surrounding trendy neighborhood. **Pros:** excellent facilities, including cinema and bowling alley; great views over neighboring rooftops from the terrace; lively bar. **Cons:** the size and scope of the public spaces can lead to some areas feeling deserted; a 20-minute Tube ride into central London; not all rooms are located in the historic former courthouse. [$] *Rooms from: £269* ✉ *335–337 Old St., Shoreditch* ☎ *020/3310–5555* 🌐 *www.shoreditch.courthouse-hotel.com* 🛏 *128 rooms* 🍴 *No Meals* [M] *Old St.*

★ The Hoxton Shoreditch
$$ | **HOTEL** | The design throughout this trendy East London lodging is contemporary—but not so modern as to be absurd; in keeping with a claim to combine a country-lodge lifestyle with true urban living, a fire crackles in the lobby. **Pros:** huge weekend discounts; cool vibe; neighborhood known for funky galleries and boutiques. **Cons:** cheapest rooms are called "shoeboxes" for a reason; away from major tourist sights; price skyrockets during the week. [$] *Rooms from: £249* ✉ *81 Great Eastern St., East End* ☎ *020/7550–1000* 🌐 *www.thehoxton.com* 🛏 *210 rooms* 🍴 *Free Breakfast* [M] *Shoreditch High St.*

Mama Shelter London Shoreditch
$$ | **HOTEL** | **FAMILY** | The first London outpost of the fashionable French hotel brand, the rooms and public areas here have the feel of an upmarket design hotel—think marble-top tables, bold fabrics, and atmospheric designed lighting—but at a fraction of the cost. **Pros:** buzzing bar and restaurant; homewares and bath products on sale at reception that make great souvenirs; dozens of free movies available in-room. **Cons:** 20-minute Tube ride from central London; bold design won't be to everyone's taste; cheapest rooms are very small. [$] *Rooms from: £132* ✉ *437 Hackney Rd., Hackney* ☎ *020/7613–6500* 🌐 *www.mamashelter.com/london-shoreditch* 🛏 *194 rooms* 🍴 *No Meals* [M] *Bethnal Green.*

Mondrian Shoreditch London
$$$ | **HOTEL** | Formerly the super-cool Curtain hotel, the Mondrian takeover has only raised the hipness stakes here, thanks to a glossy but subtle refurbishment that sees the industrial look of the place toned down to offer a more elegant feel. **Pros:** cutting-edge basement restaurant; rooftop pool great for summertime hangs; spacious rooms, some with terraces and great views. **Cons:** standard rooms small for the price; area is renowned for nightlife, so don't expect quiet nights; bar and restaurant areas can get overcrowded. [$] *Rooms from: £275* ✉ *45 Curtain Rd., Shoreditch* ☎ *020/3988–4455* 🌐 *www.sbe.com/hotels/mondrian/shoreditch* 🛏 *120 rooms* 🍴 *No Meals* [M] *Overground: Shoreditch High St.*

Town Hall Hotel
$$ | **HOTEL** | An Art Deco town hall, abandoned in the early 1980s and turned into a chic hotel 30 years later, is now a lively and stylish place, with the best of the building's elegant original features intact. **Pros:** big discounts on weekends; beautifully designed; lovely staff. **Cons:** some rooms choose style over function; a 15-minute Tube ride from central London; the area is far from the major sights. [$] *Rooms from: £220* ✉ *Patriot Sq., Bethnal Green, East End* ☎ *020/7871–0460* 🌐 *www.townhallhotel.com* 🛏 *96 rooms* 🍴 *Free Breakfast* [M] *Bethnal Green, Overground: Cambridge Heath.*

🍸 Nightlife

East London's bar scene is ever-evolving, with the trendy crowd constantly pushing farther east in search of the next big thing. Shoreditch has bars and clubs to suit nearly all tastes these days, while Dalston, the neighborhood to its north, attracts an edgier clientele. In historic neighborhoods, such as Spitalfields and Wapping, there's a cozy old drinking den around practically every corner.

BARS

Callooh Callay

BARS | Cocktails are tasty, well-executed classics, and there's also a selection of unique instant-classics at this eccentric Hoxton bar where the bells and whistles are left to the decor. ⊠ *65 Rivington St., Hoxton* ☎ *020/7739–4781* ⊕ *www. calloohcallaybar.com* Ⓜ *Old St.*

Crate Bar and Pizzeria

BARS | Enjoy canal-side craft beer and pizza at the busiest of a handful of grown-up bars in this ultra-trendy area of East London. Rub shoulders with the locals—the community still has its share of artists who made their way east following rent hikes in Shoreditch—as well as visitors who come for late-night raves in the area's many warehouses. There's a warm atmosphere inside, with quirky upcycled interior design and DJs playing on weekend evenings. The beer comes from the on-site brewery, while thin-crust pizzas emerge from the open kitchen. ⊠ *Unit 7, Queens Yard, Hackney* ☎ *0754/769–5841* ⊕ *www.cratebrewery. com* Ⓜ *Overground: Hackney Wick.*

Nightjar

BARS | The feel is moody, Prohibition-era '20s Chicago at this fabulously low-lit, tin-tiled-ceiling speakeasy and basement jazz cocktail bar in Shoreditch. Book a table or chance it on the door at this no-standing venue, where live jazz and swing bands nightly keep things lively. ⊠ *129 City Rd., Hoxton* ☎ *020/7253–4101* ⊕ *www.barnightjar.com* Ⓜ *Old St.*

Untitled

BARS | This stripped-back Dalston bar, with its design inspired by Andy Warhol's New York City Factory, is all about bold cocktails featuring unusual ingredients. Think white clay and chalk in a vodka-based Snow or leather in a champagne-based Cuir de Russie. It all somehow works, and the Korean food served alongside the drinks is delicious. ⊠ *538 Kingsland Rd., Dalston* ☎ *078/4102–2924* ⊕ *www.untitled-bar. com* Ⓜ *Overground: Dalston Junction.*

LIVE MUSIC

★ Cafe OTO

LIVE MUSIC | A relaxed café by day, and London's leading venue for experimental music by night, Cafe OTO is a Dalston institution. Its programming of free jazz, avant-garde electronica, and much more is enough of a draw that it regularly sells out, with music fans steaming up the windows and spilling out onto the pavement and road outside to smoke during breaks. Café customers are kicked out at 5 pm to make way for sound checks. It's open as a bar (no cover) on nights when no concerts are taking place. ⊠ *18–22 Ashwin St., Dalston* ☎ ⊕ *www.cafeoto. co.uk* Ⓜ *Overground: Dalston Junction.*

★ EartH (Evolutionary Arts Hackney)

LIVE MUSIC | East London's coolest performing arts venue occupies two huge spaces (one standing, one with unallocated bench seating) in an old art deco movie theater. Original architectural details add to the shabby-hip feel of the place, while in EartH Kitchen, the bar and restaurant on the venue's second floor, you'll find Scandi-modern styling (along with delicious cocktails and reasonably priced dishes from a changing roster of pop-up chefs). The wide-ranging and very much on-trend program runs from world music and hip-hop to country, folk, and dance, with stand-up comedy and free sets by leading DJs in the bar. ⊠ *11–17 Stoke Newington Rd., Dalston* ⊕ *www. earthackney.co.uk* Ⓜ *Overground: Dalston Kingsland, Dalston Junction.*

PUBS

★ Prospect of Whitby

PUBS | **FAMILY** | Named after a collier ship, this is one of London's oldest riverside pubs, dating to around 1520.

Although a regular for Dickens, Pepys, Samuel Johnson, and the American artist James Whistler, once upon a time it was called The Devil's Tavern because of the lowlifes—sailors, smugglers, footpads, and cutthroats—who congregated here. With a 400-year-old flagstone floor and ornamented with pewter ware and nautical objects, this much-loved boozer has a terrace with views of the Thames, from where boat trips often point it out. ⊠ *57 Wapping Wall, East End* ☎ *020/7481–1095* ⊕ *www.greeneking-pubs.co.uk/pubs/greater-london/prospect-of-whitby* Ⓜ *Wapping. DLR: Shadwell.*

The Ten Bells

PUBS | FAMILY | Although the number of bells in its name has varied between 8 and 12, depending on how many bells were used by neighboring Christ Church Spitalfields, this pub retains its original mid-Victorian interior and tiles, including a frieze depicting the area's French Huguenot silk-weaving tradition on the north wall and particularly fine floral tiling on two others. Urban legend says that Jack the Ripper's third victim, Annie Chapman, had a drink here before meeting her gory end. The pub is also depicted in Alan Moore's acclaimed graphic novel *From Hell*. ⊠ *84 Commercial St., Spitalfields* ☎ *020/7247–7532* ⊕ *www.tenbells.com* Ⓜ *Liverpool St.*

Performing Arts

Artists and other creative types, no longer able to afford central London rents, have been making their way eastward for years. It began in Shoreditch, but as rents increased there, too, neighborhoods farther and farther out have taken on these new residents. Go gallery hopping in Bethnal Green or catch a happening band in action at one of Shoreditch's myriad music venues.

PERFORMING ARTS CENTERS
★ Wilton's

CONCERTS | Arguably London's most atmospheric cultural space, Wilton's has been entertaining the crowds since 1743, first as an alehouse, then as a music hall. It now hosts gigs, talks, theater performances, movie screenings (often with live scores), and swing-dance evenings. The cozy Mahogany Bar, the oldest part of the building, serves a good range of quality local ales, along with snacks and meals that change according to what's playing in the theater. There's a cocktail bar upstairs, in what was once the artists' green room. ⊠ *Graces Alley, East End* ☎ *020/7702–2789* ⊕ *www.wiltons.org.uk* Ⓜ *Aldgate East, Tower Hill.*

THEATER
Hackney Empire

THEATER | FAMILY | The history of this treasure of a theater is drama in its own right. Charlie Chaplin is said to have appeared at Hackney Empire during its days as a thriving variety theater and music hall in the early 1900s. The venue now hosts traditional family entertainment and variety shows, opera, music, musical theater, dance, and drama, often with a multicultural slant. Its annual Christmas pantomime show is legendary. ⊠ *291 Mare St., Hackney* ☎ *020/8985–2424* ⊕ *www.hackneyempire.co.uk* Ⓜ *Overground: Hackney Central.*

🛍 Shopping

CLOTHING
Beyond Retro

SECOND-HAND | The more than 20,000 vintage items here—from cowboy boots to bowling shirts to prom dresses—include the largest collection of American retro fashion in the United Kingdom. The clothing isn't always in the greatest shape (missing buttons, dropped hems, etc), but prices are so low that even factoring in the price of alternations, this is a fantastic value. There are further outposts in Brixton, Dalston, and Soho.

✉ *110–112 Cheshire St., Spitalfields* ☎ *020/7297–9001* ⊕ *www.beyondretro.com* Ⓜ *Whitechapel. Overground: Shoreditch High St.*

69b Boutique
MIXED CLOTHING | This petite boutique claims to be London's first store dedicated to socially and environmentally sustainable fashion, with a strict transparency and accountability policy that all its brands must adhere to. So you can happily indulge in the likes of Marimekko, Kowtow, and Bobo Choses, plus accessories from Aspiga, ELK, and LULU Copenhagen entirely guilt-free. ✉ *69b Broadway Market, Dalston* ☎ *020/7682–0506* ⊕ *www.69bboutique.com* Ⓜ *Overground: London Fields.*

★ Retrouvé
SECOND-HAND | FAMILY | The carefully curated vintage clothing—for women, men, and kids, plus a limited range of jewelry and accessories—on sale at this atmospheric boutique is updated on a near-daily basis, meaning you'll be tempted by something new every visit. Alternations are free and can be turned around quickly. There's another branch on Broadway Market. ✉ *61 Wilton Way, Dalston* ☎ *020/3556–6273* ⊕ *www.retrouvevintage.co.uk* Ⓜ *Hackney Central.*

★ Sunspel
MEN'S CLOTHING | This British firm has been making fine men's underwear since the mid-19th century and it's still its specialty, along with luxury basics such as knitwear, outerwear, polo shirts, and swimwear. Prince Charles is a real-life customer and James Bond, a cinematic one (he wore their shorts in *Thunderball* and polo shirt in *Quantum of Solace*). The spy's creator, Ian Fleming, was another client. Sunspel also carries elegant, minimalist T-shirts, sweaters, and sweats for women. There are other branches in Marylebone, Chelsea, Notting Hill, St.

James's, and Soho. ✉ *7 Redchurch St., Shoreditch* ☎ *020/7739–9729* ⊕ *www.sunspel.com* Ⓜ *Overground: Shoreditch High St.*

HOUSEHOLD GOODS
Labour and Wait
HOUSEWARES | Although mundane items like colanders and clothespins may not sound like ideal souvenirs, this shop (something of a hipster heaven selling both new and vintage items) will make you reconsider. The owners are on a mission to revive retro, functional British household goods, such as enamel kitchenware, genuine feather dusters, bread bins, bottle brushes, and traditional Welsh blankets. There's another branch in Marylebone. ✉ *85 Redchurch St., Shoreditch* ☎ *020/7729–6253* ⊕ *www.labourandwait.co.uk* Ⓜ *Overground: Shoreditch High St.*

MARKETS
Brick Lane
MARKET | The noisy center of the Bangladeshi community is a hubbub of buying and selling on Sunday. Stalls have food, hardware, household and electrical goods, bric-a-brac, secondhand clothes, spices, and traditional saris. Some of the CDs and DVDs are pirated, and the bargain iron may not have a plug, so check carefully. Shoppers nevertheless flock to the market to enjoy the buzz, sample curries and Bangladeshi sweets, or browse at the many vintage stores lining the northern end of the street. Brick Lane's activity spills over into nearby Petticoat Lane Market, where there are similar goods but less atmosphere. ✉ *Shoreditch* Ⓜ *Aldgate E. Overground: Shoreditch High St.*

★ Broadway Market
MARKET | This parade of shops in hipster-centric Hackney (north of Regent's Canal) is worth visiting for the specialty bookshops, independent boutiques,

Did You Know?

The Columbia Road Flower Market opens at 8 am on Sunday. Arrive early to see the photogenic market at its best and to find the freshest selection. The road is lined with funky shops selling antiques, vintage clothing, horticultural accessories, and more.

On Sunday, additional clothing and craft stalls surround Spitalfields's covered market.

organic cafés, neighborhood restaurants, and welcoming community feel. But wait for Saturday (9–5), when it really comes into its own with a farmers' market and more than 70 street-food and produce stalls rivaling those of south London's famed Borough Market. Artisan breads, cheeses, pastries, organic meats, waffles, fruit and vegetables, seafood, and international food offerings: this is foodie heaven. There are also stalls selling vintage clothes, crafts, jewelry, and more. ⊠ *Broadway Market, Hackney* ⊕ *www. broadwaymarket.co.uk* Ⓜ *London Fields.*

★ Columbia Road Flower Market

MARKET | London's premier flower market is about as pretty and photogenic as they come, with more than 50 stalls selling flowers, shrubs, bulbs, and trees—everything from bedding plants to 10-foot banana trees—as well as garden tools, pots, and accessories at competitive prices. The stallholders' patter is part of the fun. It's on Sunday only, and it's all over by 3 pm. Columbia Road itself is lined with 60 interesting independent shops purveying art, fashion, furnishings (most of which are only open on weekends), and the local cafés are superb. ⊠ *Columbia Rd., Hoxton* ⊕ *www. columbiaroad.info* Ⓜ *Old St. Overground: Hoxton.*

★ Old Spitalfields Market

MARKET | Once the East End's wholesale fruit and vegetable market and now restored to its original architectural splendor, this fine example of a Victorian market hall is at the center of the area's gentrified revival. The original building is largely occupied by shops (mostly upscale brands like Jo Malone, Lululemon, and Superga, but some independents like trendy homeware-and-fashion purveyor The Mercantile), with traders' stalls in the courtyard. A modern shopping precinct under a Norman Foster–designed glass canopy adjoins the old building and holds approximately 70 traders' stalls. You may have to wade through a certain number of stalls selling cheap imports and tacky T-shirts to find the good stuff, which includes vintage and new clothing, handmade rugs and jewelry, hand-carved toy trains, vintage maps, unique baby clothes, rare vinyl, and cakes. Thursday is for antiques; Friday for a biweekly record fair; while weekends offer a little of everything. The Kitchens, 10 central dining venues showcasing small, independent chefs and restaurants, provide fresh takes on Mexican, Japanese, and other world cuisines. There are also indie street-food stalls and some superior chain outlets. ✉ *16 Horner Sq., Brushfield St., Spitalfields* ⊕ *www. oldspitalfieldsmarket.com* Ⓜ *Liverpool St. Overground: Shoreditch High St.*

Victoria Park Market

MARKET | FAMILY | Dozens of food stalls and trucks are set up in this gorgeous landscaped park (the first public park in London, opened in 1843) every Sunday, serving all manner of tasty treats from 10 am to 4 pm. Refuel after a jog around the 2.7-mile perimeter, grab a lunch to enjoy on a visit to the boating lake, or simply stock up on fresh produce and baked goods as you enjoy the free live music. ✉ *Victoria Park, Bonner Gate, Bethnal Green* ⊹ *Between Bonner Gate and Gore Gate* ⊕ *www.victoriaparkmarket.com* Ⓜ *Bethnal Green; Overground: London Fields.*

MUSIC
Rough Trade East

MUSIC | Although many London record stores are struggling, this veteran indie-music specialist in The Truman Brewery seems to have gotten the formula right. The spacious surroundings are as much a hangout as a shop, complete with a stage for live gigs and a café-bar. There's another branch on Talbot Road in Notting Hill. ✉ *Dray Walk, Old Truman Brewery, 91 Brick La., Spitalfields* ☎ *020/7392–7788* ⊕ *www.roughtrade. com* Ⓜ *Liverpool St. Overground: Shoreditch High St.*

Chapter 9

SOUTH OF
THE THAMES

Updated by
Ellin Stein

👁 **Sights**
★★★★★

🍴 **Restaurants**
★★★☆☆

🛏 **Hotels**
★☆☆☆☆

🛍 **Shopping**
★★☆☆☆

🍸 **Nightlife**
★★★★☆

SOUTH OF THE THAMES SNAPSHOT

TOP REASONS TO GO

Shakespeare's Globe: See one of Shakespeare's plays in this historically accurate replica of the Elizabethan theater where they were first performed.

Tate Modern: One of the world's great collections of post-1900 modern art, the centerpiece of this Tate branch is the huge renovated electric turbine hall, now an exhibition space used for large installations.

Sunset on Waterloo Bridge: This is one of London's most romantic views, with St. Paul's to the east and the Houses of Parliament to the west.

The London Eye: One of the city's tallest structures, this observation wheel gives you a bird's-eye view of some of London's most illustrious sights.

GETTING THERE

For the South Bank, use Embankment on the District, Circle, Northern, and Bakerloo lines and walk across the Golden Jubilee Bridges; or Waterloo on the Northern, Jubilee, and Bakerloo lines, from where it's a 10-minute walk. London Bridge on the Northern and Jubilee lines is five minutes from Borough Market and Southwark Cathedral. The station also serves Bermondsey Street, although, confusingly, the next stop on the Jubilee line is called Bermondsey. Brixton has its own stop on the Victoria line.

MAKING THE MOST OF YOUR TIME

Don't attempt to visit the area south of the Thames in one go. Tate Modern alone deserves a whole afternoon, especially if you want to do justice to both the temporary exhibitions and the permanent collection. The Globe requires about two hours for the exhibition theater tour and two to three hours for a performance. Finish with drinks at the OXO Tower or one of the Shard's restaurants, with their spectacular views. You can return across the river to central London via Southwark on the Jubilee line from Tate Modern, although it's a good walk to the station.

VIEWFINDER

■ Stand halfway between the north and south banks of the Thames on Waterloo Bridge to experience some of London's most romantic views. Facing east, you can see Christopher Wren's magnificent St. Paul's Cathedral and the elegant neoclassical terraces of Somerset House, as well as more modern landmarks like the distinctive "Gherkin" high-rise on the north side and the towering pyramid of the Shard on the south. Facing west, you can see on the north bank the distinctive Victorian Gothic towers of the Palace of Westminster (the Houses of Parliament) and Big Ben, the Edwardian splendor of The Savoy hotel and the National Liberal Club, and a bit of Westminster Abbey. Toward the south bank, the eye is immediately drawn to the wheel of the London Eye and the Brutalist Southbank Centre. If you time it right, you can see the sunset immortalized in the song by the Kinks.

This area is a magnet for tourists and residents alike, with attractions that include the IWM London, the Southbank Centre (Europe's largest arts center), and the gastronomic delight that is Borough Market.

The most important sights are clustered around the South Bank and in Bankside and Southwark, but the surrounding neighborhoods of Bermondsey and Lambeth are rising rapidly, with galleries, shops, and restaurants opening constantly. And the formerly drab Nine Elms area (near Vauxhall) is in the process of being totally transformed, with luxury high-rises and shops proliferating in the wake of the huge, fairly new U.S. Embassy in the area, as well as the opening of a new Tube station.

A borough of the City of London since 1327, Southwark first became well known for its inns (the pilgrims in Chaucer's *A Canterbury Tale* set off from one), theaters, prisons, tanneries, and brothels, as well as entertainments such as cockfighting. For four centuries, this was a sort of border town outside the city walls (and jurisdiction) where Londoners went to let their hair down and behave badly. Originally, you were just as likely to see a few bouts of bearbaiting at the Globe as you were Shakespeare's most recent work. But now that south London encompasses a world-class museum and high-caliber art, music, film, and theater venues, as well as an aquarium, a historic warship, two popular food markets, and greatly improved transportation links, this neighborhood has become one of London's leading destinations.

Today you can walk the **Thames Path** along the river from the London Eye all the way to the Thames Barrier. The segment beside the South Bank is alive with skateboarders, secondhand-book stalls, and street entertainers. At one end the **London Eye,** a 21st-century landmark that became an instant favorite with both Londoners and out-of-towners, rises next to the **London Aquarium** and the **Southbank Centre,** home to the **Royal Festival Hall,** the **Hayward Gallery,** the **BFI Southbank,** and the **National Theatre.** Farther east you'll come to a reconstruction of Sir Francis Drake's 16th-century ship the *Golden Hinde*; **Butler's Wharf,** where some notable restaurants occupy what were once shadowy Dickensian docklands; the **Shard,** the tallest building in the EU, which offers spectacular views over the city; and next to **Tower Bridge,** the massive headlight-shape **City Hall.**

Nearby Bermondsey Street (from "Beormund's Eye," as it was known in Saxon times) is home to the bright-yellow Fashion Museum, White Cube gallery, and lots of trendy shops, restaurants, and cafés. Meanwhile, younger visitors will enjoy the **London Dungeon** and **HMS Belfast,** a decommissioned Royal Navy cruiser, while food lovers should make a straight line to London's oldest food market, **Borough Market,** where the independent stallholders sell farm-fresh produce, delicious bread and cheese, and specialty fish and meat.

Even from the Shard's lofty viewing platform 1,016 feet up, the area south of the Thames still isn't one of London's most beautiful, but you'll be able to see how this patchwork of neighborhoods fits together. The heart is the South Bank, which extends east from the London Eye to Blackfriars Bridge, with the river to the north and Waterloo Station to the south. From Blackfriars Bridge east to London Bridge is Bankside, where you'll find the Globe and Tate Modern. Moving east from London Bridge is Borough, with its cobbled streets and former factories now turned into expensive lofts. Next, southeast of Borough, is buzzy, urban Bermondsey, while leafy Dulwich, with its renowned gallery and charming period streets, is quite a distance to the south.

Returning up the river to the west of the South Bank is Lambeth and then Vauxhall, with the imposing IWM London (now one of a roster of Imperial War Museums), a thriving gay scene, and scary through-traffic routes. It's a rapidly changing district, thanks to a regeneration spearheaded by the opening of the U.S. Embassy in adjacent Nine Elms and a slew of upscale riverside residential developments. South of here is Brixton, long the heartland of London's Afro-Caribbean community—with a lively club scene—and now attracting young families priced out of nearby Clapham.

Sights

Bankside Gallery

ART GALLERY | Two artistic societies—the Royal Society of Painter–Printmakers and the Royal Watercolour Society—have their headquarters in this gallery next to Tate Modern. Together they mount exhibitions of current members' work, which is usually for sale, along with art books, making this a great place for finding that unique, not too expensive gift. There are also regular themed exhibitions. ✉ *48 Hopton St., Southwark* ☎ *020/7928–7521* ⊕ *www.banksidegallery.com* ✉ *Free* Ⓜ *Mansion House, Southwark, St. Paul's.*

★ Borough Market

MARKET | There's been a market in Borough since Roman times, and this latest incarnation, spread under the arches and railroad tracks leading to London Bridge Station, is where some of the city's best food producers sell their wares, with more than 100 stands, restaurants, bars, and stalls selling street food from around the world. Fresh coffees, gorgeous cheeses, chocolates, and baked goods complement the organically farmed meats, fresh fish, condiments, fruits, and vegetables.

Don't make any other lunch plans for the day; this is where celebrity chef Jamie Oliver's scallop man cooks them fresh at Shellseekers, and Ginger Pig's free-range rare-breed sausages sizzle on grills, while for the sweets lover there are chocolates, preserves, and Whirld's handmade fudge, as well as 18 restaurants and cafés, most above average. The Market Hall hosts workshops, tastings, and demonstrations, and also acts as a greenhouse. The market is open Monday through Thursday 10–5, Friday 10–6, Saturday 8–5, and Sunday 10–2, though not all traders operate on all days; check the website for more details.

On weekends, a separate, highly regarded market specializing in produce and street food operates on nearby Maltby Street. It was originally established by eight breakaway Borough Market traders. There you'll find stalls specializing in gyoza, waffles, Scotch eggs, steak sandwiches, Ethiopian dishes, Ethiopian-Romanian-vegan dishes, Indo-Persian cuisine, brownies, and more. ✉ *8 Southwark St., Borough* ☎ *020/7402–1002* ⊕ *www.boroughmarket.org.uk* Ⓜ *London Bridge.*

The Clink Prison Museum

OTHER MUSEUM | FAMILY | This attraction devoted to shedding light on life in a medieval prison is built on the site of the original "Clink," the oldest of Southwark's five prisons and the reason why "the clink" is now slang for jail (the original medieval building was burned to the ground in 1780). Owned by the Bishops of Winchester from 1144 to 1780, it was the first prison to detain women, many for prostitution. Because of the bishops' relaxed attitude toward the endemic trade—they decided to license prostitution rather than ban it—the area within their jurisdiction was known as "the Liberty of the Clink." Subsequent prisoners included Puritans who would later sail on the *Mayflower* to find more religious freedom. Inside, you'll discover how grisly a Tudor prison could be, operating on a code of cruelty, deprivation, and corruption. The prison was only a small part of Winchester Palace, a huge complex that was the bishops' London residence. You can still see the remains of the early 13th-century Great Hall, with its famous rose window, next to Southwark Cathedral. ✉ *1 Clink St., Borough* ☎ *020/7403–0900* ⊕ *www.clink. co.uk* 🎟 *£8* Ⓜ *London Bridge.*

★ Dulwich Picture Gallery

ART MUSEUM | Designed by Sir John Soane, Dulwich (pronounced *dull*-ich) Picture Gallery was the world's first purpose-built art museum when it opened in 1811 (the recent extension was designed by Rick Mather). The permanent collection of more than 600 paintings includes landmark works by Old Masters such as Rembrandt, van Dyck, Rubens, Poussin, and Gainsborough. The museum also hosts three or so major temporary exhibitions each year devoted to more contemporary artists like Helen Frankenthaler. Check the website for its schedule of family activities; there's a lovely café here, too.

While you're in the area, take a short wander and you'll find a handful of charming clothing and crafts stores and the well-manicured Dulwich Park, which has lakeside walks and a fine display of rhododendrons in late May. Development in Dulwich Village is tightly controlled, so it feels a bit like a time capsule, with old-fashioned street signs and handsome 18th-century houses on the main street. ✉ *Gallery Rd., Dulwich* ☎ *020/8693–5254* ⊕ *www.dulwichpicturegallery.org.uk* 🎟 *£16.50* ⊙ *Museum closed Mon. and Tues. Gardens and café closed Mon.* Ⓜ *Brixton Station, then Bus P4. National Rail: West Dulwich from Victoria or North Dulwich from London Bridge.*

Fashion and Textile Museum

OTHER MUSEUM | The bright yellow-and-pink museum (it's hard to miss) designed by Mexican architect Ricardo Legorreta features changing exhibitions devoted to developments in fashion design, textiles, and jewelry from the end of World War II to the present. Founded by designer Zandra Rhodes, and now owned by Newham College, the FTM is a favorite with anyone interested in the history of style. There are weekday fashion-based workshops and lectures on design and aspects of fashion history; the excellent gift shop sells books on fashion and one-of-a-kind pieces by local designers. After your visit, check out the many restaurants, cafés, and boutiques that have bloomed on Bermondsey Street. ✉ *83 Bermondsey St., Bermondsey* ☎ *020/7407–8664* ⊕ *www.ftmlondon. org* 🎟 *£12.65* ⊙ *Closed Sun. and Mon.* Ⓜ *London Bridge.*

Florence Nightingale Museum

OTHER MUSEUM | Compact, highly visual, and engaging, this museum on the grounds of St. Thomas's Hospital is dedicated to Florence Nightingale, who founded the first school of nursing and played a major role in establishing modern standards of health care. Exhibits are divided into three areas: one is devoted

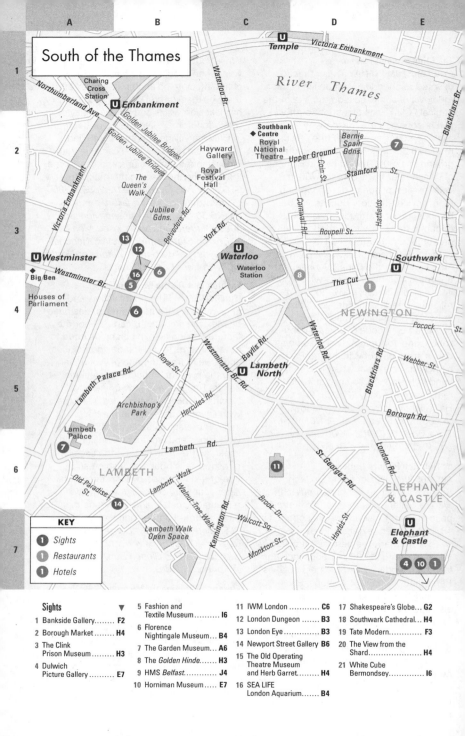

South of the Thames

KEY

- **1** Sights
- **1** Restaurants
- **1** Hotels

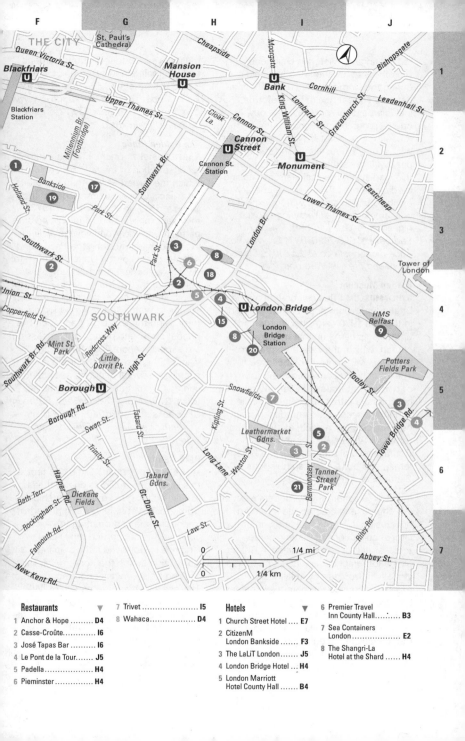

Restaurants

1 Anchor & Hope **D4**
2 Casse-Croûte **I6**
3 José Tapas Bar **I6**
4 Le Pont de la Tour **J5**
5 Padella **H4**
6 Pieminster **H4**
7 Trivet **I5**
8 Wahaca **D4**

Hotels

1 Church Street Hotel **E7**
2 CitizenM
 London Bankside **F3**
3 The LaLiT London **J5**
4 London Bridge Hotel ... **H4**
5 London Marriott
 Hotel County Hall **B4**
6 Premier Travel
 Inn County Hall **B3**
7 Sea Containers
 London **E2**
8 The Shangri-La
 Hotel at the Shard **H4**

to Nightingale's Victorian childhood, the others to her work tending soldiers during the Crimean War (1854–56) and her subsequent health-care reforms, including a display on how she developed a program for training nurses. The museum incorporates Nightingale's own books, her famous lamp, and even her pet owl (now stuffed), as well as interactive displays of medical instruments and medicinal herbs. There are temporary exhibitions and a shop with unexpectedly amusing gifts like syringe-shape highlighters. ⊠ *2 Lambeth Palace Rd., Lambeth* ☎ *020/7620–0374* ⊕ *www.florence-nightingale.co.uk* 🖾 *£10* ⊗ *Closed Mon. and Tues.* Ⓜ *Waterloo.*

Garden Museum

OTHER MUSEUM | This celebration of one of England's favorite hobbies was created in the mid-1970s after two gardening enthusiasts came upon a medieval church, which, they were horrified to discover, was about to be bulldozed. The churchyard contained the tombs of two adventurous 17th-century plant collectors, a father and son both called John Tradescant, who introduced many new species to England, as well as the tombs of William Bligh, captain of the *Bounty,* several members of the Boleyn family, and quite a few archbishops of Canterbury.

Inspired to action, the gardeners rescued the church, and created the museum now inside it. Here you'll find one of the largest collections of historic garden tools, artifacts, and curiosities in Britain, plus photographs, paintings, and films—virtually all donated by individuals. An extension houses temporary exhibitions on subjects ranging from noted garden designers like Charles Jencks to the contemporary Guerrilla Gardening movement (cultivating neglected public land). There's also a green-thumb gift shop, a glass-fronted café, and, of course, the

museum's own four beautiful gardens that are maintained year-round by dedicated volunteers. ⊠ *5 Lambeth Palace Rd., Lambeth* ☎ *020/7401–8865* ⊕ *www.gardenmuseum.org.uk* 🖾 *£12* Ⓜ *Lambeth North, Vauxhall.*

The Golden Hinde

NAUTICAL SIGHT | **FAMILY** | This is a full-size reconstruction of the little galleon in which the famed Elizabethan explorer Sir Francis Drake circumnavigated the globe in 1577–80. Launched in 1973, the exact replica made one full and one partial round-the-world voyage, calling in at ports—many along the Pacific and Atlantic coasts of the United States—to do duty as a maritime museum. Now berthed at the St. Mary Overie Dock, the ship continues its educational purpose, complete with a "crew" in period costumes and three decks of artifacts. The puppet show and pirate training sessions are especially popular with younger visitors. There are also frequent musical evenings, several featuring sea shanty choirs. Call for information on guided tours. ⊠ *St. Mary Overie Dock, Cathedral St., Bankside* ☎ *020/7403–0123* ⊕ *www.goldenhinde.co.uk* 🖾 *£5* Ⓜ *London Bridge.*

HMS *Belfast*

MILITARY SIGHT | **FAMILY** | At 613½ feet, this large light-cruiser is one of the last remaining big-gun armored warships from World War II, in which it played an important role in protecting the Arctic convoys and supporting the D-Day landings in Normandy; the ship later saw action during the Korean War. This floating museum has been moored in the Thames as a maritime branch of IWM London since 1971. A tour of all nine decks—including an engine room 15 feet below sea level, the admiral's quarters, mess decks, bakery, punishment cells, operations room, and more—gives a vivid picture of life on board the ship, while the riveting interactive gun-turret experience puts you in the middle of a World War II naval battle. ⊠ *The Queen's Walk, Borough* ☎ *020/7940–6300* ⊕ *www.iwm.org. uk* 🎫 *£22.70* Ⓜ *London Bridge.*

Horniman Museum

OTHER MUSEUM | FAMILY | Set amid 16 acres of gardens, this eclectic museum is considered something of a well-kept secret by the residents of south London—perhaps because of its out-of-the-way location. You can explore world cultures, natural history, and a fine collection of some 1,300 musical instruments (including a giant tuba) here. The emphasis is on fun and a wide range of activities, including London's oldest nature trail, which features domesticated creatures, such as sheep, chickens, and alpacas, a butterfly house, and an aquarium stocked with endangered species. It's also home to a comically overstuffed, taxidermied walrus who serves as the museum's unofficial mascot. It's a 15-minute bus ride from here to Dulwich Picture Gallery; Bus P4, heading toward Brixton, takes you from door to door. ⊠ *100 London Rd., Forest Hill, London* ☎ *020/8699–1872* ⊕ *www.horniman. ac.uk* 🎫 *Free; small charge for temporary exhibitions and aquarium* ☉ *Closed Wed.* Ⓜ *Overground: Forest Hill.*

★ IWM London

HISTORY MUSEUM | FAMILY | Despite its name, the cultural venue formerly known as the Imperial War Museum (one of five IWM branches now around the country) does not glorify either Empire or bloodshed but emphasizes understanding through conveying the impact of 20th- and 21st-century warfare on citizens and soldiers alike. A dramatic six-story atrium at the main entrance encloses an impressive amount of hardware—including a Battle of Britain Spitfire, a German V2 rocket, the remains of a car blown up in post-invasion Iraq, tanks, guns, and submarines—along with accompanying interactive material and a café. The First

World War galleries explore the wartime experience on both the home and fighting fronts, with the most comprehensive collection on the subject in the world—some 1,300 objects ranging from uniforms, equipment, and weapons to letters and diaries. The Second World War galleries shed light on that conflict through objects, film documentation, and eyewitness testimonies, as do the extensive and haunting Holocaust galleries (private tours are available for all three areas). *Peace and Security 1945–2015* looks at more contemporary hostilities, including the Cold War, Iraq, Afghanistan, and Kosovo. Other galleries are devoted to works relating to conflicts from World War I to the present day by painters, poets, documentary filmmakers, and photographers. ⊠ *Lambeth Rd., South Bank* ☎ *020/7416–5000* ⊕ *www.iwm.org. uk* 🎫 *Free (charge for special exhibitions)* Ⓜ *Lambeth North.*

The London Dungeon

OTHER ATTRACTION | FAMILY | Saved by a keen sense of its own borderline ridiculousness, this gory attraction is full of over-the-top tableaux depicting the bloody demise of famous figures alongside the torture, murder, and ritual slaughter of lesser-known victims, all to a sound track of screaming, wailing, and agonized moaning. There are lively dramatizations about the Great Plague, Henry VIII, (the fictional) Sweeney Todd, and (the real) Jack the Ripper, just to name a few, with costumed characters leaping out of the gloom to bring the information to life and add to the fear and fun. Perhaps most shocking are the crowds of children baying to get in: most kids absolutely love this place, although those with more a sensitive disposition may find it too frightening (that goes for adults as well). Expect long lines on weekends and during school holidays. There are also adults-only evening tours that include drinks. ■**TIP→ Tickets bought online and in advance can be up to 30% less than walk-up prices.** ⊠ *Riverside Bldg., County Hall,*

Westminster Bridge Rd., South Bank ☎ *0207/654–0809* ⊕ *www.thedungeons. com/london* 🚇 *From £27* Ⓜ *Waterloo.*

★ The London Eye

VIEWPOINT | FAMILY | To mark the start of the new millennium, architects David Marks and Julia Barfield devised this instant icon that allows Londoners and visitors alike to see the city from a completely new perspective. The giant Ferris wheel was the largest cantilevered observation wheel ever built at the time, and remains one of the city's tallest structures. The 30-minute slow-motion ride inside one of the enclosed passenger capsules is so smooth you'd hardly know you were suspended over the Thames. On a clear day you can see up to 25 miles, with a bird's-eye view of London's most famous landmarks as you circle 360 degrees. If you're looking for a special place to celebrate, champagne can be arranged ahead of time.

■ TIP→ **Buy your ticket online to avoid the long lines and get a 15% discount. For an extra £10, you can save even more time with a Fast Track flight (check in 15 minutes before your "departure").**

You can also buy a combination ticket for The Eye and other London attractions (check online for details) or combine with a river cruise for a 40-minute sightseeing voyage on the Thames. In December, there's a scenic ice rink just below the wheel. ⊠ *Jubilee Gardens, South Bank* ☎ *0871/781–3000* ⊕ *www.londoneye. com* 🚇 *From £27; cruise package from £41 (online only)* Ⓜ *Waterloo.*

Newport Street Gallery

ART GALLERY | Putting the seal on Vauxhall's status as an up-and-coming neighborhood, business-savvy artist Damien Hirst opened this gallery in a cavernous space that was formerly a Victorian scenery-painting workshop. It currently houses a rotating selection from his large private collection of contemporary art that includes works by Francis Bacon, Banksy, Picasso, Jeff Koons, Richard Hamilton, and Tracey Emin, to name just a few, along with six-month-long solo shows for emerging artists. There's also a shop selling artists' books, limited-edition prints, and sculptures, while snacks and drinks are available from Pharmacy 2, which takes its name and some artwork from Hirst's fashionable (and now-closed) millennium-era Notting Hill watering hole. ⊠ *Newport St., London* ☎ *020/3141– 9320* ⊕ *www.newportstreetgallery. com* 🚇 *Free* ⊗ *Closed Mon. and Tues.* Ⓜ *Vauxhall, Lambeth North.*

The Old Operating Theatre Museum and Herb Garret

OTHER MUSEUM | This rare example of a 19th-century operating theater, the oldest surviving one in Europe, dates back to 1822, when part of the large herb garret in the roof of the 17th-century St. Thomas's Church was converted for surgical use. The English Baroque church was part of St. Thomas's Hospital, which was founded in the 12th century as a monastery that looked after the sick. In 1862, the hospital moved to its present Lambeth location and the operating theater was closed. It remained abandoned until 1956, when it was restored and turned into a medical museum.

Today you can see the artifacts of early-19th-century medical practice: the wooden operating table under a skylight; the box of sawdust underneath used for absorbing blood; and the surrounding banks of seats where students crowded in to observe operations. On Saturday at 10 am, there are demonstrations of pre-anesthetic surgical practices incorporating the knives, pliers, and handsaws that were the surgeons' tools back in the day (not for the fainthearted or small children). An extra charge (£12) applies and access is by a 52-step spiral staircase, although access by elevator is available by prior arrangement. Next door is a re-creation of the 17th-century **Herb Garret,** with displays of the medicinal

Built at the site of the original theater where Shakespeare's plays were performed, the modern-day Globe is a painstaking reconstruction of an open-air theater.

herbs St. Thomas's apothecary would have used. Be sure to book in advance as admission is by timed ticket only. ✉ *9A St. Thomas St., Lambeth* ☎ *020/7188–2679* ⊕ *www.oldoperatingtheatre.com* ✉ *£7.50* ⊙ *Closed Mon.–Wed.* Ⓜ *London Bridge.*

SEA LIFE London Aquarium
AQUARIUM | FAMILY | The curved, colon-naded, neoclassical former County Hall that once housed London's municipal government is now home to a superb three-level aquarium where you can walk above sharks and stingrays and view more than 600 other aquatic species, both common and rare. There are also hands-on displays. It's not the biggest aquarium you've ever seen, but the educational exhibits are particularly well arranged, with 17 themed zones for different oceans, water environments, and climates, ranging from a stunning coral reef to a "jellyfish experience" to a rain forest. ■TIP➔ **Admission at peak periods is by 15-minute timed entry slot, but for an additional £10 you can purchase flexible priority-entry tickets that also avoid the long lines.** ✉ *County Hall, Westminster Bridge Rd., South Bank* ☎ *0871/663–1678* ⊕ *www.visitsealife.com* ✉ *From £27* Ⓜ *Westminster, Waterloo.*

★ Shakespeare's Globe
PERFORMANCE VENUE | FAMILY | This spectacular theater is a replica of Shakespeare's open-roof, wood-and-thatch Globe Playhouse (built in 1599 and burned down in 1613), where most of the Bard's greatest works premiered. American actor and director Sam Wanamaker worked ceaselessly for several decades to raise funds for the theater's reconstruction 200 yards from its original site using authentic materials and techniques, a dream that was finally realized in 1997. "Groundlings" (patrons with £5 standing-only tickets) are not allowed to sit during the performance, but you get the best view of the stage and the most authentic viewing experience. Fortunately, you can reserve an actual seat on any one of the theater's three levels, but you will want to rent a cushion for £2 (or

bring your own) to soften the backless wooden benches (cushions must be booked when you book your tickets). The show must go on, rain or shine, warm or chilly, so come prepared for anything. Umbrellas are banned, but you can bring a raincoat or buy a cheap Globe rain poncho, which doubles as a great souvenir. In the winter months and occasionally in the summer, the Sam Wanamaker Playhouse, a 350-seat re-creation of an indoor Jacobean theater lighted by candles, offers plays and concerts in a less-exposed though still atmospheric setting. Some Wanamaker benches are backless, and there are fixed standing positions in the theater's upper gallery.

Fifty-minute tours of the Globe are offered in the spring and summer until 4 pm (unless there's a matinee performance or other major event, when they're offered until noon). There are also special kid-friendly tours during school holidays (two adults, three children) for £46. Tours of the Wanamaker Playhouse are offered on an occasional basis and must be arranged directly with the theater; availability varies and is subject to change depending on performances and other events. From mid-April until October, you can also book a tour of the surrounding Bankside area, which emphasizes places Shakespeare would have frequented, including the archaeological remains of the nearby Rose Theatre, the oldest theater in Bankside. ✉ 21 New Globe Walk, Bankside ☎ 020/7401–9919 ⊕ www.shakespearesglobe.com ✆ Globe Theatre tour £17; Bankside tour £13.50; Wanamaker tour £13.50; Globe performances £5 (standing), from £25 (seated); Wanamaker performances £5 (standing), from £15 (seated) ⊗ No Globe performances mid-Oct.–mid-Apr. Ⓜ London Bridge; Mansion House, then cross Southwark Bridge.

Southwark Cathedral

CHURCH | Pronounced *suth*-uck, this is the oldest Gothic church in London, parts of it dating back to the 12th century. It remains off the beaten track, despite being the site of some remarkable memorials and a concert program that offers free half-hour organ recitals at 1:10 pm every Monday (except in August and December) and classical music at 3:15 pm every Tuesday during the school year. Originally the priory church of St. Mary Overie (as in "over the water," on the South Bank), it became a palace church under Henry VIII (when it became known as St. Saviour's) until some merchant parishioners bought it from James I in 1611. It was only promoted to cathedral status in 1905.

Look for the vivid 15th-century roof bosses (small ornamental wood carvings); the gaudily renovated 1408 tomb of John Gower, Richard II's poet laureate and a friend of Chaucer's; and the Harvard Chapel, where John Harvard, a local butcher's son who went on to found the American university, was baptized. Another notable buried here (between the choir stalls) is Edmund Shakespeare, brother of William. Free drop-in 45-minute tours are offered depending on the church's services and events. ✉ London Bridge, Bankside ☎ 020/7367–6700 ⊕ cathedral.southwark.anglican.org ✆ Free (suggested donation £4) Ⓜ London Bridge.

★ **Tate Modern**
ART MUSEUM | This spectacular renovation of a mid-20th-century power station is one of the most-visited museums of modern art in the world. Its great permanent collection, which starts in 1900 and ranges from modernist masters like Matisse to the most cutting-edge contemporary artists, is arranged in eight areas by theme (for example, "Media Networks," about artists' responses to mass media) rather than by chronology. Its blockbuster

A walk across the iconic Millennium Bridge brings you right to the Tate Modern.

temporary exhibitions have showcased the work of individual artists like Gauguin, Rauschenberg, Modigliani, Picasso, and O'Keefe, among others. Other major temporary exhibitions have a conceptual focus, like works created in response to the American Black Power movement or by Soviet and Russian artists between the Revolution and the death of Stalin.

The vast Turbine Hall is a dramatic entrance point used to showcase big audacious installations that tend to generate a lot of publicity. Past highlights include Olafur Eliasson's massive glowing sun, Ai Weiwei's porcelain "sunflower seeds," and Carsten Holler's huge metal slides.

On the ground floor of a 10-story addition, you'll find The Tanks, galleries devoted to various types of new art, including moving image, performance, soundscapes, and interactive works, while at the top is a roof terrace offering spectacular views of the London skyline. In between are three exhibition floors offering more room for large-scale installations, for art from outside Europe and North America, and for digital and interactive projects. The Start Display (Level 2) provides an introduction to the collection, highlighting art from various countries, cultures, and periods, all linked by color.

Not to be missed in the original building are the collection of Rothko murals, originally created for the Four Seasons restaurant in New York; displays devoted to Gerhard Richter (both on Level 2), Antony Gormley, Jenny Holzer, the Guerrilla Girls, and video pioneer Nam June Paik (Level 4); and a room-size installation by Yinka Shonibare (Level 2).

Head to the restaurant on Level 9, the café on Level 1, or the Espresso Bar on Level 3 for stunning vistas of the Thames. The view of St. Paul's from the Espresso Bar's balcony is one of the best in London. Near the café you'll find the Drawing Bar, which lets you create work on one of several digital sketch pads and then project your result on the gallery wall.

You can join free 45-minute guided tours starting at noon, 1, and 2. If you plan to visit Tate Britain, take advantage of the Tate Boat, which takes visitors back and forth between the two Tates every 20 to 30 minutes. Admission to Tate Modern is currently by timed ticket only, so be sure to book in advance. ⊠ *Bankside* ☎ *020/7887–8888* ⊕ *www.tate.org.uk/ modern* ⊠ *Free (charge for special exhibitions)* Ⓜ *Southwark, Blackfriars, St. Paul's.*

The View from the Shard

VIEWPOINT | At 800 feet, this addition to the London skyline currently offers the highest vantage point in Western Europe. Designed by the noted architect Renzo Piano, it has attracted both admiration and disdain. While the building itself is generally highly regarded, many felt it would have been better sited in Canary Wharf (or perhaps Dubai), as it spoils views of St. Paul's Cathedral from traditional vantage points such as Hampstead's Parliament Hill. No matter how you feel about the building, there's no denying that it offers a spectacular 360-degree perspective over London (extending 40 miles on a clear day) from viewing platforms on Level 69 and the open-air skydeck on Level 72—almost twice as high as any other viewpoint in the city. Digital telescopes provide information about 200 points of interest.

There's a weather guarantee that lets you return on a more clement day if visibility is seriously impeded, and various themed events like silent discos or early-morning yoga classes are offered at an extra charge. Admission is by timed ticket only. If you find the price as eye-wateringly high as the viewing platforms, there's a less dramatic but still very impressive (and free) view from the lobby of the Shangri-La hotel on the 35th floor, or, in the evenings, the hotel's chic Gong bar on the 52nd floor (over-18s only). ⊠ *Railway Approach, Borough* ☎ *0344/499–7222* ⊕ *www.theviewfromtheshard.com* ⊠ *From £25* ⊗ *Closed Mon. and Tues.* Ⓜ *London Bridge.*

White Cube Bermondsey

ART GALLERY | When the United Kingdom's highest-profile commercial gallery moved to this huge converted 1970s-era warehouse on Bermondsey Street, it sealed the area's reputation as a rising art-scene hot spot. This is the home gallery of some of today's top contemporary artists, including Tracey Emin, Georg Baselitz, Antony Gormley, Isamu Noguchi, Gabriel Orozco, Harland Miller, Anselm Kiefer, and several other artists with international reputations. An antiseptic central cuboid gallery, the "white cube"—also called 9 x 9 x 9 (meters, that is)—rests between two other spaces that host smaller exhibitions. There is also a bookshop and auditorium. ⊠ *144–152 Bermondsey St., Bermondsey* ☎ *0207/930–5373* ⊕ *whitecube.com* ⊗ *Closed Mon.* Ⓜ *London Bridge.*

🍴 Restaurants

First mentioned in print in 1276 and believed to have existed in Roman times, Borough Market is an established favorite with tourists, chefs, and foodies alike. Located under the Victorian wrought-iron railway arches near London Bridge, here you'll find gourmands eager to pick up produce, cheese, organically farmed meats, fresh fish, baked goods, condiments, pastries, and chocolates from the more than 120 stalls operated by some of the city's best specialty food producers. A breakaway market on Maltby Street offers stalls that are smaller in number but equally high in quality. Pubs, bars, restaurants, and specialty shops fill the surrounding streets, while a new restaurant row has sprung up on nearby Bermondsey Street, just south of the Shard, and a collection of exciting new restaurants from top chefs is filling up Borough Yards, the recently redeveloped Victorian railway arches near London Bridge.

Designed by renowned architect Renzo Piano, the Shard punctures the London skyline with its record-breaking height and spectacular modernity.

The Anchor & Hope

$$ | **MODERN BRITISH** | Exceptional Brit-focused fish and meat dishes at wallet-friendly prices fly out of the open kitchen at this permanently packed, no-reservations (apart from Sunday lunchtime) gastropub in Southwark. Pot-roast duck, braised pigs' cheeks, coastal skate with steamed spinach and crab beurre blanc, and a three-cheese and hazelnut soufflé with pumpkin, chestnuts, and cream punch above their weight in terms of taste and tenderness. **Known for:** large crowds, so prepare to wait and maybe share a table; innovative gastropub cuisine; buzzy and informal atmosphere. [$] *Average main: £18* ✉ *36 The Cut, Southwark* ☎ *020/7928–9898* 🌐 *www.anchorandhopepub.co.uk* 🕑 *Closed Mon. and Tues. No lunch Wed.–Fri. No dinner Sun.* [M] *Waterloo, Southwark.*

★ Casse-Croûte

$$$ | **BISTRO** | This bistro on Bermondsey Street near the Shard is as French as a pack of Gauloises, from the yellow walls and red-and-white checked tablecloths to the perfectly executed classics like *lapin à la moutarde* (rabbit in a creamy mustard sauce), *suprême de volaille aux mousserons* (chicken breast stuffed with mushrooms), quiche Lorraine, and Paris-Brest (decadent choux pastry stuffed with praline and whipped cream). The daily changing menu offers three reasonably priced options per course, and the wine list (French, of course) goes off the beaten path with discoveries from small local producers. **Known for:** reservations necessary for dinner; beautifully prepared bistro classics; authentic French atmosphere in tight quarters. [$] *Average main: £25* ✉ *109 Bermondsey St., Bermondsey* ☎ *020/7407–2140* 🌐 *www.cassecroute.co.uk* 🕑 *No dinner Sun.* [M] *London Bridge.*

José Tapas Bar

$$ | **TAPAS** | Renowned chef José Pizarro has managed to re-create an authentic, slightly rustic Spanish tapas-and-sherry bar. With just 30 seats and no reservations, it's always packed after 6 pm, but it's worth the wait for remarkably fresh, perfectly prepared classic tapas

plates like *patatas bravas, croquetas,* skewered prawns with lemon and garlic, and an Ibérico pork fillet with pequillo peppers. **Known for:** unique sherry menu; notoriously long waits and large crowds; daily changing menu of authentic tapas. $ *Average main: £20* ⊠ *104 Bermondsey St., Southwark* ☎ *020/7403–4902* ⊕ *www.josepizarro.com/jose-tapas-bar* Ⓜ *Borough, London Bridge.*

Le Pont de la Tour

$$$$ | **FRENCH** | This long-standing favorite specializes in French haute cuisine done right, with an emphasis on luxurious dishes like caviar, oysters, lobster, and Dover sole (served *meunière*). Standards, like the prices, remain high, and the swanky dining room takes inspiration from the Art Deco liner SS *Normandie.* **Known for:** destination and celebration meals; stunning views of Tower Bridge and the Thames; outside terrace dining in nice weather. $ *Average main: £32* ⊠ *36D Shad Thames, Bermondsey* ☎ *020/7403–8403* ⊕ *www.lepontdelatour.co.uk* Ⓜ *London Bridge, Tower Hill.*

★ Padella

$ | **ITALIAN** | Sit at the galley kitchen counter and you can watch the chefs toss hot pans of authentic handmade (on-site) Italian pasta, generally considered among the best in London. The acclaimed but amazingly affordable small plates include a ravioli with Neal's Yard ricotta and sage butter, burrata with Puglian olive oil, papardelle with a slow-cooked beef-shin ragù, and Dorset crab tagliarini with chili and lemon. **Known for:** no reservations and long waits; low priced, high-quality handmade Italian pasta; papardelle with eight-hour beef-shin ragù. $ *Average main: £7* ⊠ *6 Southwark St., Borough* ⊕ *www.padella.co* Ⓜ *Borough, London Bridge.*

Pieminister

$ | **BRITISH** | **FAMILY** | In foodie haven Borough Market, you'll find the original London home of Pieminister, now a leading purveyor of meat pies nationwide.

Ingredients like free-range chicken and bacon and tarragon are fully British and responsibly sourced. **Known for:** tasty and filling food on-the-go; fresh, responsibly sourced ingredients; range of options including choices for vegans. $ *Average main: £7* ⊠ *Borough Market, 8 Southwark St., South Bank* ☎ *020/7407–1002* ⊕ *www.pieminister.co.uk* ⊗ *No dinner* Ⓜ *Waterloo.*

Trivet

$$$$ | **MODERN EUROPEAN** | This restaurant run by two alumni of celebrated The Fat Duck in Bray was recently awarded its first Michelin star for its meticulous but unfussy modern cooking that features "prime ingredients expertly prepared" and an eclectic but outstanding wine list. Starters include sweetbreads with smoked oyster mushrooms and pickled lingonberries in a cumin-infused sauce and black winter truffles in a Madeira sauce with mushrooms and noodles, while entreés like squab breast with a pepper crust and persimmon slices or turbot poached in a Chardonnay butter sauce with confit pumpkin display a similar inventiveness. **Known for:** charming service; original dishes expertly prepared; wide-ranging, well-chosen wine list. $ *Average main: £105* ⊠ *36 Snowsfields, Southwark* ☎ *20020/3141–8670* ⊕ *trivetrestaurant.co.uk* ⊗ *Closed Sun. and Mon. No lunch Tues.* Ⓜ *London Bridge.*

Wahaca

$ | **MEXICAN FUSION** | This canteen-style outpost of the eco-conscious chain serves mildly spiced Mexican food like marinated grilled chicken and tostadas with Devon crab, plus the usual burritos, quesadillas, tacos, and salads. There's also a street-food truck parked beside the river. **Known for:** quick and affordable lunches; modern Mexican street food; good vegan options. $ *Average main: £11* ⊠ *119 Waterloo Rd., South Bank* ☎ *020/3697–4140* ⊕ *www.wahaca.co.uk* Ⓜ *Waterloo.*

Hotels

★ Church Street Hotel

$ | **HOTEL** | Like rays of sunshine in gritty south London, the rooms at this distinctive Camberwell hotel are decorated in rich colors that evoke Mexico, a theme enhanced by authentic touches like elaborately painted crucifixes, tiles handmade in Guadalajara, and handcrafted iron bed frames. **Pros:** closer to central London than it might appear; individual and fun vibe; great breakfasts. **Cons:** some rooms have shared bathrooms; a mile from a Tube station (though bus connections are handier); location very urban and busy. [$] *Rooms from: £123* ✉ *29–33 Camberwell Church St., Camberwell, South East London* ☎ *020/7703–5984* 🌐 *www.churchstreethotel.com* 🛏 *31 rooms* 🍴 *Free Breakfast* [M] *Oval St.*

citizenM London Bankside

$$ | **HOTEL** | High-concept, high-tech, and super-trendy, this Dutch budget boutique minichain has a unique selling point—nearly everything at the hotel is self-service, and that includes check-in and breakfast. **Pros:** 24-hour self-service canteen; free Wi-Fi and free movies; stylish and modern decor. **Cons:** rooms are compact; maximum two people per room; only really qualifies as "budget" on certain nights (price is higher midweek). [$] *Rooms from: £126* ✉ *20 Lavington St., Bankside* ☎ *020/3519-1680* 🌐 *www.citizenm.com/destinations/london/london-bankside-hotel* 🛏 *192 rooms* 🍴 *No Meals* [M] *Southwark.*

The LaLiT London

$$$ | **HOTEL** | A stone's throw from City Hall and just down the road from the Shard, this luxurious hotel (the first international expansion from the India-based LaLiT chain) harks back to the building's former incarnation as a Victorian grammar school, designating bedrooms as different types of classrooms and meeting rooms as laboratories. **Pros:** complimentary minibar (and stuffed elephant toys) in all rooms; decor combines English heritage with Indian warmth and color; lots of Indian dining options. **Cons:** theme might be too in-your-face for some; location a bit out of the way and dead on weekends; basic rooms are much smaller than their more expensive counterparts. [$] *Rooms from: £305* ✉ *181 Tooley St., London Bridge* ☎ *020/3765–0000* 🌐 *www.thelalit.com/the-lalit-london* 🛏 *70 rooms* 🍴 *No Meals* [M] *London Bridge.*

London Bridge Hotel

$$$ | **HOTEL** | Steps away from the London Bridge rail and Tube stations, and handy for the South Bank, this thoroughly modern stylish hotel is popular with business travelers, but leisure travelers find it just as appealing. **Pros:** good deals available online in the off-season; helpful concierge; free Wi-Fi. **Cons:** area is filled with crowds on evenings and weekends; prices rise by £100 or more midweek; small bedrooms. [$] *Rooms from: £336* ✉ *8–18 London Bridge St., Southwark* ☎ *020/7855–2200* 🌐 *www.londonbridgehotel.com* 🛏 *141 rooms* 🍴 *No Meals* [M] *London Bridge.*

London Marriott Hotel County Hall

$$$ | **HOTEL** | This grand hotel on the Thames enjoys perhaps the most iconheavy view in the city—right next door is the London Eye, and directly across the Thames are the Houses of Parliament and Big Ben. Until the 1980s this building was the seat of London's government, and the public areas are suitably imposing, full of pedimented archways, bronze doors, and acres of polished mahogany. **Pros:** good weekend discounts; handy for South Bank arts scene, the London Eye, and Westminster; great pool. **Cons:** high summer midweek rates are just ridiculous; rooms facing the river cost extra; executive-level lounge not up to usual standard. [$] *Rooms from: £365* ✉ *London County Hall, Westminster Bridge Rd., South Bank* ☎ *020/7928–5200, 888/236–2427 in U.S.* 🌐 *www.marriott.*

com/hotels/travel/lonch-london-marri-ott-hotel-county-hall ⟳ *206 rooms* ⊚| *No Meals* Ⓜ *Westminster, Waterloo. National Rail: Waterloo.*

Premier Travel Inn County Hall

$$ | **HOTEL** | **FAMILY** | The small but nicely decorated rooms at this budget choice are in the same County Hall complex as the fancier London Marriott Hotel County Hall, and, though it lacks the spectacular river views and facilities are more basic, it has the same convenient location at a fraction of the price. **Pros:** kids (sharing with adults) stay free; fantastic location for the South Bank; bargains to be had if you book in advance. **Cons:** on a busy road; cookie-cutter chain-hotel atmosphere; limited services. ⓢ *Rooms from: £139* ⊠ *County Hall, Belvedere Rd., South Bank* ☎ *0871/527–8648* ⊕ *www. premierinn.com* ⟳ *318 rooms* ⊚| *No Meals* Ⓜ *Westminster, Waterloo. National Rail: Waterloo.*

Sea Containers London

$$$ | **HOTEL** | The achingly hip Sea Containers started life as a working warehouse in London's docklands and now incorporates stylish nods to the area's history. **Pros:** short riverside walk to Tate Modern and Shakespeare's Globe; excellent bars and restaurants; beautiful river views. **Cons:** standard rooms are small; public areas can be noisy; river-view rooms are pricey (of course). ⓢ *Rooms from: £311* ⊠ *Sea Containers House, 20 Upper Ground, Southwark* ☎ *020/3747–1000* ⊕ *www.seacontainerslondon.com* ⟳ *359 rooms* ⊚| *No Meals* Ⓜ *Blackfriars, Southwark.*

★ Shangri-La the Shard

$$$$ | **HOTEL** | With its floor-to-ceiling windows, the city's highest cocktail bar and infinity pool, and unrivaled views of the London skyline from 1,016 feet above the South Bank of the Thames, Shangri-La has become one of London's most distinctive hotels, occupying floors 34 to 52 of the tallest skyscraper in Western Europe. **Pros:** superb restaurants and

cocktail bar; perhaps the city's best vistas from a hotel; great infinity pool and spa. **Cons:** restaurant, bar, and elevator can be crowded due to popularity of the view; decor may be too understated for some; design allows some guests to see into neighboring guest rooms at night. ⓢ *Rooms from: £591* ⊠ *31 St. Thomas St., South Bank* ☎ *0207/234–8000* ⊕ *www.the-shard.com/shangri-la* ⟳ *202 rooms* ⊚| *No Meals* Ⓜ *London Bridge Station.*

Nightlife

Recent years have seen an explosion in south London nightlife, as Brixton becomes more gentrified, artists flock to Peckham, and the gay scene in Vauxhall remains thriving. Head to the area around Borough Market—one of London's oldest neighborhoods—for lively historic pubs where locals and tourists jostle for craft ales and gourmet snacks.

BARS

Aqua Shard

BARS | This sophisticated bar on Level 31 of the Shard is worth a visit for the phenomenal views alone. The cocktail list is pretty special, too—big on fruit purees and unusual bitters. No reservations are taken in the bar, so be prepared to wait during busy periods. ⊠ *The Shard, 31 St. Thomas St., Level 31, London Bridge* ☎ *020/3011–1256* ⊕ *www.aquashard. co.uk* Ⓜ *London Bridge.*

Royal Vauxhall Tavern

CABARET | This former Victorian pub near the cricket grounds has been hosting drag acts since the days of World War II, with Princess Diana reportedly visiting in the late 1980s disguised as a man and accompanied by Freddy Mercury. LBGTQ+-oriented entertainment is still its mainstay, with the long-running avant-garde club night Duckie providing "queer heritage, performance art, and honky-tonk" every Saturday night. Other favorites are a bingo-cabaret night and traditional drag performance extravaganzas, some featuring alums from *RuPaul's Drag Race*. The atmosphere is welcoming, inclusive, and fun. ⊠ *372 Kennington La., London* ☎ *020/7820–1222* ⊕ *www.vauxhalltavern.com* Ⓜ *Vauxhall.*

Three Eight Four

BARS | Epitomizing a new breed of Brixton bar, Three Eight Four is known for its innovative cocktails and tapas-style shared plates. The cocktail menu changes seasonally but always involves specialty spirits and unusual mixing techniques—try the Nightshade, which comes with a pipette that you use to add the final ingredient (crème de cassis) yourself. The bare lightbulbs and stripped brick walls are a bit of a hipster bar cliché, but this place manages it with particular panache. ⊠ *384 Coldharbour La., Brixton* ☎ *020/3417–7309* ⊕ *www.threeeightfour.com* Ⓜ *Brixton.*

PUBS
The George

PUBS | Not every pub is also a Grade I–listed, National Trust property, but this is London's last surviving galleried coaching inn. Dickens once frequented the inn's Coffee Room (now the Middle Bar) and name-checked The George in *Little Dorrit*. The gallery overlooks a cobblestone courtyard where plays may have been performed in Elizabethan times (galleried inns were frequently used as production venues), although the current building dates back only to 1677 after the original was destroyed in a fire. The interior is a maze of 18th-century low-ceilinged rooms replete with wood-panel walls and period features. The cozy Parliament Bar, where passengers would have waited for the coach, is on the ground floor, while a restaurant is upstairs on the galleried level. Luckily the pub is not just a museum piece—it also has modern amenities like a beer garden and Wi-Fi. ⊠ *77 Borough High St., South Bank* ☎ *020/7407–2056* ⊕ *www.greeneking-pubs.co.uk/pubs/greater-london/george-southwark* Ⓜ *London Bridge.*

The Market Porter

PUBS | If you find yourself craving a drink at 11 am, this traditional London pub is for you. The early opening hour is not because it caters to alcoholics but for the Borough Market stallholders, who have already put in several hours by opening time. The S-shape Victorian-era bar, with its walls and ceiling covered in pump badges and beer mats, is packed when the market is busy but calms down during off-peak hours. There are 12 real ales on draught, and decent pub grub using seasonal produce from the market is served in the restaurant upstairs. The pub also provided the location for the Third Hand Book Emporium in the movie version of *Harry Potter and the Prisoner of Azkaban*. ⊠ *9 Stoney St., Borough* ☎ *020/7407–2495* ⊕ *www.themarketporter.co.uk* Ⓜ *London Bridge.*

The Mayflower

PUBS | With a solid claim to being the oldest pub on the Thames, this deeply atmospheric riverside inn dates back to the mid-16th century (although it was rebuilt in the 17th) and comes with exposed beams, mullioned windows, open fires, and nautical design touches. You can sit outside on the heated-deck jetty that overlooks the *Mayflower's* original mooring. When the ship sailed for America in 1620, it was here that Captain Christopher Jones took on the 65 passengers who became some of the original Pilgrims (Jones is buried in the nearby church of St. Mary's in Rotherhithe; legend has it that he moored here to avoid paying taxes farther down the river). The Mayflower, formerly known as The Spread Eagle, is also the only pub licensed to sell U.S. and U.K. postage stamps (inquire at the bar), a tradition dating back to the 1800s when time-pressed sailors were able to order a pint and a postage stamp at the same time. ⊠ *117 Rotherhithe St., South East London* ☎ *020/7237–4088* ⊕ *www.mayflowerpub.co.uk* Ⓜ *Overground: Rotherhithe.*

Contemporary Art: London Today

In the 21st century, the focus of the city's art scene has shifted from the past to the future. Helped by the prominence of Tate Modern, London's contemporary art scene has never been so high profile. With publicly funded exhibition spaces like the Barbican Gallery, the Hayward Gallery, and the Institute of Contemporary Arts, London now has a modern art environment on par with that of Bilbao and New York. The so-called Young British Artists (YBAs, although no longer that young) Damien Hirst, Tracey Emin, and others are firmly established in the cultural firmament.

Depending on who you talk to, the Saatchi Gallery is considered to be either the savior of contemporary art or the wardrobe of the emperor's new clothes. After a couple of moves it is now ensconced in the former Duke of York's barracks off Chelsea's King's Road.

The South Bank's Tate Modern may house the giants of modern art, but east London is where the innovative action is. There are dozens of galleries in the fashionable spaces around Old Street, and the truly hip have already moved even farther afield, to areas such as Bethnal Green, to the east, and Peckham, to the south. The Whitechapel Gallery and Jay Jopling's influential White Cube, with branches in Bermondsey and St. James's, remain essential parts of the new art establishment and continue to show exciting work by emerging British artists.

On the first Thursday of every month, more than 150 museums and galleries in east London stay open until 9 pm and host talks, workshops, and other events (more information at ⊕ *www.whitechapelgallery.org*).

⊙ Performing Arts

The South Bank and its easterly near neighbor Bankside together make up one of the richest areas in London when it comes to arts and entertainment. Whether you want to watch a play, hear a concert, or see an art exhibition, you won't have to go far to find something top class. Venture a little farther into south London for a sprinkling of fringe theaters that act as incubators for the capital's mainstream theater scene.

FILM

BFI London IMAX Cinema

FILM | FAMILY | The British Film Institute's glazed drum-shape IMAX theater (now, confusingly, operated by Odeon) has the largest screen in the United Kingdom (approximately 75 feet wide and the height of five double-decker buses). It shows state-of-the-art 2-D and 3-D films. ⊠ *1 Charlie Chaplin Walk, South Bank* ☎ *0330/333–7878* ⊕ *www.bfi.org.uk/imax* ⊠ *From £15* Ⓜ *Waterloo.*

BFI Southbank

FILM | With the best repertory programming in London, these four cinemas run by the British Film Institute are in effect a national film center. More than 1,000 titles are screened each year, with art-house and foreign-language new releases, restored classics and silents, experimental and niche interest works, and short films favored over recent Hollywood blockbusters. The center also has a gallery, bookshop, events, and a "mediatheque" where visitors can watch film and television from the National Archive for free (closed Monday). The Riverfront Bar and Kitchen offers dining with views, while the BFI Bar is informal and buzzy. This is one of the venues for the BFI London Film Festival; throughout the year there are minifestivals, seminars, and guest speakers. ✉ *Belvedere Rd., South Bank* ☎ *020/7928–3232* ⊕ *www.bfi.org. uk* 🚇 *From £10* Ⓜ *Waterloo.*

PERFORMING ARTS CENTERS

★ **Battersea Arts Centre** (*BAC*)

ARTS CENTERS | This arts center has a reputation for producing innovative new theater and dance works as well as hosting top alternative stand-up comics. It also hosts a number of community arts initiatives to develop local talent. Performances take place in quirky spaces all over this atmospheric former town hall. The bar, which serves snacks and shared plates, is open all day. ✉ *176 Lavender Hill, Battersea* ☎ *020/7223–2223* ⊕ *www. bac.org.uk* 🚇 *Pay-what-you-can (£3 suggested)–£30* Ⓜ *National Rail: Clapham Junction.*

★ **Southbank Centre**

ARTS CENTERS | **FAMILY** | The general public has never really warmed to the Southbank Centre's hulking concrete buildings (beloved by architecture aficionados),

products of the Brutalist style popular when the center was built in the 1950s and '60s—but all the same, the masses flock to the concerts, recitals, festivals, and exhibitions held here, Europe's largest arts center. The Royal Festival Hall is truly a People's Palace, with seats for 2,900 and a schedule that ranges from major symphony orchestras to pop stars. The smaller Queen Elizabeth Hall is more classically oriented. It contains the Purcell Room, which hosts lectures and chamber performances. For art, head to the Hayward Gallery, which hosts shows on top contemporary artists such as Antony Gormley and Cy Twombly. The center's riverside street level has a terrific assortment of restaurants and bars, though many are branches of upscale chains. Friday through Sunday, there's a street food market with food trucks serving cuisines from around the world. ✉ *Belvedere Rd., South Bank* ☎ *020/3879–9555* ⊕ *www.southbank-centre.co.uk* 🚇 *Free–£120* Ⓜ *Waterloo, Embankment.*

THEATER

Menier Chocolate Factory

THEATER | This converted industrial space has become celebrated for its inspired reworkings of classic musicals, with several of its productions eventually transferring to the West End and even winning Tonys on Broadway. It's not unusual for shows to feature top British talent and stars-of-tomorrow, like Sharon Horgan and Tom Hollander, before they become famous. It also hosts comedy nights and there's an excellent Modern British restaurant on-site. ✉ *53 Southwark St., London* ☎ *020/7378–1713* ⊕ *www. menierchocolatefactory.com* 🚇 *From £38* Ⓜ *London Bridge.*

★ National Theatre

THEATER | FAMILY | When this complex designed by Sir Denys Lasdun opened in 1976, Londoners were slow to warm up to the low-rise Brutalist block, with Prince Charles describing it as "a clever way of building a nuclear power station in the middle of London without anyone objecting." But whatever you think of the outside, the inside offers generally superb theatrical experiences at (relatively) friendly prices—several of which (like *War Horse* or *One Man, Two Guvnors*) have gone on to become long-running Broadway hits. Interspersed with the three theaters—the 1,150-seat Olivier, the 890-seat Lyttelton, and the 450-seat Dorfman—is a multilayered foyer with exhibitions, bars, restaurants, and free entertainment. Musicals, classics, and plays are performed by top-flight professionals, who you can sometimes catch giving foyer talks as well. Backstage, costume, and architecture tours are available daily at 9:45 am except Sunday. The Clore Learning Centre offers courses and events on different aspects of theater production, and you can watch staff at work on set building and scenery painting from the Sherling High-Level Walkway. Each weekend in August, the free outdoor River Stage Festival presents live music, dance, family workshops, and DJ sets in front of the theater. There are £10 Friday Rush tickets for some performances. ⊠ *Belvedere Rd., South Bank* ☎ *020/7452–3000* ⊕ *www.nationaltheatre.org.uk* ⊠ *From £15, tours £13* Ⓜ *Waterloo.*

The Old Vic

THEATER | In 2015, Matthew Warchus, the director behind *Matilda the Musical,* took over as artistic director of this grand venerable theater, where stage legends like John Gielgud, Vivien Leigh, Peter O'Toole, Richard Burton, and Judi Dench once trod the boards. Today, you'll still find some of the best shows in town here—both new work and revivals of modern classics—some featuring contemporary stars like Andrew Scott and Claire Foy. ⊠ *The Cut, Southwark* ☎ *0844/871–7628* ⊕ *www.oldvictheatre.com* ⊠ *From £10* Ⓜ *Waterloo, Southwark.*

Unicorn Theatre

THEATER | FAMILY | Dedicated to innovative work for young audiences, this modern theater hosts plays, musicals, and interactive theater for everyone from toddlers on up. Inclusivity is a major focus, with performances for those with visual and hearing and other impairments taking place regularly. ⊠ *147 Tooley St., Borough* ☎ *020/7645–0560* ⊕ *www.unicorntheatre.com* ⊠ *From £12* Ⓜ *London Bridge.*

Young Vic

THEATER | Just down the road from its elder sibling The Old Vic, this offshoot hosts big names performing alongside emerging talent, often in daring innovative productions of both new and classic plays that appeal to a more diverse audience than is traditionally found on the London scene. Good food is served all day at the bustling bar. ⊠ *66 The Cut, Waterloo, South Bank* ☎ *020/7922–2922* ⊕ *www.youngvic.org* ⊠ *From £10* Ⓜ *Southwark, Waterloo.*

Shopping

ART

OXO Tower Wharf

CRAFTS | The artisans creating fashion, jewelry, home accessories, textiles, prints and photographs, furniture, and other design items have to pass rigorous selection procedures to set up shop in these prime riverside studios, where they make, display, and sell their work. The OXO Tower Restaurant & Brasserie on the top floor is expensive, but with its fantastic view of London, it's worth popping up for a drink. There's also a public terrace where you can take in the view. ⊠ *OXO Tower Wharf, Bargehouse St., South Bank* ☎ *020/7021–1686 24-hr info* ⊕ *www.coinstreet.org* ☉ *Closed Mon.* Ⓜ *Waterloo.*

CLOTHING

Bermondsey 167

MIXED CLOTHING | A "lifestyle store" stocking clothing, jewelry, accessories, home decor, books, and art, this is an Aladdin's cave of one-off, beautiful, and occasionally quirky items that were carefully chosen by its welcoming owner, the former head menswear designer of Burberry. ✉ *167 Bermondsey St., Bermondsey* ☎ *020/7407–3137* ⊕ *www. facebook.com/167bermondsey* Ⓜ *London Bridge.*

MARKETS

Bermondsey Square Antiques Market

ANTIQUES & COLLECTIBLES | The early bird catches the worm at this Friday market, so come at 6 am (flashlight recommended) to bag a bargain at London's largest antiques market. Dealers also arrive before dawn to snap up the best silver, paintings, objets d'art, jewelry, and furniture, most from Georgian through Edwardian times, but there's also the odd vintage collectible like 1980s arcade games. The early start grew out of a loophole in the law (dating from when the market began on the site in 1885) that said stolen goods bought between sunset and sunrise could not be prosecuted as the origin of the goods could not be determined (stolen goods are no longer welcome). An influx of French antiques dealers has recently joined the Bermondsey veterans selling from their covered stalls. The market finishes at 2 pm. ✉ *Long La. and Bermondsey Sq., Bermondsey* ⊕ *www.bermondseysquare. net* Ⓜ *London Bridge.*

KENSINGTON, CHELSEA, KNIGHTSBRIDGE, AND BELGRAVIA

Updated by
Ellin Stein

⦿ Sights	🧳 Restaurants	💼 Hotels	🛍 Shopping	🍸 Nightlife
★★★★☆	★★★★☆	★★★★☆	★★★★★	★★☆☆☆

KENSINGTON, CHELSEA, KNIGHTSBRIDGE, AND BELGRAVIA SNAPSHOT

TOP REASONS TO GO

The V&A: The Victoria and Albert Museum offers the world's best decorative arts collection, with millions of objects to dazzle you.

The Natural History Museum: With panels depicting creatures both living and extinct, this is one of the world's most impressive natural history collections; keep an eye out for the animatronic *T. rex.*

Kensington Palace: The public areas and gardens of this royal family home show off some of the beauty enjoyed by its past and present residents, including Queen Victoria, Princess Diana, and the Duke and Duchess of Cambridge (William and Kate) and their children.

Hyde Park: Explore one of London's largest green spaces by walking, cycling (free docked bikes are available at several locations), or rowing on the Serpentine, the tranquil lake that snakes through the park.

The Serpentine Galleries: Expand your cultural horizons at one of London's foremost showcases for modern art, or just have a bite at the café in the extension to the Serpentine North Gallery, designed by famed architect Zaha Hadid and a work of art in itself.

GETTING THERE

Several Tube stations are nearby: Sloane Square and High Street Kensington on the District and Circle lines; Knightsbridge and Hyde Park Corner on the Piccadilly line; and South Kensington, and Gloucester Road on the District, Circle, and Piccadilly lines.

MAKING THE MOST OF YOUR TIME

You could fill three or four days in this borough, especially if you enjoy museums. Give yourself at least a half day for the Victoria and Albert Museum, a half day for Kensington Palace, and a half day for either the Natural History Museum or the Science Museum.

PAUSE HERE

■ Tucked away behind busy Kensington High Street is St. Mary Abbot Gardens, a charming, peaceful minipark with benches, mature lime trees, rose beds, and wildflower-sprinkled lawns. There has been a church on this site since the 12th century (you can still see medieval graves in the churchyard adjoining the park), with the current building designed by George Gilbert Scott, who also designed the Houses of Parliament. The gardens are accessed via Kensington Church Walk leading from the north side of Kensington High Street.

The Royal Borough of Kensington & Chelsea (or K&C, as the locals call it) is where you'll find London at its richest, and not just in the moneyed sense. South Kensington offers a concentration of great museums near Cromwell Road, with historic Kensington Palace and Kensington Gardens nearby in Hyde Park. Once-raffish Chelsea, where the Pre-Raphaelites painted and Mick Jagger partied, is now a thoroughly respectable home for the discreetly wealthy, while flashier Knightsbridge has become a haven for international plutocrats, with shopping to match their tastes.

Kensington

Kensington comprises the area along the southern edge of Hyde Park from Exhibition Road (where the big museum complex is) and the area to the west of the park bordered by leafy Holland Park Avenue on the north and traffic-heavy Cromwell Road on the south. This more westerly zone includes the satellite neighborhood of Holland Park, with its serenely grand villas and charming park, as well as local shopping mecca Kensington High Street and the antiques shops on Kensington Church Street.

The area's green lung is the 350-acre **Hyde Park,** an oasis offering rolling lawns, ancient trees, boating on a meandering lake, swimming, formal gardens, a playground, a leading contemporary art gallery, and even a palace.

Kensington's first royal connection was created when King William III, fed up with the dampness of his existing Thames-side palace, bought a country home there in 1689 and converted it into **Kensington Palace.** It was also William who laid out the formal **Kensington Gardens** surrounding the palace. In the gardens today is the **Diana Memorial Playground,** a children's play area dedicated to the late Princess of Wales, and, to the north (Bayswater) side, the **Italian Gardens,** an ornamental water garden with four main fountains, originally commissioned by Queen Victoria's consort, Prince Albert, and modeled on the gardens he introduced at Osborne House. Albert masterminded the Great Exhibition of 1851 and used the profits to buy the land south of the park, which became the site of a complex of colleges and museums that would eventually include the **Victoria and Albert Museum (V&A),** the **Science Museum,** and the **Natural History Museum.** During his lifetime, the area became known as the "Albertopolis," while its posthumous tributes to the prince include the **Royal Albert Hall,** with bas-reliefs that make it resemble a giant, redbrick Wedgwood teapot, and the small but lavish **Albert Memorial.**

Turn into Derry Street or Young Street and enter **Kensington Square,** one of the most complete 17th-century residential squares in London. **18 Stafford Terrace,** the perfectly preserved family home of a well-to-do, aesthetically inclined Victorian household, is nearby.

Sights

Albert Memorial

MONUMENT | After Prince Albert's early death from typhoid in 1861, his grieving widow, Queen Victoria, had Sir Gilbert Scott create this ornate, High Victorian Gothic tribute erected near the site of Albert's brainchild, the Great Exhibition of 1851. A 14-foot gilt-bronze statue of the prince (holding an Exhibition catalog) rests on a 15-foot-high pedestal, surrounded by marble figures representing his passions and interests. A frieze at the base depicts 187 exquisitely carved figures of well-known Victorian painters, poets, sculptors, musicians, and architects. ⊠ *Kensington Gardens, Kensington* Ⓜ *S. Kensington, High St. Kensington.*

18 Stafford Terrace

HISTORIC HOME | The home of *Punch* cartoonist Linley Sambourne in the 1870s, this charming house is a rare example of the "Aesthetic interior" style; it displays delightful Victorian and Edwardian antiques, fabrics, and paintings, as well as several samples of Sambourne's work for *Punch.* The Italianate house was the scene for society parties when Sambourne's granddaughter Anne Messel was in residence in the 1940s. This being Kensington, there's inevitably a royal connection: Messel's son, Antony Armstrong-Jones, was married to the late Princess Margaret, and their son has preserved the connection by taking the title Viscount Linley. On Wednesday and weekends, 75-minute guided tours are given in the morning (reservations required)—with Saturday tours given by costumed actors—but in the afternoons, you are free to wander at will. There's also a costumed evening tour the third Wednesday of every month. ⊠ *18 Stafford Terr., Kensington* ☎ *0207/602–3316* ⊕ *www.rbkc.gov.uk/linleysambournehouse* ⊉ *£9, morning tour £12, evening tour £20* ⊗ *Closed Mon., Tues., Thurs., and Fri.* Ⓜ *High St. Kensington.*

★ Hyde Park

CITY PARK | FAMILY | Along with the smaller St. James's and Green Parks to the east, the 350-acre Hyde Park once formed part of Henry VIII's hunting grounds. Along its south side runs Rotten Row—the name is a corruption of *Route du Roi* (Route of the King), as it became known after William III installed 300 oil lamps to make the busy road less attractive to highwaymen. Today it's a bridle path often used by the Household Cavalry, who are housed in the Hyde Park Barracks occupying two unattractive buildings, a high-rise and a low red block to the left. You can see the Guardsmen in full regalia leaving on horseback for guard duty at Buckingham Palace at about 10:30 (or come at noon when they return).

Hyde Park is wonderful for strolling, cycling, or just relaxing by the Serpentine, the long body of water near its southern border. On the south side, the Lido Café and Bar by the 1930s Serpentine Lido is a good spot to refuel, and close by is the Diana Memorial Fountain. On Sunday, you'll find the uniquely British tribute to free speech, Speakers' Corner, close to Marble Arch. Though not what it was in the days before people could use the Internet to vent their spleen, it still offers a unique assortment of passionate, if occasionally irrational, advocates literally getting up on soapboxes. Summer sees giant pop concerts with top artists, while during the Christmas season the park hosts a "Winter Wonderland" amusement park, Christmas market, and ice rink. ✉ *Hyde Park* ☎ *0330/061–2000* ⊕ *www.royalparks.org.uk* ✆ *Free* Ⓜ *Hyde Park Corner, Knightsbridge, Lancaster Gate, Marble Arch.*

★ **Kensington Gardens**

GARDEN | **FAMILY** | Laid out in 1689 by William III, who commissioned Sir Christopher Wren to build Kensington Palace, the gardens are a formal counterpart to neighboring Hyde Park. Just to the north of the palace itself is the Dutch-style Sunken Garden. Nearby, the 1912 bronze statue *Peter Pan* commemorates the boy in J. M. Barrie's story who lived on an island in the Serpentine and who never grew up. Kids will enjoy the magical Diana Memorial Playground, whose design was also inspired by Barrie's book. The Elfin Oak is a 900-year-old tree trunk that was carved with scores of tiny elves, fairies, and other fanciful creations in the 1920s. The Italian Gardens, an ornamental water garden commissioned by Prince Albert in 1860, is comprised of several ornamental ponds and fountains (there's also a nice café on-site), while the Round Pond attracts model-boat enthusiasts. ✉ *Kensington* ☎ *0330/061–2000* ⊕ *www. royalparks.org.uk* ✆ *Free* Ⓜ *High St. Kensington, Lancaster Gate, Queensway, South Kensington.*

★ **Kensington Palace**

CASTLE/PALACE | **FAMILY** | This is a rare chance to get a glimpse into the more domestic and personal side of royal life. Neither as imposing as Buckingham Palace nor as charming as Hampton Court, Kensington Palace is something of a royal family commune, with various close relatives of the Queen occupying large apartments in the private part of the palace. After purchasing the existing modest mansion in 1689 as a country retreat, Queen Mary and King William III commissioned Sir Christopher Wren to transform it into a palace, and over the years young royal families have made it their home. Princess Diana lived here with her sons after her divorce, and this is where Prince William now lives with his wife, Catherine, Duchess of Cambridge, and their three children. Prince Harry shared his cottage on the grounds with Meghan Markle before their marriage.

The State Apartments are open to the public. The Queen's State Apartments are the private quarters of Queen Mary II, who ruled jointly with her husband, William II. By contrast, the lavish King's State Apartments, originally built for George I, are a stage set, a circuit of sumptuous rooms where Georgian monarchs received and entertained courtiers, politicians, and foreign dignitaries. Look for the King's Staircase, with its panoramic trompe-l'oeil painting, and the King's Gallery, with royal artworks surrounded by rich red damask walls, intricate gilding, and a beautiful painted ceiling. One permanent exhibition, *Victoria Revealed,* is devoted to the private life of Queen Victoria, who was born and grew up here. A temporary exhibition explores life in the royal family as depicted in photographs.

Outside, the grounds are almost as lovely as the palace itself. You can picnic on one of the benches or head for the Baroque Orangery, serving lunch and an

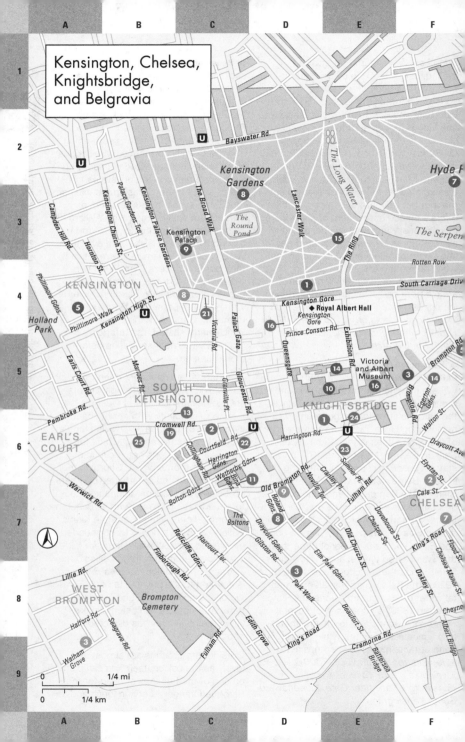

Kensington, Chelsea, Knightsbridge, and Belgravia

A B C D E F

1 2 3 4 5 6 7 8 9

Bayswater Rd.

Kensington Gardens

The Long Water

Hyde P

The Round Pond

Lancaster Walk

The Serpen

Camden Hill Rd.

Palace Gardens Tce.

Kensington Palace Gardens

Kensington Church St.

Hornton St.

The Broad Walk

KENSINGTON

Kensington Palace

Phillimore Gdns.

Phillimore Walk

Kensington High St.

Holland Park

Earls Court Rd.

Marloes Rd.

Victoria Rd.

Palace Gate

Queensgate

Kensington Gore
◆ Royal Albert Hall
Kensington Gore
Prince Consort Rd.

The Ring

Rotten Row

South Carriage Driv

Exhibition Rd.

Victoria and Albert Museum

Brompton Rd.

SOUTH KENSINGTON

Gloucester Rd.

Grenville Pl.

Brompton Rd.

Egerton Gdns.

Walton St.

EARL'S COURT

Pembroke Rd.

Cromwell Rd.

Courtfield Rd.

Harrington Rd.

KNIGHTSBRIDGE

Draycott Ave.

Elystan St.

Cale St.

CHELSEA

Warwick Rd.

Cottingham Rd.

Harrington Gdns.

Wetherby Gdns.

Old Brompton Rd.

Bolton Gdns.

Sumner Pl.

Cranley Pl.

Neville Ter.

Fulham Rd.

Dovehouse St.

Chelsea Sq.

King's Road

Flood St.

The Boltons

Roland Gdns.

Draycott Gdns.

Gilston Rd.

Old Church St.

Chelsea Manor St.

Oakley St.

Cheyne

Albert Bridge

WEST BROMPTON

Lillie Rd.

Halford Rd.

Seagrave Rd.

Redcliffe Gdns.

Finborough Rd.

Harcourt Ter.

Brompton Cemetery

Fulham Rd.

Edith Grove

Park Walk

Elm Park Gdns.

King's Road

Beaufort St.

Cremorne Rd.

Battersea Bridge

Watham Grove

0   1/4 mi
0   1/4 km

10

Sights ▼

1 Albert Memorial D4
2 Belgrave Square......... H4
3 Brompton Oratory F5
4 Duke of York Square
Fine Food Market....... G6
5 18 Stafford Terrace..... A4
6 Harrods G5
7 Hyde Park............... F2
8 Kensington Gardens..... C3
9 Kensington Palace C3
10 Natural History
Museum E5
11 Pavilion Road.......... G6
12 Royal Hospital
Chelsea H7
13 Saatchi Gallery......... G6
14 Science Museum........ E5
15 Serpentine Galleries E3
16 Victoria and Albert
Museum E5

Restaurants ▼

1 Dinner by Heston
Blumenthal G4
2 Elystan Street F6
3 The Harwood Arms...... A9
4 Marcus.................. H4
5 Mari Vanna G4
6 Pétrus H4
7 Rabbit F7
8 Stick and Bowl........... C4
9 Yashin Ocean House ... D7

Hotels ▼

1 Ampersand E6
2 Ashburn Hotel............ C6
3 At Home Inn Chelsea ... D8
4 B&B Belgravia I6
5 The Beaufort F5
6 Beaverbrook
Town House G6
7 Belmond Cadogan
Hotel..................... G5
8 The Berkeley H4
9 Bulgari Hotel London... G4
10 The Capital Hotel G4
11 The Cranley Hotel........ C6
12 The Draycott G6
13 easyHotel
South Kensington....... B6
14 The Egerton House
Hotel..................... F5
15 11 Cadogan Gardens... H6
16 The Gore Hotel.......... D4
17 The Lanesborough...... H4
18 Lime Tree Hotel I6
19 London Marriott
Kensington B6
20 Mandarin Oriental
Hyde Park............... G4
21 The Milestone Hotel..... C4
22 Millennium
Gloucester................ C6
23 Number Sixteen.......... E6
24 The Pelham Hotel........ E6
25 The Rockwell............ B6
26 San Domenico
House G6
27 Studios@82...............I6

Ice-skaters outside the Natural History Museum in South Kensington

elegant Afternoon Tea. There are more casual cafés in the Italian Gardens and on the Broad Walk. An extension adjoining the Orangery is in the works to house an educational center. ✉ *The Broad Walk, Kensington Gardens, Kensington* ☎ *0207/482–7799 for advance booking in U.K., 0203/166–6000* ⊕ *www.hrp. org.uk* 🎟 *£20* ⊗ *Closed Mon. and Tues.* Ⓜ *Queensway, High St. Kensington.*

★ Natural History Museum

HISTORY MUSEUM | FAMILY | Originally built to house the British Museum's natural history collection and bolstered by samples provided by Britain's great 19th-century explorers and scientists—notably Charles Darwin—this enormous Victorian cathedral of science is one of the world's preeminent museums of natural history and earth sciences. As might be expected given its Darwin connection, the emphasis is on evolution and conservation. The terra-cotta facade is embellished with relief panels depicting living creatures to the left of the entrance and

extinct ones to the right (although some species have subsequently changed categories). Most are represented inside the museum, which contains more than 70 million different specimens. Only a small percentage is on public display, but you could still spend a day here and not come close to seeing everything.

The skeleton of a giant blue whale dominates the vaulted, cathedral-like entrance hall. Meanwhile, similarly huge dino bones (technically rocks due to fossilization) can be found in the Dinosaur Gallery (Blue Zone), along with the only known fossil of *Spicomellus*, a type of armored dinosaur with spikes protruding from its ribs. You'll also come face-to-face with a virtual Jurassic sea dragon and a giant animatronic *T. rex* (3/4 of its actual size) that's programmed to sense when human prey is near and "respond" in character. When he does, you can hear the shrieks of fear and delight all the way across the room.

An escalator takes you into a giant globe in the Earth Galleries, where there's a choice of levels to explore. Don't leave without checking out the earthquake simulation in the Volcanoes and Earthquake Gallery. The Darwin Centre houses some 80 million items the museum itself doesn't have room to display, including "Archie," a 28-foot giant squid. If you want to see Archie and some of the other millions of animal specimens preserved (including some acquired on Darwin's *Beagle* voyage), you'll need to book one of the behind-the-scenes Spirit Collection tours (£25). These 45-minute tours take place at various dates and times and can be booked on the same day (space is limited, so come early). Night owls might prefer one of the evening talks or spending an entire night in the museum at one of the "Dino Snores" events.

The museum also has an outdoor ice-skating rink from October through January and a popular Christmas fair. ⊠ *Cromwell Rd., South Kensington* ☎ *0207/942–5000* ⊕ *www.nhm.ac.uk* ⊠ *Free (some fees for special exhibitions)* Ⓜ *South Kensington.*

★ **Science Museum**

SCIENCE MUSEUM | **FAMILY** | With attractions ranging from entertaining to educational exhibits—like the Wonderlab interactive gallery, where kids can perform their own scientific experiments, and an exhibition on the fight against superbugs—the Science Museum brings the subject alive for visitors of all ages. Highlights include Puffing Billy, the oldest steam locomotive in the world; Watson and Crick's original DNA model; and the Apollo 10 capsule. The Information Age gallery, devoted to communication networks from the telegraph to the Internet, was opened in 2014 by Queen Elizabeth, who marked the occasion by sending her first tweet. The Winton Gallery, all about mathematics and its applications, has more than 100 math-related objects, such as

a 17th-century Islamic astrolabe and an early version of Alan Turing's Enigma machine.

Overshadowed by a three-story blue-glass wall, the Wellcome Wing is an annex to the rear of the museum, devoted to contemporary science and technology. It contains a 450-seat theater (where you can visit the ocean floor or the Hubble space telescope via IMAX) and Legend of Apollo—an advanced 3-D motion simulator that combines seat vibration with other technology to re-create the experience of a moon landing. The entire first floor has been transformed into five galleries devoted to the history of medicine and the family-friendly Wonderlab (£11) is full of interactive exhibits. If you're a group of at least five, you might be able to get a place on one of the popular bi-monthly Astronight sleepovers by booking well in advance. ⊠ *Exhibition Rd., South Kensington* ☎ *0870/870–4868* ⊕ *www.sciencemuseum.org.uk* ⊠ *Free (charge for special exhibitions, IMAX, Wonderlab, and simulator rides)* Ⓜ *South Kensington.*

Serpentine Galleries

ART GALLERY | Taking its name from the artificial recreational lake that curves its way through Hyde Park, the Serpentine South Gallery, housed in a brick 1930s tea pavilion in Kensington Gardens, is one of London's foremost showcases for contemporary art. Just about everyone who's anyone has exhibited here: Louise Bourgeois, Jeff Koons, Marina Abramović, and Gerhard Richter, to name a few. A permanent work on the gallery's grounds, consisting of eight benches and a carved stone circle, commemorates its former patron, Princess Diana.

The Serpentine North Gallery, a second exhibition space that's in a small Georgian gunpowder storeroom just across a small bridge, has a dramatic extension designed by Zaha Hadid as well as a stylish restaurant. If you're in town between May and September, check out the annual Serpentine Pavilion, where each year a leading architect is given free rein to create a temporary pavilion of their choosing—always with imaginative results. Past designers have included Frank Gehry, Daniel Libeskind, and Jean Nouvel. ☒ *Kensington Gardens, Kensington* ☎ *020/7402–6075* ⊕ *www. serpentinegalleries.org* ☒ *Free* ⊘ *Closed Mon.* Ⓜ *Lancaster Gate, Knightsbridge, South Kensington.*

★ **Victoria and Albert Museum**
ART MUSEUM | **FAMILY** | Known to all as the V&A, this huge museum with more than two million items on display in 145 galleries is devoted to the applied arts of all disciplines, all periods, and all nationalities. First opened as the South Kensington Museum in 1857, it was renamed in 1899 in honor of Queen Victoria's late husband and has since grown to become one of the country's best-loved cultural institutions, with high-profile temporary exhibitions alongside an impressive permanent collection. Many collections at the V&A are presented not by period but by category—textiles, sculpture, jewelry, and so on. It's a tricky building to navigate, so use the free map.

Nowhere is the benefit of the categorization more apparent than in the Fashion Gallery (Room 40), where formal 18th-century court dresses are displayed alongside the haute couture styles of contemporary designers. The museum has become known for high-profile temporary exhibitions exploring fashion icons, such as Alexander McQueen, Balenciaga, and Christian Dior, as well as pop legends, including David Bowie and Pink Floyd.

The British Galleries (Rooms 52–58 and 118–125) survey British art and design from 1500 to 1900 and are full of rare and beautiful artifacts, such as the Tudor Great Bed of Ware (immortalized in Shakespeare's *Twelfth Night*) and silks woven by Huguenot refugees in Spitalfields. Among the series of actual rooms

that have been painstakingly reconstructed piece by piece are the glamorous rococo Norfolk House Music Room and the serenely elegant Henrietta St. Drawing Room, originally designed in 1722.

The Asian Galleries (Rooms 44–47) are full of treasures, but among the most striking items on display is a remarkable collection of ornate samurai armor in the Japanese Gallery (Room 44). Works from China, Korea, and the Islamic Middle East have their own displays. Also of note is a gallery thematically grouped around Buddhist sculptures from different regions and periods. The Europe Gallery (Rooms 1–7) brings together more than 1,100 objects created between 1600 and 1815, while the Medieval and Renaissance galleries, which document European art and culture from 300 to 1600, have the largest collection of works from the period outside of Italy.

An entrance off Exhibition Road offers access through Britain's first porcelain-tiled public courtyard, which also serves as a venue for contemporary installations and a glass-fronted café. A photography center houses books, photo equipment, and more than 270,000 prints formerly held by the Royal Photographic Society, joining the more than 500,000 photos already in the museum's collection. A room in the center has been named the Elton John and David Furnish Gallery after the couple donated some 7,000 photographs by 20th-century masters. There is a one-hour introductory tour to help you find your way around. ■ TIP→ **Whatever time you visit, the spectacular sculpture hall will be filled with artists, both amateur and professional, sketching the myriad artworks on display there. Don't be shy; bring a pad and join in.** ☒ *Cromwell Rd., South Kensington* ☎ *020/7942–2000* ⊕ *www.vam.ac.uk* ☒ *Free (charge for some special exhibitions, from £5)* Ⓜ *South Kensington.*

🍴 Restaurants

Kensington is a Victorian residential neighborhood with a wide range of restaurants, from French bistros to funky Persian hideaways.

Stick & Bowl

$ | **CHINESE** | This hole-in-the-wall restaurant, a neighborhood favorite for more than 20 years, is an amazing bargain for this pricey part of town, serving good basic Chinese food at reasonable prices. Standouts on the extensive menu include *ma-po* tofu, crispy pork belly, and seafood *ho-fun*. **Known for:** simple but delicious Chinese dishes; no-frills, speedy service; great prices. [$] *Average main: £8* ✉ *31 Kensington High St., Kensington* ☎ *020/7937–2778* 💳 *No credit cards* ⏲ *Closed weekends* [M] *High St. Kensington.*

Yashin Ocean House

$$$ | **JAPANESE** | Here at one of London's top Japanese restaurants, head chef and cofounder Yasuhiro Mineno creates fresh, colorful, and exquisite sushi, sashimi, salads, and carpaccios. Tofu-topped miso cappuccino comes in a Victorian cup and saucer, while *nigiri* might include signature flourishes such as truffle shavings on fatty tuna. **Known for:** head-to-tail seafood dishes; exquisite sushi and sashimi with creative twists; 5- to 15-piece chef-decides omakase sets. [$] *Average main: £30* ✉ *117–119 Old Brompton Rd., Kensington* ☎ *020/7373–3990* 🌐 *www.yashinocean.com* [M] *High St. Kensington.*

🛏 Hotels

From cheap and cheerful hostels for students and gleaming, efficient hotels aimed at business travelers to Victorian mansions converted to comfortable, elegant boutique hotels, this tourist-heavy part of London has accommodations to suit all tastes.

The Ampersand

$$$ | **HOTEL** | A sense of style emanates from every surface of this stylish hotel in the heart of Kensington, and the playful vintage vibe lends the property a refreshingly down-to-earth feel in a neighborhood that can feel stodgy. **Pros:** good restaurant; flawless design; great service. **Cons:** the area swarms with tourists visiting the museums on weekends; breakfast is not included in the price of a room; ground-floor rooms can be noisy. [$] *Rooms from: £286* ✉ *10 Harrington Rd., Kensington* ☎ *020/7589–5895* 🌐 *www.ampersandhotel.com* 🔑 *111 rooms* 🍽 *No Meals* [M] *Gloucester Rd.*

Ashburn Hotel

$$ | **HOTEL** | A short walk from Gloucester Road Tube station and within walking distance of Harrods and the Kensington museums, this is one of the better boutique hotels in this part of town. **Pros:** different turndown gift every night; friendly atmosphere; free Wi-Fi. **Cons:** on a very busy road; some rooms on the small side; summer prices sometimes hike the cost. [$] *Rooms from: £125* ✉ *111 Cromwell Rd., Kensington* ☎ *020/7244–1999* 🌐 *www.ashburn-hotel.co.uk* 🔑 *38 rooms* 🍽 *Free Breakfast* [M] *Gloucester Rd.*

The Cranley Hotel

$$ | **HOTEL** | Old-fashioned British propriety is the overall feeling at this small hotel made up of three Victorian town houses, where high ceilings and huge windows flood the bedrooms with light. **Pros:** free evening treats (and champagne) are a nice touch; good-size rooms; attractively decorated. **Cons:** prices rise in midsummer; some elements of the decor feel a little tired; steep stairs into lobby. [$] *Rooms from: £175* ✉ *10–12 Bina Gardens, South Kensington* ☎ *020/7373–0123* 🌐 *www.cranleyhotel.com* 🔑 *39 rooms* 🍽 *Free Breakfast* [M] *Gloucester Rd.*

easyHotel South Kensington

$ | HOTEL | London's original "pod hotel" has tiny rooms with a double bed, private shower room, and little else—each brightly decorated in the easyGroup's trademark orange and white (to match their budget airline, easyJet). **Pros:** good location; amazing rates; safe and decent-enough space. **Cons:** Wi-Fi is not included in room price; six floors and no elevator; not for the claustrophobic—rooms are truly tiny and most have no windows. [$] *Rooms from: £65* ✉ *14 Lexham Gardens, Kensington* ☎ *07951/440134* 🌐 *www.easyhotel.com* 🛏 *34 rooms* 🍴 *No Meals* [M] *Gloucester Rd.*

★ The Gore Hotel

$$$ | HOTEL | This gorgeous hotel with old-school attentive service has a mixture of the comfortable and the extraordinary. **Pros:** air-conditioning in all rooms; gorgeously designed and spacious rooms; outstanding attentive service. **Cons:** some rooms are dark; bar can be noisy; slow Wi-Fi. [$] *Rooms from: £290* ✉ *190 Queen's Gate, Kensington* ☎ *020/7584-6601, 888/757-5587 in U.S.* 🌐 *www.starhotelscollezione.com/en/our-hotels/the-gore-london* 🛏 *50 rooms* 🍴 *Free Breakfast* [M] *Gloucester Rd.*

London Marriott Kensington

$$ | HOTEL | A big favorite with the business crowd, this pleasant modern outpost of the Marriott megachain is just one of several big-name hotels on busy Cromwell Road. **Pros:** one-minute Tube ride to Kensington museums; friendly efficient service; good neighborhood. **Cons:** unattractive location on busy Cromwell Road; bedrooms are on the small side; business atmosphere feels impersonal. [$] *Rooms from: £190* ✉ *147 Cromwell Rd., Kensington* ☎ *020/7973-1000* 🌐 *www.marriott.com/hotels/travel/lonlm-london-marriott-hotel-kensington* 🛏 *216 rooms* 🍴 *Free Breakfast* [M] *Earl's Ct., Gloucester Rd.*

★ The Milestone Hotel & Residences

$$$ | HOTEL | These three intricately decorated Victorian town houses overlooking Kensington Palace provide an intimate, luxurious alternative to the city's more famous high-end hotels, offering thoughtful hospitality and opulent, distinctive rooms full of antiques. **Pros:** excellent location; beautiful and elegant; big rooms, many with park views. **Cons:** some guests might find the decor a little over-the-top; luxury and elegance comes at a high price; actual room rate discounts are rare. [$] *Rooms from: £345* ✉ *1 Kensington Ct., Kensington* ☎ *020/7917-1000* 🌐 *www.milestonehotel.com* 🛏 *56 rooms* 🍴 *Free Breakfast* [M] *High St. Kensington.*

Millennium Gloucester

$$ | HOTEL | Located next to a conference center and opposite a Tube station, this is very much a business hotel. **Pros:** good deals available if you book in advance; great location; good business facilities. **Cons:** rather bland decor will appeal more to business travelers; bathrooms are relatively small; lighting in some bedrooms is a bit too subtle. [$] *Rooms from: £161* ✉ *4-18 Harrington Gardens, Kensington* ☎ *020/7373-6030* 🌐 *www.millenniumhotels.co.uk* 🛏 *610 rooms* 🍴 *Free Breakfast* [M] *Gloucester Rd.*

★ Number Sixteen

$$$ | HOTEL | Rooms at this lovely boutique hotel, just around the corner from the Victoria and Albert Museum, look like they come from the pages of *Architectural Digest*, and the delightful courtyard garden is an added bonus. **Pros:** the Afternoon Tea is excellent; just the right level of helpful service; interiors are gorgeous. **Cons:** intimacy of a small boutique hotel may not be for everyone; elevator doesn't go to third floor; no restaurant. [$] *Rooms from: £348* ✉ *16 Sumner Pl., South Kensington* ☎ *020/7589-5232, 888/559-5508 in U.S.* 🌐 *www.firmdale.com* 🛏 *41 rooms* 🍴 *Free Breakfast* [M] *South Kensington.*

The Pelham

$$$ | HOTEL | One of the first boutique hotels ever in London, this still-stylish choice is just a short stroll away from the Natural History, Science, and Victoria and Albert museums. **Pros:** lovely staff; great location for museum-hopping; elegant interior design. **Cons:** some suites are only accessible via the stairs; some rooms are on the small side given the price; taller guests will find themselves cursing the top-floor rooms with sloping ceilings. [$] *Rooms from: £270* ✉ *15 Cromwell Pl., South Kensington* ☎ *020/7589–8288, 888/757–5587 in U.S.* 🌐 *www.starhotelscollezione.com/en/our-hotels/the-pelham-london* 🛏 *52 rooms* 🍴 *Free Breakfast* [M] *South Kensington.*

The Rockwell

$ | HOTEL | Despite being on the notoriously traffic-clogged Cromwell Road, the Rockwell is one of the best boutique hotels in this part of London—and windows have triple-soundproofing. **Pros:** helpful staff; large bedrooms; good value for neighborhood. **Cons:** decor a bit tired in places; no bathtubs; on busy road. [$] *Rooms from: £108* ✉ *181 Cromwell Rd., South Kensington* ☎ *020/7244–2000* 🌐 *www.therockwell.com* 🛏 *40 rooms* 🍴 *Free Breakfast* [M] *Earl's Ct.*

Nightlife

The Troubadour

LIVE MUSIC | A music venue since 1954, this is the last survivor of the coffeehouse scene of the 1950s and '60s that spearheaded Britain's folk revival (it also inspired the Los Angeles music club of the same name). Among the notables who have performed here either at the beginning of their careers or at informal after-gig shows are Charlie Watts (before he joined the Rolling Stones), Bob Dylan (under the name Blind Boy Grunt), Joni Mitchell, Paul Simon, and Jimi Hendrix, along with folk legends Sandy Denny and Burt Jansch. More recent headliners include Florence Welch, Paolo Nutini, Ed Sheeran, and Adele. The menu leans toward British and French-inspired comfort food. ✉ *265–267 Old Brompton Rd., Kensington* ☎ *207/341–6333* 🌐 *www.troubadourlondon.com* [M] *West Brompton.*

Performing Arts

These affluent neighborhoods just west of central London have a wide variety of galleries and performance spaces, with several located within the area's large public green spaces.

CLASSICAL MUSIC

Cadogan Hall

CONCERTS | Once a church, this spacious venue is home to the Royal Philharmonic Orchestra, and the English Chamber Orchestra performs here regularly. The hall also hosts a wide range of choral and chamber concerts, plus the occasional folk, rock, and world-music gig. ✉ *5 Sloane Terr., Kensington* ☎ *020/7730–4500* 🌐 *www.cadoganhall.com* 🎟 *Free–£100* [M] *Sloane Sq.*

★ Royal Albert Hall

CONCERTS | Opened in 1871, this splendid iron-and-glass-domed auditorium hosts everything from pop and classical headliners to Cirque du Soleil, awards ceremonies, and sumo wrestling championships, but it is best known for the annual July–September BBC Promenade Concerts. Bargain-price standing-room (or promenading or sitting-on-the-floor) tickets for "the Proms" are sold on the night of the concert. The circular 5,272-seat auditorium has a terra-cotta exterior surmounted by a mosaic frieze depicting figures engaged in cultural pursuits. The hall is open most days for daytime guided tours and Tuesday through Sunday for Afternoon Tea. ✉ *Kensington Gore, Kensington* ☎ *0207/589–8212* 🌐 *www.royalalberthall.com* 🎟 *From £7; tours £16.25* [M] *South Kensington.*

○ Shopping

HOUSEHOLD GOODS

The Conran Shop

HOUSEWARES | This is the brainchild of
the late Sir Terence Conran, who has
been a major influence on British taste
since he opened Habitat in the 1960s,
with its then-groundbreaking concept of
advanced design at an affordable price.
Although he is no longer associated
with Habitat, his Conran Shops remain
bastions of similarly clean, unfussy
modernist design. Housewares from
furniture to lighting, stemware, and
textiles—both handmade and mass-produced, by famous names and emerging
designers—are housed in a building
that is a modernist landmark in its own
right. Both the flagship store and the
branch on Marylebone High Street are
bursting with great gift ideas. ⊠ *Michelin
House, 81 Fulham Rd., South Kensington*
☎ *020/7589–7401* ⊕ *www.conranshop.
co.uk* Ⓜ *South Kensington.*

mint

HOUSEWARES | Owner Lina Kanafani has
scoured the globe to curate an eclectic
mix of conceptual statement furniture,
art, ceramics, glassware, textiles, and
home accessories. Mint also showcases
avant-garde works by an international
selection of up-and-coming designers
and sells plenty of specially commissioned limited edition and handcrafted
one-off pieces, for a price. If you don't
want to ship a couch home, consider a
miniature flower vase or a hand-painted
plate. ⊠ *2 North Terr., at Alexander Sq.,
South Kensington* ☎ *020/7225–2228*
⊕ *www.mintshop.co.uk* Ⓜ *South
Kensington.*

JEWELRY

Butler & Wilson

JEWELRY & WATCHES | Specialists in bold
costume jewelry and affordable glamour,
Butler & Wilson attracts fans including
the Duchess of Cambridge. Semiprecious
stones have been added to its foundation
diamanté, colored rhinestone, and crystal
collections. The noted British sense of
humor is reflected in items like cham-
pagne-bottle earrings or crystal studs in
the shape of an eye. ⊠ *189 Fulham Rd.,
South Kensington* ☎ *020/7352–3045*
⊕ *www.butlerandwilson.co.uk* Ⓜ *South
Kensington.*

Chelsea

Chelsea was settled before the Domes-
day Book was compiled and already
fashionable when two of Henry VIII's
wives lived there in the 16th century. On
the banks of the Thames are the vast
grounds of the **Royal Hospital,** designed
by Christopher Wren. A walk along the
riverside embankment will take you to
Cheyne Walk, a lovely street dating back
to the 18th century. Several of its more
notable residents—from J. M. W. Turner
and Henry James to Laurence Olivier and
Keith Richards—are commemorated by
blue plaques on their former houses.

The **Albert Bridge,** a sherbet-colored
Victorian confection of a suspension
bridge, provides one of London's great
romantic views, especially at night. Leave
time to explore the tiny Georgian lanes
of pastel-color houses that veer off King's
Road to the north—especially **Jubilee
Place** and **Burnsall Street,** leading to the
hidden "village square" of **Chelsea Green.**
On Saturday there's an excellent farmers'
market up from the Saatchi Gallery in
Duke of York's Square selling cheese and
chocolates, local oysters, and organic
meats, plus stalls serving international
food.

Residential Chelsea extends along
the river from Chelsea Bridge west to
Battersea Bridge and north as far as Old
Brompton Road.

👁 Sights

Duke of York Square Fine Food Market

MARKET | West London's answer to Borough Market, this Saturday open-air market is in a pedestrian-only plaza off Duke of York Square, a chic shopping precinct. It hosts 40 stalls purveying locally produced products from more than 150 small producers. Like Borough Market, this is a grazer's paradise, giving you the chance to sample fresh oysters and cooked sausages as well as yummy hot snacks from countries ranging from Brazil to Thailand. ⊠ *Duke of York Sq., Chelsea* ☎ *020/7823–5577* ⊕ *www.duke-ofyorksquare.com* ⊘ *Closed Sun.–Fri.* Ⓜ *Sloane Sq.*

Pavilion Road

PEDESTRIAN MALL | This charming pedestrianized mews is lined with Victorian stable blocks recently converted to house fashionable independent shops and specialty food providers. Here you'll find bags from Kate Spade, bikinis from Heidi Klein, nightwear from Olivia von Halle, and Sarah Chapman skincare, as well as a cheesemonger, bakery and baking school, family-run butcher, and a fishmonger. There are also dining options including a casual, all-day Australian restaurant, a plant-based restaurant, and a bar and grill, all with lots of outside tables. ⊠ *Pavilion Rd., Chelsea* ☎ *207/730–4567* ⊕ *www.pavilionroad. co.uk* ⊠ *Free* Ⓜ *Sloane Sq.*

Royal Hospital Chelsea

HOSPITAL | Charles II founded this residence for elderly and infirm soldiers in 1682 to reward the troops who had fought for him in the civil wars of 1642–46 and 1648. No sick people are treated here today; it's more of a history-packed retirement home. A creation of three of England's greatest architects—Wren, Vanbrugh, and Hawksmoor—this small enclave of brick and Portland stone set in expansive manicured grounds (which you can visit) surrounds the Figure Court (the figure being a 1682 gilded bronze statue of Charles II dressed as a Roman general). The beautiful Wren-designed chapel (a working church) and the Great Hall (the hospital's dining room) are open to the public at certain times during the day.

There is a small museum devoted to the history of the resident "Chelsea Pensioners," but the real attraction, along with the building, is the approximately 300 pensioners themselves. Recognizable by their traditional scarlet frock coats with gold buttons, medals, and tricorne hats, they are all actual veterans, who wear the uniform, and the history it represents, with a great deal of pride. On Sunday morning (10:45) from April through November, you can see groups of pensioners in full uniform on parade in the Figure Court. Individuals can visit the chapel on Sunday between 11 and 12 for services. ⊠ *Royal Hospital Rd., Chelsea* ☎ *020/7881–5298* ⊕ *www.chelsea-pensioners.co.uk* ⊠ *Free* Ⓜ *Sloane Sq.*

Saatchi Gallery

ART GALLERY | Charles Saatchi, who made his fortune in advertising, is one of Britain's canniest collectors of contemporary art, credited with discovering the likes of Damien Hirst and Tracey Emin. His current gallery, still largely devoted to contemporary art by emerging artists, is in the former Duke of York's HQ, just off King's Road. Built in 1803, its grand period exterior belies an imaginatively restored modern interior transformed into 15 exhibition spaces of varying size and shape. There is no permanent collection other than a few ongoing site-specific installations; at any one time, there are between one and three concurrent, imaginatively curated exhibitions that normally run for up to six months. There's also an excellent café, which is open late. ⊠ *Duke of York's HQ Bldg., King's Rd., Chelsea* ☎ *020/7811–3070* ⊕ *www. saatchigallery.com* ⊠ *Free; tickets for specific exhibitions £3–£10* Ⓜ *Sloane Sq.*

🍴 Restaurants

Chelsea, once the epicenter of 1960s Swinging London, today boasts restaurants ranging from top chefs' passion projects to trendy cafés perfect for a catch-up, a glass of fizz, and an organic, seasonal bite on the go.

★ Elystan Street

$$$$ | MODERN BRITISH | Chef Philip Howard is committed to seasonality, bringing together well-matched ingredients in this relaxed, loftlike space that leans toward the modernist and minimalist. The deeply flavored, accomplished dishes have earned the restaurant a Michelin star (their vegetarian game is especially strong). **Known for:** convivial vibe enhanced by a smart wine list; Michelin-level cuisine in a relaxed setting; roast grouse with celeriac and pear puree. ⓢ *Average main: £35* ✉ *43 Elystan St., Chelsea* ☎ *020/7628–5005* ⊕ *www.elystanstreet.com* ⊘ *No dinner Sun.* Ⓜ *South Kensington.*

The Harwood Arms

$$$$ | MODERN BRITISH | Despite a Michelin star and a co-owner who's also the chef at one of Britain's (and indeed the world's) top restaurants, this is a relaxed neighborhood gastropub with an unusually fine kitchen. It specializes in British produce, wild food, and especially game, with dishes like crab royale with peas and lovage and game pie with Somerset cider jelly, all served via set menus only (£42 for two courses, £55 for three). **Known for:** good-value set menus; Michelin-starred food in a gastropub setting; seasonal venison from the pub's own hunting estate. ⓢ *Average main: £55* ✉ *27 Walham Grove, Chelsea* ☎ *020/7386–1847* ⊕ *www.harwoodarms.com* ⊘ *No lunch Mon.–Thurs.* Ⓜ *Fulham Broadway.*

The Chelsea Flower Show

Run by the Royal Horticultural Society, the Chelsea Flower Show, the year's highlight for thousands of garden-obsessed Brits, is held every May (usually the third week). The huge showcase for garden design and horticultural innovation takes up all of the Royal Hospital's large grounds. You can buy all manner of gardening supplies and accessories from the many exhibitors, and the end of the last day sees a scrimmage for discount plants from the displays. For more information, check out the website at ⊕ *www.rhs.org.uk.*

Rabbit

$$ | MODERN BRITISH | FAMILY | Owned by three brothers who grew up on a farm (which supplies the restaurant with its produce and livestock), Rabbit introduces a note of rusticity to one of London's glitziest areas. The emphasis is on locality and sustainability, and the menu changes daily, depending on what's in season and available. **Known for:** English wines from owners' vineyard; fresh game, including rabbit served marinated in a bone marrow sauce and enclosed in large ravioli; shared plates with all seasonal and local ingredients. ⓢ *Average main: £17* ✉ *172 Kings Rd., London* ☎ *020/3750–0172* ⊕ *www.rabbit-restaurant.com* ⊘ *No dinner Sun. No lunch Mon.* Ⓜ *Sloane Sq.*

Hotels

At Home Inn Chelsea

$$ | **B&B/INN** | **FAMILY** | King's Road and the rest of ultra-affluent Chelsea is just a short stroll from this delightfully informal B&B, and you'd be hard-pressed to find a better room in this neighborhood for the price. **Pros:** can be booked as a whole apartment; picturesque top-floor terrace; central Chelsea location. **Cons:** one bathroom shared between both rooms; few extras; only accessible via the owners' own apartment's main entrance. [$] *Rooms from: £125* ✉ *5 Park Walk, Chelsea* ☎ *07790/844–008* 🌐 *www.athomeinnchelsea.com* 🛏 *2 rooms* 🍴 *Free Breakfast* [M] *Fulham Broadway.*

Beaverbrook Town House

$$$$ | **HOTEL** | Now a smart boutique hotel, this was not the actual London town house of Lord Beaverbrook (newspaper tycoon of the 1930s and '40s and confidante of Churchill), but its 1930s-style decor mixed with Japanese touches evokes his sophisticated life at the center of London's intellectual set. **Pros:** access to Cadogan Gardens; central location; comfortable, stylish rooms. **Cons:** not cheap; some rooms a bit dark; there's an elevator, but accessibility may be problematic for some. [$] *Rooms from: £700* ✉ *115 Sloane St., Chelsea* ☎ *207/988–6611* 🌐 *www.beaverbrooktownhouse.co.uk* 🛏 *14 rooms* 🍴 *No Meals* [M] *Sloane Square.*

The Cadogan, a Belmond Hotel

$$$$ | **HOTEL** | This elegant hotel spread out over five town houses features luxurious decor that incorporates sculptural lighting fixtures and modern art while retaining nods to The Cadogan's Edwardian past (it was the site of Oscar Wilde's infamous arrest for gross indecency with a young man). **Pros:** free Wi-Fi; luxurious but not stuffy; garden access. **Cons:** old-school clubhouse decor not for everyone; expensive rates; rooms are quite small. [$] *Rooms from: £825* ✉ *75 Sloane St., Chelsea* ☎ *0207/048–7141* 🌐 *www.cadogan.com* 🛏 *54 rooms* 🍴 *Free Breakfast* [M] *Sloane Sq.*

★ **The Draycott Hotel**

$$$ | **HOTEL** | **FAMILY** | This elegant yet homey boutique hotel near Sloane Square is the stuff London dreams are made of—if your dream is to live like a pleasantly old-fashioned, impeccably mannered, effortlessly stylish Chelsea lady or gentleman. **Pros:** access to garden square; lovely traditional town house; attentive service. **Cons:** elevator is tiny; single rooms are very small; no restaurant or bar. [$] *Rooms from: £286* ✉ *26 Cadogan Gardens, Chelsea* ☎ *020/7730–0236* 🌐 *www.draycotthotel.com* 🛏 *35 rooms* 🍴 *Free Breakfast* [M] *Sloane Sq.*

11 Cadogan Gardens

$$$ | **HOTEL** | This combination of four Victorian townhouses on a quiet street is a warren of tucked-away, intimate public rooms, where aubergine walls enlivened by gilt-framed Victorian portraits and an abundance of fresh lilies create a glamorous, luxurious, and slightly decadent atmosphere in keeping with the hotel's former owner, Elizabeth Hurley (it's now run by the owners of luxury country house hotel Chewton Glen). **Pros:** quiet location still close to the action; chic design; good bar and grill on-site. **Cons:** decor can be too dark for some; not the best soundproofing in rooms; rooms a bit on the small side. [$] *Rooms from: £350* ✉ *11 Cadogan Gardens, Chelsea* ☎ *207/730–7000* 🌐 *www.11cadogangardens.com* 🛏 *56 rooms* 🍴 *No Meals* [M] *Sloane Square.*

★ **San Domenico House**

$$$ | **HOTEL** | Discreet, beautiful, and exceptionally well-run, this converted Chelsea town house makes for a restful hideaway. **Pros:** exceptional service; unique and beautiful design; great neighborhood, with the King's Road and Saatchi Gallery a short walk away. **Cons:** only some rooms have bathtubs; no breakfast included for the (still pretty

expensive) cheapest rates; no bar or restaurant on-site. $ *Rooms from: £288* ✉ *29–31 Draycott Pl., Chelsea* ☎ *020/7581–5757* ⊕ *www.sandomenicohouse.com* 🛏 *19 rooms* ❙❁❙ *Free Breakfast* Ⓜ *Sloane Sq.*

Nightlife

The pages of society magazines are crammed with photographs of gorgeous young people dancing the night away at clubs located in these famously swanky neighborhoods. Dress up and be prepared to splurge—if you can get in (many are members-only). Pubs here range from classy modern affairs with impressive wine lists and shared plates to tiny local institutions guaranteed to make you feel like you've stepped back in time.

JAZZ AND BLUES

606 Club

LIVE MUSIC | Established in 1976, this Chelsea jazz club embraced speakeasy style long before it became a nightlife trend. Buzz the door near the far end of King's Road and you'll find a basement venue showcasing mainstream and contemporary jazz by well-known U.K.-based musicians. Alcohol can only be served if you order a "substantial meal" as well, so allow for an extra £30. Reservations are advisable. Lunchtime jazz takes place on select Sundays; call ahead. ✉ *90 Lots Rd., Chelsea* ☎ *020/7352–5953* ⊕ *www.606club.co.uk* Ⓜ *Fulham Broadway. Overground: Imperial Wharf.*

PUBS

The Anglesea Arms

PUBS | The front patio and wood-paneled bar of this traditional pub next door to Charles Dickens's former residence is invariably crowded, especially after work, but the restaurant to the rear is comfortable and more peaceful. Dishes range from traditional pub classics like burgers or fish-and-chips to more sophisticated offerings like pan-fried sea bass. Standards, of both the cooking

and the selection of beer and wines, are high. Service is friendly, if occasionally erratic. ✉ *15 Selwood Terr., Chelsea* ☎ *020/7373–7960* ⊕ *www.angleseaarms. com* Ⓜ *South Kensington.*

Performing Arts

Royal Court Theatre

THEATER | For decades, the Royal Court was one of Britain's leading showcases for exciting new theatrical voices and premieres of groundbreaking works, and it still continues to produce important British and international dramas. Ticket prices range from £14 to £45. ✉ *Sloane Sq., Chelsea* ☎ *020/7565–5000* ⊕ *www. royalcourttheatre.com* 🎟 *From £14* Ⓜ *Sloane Sq.*

⬤ Shopping

ACCESSORIES

Anya Hindmarch

HANDBAGS | Exquisite leather bags and personalized, printed canvas totes are what made Hindmarch famous, and this store sells her complete collection of bags, several with a whimsical motif. You can also order a custom piece from the "Be A Bag" collection, with its totes and wash bags imprinted with your chosen photo, or from the "I Am A Plastic Bag" collection made from recycled plastic bottles. There are branches around the corner on Pont Street in Knightsbridge and in Notting Hill. ✉ *157–158 Sloane St., Chelsea* ☎ *0207/730–0961* ⊕ *www. anyahindmarch.com* Ⓜ *Sloane Sq.*

BOOKS

John Sandoe (Books) Ltd.

BOOKS | This atmospheric warren that crams some 25,000 titles into an 18th-century building off King's Road is the antithesis of a soulless chain bookstore, so it's no surprise it has attracted equally idiosyncratic customers like Tom Stoppard and Keith Richards. Staff members are wonderfully knowledgeable (don't try to figure out how the stock is organized without their help), and there are a lot of them per customer—if a book isn't in stock, they will try to find it for you, even if it is out of print. ⊠ *10 Blacklands Terr., Chelsea* ☎ *020/7589–9473* ⊕ *www.johnsandoe.com* Ⓜ *Sloane Sq.*

CLOTHING

Brora

MIXED CLOTHING | The knitwear is cozy, but the style is cool in this contemporary Scottish cashmere emporium for men, women, and kids. There are stylish pullovers, wraps, cardigans, and adorable baby ensembles, as well as noncashmere items such as T-shirts and jersey or linen dresses. Other branches are in Marylebone and Covent Garden; plus there's a clearance store farther down King's Road. ⊠ *6–8 Symons St., Chelsea* ☎ *020/7730–2665* ⊕ *www.brora.co.uk* Ⓜ *Sloane Sq.*

Hackett

MEN'S CLOTHING | If Ralph Lauren isn't preppy enough for you, try Hackett, with additional branches in St. James's and Canary Wharf. Originally a posh thrift shop recycling cricket flannels, hunting pinks, Oxford brogues, and other staples of a British gentleman's wardrobe, Hackett now creates its own line and has become a genuine—and very good— men's outfitter. The look is traditional, and classic best buys include polo shirts, corduroys, and striped scarves. There's also a boys' line for the junior man-about-town, a made-to-measure service, and an in-house barbershop. ⊠ *137–138 Sloane St., Chelsea* ☎ *020/7730–3331* ⊕ *www.hackett.com* Ⓜ *Sloane Sq.*

Jigsaw

WOMEN'S CLOTHING | The quality of fabrics and detailing belie the reasonable prices here, where clothes are classic yet trendy and elegant without being dull—and where cuts are kind to the womanly figure. The style is epitomized by the Duchess of Cambridge, who, as Kate Middleton before her marriage, was a buyer for the company. Although there are numerous branches across London, no two stores are the same. Preteens have their own line, Jigsaw Junior. ⊠ *The Chapel, 6 Duke of York Sq., Chelsea* ☎ *020/730–4404* ⊕ *www.jigsaw-online. com* Ⓜ *Sloane Sq.*

DEPARTMENT STORES

★ Peter Jones

DEPARTMENT STORE | This tasteful department store has been a beloved local institution since it opened in 1937, and the poet John Betjeman remarked that come the end of the world he would like to be in the haberdashery department of Peter Jones "because nothing bad could ever happen there." It's the traditional default wedding-list option of Kensington and Chelsea brides thanks to its outstanding selection of bed and bath linens (many from the in-house line of John Lewis, the store's parent company), flatware, ceramics, and glassware, with offerings at all price points. There's also an extensive and eclectic beauty department, as well as kitchenware and appliances, furniture, tech stuff, a florist, and clothing, shoes, and accessories for the whole family, plus pretty much everything else you can think of, along with a restaurant and a Clarins spa. ⊠ *Sloane Sq., Chelsea* ☎ *020/7730–3434* ⊕ *www.johnlewis. com/our-shops/peter-jones* Ⓜ *Sloane Sq.*

FOOD

L'Artisan du Chocolat

FOOD | Chosen by top chefs Gordon Ramsay and Heston Blumenthal for their restaurants, L'Artisan raises chocolate to an art form, like a necklace made of chocolate-filled "pearls." "Couture" chocolates are infused with fruits, nuts, and spices (including such exotic flavorings as Szechuan pepper and tobacco). This is one of the few chocolate shops in the world that makes liquid salted caramels. There is another branch in Selfridges. ⊠ *89 Lower Sloane St., Chelsea* ☎ *0845/270–6996* ⊕ *www.artisanduchocolat.co.uk* Ⓜ *Sloane Sq.*

HOUSEHOLD GOODS
Designers Guild

HOUSEWARES | Tricia Guild's exuberantly patterned fabrics, wallpapers, paints, furniture, and bed linens have decorated design-conscious British homes for several decades, and her soft-furnishings book has taught many budget-conscious do-it-yourselfers how to reupholster a sofa or make lined draperies. The shop also stocks contemporary furniture, wallpapers, and home accessories by other designers like Christian Lacroix. There's another branch in Marylebone. ✉ *267–277 King's Rd., Chelsea* ☎ *020/351–5775* ⊕ *www.designersguild.com* Ⓜ *Sloane Sq.*

SHOES
★ Manolo Blahnik

SHOES | Blink and you'll miss the discreet sign that marks fashionista footwear central. Blahnik, the man who single-handedly managed to revive the sexy stiletto, has been trading out of this small shop on a Chelsea side street since 1973. It's a must for shoe lovers with generous budgets. If you decide to wear your new Manolos, hop on Bus No. 11 or 22 or grab a cab—the nearest Tube station is about a 20-minute totter away. There's another boutique in Mayfair. ✉ *49–51 Old Church St., Chelsea* ☎ *020/7352–8622* ⊕ *www.manoloblahnik.com* Ⓜ *Sloane Sq., South Kensington.*

Sophia Webster

SHOES | Gorgeous, fanciful shoes embellished with jeweled flowers, sequins, butterflies, and trademark wings at the heel fill Webster's first stand-alone boutique. This stylists' favorite is best known for her open-toe stilettos, but there are plenty of flat sandals, mid-height heels, platforms, and even clogs, as well as a sneaker collaboration with Puma. ✉ *86 Sloane Ave., Mayfair* ☎ *020/3150–2977* ⊕ *www.sophiawebster.co.uk* Ⓜ *South Kensington.*

SPECIALTY STORES
Green & Stone Art Materials

OTHER SPECIALTY STORE | Relocated from its original fabulous cave on King's Road, this treasure trove of artists' materials, papers, art books, easels, and mannequins began life in 1927 as part of the Chenil Gallery, run by a distinguished group that included the artist Augustus John and the playwright George Bernard Shaw. Subsequent customers have included luminaries like David Hockney, Damien Hirst, Francis Bacon, and Lucian Freud. The shop also has a framing service, antique paint boxes, and craft supplies. ✉ *251–253 Fulham Rd., Chelsea* ☎ *020/7352–0837* ⊕ *www.greenandstone.com* Ⓜ *Sloane Sq.*

Knightsbridge

There's no getting away from it: boasting high-end retail shrines **Harrods** and **Harvey Nichols,** numerous boutiques selling the biggest names in international luxury and expensive jewelry, and a summer influx of supercars like Maseratis imported from the Gulf states, London's wealthiest enclave will appeal most to those who enjoy conspicuous consumption.

Posh Sloane Street is lined with top-end designer boutiques, such as Prada, Dior, and Tod's. If it all starts to become a bit generic (expensive generic), **Beauchamp Place** (pronounced bee-*cham*) is lined with equally luxe one-off boutiques, which tend to be more distinctive and less global.

Knightsbridge is located to the east of Kensington, bordered by Hyde Park on the north and Pont Street just past Harrods on the south.

World-famous Harrods has been luring shoppers with its classic wares since 1834.

 Sights

Brompton Oratory (*London Oratory*)
CHURCH | This is a late product of the
mid-19th-century English Roman Catholic
revival led by Cardinal John Henry
Newman (1801–90), who established the
oratory in the 1840s and whose statue
you see outside. Architect Herbert Grib-
ble was an unknown 29-year-old when he
won a competition to design the church,
bringing a Baroque exuberance to his
concept for the vast, incredibly ornate
interior. It's punctuated by treasures far
older than the church itself, like the giant
Carrara marble *Twelve Apostles* in the
nave, sculpted by Giuseppe Mazzuoli
in the 1680s for Siena's cathedral. A
working church, the Oratory is known
for the quality of its organs and choir,
with exceptional music being an integral
part of services here. ⊠ *Brompton Rd.,
Knightsbridge* ☎ *0207/808–0900* ⊕ *www.
bromptonoratory.com* ☜ *Free* Ⓜ *South
Kensington.*

Harrods
STORE/MALL | With an encyclopedic assort-
ment of luxury brands, this Knightsbridge
institution, currently owned by the Qatar
Investment Authority, has more than 300
departments and 25 eating and drinking
options, all spread over 1 million square
feet on a 4½-acre site. Now populated
more by window-shopping tourists and
superrich visitors from abroad than by
the bling-averse natives, Harrods is
best approached as the world's largest,
most upscale, and most expensive
mall. The food hall offers on-site dining
options ranging from a Pasta Evangelists
restaurant to a Sushisamba deli bar. At
the center is the Wine Bar, with over a
hundred wines by the glass and food by
Caviar House and Prunier. There's also a
giant coffee-roasting station, ceiling-high
shelves of fresh bread at the Bakery, and
a vegetable butchery. The Beauty Hall
offers cult brands, innovative "Magic
Mirrors" that allow shoppers to instantly
see a new make-up look via digital
technology, an in-house "hair doctor," and
over 46,000 different lipsticks, as well as

13 treatment rooms where you can try on make-up in private. The full-service restaurant options are dazzling, including offerings from top chefs like Gordon Ramsay (a burger bar), Tom Kerridge (fish-and-chips), and Scandi superstar Björn Frantzén. There's even a breakfast café operated by—of course—Tiffany's. ✉ *87–135 Brompton Rd., Knightsbridge* ☎ *020/7730–1234* 🌐 *www.harrods.com* [M] *Knightsbridge.*

🍴 Restaurants

You can dine like a king in Knightsbridge, as long as you're prepared to spend on a regal scale and don't mind a similar level of formality. The world-class restaurants are mostly found in the area's platinum-class hotels. Come here for a celebratory dining experience, but don't expect bargains (unless it's lunchtime).

★ Dinner by Heston Blumenthal
$$$$ | **BRITISH** | Medieval English cuisine meets molecular gastronomy in this reassuringly luxurious Blumenthal flagship within the Mandarin Oriental, with two Michelin stars. Try the signature "Meat Fruit" appetizer (last popular in the 16th century, it's a ball of ultrasmooth chicken liver parfait encased in a citrus-flavored gel "peel") or the much-more-appetizing-than-it-sounds "Rice and Flesh," a 15th-century dish of yellow saffron rice with veal sweetbreads and wild smoked eel. **Known for:** pineapple Tipsy cake for dessert; handsome dining room with Hyde Park views; creative reinterpretations of historical dishes. [$] *Average main: £54* ✉ *Mandarin Oriental Hyde Park, 66 Knightsbridge, Knightsbridge* ☎ *020/7201–3833* 🌐 *www.dinnerbyheston.com* [M] *Knightsbridge.*

Marcus
$$$$ | **MODERN BRITISH** | A former Gordon Ramsay protégé and now a celebrity chef in his own right, Marcus Wareing opened this eponymous restaurant in 2008. Wareing's Michelin-starred Contemporary European cooking uses the freshest seasonal ingredients to create innovative and delicious flavor combinations like squab with beetroot, caramelized orange, hen of the woods mushrooms, and smoked almond or a baked maple custard with rum baba, caramelized pears, and a spiced flapjack. **Known for:** slightly less formal vibe than other celebrity chef restaurants; sophisticated, seasonal dishes; excellent wine list. [$] *Average main: £90* ✉ *Berkeley Hotel, 1 Wilton Pl., London* ☎ *207/7235–1200* 🌐 *www.marcusrestaurant.com* ⏲ *Closed Sun.* [M] *Hyde Park Corner.*

Mari Vanna
$$ | **RUSSIAN** | London's sizable, well-heeled Russian community flocks to this maximalist evocation of a pre-Revolution babushka's living room, overflowing with vintage chandeliers, porcelain figurines, tapestries, and nested Russian dolls. The menu leans toward traditional old-country comfort food like Siberian *pelmeni* (dumplings) filled with pork and beef, pierogi, smoked salmon blinis, creamy beef Stroganoff with wild mushrooms, and, of course, borscht, finished off with a seven-layer honey cake. **Known for:** flavored vodka shot selection; over-the-top nostalgic Russian décor; borscht, blinis, and beef Stroganoff. [$] *Average main: £20* ✉ *The Wellington Court, 116 Knightsbridge, Knightsbridge* ☎ *020/7225–3122* 🌐 *www.marivanna.ru/london* [M] *Knightsbridge.*

🛏 Hotels

The Beaufort
$$ | **HOTEL** | This family-owned boutique hotel on a quiet cul-de-sac appears in the little black books of many fashionistas—Harrods and Harvey Nicks are just a short walk from the front door. **Pros:** complimentary daily Afternoon Tea; attractive, well-designed decor; friendly and professional staff. **Cons:** no restaurant on-site; soundproofing could be better; standard doubles are much smaller than the price

might indicate. [$] *Rooms from: £175* ✉ *33 Beaufort Gardens, Knightsbridge* ☎ *020/7584–5252* 🌐 *www.thebeaufort.co.uk* 🛏 *29 rooms* 🍴 *Free Breakfast* [M] *Knightsbridge.*

★ The Berkeley

$$$$ | HOTEL | FAMILY | Convenient for Knightsbridge shopping, the very elegant Berkeley is known for its excellent restaurants, heated rooftop swimming pool with views over Hyde Park, and an excellent, if pricey, Bamford spa. **Pros:** great drinking and dining options; lavish and elegant; attentive service. **Cons:** walls on the thin side; even the cheapest rooms are expensive; you'll need your best designer clothes to fit in. [$] *Rooms from: £600* ✉ *Wilton Pl., Knightsbridge* ☎ *020/7235–6000, 800/637–2869 in U.S.* 🌐 *www.the-berkeley.co.uk* 🛏 *190 rooms* 🍴 *Free Breakfast* [M] *Knightsbridge.*

Bulgari Hotel London

$$$$ | HOTEL | This luxury hotel checks all the Knightsbridge boxes (top-of-the-range everything, ultra-fashionable design, a haven for the international rich) and brings the same attention to detail and Italian high style to the decor as it does to its eponymous jewelry line. **Pros:** lovely spa and pool; luxurious decor and atmosphere; excellent service. **Cons:** extremely expensive; restaurant not quite worth the price; somewhat anonymous surroundings of wealth. [$] *Rooms from: £800* ✉ *171 Knightsbridge, Knightsbridge* ☎ *020/7151–1010* 🌐 *www.bulgarihotels.com/en_US/london/the-hotel/overview* 🛏 *85 rooms* 🍴 *No Meals* [M] *Knightsbridge.*

The Capital Hotel

$$$ | HOTEL | Nothing is ever too much at this elegant hotel that was formerly a private house; mattresses are handmade, sheets are 450 thread count, bathrooms are marble, and everything is done in impeccable taste. **Pros:** excellent restaurant; beautiful space; handy for shopping at Harrods. **Cons:** neighborhood can be pricey; cheaper rooms are small for the price; breakfast is expensive. [$] *Rooms from: £274* ✉ *22–24 Basil St., Knightsbridge* ☎ *020/7589–5171, 800/926–3199 in U.S.* 🌐 *www.capitalhotel.co.uk* 🛏 *49 rooms* 🍴 *No Meals* [M] *Knightsbridge.*

★ The Egerton House Hotel

$$$ | HOTEL | FAMILY | This welcoming boutique hotel is an oasis of understated country-house chic in glitzy Knightsbridge, with guest rooms that don't stint on design touches like bold, rich textiles. **Pros:** striking art; personalized, attentive service; luxurious but comfortable design. **Cons:** on the pricier side; the traditional elegance won't appeal to everyone; some may find rooms overdecorated. [$] *Rooms from: £330* ✉ *17–19 Egerton Terr., Knightsbridge* ☎ *020/7589–2412, 877/955–1515 in U.S.* 🌐 *www.redcarnationhotels.com* 🛏 *29 rooms* 🍴 *Free Breakfast* [M] *Knightsbridge, South Kensington.*

★ The Lanesborough

$$$$ | HOTEL | The Lanesborough is like a beautiful, luxurious cocoon for the seriously wealthy, exuding Regency opulence from the design-magazine perfection of the bedrooms to the magnificent 19th-century antiques. **Pros:** everything—rooms, food, spa—is top-notch; beautiful and historic; great service, including a team of personal butlers. **Cons:** Hyde Park Corner is often clogged with heavy traffic; might be too fancy for some; prices are extraordinary. [$] *Rooms from: £860* ✉ *Hyde Park Corner, Knightsbridge* ☎ *020/7259–5599, 800/999–1828 in U.S.* 🌐 *www.lanesborough.com* 🛏 *93 rooms* 🍴 *Free Breakfast* [M] *Hyde Park Corner.*

★ Mandarin Oriental Hyde Park

$$$$ | HOTEL | Following an extensive renovation after a roof fire, the imposing Edwardian facade of this ultraluxe hotel on the edge of Hyde Park belies the modern and bright setting within that features spacious bedrooms filled with high-tech gadgets. **Pros:** excellent service; several rooms have balconies or terraces overlooking Hyde Park; spacious rooms and bathrooms. **Cons:** street outside often very busy; rooms on lower floors on Knightsbridge side may have traffic noise; nothing comes cheap. [$] *Rooms from: £845* ✉ *66 Knightsbridge, Knightsbridge* ☎ *020/7235–2000* 🌐 *www.mandarinoriental.com/london* 🛏 *181 rooms* 🍴 *No Meals* [M] *Knightsbridge.*

Nightlife

The Blue Bar at the Berkeley

BARS | With its Lutyens Blue walls, Edwardian plasterwork, white onyx bar, and black crocodile-print leather floor, this hotel bar oozes sultry sophistication. Immaculate service, an excellent seasonal cocktail list, and an extended glass pavilion make this an ideal spot for a romantic tête-à-tête, complete with a background soundtrack of lounge and deep house music. ✉ *The Berkeley, Wilton Pl., Knightsbridge* ☎ *020/7235–6000* 🌐 *www.the-berkeley.co.uk* [M] *Knightsbridge, Hyde Park Corner.*

Privée by Layalina

CABARET | Beneath an excellent Lebanese restaurant, you'll find this intimate nightclub space in the basement. Open only on weekends, it features a rotating program of live music, cabaret, nouveau burlesque, comedy, and karaoke. ✉ *2 Beauchamp Pl., Knightsbridge* ☎ *207/581–4296* 🌐 *www.layalina.co.uk/privee* [M] *Knightsbridge.*

Shopping

CLOTHING

egg

MIXED CLOTHING | Tucked away in a residential mews, this uncluttered shop in a former Victorian dairy is the brainchild of Maureen Doherty, once Issey Miyake's assistant who still shares his relaxed but cutting-edge aesthetic. More than half the minimalist, unstructured styles for men and women—in natural luxury fabrics such as silk, cashmere, antique cotton, or even felted Tibetan yak wool—are handmade. Garments may be casually hung on hooks or folded on wooden tables, but the price tags are anything but unassuming. The clientele includes the likes of Donna Karan and former British PM Theresa May. One-of-a-kind ceramics, scarves, blankets, bags, and jewelry are also on display. ✉ *36 Kinnerton St., Knightsbridge* ☎ *020/7235–9315* 🌐 *www.eggtrading.com* [M] *Knightsbridge.*

Rigby & Peller

LINGERIE | Many of London's most affluent women find their luxury lingerie (plus swimwear) here because the quality is excellent and the service impeccably knowledgeable—and perhaps because it's the Queen's favored underwear supplier and has provided maternity wear to the Duchess of Cambridge. Despite the upscale clientele, it's much friendlier than you might expect. Brands include PrimaDonna and Marie Jo as well as R&P's own line, and if the right fit eludes you, there's a made-to-measure service that starts at around £300. There are also branches in Mayfair, Chelsea, and St. John's Wood. ✉ *2 Hans Rd., Knightsbridge* ☎ *020/7225–4760* 🌐 *www.rigbyandpeller.com* [M] *Knightsbridge.*

DEPARTMENT STORES

Harvey Nichols

DEPARTMENT STORE | While visiting tourists flock to Harrods, local fashionistas shop at Harvey Nichols, aka "Harvey Nicks." The womenswear and accessories departments are outstanding, featuring top designers like Tom Ford, Loewe, Roland Mouret, Valentino, Tory Burch, and just about every fashionable name you can think of. The furniture and housewares are equally gorgeous (and pricey), although they become somewhat more affordable during the biannual sales in January and July. The Fifth Floor bar is the place to see and be seen, but if you're in search of food, the same floor also has an all-day Modern European café, a branch of Burger & Lobster, the carnivore-friendly Zelman Meats, or

Kenyan-Punjabi fusion from Madhu's Brasserie. To keep you looking as box-fresh as your purchases, the Beauty Lounge features a menu of treatments from brands such as La Prairie, Sisley, and La Mer, plus makeovers, LED facials, cryotherapy, thermotherapy, laser treatments, and blow-dry, nail, and brow bars. ✉ 109–125 Knightsbridge, Knightsbridge ☎ 020/7235–5000 ⊕ www.harveynichols. com Ⓜ Knightsbridge.

Belgravia

Steps away from the roaring traffic of Hyde Park Corner, lying just to the east of Kensington and Chelsea, is quiet, fashionable Belgravia, one of the most impressive set pieces of 19th-century urban planning. Street after street is lined with grand, cream-color stucco terraces, once aristocrats' town houses and most still part of the Grosvenor estate owned by the Duke of Westminster. Many buildings are leased to embassies or organizations, but a remarkable number around **Lowndes Square, Eaton Place,** and **Eaton Square** remain in the hands of private owners, whether old money or new oligarchs who put their security guards in the attached mews houses. Some people consider the area near **Elizabeth Street** to be southern Belgravia; others call it Pimlico-Victoria. Whatever its name, you'll find small, unique stores specializing in baked goods, children's wear, and gifts.

◉ Sights

Belgrave Square
PLAZA/SQUARE | This is the heart of Belgravia, once the preferred address for some of London's wealthiest, although it's now mostly occupied by organizations, embassies, and the international rich. The square and the streets leading off it share a remarkably consistent elegant architectural style thanks to all being part of a Regency redevelopment scheme commissioned by the Duke of Westminster and designed by Thomas Cubitt with George Basevi. The grand, cream-colored stucco terraced houses were snapped up by aristocrats and politicians due to their proximity to Buckingham Palace just around the corner, and still command record prices on the rare occasions when they come onto the market. The private garden in the center is open to the public once a year. Walk down Belgrave Place toward Eaton Place and you pass two of Belgravia's most beautiful mews: Eaton Mews North and Eccleston Mews, both fronted by grand rusticated entrances right out of a 19th-century engraving. Traffic can really whip around Belgrave Square, so be careful. ✉ Belgravia Ⓜ Hyde Park Corner.

🍴 Restaurants

Pétrus
$$$$ | **MODERN FRENCH** | Now in its third location, this Gordon Ramsay flagship offers fine dining to the max without being overly stuffy or cautious. The cooking combines superb technique with creativity, blending complex and intricate flavors in dishes like Orkney scallops with kombu, bacon, and sabayon; rich turbot with leeks in a seaweed beurre blanc; or Dorset beef in a charcuterie sauce. **Known for:** "preferred" business-casual dress code; Gordon Ramsay's flagship London restaurant; seasonal British ingredients with a French twist. Ⓢ Average main: £35 ✉ 1 Kinnerton St., Belgravia ☎ 020/7592–1609 ⊕ www.gordon-ramsayrestaurants.com/petrus ⊗ Closed Sun.–Tues. Ⓜ Knightsbridge, Hyde Park Corner.

Hotels

B&B Belgravia

$$ | **B&B/INN** | At this contemporary guesthouse near Victoria Station, minimalist decor, Scandinavian Modern furniture, and a lounge where a fire crackles away in the winter are all geared to homey comforts. **Pros:** superb value for money in a pricey area; nice extras like 24-hour complimentary tea and coffee; bike hire included. **Cons:** books up far in advance; some decor and mattresses tired; rooms and bathrooms are small. [$] *Rooms from: £165* ✉ *64–66 Ebury St., Belgravia* ☎ *020/7259–8570* 🌐 *www.bb-belgravia.com* 🛏 *17 rooms* 🍴 *Free Breakfast* [M] *Sloane Sq., Victoria.*

Lime Tree Hotel

$$ | **HOTEL** | In a central neighborhood where hotels veer from wildly overpriced at one extreme to grimy bolt-holes at the other, the Lime Tree gets the boutique style just about right—and at a surprisingly reasonable cost for the neighborhood. **Pros:** rooms are decent size; lovely and helpful hosts; great location. **Cons:** lack of amenities; some are up several flights of stairs and there's no elevator; cheaper rooms are small. [$] *Rooms from: £205* ✉ *135–137 Ebury St., Belgravia* ☎ *020/7730–8191* 🌐 *www.limetreehotel.co.uk* 🛏 *27 rooms* 🍴 *No Meals* [M] *Victoria, Sloane Sq.*

Studios@82

$$ | **APARTMENT** | A side operation from B&B Belgravia located eight doors down from the mothership (where you check in), these self-contained, serviced studio apartments with kitchenettes offer great value for the location. **Pros:** all the independence of self-catering; great rates; central but quiet location. **Cons:** can be subject to street noise; no major amenities; lots of stairs and no elevator. [$] *Rooms from: £157* ✉ *82 Ebury St., Belgravia* ☎ *020/7259–8570* 🌐 *www.bb-belgravia.com* 🛏 *9 studio apartments* 🍴 *Free Breakfast* [M] *Knightsbridge.*

Shopping

ACCESSORIES

★ Philip Treacy

HATS & GLOVES | Magnificent hats by Treacy are annual showstoppers on Ladies' Day at the Royal Ascot races and regularly grace the glossy magazines' party and catwalk pages. Part Mad Hatter, part Cecil Beaton, Treacy's creations always guarantee a grand entrance and are favorites with everyone from Lady Gaga to Kate Middleton. In addition to the extravagant, haute couture hats handmade in the atelier, less flamboyant ready-to-wear hats are also for sale, as are some bags. ✉ *69 Elizabeth St., Belgravia* ☎ *020/7730–3992* 🌐 *www.philiptreacy.co.uk* [M] *Sloane Sq.*

SPECIALTY STORES

Mungo & Maud

PET STORES | If you don't want to leave London without buying something for your pet, Mungo & Maud has something for your furry friend. Pick up a well-designed coat, leash, harness, bowl, toy, or comfortable bed that will make your dog the snazziest pooch in town (some collars are hand-stitched), or select from baskets, suede collars, and blankets for your cat. Even owners get a nod with luxurious merino throws (soon to be covered in pet hair), pet-themed jewelry, and leather "poop bag" pouches. ✉ *79 Elizabeth St., Belgravia* ☎ *020/7467–0823* 🌐 *www.mungoandmaud.com* [M] *Sloane Sq.*

Papouelli

OTHER SPECIALTY STORE | This small shop is full of well-made yet fun shoes for kids of all ages and genders. Your budding influencer will love the boots and shoes in leopard print or silver leather. The store also sells socks and tights, plus a small range of hats, gloves, and hair accessories. There's another branch on King's Road near Parsons Green. ✉ *51 Elizabeth St., Belgravia* ☎ *207/730–6690* 🌐 *www.papouelli.com* [M] *Sloane Sq.*

NOTTING HILL AND BAYSWATER

11

Updated by
James O'Neill

◉ Sights	🍴 Restaurants	🛏 Hotels	🛍 Shopping	🍸 Nightlife
★★☆☆☆	★★★☆☆	★★★☆☆	★★★★☆	★★★☆☆

NOTTING HILL AND BAYSWATER SNAPSHOT

TOP REASONS TO GO

Portobello Road: If you're serious about snapping up a bargain at the world-famous antiques market, it's best to go before 10 am on Saturday. Alternatively, if you're just looking to absorb the eclectic vibe, come during the week for a leisurely browse.

Holland Park: An often-overlooked gem, this is arguably London's most romantic green space, complete with woodland walks, a Jacobean mansion, open-air theater, and opera in the summer; there's even a gorgeous Japanese-style garden with a waterfall.

Notting Hill's picturesque streets and squares: From the grandeur of Lansdowne Road and Stanley Crescent to the west of Kensington Park Road, to the pastel-colored hues of Chepstow Villas to the east, this is residential London at its finest and most seductive.

GETTING THERE

For Portobello Market and environs, the best Tube stops are Ladbroke Grove and Westbourne Park (Hammersmith and City line); ask for directions when you emerge. The Notting Hill Gate stop on the District, Circle, and Central lines enables you to walk the length of Portobello Road while going slightly downhill.

MAKING THE MOST OF YOUR TIME

Saturday is the most exciting day for shopping, eating, and drinking here. The market gets crowded by noon in summer, so come early if you're serious about shopping. Head south from the north end of Portobello Road, using the parks to take a break on the way. On Sunday, the Hyde Park and Kensington Gardens railings along Bayswater Road are lined with artists displaying their work, which may slow your progress.

A GOOD WALK

■ Beginning at Lancaster Road, arguably the prettiest street in London with its colorfully painted Victorian houses, lazily snake your way down and across Portobello Road toward Notting Hill Gate tube. Wander along very cute St. Lukes Mews, home to the pink house where Keira Knightley was wooed on her doorstep by a man carrying a whole pile of cue cards in the hit rom-com *Love Actually*. Get lost among the pastel-colored houses of Westbourne Grove to the east and the stately grandeur of Kensington Park Gardens and Ladbroke Square to the west. Just beyond the Tube, more modest yet still gorgeous Hillgate Place and its surrounding streets provide a pretty pocket of unexpected tranquillity.

SAFETY

■ At night, avoid straying from the main streets north of Westbourne Park Road toward Ladbroke Grove's high-rise estates and the surrounding areas.

The center of London's West Indian community from the 1950s through the '70s, Notting Hill these days is the address of choice for the well heeled, be they bankers, rock stars, media and advertising types, or rich hippies.

Teeming with trendy restaurants, cool bars, and buzzing street markets, the area is also studded with some of London's most handsome historic residences, crescents, and terraces. Every weekend, the hordes descend on Portobello Road to go bargain hunting at one of the world's great antiques markets. Holland Park, to the west, has even grander villas, while Bayswater, to the east, has excellent world-cuisine restaurants.

Notting Hill

Notting Hill began life under the less enticing name of "The Potteries and the Piggeries," on account of the prominence of the ceramic and pig-farming industries in the area in the early 19th century. Indeed, a well-preserved brick kiln is still visible on Walmer Road, just north of aptly named Pottery Lane.

In the 1840s, the wealthy Ladbroke family decided to revamp the area into a high-end estate aimed at attracting London's wealthy elites. Their plans didn't quite work out, and soon many of the large, grand houses of Notting Hill were split into multiple occupancies and rented out to immigrant laborers. Most notably, the area saw the arrival of Irish workers lured by the Victorian building boom, and then later a wave of West Indian immigration in the 1950s.

The 1980s saw a process of gentrification that transformed Notting Hill from a lively but down-at-heel and sometimes dangerous enclave to a super-trendy fashionable neighborhood. The area's Caribbean legacy persists, however, not least in the form of the annual Notting Hill Carnival in late August.

Of course, Notting Hill's fame went global thanks to the hit rom-com of the same. name, though the movie itself was criticized by locals for downplaying the area's cultural diversity. For the Notting Hill of the silver screen, head for fashionable **Westbourne Grove** and **Ledbury Road,** lined with high-end independent boutiques offering designer goods for the home and family, as well as contemporary art.

For less rarefied shopping, try **Portobello Road**; the famous Saturday antiques market and shops are at the southern end. A little farther southwest lies the understated splendor of **Holland Park,** at the end of which you'll find the exotic delights of the **Leighton House Museum.**

Sights

Design Museum
ART MUSEUM | Located in the former Commonwealth Institute, this museum was the first in the United Kingdom to place everyday contemporary objects in a social and cultural context and to consider their role in the history of design. A

Within Holland Park, you'll find the tranquil Kyoto Garden and its Japanese maple trees, dahlias, and a koi pond.

free, permanent exhibition displays some 1,000 examples of 20th- and 21st-century design—from furniture, fashion, and domestic products to digital technology, architecture, and engineering. The temporary exhibitions may be focused on leading individual designers, such as Charles and Ray Eames, Isamu Noguchi, Terence Conran, or David Adjaye, on themes such as the global influence of Californian design, or on the role of design in related art forms, like an exhibition devoted to the work of film director Stanley Kubrick. There's also a design library and archive, two shops, a café, and a restaurant. ■TIP→ **Young designers ages 5–11 may enjoy the free, drop-in "Create and Make" workshops held the last Sunday of every month.** ⊠ *224–238 Kensington High St., Kensington* ☎ *0203/862-5900* ⊕ *www.designmuseum.org* ⊠ *Free (charge for temporary exhibitions)* Ⓜ *High St. Kensington.*

Graffik Gallery

ART MUSEUM | Not everyone thinks graffiti can be a bonus to the urban landscape, but those who do should head for this leading gallery of contemporary street art. The big name here is Banksy, but there are works for sale by several other artists in the same vein, such as TRUST, iCON and Code FC, who are more concerned with social commentary than tagging. Check out the two-hour graffiti workshops, running weekdays at 4 pm and weekends at 11 am and 1 pm (book at least a week in advance). ⊠ *284 Portobello Rd., Notting Hill* ☎ *020/8354–3592* ⊕ *www.graffikgallery.co.uk* ⊠ *Free* Ⓜ *Notting Hill Gate, Ladbroke Grove.*

Holland Park

CITY PARK | FAMILY | Formerly the grounds of a 17th-century aristocrat's manor house and open to the public only since 1952, Holland Park is an often-overlooked gem in the heart of London. The northern "Wilderness" end offers woodland walks among native and exotic trees first planted in the early 18th century. Foxes, rabbits, and hedgehogs are among the residents. The central part of the park is given over to the manicured lawns—still stalked by raucous peacocks—one would expect at a stately home, although Holland House itself, originally built by James I's chancellor and later the site of a 19th-century salon frequented by Byron, Dickens, and Disraeli, was largely destroyed by German bombs in 1940. The east wing was reconstructed and has been incorporated into a youth hostel, while the remains of the front terrace provide an atmospheric backdrop for the open-air performances of the April–September Holland Park Opera Festival (⊕ www.operahollandpark.com). The glass-walled Orangery garden ballroom now hosts events and art exhibitions, as does the Ice House, while an adjoining former granary has become the upscale Belvedere restaurant. In spring and summer, the air is fragrant with aromas from a rose garden, great banks of rhododendrons, and an azalea walk. Garden enthusiasts will also not want to miss the tranquil, traditional Kyoto Garden with its pretty waterfall, a legacy of London's 1991 Japan Festival.

The southern part of the park is devoted to sport and play: cricket and soccer pitches; a golf practice area; tennis courts; a well-supervised children's Adventure Playground (with a zip line!); and a giant outdoor chess set. ⊠ Ilchester Pl., West Holland Park ⊕ www.rbkc.gov.uk/leisure-and-culture/parks/holland-park Ⓜ Holland Park, High St. Kensington.

★ **Leighton House Museum**

ART MUSEUM | Leading Victorian artist Frederic (Lord) Leighton lived and worked in this building on the edge of Holland Park, spending 30 years (and quite a bit of money) transforming it into an opulent "private palace of art" infused with a global aesthetic sensibility. The interior is a sumptuous Middle Eastern theme:

marvel at peacock-blue tiled walls and beautiful mosaic wall panels and floors, marble pillars, and gilded ceilings. The centerpiece is the Arab Hall, its marble walls adorned with intricate murals made from 16th- and 17th-century ceramic tiles imported from the Middle East, surmounted by a domed ceiling covered in gold leaf with a gold mosaic frieze running underneath. You can also visit Leighton's studio, with its huge north window and dome, or dine in the delightful garden café. ⊠ 12 Holland Park Rd., West Holland Park ☎ 020/7602–3316 weekdays, 020/7471–9160 weekends ⊕ www.rbkc.gov.uk/subsites/museums/leightonhousemuseum1.aspx ☞ £9 ☉ Closed Tues. Ⓜ Holland Park, South Kensington.

Museum of Brands

OTHER MUSEUM | This quirky museum is a fascinating cabinet of curiosities that explores how advertising and marketing has pervaded our lives for the last 150 years. There's much to catch and delight the eyes, from branded toys, clothes, and spin-off TV show board games to the world's first portable gramophone and World War II–era products, such as a toilet paper roll that has Hitler's face on every sheet. ⊠ 111–117 Lancaster Rd., Notting Hill ☎ 020/7243–9611 ⊕ www.museumofbrands.com ☞ £9 Ⓜ Ladbroke Grove.

★ **Portobello Road Market**

MARKET | Looking for a 19th-century snuff spoon? Perhaps a Georgian salt cellar? What about a 1960s-era minidress? Then head to Portobello Road's famous Saturday market—and arrive at about 9 am to avoid the giant crowds. Stretching almost 2 miles from Notting Hill, the market is made up of four sections, each with a different emphasis: antiques, fresh produce, household goods, and a flea market. The antiques stalls are packed in between Chepstow Villas and Westbourne Grove, where you'll also find almost 100 antiques shops plus indoor

11

Notting Hill and Bayswater NOTTING HILL

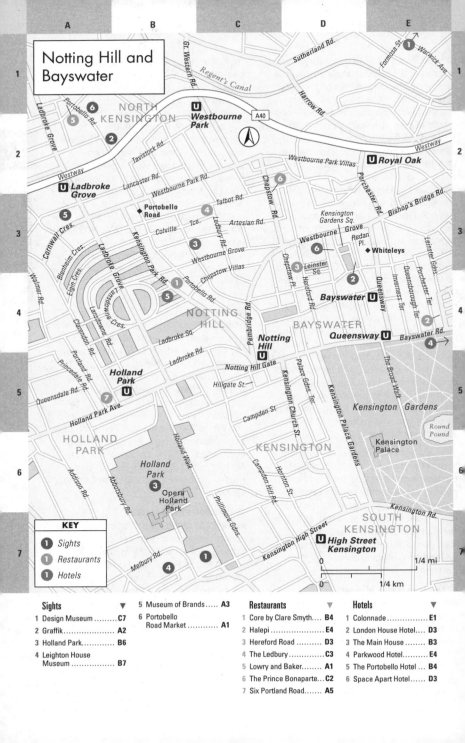

Notting Hill and Bayswater

KEY

- ❶ Sights
- ❶ Restaurants
- ❶ Hotels

markets, which are open on weekdays, when shopping is much less hectic. Where the road levels off, around Elgin Crescent, youth culture and a vibrant neighborhood life kicks in, with a variety of interesting small stores and food stalls interspersed with a fruit-and-vegetable market.

On Friday and Saturday the section between Talbot Road and the Westway elevated highway becomes one of London's best flea markets, specializing in discounted new household goods, while north of the Westway you'll find secondhand household goods and bric-a-brac. Scattered throughout, but especially under the Westway, are vendors selling a mishmash of designer, vintage, and secondhand clothing, together with jewelry, custom T-shirts, and assorted junk. There's a Trinidad-style Carnival centered on Portobello Road on the late August bank-holiday weekend, a tribute to the area's past as a center of the West Indian community. ✉ *Notting Hill* 🌐 *www.portobelloroad.co.uk* [M] *Notting Hill Gate, Ladbroke Grove.*

🍴 Restaurants

Ever since Hugh Grant and Julia Roberts starred in *Notting Hill* and put the area on the global map, Notting Hill's had a reputation as London's most glamorous neighborhood, with its myriad boutiques, chic cafés, patisseries, restaurants, bars, pubs, and the famous Portobello Road Market's collection of antiques shops, vintage-clothing stands, and food stalls. Portobello is one of London's most popular street markets, so get there early on Saturday morning (the market is open 9–7) to beat the crowds. Peruse the antiques and vintage clothes stalls, and when you want to eat, head to the north end where you'll find fresh fruit-and-veg stalls, artisan bakeries, and rare Spanish olive and French cheese purveyors, plus numerous hot-food stalls peddling savory crepes, gourmet hamburgers, spicy German chicken rolls, paella, Moroccan kebabs, and Malaysian noodles.

★ Core by Clare Smyth

$$$$ | MODERN BRITISH | FAMILY | With two Michelin stars above the door, chef Clare Smyth fuses her classical French culinary training with a devotion to quality British produce. Must-try dishes include Isle of Harris scallop tartare with sea vegetable consommé and cèpe tartlet with egg yolk, thyme, and toasted yeast. **Known for:** three-course à la carte or nine-course tasting menus; brilliant vegetable and fish dishes elevated to the highest levels; relaxed, smart, casual dining experience. [$] *Average main: £125* ✉ *92 Kensington Park Rd., Notting Hill* ☎ *020/3937–5086* 🌐 *www.corebyclaresmyth.com* ⏲ *Closed Sun. and Mon.* [M] *Notting Hill Gate, Labroke Grove.*

★ The Ledbury

$$$$ | MODERN FRENCH | FAMILY | Acclaimed Aussie chef Brett Graham and his team are known for modern European cuisine at its finest, and the sheer inventiveness and quality of the food on offer make for a very special night out. Global gourmands will struggle to find a more inventive vegetable dish than Graham's white beetroot baked in clay with goat's cheese and hazelnuts, and it's impossible to best his ultrapretty, precise, and complex mains. **Known for:** signature brown sugar tart with stem ginger ice cream for dessert; creative vegetable dishes like white asparagus soup with lemon, grapes, and ricotta; excellent game like Berkshire muntjac with endive cooked in grilled oil. [$] *Average main: £40* ✉ *127 Ledbury Rd., Notting Hill* ☎ *0207/7792–9090* 🌐 *www.theledbury.com* ⏲ *No lunch Mon. and Tues.* [M] *Westbourne Park, Ladbroke Grove.*

Lowry & Baker

$ | CAFÉ | Located on the northern stretch of Portobello Road, this quintessential neighborhood café specializes in delicious coffee, cakes, breakfast, and brunch, all served up on classic English crockery. Grab one of the outside tables and watch Notting Hill wander by. **Known for:** build-your-own breakfasts and brunches; great vegan and gluten-free options; chill, welcoming vibe. $ *Average main: £10* ⊠ *339 Portobello Rd., Notting Hill* ☎ *020/8960–8534* ⊕ *www.lowryandbaker.co.uk* ⊗ *No dinner* Ⓜ *Ladbroke Grove.*

★ Six Portland Road

$$$ | FRENCH | FAMILY | The ultimate neighborhood restaurant in west London's wealthy Holland Park section draws diners with its brilliant-but-understated French and Mediterranean classics, relaxed service, and interesting, mainly French wines. Treat yourself to bouillabaisse Provençale or ox cheek bourguignon with button mushrooms and pearl onions. **Known for:** winning boutique wine list; intimate seating; unpretentious but pitch-perfect service. $ *Average main: £24* ⊠ *6 Portland Rd., Notting Hill* ☎ *020/7229–3130* ⊕ *www.sixportlandroad.com* Ⓜ *Holland Park.*

Hotels

★ The Main House

$$ | B&B/INN | This wonderfully welcoming boutique hotel is a little gem. **Pros:** room prices decrease for longer stays; elegant and peaceful oasis in the heart of the city; charming and helpful owners. **Cons:** small number of rooms means availability can be limited; few in-house services; not for those who like the hustle and bustle of a big hotel. $ *Rooms from: £130* ⊠ *6 Colvile Rd., Notting Hill* ☎ *020/7221–9691* ⊕ *www.themainhouse.co.uk* ⇴ *4 rooms* ⌾ *No Meals* Ⓜ *Notting Hill Gate.*

The Portobello Hotel

$$ | HOTEL | One of London's quirkiest hotels, The Portobello (formed from two adjoining Victorian houses) has attracted scores of celebrities to its small but stylish rooms over the years, and the decor reflects these hip credentials with joyous abandon. **Pros:** guests have use of nearby gym and pool; stylish and unique; pets are allowed. **Cons:** a continental breakfast is included in the price, but cooked breakfasts are extra; may be too eccentric for some; all but the priciest rooms are quite small. $ *Rooms from: £180* ⊠ *22 Stanley Gardens, Notting Hill* ☎ *020/7727–2777* ⊕ *www.portobellohotel.com* ⇴ *21 rooms* ⌾ *Free Breakfast* Ⓜ *Notting Hill Gate.*

Nightlife

The focus is more on bars than clubs in this west London neighborhood, although late-night fun is on offer at a few notable exceptions. In general, you can expect a young moneyed crowd making this their first stop on a wild night out elsewhere. The line between pub and bar is frequently blurred here, with an emphasis on good—often haute—food, sleek style, and extensive wine lists.

BARS

★ Beach Blanket Babylon

BARS | In a Victorian mansion house close to Portobello Market, this always-packed bar is distinguishable by its eclectic indoor-outdoor spaces with Gaudí-esque curves and snug corners—like a candlelit fairy-tale grotto, folly, or medieval crypt. Also perfect for an alfresco lunch or intimate dinner, the cocktails here are the star of the show. ⊠ *45 Ledbury Rd., Notting Hill* ☎ *020/7229–2907* ⊕ *www.beachblanket.co.uk* Ⓜ *Notting Hill Gate.*

Electric Diner

BARS | FAMILY | A huge selection of bottled beers and quirky twists on classic cocktails are the big attractions at this bar and diner next to Notting Hill's famed Electric Cinema on Portobello Road. Run by the people behind the members-only Soho House, the place exudes the same effortless mixture of posh and cool, but it is open to anyone and everyone. Sit in the window and watch the world go by or opt for one of the luxury takes on classic diner fare at a booth in the moody, vaulted interior. ⊠ *191 Portobello Rd., Notting Hill* ☎ *020/7908–9696* ⊕ *www.electricdiner.com* Ⓜ *Ladbroke Grove.*

The Tabernacle

GATHERING PLACES | The Victorian Gothic interior of this bar, café, and arts center combo hosts intimate music gigs, art exhibitions, and 15-minute talks with speakers such as historian Niall Ferguson. The food is Caribbean-influenced, and the atmosphere, especially in the outdoor courtyard, is friendly and relaxed. ⊠ *34–35 Powis Sq., Notting Hill* ☎ *020/7221–9700* ⊕ *www.thetabernaclew11.com* Ⓜ *Notting Hill Gate.*

PUBS

The Cow

PUBS | **FAMILY** | This boho-chic Irish pub is all about the Guinness and the superb, if pricey, seafood. Whether you're in the unpretentious downstairs saloon bar or the more formal dining rooms upstairs, the atmosphere is always warm, welcoming, and buzzing. It's also a favorite haunt of fashion glitterati such as Stella McCartney, Victoria Beckham, and Alexa Chung. ⊠ *89 Westbourne Park Rd., Notting Hill* ☎ *020/7221–0021* ⊕ *www.thecowlondon.co.uk* Ⓜ *Westbourne Park, Royal Oak.*

⏣ Performing Arts

This cosmopolitan west London neighborhood, shown to advantage in the 1999 film of the same name, is best known for the Notting Hill Carnival, a lively music-focused street festival that takes over the wider area on the final weekend of August each year. There's a year-round culture scene, too, catering mainly to the neighborhood's trendy young professionals.

FILM

The Electric Cinema

FILM | **FAMILY** | One of the oldest cinemas in the country, this refurbished Portobello Road art house screens mainstream and international movies. The emphasis is on comfort, with leather sofas, armchairs, side tables for your wine and appetizers, cashmere blankets, and even double beds in the front row. ⊠ *191 Portobello Rd., Notting Hill* ☎ *020/7908–9696* ⊕ *www.electriccinema.co.uk* ⊠ *From £25* Ⓜ *Ladbroke Grove, Notting Hill Gate.*

OPERA

Opera Holland Park

OPERA | **FAMILY** | In summer, well-loved operas and imaginative productions of lesser-known works are presented under a spectacular canopy against the remains of Holland House, one of the first great houses built in Kensington. The company has successfully branched out into opera for families in recent years, too. There are 1,200 tickets offered free to those ages 7–18 every season. Tickets go on general sale in April (earlier for members). After the opera season is over in August, the venue hosts under-the-stars showings of recent movies on a giant screen. ⊠ *Holland Park, Kensington High St., Kensington* ☎ *0300/999–1000 for box office (opens Apr.), 020/3846–6222 for inquiries* ⊕ *www.operahollandpark.com* ⊠ *From £20* Ⓜ *High St. Kensington, Holland Park.*

Shopping

BOOKS

★ Books for Cooks

BOOKS | It may seem odd to describe a bookshop as delicious smelling, but on several days you can't help but notice the aromas wafting out of the tiny café in the back of this cookbook shop, where the resident chef cooks a three-course set lunch for only £7, served from noon on Tuesday through Friday (it's first come, first served, so get there early). The dishes are drawn from recipes in the 8,000 cookbooks on the shelves. Just about every world cuisine is represented, along with a complete lineup of works by celebrity chefs. Before you come to London, visit the shop's website to sign up for a specialized cooking workshop in the upstairs demonstration kitchen. ⊠ *4 Blenheim Crescent, Notting Hill* ☎ *020/7221–1992* ⊕ *www.booksforcooks.com* Ⓜ *Notting Hill Gate, Ladbroke Grove.*

CLOTHING

Aimé

MIXED CLOTHING | French-Cambodian sisters Val and Vanda Heng-Vong launched this shop to showcase the best of French clothing and designer housewares. Expect to find cult French labels like Isabel Marant, forte_forte, and A.P.C., along with housewares and gorgeous ceramics. Aimé has now launched its first in-house label that promises everyday style with a French twist. There's also a Shoreditch branch. ✉ *32 Ledbury Rd., Notting Hill* ☎ *020/7221–7070* ⊕ *www.aimelondon.com* Ⓜ *Notting Hill Gate.*

Caramel Baby & Child

CHILDREN'S CLOTHING | FAMILY | This is the place for adorable yet understated clothes for children six months and up. You'll find everything from 100% cotton baby romper suits to a fab selection of floral dresses, gingham shirts, and handcrafted alpaca and merino jerseys, as well as twill, corduroy, and cotton pants. Kids' accessories range from charming mittens and beanies to cool sunglasses and superchic hair bands and clips. A sister shop farther along Ledbury Road (No. 38b) offers moms the chance to buy clothing in a similar vein. Caramel also sells a small selection of children's books as well as decorative functional items like sleeping bags, lamps, and quilts. Prices aren't cheap, but the quality is superb. Every Tuesday and Saturday, the shop offers a hair salon for little customers. There's another branch in South Kensington and outlets in Selfridges and Harrods. ✉ *77 Ledbury Rd., Notting Hill* ☎ *020/7727–0906* ⊕ *www.caramel-shop.co.uk* Ⓜ *Westbourne Park, Notting Hill Gate.*

The Cross

MIXED CLOTHING | Exquisitely situated on a corner of Portland Road, this west London gem was one of the city's first "lifestyle boutiques" and is still one of the best. The shop carries luxury casual fashion from the likes of Vanessa Bruno and Velvet, plus housewares, accessories, and jewelry. The accent here is on feminine, quirky boho chic. ✉ *141 Portland Rd., Notting Hill* ☎ *020/7727–6760* ⊕ *www.thecrossshop.co.uk* Ⓜ *Holland Park.*

Rellik

SECOND-HAND | Now in the modernist landmark known as the Trellick Tower and favored by the likes of Kate Moss, Rellik began as a stall in Portobello Road Market. Vintage hunters looking to splurge can find a selection of YSL, Dior, Pierre Cardin, and Ossie Clark as well as items from lesser-known designers. ✉ *Trellick Tower, 8 Golborne Rd., Notting Hill* ☎ *020/8962–0089* ⊕ *www.relliklondon.co.uk* Ⓜ *Westbourne Park.*

MUSIC

Music & Video Exchange

MUSIC | This store is a music collector's treasure trove, with a constantly changing stock refreshed by customers selling and exchanging as well as buying. The ground floor focuses on rock, pop, indie, and punk, both mainstream and obscure, in a variety of formats ranging from vinyl to CD, cassette, and even minidisk. Don't miss the classical music in the basement and the soul, jazz, house, techno, reggae, and more upstairs. Like movies? There's a wide variety of Blu-ray and DVD box sets, as well as bargain classic and cult films. Keep an eye out for rarities—including first pressings and one-offs—in all departments. Similar exchanges for comics (No. 32) and books (No. 30) are on nearby Pembridge Road (also a destination for vintage clothing for men [No. 28] and women [Nos. 16 and 20]). Just keep in mind that stock depends on what customers bring in to exchange, so you'll surely find many more DVDs with European (PAL) formatting than the North American–friendly NTSC format, but the store does get the latter occasionally. ✉ *38 Notting Hill Gate, Notting Hill* ☎ *020/3404–5200* 🌐 *www.mgeshops.com* [M] *Notting Hill Gate.*

SHOES

Emma Hope

SHOES | The signature look of the footwear here is elegant and feminine, with pointed toes and kitten heels, often ornamented with bows, lace, crystals, or exquisite embroidery (such craftsmanship doesn't come cheap, unfortunately). Ballet flats and sneakers in velvet or animal prints provide glamour without sacrificing comfort. There's also a selection of shoes and sneakers for men. ✉ *207 Westbourne Grove, Notting Hill* ☎ *020/7792–7800* 🌐 *www.emmahope.com* [M] *Notting Hill Gate.*

Bayswater

East of Notting Hill Gate Tube station, Notting Hill turns into Bayswater, with its wide streets and imposing white stucco terraced houses. Known in medieval times as Bayswatering on account of the stream where you could literally lead your horse to water, the neighborhood as we know it burst into life in the 1850s. Once the preserve of cheap bed-and-breakfasts, the area has begun to gentrify in recent years, drawing people to its excellent world cuisine restaurants.

Nearby **Paddington Station** is as well known for its association with the world's most famous marmalade fan, Paddington Bear, as it is for being one of London's more handsome rail terminals.

🍴 Restaurants

Halepi

$ | **GREEK** | Run by the same Greek-Cypriot family since 1966, this friendly taverna is a local institution. With its rustic interior and a mouthwatering menu of Greek culinary classics, it's the perfect spot for a leisurely lunch or a memorable evening out. **Known for:** authentic Greek food, perfectly done; relaxed, informal vibe; excellent oven-cooked lamb. [$] *Average main: £15* ✉ *18 Leinster Terrace, Bayswater* ☎ *020/7262–1070* 🌐 *halepi-restaurant.co.uk* [M] *Bayswater, Queensway.*

Hereford Road

$$ | **MODERN BRITISH** | **FAMILY** | A Bayswater favorite with the well-connected Notting Hill set, Hereford Road is renowned for its pared-down, pomp-free, and ingredient-driven seasonal British fare, with an emphasis on well-sourced regional British produce. Work your way through uncluttered combos like smoked cod's roe with rocket and breadcrumbs, braised duck leg and carrots, or buttermilk pudding with poached pear. **Known for:** famously affordable two- and three-course set lunches; pared-back Modern British nose-to-tail dining; deceptively simple-sounding dishes like duck livers with green beans. [$] *Average main: £18* ✉ *3 Hereford Rd., Bayswater* ☎ *020/7727–1144* 🌐 *www.herefordroad.org* ⏲ *No lunch Mon.–Wed.* [M] *Bayswater, Queensway.*

The Prince Bonaparte

$ | **BRITISH** | A laid-back, airy, art deco–inspired gastropub serving up quality Modern British food, the Prince Bonaparte offers a fine selection of ales and carefully chosen wines. A stone's throw from Portobello Market, it's the perfect place for a drink or a bite to eat. **Known for:** legendary Sunday roasts; relaxed and friendly atmosphere; super-helpful wait and bar staff. [$] *Average main: £15* ✉ *80 Chepstow Rd., Bayswater* ☎ *020/7313–9491* 🌐 *www.theprincebonapartew2.co.uk* [M] *Notting Hill Gate, Royal Oak.*

🛏 Hotels

The Colonnade Hotel

$$ | **HOTEL** | Near a canal filled with colorful narrow boats in the Little Venice neighborhood, this lovely town house offers individually styled rooms, some with rich brocades, velvets, and antiques,

others with balconies. **Pros:** cool history; beautifully decorated; unique and little-known part of London by Regent's Canal. **Cons:** not the closest location for visiting major sights; rooms are small; you have to go through shoddier parts of town to get here. [$] *Rooms from: £150* ✉ *2 Warrington Crescent, Bayswater* ☎ *020/7286–1052* 🌐 *www.colonnadehotel.co.uk* 🛏 *43 rooms* 🍴 *Free Breakfast* [M] *Warwick Ave.*

London House Hotel
$ | **HOTEL** | Set in a row of white Georgian town houses, this excellent budget option in hit-or-miss Bayswater is friendly, well run, and spotlessly clean. **Pros:** good location; complimentary Wi-Fi; emphasis on value. **Cons:** the area isn't quite as vibrant as neighboring Notting Hill; smallest rooms are tiny; basement rooms lack sunlight. [$] *Rooms from: £110* ✉ *81 Kensington Garden Sq., Bayswater* ☎ *020/7243–1810* 🌐 *www.londonhousehotels.com* 🛏 *103 rooms* 🍴 *No Meals* [M] *Queensway, Bayswater.*

Parkwood Hotel
$$ | **B&B/INN** | Perfectly located just steps from the tranquility of Hyde Park to the south and the hustle and bustle of Oxford Street to the east, this sweet guesthouse oozes warmth, homeliness, and good value. **Pros:** hotel guarantees to match or beat rate of any other hotel of its class in the area; fascinating but ghastly nearby history; free Wi-Fi. **Cons:** front-facing rooms can be noisy; no elevator and no ground-floor bedrooms; often booked up in advance. [$] *Rooms from: £130* ✉ *4 Stanhope Pl., Bayswater* ☎ *020/7402–2241* 🌐 *www.london-parkwood.com* 🛏 *16 rooms* 🍴 *Free Breakfast* [M] *Marble Arch.*

Space Apart Hotel
$ | **APARTMENT** | These studio apartments near Hyde Park are done in soothing tones of white and gray, with polished wood floors and attractive modern kitchenettes equipped with all you need to make small meals. **Pros:** handy location; especially good value; the larger suites have space for four people. **Cons:** standard apartments are small; two-night minimum stay; no in-house restaurant or bar. [$] *Rooms from: £120* ✉ *36–37 Kensington Gardens Sq., Bayswater* ☎ *020/7908–1340* 🌐 *www.aparthotel-london.co.uk* 🛏 *30 rooms* 🍴 *No Meals* [M] *Bayswater.*

REGENT'S PARK AND HAMPSTEAD

12

Updated by
Ellin Stein

⊙ **Sights** 🍴 **Restaurants** 🛏 **Hotels** 🛍 **Shopping** 🍸 **Nightlife**

★★★★☆   ★★☆☆☆   ★★☆☆☆   ★★★☆☆   ★★★☆☆

REGENT'S PARK AND HAMPSTEAD SNAPSHOT

TOP REASONS TO GO

Hampstead Heath: Londoners adore the Heath for providing an escape to the countryside without leaving the city.

Keats House: Visit the rooms where one of England's greatest poets wrote some of his major works, inspired by his love for the girl next door, Fanny Brawne.

Regent's Park: Cycle past Nash's grand neoclassical stucco terraces or walk up Primrose Hill for a great view over the city.

Kenwood House: See one of Britain's best art collections at this 18th-century gentleman's estate largely designed by Robert Adam.

London Zoo: A VIP ticket will let you get up close and personal with the penguins at the city's zoo.

GETTING THERE

To get to Hampstead by Tube, take the Northern line (the Edgware branch) to Hampstead or Golders Green Station, or take the London Overground to Hampstead Heath Station. The south side of Hampstead Heath can also be reached by the London Overground Gospel Oak Station. To get to Regent's Park, take the Bakerloo line to Regent's Park Tube station or, for Primrose Hill, the Chalk Farm stop on the Northern line. Little Venice is reachable by the Warwick Avenue stop on the Bakerloo line, and St. John's Wood has its own stop on the Jubilee line.

MAKING THE MOST OF YOUR TIME

■ Regent's Park, Primrose Hill, and Hampstead can be covered in a day. Spend the morning in Hampstead, with a brief foray onto the Heath, then head south to Regent's Park in the afternoon so that you're closer to central London come nightfall, if that is where your hotel is located. (You'll also be heading downhill instead of up.) You can always return to Hampstead another day for a long walk across the Heath or to head west to Little Venice's canals.

SAFETY

■ Avoid Hampstead Heath, Primrose Hill, and Regent's Park at night unless there's an event; all are perfectly safe during the day. Also to be avoided after dark: the canal towpath in Primrose Hill and Camden Town.

Regent's Park, Primrose Hill, Belsize Park, and Hampstead are four of London's prettiest and most genteel neighborhoods. The city becomes noticeably calmer and greener as you head uphill from Marylebone Road through Regent's Park to the refreshing greenery of Primrose Hill and the handsome Georgian houses and Regency villas of Hampstead. To the west, the less bucolic but equally elegant St. John's Wood and Little Venice also provide a taste of moneyed London.

Leaving the park at London Zoo, walk up adjoining **Primrose Hill** for one of the most picturesque views of London. Long a magnet for the creative (though these days within reach of only the most well-heeled creatives), this is the kind of neighborhood where the local library's screening of *The Madness of King George* is introduced by its writer, long-time resident Alan Bennett. Peel off from the Hill to explore Regent's Park Road and its attractive independent shops and cafés, as well as the surrounding streets with their pastel Victorian villas.

Alternatively, continue hugging the Hill heading north along Primrose Hill Road. This will take you to Belsize Park, itself a celebrity hot spot (Tim Burton and Hugh Laurie have houses here), with a mixture of Victorian, Arts and Crafts, and Art Deco buildings. Turn right onto England's Lane, another street full of independent

shops and nice cafés, then left onto Haverstock Hill and head farther uphill. At the corner of Pond Street you will see two enormous Victorian Gothic buildings: one, St. Stephen's Church, is now a community arts center. The other, AIR Studios, founded by the Beatles' producer, Sir George Martin, is where scores for movies, including *Iron Man 3*, *Paddington 2*, and *Dunkirk* have been recorded.

Turn right onto Pond Street and go downhill past the unlovely Royal Free Hospital to South End Green and the entrance to **Hampstead Heath.** Or go straight to stay on Rosslyn Hill and then Hampstead High Street, the neighborhood's main drag. Turn left onto Church Row, with its unspoiled early Georgian terraced houses leading to **St John-at-Hampstead,** where the painter John Constable is buried. To the northeast of Hampstead Heath is Highgate, another upscale north London "village," with a large concentration of Georgian and early Victorian buildings, particularly around The Grove (home to Kate Moss [who lives in Samuel Taylor Coleridge's former residence] and Jude Law).

To reach **Little Venice,** go to the west entrance of Regent's Park by the gold-domed London Central Mosque and then north past **Lord's Cricket Ground** to the St. John's Wood Tube stop. Turn left onto Grove End Road, which will bring you to the famous Abbey Road crosswalk featured on the Beatles' album of the same name. Head southwest for Little Venice, known as the Belgravia of north London due to its stucco terraces (found on streets such as Randolph Avenue, Clifton Avenue, and Randolph Road) that are very similar to the other neighborhood's. The "Venice" comes from its proximity to a picturesque stretch of the Grand Union Canal along Blomfield Road, where highly decorative houseboats are moored. If you happen to be here on the second Sunday in May, you'll be able to see houseboats from all over London's canals gather here in Paddington Basin for the Blessing of the Boats.

Regent's Park with Primrose Hill and Camden Town

Commissioned by his patron the Prince Regent (later George IV) to create a master plan for this part of London, formerly a royal hunting ground, London's great urban planner and architect John Nash laid out the plans for the 410-acre Regent's Park in 1812. Bordered by grand neoclassical terraces, the park holds many attractions, including London Zoo and the summer display of more than 400 varieties of rose in Queen Mary's Gardens.

 Sights

Cecil Sharp House

ARTS CENTER | The home of the English Folk Dance and Song Society, this soaring building from 1930 hosts concerts by artists ranging from Mumford & Sons and Laura Marling to the Ukulele Orchestra of Great Britain, as well as family barn dances and céilidhs (Irish barn dances). Meet the locals at one of the drop-in dance classes offering English and Irish folk dancing as well as international traditional dances. There are also temporary exhibitions on British folk art, a café and bar, and an outstanding specialist library with an extensive collection of recordings, manuscripts, sheet music, and images relating to British folk songs, dances, and regional cultures in general. ⊠ *2 Regent's Park Rd., Primrose Hill* ☎ *020/7485–2206* ⊕ *www.cecilsharphouse.org* 🎟 *Free, classes from £8* ⊗ *Library closed Aug., Sun., Mon., and 2nd and 4th Sat. of each month* Ⓜ *Chalk Farm, Camden Town.*

Jewish Museum

OTHER MUSEUM | This fascinating museum tells the story of Britain's Jewish community through a combination of art, religious artifacts, photographs, manuscripts, and interactive displays. Its permanent exhibitions include an exploration of Jewish history in Britain from 1066 to today, including the period between the 13th and 17th centuries when Judaism was outlawed in England. It also features a recreation of a Jewish East End street from the Victorian era and displays relating to refugees from Nazism, including the 10,000 Jewish Kindertransport children who came to Britain as World War II loomed. Other permanent exhibitions include the story of a Britain-based Holocaust survivor and a medieval *mikveh* (ritual bath) excavated a few miles from here in 2001. A free overview of the museum can be found on the ground floor, along with rotating temporary exhibitions and a collection of personal diaries, letters, medals, uniforms, and souvenirs from Jewish soldiers who served in the British military. The extensive research library is now open to the public. ✉ *Raymond Burton House, 129–131 Albert St., Camden Town* ☎ *020/7284–7384* ⊕ *www.jewishmuseum.org.uk* 🎟 *£7.50* ⊗ *Closed Wed., Fri., Sat., and major Jewish holidays* ⬥ *Online advance booking for timed slots required* Ⓜ *Camden Town.*

Lord's Cricket Ground & MCC Museum
SPORTS VENUE | The spiritual home of this most English of games—and the headquarters of the MCC (Marylebone Cricket Club)—opens its "behind the scenes" areas to visitors during a 100-minute tour. Highlights include the beautiful Long Room, a VIP viewing area where portraits of cricketing greats are on display (you can also book a traditional Afternoon Tea here); the players' dressing rooms; and the world's oldest sporting museum, where cricket's 400-year progress from gentlemanly village-green game to worldwide sport is charted via memorabilia, equipment, trophies, and footage of memorable performances.

Don't miss the prize exhibit: the urn known as the Ashes—allegedly the remains of a cricket bail (part of the wicket assembly) presented to the English captain in 1883 by a group of Australian women, a jokey allusion to a newspaper's satirical obituary for the death of English cricket published after a resounding defeat. It's been a symbol of the two nations' long-running rivalry ever since. They still play for possession of the Ashes—an official (as opposed to joke) trophy only since 1998—every two years. A Waterford crystal version changes hands these days, although the winners still hold a replica of the original urn aloft.

There is no separate non-tour admittance to the museum, except for match ticket holders. All tours must be booked in advance and are not available during matches. Tour itineraries can change due to grounds maintenance.

✉ *St. John's Wood Rd., St. John's Wood* ☎ *020/7616–8595* ⊕ *www.lords.org* 🎟 *Tour £25; museum £3 with county match ticket, free with major match or grounds tour ticket* ⊗ *Closed late Dec. No tours Apr.–Sept. on major match days, preparation days, and event days and limited availability on other match days* Ⓜ *St. John's Wood.*

★ **Primrose Hill**
CITY PARK | FAMILY | More conventionally parklike than Hampstead Heath, the rolling lawns of Primrose Hill, the northerly extension of Regent's Park, rise to 213 feet and provide outstanding views over the city to the southeast, encompassing Canary Wharf and the London Eye. Formerly the site of boxing matches and duels but now filled with families and picnickers in nice weather, it has been featured in several books—it was here that Pongo engaged in "twilight barking" in *The Hundred and One Dalmatians* and the Martians set up an encampment in H. G. Wells's *The War of The Worlds*. It's also been mentioned in songs by Blur, Madness, and Paul McCartney, among others, and served as a location for films, including *Bridget Jones: The Edge of Reason* and *Paddington*. ✉ *Regent's Park Rd., Regent's Park* ☎ *0300/061–2300* ⊕ *www.royalparks.org.uk* 🎟 *Free* Ⓜ *Chalk Farm.*

★ **Regent's Park**
CITY PARK | FAMILY | The formal cultivated Regent's Park, more country-house grounds than municipal amenity, began life in 1812, when John Nash was commissioned by the Prince Regent (later George IV) to create a master plan for the former royal hunting ground. Nash's original plan included a summer palace for the prince and 56 villas for friends, none of which were realized except for eight villas (only two survive). But the grand neoclassical terraced houses on the south, east, and west edges of the park were built by Nash and reflect the scope of his ambitions.

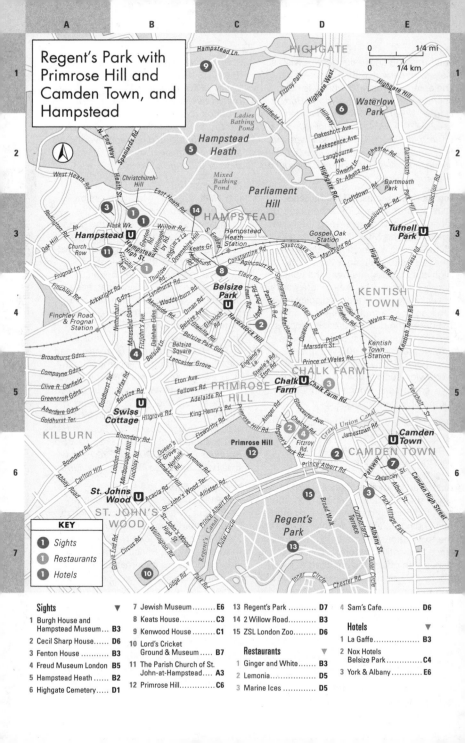

Regent's Park with Primrose Hill and Camden Town, and Hampstead

Today the 395-acre park, with the largest outdoor sports area in central London, draws the athletically inclined from around the city. At the center of the park is Queen Mary's Gardens, created in the 1930s, a fragrant 17-acre circle containing more than 400 varieties of roses that is a favorite spot for weddings. Just to the east of the gardens is the Regent's Park Open Air Theatre and the Boating Lake, which you can explore by renting a peda-lo or a rowboat. Heading east from the rose gardens along Chester Road past the Broad Walk will bring you to Nash's renowned white-stucco Cumberland Ter-race, with its central Ionic columns sur-mounted by a triangular Wedgwood-blue pediment. At the north end of the Broad Walk, you'll find London Zoo, while to the northwest of the central circle is The Hub, a state-of-the-art community sports center that has changing rooms, exercise classes, and a café with 360-degree views of the surrounding sports fields, used for soccer, rugby, cricket, field hockey, and softball. There are also tennis courts toward the park's southeast (Baker Street) entrance, and the park is a favorite north–south route for cyclists.

Regent's Park also hosts two annual events: the prestigious Frieze London art fair and Taste of London, a foodie-oriented extravaganza. ⊠ *Chester Rd., Regent's Park* ☎ *0300/061–2300* ⊕ *www.royal-parks.org.uk* ⊡ *Free* Ⓜ *Baker St., Regent's Park, Great Portland St.*

★ **ZSL London Zoo**

ZOO | FAMILY | With an emphasis on education, wildlife conservation, and the breeding of endangered species, London Zoo offers visitors the chance to see tigers, gorillas, meerkats, and more in something resembling a natural environ-ment rather than a cage. Operated by the nonprofit Zoological Society of London, the zoo was begun with the royal animals collection, moved here from the Tower of London in 1828; the zoo itself did not open to the public until 1847. Big

attractions include Land of the Lions, a walk-through re-creation of an Indian forest where you can see three resident Asiatic lions relaxing at close range; Gorilla Kingdom, which provides a similar re-created habitat (in this case an African rain forest) for its colony of six Western Lowland Gorillas; and the Attenborough Komodo Dragon House, renamed to honor the renowned naturalist. The zoo also offers the chance to get up close and personal with 15 ring-tailed lemurs. The huge B.U.G.S! pavilion (Biodiver-sity Underpinning Global Survival) is a self-sustaining, contained ecosystem for 140 less-cuddly species, includ-ing invertebrates such as spiders and millipedes, plus some reptiles and fish. Rainforest Life is an indoor tropical rain forest (complete with humidity) inhabited by the likes of armadillos, monkeys, and sloths. A special nighttime section offers glimpses of nocturnal creatures like slow lorises and bats. The Animal Adventures Children's Zoo allows kids to closely observe coatis, as well as to interact with llamas, donkeys, small pigs, sheep, and goats. Two of the most popular attrac-tions are Penguin Beach, especially at feeding time (1:30 and 4:30), and meer-kat snack time (11:15), where you can see the sociable animals keeping watch over their own sandy territory.

If you're feeling flush, try to nab one of the six daily "Meet the Penguins" VIP tickets (noon and 2:30 pm) that offer a 20-minute guided close encounter with the locals (£54); there are similar VIP encounters with gorillas, giraffes, meerkats, and various denizens of the rain forest. Other zoo highlights include Butterfly Paradise and Tiger Territory, an enclosure for four beautiful endan-gered Sumatran tigers (including two cubs born at the zoo). There are also early (8:30 am) opening mornings for the neurodiverse to ensure a calmer experience and Adults-only Zoo Nights held Friday nights in June and July that offer street food, alcoholic drinks, and entertainment. You can also experience the zoo after-hours by booking an overnight stay in one of the cozy cabins near (not *in*) the lion enclosure. Check the website or the information board out front for free events, including creature close encounters and "ask the keeper" sessions. Booking in advance online for all tickets is required. ✉ *Outer Circle, Regent's Park* ☎ *0844/225–1826* 🌐 *www.zsl.org* 🎟 *From £26* [M] *Camden Town, then Bus 274.*

🍴 Restaurants

The high-profile but low-key residents of Primrose Hill love the unpretentious, family-friendly neighborhood restaurants like Lemonia. Meanwhile farther north, leafy Hampstead is known for its cozy, atmospheric pubs converted from 17th-century coaching inns, with wood beams, open fireplaces, and hearty Sunday roast lunches.

Lemonia

$$ | **GREEK** | **FAMILY** | This consistently popular, family-run, taverna-style restaurant has been serving local families and celebrities alike in its large, vine-decked premises for more than 40 years. Besides a large selection of Greek Cypriot small-dish meze dips, hot breads, and starters, there are rustic mains like moussaka or slow-baked *kleftiko* lamb in lemon. **Known for:** great weekday set lunches; Greek taverna-style atmosphere; meze, moussaka, and grilled sea bass. [$] *Average main: £16* ✉ *89 Regent's Park Rd., Primrose Hill* ☎ *020/7586–7454* 🌐 *www.lemonia.co.uk* 🕓 *No dinner Sun.* [M] *Chalk Farm.*

Marine Ices

$ | **ICE CREAM** | **FAMILY** | This long-established ice cream parlor near Camden Lock has been serving authentic artisanal gelato and sorbet since the 1930s (originally a few doors down) and ranks among London's best. Cones and scoops made from an Italian family recipe come in flavors like Cinnamon and Honey, Dulce de Leche, and Toffee Crunch, as well as more conventional choices, and make the perfect accompaniment to strolling through Camden Market. **Known for:** authentic Italian gelato; fresh ingredients, many from Italy; wide range of flavors. [$] *Average main: £4* ✉ *Old Dairy Mews, 61 Chalk Farm Rd., Camden Town* ☎ *020/7428–9990* 🌐 *www.marineices.co.uk* [M] *Chalk Farm.*

Sam's Cafe

$ | **BRITISH** | This "greasy spoon without the grease" has become a neighborhood hot spot thanks to its modern reinterpretation of traditional British "caff" food (with the non-traditional additions of a wine list, vegan options, newspapers, and books) as well as its well-connected owners (the restaurant was officially opened by local resident Helena Bonham Carter and the vintage jukebox is "curated" by none other than Robert Plant). Lunch and dinner options feature healthy takes on British comfort food like bangers-and-mash with onion gravy, salmon fishcakes, and mac-and-cheese. **Known for:** healthy takes on British comfort food; upscale but friendly ambience; excellent all-day breakfasts. [$] *Average main: £14* ✉ *40 Chalcot Rd., Primrose Hill* ☎ *207/916–3736* 🌐 *www.samscafeprimrosehill.com* 🕓 *No dinner Wed.* [M] *Chalk Farm.*

🛏 Hotels

You'll find a few outposts of the megachains in north London, but accommodations with character are surprisingly hard to find in this area otherwise so laden with it.

York & Albany

$$ | **HOTEL** | Located on the northern edge of Regent's Park opposite the zoo entrance, this town house hotel with stylish, individually decorated rooms is owned by noted chef Gordon Ramsay, who also operates the restaurant on the ground floor. **Pros:** charming decor that is both traditional and modern; location

close to Regent's Park and Camden Town; excellent restaurant on-site. **Cons:** rooms not spacious for the price; hotel located at busy intersection; some traffic noise from outside road. $ *Rooms from: £230 ⊠ 127–129 Parkway, London ☎ 207/387–5700 ⊕ www.gordonramsay-restaurants.com/york-and-albany ⇆ 9 rooms* ⦿ *No Meals* Ⓜ *Camden Town.*

⑨ Nightlife

London's villagelike northern neighborhoods all boast atmospheric local pubs where you can easily while away an afternoon. Camden Town has more of a buzz and attracts a younger international crowd with its dance clubs and music venues. Every genre is covered, from folk and indie to jazz and world music, with interesting gigs taking place every night of the week. In short, the spirit of the area's most well-known musical daughter, Amy Winehouse, is still venerated here (she even has a statue in Camden Town).

DANCE CLUBS
KOKO

DANCE CLUBS | Once known as the Camden Palace, this legendary venue has lush red decor and gilt-trimmed boxes that recall its past as a Victorian theater, but now packs the dance floor with genres from hip-hop to funky house, club classics, and indie. Headliners who have performed "secret" gigs here include Madonna, Prince, Kanye West, Bruno Mars, Dua Lipa, the Red Hot Chili Peppers, and Amy Winehouse. A recent renovation following a 2020 fire has added a four-story extension to the original theater and two adjoining buildings, incorporating a pizzeria and tap bar for intimate performances, a cocktail bar in the large roof dome, a roof terrace, more performance spaces, and a recording studio. ⊠ *1A Camden High St., Camden Town ☎ 020/7388–3222 ⊕ www.koko. uk.com* Ⓜ *Mornington Crescent.*

LIVE MUSIC
The Camden Assembly

LIVE MUSIC | Drawn by its reputation for featuring indie stars of tomorrow (think the likes of Jessie J, Laura Marling, The Killers, and Foals), non-mainstream crowds flock here, one of the finest small clubs in London. Weekend pop-punk and hip-hop club nights upstairs host live bands as well as DJs who rock the decks. ⊠ *49 Chalk Farm Rd., Camden Town ☎ 020/7424–0800 for venue, 020/7424–0800 for tickets ⊕ www.camdenassembly.com* Ⓜ *Chalk Farm.*

The Dublin Castle

LIVE MUSIC | Run by the same family for nearly three decades, The Dublin Castle has hosted almost every British rock group you care to name, from Madness to Blur. With four bands on the bill almost every night, and DJs taking over afterward on Friday and weekends, there's something for most tastes at this legendary venue. ⊠ *94 Parkway, Camden Town ☎ 07949/575–149 ⊕ www.thedublincastle.com* Ⓜ *Camden Town.*

★ Jazz Café

LIVE MUSIC | A long-standing hotbed of cool in Camden, the Jazz Café hosts top acts in mainstream jazz as well as hip-hop, funk, world music, soul, and Latin fusion. On Saturday night, a DJ plays disco, house, and soul. Book ahead if you want a table in the balcony restaurant overlooking the stage; otherwise you'll be standing (and probably dancing). ⊠ *5 Parkway, Camden Town ☎ 020/7485–6834 for venue info, 020/7485–6834 for tickets (Ticketmaster) ⊕ www.thejazzcafelondon.com* Ⓜ *Camden Town.*

O2 Forum Kentish Town

LIVE MUSIC | The best up-and-coming and medium-to-big-name music acts (recent bookings have included Beck, The Libertines, and Paul Weller) consistently play at this 2,000-capacity club. It's a converted 1930s Art Deco movie theater, with a balcony (the only area with seats) overlooking the grungy dance floor.

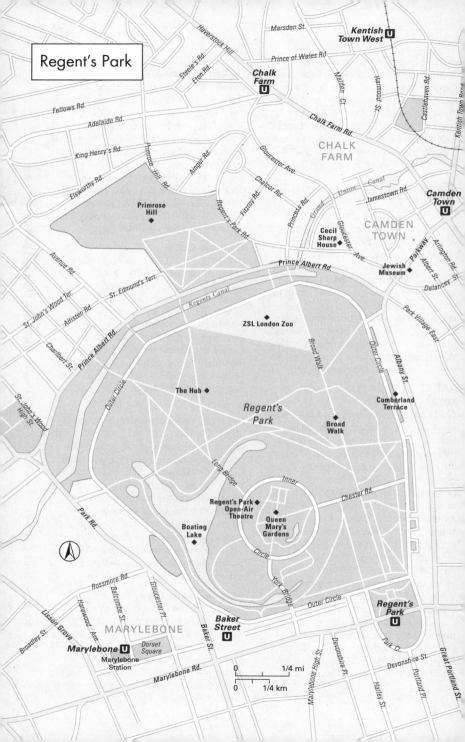

Regent's Park

Marsden St.

Kentish Town West Ⓤ

Haverstock Hill

Prince of Wales Rd.

Chalk Farm Ⓤ

Steele's Rd.

Eton Rd.

Maiden Ct.

Harmood St.

Castlehaven Rd.

Kentish Town Road

Chalk Farm Rd.

Fellows Rd.

Adelaide Rd.

CHALK FARM

King Henry's Rd.

Primrose Hill Rd.

Ainger Rd.

Gloucester Ave.

Chalcot Rd.

Fitzroy Rd.

Princess Rd.

Grand

Union

Canal

Jamestown Rd.

Camden Town Ⓤ

Elsworthy Rd.

Regent's Park Rd.

CAMDEN TOWN

◆ **Primrose Hill**

Cecil Sharp House ◆

Gloucester Ave.

Parkway

Albert St.

Arlington Rd.

Delancey St.

Avenue Rd.

Prince Albert Rd.

Jewish Museum ◆

St. Edmund's Terr.

Regents Canal

Park Village East

St. John's Wood Ter.

Allitsen Rd.

Prince Albert Rd.

◆ **ZSL London Zoo**

Broad Walk

Outer Circle

Albany St.

Charlbert St.

Regent's Park

The Hub ◆

◆ **Cumberland Terrace**

St. John's Wood High St.

Outer Circle

Broad Walk ◆

Long Bridge

Inner

Chester Rd.

Regent's Park Open-Air Theatre ◆

◆

Park Rd.

Boating Lake ◆

Queen Mary's Gardens

Circle

York Bridge

Rossmore Rd.

Balcombe St.

Gloucester Pl.

Outer Circle

Regent's Park Ⓤ

Lisson Grove

Harewood Ave.

Park Cr.

Baker St.

Baker Street Ⓤ

Devonshire Pl.

Devonshire St.

Great Portland St.

Broadley St.

MARYLEBONE

Dorset Square

Marylebone High St.

Portland Pl.

Marylebone Ⓤ

Marylebone Station

Marylebone Rd.

Harley St.

0   1/4 mi

0   1/4 km

✉ *9–17 Highgate Rd., Kentish Town* ☎ *0844/477–2000 for tickets* ⊕ *www.academymusicgroup.com/o2forum-kentishtown* Ⓜ *Kentish Town.*

Roundhouse

LIVE MUSIC | This 1840s former railway terminus and onetime gin warehouse in Chalk Farm now hosts a varied program of live music, circus, theater, cabaret, spoken word, and even a bit of Lucha Libre (Mexican wrestling). Usually there's a genre-busting assortment of new and familiar musical acts, most of them cult favorites ranging from world and electronica to indie and emo. Standing tickets offer good value. There's a nice restaurant on the first floor, and in the summer, the terrace bar is transformed into a popular "urban beach," complete with sand, a retro bar, palm trees, and outdoor film screenings. ✉ *Chalk Farm Rd., Chalk Farm* ☎ *0300/6789–222* ⊕ *www.roundhouse.org.uk* Ⓜ *Chalk Farm.*

🎭 Performing Arts

Leafy north London has long been a stomping ground for the capital's cultural elite—stroll through Primrose Hill and you're practically guaranteed to spot a film star or musician—but there's diversity here, too. Camden Town is justifiably famous for its indie music scene, as well as leading stand-up comedy venues.

THEATER

Open Air Theatre

THEATER | FAMILY | Works by Shakespeare have been performed here every summer (from mid-May to mid-September) since 1932, with casts including luminaries such as Vivien Leigh, Dame Judi Dench, and Damien Lewis. Today the theater also mounts productions of classic plays, Broadway musicals, and shows for family audiences among its four annual productions. *A Midsummer Night's Dream* is the one to catch, if it's on—never has that enchanted Greek wood been better

evoked, especially when enhanced by genuine birdsong and a rising moon.

There's a covered restaurant for pretheater dining, an informal café, and, of course, a bar. You also can order picnic hampers in advance. The park can get chilly, so bring a blanket. Performances proceed rain or shine (umbrellas aren't allowed), with refunds only in case of a very heavy downpour. ✉ *Inner Circle, Regent's Park* ☎ *0844/826–4242* ⊕ *www.openairtheatre.com* 🎟 *From £25* Ⓜ *Baker St., Regent's Park.*

🛍 Shopping

HOUSEHOLD GOODS

Graham & Green

HOUSEWARES | Combining style with practicality and a whimsical twist, this delightful interiors shop carries a broad but carefully curated selection of faux-fur throws, elegant lamps and lampshades, embroidered cushions, sheepskin rugs, agate or Venetian glass doorknobs, folding deck chairs (as found in the Royal Parks), shabby-chic sofas, ceramics and cutlery, dinosaur string lights, and more. There are branches in Notting Hill and Bayswater. ✉ *164 Regent's Park Rd., Primrose Hill* ☎ *020/7586–2960* ⊕ *www.grahamandgreen.co.uk* Ⓜ *Chalk Farm.*

MARKETS

The Camden Markets

MARKET | Begun in the early 1970s, when weekend stalls sold the output of nearby craft workshops, Camden Lock Market later expanded to four markets: Camden, Camden Lock, The Stables, and the Canal Market, all grouped around two locks on Regent's Canal. Though much of the merchandise is targeted at young street-fashion aficionados as well as aging hippies, anyone with a taste for alternative culture will also find plenty that appeals. This shopping experience is best suited to those who don't mind large crowds and a boisterous atmosphere (i.e. teenagers), especially on weekends. For many years, the markets have hosted more than 1,000 stalls offering a wide-ranging array of merchandise—vintage and new clothes, antiques and junk, rare vinyl, vintage board games, ceramics, Indian bedspreads, fetishwear, obscure band memorabilia, and toys.

The outdoor Camden Market on Camden High Street mainly sells cheap jeans, secondhand clothes, and tacky pop-culture paraphernalia; Camden Lock Market is the place to go for crafts, clothes, and jewelry, plus loads of street food stalls; and The Stables Market, which has expanded into the so-called Catacombs (Victorian brick arches), has more than 700 shops and stalls and is where you go for furniture and vintage items. The former Canal Market is now known as Hawley Wharf, a mixed-use development with luxury apartment buildings plus retail and dining outlets, a canal-side farmer's market, and an arthouse cinema. The other three markets are currently ear-marked for further redevelopment, so more gentrification is in the cards—if the original scrappy, bohemian atmosphere of the area appeals to you, enjoy it while you can. ✉ *Camden High St. to Chalk Farm Rd., Camden Town* ⊕ *www.camdenmarket.com* Ⓜ *Camden Town, Chalk Farm.*

SHOES
Spice
SHOES | Touring London requires a lot of walking, so if your feet are crying out for mercy, stop in at this long-established boutique that specializes in shoes, sandals, and boots for men and women that hit the sweet spot between comfy and stylish. Brands include 4CCCCEES, Arche, and Chie Mihara, as well as the store's own Spice line. ✉ *162 Regent's Park Rd., Primrose Hill* ☎ *020/7722–2478* ⊕ *www.spiceshu.co.uk* Ⓜ *Chalk Farm.*

Hampstead

Back in 1818, even impoverished Romantic poets like John Keats could afford to live in **Hampstead**. His former residence, now known as **Keats House,** is a pretty Regency villa where he spent two years and wrote several of his most famous works. These days Hampstead's bohemian past is long gone, although several distinguished writers, actors, and musicians still live here. Specialty food shops and boutiques cluster along Hampstead High Street, where upscale high-street chains proliferate the closer you get to Hampstead Tube station. Be sure to leave the beaten path to explore the numerous narrow charming roads, like Flask Walk, Well Walk, and New End Road. Also hidden among Hampstead's winding streets are **Fenton House,** a Georgian town house with a lovely walled garden, and **Burgh House,** the oldest (1704) house in the village and a repository of local history.

Hampstead's biggest claim to fame, however, is **Hampstead Heath** (known locally as "The Heath"), 791 acres of verdant open space, woods, spring-fed swimming ponds, and some of Europe's oldest oaks. It's also home to one of London's highest vantage points (321 feet), Parliament Hill. On the Highgate end of Hampstead Heath, you'll find **Kenwood House,** an 18th-century mansion that was designed by Robert Adam and is noted for its remarkable art collection and grounds.

Sights

Burgh House and Hampstead Museum
HISTORIC HOME | One of Hampstead's oldest buildings, Burgh House was built in 1704 to take advantage of the natural spa waters of the then-fashionable Hampstead Wells. A private house until World War II, it was saved from dereliction in the 1970s by local residents, who have maintained it ever since. The building is

The more residential neighborhoods of London, like Hampstead, are marked by rows of colorful houses called terraces.

a fine example of the genteel elegance typical of the Queen Anne period, with brick frontage, oak-paneled rooms, and a terraced garden that was originally designed by Gertrude Jekyll. Today the house contains a small but diverting museum on the history of the area, and also hosts regular talks, concerts, and recitals. The secluded garden courtyard of the café is a lovely spot for lunch, tea, or a glass of wine on a summer's afternoon. ⊠ *New End Sq., Hampstead* ☎ *020/7431–0144* ⊕ *www.burghhouse. org.uk* ✉ *Free* ⊗ *House closed Mon., Tues., and Sat. Café closed Mon. and Tues.* Ⓜ *Hampstead.*

Fenton House

HISTORIC HOME | This handsome 17th-century merchant's home, Hampstead's oldest surviving house, has fine collections of porcelain, Georgian furniture, and 17th-century needlework. The 2-acre walled garden, with its rose plantings and apple orchard, has remained virtually unchanged for 300 years. Booking tickets in advance for a visit to the house is

required as entry is by timed ticket only; you can stop by and visit the garden without booking in advance. ⊠ *Hampstead Grove, Hampstead* ☎ *020/7435–3471* ⊕ *www.nationaltrust.org.uk* ✉ *£10* ⊗ *Closed Sun.–Thurs.* Ⓜ *Hampstead.*

Freud Museum London

OTHER MUSEUM | The father of psychoanalysis lived here with his family for a year, between his escape from Nazi persecution in his native Vienna in 1938 and his death in 1939. His daughter Anna (herself a pioneer of child psychoanalysis) remained in the house until her own death in 1982, bequeathing it as a museum to honor her father. The centerpiece is Freud's unchanged study, containing his remarkable collection of antiquities and his library. Also on display is the family's Biedermeier furniture—and, of course, the couch. As well, there are lectures, study groups, and themed exhibitions, in addition to a psychoanalysis-related archive and research library. Looking for a unique souvenir for the person who has everything? The

Thanks to the Beatles' album, Abbey Road has become the world's most famous traffic crossing.

gift shop here sells "Freudian Slippers." ✉ *20 Maresfield Gardens, Swiss Cottage* ☎ *020/7435–2002* ⊕ *www.freud.org. uk* 🖃 *£9* ⊗ *Closed Tues. year-round and Mon. Oct.–Feb.* Ⓜ *Swiss Cottage, Finchley Rd.*

★ Hampstead Heath

CITY PARK | FAMILY | For generations, Londoners have headed to Hampstead Heath to escape the dirt and noise of the city, and this unique 791-acre expanse of *rus in urbe* ("country in the city") is home to a variety of wildlife and habitat: grassy meadows, woodland, scrub, wetlands, and some of Europe's most venerable oaks. Be aware that, aside from the Parliament Hill area to the south and Golders Hill Park in the west, it is more like countryside than a park, with signs and amenities in short supply. Pick up a map at Kenwood House or at the "Enquiries" window of the Staff Yard near the tennis courts off Highgate Road, where you can also find details about the history of the Heath and its flora and

fauna. An excellent café near the Edwardian bandstand serves Italian food.

Coming onto the Heath from the Savernake Road entrance on the southern side, walk past the children's playground and paddling pool and head uphill to the top of Parliament Hill. At 321 feet above sea level, it's one of the highest points in London, providing a stunning panorama over the city. On clear days you can see all the way to the Surrey Hills beyond the city's southern limits. Keep heading north from Parliament Hill to find the more rural parts of the Heath.

If you keep heading east from the playground instead, turn right past the Athletics Track and you'll come to the Lido, an Olympic-size, outdoor, unheated swimming pool that gets packed on all-too-rare hot summer days. More swimming options are available at the Hampstead ponds, which have been refreshing Londoners for generations. You'll find the "Mens" and "Ladies" ponds to the northeast of Parliament Hill, with a "Mixed" pond closer to South

A Trip to Abbey Road

The black-and-white crosswalk (known as a "zebra crossing") near the Abbey Road Studios at No. 3, where the Beatles recorded their entire output from "Love Me Do" onward, is a place of pilgrimage for Beatles fans from around the world, many of them teenagers born long after the band split up. They converge here to re-create the cover of the Beatles' 1969 *Abbey Road* album, posing on the crossing despite the onrushing traffic.

■TIP➔ Be careful if you're going to attempt this; traffic on Abbey Road is busy.

One of the best ways to explore landmarks in the Beatles' story is to take one of the excellent walking tours offered by **Original London Walks** (☎ 020/7624–3978). Try **The Beatles In-My-Life Walk** (Saturday and Tuesday at 11 am outside Marylebone Railway station) or **The Beatles Magical Mystery Tour** (Sunday and Thursday, except for December and January, at 11 am, at Underground Exit 1, Tottenham Court Road).

End Green. A £2 donation is requested.
■TIP➔ **Golders Hill Park, on the Heath Extension to the northwest, offers a good café, tennis courts, a duck pond, a croquet lawn, and a walled flower garden, plus a Butterfly House (May–September) and a small zoo with native species including muntjac deer, rare red squirrels, and a Scottish wildcat.** ✉ *Hampstead* ☎ *020/7332–3322* ⊕ *www.cityoflondon. gov.uk/hampstead* ✆ *Free* Ⓜ *Overground: Hampstead Heath for west of Heath or Gospel Oak for south and east of Heath and Lido. Northern line: Golders Green, then Bus 210 or 268 to Whitestone Pond for north and west of Heath and Golders Hill Park.*

Highgate Cemetery

CEMETERY | Highgate is not the oldest cemetery in London, but it is probably the best known, both for its roster of famous "inhabitants" and the quality of its funerary architecture. After it was consecrated in 1839, Victorians came from miles around to appreciate the ornate headstones, the impressive tombs, and the view. Such was its popularity that 19 acres on the other side of the road were acquired in 1850, and this additional

East Cemetery is the final resting place of numerous notables, including the most visited, Karl Marx (1818–83), as well as George Eliot and, a more recent internment, George Michael. At the summit is the Circle of Lebanon, a ring of vaults built around an ancient cypress tree, a legacy of the 17th-century gardens that formerly occupied the site. Leading from the circle is the Egyptian Avenue, a subterranean stone tunnel lined with catacombs, itself approached by a dramatic colonnade that screens the main cemetery from the road. Both sides are impressive, with a grand (locked) iron gate leading to a sweeping courtyard built for the approach of horses and carriages.

By the 1970s the cemetery had become unkempt and neglected until a group of volunteers, the Friends of Highgate Cemetery, undertook the huge upkeep. Tours are conducted by the Friends, who will show you the most interesting graves among the numerous statues and memorials once hidden by overgrowth. The West Cemetery tour is 70 minutes, while the East Cemetery tour (Saturday only) is 75 minutes. Alternatively, you can go on a self-guided ramble, but entrance to both sides of the cemetery is by pre-booked timed slot only, and the catacombs can only be seen on a tour. You're expected to dress respectfully, so skip the shorts and the baseball cap; children under eight are not admitted and neither are dogs, tripods, or video cameras. ⊠ *Swains La., Highgate* ☎ *020/8340–1834* ⊕ *www. highgatecemetery.org* ◻ *East Cemetery £4.50, tours £8.50; West Cemetery £10, tours £14, includes admission to East Cemetery* Ⓜ *Archway, then Bus 210, 271, or 143 to Waterlow Park; Belsize Park, then Bus C11 to Brookfield Park.*

Keats House
HISTORIC HOME | It was while lodging in this house between 1818 and 1820 that the leading Romantic poet John Keats (1795–1821) fell in love with girl-next-door Fanny Brawne and wrote some of his best-loved poems. (Soon after, ill health forced him to move to Rome, where he died the following year.) After a major refurbishment to make the rooms more consistent with their original Regency style, the house now displays all sorts of Keats-related material, including portraits, letters, many of the poet's original manuscripts and books, the engagement ring he gave to Fanny, and items of her clothing. A pretty garden contains the plum tree under which Keats supposedly composed *Ode to a Nightingale.* There are frequent Keats-theme events, including evening poetry readings, concerts, and special talks featuring local literary luminaries. Picnics can be taken onto the grounds during the summer. Admission is by timed ticket only. ⊠ *10 Keats Grove, Hampstead* ☎ *020/7332–3868* ⊕ *www. cityoflondon.gov.uk/things-to-do/keats-house* ◻ *£7.50* ⊙ *Closed Mon.–Wed. and Sat.* Ⓜ *Overground: Hampstead Heath.*

★ Kenwood House
HISTORIC HOME | This largely Palladian villa offers an escape to a gracious country house with a magnificent collection of Old Masters and beautiful grounds, all within a short Tube ride from central London. Originally built in 1616, Kenwood was expanded by Robert Adam starting in 1767 and later by George Saunders in 1795. Adam refaced most of the exterior and added the splendid library, which, with its vaulted ceiling and Corinthian columns, is the highlight of the house's interior. A major renovation restored four rooms to reflect Adam's intentions as closely as possible, incorporating the furniture he designed for them and his original color schemes.

Kenwood is also home to the Iveagh Bequest, a world-class collection of some 60 paintings that includes masterworks like Rembrandt's *Self-Portrait with Two Circles* and Vermeer's *The Guitar Player,* along with major works by Reynolds, van Dyck, Hals, Gainsborough, Turner, and more. Knowledgeable room guides are present to answer any questions on the rooms and the works inside. The grounds, designed by Humphry Repton and bordered by Hampstead Heath, are equally elegant and serene, with lawns sloping down to a little lake crossed by a trompe-l'oeil bridge. All in all, it's the perfect home for an 18th-century gentleman. In summer, the grounds host a series of popular and classical concerts, culminating in fireworks on the last night. The Brew House café, occupying part of the old coach house, has outdoor tables in the courtyard and a terraced garden. ⊠ *Hampstead La., Highgate* ☎ *0870/333–1181* ⊕ *www.english-heritage.org.uk/ visit/places/kenwood* ◻ *Free* Ⓜ *Golders Green or Archway, then Bus 210. Overground: Gospel Oak.*

The Parish Church of St John-at-Hampstead
CHURCH | There has been a church here since 1312, but the current building—consecrated in 1747 and later extended in 1877—is a fine example of neoclassical serenity, enhanced by Ionic columns and vaulting arches. Also known as the Hampstead Parish Church, it stands at the end of Church Row, a narrow street lined

with flat-fronted brick Georgian houses that gives you a sense of what Hampstead was like when it truly was a rural village as opposed to a traffic-clogged north London neighborhood. Many local notables are buried in the picturesque churchyard, including painter John Constable (some of whose most famous works depict the Heath), John Harrison (the inventor of the marine chronometer at the heart of the book *Longitude*), members of the artistic du Maurier family, Jane Austen's aunt, and comedy god Peter Cook. ⊠ *Church Row, Hampstead* ☎ *020/7794–5808* ⊕ *www. hampsteadparishchurch.org.uk* ✉ *Free* Ⓜ *Hampstead.*

2 Willow Road

HISTORIC HOME | Among the many artists and intellectuals fleeing Nazi persecution who settled in the area was noted architect Ernö Goldfinger, who built this outstanding and influential modernist home opposite Hampstead Heath in 1939 as his family residence. (His plans drew the ire of several local residents, including novelist Ian Fleming, who supposedly got his revenge by naming the Bond villain after his neighbor.) Along with design touches and building techniques that were groundbreaking at the time, the unique house, a place of pilgrimage for 20th-century architecture enthusiasts, also contains Goldfinger's impressive collection of modern art and self-designed innovative furniture. Admission is between 11 am and 2 pm, by prebooked hourly tour only. ⊠ *2 Willow Rd., Hampstead* ☎ *020/7435–6166* ⊕ *www.nationaltrust.org.uk* ✉ *£9* ⊙ *Closed Mon.–Wed., Fri., and Sun.* Ⓜ *Overground: Hampstead Heath.*

Restaurants

Ginger & White

$ | **CAFÉ** | **FAMILY** | Family-friendly and tucked away on a pretty mews, Ginger & White is a delightful fusion of a Continental-style café and traditional British "caff"—all bound up with a modern, sophisticated Hampstead vibe. Specialties include homemade peanut butter and cakes, farm-sourced free-range eggs, rare breed bacon, and artisanal espresso. **Known for:** family and dog-friendly atmosphere; weekend crowds; excellent coffee. Ⓢ *Average main: £7* ⊠ *4A–5A Perrins Ct., Hampstead* ☎ *020/7431–9098* ⊕ *www.gingerandwhite. com* ⊙ *No dinner* Ⓜ *Hampstead.*

Hotels

La Gaffe

$ | **B&B/INN** | The name of this unpretentious, family-run restaurant with rooms means "the mistake" in Italian, and it also provides the punchline to the unlikely tale of how the original owners (the parents of the current proprietor) met in the 1950s. **Pros:** comes with the convenience of a traditional Italian restaurant below; unusual place with a cheerful atmosphere; great price. **Cons:** small rooms; no elevator; few amenities. Ⓢ *Rooms from: £110* ⊠ *107–111 Heath St., Hampstead* ☎ *020/7435–8965* ⊕ *www.lagaffe.co.uk* ⇩ *18 rooms* ⏉ *Free Breakfast* Ⓜ *Hampstead.*

Nox Hotels Belsize Park

$ | **HOTEL** | Just down the hill from Hampstead Village is this stylish boutique hotel, part of a small chain, located in a converted pub and the Victorian building above it. **Pros:** free Wi-Fi; clean, minimalist decor; convenient to Hampstead, Belsize Park, and Primrose Hill. **Cons:** some rooms can be noisy; rooms on the small side; no elevator. Ⓢ *Rooms from: £75* ⊠ *154 Haverstock Hill, Hampstead* ☎ *020/7722–5097* ⊕ *www.noxhotels. co.uk/en/hotel-belsize-park-in-belsize-park* ⇩ *22 rooms* ⏉ *No Meals* Ⓜ *Belsize Park.*

ⓨ Nightlife

PUBS

The Holly Bush

PUBS | A short walk up the hill from Hampstead Tube station, the friendly Holly Bush dates back to the 18th century and retains something of the country pub it was before London spread this far north, thanks to the stripped wooden floors, walls paneled in dark wood, and big open fires. The combination of great ales and organic, free-range gastropub food makes it perennially packed with locals. Try the pumpkin tart or the Guinea fowl with a leek and artichoke risotto, and don't miss the hot cider in the wintertime. ⊠ *22 Holly Mount, Hampstead* ☎ *020/7435–2892* ⊕ *www.hollybush-hampstead.co.uk* Ⓜ *Hampstead.*

The Spaniards Inn

PUBS | Ideal as a refueling point when you're hiking over Hampstead Heath, this atmospheric oak-beamed pub has been serving customers since 1585 and comes with a gorgeous garden that was immortalized in Dickens's *Pickwick Papers.* Other notable former patrons include infamous highwayman Dick Turpin as well as local resident Keats and fellow poets Shelley, Blake, and Byron. Fresh takes on traditional pub food and a wide selection of cask beer ensure a crowd, especially on Sunday. And if you've brought your furry friend along, there's a doggy bath in the garden. ⊠ *Spaniards Rd., Hampstead* ☎ *020/8731–8406* ⊕ *www.thespaniards-hampstead.co.uk* Ⓜ *Hampstead.*

🎭 Performing Arts

FILM

Everyman Hampstead

FILM | The antithesis of a noisy, sticky-floored multiplex, the Everyman arthouse chain offers a premium cinema-going experience with ticket prices to match. But many say it's worth it for the large leather armchairs, loveseats, and waitstaff that bring tapas and champagne to your seat. Along with recent releases, the cinema screens live ballet and opera performances from the Royal Opera House and plays from the National Theatre. There's another branch down the hill in Belsize Park. ⊠ *5 Holly Bush Vale, Hampstead* ☎ *0871/906–9060* ⊕ *www.everymancinema.com* 🎫 *From £18.90* Ⓜ *Hampstead.*

THEATER

Hampstead Theatre

THEATER | Located in nearby Swiss Cottage, this handsome theater specializes in commissioning and producing new work. Established names like Mike Bartlett, Terry Johnson, and Joe Penhall debut their creations in the upstairs theater (with several productions eventually going on to the West End), while fresh voices are produced in the downstairs studio theater at friendly ticket prices. It's also known for its productions of recent Pulitzer Prize–winning plays imported from the United States. There's a good café that's open all day as well as during performances. ⊠ *Eton Ave., Swiss Cottage* ☎ *207/722–9301* ⊕ *www.hampsteadtheatre.com* 🎫 *Downstairs theater from £5 , main theater from £12* Ⓜ *Swiss Cottage.*

Shopping

Susan Wainwright

SOUVENIRS | **FAMILY** | If you're looking for an alternative to the cheesy and the mass-produced, this eclectic shop packs loads of distinctive, stylish, affordable gifts into a small space. The assortment includes handsome gloves and fake-fur accessories, handmade silver jewelry, tweed travel blankets, cashmere shawls, leather handbags, comfy yet attractive robes and pajamas, natural-fiber baby and children's clothes and accessories, retro toys, sophisticated stationery, specialty creams and lotions, and flasks and leather goods for him. Best of all, prices are reasonable. ⊠ *31 South End Rd., Hampstead* ☎ *020/7431–4337* Ⓜ *Overground: Hampstead Heath.*

Chapter 13

GREENWICH

Updated by
Jo Caird

⊙ Sights	🍴 Restaurants	🛏 Hotels	🛍 Shopping	🍸 Nightlife
★★★★☆	★★☆☆☆	★☆☆☆☆	★★☆☆☆	★☆☆☆☆

GREENWICH SNAPSHOT

TOP REASONS TO GO

The Greenwich meridian line: At the Royal Observatory—where the world's time is set—you can be in the Eastern and Western Hemispheres simultaneously.

The Queen's House: Sir Inigo Jones's 17th-century building was the first in England to embrace the styles of the Italian Renaissance.

The National Maritime Museum: Discover Britain's seafaring past, and see how Britannia ruled the waves and helped shape the modern world.

Cutty Sark: Take a stroll along the deck of the last surviving 19th-century tea clipper, now shipshape after years of renovation.

GETTING THERE

The Docklands Light Railway (DLR) is a zippy way to get to Cutty Sark Station from Canary Wharf or Bank Tube station in The City. Or take the DLR to Island Gardens and walk the old Victorian foot tunnel under the river. (Sitting at the front of a train can be disconcerting, as you watch the controls in the fully automated driver's cab move about as if a ghost were at the helm.) The best way to arrive, however—time and weather permitting—is like a sea captain of old: by water (it takes an hour from central London).

MAKING THE MOST OF YOUR TIME

Set apart from the rest of London, Greenwich is worth a day to itself—those who love maritime history will want to spend two—in order to make the most of walks in the rolling parkland and to immerse yourself in the richness of Greenwich's history, science, and architecture. The boat trip takes about an hour from Westminster Pier (next to Big Ben) or 25 minutes from the Tower of London, so factor in enough time for the round-trip.

PAUSE HERE

■ Tucked away on the Greenwich Park side of the National Maritime Museum (an ideal stop en route to or from the Royal Observatory) is Yinka Shonibare's 2010 artwork *Nelson's Ship in a Bottle*. The scaled-down replica of HMS *Victory* was first seen in Trafalgar Square, before being relocated to Greenwich in 2012, just in time for the NMM's 75th anniversary. Along with being just delightful to gaze upon, the work prompts questions of colonialism, trade, and power—note the sails inspired by the mass-produced Indonesian batik fabrics associated with African dress.

NEAREST PUBLIC RESTROOMS

■ Duck into the visitor center at the Old Royal Naval College, where the facilities are free.

About 8 miles downstream (meaning seaward, to the east) from central London, Greenwich is a small borough that looms large across the world. Once the seat of British naval power, it is not only home to the Old Royal Observatory, which measures time for our entire planet, but also the Greenwich meridian, which divides the world into two—you can stand astride it with one foot in each hemisphere.

Bear in mind that the journey to Greenwich is an event in itself. In a rush, you can take the driverless DLR train, but many opt for arriving by boat along the Thames. This way, you glide past famous sights on the London skyline—there's a guaranteed spine chill on passing the Tower—and ever-changing docklands, and there's usually a chirpy Cock-er-ney navigator enlivening the journey with fun commentary.

A visit to Greenwich feels like a trip to a rather elegant seaside town—albeit one with more than its fair share of historic sites. The grandiose **Old Royal Naval College,** designed by Sir Christopher Wren, was originally a home for veteran sailors. Today it's a popular visitor attraction, with a more glamorous second life as one of the most widely used movie locations in Britain.

Greenwich was originally home to one of England's finest Tudor palaces, and the birthplace of Henry VIII, Elizabeth I, and Mary I. Inigo Jones began what is considered the first "classical" building in England in 1616: the **Queen's House,** which now houses a collection of fine art. Britain was the world's preeminent naval power for more than 500 years, and the excellent **National Maritime Museum** details that history in an engaging way. Its prize exhibits include the coat worn by Admiral Lord Nelson (1758–1805) in his final battle—bullet hole and all. The 19th-century tea clipper *Cutty Sark* was nearly destroyed by fire in 2007 but reopened in 2012 after a painstaking restoration. Now it's more pristine than ever and has an impressive visitor center.

Greenwich Park, London's oldest royal park, is still home to fallow red deer, just as it has been since they were first introduced here for hunting by Henry VIII. The **Ranger's House** now houses a private art collection, next door to a beautifully manicured rose garden. Above it all is the **Royal Observatory,** where you can be in two hemispheres at once by standing along the **Greenwich meridian line,** before seeing a high-tech planetarium show.

Toward north Greenwich, the hopelessly ambitious Millennium Dome has been successfully reborn as The O2 and now hosts major concerts and stand-up comedy gigs. More adventurous visitors can also go **Up at The O2** on a climbing expedition across the massive domed surface. Meanwhile, those who prefer excursions of a gentler kind may want to journey a couple of miles south of the borough, farther out into London's southern suburbs, to the shamefully underappreciated **Eltham Palace,** once a favorite of Henry VIII. Parts of the mansion were transformed into an Art Deco masterpiece in the 1930s.

Sights

★ *Cutty Sark*

NAUTICAL SIGHT | FAMILY | This sleek, romantic clipper was built in 1869, one among a vast fleet of tall-masted wooden ships that plied the oceanic highways of the 19th century, trading in exotic commodities—in this case, tea. *Cutty Sark* (named after a racy witch in a Robert Burns poem) was the fastest in the fleet, sailing the London–China route in 1871 in only 107 days. The clipper has been preserved in dry dock as a museum ship since the 1950s, but was severely damaged in a devastating fire in 2007.

Yet up from the ashes, as the song goes, grow the roses of success: after a major restoration project, the visitor facilities are now better than ever. Not only can you tour the ship in its entirety, but the glittering visitor center (which the ship now rests directly above) allows you to view the hull from below. There's plenty to see here, and the cramped quarters form a fantastic time capsule to walk around in—this boat was never too comfortable for the 28-strong crew (as you'll see). Don't miss the amusing collection of figureheads. The ship also hosts comedy, cabaret, and theater shows. More adventurous visitors can get an entirely different perspective on the ship via the rig-climbing experience. ⊠ *King William Walk, Greenwich* ☎ *020/8858–4422* ⊕ *www.rmg.co.uk/cuttysark* 💷 *From £15* Ⓜ *DLR: Cutty Sark.*

★ Eltham Palace

CASTLE/PALACE | FAMILY | Once a favorite getaway for Henry VIII (who liked to spend Christmas here), Eltham Palace has been drastically remodeled twice in its lifetime: once during the 15th and 16th centuries, and again during the 1930s, when a grand mansion was annexed onto the Tudor great hall by the superwealthy Courtauld family. Today it's an extraordinary combination of late medieval grandeur and art deco masterpiece, laced with an eccentric whimsy— the Courtaulds even built an entire room to be the personal quarters of their beloved pet lemur. The house and its extensive gardens were fully restored when the palace finally entered public ownership in the late 1990s. Be sure to get a glimpse of the Map Room, where the Courtaulds planned their round-the-world adventures, and the reconstruction of a lavish 1930s walk-in wardrobe, complete with genuine dresses from the time period. ⊠ *Court Rd., Eltham* ☎ *020/8294–2548* ⊕ *www.english-heritage.org.uk/eltham-palace* 💷 *£17.60* 🕒 *Closed weekdays Nov.–Jan. and Mon. and Tues. in Mar.* Ⓜ *Eltham.*

Emirates Air Line

VIEWPOINT | FAMILY | It may not have become the essential commuter route its makers envisioned, but this cable car, which connects Greenwich Peninsula with the Docklands across the Thames, offers spectacular views from nearly 300 feet up. The journey takes about 10 minutes each way and cable cars arrive every 30 seconds. Entrance to the Emirates Aviation Experience, a small exhibition about commercial air travel that includes life-size models of aircraft and flight simulators, is included with "Discovery Experience" round-trip tickets. ⊠ *Edmund Halley Way* ⊕ *www.aviation-experience.*

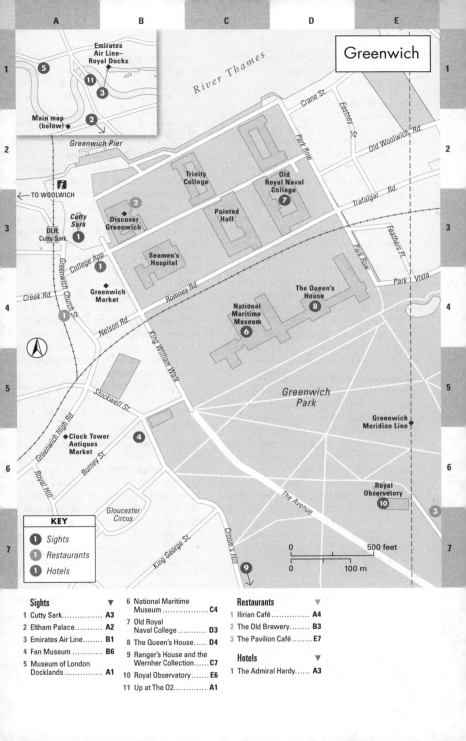

Greenwich

KEY
- ① Sights
- ① Restaurants
- ① Hotels

Sights ▼
1 Cutty Sark................. A3
2 Eltham Palace............ A2
3 Emirates Air Line........ B1
4 Fan Museum B6
5 Museum of London Docklands A1
6 National Maritime Museum C4
7 Old Royal Naval College D3
8 The Queen's House..... D4
9 Ranger's House and the Wernher Collection...... C7
10 Royal Observatory....... E6
11 Up at The O2............. A1

Restaurants ▼
1 Ilirian Café A4
2 The Old Brewery........ B3
3 The Pavilion Café E7

Hotels ▼
1 The Admiral Hardy...... A3

com ✉ One-way ticket £5, Discovery Experience £9.40 Ⓜ North Greenwich, Royal Victoria.

The Fan Museum

OTHER MUSEUM | This quirky little museum is as fascinating and varied as the uniquely prized object whose artistry it seeks to chronicle. The simple fan is more than a mere fashion accessory; historically, fans can tell as much about craftsmanship and social mores as they can about fashion. There are 5,000 of them in the collection, dating from the 17th century onward, often exquisitely crafted from ivory, mother-of-pearl, and tortoiseshell. It was the personal vision of Hélène Alexander that brought this enchanting museum into being, and the workshop and conservation–study center that she has also set up ensure that this art form continues to have a future. ✉ 12 Crooms Hill, Greenwich ☎ 020/8305–1441 ⊕ www.thefanmuseum.org.uk ✉ £5 ⊘ Closed Sun.–Tues. Ⓜ DLR: Cutty Sark.

Museum of London Docklands

HISTORY MUSEUM | This wonderful old warehouse building, on a quaint cobbled quayside near the tower of Canary Wharf, is worth a visit in its own right. With uneven wood floors, beams, and pillars, the museum used to be a storehouse for coffee, tea, sugar, and rum from the West Indies, hence the name: West India Quay. The fascinating story of the old port and the river is told using films, together with interactive displays and reconstructions. Excellent permanent exhibitions include *City and River*, which chronicles the explosion of trade and industry that, by the mid-19th century, had transformed this district into the world's most important port. *Sailortown* is an effective reconstruction of the Wapping district in Victorian times, complete with period shops, a pub, spooky alleys, and costumed guides. Young kids can hunt for treasure and let off some steam in the soft play area in the Mudlarks Gallery. Special events and exhibitions happen

year-round; check the museum's website for details. ✉ No. 1 Warehouse, West India Quay, Canary Wharf ☎ 020/7001–9844 ⊕ www.museumoflondon.org.uk/docklands ✉ Free, special exhibitions sometimes extra Ⓜ Canary Wharf. DLR: West India Quay.

★ National Maritime Museum

HISTORY MUSEUM | **FAMILY** | From the time of Henry VIII until the 1940s, Britain was the world's preeminent naval power, and the collections here trace half a millennia of that seafaring history. The story is as much about trade as it is warfare: in the Atlantic gallery, *Slavery, Trade, Empire* explores how trade in goods (and people) irrevocably changed the world, while in the Traders gallery, *The East India Company and Asia* focuses on how the epoch-defining company shaped trade with Asia for 250 years. One gallery, Polar Worlds, includes a sledge from one of Shackleton's expeditions, while another is devoted to Admiral Lord Nelson, Britain's most famous naval commander; among the exhibits there is the uniform he was wearing, complete with bloodstains, when he died at the Battle of Trafalgar in 1805.

Temporary exhibitions here are usually fascinating—those in recent years have included personal accounts of the First World War at sea. Borrow a tablet computer from the front desk and take it to the giant map of the world in the courtyard at the center of the museum; here, a high-tech, interactive app opens up hidden stories and games as you walk between continents. The Ahoy! gallery is filled with interactive fun for kids, where they can learn about polar exploration, pirates, and more. ✉ Romney Rd., Greenwich ☎ 020/8312–6608 ⊕ www.rmg.co.uk/national-maritime-museum ✉ Free; tours £10; fee for special exhibitions Ⓜ DLR: Greenwich.

★ Old Royal Naval College

COLLEGE | Built by Sir Christopher Wren between 1696 and 1751 as a rest

Did You Know?

Once sailors could determine their distance from the Greenwich meridian (longitude), maritime navigation was greatly improved. Look for the brass line marking the two hemispheres throughout the cobblestone streets.

home for ancient mariners, the college became a naval school in 1873. The site is still used for classes by the University of Greenwich and the Trinity Laban Conservatoire of Music and Dance, although you're more likely to recognize it as a film location: blockbusters to have made use of its elegant interiors include *Skyfall, Les Misérables,* and *The King's Speech.* Architecturally, you'll notice how the structures part to reveal the Queen's House across the central lawns. The Painted Hall, the college's dining hall, derives its name from the Baroque murals of William and Mary (reigned jointly 1689–94; William alone 1695–1702) and assorted allegorical figures. James Thornhill's frescoes, depicting scenes of naval grandeur with a suitably pro-British note, were painstakingly completed 1707–12 and 1718–26, and were good enough to earn him a knighthood. Next door, the Sackler Gallery tells the story of the frescoes.

In the opposite building stands the College Chapel, which was rebuilt after a fire in 1779 in an altogether more restrained, neo-Grecian style. It hosts free lunchtime concerts by Trinity students each Tuesday and Friday, beginning at 1:05 pm. The underground passage connecting the two buildings also leads to Skittle Alley, where naval veterans, known as Greenwich Pensioners, played skittles to pass the time. The college's free visitor center includes interactive exhibits on the history of Greenwich, plus an assortment of local treasures and artifacts. Most intriguing among them is a 17th-century "witch bottle," once used to ward off evil spirits. High-tech scans have revealed it to contain a mixture of human hair, fingernails, and urine. ✉ *King William Walk, Greenwich* ☎ *020/8269–4747* ⊕ *www. ornc.org* ☞ *Visitor center and chapel free; grounds tours and Painted Hall £12.50* Ⓜ *DLR: Greenwich, Cutty Sark.*

Greenwich Foot Tunnel 👁

In 1849, Greenwich Hospital bought Island Gardens, on the other side of the Thames, to guard against industrial sprawl and to preserve one of the most beautiful views in London. Take the stone spiral steps down into Greenwich Foot Tunnel and head under the Thames (enjoying the magnificently creepy echo) to Island Gardens, at the southern tip of the Isle of Dogs. Then look back over the river for a magnificent vista: the Old Royal Naval College and the Queen's House in all their glory, framed by the verdant green borders of the park.

★ The Queen's House
ART MUSEUM | Next to the National Maritime Museum, you'll find the Queen's House, home to a changing selection of the extraordinary Royal Museums Greenwich art collection. The largest collection of maritime art in the world, it includes artwork by William Hogarth, Canaletto, and Joshua Reynolds. These names alone would make the Queen's House worthy of your time, but there's so much more here to enjoy, from the glorious architecture of Inigo Jones to the sensitive and thought-provoking contemporary artist responses commissioned to contextualize the collection's works. ✉ *Romney Rd., Greenwich* ☎ *020/8312–6608* ⊕ *www.rmg.co.uk/queens-house* ☞ *Free* Ⓜ *DLR: Greenwich.*

Ranger's House and the Wernher Collection
HISTORIC HOME | This handsome, early 18th-century villa, which was the Greenwich Park ranger's official residence during the 19th century, is hung with Stuart and Jacobean portraits, but the most interesting diversion is the Wernher Collection, which contains nearly 700

Without a central support, the Tulip Stairs spiral up to the Great Hall of the Queen's House.

artworks that were amassed by the diamond millionaire Sir Julius Wernher (1850–1912) and were once housed in his fabulous stately house, Luton Hoo, in Bedfordshire. The collection ranges from Old Master paintings to Renaissance jewelry and assorted pieces of decorative art and curios from the medieval period onward, including the gorgeous *Madonna of the Pomegranates* from the workshop of Sandro Botticelli. The Ranger's House is just under a mile's walk from the DLR station at Greenwich, or you can catch a bus there from Greenwich or Deptford DLR. ⊠ *Blackheath, Chesterfield Walk, Greenwich Park, Greenwich* ☎ *020/8294–2848* ⊕ *www.english-heritage.org.uk* 🎫 *£11.20* ⊗ *Closed Nov.–Apr., Mon., and Tues.* Ⓜ *DLR: Deptford Bridge, then Bus 53; or Greenwich, then Bus 386.*

★ Royal Observatory

OBSERVATORY | Greenwich is on the prime meridian at 0° longitude, and the ultimate standard for time around the world has been set here at the Royal Observatory since 1884, when Britain was the world's maritime superpower. The observatory is actually split into two sites, a short walk apart: one devoted to astronomy, the other to the study of time. The enchanting Peter Harrison Planetarium is London's only planetarium, its bronze-clad turret glinting in the sun. Shows on black holes and how to interpret the night sky are enthralling and enlightening, and there are dedicated shows for young children, too.

Across the way is Flamsteed House, designed by Sir Christopher Wren in 1675 for John Flamsteed, the first Royal Astronomer. The Time Ball atop Flamsteed House is one of the world's earliest public time signals. Each day at 12:55, it rises halfway up its mast. At 12:58 it rises all the way to the top, and at 1 exactly, the ball falls. A climb to the top of the house also reveals a 28-inch telescope, built in 1893 and now housed inside an onion-shape fiberglass dome. It doesn't compare with the range of modern optical telescopes, but it's still the largest in the United Kingdom. Regular wintertime viewing evenings reveal startlingly detailed views of the lunar surface.

In the Time Galleries, linger over the superb workmanship of John Harrison (1693–1776), whose famous maritime clocks won him the Longitude Prize for solving the problem of accurate time-keeping at sea, paving the way for modern navigation. Don't miss the Camera Obscura, which showcases views down to the river below. Outside, a brass line laid among the cobblestones marks the meridian. As darkness falls, a green laser shoots out, following exactly the path of the meridian line. The hill that is home to the observatory gives fantastic views across London, topped off with £1-a-slot telescopes to scour the skyline. ✉ *Romney Rd., Greenwich* ☎ *020/8858–4422* 🌐 *www.rmg.co.uk/royal-observatory* 🎫 *Royal Observatory £16, planetarium shows £10; special exhibitions £10* [M] *DLR: Greenwich.*

Up at The O2

VIEWPOINT | FAMILY | Certainly one of the most original ways to see London, this thrilling urban expedition takes you on a 90-minute journey across the giant dome of The O2 arena. After a short briefing, you're dressed in safety gear and taken in small groups across a steep walkway, running all the way to the summit and down the other side. The high point (literally) is a viewing platform, 171 feet aboveground, with magnificent views of the city. On a clear day you can see for 15 miles (that's as far as Waltham Abbey to the north and Sevenoaks to the south). Climbs at sunset and twilight are also available, but the best trips are on nights when London is lit up by fireworks, such as New Year's Eve, Fireworks Night, and Diwali.

It's quite an experience, but unsurprisingly there are restrictions: you have to be at least 8 years old, taller than 4 feet, have a waist measurement that's less than 49 inches, weigh less than 286 pounds, and pregnant women can't make the climb at all. Wheelchairs can be accommodated on a few tours. Advance booking is essential. ✉ *Peninsula Sq., London* ☎ *020/8463–2680* 🌐 *www.theo2.co.uk/do-more-at-the-o2/up-at-the-o2* 🎫 *From £32* 🕓 *Closed Mon.–Thurs. in Jan.* [M] *North Greenwich.*

🍴 Restaurants

Ilirian Cafe

$ | CAFÉ | FAMILY | One of a handful of independent businesses in the midst of food chain–dominated Greenwich, this Greek-run café serves filling savory baked goods (the spinach and feta is a winner), generous slices of cake, and good coffee, all in bright and friendly surroundings. **Known for:** traditional Greek pastries such as baklava; central location; homemade cakes. [$] *Average main: £6* ✉ *21 Greenwich Church St., Greenwich* ☎ *020/8858–2858* 🕓 *No dinner* [M] *Cutty Sark.*

The Old Brewery

$$ | MODERN BRITISH | Right next to the Old Royal Naval College Visitor Centre, The Old Brewery is a great spot for a laid-back summer drink with a view of the river and the grand buildings of the college. The all-day menu is mainly British pub classics, but with a focus on locally sourced ingredients. **Known for:** attractive, walled garden; terrace with buzzy vibe in good weather; nice Sunday brunch. [$] *Average main: £16* ✉ *Pepys Bldg., Old Royal Naval College, King William Walk, Greenwich* ☎ *020/3437–2222* 🌐 *www.oldbrewerygreenwich.com* [M] *Cutty Sark, Greenwich.*

The Pavilion Café

$ | CAFÉ | Healthy snacks and lunches are served at this bright café next to the Royal Observatory. Homemade soups and sandwiches are good for a quick refuel, or try one of the delicious stone-baked pizzas for something more substantial. **Known for:** ideal location at the top of Greenwich Park; large garden seating area; family-friendly atmosphere.

$ *Average main: £7* ✉ *Charlton Way, Greenwich* ☎ *020/8305–2896* 🌐 *www.royalparks.org.uk* [M] *Cutty Sark, Greenwich.*

Hotels

The Admiral Hardy

$$ | **B&B/INN** | Those keen to explore Greenwich at a more leisurely pace than a day trip from central London permits should seek out these unexpectedly elegant rooms above a pub, a quick walk from the Old Royal Naval College in one direction and the National Maritime Museum in the other. **Pros:** vintage furniture gives each room a unique feel; lovely views from rooms, including some of the *Cutty Sark*; one-minute walk from most Greenwich sights. **Cons:** no elevator; some rooms prone to traffic noise; no room service. $ *Rooms from: £143* ✉ *7 College Approach, Greenwich* ☎ *020/8293–9535* 🌐 *www.admiralhardygreenwich.co.uk* 🛏 *7 rooms* 🍴 *No Meals* [M] *Cutty Sark.*

Nightlife

Oliver's Jazz Bar

LIVE MUSIC | The scuffed carpet and peeling paintwork only add to the atmosphere at this tiny basement jazz bar, one of London's leading music venues. There's live music every night of the week, with tickets for just £10. It's a phenomenal bargain given the level of talent that regularly performs, from international acts in town for the London Jazz Festival each November to the weekly free Beats in the Bar nights, where students from nearby Trinity Laban Conservatoire try out new material in a low-pressure environment. Walk-ins are always welcome, but if you're planning a weekend visit, it's a good idea to reserve a table a few days ahead of time. ✉ *9 Nevada St., Greenwich* ☎ *020/8858–3693* 🌐 *oliversjazzbar.com* [M] *Cutty Sark.*

Trafalgar Tavern

PUBS | With its excellent vista of the Thames, there is no more handsomely situated pub in Greenwich than the Trafalgar Tavern. Open at 11 am every day, it's still as grand a place as it ever was to have a pint and a quick tasty meal. ✉ *Park Row, Greenwich* ☎ *020/3887–9886* 🌐 *www.trafalgartavern.co.uk* [M] *Cutty Sark, Greenwich.*

Shopping

Greenwich Market

MARKET | Established as a fruit-and-vegetable market in 1700, the covered market now offers around 120 mixed stalls of art and crafts on Monday, Wednesday, Friday, and weekends, and vintage antiques on Tuesday, Thursday, and Friday. You can buy food on each day, although the offerings are usually best on weekends. Shopping for handicrafts is a pleasure here, as in most cases you're buying directly from the artist. ✉ *College Approach, Greenwich* ☎ *020/8269–5096* 🌐 *www.greenwichmarketlondon.com* [M] *DLR: Cutty Sark.*

Music & Video Exchange

MUSIC | This London institution (there are other branches in Notting Hill) carries a remarkable range of secondhand vinyl records, with everything from bargain 25-pence records to treasured first editions costing more than £1,000. ✉ *23 Greenwich Church St., Greenwich* ☎ *020/8858–8899* 🌐 *www.mgeshops.com* [M] *Cutty Sark, Greenwich.*

Chapter 14

THE THAMES UPSTREAM

Updated by
Toby Orton

👁 Sights	🍽 Restaurants	🛏 Hotels	🛍 Shopping	🍸 Nightlife
★★★★☆	★★☆☆☆	★☆☆☆☆	★☆☆☆☆	★★☆☆☆

THE THAMES UPSTREAM SNAPSHOT

TOP REASONS TO GO

Hampton Court Palace: Go ghost hunting or just admire the beautiful Tudor architecture at Henry VIII's beloved home, then lose yourself in the maze as night begins to fall.

Strawberry Hill House: The 19th-century birthplace of connoisseur Horace Walpole's Gothic style, this mock castle is a joyous riot of color and invention.

Kew Gardens: See the grounds from above by visiting Kew's treetop walkway at the famous Royal Botanic Gardens.

The River Thames: Enjoy a pint from the creaking balcony of a centuries-old riverside pub as you watch the boats row by on the loveliest stretch of England's greatest river.

GETTING THERE

The District line is your best Tube option, stopping at Turnham Green (in the heart of Chiswick but a walk from the houses), Gunnersbury (for Syon Park), Kew Gardens, and Richmond. For Hampton Court, overland train is quickest: South West trains run from Waterloo four times an hour, with roughly half requiring a change at Surbiton. There are also regular direct trains from Waterloo to Chiswick Station (best for Chiswick House), Kew Bridge, St Margarets (for Marble Hill House), and Richmond (for Ham House). London Overground trains also stop at Gunnersbury, Kew Gardens, and Richmond.

A pleasant way to go is by river. Boats depart from Westminster Pier, by Big Ben, for Kew (1½ hours), Richmond (2 hours), and Hampton Court (3 hours). The trip is worth taking if you make it an integral part of your day, and know that it gets breezy. Round-trip tickets run £22–£27. For more details, contact Thames River Boats (☎ *020/7930–2062* ⊕ *www. wpsa.co.uk*).

MAKING THE MOST OF YOUR TIME

■ Hampton Court Palace requires half a day to experience its magic, although you could make do with a few hours for the other attractions. Because of the distance between sights, it's best to focus on one, add in some others within the area, then a riverside walk and a pint at a pub.

A GOOD WALK IN CHISWICK

■ From Chiswick House, follow Burlington Lane and take a left onto Hogarth Lane—which, in reality, is anything but a lane—to reach Hogarth's House. Chiswick's Church Street (reached by a rather unappealing underpass from Hogarth's House) is the nearest thing to a sleepy country village street you're likely to find in London. Follow it down to the Thames and turn left at the bottom to reach the 18th-century riverfront houses of Chiswick Mall, referred to by locals as "Millionaire's Row."

The upper stretch of the Thames links a string of upmarket districts—Chiswick, Kew, and Richmond—with winding old streets, horticultural delights, cozy riverside pubs, and Henry VIII's Hampton Court Palace. The neighborhoods along the way are as proud of their villagey feel as of their stately history, witnessed by such handsome estates as Strawberry Hill and Syon House. After the sensory overload of the West End, it's easy to forget you're in a capital city.

Chiswick

On the banks of the Thames just west of central London, far enough out to escape the crush and crowds you're just getting used to, Chiswick is a low-key, upscale district, content with its run of restaurants, stylish shops, and film-star residents. No doubt its most famous son wouldn't approve of all the conspicuous wealth, though; Chiswick was home to one of Britain's best-loved painters, William Hogarth, who tore the fabric of the 18th-century nation to shreds with his slew of satirical engravings. **Hogarth's House** has been restored to its former glory.

Incongruously stranded among Chiswick's row houses are a number of fine 18th-century buildings, which are now some of the most desirable suburban houses in London. By far the grandest of all is **Chiswick House,** a unique Palladian-style mansion born from the 3rd Earl of Burlington's love of classical and Renaissance architecture—a radical style at the time.

 Sights

⭐ **Chiswick House**

HISTORIC HOME | Completed in 1729 by the 3rd Earl of Burlington (also known for Burlington House—home of the Royal Academy—and Burlington Arcade on Piccadilly), this extraordinary Palladian mansion was envisaged as a kind

of temple to the arts. Burlington was fascinated by the architecture he saw in Italy while on the Grand Tour as a young man and loosely modeled this building on the Villa Capra, "La Rotonda," near Vicenza and the Pantheon in Rome (note the colonnaded frontage and the domed roof, which is visible from the inside in the Upper Tribunal).

The sumptuous interiors were the work of William Kent (1685–1748), and it's easy to see how they made such a profound impact at the time; the astonishing Blue Velvet Room, with its gilded decoration and intricately painted ceiling, is an extraordinary achievement, as are the gilded domed apses that punctuate the Gallery (an homage to the Temple of Venus and Roma from the Forum Romanum in Rome). Such ideas were so radical in England at the time that wealthy patrons clamored to have Kent design everything from gardens to party frocks.

The rambling grounds are one of the hidden gems of West London. Italianate in style (of course), they are filled with classical temples, statues, and obelisks. Also on the grounds are a café and a children's play area. ⊠ *Burlington La., Chiswick* ☎ *020/3141–3350* ⊕ *www. chiswickhouseandgardens.org.uk* ✉ *£11, grounds free* ⊗ *House closed Nov.–Mar. and Tues., Thurs., and Fri. in summer* Ⓜ *Turnham Green, Chiswick. National Rail: Chiswick.*

Hogarth's House

HISTORIC HOME | The satirist and painter William Hogarth (1697–1764), little known in the rest of the world, is hugely famous in Britain. His witty, acerbic engravings, which railed against the harsh injustices of the time, may be called the visual equivalent of the satires of Jonathan Swift and were no less influential in their time. Unfortunately his beloved house has had an appalling streak of bad luck; as if the decision, in the 1960s, to route one of the nation's

busiest highways outside the front gates wasn't ignoble enough, the house was closed after a fire in 2009.

Now fully restored, the rooms contain absorbing exhibitions, featuring many of Hogarth's 18th-century prints, together with replica furniture of the period. Look out for the 300-year-old mulberry tree outside; Hogarth and his wife used its fruit to bake pies for destitute children. The original copies of some of Hogarth's most famous works can be seen elsewhere in the city: *A Rake's Progress* at Sir John Soane's Museum; *Marriage A-la-Mode* at the National Gallery; and *Gin Lane* at the British Museum. His tomb is in the cemetery of St. Nicholas's Church on nearby Chiswick Mall. ⊠ *Hogarth La., Great West Rd. (A4), Chiswick* ☎ *020/8994–6757* ⊕ *www. hogarthshouse.org* ✉ *Free* ⊗ *Closed Mon.* Ⓜ *Turnham Green. National Rail: Chiswick.*

Kew

A mile or so beyond Chiswick is Kew, a leafy suburb with little to see other than its two big attractions: the lovely **Kew Palace** and the **Royal Botanic Gardens**—anchored in the landscape for several miles around by a towering, mock-Chinese pagoda.

◉ Sights

★ Kew Gardens

GARDEN | FAMILY | Enter the Royal Botanic Gardens, as Kew Gardens are officially known, and you are enveloped by blazes of color, extraordinary blooms, hidden trails, and lovely old follies. Beautiful though it all is, Kew's charms are secondary to its true purpose as a major center for serious research: more than 200 academics are consistently hard at work here on projects spanning 110 countries. First opened to the public in 1840, this 326-acre site has been supported by royalty and nurtured by landscapers,

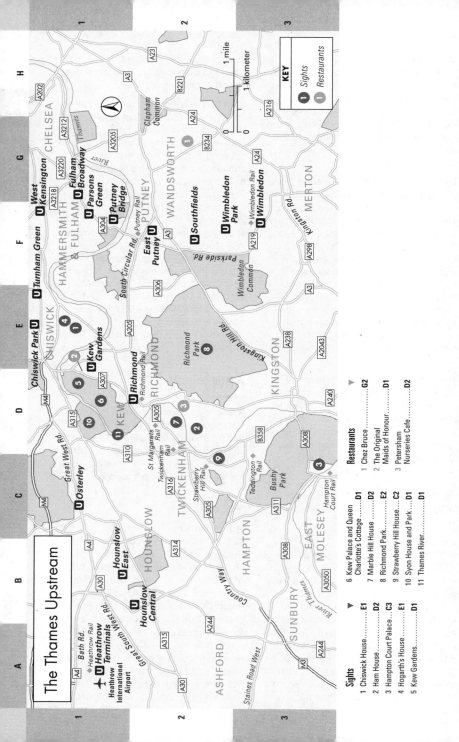

The Thames Upstream

Sights ▶

1 Chiswick House............**E1**
2 Ham House...............**D2**
3 Hampton Court Palace....**C3**
4 Hogarth's House.........**E1**
5 Kew Gardens............**D1**

6 Kew Palace and Queen
  Charlotte's Cottage.......**D1**
7 Marble Hill House........**D2**
8 Richmond Park...........**E2**
9 Strawberry Hill House....**C2**
10 Syon House and Park.....**D1**
11 Thames River...........**D1**

Restaurants ▶

1 Chez Bruce..............**G2**
2 The Original
  Maids of Honour.........**D1**
3 Petersham
  Nurseries Cafe..........**D2**

KEY

1 Sights

1 Restaurants

0   1 mile

0   1 kilometer

botanists, and architects since the 1720s. Today the gardens, now a UNESCO World Heritage Site, hold more than 30,000 species of plants from every corner of the globe.

Architect Sir William Chambers built a series of temples and follies, of which the crazy 10-story Pagoda, visible for miles around, is the star. The Princess of Wales Conservatory houses 10 climate zones, and the Treetop Walkway takes you 59 feet up into the air. Two great 19th-century greenhouses—the Palm House and the Temperate House—are filled with exotic blooms, and many of the plants have been there since the final glass panel was fixed into place, including the largest greenhouse plant in the world, a Chilean wine palm planted in 1846 (it's so big you have to climb the spiral staircase to the roof to get a proper view of it).

To get around the gardens, the Kew Explorer bus runs on a 40-minute, hop-on, hop-off route, starting at the Victoria Gate, every 30 minutes, 11–4:30 (£6.50). Free guided tours, run by volunteers, are given daily at 11 and 1:30, plus special seasonally themed tours at other times. Discovery Tours, fully accessible for visitors in wheelchairs, are also available daily with advance booking. ⊠ *Kew Rd. at Lichfield Rd., for Victoria Gate entrance, Kew* ☎ *020/8332–5000* ⊕ *www.kew. org* 🎫 *£21.45, Explorer Land Train £6.50* Ⓜ *Kew Gardens. National Rail: Kew Gardens, Kew Bridge.*

★ **Kew Palace and Queen Charlotte's Cottage**
CASTLE/PALACE | The elegant redbrick exterior of the smallest of Britain's royal palaces seems almost humble when compared with the grandeur of, say, Buckingham or Kensington Palace. Yet inside is a fascinating glimpse into life at the uppermost end of society from the 17th to 19th centuries. This is actually the third of several palaces that stood here; once known as Dutch House, it was one

of the havens to which George III retired when insanity forced him to withdraw from public life. Queen Charlotte had an *orné* (a rustic-style cottage retreat) added in the late 18th century. In a marvelously regal flight of fancy, she kept kangaroos in the paddock outside. The main house and gardens are maintained in the 18th-century style. Entry to the palace itself is free, but it lies within the grounds of Kew Gardens, and you must buy a ticket to that to get here. ⊠ *Kew Gardens, Kew Rd. at Lichfield Rd., Kew* ☎ *020/3166–6000* ⊕ *www.hrp.org.uk/ kew-palace* 🎫 *Free with entry to Kew Gardens* ⊘ *Closed Oct.–Apr.* Ⓜ *Kew Gardens.*

🍴 Restaurants

The Original Maids of Honour
$$ | CAFÉ | This most traditional of old English tearooms is named for a kind of cheese tart invented near here in Tudor times. Legend has it that Henry VIII loved them so much he had the recipe kept under armed guard; this place has specialized in the authentic royal recipe for more than 120 years now, and still bakes the maids by hand on the premises.
Known for: nostalgic mock Tudor decor rebuilt following bomb damage during WWII; traditional baking techniques that date back over centuries; excellent full English breakfast. 💲 *Average main: £18* ⊠ *288 Kew Rd., Kew* ☎ *020/8940–2752* ⊕ *www.theoriginalmaidsofhonour.co.uk.*

Richmond

Named after the (long-vanished) palace Henry VII started here in 1500, Richmond is still a welcoming suburb with a small-town feel, marred only by choking levels of traffic. Duck away from the main streets to find many handsome Georgian and Victorian houses, antiques shops, a Victorian theater, a grand stately home—and, best of all, the largest of London's royal parks.

Sights

Ham House

HISTORIC HOME | To the west of Richmond Park, overlooking the Thames and nearly opposite the memorably named Eel Pie Island, Ham House was built in 1610 and remodeled 60 years later. It's one of the most complete examples in Europe of a lavish 17th-century house, and as such you can get a clear sense of how the English aristocracy really lived during that period (in short: comfortably). The beautiful formal gardens, with their distinctive spherical and conical topiary, have become an influential source for other palaces and grand villas seeking to restore their gardens to how they were in their heyday. The original decorations in the Great Hall, Round Gallery, and Great Staircase have been replicated, and most of the furniture and fittings are on permanent loan from the Victoria and Albert Museum.

Note that from January to March, visits are by guided tour only, lasting around 30 minutes (no need to book). A tranquil and scenic way to reach the house is on foot, which takes about 30 minutes, along the eastern riverbank south from Richmond Bridge. ✉ *Ham St., Richmond* ☎ *020/8940-1950* ⊕ *www.nationaltrust. org.uk/hamhouse* 🎟 *£13* Ⓜ *Richmond, then Bus 65 or 371.*

★ Hampton Court Palace

CASTLE/PALACE | **FAMILY** | The beloved seat of Henry VIII's court, sprawled elegantly beside the languid waters of the Thames, Hampton Court is steeped in more history than virtually any other royal building in England. The Tudor mansion, begun in 1515 by Cardinal Wolsey to curry favor with the young Henry, actually conceals a larger 17th-century Baroque building, which was partly designed by Sir Christopher Wren. The earliest dwellings on this site belonged to a religious order founded in the 11th century and were expanded over the years by its many subsequent residents, until George II moved the royal household closer to London in the early 18th century.

After entering through the magnificent Tudor courtyard, start with a look through the State Apartments, decorated in the Tudor style, and on to the wood-beamed magnificence of Henry's Great Hall, before taking in the strikingly azure ceiling of the Chapel Royal. Watch out for the ghost of Henry VIII's doomed fifth wife, Catherine Howard, who lost her head yet is said to scream her way along the Haunted Gallery. (Believe it or not, what is certainly true is that the corridor is prone to sudden drops in temperature—and no one quite knows why.) Latter-day masters of the palace, the joint rulers William and Mary (reigned 1689–1702), were responsible for the beautiful King's and Queen's Apartments and the elaborate Baroque of the Georgian Rooms.

Well-handled reconstructions of Tudor life take place all year, from live appearances by "Henry VIII" to cook-historians preparing authentic feasts in the Tudor Kitchens. (Dishes on offer in the adjacent café include a few of these traditional recipes.) The highlight of the formal grounds is undoubtedly the famous maze (the oldest hedge maze in the world), its half mile of pathways among clipped hedgerows still fiendish to negotiate. There's a trick, but we won't give it away here; it's much more fun just to go and lose yourself. Meanwhile, the Lower Orangery Garden shows off thousands of exotic species that William and Mary, avid plant collectors, gathered from around the globe. Family ghost tours are given on evenings from October to February. Not only are they entertainingly spooky, but they're a great opportunity to see the older parts of the palace without the crowds. Scarier, adults-only versions last two hours. Note that tours can sell out several weeks in advance. ✉ *Hampton Court Rd., East Molesey* ☎ *020/3166–6000* ⊕ *www.hrp.org.uk/*

Hampton Court Palace, the seat of Henry VIII's court, is a prime example of a Tudor mansion and features the oldest hedge maze in the world.

hamptoncourtpalace ✉ £25.30 palace, maze, and gardens Ⓜ Richmond, then Bus R68. National Rail: Hampton Court, 35 mins from Waterloo (most trains require change at Surbiton).

Marble Hill House

HISTORIC HOME | This handsome Palladian mansion is set on 66 acres of parkland on the northern bank of the Thames, almost opposite Ham House. It was built in the 1720s by George II for his mistress, the "exceedingly respectable and respected" Henrietta Howard. Later the house was occupied by Mrs. Fitzherbert, who was secretly (and illegally) married to the Prince Regent (later George IV) in 1785. The house was restored and opened to the public in 1903, looking very much like it did in Georgian times, with extravagant gilded rooms in which Mrs. Howard entertained the literary superstars of the age, including Alexander Pope and Jonathan Swift. A ferry service from Ham House operates during the summer; access on foot is a half-hour walk south along the west bank of the Thames from Richmond Bridge. Note that entry is by guided tour only, run by English Heritage and volunteers from a local history group. ✉ Richmond Rd., Twickenham ☎ 037/0333–1181 ⊕ www.english-heritage.org.uk/visit/places/marble-hill-house ✉ £8 ⊘ Closed Nov.–Apr. and weekdays Ⓜ Richmond. National Rail: St. Margaret's.

★ Richmond Park

CITY PARK | FAMILY | This enormous park was enclosed in 1637 for use as a royal hunting ground—like practically all other London parks. Unlike the others, however, Richmond Park still has wild red and fallow deer roaming its 2,500 acres (three times the size of New York's Central Park) of grassland and heath. Its ancient oaks are among the last remnants of the vast, wild forests that once encroached on London in medieval times. The Isabella Plantation (near the Ham Gate entrance) is an enchanting and colorful woodland garden, first laid out in 1831. There's a splendid protected view of St. Paul's Cathedral from King Henry

Another highlight of Richmond is the dazzling and bold Strawberry Hill House.

VIII's Mound, the highest point in the park; find it, and you have a piece of magic in your sights. The park is also home to White Lodge, a 1727 hunting lodge that now houses the Royal Ballet School. ✉ *Richmond* ☎ *030/0061–2200* ⊕ *www. royalparks.org.uk* ✉ *Free* Ⓜ *Richmond, then Bus 371 or 65.*

★ Strawberry Hill House

HISTORIC HOME | From the outside, this rococo mishmash of towers, crenellations, and white stucco is dazzling in its faux-medieval splendor. Its architect and owner, Sir Horace Walpole (1717–97), knew a thing or two about imaginative flights of fancy; the flamboyant son of the first British prime minister, Robert Walpole, he all but single-handedly invented the Gothic novel with *The Castle of Otranto* (1764).

Once you pass through Strawberry Hill's forbidding exterior, you'll experience an explosion of color and light, for Walpole boldly decided to take elements from the exteriors of Gothic cathedrals and move them inside. The detail is phenomenal,

from the cavernous entrance hall with its vast Gothic trompe-l'oeil decorations, to the Great Parlour with its Renaissance stained glass, to the Gallery, where extraordinary fan vaulting is a replica of the vaults found in the Henry VII Chapel at Westminster Abbey. The gardens have been meticulously returned to their original 18th-century design, right down to a white marble loveseat sculpted into the shape of a shell. Opening days can vary, so call ahead to check times. ✉ *268 Waldegrave Rd., Twickenham* ☎ *020/8744–1241* ⊕ *www.strawberryhill-house.org.uk* ✉ *£14* ⊙ *Property closed Jan.–Mar.; house closed Thurs.–Sat. Apr.–Dec.* Ⓜ *Richmond, then Bus 33 or R68. National Rail: Strawberry Hill.*

★ Syon House and Park

HISTORIC HOME | **FAMILY** | The residence of the Duke and Duchess of Northumberland, this is one of England's most lavish stately homes. Set in a 200-acre park landscaped by the great gardener "Capability" Brown (1716–83), the core of the house is Tudor—it was one of the last stopping places for Henry VIII's fifth wife, Catherine Howard, and the extremely short-lived monarch Lady Jane Grey before they were sent to the Tower. It was remodeled in the Georgian style in 1762 by famed decorator Robert Adam. He had just returned from studying the sights of classical antiquity in Italy and created two rooms sumptuous enough to wow any Grand Tourist: the entryway is an amazing study in black and white, pairing neoclassical marbles with antique bronzes, and the Ante Room contains 12 enormous verd-antique columns surmounted by statues of gold—and this was just a waiting room for the duke's servants and retainers. The Red Drawing Room is covered with crimson Spitalfields silk, and the Long Gallery is one of Adam's noblest creations. ✉ *Syon Park, Brentford* ☎ *020/8560–0882* 🌐 *www.syonpark.co.uk* 🎟 *£13.50, £8 gardens and conservatory only* 🕒 *Property closed Nov.–mid-Mar.; house closed Mon., Tues., Fri., and Sat. mid-Mar.–Oct.* [M] *Gunnersbury, then Bus 237 or 267 to Brentlea.*

Thames River

BODY OF WATER | The twists and turns of the Thames through the heart of the capital make it London's best thoroughfare and most compelling viewing point. Every palace, church, theater, wharf, museum, and pub along the bank has a tale to tell, and traveling on or alongside the river is one of the best ways to soak up views of the city. Frequent daily tourist-boat services are at their height April through October. In most cases you can turn up at a pier, and the next departure won't be far away; however, it never hurts to book ahead if you can. The trip between Westminster Pier and the Tower of London takes about 40 minutes, while that between the Tower and Greenwich takes around half an hour. A full round-trip can take several hours. Ask about flexible fares and hop-on, hop-off options at the various piers. ✉ *London.*

🍴 Restaurants

Chez Bruce

$$$ | MODERN FRENCH | Top-notch French and Mediterranean cuisine, faultless service, and a winning wine list make this one of London's all-star favorite restaurants. At this cozy haunt overlooking Wandsworth Common, prepare for unfussy grown-up gastro wonders ranging from homemade charcuterie to lighter, simply grilled fish dishes. **Known for:** impressive sommelier; elegant neighborhood salon; luxe classics like lobster and scallop ravioli. [$] *Average main: £30* ✉ *2 Bellevue Rd., Wandsworth Common, Battersea* ☎ *020/8672–0114* 🌐 *www.chezbruce.co.uk* [M] *Overland: Wandsworth Common.*

Petersham Nurseries Café

$$$ | ITALIAN | Bucolic beauty and rustic Italian cuisine combine wonderfully at Petersham Nurseries Café, a delightfully charming and informal dining experience housed within the serene environ of Richmond's poshest garden center. Prices are high, but your farm-fresh dishes do come surrounded by a backdrop of hanging plants, succulents, shrubs, and climbers that create London's most whimsical greenhouse dining room. **Known for:** relaxed, rustic fine dining; sustainable ingredients and Slow Food philosophy; stunning ramshackle interiors filled with plants. [$] *Average main: £30* ✉ *Church La., off Petersham Rd., London* ☎ *020/8940–5230* 🌐 *www.petershamnurseries.com* 🕒 *Closed Mon. No dinner Sun., Tues., and Wed.* [M] *Richmond Station, 65 bus.*

🍸 Nightlife

A pint in a riverside pub is a London must, and the capital's western reaches (including the Richmond and Hammersmith neighborhoods) offer some truly picturesque drinking opportunities. Pick a traditional establishment and you'll feel like you've ventured far from the Big Smoke.

PUBS

★ The Dove

PUBS | FAMILY | Read the list of famous ex-regulars, from Charles II and Nell Gwyn to Ernest Hemingway and Dylan Thomas, as you wait for a beer at this smart, comely, and popular 16th-century Thames riverside pub on the Upper Mall towpath in Hammersmith. If—as is often the case—The Dove is too full, stroll upstream along the bank to The Old Ship or The Blue Anchor. ✉ *19 Upper Mall, Hammersmith* ☎ *020/8748–9474* ⊕ *www.dovehammersmith.co.uk* Ⓜ *Hammersmith.*

The Roebuck

PUBS | FAMILY | Perched on top of Richmond Hill, The Roebuck has perhaps the best view of any pub in London. The most sought-after seats are the benches found directly across the road, which look out over the Thames as it winds its way into the countryside below. Friendly and surprisingly unpretentious, given its lofty surrounds, it is well worth the long climb up the hill from the center of Richmond. ✉ *130 Richmond Hill, Richmond* ☎ *020/8948–2329* ⊕ *www.greeneking-pubs.co.uk* Ⓜ *Richmond.*

SIDE TRIPS FROM LONDON

15

Updated by
Toby Orton

 Sights
★★★★☆

 Restaurants
★★★☆☆

 Hotels
★☆☆☆☆

 Shopping
★☆☆☆☆

 Nightlife
★☆☆☆☆

WELCOME TO SIDE TRIPS FROM LONDON

TOP REASONS TO GO

★ **Shakespeare in Stratford:** To see a play by Shakespeare in the town where he was born—and perhaps after you've visited his birthplace or other sights—is a magical experience.

★ **Cambridge:** A walk through the colleges is grand, but the best views of the university's buildings and immaculate lawns (and some famous bridges) are from a punt on the river.

★ **Stonehenge:** The power and mystery of this Neolithic stone circle on Salisbury Plain are still spellbinding.

★ **Oxford:** While scholars' noses are buried in their books, you get to sightsee among Oxford University's ancient stone buildings and memorable museums.

★ **Windsor Castle:** The mystique of eight successive royal houses of the British monarchy permeates Windsor and its famous castle, where a fraction of the current Queen's vast wealth is displayed.

1 Cambridge. Home to one of the world's most prestigious universities.

2 Stratford-upon-Avon. Shakespeare's famous hometown.

3 Oxford. One of the world's oldest and greatest centers of learning.

4 Stonehenge. An enigmatic prehistoric monument that has baffled the world for millennia.

5 Windsor. A gorgeous town with one of England's most famous castles.

6 Warner Bros. Harry Potter Studio Tour. An attraction that brings you up close and personal to some of the most famous scenes in the world of Harry Potter.

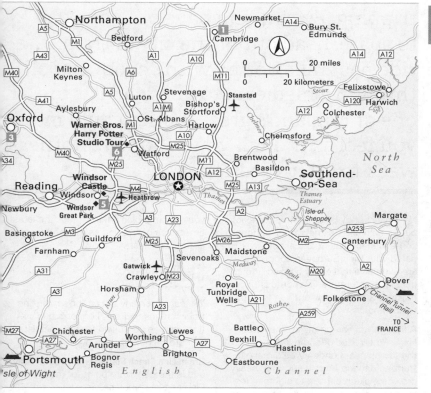

Londoners are undeniably lucky. Few urban populations enjoy such glorious—and easily accessible—options for day-tripping. Even if you have only one day to spare, head out of the city. A train ride past hills dotted with sheep, a stroll through a medieval town, or a visit to one of England's great castles could make you feel as though you've added another week to your vacation.

Not only is England extremely compact, but its train and bus networks, although somewhat inefficient and expensive compared with their European counterparts, are extensive and easily booked (though pricing structures can be confusing), making "a brilliant day out" an easy thing to accomplish.

Although you can do the Warner Bros. Harry Potter Studio Tour in a day, many of the towns near London would make for a frenzied day trip. And in summer, heavy crowds make it difficult to sightsee in a relaxed manner, so consider staying for a day or two instead. You'd then have time to explore a different England—one with quiet country pubs, tree-lined lanes, and neat fields.

Planning

Getting Around

Normally the towns near London are best reached by train. Bus travel costs less, but can take twice as long. Wherever you're going, plan ahead: check the latest timetables before you set off, and try to get an early start.

Station Tips

You can reach any of London's main-line train stations by Tube. London's bus stations can be confusing for the uninitiated, so here's a quick breakdown:

Green Line Coach Station is on Bulleid Way and is the departure point for most Green Line and Megabus services.

Victoria Bus Station is where many of the local London bus services arrive and depart, and is directly outside the main exits of the train and Tube stations.

Victoria Coach Station is on Buckingham Palace Road: it's a five-minute walk from Victoria Tube station. This is where to go for coach departures; arrivals are at a different location, a short walk from here.

To Get to ...	Take the Train from ...	Take the Bus from ...
Cambridge	King's Cross (45–90 minutes, every 10 or 20 minutes); Liverpool St. (80 minutes, every 30 minutes)	Victoria Coach (about 3 hours, every 60–90 minutes)
Oxford	Paddington (55–110 minutes, every 3–20 minutes)	Victoria Coach (100 minutes, every half hour) or Oxford Tube, Buckingham Palace Rd. (100 minutes, every 12–20 minutes)
Stonehenge	Waterloo to Salisbury (90 minutes, every hour)	Victoria Coach to Amesbury (2 hours, about 3 times daily)
Stratford-upon-Avon	Marylebone (2–2½ hours, every 2 hours); or Euston (1½ hours, every 20 or 40 minutes or hourly)	Victoria Coach (3 hours 25 minutes, about 3 times daily)
Warner Bros. Harry Potter Studio Tour	Euston (20 minutes) to Watford, then shuttle bus to attraction	Watford (15 minutes, every 20 minutes), after taking London train from Euston
Windsor	Paddington (25–50 minutes, every 5–30 minutes) or Waterloo (1 hour 5 minutes, every half hour)	Green Line Coach, Victoria (1 hour 5 minutes, hourly)

15

Side Trips from London   CAMBRIDGE

Restaurants

Prices in the reviews are the average cost of a main course at dinner or, if dinner is not served, at lunch. Note: If a restaurant offers only prix-fixe (set-price) meals, it has been given the price category that reflects the full prix-fixe price.

WHAT IT COSTS in Pounds			
$	$$	$$$	$$$$
RESTAURANTS			
Under £16	£16–£23	£24–£31	Over £31

Cambridge

60 miles northeast of London.

With the spires of its university buildings framed by towering trees and expansive meadows, its medieval streets and passages enhanced by gardens and riverbanks, the city of Cambridge is among the loveliest in England. The city predates the Roman occupation of Britain, but there's confusion over exactly how the university was founded. The most widely accepted story is that it was established in 1209 by a pair of scholars from Oxford, who left their university in protest over the wrongful execution of a colleague for murder.

This university town may be beautiful, but it's no museum. Even when the students are on vacation, there's a cultural and intellectual buzz here. Well-preserved medieval buildings sit cheek-by-jowl with the latest in modern architecture (for example, the William Gates Building, which houses Cambridge University's computer laboratory) in this growing city—dominated culturally and architecturally by its famous university, whose students make up around one fifth of the city's 109,000 inhabitants, and beautified by parks, gardens, and the quietly flowing River Cam. One quintessential Cambridge pursuit is punting on the Cam (one occupant propelling the narrow, square-end, flat-bottom boat with a long pole), followed by a stroll along The Backs, the left bank of the river fringed by St. John's, Trinity, Clare, King's, and Queens' colleges, and by Trinity Hall.

GETTING HERE AND AROUND

Good bus (three hours) and train (one hour) services connect London and Cambridge. The city center is very amenable to explorations on foot, or you could join the throng by renting a bicycle.

VISITING THE COLLEGES

College visits are certainly a highlight of a Cambridge tour, but remember that the colleges are private residences and workplaces, even when school isn't in session. Each is an independent entity within the university; some are closed to the public, but at others you can see the chapels, dining rooms (called halls), and sometimes the libraries, too. Some colleges charge a fee for the privilege of nosing around. All are closed during exams (usually mid-April–late June), and the opening hours often vary. Additionally, all are subject to closure at short notice (especially King's); check the websites in advance. For details about visiting specific colleges not listed here, contact Cambridge University.

TOURS
City Sightseeing
BUS TOURS | This company operates open-top bus tours of Cambridge, including The Backs, colleges, and Botanic Gardens. Tours can be joined at marked bus stops in the city. Ask the tourist office about additional tours. ⊠ *Silver, Street East, Cambridge* ☎ *01789/299123* ⊕ *www.city-sightseeing.com* ▨ *From £16.50.*

Society of Cambridge Tourist Guides
WALKING TOURS | Walking tours are led by official Blue or Green Badge guides. The 1½- or 2-hour tours range from the Cambridge Highlights tour, which takes in the city's central landmarks, to the self-explanatory Haunted Cambridge tour. Hours vary according to the tour, with the earliest leaving at 10:30 am and the latest departing in the early evening. ⊠ *185 East Rd., Cambridge* ⊕ *sctg.org.uk/tours* ▨ *From £20.*

◉ Sights

Emmanuel College
COLLEGE | The master hand of architect Sir Christopher Wren (1632–1723) is evident throughout much of Cambridge, particularly at Emmanuel, built on the site of a Dominican friary, where he designed the chapel and colonnade. A stained-glass window in the chapel has a likeness of John Harvard, founder of Harvard University, who studied here. The college, founded in 1584, was an early center of Puritan learning; a number of the Pilgrims were Emmanuel alumni, and they remembered their alma mater in naming Cambridge, Massachusetts. ⊠ *St. Andrew's St., Cambridge* ☎ *01223/334200* ⊕ *www. emma.cam.ac.uk* ▨ *Free* ⊗ *Closed during exam periods.*

★ The Fitzwilliam Museum

ART MUSEUM | In a classical-revival building renowned for its grand Corinthian portico, "The Fitz," founded by the 7th Viscount Fitzwilliam of Merrion in 1816, has one of Britain's most outstanding collections of art and antiquities. Highlights include two large Titians, an extensive collection of French impressionist paintings, and many works by Matisse and Picasso. The opulent interior displays these treasures to marvelous effect, from Egyptian pieces like inch-high figurines and painted coffins to sculptures from the Chinese Han dynasty of the 3rd century BC. Other collections of note here include a fine collection of flower paintings, an assortment of medieval illuminated manuscripts, and a fascinating room full of armor and muskets. ⊠ *Trumpington St., Cambridge* ☎ *01223/332900* ⊕ *www.fitzmuseum. cam.ac.uk* ☎ *Free* ☉ *Closed Mon. except bank holidays.*

King's College

COLLEGE | Founded in 1441 by Henry VI, King's College has a magnificent late 15th-century chapel that is its most famous landmark. Other notable architecture includes the neo-Gothic Porters' Lodge, facing King's Parade, which was a comparatively recent addition in the 1830s, and the classical Gibbs Building. Head down to the river, from where the panorama of college and chapel is one of the university's most photographed views.

Past students of King's College include the novelist E. M. Forster, the economist John Maynard Keynes, and the World War I poet Rupert Brooke. ⊠ *King's Parade, Cambridge* ☎ *01223/331100* ⊕ *www.kings.cam.ac.uk* ☎ *£10, includes chapel.*

★ King's College Chapel

CHURCH | Based on Sainte-Chapelle, the 13th-century royal chapel in Paris, this house of worship is perhaps the most glorious flowering of Perpendicular Gothic in Britain. Henry VI, the king after

A Gift for Science

For centuries Cambridge has been among the country's greatest universities, rivaled only by Oxford. Since the time of one of its most famous alumni, Sir Isaac Newton, it's outshone Oxford in the natural sciences. The university has taken advantage of this prestige, sharing its research facilities with high-tech industries. Surrounded by technology companies, Cambridge has been dubbed "Silicon Fen," a comparison to California's Silicon Valley.

whom the college is named, oversaw the work. From the outside, the most prominent features are the massive flying buttresses and the fingerlike spires that line the length of the building. Inside, the most obvious impression is of great space—the chapel was once described as "the noblest barn in Europe"—and of light flooding in from its huge windows. The brilliantly colored bosses (carved panels at the intersections of the roof ribs) are particularly intense, although hard to see without binoculars. An exhibition in the chantries, or side chapels, explains more about the chapel's construction. Behind the altar is *The Adoration of the Magi,* an enormous painting by Peter Paul Rubens.

The chapel, unlike the rest of King's College, stays open during exam periods. Every Christmas Eve, a festival of carols is sung by the chapel's famous choir. It's broadcast on national television and considered a quintessential part of the traditional English Christmas. To compete for the small number of tickets available, join the line at the college's main entrance in the early hours—doors open at 7 am. ⊠ *King's Parade, Cambridge* ☎ *01223/331212* ⊕ *www.kings.cam.ac.uk*

🎟 *£10, includes college and grounds* ⏲ *Sometimes closed for events; check ahead to confirm.*

★ Polar Museum

HISTORY MUSEUM | Beautifully designed, this museum at Cambridge University's Scott Polar Research Institute chronicles the history of polar exploration. There's a particular emphasis on the British expeditions of the 20th century, including the ill-fated attempt by Robert Falcon Scott to be the first to reach the South Pole in 1912. Norwegian explorer Roald Amundsen reached the pole first; Scott and his men perished on the return journey, but their story became legendary. There are also collections devoted to the science of modern polar exploration; the indigenous people of northern Canada, Greenland, and Alaska; and frequently changing art installations. ✉ *Scott Polar Research Institute, Lensfield Rd., Cambridge* ☎ *01223/336540* 🌐 *www.spri.cam.ac.uk/museum* 🎟 *Free* ⏲ *Closed Mon. except bank holidays.*

Queens' College

COLLEGE | One of the most eye-catching colleges, with a secluded "cloister court" look, Queens' is named after Margaret, wife of Henry VI, and Elizabeth, wife of Edward IV. Founded in 1448 and completed in the 1540s, the college is tucked away on Queens' Lane, next to the wide lawns that lead down from King's College to The Backs. The college's most famed piece of architecture is the wooden lattice Mathematical Bridge, first built in 1749. The original version is said to have been built without any fastenings, though the current bridge (reconstructed in 1902) is securely bolted. ✉ *Queens' La., Cambridge* ☎ *01223/335500* 🌐 *www.quns.cam.ac.uk* 🎟 *£3.50* ⏲ *Closed weekends Jan. and Feb. and during exam periods, certain wks Apr.–July; call to confirm.*

Trinity College

COLLEGE | Founded in 1546 by Henry VIII, Trinity replaced a 14th-century educational foundation and is the largest college in either Cambridge or Oxford, with nearly 1,000 undergraduates. In the 17th-century great court, with its massive gatehouse, is Great Tom, a giant clock that strikes each hour with high and low notes. The college's true masterpiece is Sir Christopher Wren's library, colonnaded and seemingly constructed with as much light as stone. Among the things you can see here is A. A. Milne's handwritten manuscript of *The House at Pooh Corner.* Trinity alumni include Sir Isaac Newton, William Thackeray, Lord Byron, Lord Tennyson, and 34 Nobel Prize winners (to date). ✉ *St. John's St., Cambridge* ☎ *01223/338400* 🌐 *www.trin.cam.ac.uk* 🎟 *£3.50* ⏲ *College and chapel closed exam period and event days; Wren library closed Sun.*

🍴 Restaurants

Loch Fyne

$$ | SEAFOOD | Part of a Scottish chain that harvests its own oysters, this airy, casual place across from the Fitzwilliam Museum is deservedly popular. The seafood is fresh and well prepared, served in a traditional setting with a modern charm. **Known for:** great Scotch whiskey menu; Bradan Rost smoked salmon; Scottish oysters. [$] *Average main: £17* ✉ *37 Trumpington St., Cambridge* ☎ *01223/362433* 🌐 *www.lochfyneseafoodandgrill.co.uk.*

★ Midsummer House

$$$$ | FRENCH | Beside the River Cam on the edge of Midsummer Common, this gray-brick 19th-century villa holds a two–Michelin star restaurant set in a comfortable conservatory. Fixed-price menus for lunch and dinner (with five to eight courses) present innovative dishes that place a focus on seasonal, often local, ingredients. **Known for:** special-occasion dining; great river views; beautiful historic setting. [$] *Average main: £135* ✉ *Midsummer Common, Cambridge* ☎ *01223/369299* 🌐 *www.midsummerhouse.co.uk* ⏲ *Closed Sun.–Tues.*

River Bar Steakhouse & Grill

$$$ | **MODERN BRITISH** | Across the river from Magdalene College, this popular waterfront bar and grill serves delicious steak, burgers, and pies, plus specialties such as lobster mac and cheese or salmon steak with molasses and spices. There's an extensive cocktail menu as well. **Known for:** huge cocktail menu; classic British mains; rooftop terrace dining. ⓢ *Average main: £27* ✉ *Quayside, 3 Thompsons La., off Bridge St., Cambridge* ☎ *01223/307030* ⊕ *www.riverbarsteakhouse.com.*

Stratford-upon-Avon

104 miles north of London.

Stratford-upon-Avon has become adept at accommodating the hordes of people who stream in for a glimpse of William Shakespeare's world. Filled with distinctive, Tudor half-timber buildings, this is certainly a handsome town, and the Royal Shakespeare Theatre is a don't-miss for those who want to see Shakespeare performed in England. But the town can feel, at times, like a literary amusement park, so if you're not a fan of the Bard, you may want to explore elsewhere.

GETTING HERE AND AROUND

Chiltern Railways serves the area from London's Marylebone Station and takes on average two hours; some trains are direct, but most have one change.

TOURS AND TICKETS

★ City Sightseeing

GUIDED TOURS | Running from early April to early November, these double-decker tour buses offer two options: a hop-on, hop-off bus tour that allows you to create your own itinerary around 11 landmarks in and around the town or a ticket that includes entry to each of the five Shakespeare family homes. ✉ *Birmingham Rd., Stratford-upon-Avon* ☎ *01789/299123* ⊕ *www.city-sightseeing.com/en/100/stratford-upon-avon* ⤷ *From £15.*

★ Shakespeare Birthplace Trust

OTHER TOURS | FAMILY | The main places of Shakespearean interest (Anne Hathaway's Cottage, Hall's Croft, Mary Arden's Farm, Shakespeare's New Place, and Shakespeare's Birthplace) are run by the Shakespeare Birthplace Trust, an independent charity that aims to preserve and promote the properties. By far the most economical way to visit the properties is to get a Full Story ticket (£23), which gives unlimited access to all five houses for a year. ✉ *The Shakespeare Centre, Henley St., Stratford-upon-Avon* ☎ *01789/204016* ⊕ *www.shakespeare.org.uk.*

Stratford Town Walk

WALKING TOURS | This walking tour runs every day of the year, even on Christmas Day, at 11 am, with an extra tour on Saturday at 2 pm. There's no need to book in advance; you can just show up. The tours, which take around two hours, will take you on a journey through the town, unravelling Shakespeare's story as you go. The meeting point is by the yellow sign outside the Royal Shakespeare Company, opposite the junction with Sheep Street. ✉ *20 Waterside, Stratford-upon-Avon* ☎ *07855/760377* ⊕ *www.stratfordtownwalk.co.uk* ⤷ *From £10.*

ESSENTIALS

VISITOR INFORMATION Stratford-upon-Avon Tourist Information Centre. ✉ *Bridgefoot, Stratford-upon-Avon* ☎ *01789/264293* ⊕ *www.visitstratforduponavon.co.uk.*

 ## Sights

Hall's Croft

HISTORIC HOME | One of the finest surviving Jacobean (early 17th-century) town houses in England, this impressive residence (one of the best preserved of the Shakespeare family homes) has a delightful walled garden and was once the home of Shakespeare's eldest daughter, Susanna, and her husband, Dr. John Hall. John Hall was a wealthy physician who,

Stratford-upon-Avon honors Shakespeare's birthday with an annual procession.

by prescribing an herbal cure for scurvy, was well ahead of his time. One room is furnished as a medical dispensary of the period, and throughout the building are fine examples of heavy oak Jacobean furniture, including a child's high chair and some 17th-century portraits. The café serves light lunches and afternoon teas. ⊠ *Old Town, Stratford-upon-Avon* ☎ *01789/338533* ⊕ *www.shakespeare. org.uk* ⊠ *£9; Full Story ticket (includes Anne Hathaway's Cottage and Gardens, Shakespeare's Birthplace, Shakespeare's New Place, and Mary Arden's Farm) £23.*

★ **Holy Trinity Church**

CHURCH | This 13th-century church on the banks of the River Avon is the final resting place of William Shakespeare. He was buried here not because he was a famed poet but because he was a lay rector of Stratford, owning a portion of the township tithes. On the north wall of the sanctuary, over the altar steps, is the famous marble bust created by Gerard Jansen in 1623 and thought to be a true likeness of Shakespeare. The bust offers a more

human, even humorous, perspective when viewed from the side. Also in the chancel are the graves of Shakespeare's wife, Anne; his daughter, Susanna; his son-in-law, John Hall; and his granddaughter's first husband, Thomas Nash. Also here is the christening font in which Shakespeare was baptized. ⊠ *Old Town, Stratford-upon-Avon* ☎ *01789/266316* ⊕ *www.stratford-upon-avon.org* ⊠ *£4 donation requested.*

★ **Royal Shakespeare Company**

THEATER | One of the finest repertory troupes in the world and long the backbone of England's theatrical life, the Royal Shakespeare Company (RSC) performs plays year-round in Stratford and at venues across Britain. The stunning Royal Shakespeare Theatre, home of the RSC, has a thrust stage based on the original Globe Theatre in London. The Swan Theatre, part of the theater complex and also built in the style of Shakespeare's Globe, stages plays by Shakespeare and his contemporaries, such as Christopher Marlowe and Ben Jonson. Contemporary works are staged at The Other Place, nearby. Prices start from £5 for rehearsals and previews. ■ TIP→ **Seats book up fast, but day-of-performance and returned tickets are sometimes available.** ✉ *Waterside, Stratford-upon-Avon* ☎ *01789/331111* ⊕ *www.rsc.org.uk* ✎ *General tickets from £16.*

★ Shakespeare's Birthplace

HISTORIC HOME | A half-timber house typical of its time, the playwright's birthplace is a much-visited shrine that has been altered and restored since Shakespeare lived here. Passing through the modern visitor center, you are immersed in the world of Shakespeare through a state-of-the-art exhibition that includes evocative audio and visuals from contemporary stagings of his plays. The house itself is across the garden from the visitor center. Colorful wall decorations and furnishings reflect comfortable, middle-class Elizabethan domestic life. You can view his father's workshop and you can see the very room where Shakespeare was born. Mark Twain and Charles Dickens were both pilgrims here, and you can see the signatures of Thomas Carlyle and Walter Scott scratched into the windowpanes. In the garden, actors present excerpts from his plays. There's also a café and bookshop on the grounds. ✉ *Henley St., Stratford-upon-Avon* ☎ *01789/204016* ⊕ *www.shakespeare.org.uk* ✎ *£20; Full Story ticket (includes Anne Hathaway's Cottage and Gardens, Hall's Croft, Shakespeare's New Place, and Mary Arden's Farm) £23.*

★ Shakespeare's New Place

HISTORIC HOME | This is the spot where Shakespeare lived for the last 19 years of his life and where he wrote many of his plays, including *The Tempest*. Though the actual 15th-century building he inhabited was torn down in the 18th century, the site was imaginatively reinterpreted in 2016 as an outdoor space where the footprint of the original house can be traced. Each of his 38 plays is represented by a pennant in the Golden Garden, and his sonnets are engraved into the stone paving. Highlights include a mulberry tree that some believe was given to Shakespeare by King James I and a restored Elizabethan knot garden. A permanent exhibition inside the neighboring Nash's House tells the story of the New Place and Shakespeare's family life within it; there's also a roof terrace, which provides views of the gardens. Nash's House was once home to Thomas Nash, the husband of Shakespeare's granddaughter, Elizabeth Hall. ✉ *22 Chapel St., Stratford-upon-Avon* ☎ *01789/204016* ⊕ *www.shakespeare.org.uk* ✎ *£13; Full Story ticket (includes Anne Hathaway's Cottage and Gardens, Shakespeare's Birthplace, Hall's Croft, and Mary Arden's Farm) £23.*

Around Stratford

Two additional stops on the Shakespeare trail are just outside Stratford; also nearby is spectacular Warwick Castle.

★ Anne Hathaway's Cottage

HISTORIC HOME | The most picturesque of the Shakespeare Birthplace Trust properties, this thatched cottage on the western outskirts of Stratford is the family home of the woman Shakespeare married in 1582. The "cottage," actually a substantial Tudor farmhouse with latticed windows, is astonishingly beautiful. Inside, it is surprisingly cozy with lots of period furniture, including the loveseat on which Shakespeare reputedly conducted his courtship and a rare carved Elizabethan bed. The cottage garden is planted in lush Edwardian style with herbs and flowers. Wildflowers are grown in the adjacent orchard (a nod to what was grown in the garden in the Hathaways' time), and the neighboring arboretum has trees, shrubs, and roses mentioned in Shakespeare's works.

The best way to get here is on foot, especially in late spring when the apple trees are in blossom. The signed path runs from Evesham Place (an extension of Grove Road) opposite Chestnut Walk. Pick up a leaflet with a map from the tourist office; the walk takes 25–30 minutes. ⊠ *Cottage La., Stratford-upon-Avon* ☎ *01789/338532* ⊕ *www.shakespeare. org.uk* ⊠ *£13; Full Story ticket (includes entry to Hall's Croft, Mary Arden's Farm, Shakespeare's New Place, and Shakespeare's Birthplace) £23.*

★ Mary Arden's Farm

HISTORIC HOME | FAMILY | This charming working farm was the childhood home of Shakespeare's mother, Mary Arden, and offers great insight into the farming methods employed in Tudor England. The rural heritage attraction, just three miles outside Stratford, is great for kids, who can try their hand at basket weaving and gardening, listen as the farmers explain their work in the fields, watch the cooks prepare food in the Tudor farmhouse kitchen, or play in the amazing timber-framed adventure playground. There are also daily falconry and archery displays and opportunities to meet the farm animals, as well as a good café. ⊠ *Station Rd., Wilmcote* ☎ *01789/338535* ⊕ *www.shakespeare.org.uk* ⊠ *Adult £15.50; Full Story ticket (includes Anne Hathaway's Cottage and Gardens, Hall's Croft, Shakespeare's New Place, and Shakespeare's Birthplace) £23* ⊗ *Closed Nov.–mid-Mar.*

★ Warwick Castle

CASTLE/PALACE | FAMILY | The vast bulk of this medieval castle rests on a cliff overlooking the Avon River and is considered "the fairest monument of ancient and chivalrous splendor which yet remains uninjured by time," to use the words of Sir Walter Scott. Today, the company that runs the Madame Tussauds wax museums owns the castle, and it has become more theme park than authentic heritage site, but it is still a lot of fun.

Warwick's two soaring towers, bristling with battlements, can be seen for miles: the 147-foot-high Caesar's Tower, built in 1356, and the 128-foot-high Guy's Tower, built in 1380.

Warwick Castle's monumental walls enclose an impressive armory of medieval weapons, as well as state rooms with historic furnishings and paintings. Other exhibits explore the castle's history through the ages, display the sights and sounds of a great medieval household as it prepares for an important battle, and tell the story of a princess's fairy-tale wedding. Be prepared both to play your part and be spooked in the gruesome dungeon experience (50 minutes and not recommended for under-10s) as you travel through scenes of torture, poisonings, and death sentences. Elsewhere, a working trebuchet (a kind of catapult), falconry displays, and rat-throwing (stuffed, not live) games add to the atmosphere. Below the castle, strutting peacocks patrol the 64 acres of grounds elegantly landscaped by Capability Brown in the 18th century.

Arrive early to beat the crowds. If you book online, you save 30% on ticket prices. Lavish medieval banquets take place throughout the year, and plenty of food stalls serve lunch. For the ultimate castle experience, you can "glamp" (glamorously camp) in a medieval tent, stay in a wooden lodge in the Knight's Village, or spend the night in your own luxury suite in the 14th-century Caesar's Tower. ⊠ *Castle La. off Mill St., Warwick* ☎ *0371/265–2000* ⊕ *www.warwick-castle.com* ⊠ *Castle £22, £16 in advance; dungeon experience £10.*

🍽 Restaurants

The Dirty Duck/The Black Swan

$ | BRITISH | The only pub in Britain to be licensed under two names (the more informal one came courtesy of American GIs who were stationed here during

World War II), this is one of Stratford's most celebrated and consistently rated pubs, attracting actors since the 18th-century days of thespian David Garrick. Along with your pint of bitter, you can choose from the extensive pub-grub menu of fish-and-chips, steaks, burgers, and grills; there are also good-value light bites. **Known for:** veranda overlooking the river; classic English pub atmosphere; reservations-only for dinner. [$] *Average main: £12* ✉ *Waterside, Stratford-upon-Avon* ☎ *01789/297312* 🌐 *www.greeneking-pubs.co.uk.*

The Opposition

$$ | **MODERN BRITISH** | Hearty, warming meals are offered at this informal, family-style restaurant in a 16th-century building on the main dining street near the theaters. The English and international dishes win praise from the locals. **Known for:** summertime crowds; historical setting; plenty of vegetarian and healthy options. [$] *Average main: £18* ✉ *13 Sheep St., Stratford-upon-Avon* ☎ *01789/269980* 🌐 *www.theoppo.co.uk* 🕒 *Closed Sun.*

Oxford

55 miles northwest of London.

With arguably the most famous university in the world, Oxford has been a center of learning since 1167, with only the Sorbonne preceding it. It doesn't take more than a day or two to explore its winding medieval streets, photograph its ivy-covered stone buildings and ancient churches and libraries, and even take a punt down one of its placid waterways. The town center is compact and walkable, and at its heart is Oxford University. Alumni of this prestigious institution include more than 60 Nobel Prize winners, 28 British prime ministers, and at least 30 international leaders, along with poets, authors, and artists, such as Percy Bysshe Shelley, Oscar Wilde, and W. H. Auden.

Oxford is northwest of London, at the junction of the Rivers Thames and Cherwell. The city is more interesting and more cosmopolitan than Cambridge, and although it's also bigger, its suburbs aren't remotely interesting to visitors. The interest is all at the center, where the old town curls around the grand stone buildings, great restaurants, and historic pubs. Victorian writer Matthew Arnold described Oxford's "dreaming spires," a phrase that has become famous. Students rush past on the way to exams, clad with antiquarian style in their requisite mortar caps, flowing dark gowns, stiff collars, and crisp white bow ties.

■ **TIP→ Bikes are everywhere, so watch your back when crossing roads.**

GETTING HERE AND AROUND

Megabus, Oxford Bus Company, and Stagecoach Oxford Tube all have buses traveling from London 24 hours a day; the trip takes between one hour 40 minutes and two hours. In London, Megabus departs from Victoria Coach Station, while Oxford Bus Company and Stagecoach Oxford Tube have pickup points on Buckingham Palace Road; Oxford Tube also picks up from the Marble Arch underground station. Oxford Bus Company runs round-trip shuttle service from Gatwick Airport every hour and Heathrow every half hour. Trains to Oxford depart from London's Paddington Station for the one-hour trip. Once here, you can easily traverse the town center on foot, but the Oxford Bus Company has a one-day ticket for unlimited travel in and around Oxford.

VISITING THE COLLEGES

You can explore the town's major sights in a day, but it takes more than a day to spend an hour in each of the key museums and absorb the college scene. Some colleges are open only in the afternoons during university terms. When undergraduates are in residence, access is often restricted to the chapels, dining rooms, and libraries, and you're requested to

Radcliffe Camera is an unmissable circular library at Oxford University.

refrain from picnicking in the quadrangles. All are closed certain days during exams, usually mid-April–late June.

TOURS
City Sightseeing
BUS TOURS | FAMILY | This company runs hop-on, hop-off bus tours with 20 stops around Oxford. Your ticket, purchased from the driver, is good for 24 hours. ☎ 01865/790522 ⊕ www.citysightseeingoxford.com ⊠ From £16.50.

Sights

★ Ashmolean Museum
HISTORY MUSEUM | What might be Britain's greatest museum outside London is also the oldest public museum in the United Kingdom. "The Ash," as locals call it, displays its rich and varied collections from the Neolithic to the present day over five stunning floors. Innovative and spacious galleries explore connections between priceless Greek, Roman, and Indian artifacts, as well as Egyptian and Chinese objects, all of which are among the best in the country. In the superb art collection, don't miss drawings by Raphael, the shell-encrusted mantle of Powhatan (father of Pocahontas), the lantern belonging to Guy Fawkes, and the Alfred Jewel, set in gold, which dates from the reign of King Alfred the Great (ruled 871–899). ⊠ Beaumont St., Oxford ☎ 01865/278000 ⊕ www.ashmolean.org ⊠ Free.

The Bodleian Library and Radcliffe Camera
LIBRARY | A vast library, the domed Radcliffe Camera is Oxford's most spectacular building, built in 1737–49 by James Gibbs in Italian Baroque style. It's usually surrounded by tourists with cameras trained at its golden-stone walls. The Camera contains part of the Bodleian Library's enormous collection, begun in 1602 and one of six "copyright libraries" in the United Kingdom. Like the Library of Congress in the United States, this means it must by law contain a copy of every book printed in Great Britain. In addition, the Bodleian is a vast repository for priceless historical documents—including a Gutenberg Bible and

a Shakespeare *First Folio*. The collection continues to grow by more than 5,000 items a week.

Tours reveal the magnificent Duke Humfrey's Library, which was the original chained library, completed in 1488 (the ancient tomes are dusted once a decade) as well as the spots used to create Hogwarts in the Harry Potter films. Arrive early to secure tickets for the three to six daily tours. The standard tours can be prebooked, as can the extended tours on Wednesday and Saturday; otherwise, tours are first-come, first-served. Audio tours don't require reservations. ✉ *Broad St., Oxford* ☎ *01865/287400* ⊕ *www. bodleian.ox.ac.uk* ✆ *From £4* ⊙ *Sometimes closed for events; call to confirm.*

Christ Church
COLLEGE | Built in 1546, the college of Christ Church is referred to by its members as "The House." This is the site of Oxford's largest quadrangle, Tom Quad, named after the huge bell (6¼ tons) that hangs in the Sir Christopher Wren–designed gate tower and rings 101 times at 9:05 every evening in honor of the original number of Christ Church scholars. The vaulted, 800-year-old chapel in one corner has been Oxford's cathedral since the time of Henry VIII. The college's medieval dining hall contains portraits of many famous alumni, including 13 of Britain's prime ministers, but you'll recognize it from its recurring role in the Harry Potter movies (although they didn't actually film here, the room was painstakingly re-created in a studio). Plan carefully, as the dining hall is often closed between noon and 2 pm during term time. Lewis Carroll, the author of *Alice in Wonderland*, was a teacher of mathematics here for many years; a shop opposite the meadows on St. Aldate's sells Alice paraphernalia. ✉ *St. Aldate's, Oxford* ☎ *01865/276492* ⊕ *www.chch. ox.ac.uk* ✆ *£16* ⊙ *Sometimes closed for events; check website to confirm.*

★ Magdalen College
COLLEGE | Founded in 1458, with a handsome main quadrangle and a supremely monastic air, Magdalen (pronounced *maud*-lin) is one of the most impressive of Oxford's colleges and attracts its most artistic students. Alumni include such diverse people as P. G. Wodehouse, Oscar Wilde, and John Betjeman. The school's large, square tower is a famous local landmark. ■TIP➜ **To enhance your visit, take a stroll around the Deer Park and along Addison's Walk; then have tea in the Old Kitchen, which overlooks the river.** ✉ *High St., Oxford* ☎ *01865/276000* ⊕ *www.magd.ox.ac.uk* ✆ *£8* ⊙ *Closed mornings Oct.–June.*

Oxford Botanic Garden & Arboretum
GARDEN | **FAMILY** | Founded in 1621 as a healing garden, this is the oldest of its kind in the British Isles. Set on the river, the University of Oxford's diverse garden displays 6,000 species ranging from lilies to citrus trees. There are a spacious walled garden, six luxuriant glass houses, including insectivorous and lily houses, and interesting medicinal, rock, and bog gardens to explore. Picnics are allowed, but you must bring your own food and drinks, as there's nowhere to buy them inside. ✉ *Rose La., Oxford* ☎ *01865/610300* ⊕ *www. obga.ox.ac.uk* ✆ *£6.30.*

Oxford University Museum of Natural History
HISTORY MUSEUM | **FAMILY** | This highly decorative Victorian Gothic creation of cast iron and glass, more a cathedral than a museum, is worth a visit for its architecture alone. Among the eclectic collections of entomology, geology, mineralogy, and zoology are the towering skeleton of a *Tyrannosaurus rex* and casts of a dodo's foot and head. There's plenty for children to explore and touch. ✉ *Parks Rd., Oxford* ☎ *01865/272950* ⊕ *www.oumnh. ox.ac.uk* ✆ *Free.*

★ Pitt Rivers Museum

OTHER MUSEUM | FAMILY | More than half a million intriguing archaeological and anthropological items from around the globe, based on the collection bequeathed by Lieutenant-General Augustus Henry Lane Fox Pitt Rivers in 1884, are crammed into a multitude of glass cases and drawers. In an eccentric touch that's surprisingly thought-provoking, labels are handwritten, and items are organized thematically rather than geographically—a novel way to gain perspective. Give yourself plenty of time to wander through the displays of shrunken heads, Hawaiian feather cloaks, and fearsome masks. ✉ *S. Parks Rd., Oxford* ☎ *01865/613000* 🌐 *www.prm.ox.ac.uk* 🎟 *Free (donations welcome).*

St. John's College

COLLEGE | One of Oxford's most attractive campuses, St. John's has seven quiet quadrangles surrounded by elaborately carved buildings. You enter the first through a low wooden door. This college dates to 1555, when Sir Thomas White, a merchant, founded it. His heart is buried in the chapel (it's a tradition for students to curse as they walk over it). The Canterbury Quad represented the first example of Italian Renaissance architecture in Oxford, and the Front Quad includes the buildings of the old St. Bernard's Monastery. ✉ *St. Giles', Oxford* ☎ *01865/277300* 🌐 *www.sjc.ox.ac.uk* 🎟 *Free.*

University Church of St. Mary the Virgin

CHURCH | Seven hundred years' worth of funeral monuments crowd this galleried and spacious church, including the alter-step tombstone of Amy Robsart, the wife of Robert Dudley, who was Elizabeth I's favorite suitor. One pillar marks the site where Thomas Cranmer, Anglican author of *The Book of Common Prayer,* was brought to trial for heresy by Queen Mary I (Cranmer had been a key player in the Protestant reforms). He was later burned at the stake nearby on Broad Street. The top of the 14th-century tower has a panoramic view of the city's skyline—it's worth the 127 steps. The Vaults and Garden café, part of the church accessible from Radcliffe Square, serves breakfasts and cream teas as well as good lunches. ✉ *High St., Oxford* ☎ *01865/279111* 🌐 *www.universitychurch.ox.ac.uk* 🎟 *Church free, tower £5.*

🍴 Restaurants

Branca

$$ | ITALIAN | FAMILY | While visitors don't need much persuading to venture out of the town center to the trendy nearby enclave of Jericho, Branca's charming interior, vibrant atmosphere, and solid menu of Italian classics provides yet more allure for the neighborhood. À la carte options inside the rustic, airy corner restaurant include everything from stone-baked pizza to risotto along with a wide selection of meat and fish dishes. Look out for the lunchtime and supper specials and be sure to check out the next-door deli. **Known for:** deli next door provides perfect picnic food; great lunchtime and dinner set menu deals; popular weekend brunches. [$] *Average main: £17* ✉ *111 Walton St., Oxford* ☎ *01865/807745* 🌐 *www.branca.co.uk.*

Brasserie Blanc

$$ | FRENCH | Raymond Blanc's sophisticated brasserie in the Jericho neighborhood is the more affordable chain restaurant cousin of Le Manoir aux Quat'Saisons in Great Milton. The changing menu always lists a good selection of steaks and innovative adaptations of bourgeois French fare, sometimes with Mediterranean or Asian influences. **Known for:** good wine selection; French classics like moules marinières; affordable prix-fixe lunch menu. [$] *Average main: £17* ✉ *71–72 Walton St., Oxford* ☎ *01865/510999* 🌐 *www.brasserieblanc.com.*

Gee's

$$ | **MEDITERRANEAN** | With its glass-and-steel framework, this former florist's shop just north of the town center makes a charming conservatory dining room, full of plants and twinkling with lights in the evening. The menu concentrates on the best of Oxfordshire produce and changes daily, but you can expect to find the likes of delicate seafood linguine, farm-fresh roasted vegetables, and wood-fired octopus. **Known for:** affordable lunch and early dinner menus; sophisticated Mediterranean dishes with local produce; chocolate nemesis and pistachio ice cream dessert. $ *Average main: £18* ✉ *61 Banbury Rd., Oxford* ☎ *01865/553540* ⊕ *www.geesrestaurant.co.uk.*

Stonehenge

85 miles southwest of London.

Almost five millennia after their construction, these stone circles on the Salisbury Plain continue to pose fascinating questions. How were the giant stones, some weighing as much as 45 tons, brought here, possibly from as far away as Wales? What was the site used for? Why were the stones aligned with the midsummer sunrise and the midwinter sunset? But Stonehenge is more than just the megaliths; the surrounding landscape is dotted with ancient earthworks, remains of Neolithic settlements, and processional pathways, creating a complex of ceremonial structures that testifies to the sophisticated belief system of these early Britons.

GETTING HERE AND AROUND

From London, you need to first take a train or bus to Salisbury or Avebury. Stonehenge Tour buses leave from Salisbury's train and bus stations every half hour from 9:30 to 2:30, and then hourly from 3 to 5, from early June to August; hourly from 10 to 4 from April to early June and September through October;

and 10 to 2 in November through March. Tickets cost £16 (bus to site only) or £38 (includes Stonehenge and a visit to Old Sarum). Other options are a taxi or a custom tour. Drivers can find the monument near the junction of A303 with A344.

 ## Sights

★ Stonehenge

RUINS | FAMILY | Mysterious and ancient, Stonehenge has baffled archaeologists, not to mention the general public, for centuries. One of England's most visited monuments (attracting over a million visitors a year) and a UNESCO World Heritage Site, the circle of giant stones standing starkly against the wide sweep of Salisbury Plain still has the capacity to fascinate and move those who view it. Unattractive visitor facilities have been removed to better establish the stones in their original context of grass fields, other nearby monuments, and their original processional approach, the Avenue. Although general visitors can no longer enter the stone circle itself (except by special arrangement; call for further information), you can roam free over the surrounding landscape with its Neolithic earthworks, some of which predate the stones. To best experience the awe and mystery of Stonehenge, visit the circle in the early morning or in the evening, when the crowds have dispersed.

Stonehenge was begun as early as 3000 BC with the construction of a circular earthwork enclosure. The nearby Cursus, long rectangular earthwork banks, were also created around this time. The stone circle itself was completed in stages, beginning around 2500 BC with the inner circle of bluestones, and continued to be changed and in use until around 1600 BC. The early inner circle was later surrounded by an outer circle of 30 sarsen stones, huge sandstone blocks weighing up to 25 tons, which are believed to have originated from the Marlborough Downs. Within these two circles was a horseshoe-shape group of sarsen trilithons (two large vertical stones supporting a third stone laid horizontally across it) and within that another horseshoe-shape grouping of bluestones. The sarsens used in the trilithons averaged 45 tons. Many of the huge stones were brought here from great distances before the invention of the wheel, and it's not certain what ancient form of transportation was used to move them. Every time a reconstruction of the journey has been attempted, it has failed. The labor involved in quarrying, transporting, and carving these stones is astonishing, all the more so when you realize that it was accomplished about the same time as the construction of Egypt's major pyramids.

Stonehenge (the name derives from the Saxon term for "hanging stones") has been excavated several times over the centuries, but the primary reason for its erection remains unknown. It's fairly certain that it was a religious site, and that worship here involved the cycles of the sun; the alignment of the stones on the axis of the midsummer sunrise and midwinter sunset makes this clear. Viewed from the center of the stone circle, the sun rises adjacent to the Heel Stone at midsummer and sets between the stones of the tallest trilithon at midwinter. The Druids certainly had nothing to do with the construction: the monument had already been in existence for nearly 2,000 years by the time they appeared. Some historians have maintained that Stonehenge was a kind of Neolithic computer, with a sophisticated astronomical purpose—an observatory of sorts—though evidence from excavations in the early 20th century shows that it had once been used as a burial ground. Another possibility is that this Neolithic village was home to those who performed the religious rites at Stonehenge, where people gathered from far and wide to feast and worship.

Without direct access to the stones, it is not possible to closely examine their prehistoric carvings, some of which show axes and daggers, so bring a pair of binoculars to help make out the details on the monoliths. To fully engage your imagination or to get that magical photo, it's worth exploring all aspects of the site, both near and far. An informative visitor center is located 1½ miles away (access to the stone circle is via a frequent shuttle), with parking, audio guide rental, a café, loads of branded merchandise, and an exhibition of prehistoric objects found at the site. There's also a dramatic display using time-lapse photography that puts you (virtually) in the center of the circle as the seasons change. Next to the visitor center are some re-created Neolithic huts that show how the people who built and used Stonehenge might have lived. Visits are by timed admission slots only. ✉ *Amesbury* ✣ *Junction of A360 and Airman's Corner* ☎ *0370/333–1181* 🌐 *www.english-heritage.org.uk* 🎫 *£22.80 (walk-up); £21.50 (advance).*

🍴 Restaurants

★ Allium

$$ | MODERN BRITISH | This family-run, centrally located restaurant has been winning rave reviews for both the taste and presentation of its creative Modern British dishes. Produce is largely fresh and local while meats and poultry are free-range and sustainably farmed. **Known for:** reasonable prices; high-quality, creative dishes; nice wine selection. [$] *Average main: £20* ✉ *6–7 Ox Row, Salisbury* ☎ *01722/326057* 🌐 *alliumsalisbury.restaurant* 🕒 *Closed Sun. and Mon.*

Windsor

21 miles west of London.

The tall turrets of Windsor Castle, one of the homes of the royal family, can be seen for miles around. The grand stone building is the star attraction in this quiet town with some remaining medieval elements—although Eton College, England's most famous public (what Americans would call private) school, is also just a lovely walk away across the Thames.

GETTING HERE AND AROUND
Fast Green Line buses leave opposite London's Victoria Coach Station every half hour for the 70-minute trip to Windsor. Trains travel from London Waterloo every 30 minutes, or you can catch more frequent trains from Paddington and change at Slough. The trip takes less than an hour from Waterloo and around 30 minutes from Paddington.

ESSENTIALS
VISITOR INFORMATION Royal Windsor Information Centre. ✉ *Old Booking Hall, Windsor Royal Station, Thames St., Windsor* ☎ *01753/743900, 01753/743907 for accommodations* ⊕ *www.windsor. gov.uk.*

⊙ Sights

★ Eton College
COLLEGE | Signs warn drivers of "Boys Crossing" as you approach the splendid Tudor-style buildings of Eton College, the distinguished boarding school for boys ages 13–18 founded in 1440 by King Henry VI. It's all terrifically photogenic—during the college semester students still dress in pinstripe trousers, swallowtail coats, and stiff collars. Rivaling St. George's at Windsor in terms of size, the Gothic **Chapel** contains superb 15th-century grisaille wall paintings juxtaposed with modern stained glass by John Piper. Beyond the cloisters are the

15

Side Trips from London **WINDSOR**

school's playing fields where, according to the Duke of Wellington, the Battle of Waterloo was really won, since so many of his officers had learned discipline and strategy during their school days. Boris Johnson is the most recent of the country's many prime ministers to have been educated here. The **Museum of Eton Life** has displays on the school's history and vignettes of school life. The school gives public tours on Friday afternoon from early April through August, bookable online. ✉ *Brewhouse Yard, Eton* ☎ *01753/370100* ⊕ *www.etoncollege. com* 🎫 *£10* ⊙ *Closed Sept.–early Apr.*

★ Windsor Castle
CASTLE/PALACE | From William the Conqueror to Queen Victoria, the kings and queens of England added towers and wings to this brooding, imposing castle that is visible for miles. It's the largest inhabited castle in the world and the only royal residence in continuous use by the British royal family since the Middle Ages. Despite the multiplicity of hands involved in its design, the palace manages to have a unity of style and character. The most impressive view of Windsor Castle is from the A332 road, coming into town from the south. Admission includes an audio guide and, if you wish, a guided tour of the castle precincts. Entrance lines can be long in season, and you're likely to spend at least half a day here, so come early.

As you enter, Henry VIII's gateway leads uphill into the wide castle precincts, where you're free to wander. Across from the entrance is the exquisite St. George's Chapel (closed Sunday). Here lie 10 of the kings of England, including Henry VI, Charles I, and Henry VIII (Jane Seymour is the only one of his six wives buried here). One of the noblest buildings in England, the chapel was built in the Perpendicular style popular in the 15th and 16th centuries, with elegant stained-glass windows; a high, vaulted ceiling; and intricately carved choir stalls. The colorful heraldic banners of the Knights of the Garter—the oldest British Order of Chivalry, founded by Edward III in 1348—hang in the choir. The ceremony in which the knights are installed as members of the order has been held here with much pageantry for more than five centuries. The elaborate Albert Memorial Chapel was created by Queen Victoria in memory of her husband.

The North Terrace provides especially good views across the Thames to Eton College, perhaps the most famous of Britain's exclusive public schools (confusingly, "public schools" in Britain are highly traditional, top-tier private schools). From the terrace, you enter the State Apartments, which are open to the public most days. On display to the left of the entrance to the State Apartments, Queen Mary's Dolls' House is a perfect miniature Georgian palace-within-a-palace, created in 1923. Electric lights glow, the doors all have tiny keys, and a miniature library holds Lilliputian-size books written especially for the young queen by famous authors of the 1920s. Five cars, including a Daimler and Rolls-Royce, stand at the ready. In the adjacent corridor are exquisite French couturier–designed costumes made for the two Jumeau dolls presented to the Princesses Elizabeth and Margaret by France in 1938.

Although a fire in 1992 gutted some of the State Apartments, hardly any works of art were lost. Phenomenal repair work brought to new life the Grand Reception Room, the Green and Crimson Drawing Rooms, and the State and Octagonal Dining Rooms. A green oak hammer-beam (a short horizontal beam that projects from the tops of walls for support) roof looms magnificently over the 600-year-old St. George's Hall, where the Queen gives state banquets. The State Apartments contain priceless furniture, including a magnificent Louis XVI bed and Gobelin tapestries; carvings by Grinling Gibbons; and paintings by Canaletto, Rubens, van Dyck, Holbein, Dürer, and Bruegel. The tour's high points are the Throne Room and the Waterloo Chamber, where Sir Thomas Lawrence's portraits of Napoléon's victorious foes line the walls. You can also see arms and armor—look for Henry VIII's ample suit. A visit October to March also includes the Semi-State rooms, the private apartments of George IV, resplendent with gilded ceilings.

To see the castle come magnificently alive, check out the Changing the Guard ceremony, which takes place daily at 11 am April to July and on alternate days at the same time August to March. Confirm the exact schedule before traveling to Windsor. Note that the State rooms (and sometimes the entire castle) are closed during official state occasions; dates of these closures are listed on the website, or you can call ahead to check. Oh, and if the Royal Standard flag is being flown, you'll know the Queen is in residence. ⊠ *Castle Hill, Windsor* ☎ *0303/123–7304 for tickets* ⊕ *www.rct.uk/visit/windsor-castle* ⊠ *£26.50 for Precincts, State Apartments, Gallery, St. George's Chapel, and Queen Mary's Dolls' House; £12.90 when State Apartments are closed.*

★ Windsor Great Park

CITY PARK | The remains of an ancient royal hunting forest, this park stretches for some 5,000 acres south of Windsor Castle. Much of it is open to the public and can be explored by car or on foot. Its chief attractions are clustered around the southeastern section, known (or at least marketed) as the Royal Landscape. These include Virginia Water, a 2-mile-long lake that forms the park's main geographical focal point. More than anything, however, the Royal Landscape is defined by its two beautiful gardens. Valley Gardens, located on the north shore of Virginia Water, is particularly vibrant in April and May, when the dazzling multicolor azaleas are in full bloom. If you're feeling fit, the romantic Long Walk is one of England's most photographed footpaths—the 3-mile-long route, designed by Charles II, starts in the Great Park and leads all the way to Windsor Castle.

Divided from the Great Park by the busy A308 highway, the smaller Windsor Home Park, on the eastern side of Windsor Castle, is the private property of the Royal Family. It contains Frogmore House, a lavish royal residence. Completed in 1684, Frogmore was bought by George III as a gift for his wife, Queen Charlotte. The sprawling white mansion later became a beloved retreat of Queen Victoria. It was also formerly home to the Duke and Duchess of Sussex, otherwise known as Prince Harry and Meghan Markle, and can still only be visited by guided tour on a handful of days throughout August; see ⊕ *www.rct.uk* for more information. ⊠ *Entrances on A329, A332, B383, and Wick La., Windsor* ☎ *01753/860222* ⊕ *www.windsorgreatpark.co.uk* ⊠ *Savill Garden £7.50* ☉ *Windsor Home Park closed Sept.–July and Mon. and weekends in Aug.*

Warner Bros. Harry Potter Studio Tour

20 miles northwest of London.

Popular and family-friendly, the Warner Bros. Harry Potter Studio Tour has sets and props from the successful films, and plenty of engaging interactive diversions for all ages. The train and a special shuttle bus from Watford get you here.

Sights

★ Warner Bros. Harry Potter Studio Tour

FILM/TV STUDIO | **FAMILY** | Attention all Muggles: this spectacular attraction just outside Watford immerses you in the magical world of Harry Potter for hours. From the Great Hall of Hogwarts—faithfully re-created, down to the finest detail—to magical props beautifully displayed in the vast studio space, each section of this attraction showcases the real sets, props, and special effects used in the eight movies.

Visitors enter the Great Hall, a fitting stage for costumes from each Hogwarts house. You can admire the intricacies of the huge Hogwarts Castle model, ride a broomstick, try butterbeer, explore the Forbidden Forest, and gaze through the shop windows of Diagon Alley. The Hogwarts Express section—at a faithfully reproduced Platform 9¾—allows you to walk through a carriage of the actual steam train and see what it's like to ride with Harry and the gang. Tickets, pegged to a 30-minute arrival time slot, must be prebooked online. The studio tour is a 20-minute drive from St. Albans. You can also get here by taking a 20-minute train ride from London's Euston Station to Watford Junction (then a 15-minute shuttle-bus ride, free with a valid Studio Tour ticket). Via car from London, use M1 and M25—parking is free. ⊠ *Studio Tour Dr., Leavesden Green* ☎ *0345/084–0900* ⊕ *www.wbstudiotour.co.uk* ⊠ *£49.95.*

Index

Photo Credits

Front Cover: Tetra Images [Description: UK, England, London, Big Ben and Boadicea Statue at dusk]. **Back cover, from left to right:** Gbphoto27/Dreamstime. Victor10947/Dreamstime. Piotreknik / Shutterstock. **Spine:** Kim Pin/Shutterstock. **Interior, from left to right:** Songquan Deng/Shutterstock (1). Jarek Kilian/iStockphoto (2-3). Beataaldridge/Dreamstime.com (5). **Chapter 1: Experience London:** Daniel Lange/iStockphoto (6-7). Mistervlad/Shutterstock (8-9). Robertharding / Alamy Stock Photo (9). Danbreckwoldt/Dreamstime (9). Alexeyfedoren/Dreamstime (10). PA Images / Alamy Stock Photo (10). Mirohasch/Dreamstime (10). Mariagroth/Dreamstime (10). Ml12nan/ Dreamstime (11). Matt Child / Alamy Stock Photo (11). Lucidwaters/Dreamstime (12). Tony french / Alamy Stock Photo (12). Peter D Noyce / Alamy Stock Photo (12). Gavin Bates/Dreamstime (12). Dan Breckwoldt / Shutterstock (13). Tupungato / Shutterstock (13). Lowerkase/ Dreamstime (14). VV Shots / iStock (14). Ross Brinkerhoff / Fodors Travel (14). Tim Gartside London / Alamy Stock Photo (14). Kiev.Victor/ Shutterstock (15). Hawksmoor (22). Gordon's Gin (23). Camden Market (24). James Smith & Sons Umbrellas (25). Trustees of the Natural History Museum (26). Victoria and Albert Museum, London (26). Kiev.Victor/Shutterstock (26). Imperial War Museum (27). Plastiques. Photography Limited (27). TomasSereda/iStockphoto (28). Vladislav Zolotov/iStockphoto (28). Royal Collection Trust /Her Majesty Queen Elizabeth II (28). Dean and Chapter of Westminster (28). Aerial-motion/Shutterstock (29). Afflamen/Shutterstock (29). Historic Royal Palaces (29). Vladislav Zolotov/iStockphoto (29). S.Borisov/Shutterstock (30). Stockinasia/iStockphoto (30). Kornelija Cakarun/Shutterstock (30). The City of London Corporation (30). Courtesy_Historic Royal Palaces (31). Pajor Pawel/SHutterstock (31). I Wei Huang/Shutterstock (31). I Wei Huang/ Shutterstock (31). Roberto Garagarza/Nicholson's Pubs (32). Greene King (32). CC-by-SA Photo by George Rex (32). Annabel Staff (32). Tayo Lee Nelson/ Fullers (33). Geffrye Museum (34). Nate Luebbe/Shutterstock (34). Nicole Engelmann Photography (34). Jonathan Reid/Vsit London (34). Max Colson (35). **Chapter 3: Westminster and St. James's:** Peter Phipp/Travelshots.com / Alamy (73). Mistervlad/Shutter-stock (82-83). Kiev.Victor/Shutterstock (85). Chlodvig/Dreamstime (88). Ktylerconk/Flickr (93). **Chapter 4: Mayfair and Marylebone:** Derek Croucher / Alamy (105). Travelview/Shutterstock (109). Benedict Johnson (111). Alex Segre/Shutterstock (118). PCL / Alamy (125). **Chapter 5: Soho and Covent Garden:** Courtauld Gallery (131). British Tourist Authority (149). Anatoleya/iStock (151). **Chapter 6: Bloomsbury and Holborn:** Michael Jenner / Alamy (161). Alex Segre/ Shutterstock (170). British Museum (171). British Museum (172). Francisco Javier Diaz/ Shutterstock (172). British Museum (174). Britainonview/ McCormick-McAdam (175). Eric Nathan / Alamy Stock Photo (176). Alexey Fe-dorenko/Shutterstock (189). **Chapter 7: The City:** PSL Images / Alamy (191). Tomas111J/Dreamstime (201). Vladislav Zolotov/ iStock (203). Beataaldridge/Dreamstime.com (205). PA Images / Alamy Stock Photo (205). HRP/newsteam.co.uk (206). Will Rodrigues (207). Chenyujie1898 | Dreamstime (208). Sergey Goryachev/Shutterstock (208). Eden, Janine and Jim/Flickr (208). Inguskruklitis/ Dreamstime (209). **Chapter 8: East London:** Leklek73/Dreamstime (215). ElenaChaykinaPhotography/ Shutterstock (231). Elly Godfroy / Alamy (232). **Chapter 9: South of the Thames:** Mike Peel, [Creative Commons Attribution ShareAlike 2.5 License]/wikipedia (235). Lance Bellers / Shutterstock (245). Coward-lion/Dreamstime (247). Piotreknik / Shutterstock (249). **Chapter 10: Kensington, Chelsea, Knightsbridge, and Belgravia:** Ttatty/ Shutterstock (259). Londonstills.com / Alamy (266). Kiev.Victor / Shutterstock (279). **Chapter 11: Notting Hill and Bayswater:** Roger Cracknell 01/classic / Alamy (285) Robin Nieuwenkamp/Shutterstock (288). **Chapter 12: Regent's Park and Hampstead:** VisitEngland Images (297). I-Wei Huang/ Dreamstime (309). Immagambardella/Dreamstime (310). **Chapter 13: Greenwich:** Michael Booth / Alamy (315). Alicephotography/Dreamstime (321). Jon Arnold Images Ltd / Alamy (322). Mcginnly,[GNU Free Documentation License]/wikipedia (324). **Chapter 14: The Thames Upstream:** Mark6138/Dreamstime (327). Terry Harris / Alamy (330). Emotionart/Dreamstime (335). Hilsdon25/Dreamstime (336). **Chapter 15: Side Trips from London:** Andrew Holt / Alamy (339). John Martin / Alamy (348). British Tourist Authority/ Tourism South East (352). **About Our Writers:** All photos are courtesy of the writers except for the following: Courtesy of James O'Neill (367). Paul Rider (367). Courtesy of Heathcliff O'Malley (367). Courtesy of Jo Caird (367).

*Every effort has been made to trace the copyright holders, and we apologize in advance for any accidental errors. We would be happy to apply the corrections in the following edition of this publication.

Fodor's LONDON 2023

Publisher: Stephen Horowitz, *General Manager*

Editorial: Douglas Stallings, *Editorial Director*; Jill Fergus, Amanda Sadlowski, *Senior Editors*; Kayla Becker, Alexis Kelly, Brian Eschrich, *Editors*; Angelique Kennedy-Chavannes, *Assistant Editor*

Design: Tina Malaney, *Director of Design and Production*; Jessica Gonzalez, *Graphic Designer*; Erin Caceres, *Graphic Design Associate*

Production: Jennifer DePrima, *Editorial Production Manager*; Elyse Rozelle, *Senior Production Editor*; Monica White, *Production Editor*

Maps: Rebecca Baer, *Senior Map Editor*; David Lindroth, Mark Stroud (Moon Street Cartography), *Cartographers*

Photography: Viviane Teles, *Senior Photo Editor*; Namrata Aggarwal, Payal Gupta, Ashok Kumar, *Photo Editors*; Eddie Aldrete, *Photo Production Intern*

Business and Operations: Chuck Hoover, *Chief Marketing Officer*; Robert Ames, *Group General Manager*; Devin Duckworth, *Director of Print Publishing*

Public Relations and Marketing: Joe Ewaskiw, *Senior Director of Communications and Public Relations*

Fodors.com: Jeremy Tarr, *Editorial Director*; Rachael Levitt, *Managing Editor*

Technology: Jon Atkinson, *Director of Technology*; Rudresh Teotia, *Lead Developer*

Writers: Jo Caird, James O'Neill, Toby Orton, Ellin Stein, Alex Wijeratna

Editor: Amanda Sadlowski

Production Editor: Monica White

ISBN 978-1-64097-517-0

ISSN 0149-631X

All details in this book are based on information supplied to us at press time. Always confirm information when it matters, especially if you're making a detour to visit a specific place. Fodor's expressly disclaims any liability, loss, or risk, personal or otherwise, that is incurred as a consequence of the use of any of the contents of this book.

SPECIAL SALES

This book is available at special discounts for bulk purchases for sales promotions or premiums. For more information, e-mail SpecialMarkets@fodors.com.

PRINTED IN CANADA

10 9 8 7 6 5 4 3 2 1

MIX
Paper from responsible sources
FSC® C016245
www.fsc.org

About Our Writers

Jo Caird is a travel and arts journalist who writes on theater, visual arts, film, literature, and food and drink, as well as cycling and scuba diving. Her travel stories, city guides, and arts features appear regularly in the *Guardian*, the *Independent*, the *Sunday Telegraph*, the *Economist*, *Condé Nast Traveler*, and *World of Interiors*. Born and raised in London, Caird has an endless fascination for the city and is delighted to write about it whenever the opportunity arises. For this edition, she updated the Westminster and St. James's; East London; and Greenwich chapters. Follow her on Twitter @jocaird or visit her website, jocaird.com.

James O'Neill loves London and—as his work updating our chapters on Bloomsbury and Holborn; Notting Hill and Bayswater; and Travel Smart for this edition proves—loves rediscovering it, too. Although originally from Ireland, he's lived in London for almost 20 years—and still loves it just as much now as he did back then. He has written extensively for TV (BBC and Channel 4), the stage, and the page. He is currently finishing his debut novel, which is set in—where else?—London.

Having studied in London and never left—aside from a brief sojourn in Madrid—**Toby Orton** has experienced everything in the capital from Hackney to Notting Hill, Highgate to Peckham, and still finds it the most inspiring city in the world. He credits the bookshops, bars, galleries, clubs, and streets of London with making him the person he is today.

He has written about travel, cycling, food, and drink for a range of websites and publications. He updated the Experience; Mayfair and Marylebone; The City; The Thames Upstream; and Side Trips from London chapters of this edition.

Ellin Stein has written for publications on both sides of the Atlantic, including the *New York Times*, the *Times* (London), the *Guardian*, the *Telegraph,* and *InStyle,* for whom she was European correspondent. Her book *That's Not Funny, That's Sick: The National Lampoon and the Comedy Insurgents Who Captured the Mainstream,* was published by W. W. Norton & Co. in 2013. Originally from Manhattan, she has lived in London for two decades. For this edition, she updated the Kensington, Chelsea, Knightsbridge, and Belgravia; South of the Thames; and Regent's Park and Hampstead chapters.

London restaurant maven **Alex Wijeratna** is permanently blown away by the capital's rocket-fueled restaurant scene. From locavore heroes and street-food gourmet democrats, to global gastro-panjandrums, Alex tickles out the best joints that restaurant-mad London has to offer. Alex has also written for the *Times* (London), the *Guardian,* the *Independent,* the *Daily Mail,* the *Daily Express,* and the *Face.* For this edition, he updated the Soho and Covent Garden chapter.

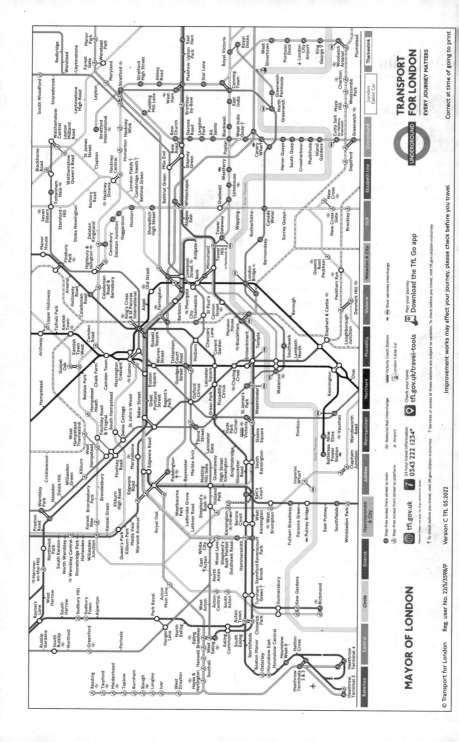